NEW MEXICO

A Brief Multi-History

By
Rubén Sálaz Márquez

COSMIC HOUSE
Albuquerque

NEW MEXICO: A BRIEF MULTI-HISTORY

Copyright ©1999 by Rubén D. Sálaz

All Rights Reserved.

Limited First Edition.

Sálaz Márquez, Rubén, 1935-
   New Mexico: A Brief Multi-History: a general history of New Mexico/Rubén Sálaz Márquez.

   692 pages.
   Includes Profile Biographies, 123 Illustrations, 4 Maps, Glossary, Annotated Bibliography,
   Recommended Books and Authors of N.M., Hall of Fame, and Index.

   ISBN 0-932492-05-3

   Layout and Design: Stan Anglen and the Author.
   Cover design by David Wilson and the Author.
   Printed in New Mexico by Albuquerque Printing Company.
   Photos/drawings:
         "San José Church in Los Ojos with Brazos Cliffs" courtesy of Atencio Photography, P.O.
         Box 115, Tierra Amarilla, N.M. 87575;
         Museum of New Mexico, negatives #2326 (T. Harmon Parkhurst photo) and #30769
         (drawing by Clarence Batcheller);
         "Great-Grandparents" from the Justiniano and Juanita Márquez family;
         Spanish drawings courtesy of Stephen Gallegos of Atlanta, Georgia;
         Petroglyph drawings courtesy of George Berry;
         Autograph calligraphy by Jimmy Ning.

Cosmic House
P.O. Box 10515
Alameda, N.M. 87184

WORKS by RUBEN SALAZ M.

Tabloid
Tierra Amarilla Shootout

History
Cosmic: The La Raza Sketchbook

Educational Materials
Cosmic Posters (bilingual)
Indian Saga Posters

Children's Books
The Cosmic Reader of the Southwest - For Young People

In Spanish
La lectura cósmica del suroeste - para los jóvenes

Short Stories
Heartland: Stories of the Southwest

Novels (trilogy)
I am Tecumseh! (Books I and II)

Dramas
Embassy Hostage: The Drama of Americans in Iran
Tonight or Never!

Essays
USA Today (Guest Editorials)

Anthologies
Included in: *The Language of Literature* (McDougal Littell); *Cuento Chicano del siglo XX* (Universidad Nacional Autónoma de México, Ediciones Coyoacán, New México State University); *Voces: An Anthology of Nuevo Mexicano Writers* (El Norte Publications); *Tierra: Contemporary Short Fiction of N.M.* (Cinco Puntos Press)

To Claressa and Jason,
my Aunt Dulcinea and primas Josephine and Dolores,
with thanks to Chris and Sean who introduced me to the computer,
and for the pioneering people of New Mexico from the San Luis Valley to El Paso,
especially those who have been neglected in the historical record.

Our conquering ancestors have outlived their mortal days
but now in you and I have come home to be enshrined
within our hearts and souls.

Their deeds shall be a heritage for all good men and women
to teach their sons and daughters
so that they, and we, shall be remembered
to the ending of the world.

Table of Contents

GOVERNORS

and the Years of their Administrations:

Part III   MEXICAN   REPUBLIC

Part IV   AMERICAN OCCUPATION

Part V   TERRITORIAL GOVERNMENT

Part VI   STATEHOOD TO PRESENT

Illustrations

Maps

INTRODUCTION

The quest by author Rubén Sálaz M. to arrive at the publication of *New Mexico: A Brief Multi-History* could be described as almost as formidable a saga as some of those related in the *Multi-History* itself. Sálaz' tenacity can be described as truly heroic. I personally observed his encounters with a variety of obstacles before and after an editorial review process which was intended as a standard professional academic procedure. Each time these situations presented themselves he passionately agreed or disagreed but always continued to pursue the quest of having his work published. Re-write after re-write he improved his manuscript, persevering until he realized the work represented his best effort. I remember him telling me: "The work is now the first comprehensive general New Mexico history book produced by a Spanish surnamed, native Hispanic New Mexican author…For me it is the culmination of a lifelong aspiration to tell the true history of New Mexico." The reader will soon agree that the immense variety of documented historical and cultural information in this *Multi-History* cannot be found under one cover in any other book. It is indeed an asset to be valued by history buffs, students, and historians alike for many years to come. The many pictures in the work, pictures that somehow have a vital freshness about them, are priceless because they put a face on New Mexico's long history.

At a time when Hispanic students are dropping out of school at alarming rates throughout our country and achievement motivation is at dismally low levels, this work represents the excellence that can be realized when one is determined to accomplish a goal. Although it is a book for everyone, it is my perspective that some will glean more from it than others. As we look into the new millennium and the cultural developments occurring in our society there is hope that a book of the magnitude of this *Multi-History* will inspire students and others to set higher standards, accomplish more, and promote elevated levels of self-esteem.

To complement the fascinating people, events and places of New Mexico, Sálaz provides us with the "Timeline" comparative history feature. The reader thus has access to the turn of events simultaneously unfolding in Europe and eastern North America where the United States was born. The "Timeline" provides us with comparative analysis so the feature is not without risks, which makes the work even more exciting and valuable. I appreciate the Sálaz historical range and encourage readers to research items that may raise their ire because they might not have been exposed to a broad historical spectrum in the same volume as in this chronologically structured *Multi-History*.

The chronology quickly takes you from pre-contact with the indigenous people of this region to the European contacts made by the various Spanish adelantados and their expeditions to Oñate's colonization. One gains an understanding of the societal evolution of colonization, military conflicts, peace, cultural blending, population growth, commerce, property law, government, politics, etc., as well as just living through the periods of Spanish sovereignty (1540-1821), the Mexican Republic (1821-1846), the American Occupation, (1846-1850), the Territorial Government (1851-1912) and Statehood from 1912 to the present.

At a minimum, the *Multi-History* represents a unique format which allows us to look comprehensively at our New Mexican history as well as other events occurring in other places in what is now the contiguous United States. For example, how many of us realize that at the time the Declaration of Independence was created, a great part of the Spanish Trail was discovered by the Domíniguez/Escalante expedition? For readers that hail from the Southwest, Sálaz' description of the people, places, events, social systems, war, diplomacy, religion, business, etc, evokes strong responses from our senses. One can feel the excitement Oñate and his caravan of colonists must have felt as they left El Paso in 1598, visualize the semiarid land and beautiful vistas as they made their way up what was to become the Camino Real some 300 miles north to the base of majestic mountains where they settled on the west side of the confluence of the Rio Grande and Rio Chama in what they named San Juan de los Caballeros just north of present Española. Those readers who have not been to this part of our country have been guided by various artistic depictions, photos and maps that in their minds eye give them a glimpse of what it was like some 400 years ago and now they can add the *Multi-History* to their basic resources.

I believe in the adage that tells us: **To understand today you have to study yesterday**. It is incumbent upon us who reside in New Mexico to read, study and analyze this *Multi-History* for a better understanding of how we came to be and who we are as a people. Suggestions that Sálaz make every effort to have this work adopted as a textbook to be studied in the public schools have been made on numerous occasions. Those folks throughout the country who have a deep or even a passing interest in the Southwest will delight in the vastness of facts, the chronology of events and the interesting characters that had their time in building this precious Southwestern area of our USA.

My heartiest congratulations to Rubén Sálaz M. for this timeless triumph!

J. Ronald Vigil

FOREWORD

The reading of New Mexico history is rewarding for a number of reasons. Pueblo culture was the first civilization in what is now called the USA. The Pueblos are still living in areas where they were first encountered by Hispanic Europeans, with much of their culture still intact, because of the unique alliance created between the two societies.

Hispanic New Mexico was the first European settlement in the present United States. It reveals, among other things, how pioneering Hispanic Europeans, their culture and their religion, interacted with and affected Native Americans. History records how a tiny island of Hispanics survived, endured, and prevailed in this northernmost frontier outpost of the Spanish empire and *la Nueva México* provides much information on how Spain and its people operated in the New World.

New Mexico history also provides a wealth of information on how a frontier society functioned, not only its trials and tribulations, but how real people lived, worked, and died in a folk society which was so closely surrounded by strong cultures of the Pueblo, Comanche, Apache, Navajo, Ute. These Native Americans are an inextricable part of the story and deserve to be understood in the context of New Mexican history.

The entrance of the United States into the Southwest adds yet another layer to the rich civilizations and cultures of New Mexico, affording the reader yet another perspective in the study of American history, character, and life styles.

This particular volume is intended as a **quick read** popular history, an *introduction* to the histories, cultures, societies, arts, literatures, etc., and peoples of New Mexico. Structure is an integral part of the work and a conscientious effort has been made to keep units of information in close proximity on the printed pages. (Consequently some pages might give the appearance of having "gaps" but the reader is assured the blank spaces aren't a signal of missing information). There are **SUBJECT** headings to introduce each item; **TIMELINE** items establish **comparative history perspectives** into what was happening outside New Mexico during a particular period; **PROFILE** signals short biographies. The ANNOTATED BIBLIOGRAPHY at the end of the *Multi-History* is for readers who wish to explore more widely. Emphasis from **bold** or *italicized* script is from the present author. The GLOSSARY contains definitions of Spanish and other terms that might not often be encountered by the general reader, and the INDEX is the quickest way to locate a desired item. The HALL OF FAME listing is an effort to recognize various individuals for their accomplishments, some of them heroic while others are representative of worthwhile behavior. Some of the author's favorite works can be found in the RECOMMENDED BOOKS AND AUTHORS OF NEW MEXICO.

It is no exaggeration to say this book had its genesis when I read about Pablo Apodaca and his hand-to-claw fight with a bear in the Seboyeta (Cebolleta) mountains. I was in elementary school at the time and I had no idea of who the author C.F. Lummis was. I knew next to nothing of New Mexican history but, striving toward optimism, now Lummis and his engaging *A New Mexico David* are a part of this inclusive *Multi-History.*

All books have a story of their own and this volume is no exception. Despite the "slings and arrows of outrageous machinations," if I may paraphrase The Bard, the *Multi-History* is a reality thanks to the efforts of many people, not the least of which have been various culture groups and their leaders but also printing professionals like Stan Anglen and Mike Bridge. While many individuals offered encouragement for this volume, I am convinced our *Multi-History* would never have seen the light of day had it not been for J. Ronald *(Capitán)* Vigil, formerly of the Office of Cultural Affairs. His efforts to create the Hispanic Cultural Center, the Hispanic Cultural Center Press, and this *Multi-History* are perhaps inextricable from each other but I am fully aware this history might never have become a reality if *Capitán* had been lacking in commitment to the people and State of New Mexico, the HCC, or the publication of this book. As always, the poet expresses our innermost feelings with the grandest sensitivity:

> *There was a time when meadow, grove, and stream,*
> *The earth and every common sight*
> *To me did seem the glory and freshness of a dream.*
> *It is not now as it has been of yore,*
> *Turn wheresoever I may, by night or day,*
> *The things which I have seen I now can see no more...*
> *The clouds that gather round the setting sun*
> *Do take a sober colouring from an eye*
> *That has kept watch oer man's mortality...*
> *At length the man perceives it die away*
> *And fade into the light of common day...*
> *Though nothing can bring back the hour*
> *Of splendor in the grass, of glory in the flower,*
> *To me the meanest flower that blows can give*
> *Thoughts that do often lie too deep for tears.*

> *W. Wordsworth*

Drawing by George Berry

PRECONTACT

Ca. 12,000-10,000 B.C.

A group of *Amerinds* known as the **SANDÍA** people is thought to be the earliest residents of N.M. Traditional beliefs of the Pueblo people teach that humanity emerged from the earth via a beautiful lake in a place referred to as *Shibapu*. **Joe Sando** tells us that the Ancients, led by their *caciques,* war chiefs, and the Great Spirit, traveled south to many places (in what is now called North America) and some settled in (what is now called) the Four Corners area. In time their way of life spreads throughout the land.

Ca. 10,000-9,000 B.C.

Amerind hunters referred to as **CLOVIS** people roam N.M. in search of mammoth, bison, and other game animals.

Ca. 10,000-500 B.C.

The **COCHISE** people are thought to be the first cultivators of corn, squash, and beans, the first systematized agriculture in the Southwest. It is believed the Cochise people lived in permanent settlements, that they wove baskets and at some point in time raised tobacco.

Ca. 9,000-8,000 B.C.

The Ice Age ends and the Amerind **FOLSOM** people flourish throughout the Southwest.

Drawing by George Berry

TIMELINE

1200 B. C.: The Phoenicians make contact with a people in a "remote" country they refer to as *Hispalis* (Spain). The people they call *Hispani*.

800 B.C.: The various Greek city-states are emerging.

500 B.C.: The Greek city-states are at the height of their power and culture.

236 B.C.: Carthaginians led by Hamilcar Barca and his son-in-law Hrasdrubal, in which group is Hamilcar's nine-year-old son Hannibal, arrive in Spain with a large army and war elephants. Hannibal takes charge of the army at the age of 26 and declares war on Rome, the beginning of the Second Punic War.

201 B.C.: Rome conquers Hispalis, which becomes Hispaniarium then *Hispania* (modern España, Spain). In time Spain becomes the most latinized country in Europe after Rome itself. Rome is now dominant in the western Mediterranean.

146 B.C.: Rome is master of the Mediterranean world.

[Greek and Roman cultures lay the foundation for what comes to be known as Western civilization.]

Anno Domini

Ca. 1-700 A.D.

ANASAZI, thought to be ancestors of the modern Pueblos, elevate weaving to a fine art while they also produce utensils, sandals, clothing and baskets.

Ca. 300-1400

MOGOLLON culture is characterized by early pit house architecture and highly artistic pottery.

TIMELINE

Barbaric tribes of Vandals, Angles [from which the modern term "Anglos" is derived; the Angles settled in eastern England in the fifth century A.D.; the name England is derived from *Englaland*, "land of the Angles," as opposed to "land of the Saxons," a rival group; and English (from Englisc) means "of the Angles"], **Saxons, Goths,** etc. destroy the Roman Empire, plunging Europe into the **Dark Ages.** The barbarians especially target libraries and destroy all books.

378: Romans are defeated at Adrianople.

410: Alaric's army sacks Rome.

455: Gaiseric and the Vandals sack Rome. Odoacer (Odovacar) deposes Romulus Augustulus, the last Roman emperor in the West.

Ca. 700-1300

Anasazi culture reaches its zenith and is referred to as the **CHACO** civilization. Trade for seashells, parrot feathers, etc., is carried on with populations far to the south. Horizontal masonry appears at some point in time, as do the bow and arrow.

711-1493

TIMELINE

711: A force of 12,000 Moslems (Muslims), **Arabs, Berbers,** and **Syrians** led by the Berber chieftain **Tarik** land in the badly divided Visigothic kingdom of Spain and defeat the army of **Roderick,** the last Visigothic king. **Musa,** Governor of Moslem Africa, joins him with a larger army and within seven years virtually all of **Iberia** is under Moslem rule. Spain is now under the rule of the **Caliph of Damascus** with **Saracens** in charge of its destiny.

718: **Pelayo,** King of Asturias and first of the Christian kings bent on reconquest of their country, meet and defeat a Moslem army at **Covadonga.** The Christians have little to resist with except their independence of spirit and faith in their Christian God. Most of their former country is now a frontier and the people, nobility and peasant alike, live the hard life of frontiersmen. When the tomb of **Saint James** is discovered in Compostela in northwestern Spain, St. James becomes the country's patron and symbol, mounted on a great white horse and wielding his sword, of the Reconquest.

758: **Abdu-r-Rahman I** of the **Omayyad dynasty** raises a small army, defeats the emir Yusuf of Córdova and establishes the Omayyad dynasty in Spain, now independent from Damascus where the Abbasids had overthrown the Omayyads. Because of his military and administrative abilities Abdu-r-Rahman I stabilizes the various kingdoms.

912: By the time of **Abdu-r-Rahman III,** Moslem Spain is the richest, most cultured and powerful state in all Europe. The Moslems bring in their highly developed culture characterized by aspects like their language [which influences the Spanish language], the hot-blooded Arabian horse and the Moslem "horse culture," to items like paper which replaces the more expensive and cumbersome papyrus. They introduce practices like bathing [Europeans of the day didn't believe in or practice it; Queen Elizabeth of England was later to "brag" that she had taken a bath only twice in her life] as well as the concept of zero along with higher mathematics, advanced irrigation techniques, a highly developed love for poetry and books on subjects like religion, astronomy, law, medicine, philosophy, architecture, etc. Christian, Jewish, and Moslem scholars work together without problems. Christians and Jews have to pay a small additional tax but otherwise people are allowed to live their lives without persecution. In time the Moslems build the Alcázar in Seville, the incomparable Alhambra in Granada, and the great Mosque of Córdova with its 21 gates and 1,293 columns of jasper and porphyry. All become famous throughout the Moslem world. The city of Córdova has 200,000 houses, 900 bathhouses, and 600 mosques. Libraries are built and the famous school of translators at Toledo brings in great works from Greek, Roman, and Arabic writers (books which later prompt the Renaissance; they had been destroyed in the rest of Europe with the destruction of the Roman Empire by the barbaric tribes).

1000: The famous general **Almanzor** has battled Christian forces to a standstill but toward the end of the century Christians are achieving military successes. At this time emerges *El Cid*, **Rodrigo Díaz de Vivar,** the most famous knight of the Middle Ages.

1031: The Omayyad caliphate comes to an end and Moslem Spain disintegrates into various independent, often rival, kingdoms which enable Christians to battle them more successfully. As territory is reconquered from the Moslems it is awarded to various individuals as **land grants**.

1150s: The military orders of the **Knights of Santiago** and the **Knights of Calatrava** are created. Fortified towns become a necessity and in León the Cortes parliament is created [thus Spain became the first country to experience a measure of democracy, much sooner than any other nation in Europe] to advise the king. Other kingdoms follow the example.

1212: Moslems are defeated at **Navas de Tolosa**.

1340: Christian forces win the day in a decisive battle at the Salado River.
January, 1492: Christian armies under Ferdinand and Isabel conquer Granada, the last

3

Moslem stronghold in Spain. The country is now united politically and religiously. [Spain is the first European nation to be so united.] The year of 1492, the dawn of what would be described as the "Modern Age" and Spain's "Golden Century," is exceptionally notable for other achievements: Cardinal Francisco Jiménez de Cisneros (founder of the University of Alcalá and later to be Regent of Spain) becomes the confessor of Queen Isabel; Antonio de Nebrija publishes his grammar of the Spanish language (the first for any modern European language); Juan del Encina presents his first drama, becoming "Father of Spanish Theater;" and one of the greatest achievements in the history of mankind, discovery of the Americas by Cristóbal Colón on October 12th. Spain now turns its attention to the "New World" discovered by Columbus.

1493: Pope Alexander VI decides on a line to divide lands discovered by Spain and Portugal, with the injunction that *natives of all lands should not be exterminated but rather assimilated into the Christian fold.*

Ca. 750

Pikuri, "Those Who Paint," **Picurís Pueblo** is thought to have been founded around this period

TIMELINE

771 - 814: By this era of **Charlemagne** (Charles the Great) Europe has worked its way out of the Dark Ages. Charlemagne, a real life Christian king, and his paladin knights expand the **Carolingian Empire** and establish the foundations of medieval Christian unity. [For whatever the reasons, speakers of English are often more aware of the imaginary King Arthur and his imaginary knights of the round table than of historical Charlemagne and his authentic paladins.]

800s: **Raiders** known as Norsemen, Northmen, and Vikings, are coming out of Scandinavian countries in their streamlined "dragon ships" to sow a reign of destruction in coastal villages and towns where they loot anything valuable and burn what they can't carry off. They generally defeat small local armies and after decapitating their victims they clean out their skulls in order to drink a toast which they refer to as **SKOAL!** and then escape in their dragon ships before large military forces can engage them. The Norseman are the terror of coastal Europeans (except in Moslem Spain where the raiders are so terribly defeated they never attack any part of Spain again).

Ca. 950-1000

Tiwa people migrate to the northern and southern areas of the Río Grande Valley.

Ca. 1000-1450

Tua-Tah, "Our Village," **Taos Pueblo** is founded and built during this period. *[Hlauuma* (north house) and *Hlaukwima* (south house) are sometimes described as the oldest continuously inhabited communities in the USA.]

Ca. 1150-1250

Keresan people move from Chaco Canyon into the Río Grande area. The people of [present] Santa Ana and Zía migrate to the Río Puerco area.

Ca. 1150-1350

The "golden age" of Pueblo culture is taking place during these years. An identifiable culture, religion, and government evolve in the Pueblo city-states.

Ca. 1200

Cultures of the **Pueblo people, the first pioneers** [of what is now called the Southwest] is highly developed in independent **city-states** along the Río Grande River and its tributaries.

TIMELINE

Monasticism is a vital part of European life. Monks are considered the heroes of Christian civilization because of their dedication to God and a spiritual life based on asceticism, mystical experience, and denial of worldly pleasures. Because of their stature they are also responsible for the intellectual, social, cultural, and medical needs of Europeans.

Ca. 250-350: **Saint Anthony**, a well-to-do Egyptian peasant who gave all his worldly possessions to the poor, establishes the basic tenets of eremitical monasticism when he becomes a solitary hermit in pursuit of spirituality. Without intending it, Anthony and other monks attract followers.

Ca. 290-346: **Saint Pachomius** organizes communities of monks and writes the first rules, which emphasize obedience and manual labor, for them.

306-337: **Constantine** is the first Román Emperor to become a Christian. He also builds a new capital city, **Byzantium,** in the eastern portion of the Empire which in time is renamed Constantinople [modern lstanbul].

Ca. 329-379: **Saint Basil**, a Palestinian, visits Egypt and establishes a monastic life that emphasizes fellowship and work. Monastic communities come to be considered as the ideal Christian society.

378-395: During the rule of Theodosius, **Christianity** becomes the official religion of the Empire.

Ca. 480-543: **Saint Benedict**, born to a noble Roman family, founds a monastic house at Monte Cassino where he writes the *"Benedictine Rule"* which is adopted by most monastic groups in the Western world. Benedict promotes a disciplined existence based on poverty, chastity, obedience, etc., and de-emphasizes the eastern influence of severe fasting and self-inflicted torments.

910: Duke **William of Aquitaine** founds the abbey of **Cluny** in Burgundy in eastern France in an effort to combat abuses that had crept into monastic life. **Cluniac reforms** stress the need for work, replacing manual labor with the copying of manuscripts, more community worship and less private prayer. The Abbot of Cluny was responsible for supervising the hundreds of Cluniac monasteries in an effort to promote rigid discipline and the highest possible Christian standards.

1054: The final separation occurs between Roman Catholicism and Greek Orthodoxy.

1098: Dissatisfied with what they consider to be a lack of strict discipline at their Benedictine monastery, a group of monks found the **Cistercian** order at Citeaux in Burgundy and spreads rapidly from France into Italy, Spain, England, Germany, and the eastern European countries. In 1113 **Bernard of Clairvaux** joins the Cistercians, becomes the abbot of the monastery at Clairvaux, and then goes on to be the most important religious personality of the 12th century. By 1150 there are more than three hundred Cistercian monasteries. Because of their dedication to labor and agriculture, the virgin lands they occupy become fantastically successful farms and vineyards, many monasteries becoming quite wealthy.

1098-1179: **Hildegard of Bingen** is the abbess of a convent for nuns at Disibodenberg in Germany. During her lifetime she writes books on science, theology, philosophy, medicine, etc., paints, and composes more than 70 songs.

1170-1221: **Dominic de Guzmán**, a Spanish priest, founds the *Order of Preachers*, the **Dominicans** (called *Black Friars* because of the color of their robes) in 1215. They take vows of poverty but their major emphasis is learning and effective preaching to combat heresy.

1182-1286: **Saint Francis of Assisi**, born to a wealthy Italian merchant family, founds the *Order of Friars Minor*, the **Franciscans** (*Grey Friars*). They take vows of poverty; they preach, work, and beg for their food. **Saint Clare**, an aristocratic lady also from Assisi, founds the **Poor Clares**, the Franciscan female group.

1200: The **Beguines**, communities of devout women dedicated to prayer, dwelling together in poverty and begging or working at menial tasks, originate in the Low Countries and become strong in the Rhineland area of Germany. They take no vows and are free to leave the group at any time.

1491-1556: **Ignatius of Loyola,** a Spanish nobleman, founds the *Society of Jesus,* the **Jesuits**, who become the most important instrument of the Catholic Reformation. They pursue three basic activities: establishing schools in which are employed humanistic methods (by 1600 they are the most famous educators in Europe); propagating the Faith around the world; working to restore Catholicism in Germany and eastern Europe.

1515-1582: **Saint Teresa of Avila,** a Spanish Carmelite nun and proponent of mysticism, founds a new order of barefoot Carmelite nuns.

1522: **Martín Luther** organizes a "reformed" church which begins the movement known as the **Reformation**. Civil authorities in various German states take charge of reforms. **Lutheranism** begins to spread. **Ulrich Zwingli** (1484-1531) begins the Reformation in Switzerland. **Anabaptists** favor more radical reforms like complete separation of Church and State.

1532: **Pope Clement VII** will not give **Henry VIII** of England an annulment of his marriage to Catherine of Aragón so the following year he has the Archbishop of Canterbury annul the marriage. Henry declares himself head of the Church of England and humanist protesters like Bishop John Fisher, Chancellor Sir Thomas More, etc., are murdered on Henry's orders through the *Star Chamber*. Henry (who has been accused of hanging some 72,000 persons during his reign, 1509-1547) confiscates all church lands and possessions, selling them off and enriching himself further.

[**Star Chamber** courts are generally carefully hidden in English history. They were set up by Henry VII, conducted in secret, used torture to extract confessions, there was no jury, the accused were not permitted to see any evidence presented against them, records were either never written down or immediately destroyed, and its victims were beheaded. By comparison the "notorious" **Spanish Inquisition**, which kept records and had to abide by certain established rules which were typical of the historical era, could almost be described as a reputable tribunal.]

1536: **John Calvin** (1509-1564), a Frenchmen, becomes perhaps the most important theologian and organizer of the **Protestant** ("protester") movement. **Calvinism** becomes the militant international form of Protestantism.

[Friars from Europe will become an integral part of New Mexican history. Catholic Spain, *"Defender of the Faith,"* and her Hispanic people will be targeted with the **Black Legend** by non-Catholics for centuries to come, thereby becoming an important factor in American and New Mexican history.]

Ca. 1250-1400

In the **Zuñi** area alone it is estimated that Amerind villages containing a total of 13,000 rooms are built and abandoned, indicating a very mobile society.

Ca. 1275-1300

The **Four Corners** area is vacated.

Ca. 1300

Acoma [sometimes described as the oldest continuously inhabited town in the present USA] is settled around this period.

Nambé, "*Mound of Earth in the Corner*," is thought to have been founded during this period.

Ca. 1300s

Po-Woh-Ge-Oweenge, "Where the Water Cuts Down Through," **San Ildefonso Pueblo** is
  founded around this period.

1350-1700

The maximum expansion of Pueblo Indian culture is experienced during this period. By 1700 there is also
  the beginning of an enduring alliance with the Spanish against viking tribes.

1400-1525

An Athabascan people later to be known as **Apache** and **Navajo** enter the (present) Southwest.

T I M E L I N E

**1444-1450: Printing with movable metal type becomes a reality during this period and
immediately makes a permanent impact on European life.** Johannes Gutenberg **of Mainz,
Germany, plays an important role in developing the final process.**

1455 or 1456: **Gutenberg's Bible** is the first real book printed from movable type.

1460s: **Printing presses** spread throughout the **Holy Román Empire** and then throughout
Europe.

1500: **Venice** becomes known as a **printing center** because it has nearly 100 professional
printers who have produced almost two million volumes. There are more than 1,000 printers in
Europe, they have printed more than 40,000 books (some eight to ten million copies). Perhaps
half are of a religious nature, then Greek and Latin classics, etc., and popular romances. Books
encourage the development of research and the pursuit of knowledge but also stimulate an
expanding reading public. Printing becomes a basic European industry.

1450-1550: This period of European history is described as the **Renaissance** ("rebirth").
Beginning in **Italy**, especially the city of **Florence**, then spreading to the rest of Europe, the
Renaissance is characterized by an intense interest in Greek and Roman cultures, their writers
and artists, but also emphasizes the *individual* and development of all his abilities. Towering
figures of the age include Petrarch, Leonardo da Vinci, Michelangelo, Lorenzo Medici (il
Magnifico), Isabella d'Este, Machiavelli, Boticelli, Donatello, Raphael, Jan van Eyck, Francisco
de Vitoria, Albrecht Durer, Guillaume Dufay, Garcilaso de la Vega, Desiderius Erasmus,
Thomas More, Gonzalo de Córdova (el Gran Capitán), etc.

Ca. 1450-1850

A climactic period known as the "Little Ice Age" brings colder temperatures to most parts of the Northern Hemisphere.

SPAIN
1492

Christopher Columbus (Cristóbal Colón, **Admiral of the Ocean Sea)** and the Spanish crews of three ships, led by the **Pinzón** brothers **Martín and Vicente,** sail west in hopes of reaching the Orient. Instead they stumble onto the continents of the Americas, changing the course of human history for all time.

[J.A. Crow has written that the *"discovery of America represents the greatest revolution ever effected in the history of mankind"* because it shifted emphasis from the East to the West, ended the Middle Ages and began the modern era. It ended the *"inward, mystical life"* in favor of exploration which would take humanity to the stars, changed the value of money and gave birth to capitalism in a new world where men of action and enterprise would replace men of birth as leaders of society.]

Almost immediately a liberal Spanish immigration policy to America is enacted: **Catholic Christians** are eligible for free passage, they are exempt from taxes, they will be granted title to all lands they cultivate for four years, that will be supplied with stock and grain from the Royal Treasury, there will be no tax on imports or exports. (Foreigners, Jews, and Moors are prohibited from even visiting the New World.)

1493

Pope Alexander VI (a Spaniard of the Borgia family) proclaims that all lands discovered west of a line of demarcation 100 leagues beyond the Azores would belong to Spain and in a second bull declared that *"all islands and mainlands whatsoever found and to be found in sailing or travel toward the west or south"* would also be Spanish on the **condition that aboriginal populations be Christianized and not harmed.**

1494

King John II of Portugal, head of the best navy in the world of the day, negotiates the **Treaty of Tordesillas** with Fernando and Isabel of Spain: the line of demarcation is moved to the meridian 370 leagues west of the Azores.

[While it was unknown at the time, moving the line so far to the west put Brazil into the Portuguese sphere of influence.]

1500

Pueblo people speak in seven languages that belong to four language groups: Tanoan, Keresan, Zuñi, and Uto-Aztecan.

1503

1503: **Amerigo Vespucci**, a Florentine clerk who travels to the New World, writes his *Mundus Novus* description of the new lands. Because the work is written in Latin it circulates all over Europe and Amerigo becomes "famous."

1507: A German cartographer by the name of **Martín Waldseemüler** publishes a map of the newly discovered lands and labels them America in honor of Amerigo Vespucci. The name catches on and the Western Hemisphere becomes known as *America* for all time.

[The journals of **Christopher Columbus** aren't published immediately so the new lands he discovered bear his name only in the country of **Columbia**.]

1504

Queen Isabel (Elizabeth) **of Spain** decrees that the grant made by Pope Alexander VI obligates the Spanish Crown and all its citizens to convert the Indians *"...to our holy catholic faith, to teach and instruct them in good morals, and to do it with great diligence ... and that they should not permit or give an occasion that the Indian citizens and dwellers of the said islands and firm land, acquired or to be acquired, receive any harm in their persons or in their possessions, even more they must order that they should be well and justly treated, and if they have received any harm they should amend it and see to it that in no way they should go beyond what is urged and commanded to us by the apostolic Letters...And I say and declare that this is my will...And so that this be firm and there be no doubt ... I sign it with my name before witnesses and I order it to be sealed with my seal.* (sig.) **I, the Queen Isabel**

1516

The Dominican Fray **Bartolomé de Las Casas** is the first individual to be appointed (by regent Cardinal **Francisco Jiménez de Cisneros**) to the post of *Protector of the Indians,* the Catholic clergy thus becoming the first protectors of American Indians according to C.R. Cutter. [This office is to be a factor in the government of N.M.]

1519-1521

Hernán Cortés and a handful of Spaniards lead a number of Mexican Indian nations, especially the Tlaxcalans, against their ancient enemies, the **Aztecs** of Mexico City, and finally conquer them. Cortés asks the King to exempt the Tlaxcalans from tribute, slavery or mandatory servitude for all time because of their invaluable services to the Crown. The King so decrees.

[Some **Tlaxcalans** were to be in Oñate's expedition in 1598, taking up

Hernán Cortés
Courtesy Museum of New
Mexico #112517

residence in the **Analco,** *"across the water,"* section of Santa Fe as vassals of the King.]

When **Motolinía** and the other first missionaries enter Mexico City, Cortés declares a celebration during which he and all his Captains kneel to kiss the hand of each holy man. The Mexican warriors are amazed to see their conquerors kneeling to a group of men who are so obviously impoverished and Cortés thus makes the point of the importance of Christianity.

1533

TIMELINE

The *University of Mexico City* **is founded, the first university in the Americas.**

1536

It is conjecture that **Alvar Nuñez Cabeza de Vaca, Esteban the Moor, Andrés Dorantes, and Alonso de Castillo Maldonado** wander through parts of southern New Mexico before reaching Culiacán, Mexico. Conjecture notwithstanding, their reports give rise to the legend of the *Seven Cities of Cíbola.*

[A medieval legend had it that seven Spanish bishops fled Spain with their congregations because of the Arab conquest of their native land. They founded the cities of Antilia (hence the name **Antilles**) somewhere in the Western Ocean. After the discovery of Mexico and its fabulous riches it was thought that perhaps the Seven Cities were located in what is now referred to as New Mexico.]

The story of Alvar Nuñez C. de Baca is first printed in 1542 in Zamora, Spain.

1539

TIMELINE

1539: The first book is printed in the New World. **Bishop Zurnárraga** causes a bilingual (Spanish and Nahuatl) catechism to be published in order to facilitate Christianization of native inhabitants.

[American publishing thus begins 18 years after Hispanics conquer Mexico, 47 years after the landing of Columbus, and it is done in the Spanish and Aztec languages.]

EXPLORATION

Fray **Marcos de Niza,** a Franciscan who had been with Pizarro in Perú, and **Esteban** lead a small expedition of discovery to **Cíbola.** Esteban arrives at Zuñi (Hawikuh), where he is killed, but Fray Marcos believes he has discovered cities of gold. He returns to Mexico with his reports and a well-equipped expedition is organized to investigate.

INTERNATIONAL LAW

Francisco de Vitoria lectures at the University of Salamanca. He espouses the philosophy that the men and women of the New World are free people who can't be enslaved by a genuinely Christian society merely because it has the weapons to do so.

1540-42
Coronado Expedition

While in search of the fabled riches of the *Seven Cities of Cíbola* and *Grand Quivira*, **Francisco Vásquez de Coronado** and members of his expeditionary force [which includes at least three women according to H.E. Bolton: **Francisca de Hozes,** wife of Alonso Sánchez; **María Maldonado,** wife of Juan de Paradinas; Sra. **Caballero,** wife of Lope de Caballero] discover and/or explore parts of (what is now called) northern Mexico, Arizona, the Grand Canyon, the Colorado River, California, New Mexico, Texas, Oklahoma, and Kansas. They are the first Europeans to meet the Pueblo people, see vast herds of bison, and draw back the curtain of what is now the Southwest.

Coronado's feat of discovery and adventure leaves an indelible stamp on the map of the Americas because he blazes trails that others will follow and discovers lands where others will live. (Coronado's force and De Soto's expedition coming from the east get within 300 miles of each other.) Coronado's headquarters are thought to have been at **Tiguex,** present-day Bernalillo, New Mexico.

Pedro Castañeda is chronicler of the Coronado expedition and documents all events, (which take place some 48 years after Columbus lands in the New World.) He records that the Spaniards are impressed with the Pueblo Indians; of the Zuñis he writes: *"There is no drunkenness among them, nor sodomy nor sacrifices, neither do they eat human flesh nor steal, but they are usually at work."* Missionaries Fr. **Juan Padilla,** Fr. Luis de Escalona (Ubeda), and Fr. Juan de la Cruz remain behind to teach Christianity but when Coronado returns to Mexico they are soon martyred by the Amerinds.

[Stewart L. Udall has written that *"1542 was the apex of the Spanish age of discovery"* because Spain had expeditions in progress that stretched halfway around the globe *from California to New Mexico to Kansas to North Carolina to the Mississippi and Amazon Rivers to the pampas of southern Brazil to Chile's Atacama Desert to Luzon in the Philippine Islands, and back across the Pacific to the shores of Oregon.* He believes *"One must telescope two centuries of history ... to include the quests of Captain Cook, Vitus Bering, Lewis and Clark, Luis Vaez de Torres, and David Livingstone, consider them all as from a single nation and doing everything in a single year, to amass a list that can be compared with the achievements of **Spain's class of** 1542."* He further states these achievements haven't been properly *"recognized in North America"* because of the *"anti-Spanish blinders worn for so long by many students of history..."*]

1546

Francisco de Vitoria, a Dominican, dies in Spain but his theory and philosophy concerning the New World and its native inhabitants lay the groundwork for New World legal perspectives (and for *international law* according to L. Hanke). He is the first Spaniard to assert the papal grant of **Alexander VI** to Spain for conversion of the Indians has no temporal value. He declares that neither the Emperor nor the Pope own the whole world and therefore neither can require allegiance. War can't be waged against

Indians or unbelievers merely because they aren't Christians or refuse to become so. The Emperor may not seize Indian provinces, erect new governments, or levy taxes merely because he has the military power to do so, for that would be immoral and unworthy of a civilized nation. Spaniards may go to the Americas, travel and/or live there, so long as they do no harm to the Indians who reside there, just as Indians may do the same in Spain. Spaniards may preach the Gospel but Indians aren't required to accept it and must not be forced to do so. If Spaniards are attacked then war *"...in moderation and proportion..."* may be waged, which may also be done if Indian converts are persecuted by unconverted heathen. Spaniards may wage war to put a stop to practices like **human sacrifices** and **cannibalism**, thus protecting innocent victims from such practices, and they may help allies to fight their enemies if the allies so request. Spaniards may also prepare the Indians to function in the international community of nations, so long as it is to the benefit of the aborigines to do so.

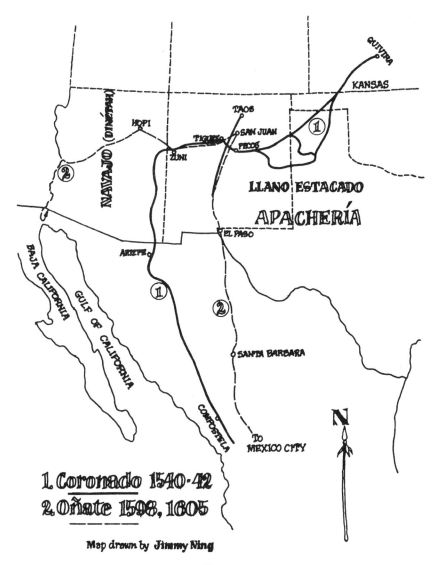

1. Coronado 1540-42
2. Oñate 1598, 1605

Map drawn by Jimmy Ning

15

1550-1551

Debates rage in Spain, as well as the Americas, as to Spanish responsibilities in the New World. [Debates of this nature were not to be characteristic of later powers like England, France, or the USA.] The learned and highly respected Dr. **Juan Ginés de Sepúlveda** writes a treatise, sponsored by Cardinal García de Loaysa of Seville and referred to as "*a service to God and King*," in which he shows why the wars waged in the Americas are justified because so many aboriginal societies revolve around abominations like **cannibalism and human sacrifice**.

Father **Bartolomé de Las Casas,** official *"Protector of the Indians"* who has had firsthand missionary experiences in the Indies, opposes Sepúlveda in favor of the Native American point of view: the conquest has no moral justification, it is laced with brutality unworthy of a Christian nation, and all licenses for expeditions should be revoked immediately until colonization can be effected by peace, Christian love and good example. He declares that American Indians compare favorably with the peoples of ancient times and that they are rational beings like Europeans. The two men debate the issues before the **Council of Fourteen** in Valladolid and at the end both claim victory.

[Father De Las Casas denigrated Spanish atrocities and defended Native American aboriginal populations in his writings which were then utilized by the enemies of Hispanics and Catholic Christians in Europe. No other country produced a champion like Bartolomé de Las Casas. The philosophies of Vitoria, Sepúlveda, and Las Casas are to be vital factors in New Mexican history.]

1572

1573

Royal Ordinances define conditions for exploration and settlement of new lands. J.M. Espinosa writes that because there is now awareness of brutalities perpetrated by military conquests, the Crown decrees that henceforth there shall be no more conquest but instead, pacification.

1581

Rodríguez/Chamuscado Expedition.

Missionaries led by Fr. **Agustín Rodríguez** and a few soldiers led by Francisco Sánchez Chamuscado go up the Río Grande Valley, making their headquarters at Puaray (Coronado's Tiguex, near the area of present Bernalillo, N.M.) When the soldiers depart for Mexico the missionaries, Fathers Rodríguez, López, and Santa María, remain behind to missionize but are quickly martyred by the Native Americans.

1582-1583

Espejo Expedition.

Wealthy **Antonio de Espejo** finances a small group for this *entrada* into New Mexico, with himself as commander, to ascertain the fate of missionaries who had remained behind the previous year. Up to 74 Pueblos are visited, including Zía, Jémez, Acoma, Zuñi, and the Moqui towns. (Espejo is credited as being the first to use the term *Nuevo México* and **Casilda de Anaya Espejo Valenciano,** wife of one of the soldiers, is among the first white women to enter N.M. after those with Coronado.)

TIMELINE

1589: **Reverend Richard Hakluyt** (1552?-1616), a member of the Virginia Company of London, compiles his *Principall Navigations, Voiages and Discoveries of the English Nation* **(enlarged to three volumes between 1598 and 1600).**

[**Stewart L. Udall** writes that Hakluyt, an *"evangelist patriot of immense persistence, imagination, and force"* became Europe's most successful **political propagandist** when he *"distorted Spain's great age of discovery and denigrated the character of her people"* with the **Black Legend of innate cruelty and depravity.** Because of *"his skill with words"* Hakluyt was able to *"convey the false impression that English exploration ran on a track parallel to that followed by Spain's great discoverers."* Reverend Hakluyt and his successors *"distorted 16th century history"* by glorifying English accomplishments which came much later than those of Spain. *"He altered the outlines of 16th century history by muddling events, dates, and the deeds of individual nations"* to the point that the achievements of Spain were all but lost in the **"European experience" propaganda** of *"an ongoing age of discovery"* in which England played the major role. The self-serving "European experience" concept *"gave a permanent distortion to Anglo-Saxon interpretation of 16th century events."* Because of this historical distortion, **Francis Drake** is often considered alongside the great Spanish explorers like Magellan and Cabrillo who were dead before Drake was even born. Many people have the *"mistaken impression that Walter Raleigh was the first European to attempt to plant colonies along the Atlantic coast when Spaniards had mounted much more vigorous colonizing efforts a half century earlier."* Udall asserts the *"Spanish Age of Discovery is an historical*

reality" and in 1600 *"not a single Anglo-Saxon was living in North America ... yet even in our time most Anglo-Saxons are convinced their ancestors were in the vanguard of the great pageant of New World exploration."*
Udall further states that American **historians out of New England,** men like Francis Parkman, Jared Sparks, John L. Motley, George Bancroft, Charles A. Beard, etc. (with a few exceptions like William H. Prescott or Herbert E. Bolton and his school of historians), *"adopted the anti-Spanish attitudes so popular in Britain"* and ignored Hispanic achievements or were influenced by Black Legend propaganda. This channeled American historiography into the mold that *"England was the mother country"* and nothing important happened unless accomplished by England or the USA.]

1590-1591
Sosa Expedition.

More than 170 men, women, and children travel to settle New Mexico under the leadership of **Gaspar Castaño de Sosa.** Many Pueblos are visited but no permanent settlement is made because a detachment of soldiers appears and arrests Sosa for entering New Mexico without proper authority. With Sosa in shackles, the entire group is returned to Mexico.

1595
Leyva Bonilla/Gutiérrez Humaña Expedition.

After subduing rebellious Indians in Nueva Vizcaya (present-day Durango and Chihuahua) a small party led by these two soldiers continues up the Río Grande valley and settles in the pueblo of (present-day) San Ildefonso. They hunt for precious metals then move out into the plains where Gutiérrez kills Leyva in a dispute over command. Some of the Indians in the group desert (including Jusepillo Gutiérrez, who is later found by Oñate at San Juan). Indians attack the party and all but two are slain.

1598-1608
Juan de Oñate is Governor

COLONIZATION
Colonists going into the northern lands referred to as *la Nueva México* have already waited a year for the Oñate expedition to get started. They are spread over a 30 mile area and rumor has it even the soldiers are ready to abandon the effort. Doña **Eufemia Sosa de Peñalosa,** wife of the Royal Ensign, issues a call for the troops and asks them:
Tell me noble soldiers, where is that courage which you promised when you enlisted in this noble cause? You promised nothing could resist the might of your arms but now you wish to turn back and ignobly desert? What explanation could you have for this conduct if you consider yourselves men? For Shame! Such are not the actions of Spaniards! Even though everything else might be lost there

is yet land on the bank of some mighty river where we might raise a great city and thus immortality. To such a place we can go and it is better to halt and rest than to retrace our steps and weave upon ourselves and our posterity a stigma which can never be erased...

1598

April 30, 1598: After exasperating and expensive delays **Juan de Oñate** leads an expedition that enables him to claim northern lands [now the American Southwest] for Spain [from the area of present day Juárez/El Paso]. The entire northern lands are called **"New Mexico."**

PROFILE

Juan de Oñate

HEROIC FOUNDER OF NEW MEXICO

1524: (Juan's father) **Cristóbal de Oñate**, a Basque, arrives in New Spain. He isn't flamboyant but works toward his goals with steady determination in the service of king, country, and Christianity.

1546: With several other energetic Basque partners, Oñate discovers rich silver deposits and founds the town of **Zacatecas**.

1550: Zacatecas is second in importance only to Mexico City. Many fortune seekers enter the Zacatecas mining area, some of them destitute, and Cristóbal grubstakes them all, friend and stranger alike.

1549 or 1550: Cristóbal marries **Catalina de Salazar** y de la Cadena. In time they have seven children.

1550 or 1552: **Juan de Oñate is** born in the Pánuco area of Zacatecas. (Some sources say he had a twin brother.) The Oñate family spends as much time in Mexico City as in Zacatecas so Juan becomes familiar with sophisticated urban life as well as the challenges of a raw mining frontier. Juan acquires a good education.

1550: The **Chichimeca Wars** begin (and last almost half a century). Juan often accompanies his father Cristóbal on expeditions against the cannibalistic Chichimecas who routinely torture and scalp their captives before decapitating them. Captive children are forced to drink the blood and eat the brains of their murdered parents who are then roasted on spits and eaten by the tribesmen.

October 6, 1567: Cristóbal de Oñate dies.

1572(?)-1792: Juan is now in command of expeditions against hostile Chichimecas. He also pays all expenses out of his own pocket.

1574: Charcas is one of the mining centers believed to have been opened by Juan de Oñate. As new settlements sprout up wealthy patrons like the Oñate family spend millions of pesos to finance military campaigns. They also sponsor the construction of churches, missions, monasteries, etc., so they continually serve their Church and Crown.

1588: Juan marries **Isabel de Tolosa Cortés Moctezuma,** granddaughter of the incomparable *conquista*dor Hernán Cortés and Isabel Moctezuma, daughter of the emperor Moctezuma.

1590: A son is born to Juan and Isabel. He is named **Cristóbal** de Naharriondo Pérez Oñate y Cortés Moctezuma. In 1598 (or 1599) a daughter, **María** *(Mariquita)* de Oñate y Cortés Moctezuma is born.

1592: Soldier and frontiersman **Miguel Caldera** discovers a rich bonanza at **San Luis Potosí.** When the time comes to establish the municipality there **Viceroy Velasco** assigns Juan de Oñate to preside over the founding. Juan organizes a municipal council, enforces royal mining ordinances, adjudicates claims, sees to the welfare of Indians who settle in the area, etc. His skill in civil duties impresses Velasco who believes that Oñate is ready for greater challenges.

September 21, 1595: Juan de Oñate signs a formal contract to colonize New Mexico. Among others, blood-related family members like the **Zaldívar** clan, also of Basque origin, become part of the expedition.

The momentous event is marked and consecrated by a **Thanksgiving** ceremony: a solemn high mass is celebrated with everyone in attendance then with the soldiers donned in shining armor for the occasion, on horseback and in military formation, Oñate reads the **official act of possession** which begins:

> *In the name of the most holy Trinity and of the eternal Unity, Deity, and Majesty, God the Father, the Son, and the Holy Ghost ... and in honor of His most holy and venerable Mother, the holy Virgin Mary, our Lady, Gate of Heaven, Ark of the Covenant, in whom the manna of heaven, the divine rod of justice and His law of grace and love were placed, as the Mother of God, sun, moon, north star, the Guide and Advocate of all human kind ... I, don Juan de Oñate, Governor, Captain General and Adelantado of New Mexico, and of its kingdoms ... do take possession of this land*

this 30th day of April, the feast of the Ascension of our Lord, in the year 1598...
There is much merrymaking for the rest of the day which closes with the enactment of an original drama written by Captain **Farfán de los Godos,** performed by and for members of the expedition.

[Thanks to Capt. **Gaspar de Villagrá,** who chronicles all events in the form of an epic poem, New Mexico is the *only colony in history* to have an epic like "The Iliad," "The Odyssey" or "The Aeneid" as a source for its incipient annals.

According to R.L. Nostrand, one of the promised benefits for the colonists who stay in New Mexico for five years is to be entitled to use **Don (Doña)** (*de origin noble:* **of noble origin**) with their name.]

PIONEERS
The following are some of the people who accompany Oñate, many of them with families:

Stephen Gallegos, Illustrator
Atlanta, Georgia

A: Pablo de Aguilar; Araujo; Ascencio de Archuleta; Ayarde;

B: Dionisio de Bañuelos; Bartol; Juan Benitez; Bibero; Juan Gutiérrez de Bocanegra; Juan Pérez de Bustillo (with his wife, María de la Cruz, a son, and three daughters);

[It is a popular misconception that Spanish women didn't colonize with their men. H.H. Bancroft states there were "...400 men, 130 of whom were accompanied by their families." Yet D.J. Boorstin and B.M. Kelley tell us in their popular classroom textbook: *"Nearly all"* Spaniards who came to the Americas were males. *"Unmarried girls"* weren't *"allowed to come to America alone"* so Spanish settlers *"married Indian women."*]
C: Cesar Ortíz Cadimo; Juan Camacho; Esteban Carabajal; Carrera; Juan de Caso; Bernabé de las Casas; Castillo; Juan Catalán; Cavanillas; Gregorio César; Cordero; Juan Cortés; Marcos Cortés;

D: Pedro Sánchez Damiero; Juan Díaz; Juan Pérez de Donis;

E: Felipe Escalte; Juan Escarramal; Marcelo de Espinosa;
F: Marcos Farfán de los Godos; Juan Fernández; Manuel Francisco;
G: Alvaro García; Francisco García; Francisco García; Marcos García; Simón García; Luis Gascon; Bartolomé González; Juan González; Juan Griego; Guevara; Francisco Guillén; Antonio Gutiérrez;

H: Gerónimo de Heredia; Antonio Hernández; Francisco Hernández; Gonzalo Hernández; Pedro Hernández; Antonio Conde de Herrera; Cristóbal de Herrera; Juan de Herrera; Alonzo Nuñez de Hinojosa;

Stephen Gallegos, Illustrator
Atlanta, Georgia

I: León de Isati;

J: Jiménez;

K:

L: Diego Landin; Francisco de Ledesma; Juan de León; Domingo de Lizana; Cristóbal López; Juan López; Alonso Lucas; Lucio;

M: Mallea; Francisco Márquez; Gerónimo Márquez; Hernán Martín; Juan Martínez; Juan Medel; Medina; Monroi; Alonso Gómez Montesinos; Baltazar de Monzon; Morales; Juan Moran; Munera;

N: Naranjo; Diego Nuñez;

0: Juan de Olague; Cristóbal de Oñate; Juan de Ortega; Ortiz;

P: Regundo Paladin; Simón de Paz; Juan de Pedraza; Pereya; Simón Pérez; Juan Pinero; Francisco de Posa y Peñalosa;

Q: Alonso de Quesada; Francisco Guillén de Quesada;

R: Martín Ramiréz; Juan Rangel; Rascón; Pedro de los Reyes; Pedro de Ribera; Alonso del Rio; Diego Robledo; Francisco Robledo; Pedro Robledo (*the first colonist to die in N.M.*) with his wife, Catalina López; Pedro Rodríguez; Sebastián Rodríguez; Bartolomé Romeros; Moreno de la Rua; Capt. Ruiz; Juan Ruiz;

S: Lorenzo Salado; Juan de Salas; Alonso Sánchez; Cristóbal Sánchez; Francisco Sánchez; Antonio Sarinana; Juan de Segura; Serrano; Sosa;

T: Capt. Tabora;

V. Francisco Vaca; Varela; Francisco Vásquez; Jorge de la Vega; Juan Velarde; Francisco Vido; Juan de Victoria Vido; Gaspar Pérez de Villagrá; Villalba; Villaviciosa;

Z: Juan de Zaldívar; Vicente de Zaldívar; León Zapata; Zubia; Zumaia.

[**Women** are not mentioned by name according to R.A. Gutiérrez. There are eight **Franciscan friars** with the group.]

NEW MEXICO (First European) COLONY

July 11, 1598: **San Juan de los Caballeros,** *Knights of St. John,* [in the present Española Valley] is established as the capital of N.M. across the river from **San Juan Pueblo.**

Stephen Gallegos, Illustrator
Atlanta, Georgia

Oñate Monument
Courtesy Museum of NM #16739

Donfuan de Oñate

Calligraphy by Jimmy Ning

 A week-long celebration is declared during which two theatrical events are staged: a happy (perhaps comical) play and a dramatic pageant of Christian victory over the Moors.

El Camino Real (*The Royal Road*, *The Kings Highway*) now extends nearly 2,000 miles from Mexico City [and remains the longest road in North America for several centuries].

August: Disgusted colonists, including 45 officers and soldiers, want to leave New Mexico (according to Oñate's later testimony) because they don't find "silver lying on the ground" or because he prevents them from enslaving the Indians. Mutiny is now a definite possibility.

September 12: Four men steal horses and flee south toward Nueva Vizcaya. Oñate feels this desertion in the line of duty must be punished harshly. Pursuers Villagrá and Márquez catch two and execute them immediately but the other two make good their escape.

PUEBLOS

JuandeOñate meets with 38 Pueblo leaders at *Khe-wa* (now **Santo Domingo**) to advise them about his colonizing efforts.

[This meeting is said to be the first recorded gathering of the modern **All Indian Pueblo Council,** which currently displays "1598" on its official logo.]

Oñate estimates that the **Pueblo Indians** number about 60,000 and they receive much attention: The Pueblos are **polygamous**, each man having as many wives as he can support and it is prestigious to have many wives. **Elders** have the most authority in Pueblo society. Pueblo **society is matrilineal** and females own the homes and have final authority in them. Corn, beans, and squash are dietary staples. The *kiva* is identified as a ceremonial chamber and the physical symbol of political as well as religious society.

BUFFALO HUNTING

September-October: **Vicente de Zaldívar** leads 60 men onto the eastern plains for an immensely successful **bison** hunt. A chronicler writes: *"Their shape and appearance are so amazing and amusing or frightening, that one never tires of looking at them."* Vicente has his men create a corral but the bison are so wild none can be driven into it. The *"wild and fierce"* bison kill three horses and wound 40 others. Calves are captured with the hope of taking them back home for domestication but they fight the ropes so furiously they quickly die from the exertion. So the soldiers-turned-hunters down the new American cattle to supply enough meat and tallow for the colony's winter needs. The meat is said to be better than beef.

ACOMA VISIT

October, 1598: With **Juan de Zaldívar** in charge at San Juan and with instructions to wait for his brother, **Vicente de Zaldívar,** to return from the buffalo hunt whereupon Juan is to join him at Zuñi, Oñate is touring the kingdom of N.M. to receive submission of the Pueblos and investigating for trace precious minerals. During the tour he decides to go west in quest of the **South Sea** and toward the end of the month he is at Acoma. One of his men describes the Pueblo as *"the best situated Indian stronghold in all Christendom."*

Unknown to the Christians, a minor chieftain by the name of **Zutucapán** has been speaking for a war of extermination against the newcomers. Cooler heads prevail and instead the Acomas bid them welcome and invite them to climb to the top of the stronghold. Oñate and many of his men do so. One of Zutucapán's warriors leads Oñate to the entrance of an underground kiva and urges him to descend via the ladder in order to see a glorious treasure. Oñate, a veteran Frontiersmen with much combat experience, becomes suspicious and declines the invitation. (**Unknown to Oñate at the moment, a dozen of Zutucapán's armed warriors wait in the kiva to assassinate the Christian leader in hopes of forcing a war.**) The Hispanics descend to the plain below and later conduct the ceremony that makes the Acomas vassals of the King. Oñate then leads his men westward to Zuñi.

Oñate is greeted warmly by the six pueblos of Zuñi Indians where he decides to wait for Zaldívar's reinforcements before going on in quest of the Pacific Ocean. He sends a small reconnaissance force south to map the existence of a salt lake that is described as the "best saline in the world."

VILLAGRÁ & ACOMAS

Oñate is visiting the various pueblos when Captain Villagrá sets out to locate him to inform him about the deserters. Riding his purebred horse he goes west after Oñate but while approaching Acoma he encounters a war party, led by **Zutucapán,** guarding the trail...*"like so many crouching tigers ready to pounce upon their prey."* The Acomas are ready to attack so he quickly rides away because *"they were out for blood."* It snows early the next morning and Villagrá fails to see the trap the Acomas had set, a camouflaged pit in the middle of the trail. Horse and rider plunge into the pit, killing the horse immediately, though Villagrá isn't wounded. He believes the Acomas will soon be after him so he sets out on foot, walking for four days until he is chanced upon by Oñate's soldiers looking for stray horses. Villagrá is reunited with Oñate at Zuñi and makes his reports, including the incident at Acoma.

November 8, 1598: Oñate and his men leave Zuñi for the Moqui (**Hopi**) villages where they are received cordially. He sends out small expeditions and wonders why **Zaldívar hasn't arrived.** In time all return to Zuñi.

December 12, 1598: With Christmas coming up and no word from his nephew, Oñate decides to return home so his men may celebrate the holidays with their families and then later set out for the South Sea. At El Morro Oñate hears the news about his nephew Juan de Zaldívar.

AMBUSH AT ACOMA

December: **Juan de Zaldívar** and 31 men stop to trade hatchets, hawk bells and other items for provisions like flour at **Acoma Pueblo.**

[On their way to Acoma, Zaldívar had instructed his men to treat all Indians with utmost courtesy and respect, which they did according to the depositions published in the Hammond and Rey work.]

Unknown to the Spaniards, **Zutucapán** and the war faction have gained dominance in the Pueblo and the intent is to exterminate the Christians. The Acomas say they will trade and so invite them up to their Sky City. Zaldívar and 18 men climb to the top only to be told the flour is at various houses in the Pueblo so the men have to separate. *"The Indians led us through small plazas and narrow streets."* Suddenly the Acomas rise in large numbers and ambush the Spaniards from all sides and terraces, warriors shooting arrows, men and women hurling stones and wielding war clubs, all of which had been prepared beforehand. Zaldívar orders that no one should fire at the Indians, but to shoot their harquebuses into the air to scare them in order to calm them with *"words and kindness."* Then Zaldívar receives an arrow in the leg and the Christians realize they must fight back in order to preserve their lives but in the end they are forced against a rock wall and fall in bloody hand-to-hand combat. This includes Juan, Oñate's nephew, not yet 30 years of age, who receives the final blow from Zutucapán. (Survivors later were to testify they saw the Spaniards who had fallen to the ground had their heads split open with large stones.) Only five Hispanics survive, some by jumping from the top of the Sky City and landing on sand dunes below. Bodies of dead Christians are hurled down the cliff where a small number of men are guarding the horses. The victorious Acomas are wearing the helmets, coats of mail, and brandishing the swords of the dead Spaniards. The Christian survivors hurry to where iron articles and horse shoeing materials had been cached only to find the items gone and when couriers go to seek Oñate in the Zuñi country some horses are killed with arrows by the warriors.

Hispanic New Mexico is now teetering on the brink of extermination if Amerinds unite with Acoma to attack the small colony of Christians.

[**New Mexico's first Christmas** is one of gloom and heartfelt sadness but the pageantry of Christmas Mass in the church of San Juan Bautista is a ray of optimism that works to alleviate grief and Christian spirit thus illuminates the path toward survival.]

1599
CONFERENCE
January: A tribunal convenes to decide if a just war can be waged against Acoma.

[According to **Mark Simmons**, contrary to what *"many writers would have us believe,"* Spaniards weren't reckless or given to unprovoked reprisals. The King's law and Church doctrine required rational deliberation. A *"highly formalized and legalistic procedure"* was in place by this time and it had to be observed before launching a war.]

Oñate weighs and considers all testimony and recommendations:

Capt. **Gerónimo Márquez** states that if Acoma is not captured *"...there will be no security in all New Mexico, nor can it be settled as the natives of other Pueblos are watching what we do at Acoma and whether we punish them..."*

Juan de Olague (who saved his life only by leaping onto the sand dunes below) testifies under oath that the Acomas have acted with treacherous premeditation in order to kill the Spaniards.

The **friars** testify that Oñate may wage war because the Acomas have sworn allegiance to the King and as subjects have no right to revolt; but war for revenge would be illegal.

Several **married soldiers** testify that unless the rebellion is crushed immediately they will be forced to ask permission to take their women and children back to New Spain for there will be no security for them in N.M.

The decision being agreed to democratically by all present, Oñate declares that *guerra de sangre y fuego* will be waged against Acoma and he will lead it personally. The colonists convince Oñate he mustn't participate in the attack for in case of failure he will have to lead everyone out of New Mexico. The governor selects his other nephew, **Vicente de Zaldívar,** to lead the Christian army, including in his general orders: *"Make more use of clemency than severity if it should turn out that the Acomas have committed their crimes more from incapacity of reason than from malice ... If you should want to show lenience after they are arrested you should seek all possible means to make the Indians believe that you are doing so at the request of the friar with your forces. In this manner they will recognize the friars as their benefactors and protectors and come to love and esteem them, and to fear us."*

MILITARY

Sargento Mayor **Vicente de Zaldívar,** 25 years of age and the fate of Hispanic New Mexico hanging in the balance, leads 72 men to Acoma where, through the **interpreter Tomás**, he states he wants to make peace and demands to know why they have killed the Spaniards. From atop their Sky City the Acomas jeer and insult (*llorones, cornudos*) the tiny army far below, promising to annihilate it, their puny colony, and all *"the Queres and the Tiguas and everyone at Zía because they have failed to kill the Spaniards."*

Zaldívar demands surrender the required three times then, upon continued jeering, informs the Acomas to prepare for battle in which no quarter will be given or expected.

WOMEN

Scouts from San Juan Pueblo inform Oñate that many **Pueblos** are massing for an attack on the weakened Hispanic colony. All men prepare for defense and the **women of the colony,** led by **doña Eufemia,** wife of E. Sosa Peñalosa, have a meeting with Oñate in which they volunteer to fight. Henceforth the women appear on the rooftops throughout the crisis alongside their men, thus giving the impression that there are more Spanish defenders than there really are. Aware of Spanish readiness, the Indians delay their attack until they receive news from Acoma.

COMBAT

January 22-24, 1599: Like the knights of old, Zaldívar rides up to the base of the rock and shouts to his enemies to prepare themselves for they are going to be attacked. Then there are three days of desperate hand-to-hand fighting at Acoma. At first the Spaniards are on the verge of being overcome by sheer numbers but once again Hispanics prove themselves fierce fighters and the tide is turned against the valiant warriors. [Legend has it that Santiago, **St. James,** appeared and turned the tide of battle.] With so many warriors killed Zaldívar sends the interpreter Tomás to urge the chiefs to surrender, *"promising that he would do justice to all who surrendered and placed themselves in his care."* The leaders reply that they and their women and children want only to die, that the Spaniards are scoundrels, and they attack Tomás with arrows and stones. The battle continues until the Acomas know they are defeated so they ask for peace. Zaldívar accepts their surrender and incarcerates them in their kivas. The Acomas *"broke away through many tunnels and mines concealed in the estufas and which opened out into adjoining houses ... Indians ran from house to house and killed each other without sparing their children, however small, or their wives."* Zaldívar orders the battle to resume, setting fire to all houses, and orders that *"all Indian women and children who could be found should be taken prisoners to save them from being killed by the Indian warriors."* Some 500 Acomas, men and women, young and old, are saved.

Acoma is destroyed to prevent it being used as a fortress for rebellion.

TRIAL
February 9-12: Acoma survivors are put on trial for the murders of 27 Christians.

Caoma, a native from Acoma, testifies through the interpreter Tomás that he was not present when the Spaniards were killed but they were killed because they asked for such large amounts of provisions.

Cat-ticati testifies the Christians were killed because they asked for maize, flour, and blankets. Some Acomas had not wanted to fight.

Taxio testifies that he was at home when he heard shouting and went outside where he saw the Spaniards were being killed.

Xunusta testifies that the Spaniards first killed an Indian and then the Indians became very angry and killed them.

Excasi testifies that it was said the Spaniards were killed because a soldier either asked for or took a turkey.

Caucachi testifies that the Spaniards wounded an Acoma and the people became angry and killed them.

Captain **Alonso Gómez Montesinos,** in charge of their defense, pleads for clemency on the grounds that these Acomas were absent when the Spaniards were killed, that Indians aren't "civilized," that they should be acquitted, set free, allowed to go wherever they wish, and order compensation for the expenses resulting from their arrest. But the rebels are found guilty.

No Acoma is given a death sentence;
> **24 males** over the age of 25 are sentenced to have ***puntas de pies*** (*toes, not feet*) cut off (according to researcher/author E.J. Gallegos) and then must render 20 years of servitude;

[April 2, 1998, St. Francis Auditorium, Santa Fe, N.M.: In a keynote speech titled "A *Foot For A Foot,"* historian Dr. **John Kessell** states that he and colleague researchers have been unable to find documentation that verifies the dismembering portion of the sentence was ever carried out. Archival documentation indicates that the friars, with or without the prompting of Oñate, went to the Governor with pleas to suspend the dismemberment, that Oñate was thereby encouraging the Pueblos to seek out Christian friars as protectors while saving face but instilling respect for Spanish law. Spaniards have been described as the *best record keepers in the world* and if the sentence had been carried out, especially one of that magnitude, it would have been recorded and despite concerted efforts no such record has surfaced, according to Dr. Kessell. This flies in the face of the work by **Hammond and Rey** where no mention is made of the friars' pleading for clemency but which states the sentences were carried out. It must also be pointed out that in English-language translations it is written that feet were ordered cut off, not toes. It is more logical that toes were targeted because the rebels were also sentenced to years of servitude and they would be of little use if they were missing a foot. *Puntas de pies* aren't feet just like *Llano Estacado* isn't Staked Plains, another popularly accepted mistranslation.]

> two Moquis (Hopis) in the fight are to have a hand (*fingertips?*) cut off then set free;
> males 20 to 25 years of age are condemned to slavery for 20 years;
> females over 12 years of age are condemned to slavery for 20 years;

Oñate then states: *"All of the **children under twelve years of age** I declare free and innocent of the grave offense for which we punish their parents. And because of my duty to aid, support, and protect both the boys and girls ... I place the girls under the care of our father commissary, Fray Alonso Martínez, in order that he, as a Christian and qualified person, may distribute them in this kingdom or elsewhere in monasteries or other places where he thinks they may attain the knowledge of God and the salvation of their souls. The boys under twelve years of age I entrust to Vicente de Zaldívar Mendoza, my sargento mayor, in order that they may attain the same goal. The old men and women, disabled in the war, I order freed and entrusted to the Indians of the province of the Querechos where they may be supported and may not allow them to leave their pueblos..."*

[These punishments, especially the dismemberments if they actually occurred, must be understood in the context of the historical age in which they transpired. For example, at that time if a Pueblo woman was found guilty of adultery the Pueblo punishment was to have *her ears and nose cut off*. Physical torture was also an integral part of the European legal process and in 1692, almost a century after Oñate, women were being tortured and executed for being *witches* in Salem, Massachusetts. As for New Mexico's Acomas they escaped their servitude and by 1604 rebuilt their Sky City, which suggests that if they were not forced to abide with the servitude portion of their sentence, it is quite possible the dismemberment never took place either but was used as a strategy to impress the Indians. Acoma still exists as one of the most popular tourist attractions in New Mexico to the present day. Compare this to the many villages found by Captain **John Smith** in the Jamestown, Virginia, region or the numerous aboriginal settlements encountered by the **Puritans** around Plymouth, Massachusetts, and the rest of New England: while all were wiped off the earth so completely that few people even wonder as to what happened to them, the 1599 brutalities at Acoma, generally portraying the Acomas as victims, are often singled out as if they were unique in the history of the USA.]

1600
AMERIND NATIONS
Native American groups that come to be known as *indios de pueblo,* village Indians (as opposed to the
viking tribes of nonsedentary *indios bárbaros)* are described by E. Spicer as:
Northern Tiwas: Taos, Picurís;
Tewas: San Juan, Pojoaque, Santa Clara, San Ildefonso, Nambé, Tesuque;
Keres: 8 to 14 villages that include Acoma;
Towas: Pecos, Jémez, Patoqua, etc., (eight others);
Tanos: 5 to 10 villages;
Southern Tiwas: some 8 to 20 villages, including Isleta;
Piros: 9 to 14 villages that include Abo and Quarai.

These "village Indians" speak dialects from five general language groups and often citizens of one Pueblo
can't be understood easily or at all by those of another. All are politically independent of each
other and alliances change constantly.

HISPANIC SOCIETY
Oñate moves his capital a short distance to **San Gabriel.** Hispanic colonists introduce **Christianity, the
wheel, adobe, log housing, fireplaces, and hornos** [outdoor baking ovens popularly known as
"Indian ovens"] for the first time in N.M. **New crops** like wheat, chile, watermelon, lettuce,
cabbage, peas, chickpeas, cumin-seed, carrots, turnips, garlic, onions, artichokes, radishes,
cucumbers, various varieties of melons, new varieties of corn (such as sweet corn, the large cob,
Cristalina de Chihuahua, Mexican dent) etc., and **stock animals** like horses, mules, cows, sheep,
goats, etc. are also introduced (and in time revolutionize the lives of Native Americans). Domesti-
cated amaranth and tobacco, called *punche* by Hispanic settlers, are also introduced.

There are at least seven carpenters among the colonists. These craftsmen (specialists in
carpintería de lo blanco, **joinery)** produce furniture, doors, windows, etc. When **Franciscans**
establish missions for the Indians they bring in Hispanic artisans to teach joinery to the Indians.

Chief activities in New Mexico are staying alive, converting Indians to Christianity,
exploring and prospecting for mines. There are shortages of every kind, especially food. Some
want to "abandon the land" and its privations.

JUMANO WAR
Before leaving on explorations toward the west, **Vicente de Zaldívar** is ordered to collect corn
from the Jumano (Humano) villages. The Jumanos give him *stones* instead. Vicente
informs Oñate then goes west on his explorations.

Oñate takes 50 men to the Jumano village and demands tribute in cotton mantas. They give him a dozen,
grudgingly. The next day he informs them they will be punished for giving Vicente and his men
"stones to eat." A corner of the pueblo is burned and an harquebus volley is discharged into a
crowd on the rooftops. Five or six are killed, others wounded. Two war leaders are captured and
executed by hanging.

Christmas, 1600: Five Spaniards travelling south for Santa Bárbara are **attacked by Jumano warriors**. Two Christians are killed and rumors are rampant that another uprising is in the making. The Franciscan friars urge Oñate to take immediate action to prevent another rebellion. A general war council is convened and it is decided to fight the Jumanos.

In the spring **Vicente de Zaldívar,** perhaps remembering the incidents which led to the Acoma war and the deaths of so many Christians, including his brother, leads a successful expedition against the Jumano villages (though Vicente is seriously wounded), burns them and distributes adult Indian males to serve his soldiers as servants. (**Fray Juan de Escalona,** later one of Oñate's enemies, wrote that some 800 men, women, and children were killed in three Jumano pueblos.)

AGRICULTURE
1599: Seven fanegas of wheat are planted.
1600: Fifty fanegas of wheat are planted and almost 1,000 are harvested.
1601: The wheat yield is around 1,500 fanegas.

COLONISTS
August: For reasons known only to them, Gaspar Pérez de Villagrá, Marcos Farfán de los Godos, and Juan Pinero refuse to return to New Mexico from Santa Bárbara after recruiting more colonists.

PIONEERS
December 24: Capt. **Bernabé de las Casas** arrives at San Gabriel with new soldiers, **colonists with families,** six Franciscans, stock and supplies. Christmas is a joyful celebration. Angélico Chávez writes that among the new colonists are:

Cristóbal Baca (with wife Ana Ortiz, their three grown daughters and one son; Cristóbal is the progenitor of the Baca family in *N.M.*); **Pedro Durán y Chaves** (with wife Isabel de Bohorquez Baca and children; Pedro and Isabel are the progenitors of the Chávez clans in *N.M.*); **Cristóbal Enriquez; Alvaro García Holgado; Domingo Gutiérrez; Antonio Hernández; Juan de Herrera; Juan Jorge; Juan López Mederos; Juan Luján; Bartolomé de Montoya** (with wife María de Zamora and family which includes three boys and two girls, all under 16 years of age); **Alonso Naranjo; Juan López Holguín (Olguín); Juan Rodríguez Bellido; Juan Ruiz Cáceres** ...There are *"...some 45 wives,* sisters, *children, and servants"* in this group.

1601
EXPLORATION & DISCONTENT
June: Oñate leads an expedition some 600 miles east to the **Quivira** plains, although in N.M. some Indian nations are considering rebellion and many colonists express their discontent, especially at food shortages. They want to leave N.M. and its hardships.

Captain Pablo de Aguilar, who twice before had been sentenced to death and twice had been pardoned by Oñate, is executed for another offense [the nature of which is unknown].

DESERTION

October: **Many soldiers, friars, and colonists desert N.M.** with their families, fleeing south. They also steal horses and personal property from the men who are with Oñate in the Quivira country. Remaining at San Gabriel are a mere 25 soldiers. (Cristóbal Baca later states that the Franciscan friars had fomented the desertion.) Native Americans can destroy the colony whenever they wish.

November 24: Oñate returns from Quivira to find most of his colony gone. He convenes a tribunal which finds the deserters guilty of mutiny and treason; they are condemned to death. Zaldívar is sent with a detachment of soldiers to bring back the deserters but their headstart enables them to reach Santa Bárbara and safety.

1602
SOCIETY

Colonists now dress in clothes made of gamuza, the soft tanned hide of deer or antelope. This **buckskin** is so valuable that it becomes a medium of exchange. The finest buckskin is set aside to be used as canvas on which to paint. [T.J. Steele tells us the *Segesser hide* paintings (named for the person who collected them) are the earliest extant religious paintings in N.M. and the USA.]

May: **Vicente de Zaldívar** testifies before the Viceroy and Audiencia regarding the dire needs of the N.M. colony.

T I M E L I N E

July 8, 1602: To all persons who undertake the settlement [of New Mexico], once they have settled the land and met their contractual obligations, in honor of their persons and their descendants, and from them, as the first settlers that they be a praiseworthy memory, we confer upon them nobility of solar conocidos for themselves and their legitimate heirs.
[New Mexicans who complied with their contract could now use the honorific DON when they signed their name.]
So that in any town that they settle in all other parts of the Indies they are recognized as nobility and persons of noble lineage and members of landed gentry. That they be recognized, honored and esteemed, and that they enjoy all honors and distinctions. That they may do all things that all noble men and knights of the kingdoms of Castile, according to the privileges, laws and customs of Spain that they are allowed to do and should do... it is my wish and my will that this have the force of law the same as if it had been decreed and promulgated in the Cortes. Let it be proclaimed in all parts and places where this applies.
[signed] Yo, el Rey, Felipe III

1603
TAOS REVOLT

Oñate quells a revolt at Taos Pueblo.

1604
ACOMA RESETTLED

Oñate sends a peace mission to the newly reestablished pueblo of **Acoma.** The three missionaries report that lingering wounds from the terrible war of five years ago must be healed.

EXPLORATION

October: Oñate leads an expedition west to discover the **South Sea** (Pacific Ocean). By January of 1605 he is at the estuary of the Colorado River in the Gulf of California.

1605

April 16: Oñate leaves an inscription on **El Morro** [now Inscription Rock National Monument]: *Pasó por aquí el adelantado don juan de Oñate del descubrimiento de la mar del sur a 16 de abril de 1605.*
[It is the oldest inscription by a European in the present USA.]

GOVERNMENT

A **Cabildo,** Town Council, is elected at San Gabriel.

[The Cabildo consists of four councilmen (*regidores*) who are elected annually by the citizenry, and two magistrates (*alcaldes ordinarios*) elected by the councilmen. They are assisted by a bailiff (*alguacil*) and a notary, who are also elected by the councilmen. The Cabildo represents the entire community and its ordinances are subject to the Governors approval.]

TIMELINE

1605: **Part I** of *El ingenioso Hidalgo Don Quijote de la Mancha* is published in Spain. Written by Miguel de Cervantes y Saavedra, **Part II** follows 10 years later and the entire work becomes one of the most popular books ever written.

1606
RAIDS

Apaches and Navajos are attacking the more isolated **Pueblos,** killing the inhabitants. They also steal Spanish stock and attack San Gabriel itself.

1607
ONATE RESIGNS

August 24: Oñate writes to the Viceroy: *"Finding myself helpless in every respect, because I have used up on this expedition my estate and the resources of my relatives and friends, amounting to more than 600,000 pesos, I find no other means than to renounce my office, which resignation I am sending your Excellency."* He continues that no one in authority has bothered even to acknowledge the monumental sacrifices made by his soldiers, friars, and colonists. The deserters of 1601 not only haven't been punished but have used their freedom to spread lies, justify their treason, and attack his personal honor. He will hold his colonists only until the summer of 1608 then he will release them from all obligations to remain.

TIMELINE

May 23,1607: **One hundred and four (104) males found an English trading post at (James Fort) Jamestown, Virginia**. (There are no women in the colony.) Indian warriors attack to test their strength but muskets and cannons win the day. The colonists, mostly "gentlemen adventurers" ignorant of farming and unaccustomed to hard physical work, are soon categorized as *"those who could not and those who would not work."* **Captain John Smith** writes: *"In Virginia, a plain Souldier* [sic] *that can use a Pick-axe and spade, is better than five Knights"* and in time a law has to be made that he who doesn't work, doesn't eat.

[S.E. Morison writes that the English had a number of reasons behind their efforts at colonization in the New World: England is overpopulated so the poor and unemployed could get a new lease on life overseas; England needs new markets for its woolens, needs precious metals like gold and silver, wants lands to produce items like olive oil, timber, etc.; a short route is needed to the Orient; and *"a place of safetie"* [sic] might be necessary *"if change of relligion or civil warres should happen in this Realme."*

Making money for stockholders being the primary motivation for English activities in the New World, the **joint stock company** is set up as the vehicle for English efforts: the King grants an association of stockholders a charter and the company stockholders select a governor, treasurer, assistants, etc., for what is basically a trading post settlement. The "Governor" is responsible to the stockholders living in England. "Settlers" are employees working for their absentee stockholders. No private property is allowed (until communal ownership proves to be a failure) so the people lack incentive.]

September, 1607: **Half of the original settlers are dead**. Local **Powhatans** show compassion for the survivors and bring them food *"such plenty of their fruits and provisions as no man was in want."* When more provisions are needed **Captain John Smith** and others go to Indian towns to trade for food. But the Indians will trade only for muskets so **Smith's men kill several Indians** and take all the corn they can carry. Finally **Chief Wahunsonacock** (referred to as **Powhatan** by the English) has his warriors bring Smith in, feasting him for several days, and decides to keep the English as trading partners for muskets and metal knives. Then he returns Smith to James Fort.

[The story of Pocahontas saving Smith's life wasn't mentioned by Smith in his correspondence related to the incident. But according to his later writings and **16 years after the death of Pocahontas**, Smith was *"saved from a horrible death"* by the princess. It has been written that he promoted the same story three different times, saying he was saved by (three different) beautiful women in adventures from India to America.]

Colonists arrive in 1608 ad 1609, numbering more than 500, this time including woman and children.

January, 1609: Smith leads his man to the capital town of the **Pamunkey** nation and demands corn of the powerful chief **Opechancanough**. The chief refuses whereupon Smith grabs him by the hair and holds a gun on him while the English take all the corn they want. Smith then demands a regular tribute in corn and if the Pamunkeys refuse he promises to load his ships with their *"dead carkasses,"* boasting that *"warres are the chiefest pleasure of the English."*

The Pamunkeys weary of English aggressions and a full-scale war breaks out, the English holding out at first but soon they have to retreat to James Fort which is under siege.

1610: More colonists arrive and the English go on the offensive, killing all Indian men, women, and children they encounter. But the situation worsens and after the **"Starving Time"** which sees the emergence of cannibalism, only 60 people survive. More colonists are needed.

[Of the **900** English who have settled in Virginia since 1607 only **150** are still alive by the end of 1610.]

1611: Governor Sir Thomas Dale writes:
[sic] *Every man allimost laments himself of being here and murmurs against his present state. These colonists are sutch disordered persons, so prophane, so rioutous, so full of treasonable intendments, besides of sutch diseased and crased bodies ... as of 300 not three score may be called forth or imploied upon any labor or service ... If it will please his Majestie to banish hither all offenders condemned to die, it would be a readie way to furnish us with men, and not allwayes with the worst kinde of men either for birth, spiritts or Bodie...*

1613: **Pocahontas**, daughter of Wahunsonacock, is captured by the English who offer to exchange her for English prisoners held by the Powhatans. The Indians release their prisoners but Pocahontas is not freed by the English. (It is during this time that she meets **John Rolfe** and is baptized as *Lady Rebecca*.)

1614: Hoping to rescue his daughter, Wahunsonacock agrees to sign a peace treaty. (**John Rolfe marries Pocahontas**, even if she is married to a man of her tribe, and sails to England where, at the age of 22, she dies of smallpox in 1617.)

1618: Wahunsonacock (Powhatan) dies and his brother, **Opechancanough**, becomes chieftain. **Tobacco** becomes very popular in England and more colonists arrive and appropriate more Indian land. The English treat the Indian nations harshly and the Native Americans begin to understand that the mounting English population (now around 1,000) portends their annihilation.

March 22,1622: The English execute an Indian named Nemattanou for the suspected murder of an English trader. Opechancanough's retaliatory strike leaves 347 men, women, and children dead, as well as wasted tobacco fields.
English policy is now extermination of every Native American by any means available.
Regular patrols attack and burn villages and crops, driving the Indians westward. The

colonists finally invite hundreds of Indian leaders in for a **peace conference** and to conclude all ceremonies the English pass around wine and propose a toast *to eternal friendship.* **But the English wine has been poisoned and all Indians who drink fall down dead. Those remaining are slaughtered on the spot.** Opechancanough is one of the few to escape.

1623: The **Dutch** "buy" [Indians didn't believe land could be "sold or bought" any more than the sky, sun, clouds, air, etc. could] **Manhattan Island** to use as a base for trading. They pay 60 Dutch guilders, or about $24, for the island.

[**Boornstin and Kelly** tell us in their U.S. history textbook: Of course, in those days $24 was worth several thousand dollars in today's money.]

1625: The English attack the village of **Pamunkey** and kill around 1,000 Indians.

1632: Raid and counter-raid finally exhaust both sides so a peace treaty is agreed upon.

1644: The English population is now around 8,000.

April 18, 1644: The harsh English tyranny causes Opechancanough (who is reported to be more than 100 years old) to send his warriors out to attack English encroachers on the York and Pamunkey rivers. **Governor William Berkeley** of Virginia launches a counteroffensive.

1646: Opechancanough is captured by Governor Berkeley and carried on a litter to Jamestown where a guard shoots him in cold blood. As he lay dying, Opechancanough is recorded as saying: *"If it had been my fortune to take Berkeley prisoner, I would not have meanly exposed him as a show to my people."* A fragile peace ensues after Opechancanough's murder but the English continue to demand more and more Indian land.

1675: An Englishman refuses to pay a debt owed an Indian so the Indian takes the man's hogs as payment. The English kill some Indians because of it and the Indians retaliate. The English gather a force of militia, cross the Potomac River and kill some 11 **Nanticokes.** Then they encounter a cabin with **Susquehannocks** (who were totally unrelated and had nothing to do with the original incident) and murder 14 of them. The Susquehannock nation now retaliates.

In short order a combined force of **Maryland and Virginia militia** surround the main Susquehannock village. When five chieftains come out to parley under a flag of truce they are shot down in cold blood. Susquehannock warriors retaliate, killing five English for every chieftain who has been murdered.

English atrocities against the Indians are investigated: *one Maryland major is fined.* Vigilantes under the leadership of **Nathaniel Bacon** (cousin of Governor Berkeley) decide to take matters into their own hands. The innocent and peaceful **Ocaneechl** and **Monacan** tribes are attacked along with the warring Susquehannocks. The **Virginia House of Burgesses** commissions young Bacon commander-in-chief for the Indian war. He and his followers march off against the **Pamunkey** Indians, who had always been loyal to the English, and drive them off into the Great Dragon Swamp between the Potomac and Rappahannock rivers. The militia pursues them and when discovered they offer no resistance. *Bacon's force slaughters them to the last man, woman, and child.*

1607-1640
RELIGION

Christianization of Pueblo Native Americans is progressing rapidly under the direction of the **blue-robed Franciscans.** The most heated Pueblo objection to Christianity is its prohibition of polygamy. Some 50 churches are built during this period according to R.E Gavin.

Fray **Alonso de Lugo** works at Christianizing the **Navajos** but all efforts fail (including those of Benavides and other missionaries for decades to come according to E. McNitt).

1608
GOVERNMENT

February 27: **Viceroy Velasco** accepts Oñate's resignation but orders him to remain in N.M. until further notification.

The fate of N.M. is reviewed in Mexico City. It wouldn't be an impossibility to recall all colonists but what would happen to Christian converts? **The decision is made to keep N.M. as a missionary field.** Capt. Juan Martínez de Montoya is appointed by Viceroy Velasco to replace Oñate but the Cabildo deposes Martínez de Montoya in favor of **Cristóbal Oñate,** don Juan's son, who is now Acting Governor at the age of 18.

1608-1610
Bernardino de Ceballos is Governor.

1608
CARAVAN

March: Viceroy Velasco dispatches a **caravan** to N.M., at royal expense, which includes wagonloads of clothing and 500 head of horses, cattle, and sheep.

[This is the beginning of the supply caravans whose appearance in isolated N.M. comes to be a joyful event.]

TIMELINE

July 3, 1608: **Samuel de Champlain** founds the French settlement of **Quebec.**

1608-1610
SETTLEMENTS

La Villa Real de la Santa Fe de San Francisco de Asís, **Santa Fe,** is founded during this period some 20 miles south of San Gabriel, in a narrow valley unoccupied by Native Americans. The **mission supply service** is started between Santa Fe and points south to Mexico City.

[A *villa* or town is laid out according to rules and tradition. It must have a plaza in the shape of a parallelogram 100 *varas* (a vara is 32.99 inches) long and 75 varas wide. Streets, which must be 10 varas wide, run into the plaza at right angles and the settlement extends one league (about three miles) from the plaza, in each of the four directions, thus containing about 17,700 acres. The church entrance should be from the east and facing the plaza.]

Valencia is founded by **Francisco de Valencia.**

1610-1614

Pedro de Peralta is Governor.

1610
GOVERNMENT

Peralta receives 1,000 sheep and goats, valued at 1,375 pesos, from Oñate as part of the official transition.

HISTORIOGRAPHY

1610: The epic **"History of New Mexico,"** *Historia de la Nueva México* by **Gaspar Pérez de Villagrá** is published in Spain, the only founding chronicle in the history of any colony to be written as an epic poem. It begins:

I sing of arms and the heroic man,
The being, courage, care, and high emprise
The deeds of those brave Spaniards
Who, in the far...West...go bravely....
By force of valor and strong arms...

[It is also the first published history of any part of the present USA, preceding by 14 years the well known *General History of Virginia* by Captain John Smith.]

TIMELINE

1610: Juan de Oñate and his son Cristóbal leave N.M., never to return.

1612: Cristóbal de Oñate dies at the age of 22.

1614: Oñate is arraigned on 30 charges related to his tenure as Governor of N.M. He is under house arrest for the duration of the lengthy trial. His basic defense is that his accusers are the mutineers and traitors who deserted N.M., contrary to their contract and responsibilities as soldier/colonists, individuals whom Oñate had sentenced to death.

May 13, 1614: **Oñate is found guilty on 12 charges**. He is sentenced to perpetual exile from N.M. and a four-year exile from Mexico City; he must pay a fine of 6,000 ducats and all court costs.

1619-1620: Don Juan goes to Spain and continues to petition **King Philip IV** to exonerate him of all charges.

August 11,1623: Oñate is reimbursed for the 6,000 ducats fine he had to pay in 1614, thus winning **exoneration**.

1624: Oñate is appointed Mining Inspector for all of Spain.

1625: Oñate is made a member of the prestigious and exclusive **Military Order of Santiago,** proof that he has won complete exoneration in the eyes of his countrymen.

June 3, 1626 : Juan de Oñate dies while inspecting a mine in Spain. (His will stipulates that one-fifth of his vast estate will go to the Jesuit *Colegio Imperial* of Madrid.)

[Not considered successful in his own day, victimized by royal bureaucrats, jealous rivals, and lack of mineral wealth in N.M., the contemporary perspective on Oñate acknowledges that he founded a new kingdom which is today the oldest colony in the present USA, sponsored permanent Christianization of Native Americans from Texas to California, laid the foundations for ranching and mining, and brought to light the geography of much of western America in his explorations, which includes extending the Camino Real into what is now the USA. In some quarters he is now honored as the founding father of N.M., fountainhead of the Southwest. In the view of some he is also representative of Spain's **Black Legend** of "greed, cruelty, religious fanaticism," etc. For example it has been asserted by **W.A. Beck** that *"the most important crime Oñate had committed in the eyes of Spain's rulers"* was that he failed to find rich Indians from which *"to swell the bottomless coffers at Madrid."* Needless to say, this was not one of the charges on record though Beck makes the assertion anyway. To this day Spanish archival resources, especially those which are of a negative nature, are utilized to promote the Black Legend. But for those who wish to investigate seriously the work by Hammond and Rey states: *"Oñate, striving against bitter odds to conquer and Christianize, carried his mission to success with a Spaniard's traditional courage and ability-but the country proved too poor to justly reward his efforts. And so the land remained, for two centuries, Spain's peaceful missionary province."*]

1612
CARAVAN
The supply caravan shipment for the missions includes tabernacles, carved and gilded crosses, carved and
painted images of Christ, and oil paintings of the saints. The caravan is the only way into or out of
N.M.

CHURCH &STATE
Fray **Isidro Ordoñez,** the first Franciscan prelate and commissary of the **Inquisition,** arrives in N.M. Conflict
between religious and civil/military authorities begins to rise and worsens with the passage of time.
Disputes center around political power, religious doctrine, and economic matters like the use of
fields and pastures. Fray Isidro denounces Governor Peralta for using unpaid Indian labor to
construct government buildings. The friar decrees that any settler who wishes to leave N.M. may
do so; when a large percentage leaves Gov. Peralta warns that weakened defenses will lead to the
demise of the entire colony. One Sunday Ordoñez throws Peralta's canopied church chair out into
the street. Peralta tells his men to put it back in church at the rear with the Indian portion of the
congregation.

Fray **Andrés Juárez** believes Ordoñez has gone beyond reason in exercising religious authority in N.M. so
he plans to escape and inform his superiors in Mexico City. Ordoñez gets wind of the "plot," waits
for him down the road where he is grabbed, then returns him to Santo Domingo where he is under
house arrest for some four months.

1613
Fray **Isidro Ordoñez** charges that tribute levied on the Indians is too burdensome and that several soldiers
have sexually abused Indian women; the Governor will correct these abuses or he will be excommunicated from Holy Mother Church. Peralta states Ordoñez doesn't have the authority to do so, so
Ordoñez excommunicates the Governor and threatens to excommunicate anyone who aids Peralta.

July 23: Ordoñez sends dispatches to Mexico City describing the *"godlessness that exists in New Mexico."*
Peralta decides to go to Mexico City and plead his case to the Viceroy.

August 12: Fray Isidro Ordoñez and a group of partisans arrest Governor Peralta at Isleta Pueblo and hold
him prisoner for the next nine months. **Fray Isidro is in charge of the kingdom of N.M.,** exercising
secular as well as ecclesiastical power until a new governor arrives.

[Peralta finally escapes from N.M. in November of 1614 and goes to Mexico City where in 1617 he is exonerated of all charges levied against him while in N.M. **John L. Kessell** writes: *"Thus, from the arrival of
Peralta in early 1610 until the Pueblos revolted in 1680, the single most notorious feature of life in
colonial New Mexico was the war between civil governors and the Franciscans."*]

RELIGIOUS ARCHITECTURE
The Mission (church) of San Agustín is built at **Isleta Pueblo.**

1614-1618
Bernardino de Ceballos is Governor.

MANUFACTURES

Along with **blankets, footless wool stockings** [tube socks] become one of the chief products manufactured in N.M. Weaving of these textiles becomes a cottage industry.

[The blankets are the beginning of what is to be called the **Río Grande blanket.**]

1616
CHRISTIANIZATION

Seven new friars arrive in N.M. which is now designated a Franciscan custody and named *Custody of the Conversion of Saint Paul of New Mexico.* Fray **Estevan de Perea** is Custodian and **Santo Domingo** is the ecclesiastical headquarters of N.M. There are 10 mission centers: Santa Fe and the nine Pueblo villages of San Ildefonso, Nambé, Galisteo, San Lázaro, Santo Domingo, Zía, Sandía, Isleta, and Chililí. There are *visitas* (missions) at San Juan, Cochití, San Felipe, and Santa Ana.

Franciscan friars endeavor to combat what they term animalistic *(more canino)* or pagan sexuality [the Indian female is described as being very aggressive] that is so much a part of Pueblo ritual and life. Missionaries also vigorously condemn brutal practices like cutting off the nose and ears of adulterous women. For violating Christian laws of sexual morality some men are publicly whipped, placed in stocks, or have their **hair cut off,** the latter being one of the most serious of punishments. Of all the Christian reforms, Pueblo men are most angered by the friars' control of marriage and the imposition of monogamy.

CHURCH &STATE

Because of conflicts with the Franciscans, **Governor Ceballos is excommunicated.**

1617
RELIGIOUS

Friar **Isidro Ordoñez** is ordered to Mexico City. He is officially reprimanded and denied permission ever to return to N.M.
["In just four years, he had indeed established the precedent--doubtless justified to some extent by outrages on the other side--for a malignant, divisive tradition of CHURCH & STATE discord.]

LABOR

The **encomienda system** is permitted in N.M., though no more than 35 *encomiendas* may be awarded. Authority is thereby granted to a citizen who is entrusted with the spiritual and temporal welfare of specific Native American groups. In exchange for the care and protection supplied by the *encomendero* he has the right to exact labor from the Indians "commended" to him. Tribute, which comes due every May and October, in local products can also be collected. In return for the encomienda award the encomendero is required to defend the land at his own expense.

The **repartimiento** is also used in N.M.: any Spaniard can petition the governor for Indian labor, up to 100 Indians at a time, who are paid a specified wage and provided with meals for a specified period of work time.

FRANCISCANS
January: Fray **Esteban de Perea** arrives as the *Father Custos* for N.M. With Fr. Perea are seven other Franciscans.

1618
T I M E L I N E

1618: Sir Walter Raleigh had written that the New World was the place for England to acquire **gold and silver.** When he didn't find it in **Virginia** (the name used at the time for all of English North America) he was imprisoned in the Tower of London by Elizabeth I and then King Jarnes I. James gave Raleigh another chance to find gold and silver in Guiana in 1616 and when he didn't King James I had *Raleigh beheaded for treason* in 1618.

1618-1625
Juan de Eulate is Governor.

CHURCH & STATE
Upon arriving in N.M. Governor Eulate announces that the **King is ruler, not the Pope** or the Church. He forbids *encomenderos* to give military escort to the friars and informs the Pueblos they can perform their ancient rituals with masks and kachinas. The friars attack him constantly in their correspondence to Mexico City, saying he is *"...more suited to a junk shop than the office of governor he holds."*

[Eulate is characterized by **France V. Scholes** as *"...a petulant, tactless, irreverent soldier whose actions were inspired by open contempt for the Church and its ministers and by an exaggerated conception of his own authority as representative of the royal Crown."*]

T I M E L I N E

1619: The drama *Fuente Ovejuna* by **Lope de Vega** is produced in Spain.

1619: A Dutch privateer puts into the James River in **Virginia** and 20 **Africans** disembark and are sold as **slaves, the first in Virginia** where **tobacco** is becoming the cash crop.
1649: There are some 300 black slaves in Virginia which has a total population of around 15,000. The tobacco industry requires many laborers so black slavery grows hand in hand with the tobacco industry.
1670: Virginia has around 2,000 blacks out of a population of 40,000.

1700: There are 6,000 black slaves in Virginia.
1730: Virginia has 30,000 black slaves in a population of 114,000.
1776: Blacks are nearly 40% of the Virginia population.

1620
CHRISTIANIZATION
Mission Indians number about 17,000.

[V. Westphall believes the mission program *"must be recognized as a monumental contribution of mind, body, and spirit by a few indomitable friars who simply would not recognize the impossibility of their tasks."*]

Fray **Pedro de Ortega** determines to stamp out idolatry in Pecos Pueblo, the largest in N.M. with about 2,000 inhabitants. In a bold maneuver he rounds up all clay, stone, or wooden "idols" and smashes them to pieces. The Pecos people acquiesce, though a man named **Mosoyo** goes about the pueblo saying Gov. Eulate is their friend, not Fray Ortega.

T I M E L I N E

December 16, 1620: A group of **Separatists** (**Puritans** who had seceded from the Church of England) sailing for Virginia in the *Mayflower* land further north [thus making it an illegal venture] at Cape Cod. They have no *patent* for a land grant and no *charter* for authority to establish a government so they create the **Mayflower Compact** as a basis for government in their **Plymouth Colony** which is first and foremost a trading post owned by merchants back in England. **William Bradford** writes in his history *Of Plymouth Plantation* of the continuous toil and dangers endured by the colonists as well as of their *"sundry notorious sins"* like drunkenness, incontinency, *"sodomy and buggery of things too fearful to name."* Because there is so much labor *"many untoward servants,"* both men and women, are sent over *"and by this means the country becomes pestered with many unworthy persons."* He wonders *"whether the greater part be not grown the worse."*

March, 1621: **Samoset**, who could speak some English, and **Squanto** (Tisquantum), an Indian who had been kidnapped by an English sea captain and therefore spoke English well, teaches the English how to plant corn, catch fish, trap beaver, etc., to survive in the wilderness. Squanto helps the English establish a friendly relationship with the sachem **Massasoit** of the **Wampanoag Confederacy**. (Because of this there is peace for 40 years until the English have developed superior military power.)

October, 1621: A **Thanksgiving** feast is shared with the friendly Wampanoag Indians.

June, 1625: **Governor William Bradford** writes to a friend in England that the Pilgrims *"never felt the sweetness of the country till this year."*

1630s: Thousands of Puritans flock to New England.
1634: There are some 10,000 Puritans in New England.
1637: The   Pequots are virtually wiped off the face of New England.

1638: In a small house in a cow-yard given by the town, **Harvard College** is opened at Cambridge.

1639: A **printing press** is set up in the Harvard College Yard, the first in the English colonies and the second in North America.

1644: Only **male church members** in good standing have the right to **vote in elections**. Four settlements are started on Narragansett Bay, founded by **Roger Williams, Samuel Gorton**, and **Anne Hutchinson**, all of whom had been banished from Massachusetts Bay or Plymouth as *troublemakers*. (Roger Williams had spoken out against robbing Indians of their land so he was "kicked out" by his community.)

1662: Massasoit dies. English "settlers," now numbering around 40,000, and their leaders assert a "stern and disrespectful rule" over all Indians, Wampanoags (who had preserved the first English "settlers") included. Indians are vigorously prosecuted for hunting or fishing on the Sabbath, using native medicines, or marrying according to native custom. **Indians denying the Puritan religion face an automatic sentence of death.**

1675-1676: The Wampanoags, former friends who helped the Puritans survive and found New England, and most of their allies are destroyed in a bloody war. Surviving Indian women and children are enslaved by English families and all warriors are sold into slavery in the various English colonies from whence they never return. Capturing Indians and selling them into slavery becomes a basic industry until the coastal tribes are no more (by around 1730, so the colonists expand the importation of captured Africans).

1691: Plymouth Colony is absorbed into the Massachusetts Bay Colony.

PROFILE

Andrés Juárez

L E G E N D A R Y   M I S S I O N A R Y

1582: Andrés Juárez is born to **Sebastián Rodríguez Galindo** and **María Juárez Rodríguez** in Fuenteovejuna, Spain. (Andrés, who carried his mother's surname, and the great Lope de Vega, who wrote the enduring theater classic of heroic community solidarity, *Fuente Ovejuna*, were contemporaries.)

1608: The investiture of Juárez takes place in the diocese of Córdova, Spain.

1609: His novitiate coming to an end, Juárez takes his vows as a Franciscan.

1612: Recruited by Fray Isidro Ordoñez, Fray Andrés enters N.M. for the first time. He is assigned to Santa Fe where he is tongue-lashed by Ordoñez on various occasions. Deciding the situation as intolerable, Juárez plans to escape and inform his superiors about the regime of Comisario Ordoñez. He feels his only other options are to hang himself or kill the Father Comisario. Fray Andrés hires a manservant for the journey back to Mexico but the man betrays him and Ordoñez traps him before he has traveled very far. Juárez is taken to Santo Domingo and held virtually in jail for four months. Fray Andrés calms down during this period of incarceration. When Ordoñez is removed from N.M. Juárez becomes the guardian at Santo Domingo.

1621: Governor Eulate labors to stop all church building in N.M. He charges that the missionaries demand unending free labor from the Indians to build unneeded grandiose structures, that so much building keeps them from working their farms, and that building demands monopolize too many oxen and the construction skills of too many colonists. In an effort to keep the peace, Father Custos Esteban de Perea tells his missionaries to halt all building or repair work. Sunday, August 1, 1621: After listening to a Juárez sermon, Capt. Pedro Durán y Chávez, a partisan of Governor Eulate, states that what Father Juárez needs is a good punch in the nose.

1621-1634: Fray Andrés is assigned to the village of Pecos (probably the largest in the entire province at that time).

1622: Construction of the Pecos church resumes under the direction of Juárez. The job requires some 300,000 adobes that weigh around 40 pounds each. The nave is 41 feet high at the entrance and the length of the edifice is 145 feet. Walls vary in thickness from 8 to 10 feet down the sides between buttresses and where the walls are to hold the towers they are 22 feet thick.

1625: The Pecos church is completed. It looks like a fortress and any Hispanic, Pueblo, or Vaquero Apache who sees it is greatly impressed. Most importantly it epitomizes the ministry of Andrés Juárez (and the other New Mexican missionaries). His fluency in the Pecos language enhances his work as evangelist and teacher. [The Pecos people become famous for their carpentry skills and many earn their livings as carpenters throughout the province.] He also labors mightily to convert the Vaquero Apaches who come to Pecos to trade from August to October.

1634: Juárez ventures out to the eastern plains in an effort to missionize the Vaquero Apaches (probably with the expedition of Capt. Alonso Baca).

1635: Fray Andrés is no longer ministering at Pecos. (Historians can't say why.) At the age of

53 he has already missionized in N.M. for 22 years and he is still working in the province at the village of Nambé (where he would labor for at least 12 more years).

1640: Governor Rosas attacks the Franciscan power structure. An aging Fray Andrés, as well as other missionaries, is targeted by Rosas' henchmen (according to missionary reports).

1647: Fray Andrés Juárez, the dean of New Mexican missionaries, informs the King that "self-serving" governors are keeping New Mexico in turmoil and impeding the Christianization process, thus encouraging the Pueblos to return to idolatry.

1621
AMERIND GOVERNMENT
Town government is established at all Pueblos, with a Governor, Sheriff, Mayordomo, Church wardens, etc., all under supervision of the friars. Silver crowned **canes** are given to Pueblo governors as symbols of leadership and justice that will be supported by the Spanish government. A Christian cross is engraved on the head of each cane, indicating a blessing from the Church.

CHURCH & STATE
October: Newly appointed Custos Fray **Miguel de Chavarría** and six new friars arrive with explicit orders from the Viceroy himself: *conciliate the situation in N.M.; the friars will cease interfering in civil affairs; the governor will provide military escorts for missionary activities...*

Heads of Church and State now greet each other in public.

1622
MISSION ARCHITECTURE
Fray **Andrés Juárez** brings in Spanish carpenters to teach the **Pecos** the craft of carpentry and directs the building of a monumental church in **Pecos Pueblo.** The massive structure requires 300,000 adobes. The ceiling is 40 feet high and walls measure from 8 to 10 feet thick.

1623
MARTYRDOM
The **Jémez** people kill their friars, burn the church, and flee to the hills.

1625-1629
Felipe Sotelo Ossorio is Governor.

1625
RELIGION
La Conquistadora, Our Lady of the Rosary [now called *Our Lady of Peace*], is brought to N.M.

AGRICULTURE
Major **Pueblo Indian crops** are corn, beans, and squash. Pueblos are highly accomplished farmers and they

La Conquistadora, Our Lady of Peace
Courtesy Museum of NM, #41984

own the richest farmlands in N.M. New crops introduced by Hispanic settlers are added to Pueblo production over the years and wheat, chile, and watermelons become integral parts of official Pueblo festivities. "Kitchen gardens" become popular as do orchards of peach, apricot, plum, and cherry.

RELIGIOUS ARCHITECTURE

The **Pecos Pueblo** church is dedicated. The towering structure impresses Spaniard and Native American alike. Even the plains people, called **Vaquero Apaches,** who come to trade at Pecos are struck by the grandeur of the monumental edifice.

[Possibly due to the construction effort, Pecos men are now in demand throughout the province because of their highly developed carpentry skills. A certain style of chair and bed are referred to as *silla de Pecos, cama de Pecos.* These craftsmen are commissioned from as far away as Taos because of their skills.]

AGRICULTURE

Hispanic crops (through the years) include wheat, barley, cabbage, onions, lettuce, radishes, a variety of melons which include cantaloupe and watermelon, **chile** (from Mexico), cultivated tobacco, Mexican varieties of beans and corn [especially the Mexican Dent, ancestor of the American Corn Belt Dent], tomatoes, grapes, and cultivated fruit trees like quince, apricot, peach, pear, plum, and apple.

Pueblo farmers are in the process of adopting the new Hispanic technology of plowed fields, irrigated wheat fields and fruit orchards.

1626
FRANCISCANS

Fray **Alonso de Benavides** *("...New Mexico's seventeenth century promoter par excellence"),* custodian of Franciscan missions and agent for the Inquisition, arrives in Santa Fe with 11 additional friars. He stays more than three years and is a most vital factor in stimulating the missionary effort.

[As *Custodio* for the Custody of the Conversion of Saint Paul and Commissary of the Holy Office in N.M. Benavides had immense power, enjoying even quasi-episcopal authority.]

Governor Sotelo Ossorio is charged by the **Inquisition** for heresy, blasphemy, and immorality.

1629-1632

Francisco Manuel de Silva Nieto is Governor.

1629
MISSIONARIES

Fray **Esteban de Perea** returns to N.M. along with 30 additional friars. By the end of the year 25 Pueblos have missions with resident friars. The **46 Franciscans** in N.M. are the intelligentsia of the province. Many were born in Spain. While they Christianize the Pueblos they also function like a community college for they teach various trades like construction with adobe, growing European crops, ranching, animal husbandry, tailoring, shoemaking, carpentry, smithery, jewelry design and manufacture, as well as music, reading, and writing. The Franciscan custody owns lands on which to raise horses, cattle, sheep, mules, oxen, hogs, and a few chickens. They raise corn, beans, chile, grapes, wheat, etc., various kinds of fruits in their orchards, as well as cotton in some areas.

RELIGION

The **Jumanos,** a nation living east of the **Vaquero Apaches,** relate to **Fray Juan de Salas** that they have been missionized by a *youthful lady dressed in blue.* Superiors in Mexico City order that the matter be investigated because they are familiar with the story that **María de Jesús de Agreda,** a Spanish Conceptionist Franciscan nun, has claimed to be transported to the New World in order to instruct the neglected heathens.

SOCIETY

A medicine man from **Chililí** shouts violently at Fray Alonso de Benavides on **Good Friday**: *You Christians are crazy and you desire that we in this village also go crazy! You go through the streets in groups, whipping yourselves until you bleed and you want everybody to do the same! You are all madmen! I will not go mad for your benefit! You Christians are crazy! I will not go crazy!*

1630
REPORT

Fray **Alonso de Benavides** is sent to the court of Philip IV in Madrid where his *Memorial de 1630* is published by royal authority. The work proves to be very popular and he becomes an influential lobbyist for the missions of N.M.

1631
MARTYRDOM

Fray **Pedro de Miranda** is killed at **Taos.**

CHRISTIANIZATION & PUEBLOS

Mission Indians are reported to number about 60,000 and there are **66 Franciscans** in N.M.

CARAVAN

April 30: A **Mission Supply Contract** is signed, detailing to the last *peso* what the Crown will spend for the missions in N.M. [The agreement endures for 33 years.] The contract calls for 32 wagons, the heavy, four-wheeled freight wagons with iron tires, drawn by eight mules and capable of hauling

---

PROFILE

Sor María de Jesús de Agreda

THE LADY IN BLUE

1602: **María Coronel y Arana**, later to be known as Sor María de Jesús de Agreda, is born in the village of Agreda in northern Spain. As María is growing up her mother converts the family home into a convent for **Conceptionist** nuns.

1618: María enters the Conceptionist order.

1620: María reveals to her confessor that she is confused because somehow she has been transported to the New World to help in propagating Christianity. Fellow nuns also report that María enters deep trances and levitates.
The confessor later reports that, according to Sor María, her body is in the convent while her spirit *visits Indians in New Mexico*, that she is praying to put a stop to the "visits."

1629: **Fray Alonso de Benavides** in New Mexico is instructed to investigate Sor María allegations concerning the Jumano Indians who visit the mission at Isleta Pueblo and repeatedly ask for missionaries because of the "Lady in Blue" visitations.

1631: Benavides is ordered to return to Spain with his findings. He and other Church officials interview Sor María for a period of two weeks and the nun accurately describes Fray Pedro de Ortega, "Apostle of the Plains Indians," as well as scenes in New Mexico though she has never left the convent.
Sor María writes the story of the life of the Virgin Mary, describing her daily habits, what she ate, the hidden life of Jesús, etc. It is titled *The Mystical City of God.*
1665: Sor María dies.

1670: Sor María's four volume work *The Mystical City of God is* published. (Missionaries are said to be very inspired by it.)

---

two tons of goods, to supply the missions and the 66 missionaries in them. It takes six months for the wagons to get to N.M., they stay there another six, then still another six to return to Mexico City. The system runs smoothly so long as Fray **Tomás Manso** is in charge. **This mission supply service is New Mexico's lifeline,** the only regularly scheduled freight, mail, and passenger service into and out of the province.

[The appearance of the caravan at the end of the   Camino Real is as joyous an event as the later appearance of the riverboat on the Mississippi.]

INQUISITION
Fray **Esteban de Perea** is commissioned Agent of the Inquisition. He investigates charges on the use of love potions and powders, witch curses, visions, bigamy, etc. Because they are neophytes, Indians are exempt from prosecution by the Holy Office.

1632-1635
Francisco de la Mora y Ceballos is Governor.

1632
MARTYRDOM
Zuñis kill friars **Francisco de Letrado** and **Martín de Arvide,** scalp and decapitate them, then take their hands and feet as trophies.

REPORT
True Relation of the Great Conversion in New Mexico by Fray **Esteban de Perea** is published in Seville, Spain.

1634
REPORT
In his *Memorial* addressed to Pope Urban VII, Fray **Alonso de Benavides** describes life in N.M.: mission agriculture is a source of food for the poor during periods of scarcity. The friars use farm products to pay workmen in the building of Pueblo churches. Woolen textiles are being manufactured by the friars and their Indian charges. The Church is growing prosperous (and it is said civil authorities resent it). *"This land ... is the most abundant and fertile of all the Indies ... and produces an incredible quantity."* He also reports that when Indians martyr their friars they cut off their heads and sometimes their hands.

CHRISTIANIZATION & PUEBLOS
Fray **Andrés Juárez** of   Pecos accompanies trading expeditions onto the eastern plains in his efforts to missionize the Apaches. (Various expeditions are led by men like Antonio Alonso **Baca**, Francisco **Luján,** Gaspar **Pérez,** etc.)

GOVERNMENT
February: An investigation of **Gov. de la Mora y Ceballos** is initiated for exporting foodstuffs and large numbers of horses, cows, sheep, and goats to Santa Bárbara, thus stripping N.M. of breeding stock and staple food supplies.

1635-1637

Francisco Martínez de Baeza is Governor.

1635
MISSIONARIES & INDIANS

Fray **Estevan de Perea** petitions **Philip IV** to free Christianized Pueblo Indians from the obligations of paying tribute or rendering personal service. **Philip IV grants the petition and thereafter Pueblos must be paid for their labors.**

[The period from approximately 1610 to 1635 has been referred to as the *Golden Age of Franciscan Missions* in N.M.]

CHURCH & STATE

Franciscan friars charge that **sweatshops** are being created by civil authorities, including Governor Martínez de Baeza, that they are involved in illegal ranching operations, and are monopolizing export items like salt, hides, livestock and piñon nuts. Civil officials make counter charges.

1636
HEALTH

A **smallpox** epidemic hits N.M. Hispanic and Pueblo populations decline.

TIMELINE

1636: After Indians kill trader **John Oldham**, officials of **Massachusetts Bay** order a punitive attack against the **Pequots** (though it wasn't certain they had committed the murder). "A *force of some 90 men led by Capt.* **John Endecott** *descended upon Block Island and killed every Indian male they could find ..* "who were mostly **Narragansetts**, and burned their villages. Then they go looking for Pequots, kill one, and burn several villages.

1636-37: Led by their sachem **Sassacus** (who failed to enlist the Narragansetts in the war) the Pequots lay siege to Fort Saybrook and attack outlying settlements. Colonists from all over New England gather under Capts. **John Mason** and **John Underhill**. They are joined by a contingent of **Mohegans**, with Narragansetts under Miantinomo and **Niantics** under Ninigret.

May 25,1637: The stockaded Pequot village is attacked at dawn. The New Englanders are thrown back but dwellings are fired and all Indians are cut down as they try to flee or are burned to death, some 600 to 1,000 Pequots dying that day.

July, 1637: A large group of Pequots is trapped in a swamp near New Haven. Sassacus and others escape to **Mohawk** territory where they are beheaded by the Mohawks in an effort to prove they had nothing to do with the uprising. *Colonial English authorities sell all known Pequots into slavery in their Caribbean colonies like Bermuda or among their Indian allies. Use of the Pequot tribal name is forbidden and Pequot place names are abolished for all time.*

1637-1641

Luis de Rosas is Governor.

CHURCH & STATE

Governor Rosas is determined to empower civil authority above that of ecclesiastical forces. During the required *residencia* of his predecessor he finds no grievous faults. Then he takes over where Martínez de Baeza left off, determined to make his fortune in this remote colony. He begins trading with the Indians but the friars foil his strategy so he has one arrested at Pecos.

[Rosas is a *"...tough, two-fisted, damn-the-hindmost..."* military man who would *"...knock down the man, colonist or missionary, who got in his way."*]

MISSIONARIES & INDIANS

There is constant resistance to Christianization in Pueblos like Acoma, Zuñi, Hopi to the west, as well as in Jémez, Picurís, and Taos. Among the worst difficulties is the Christian rule against polygamy which is an integral part of Pueblo culture.

PROFILE

Fray Estevan de Perea

FATHER OF THE NEW MEXICAN CHURCH

1610: Estevan de Perea arrives in N.M.

1616: Fray Estevan is selected *Custodian* of the Franciscan Custody of the Conversion of Saint Paul in N.M. He supervises 10 mission centers: Santa Fe, San Ildefonso, Nambé, Galisteo, San Lázaro, Santo Domingo, Zía, Sandía, Isleta, Chililí and *visitas* (missions) at San Juan, Cochití, San Felipe, Santa Ana.

1621: Perea serves as Custodian until this year and receives six more friars.

1626-29: Perea is away from N.M.

1629: Fray Estevan returns to N.M. with 30 more friars and is reelected Custodian. By the end of the year there are 46 friars ministering to some 35,000 Christian Indians at some 35 missions and *visitas*. Through the years Perea makes great efforts to establish missions at Acoma, Zuñi, and the Hopi Pueblos. He establishes his 10th (and last) church-convent complex at Santa Clara.

1632: Perea's *Verdadera Relación is* published in Seville.

1638: Fray Estevan de Perea dies.

[The period from 1610 to 1638 is sometimes referred to as the "Golden Age" of Franciscan missions in N.M. **France V. Scholes** has written that Alonso de Benavides and Estevan de Perea have been the two most important religious leaders in early N.M. and he considers Perea the *"Father of the New Mexican Church"* because he was the dominant figure in the religious life of N.M. through his long service and influence.]

1638
SOCIETY
New Mexico's Hispanic population totals about 800 with about 200 of these being soldier-settlers able to bear arms. In the highly charged quarrels between civil and religious authorities it is these soldier-settlers who hold the balance of power.

MILITARY
Gov. Rosas wars on the **Vaquero Apaches** and **Utes,** enslaving the survivors. The friars object vociferously to the Governor's actions. The Apaches retaliate on settled communities.

MISSIONARIES
Taos Pueblo complains vigorously about **Fray Nicolás Hidalgo**, who is relieved of duty the following year.

Fray Estevan de Perea has been missionizing in N.M. for 28 years.

TRADE
According to H.P. Mera, Gov. Rosas ships woolen textiles for sale in Mexico.

[According to W.A. Beck a *"staple export ... overlooked by historians"* is the *"Indian slaves driven along with the sheep."* Beck provides no documentation to support his discovery.]

TIMELINE

1639: **William Kieft** becomes Governor General of **New Netherland**. His policy for Native Americans is *"harassment and extermination ... he set about the task with cruel efficiency."* First he levies a protection tax, payable in corn, furs, or wampum, on down river Indians as the cost for protecting them from hostile tribes.

1641: Dutch livestock destroy **Raritan** Indian cornfields on Staten Island and the Indians retaliate. Governor Kieft offers bounties for their **heads** and when they are seen as too cumbersome to carry he deems **scalps** to be sufficient proof for payment. [*This is the introduction of taking* *scalps in North America. Indians then take up the practice.*]

1643: A war party of **Mohawks** comes into the vicinity to exact tribute from the **Wappingers** who flee to Pavonia and **New Amsterdam** for safety. Governor Kieft allows the Mohawks free reign: they kill 70 Wappingers and take others as slaves. When the Mohawks leave Kieft sends in Dutch soldiers to finish off the remaining Wappingers, including women and children. The soldiers take 80 heads and herd some 30 prisoners back to New Amsterdam. The heads are used as decorations and kickballs. For additional entertainment, the 30 captives are tortured to death.

Native Americans now rise and raid outlying settlements from Delaware Bay to the Connecticut River Valley, disrupting trade and farming. New Amsterdam itself is under siege. Then Capt. **John Underhill** leads an army of Dutch and English soldiers who campaign against the Indians, killing any encountered and destroying their villages and crops. Underhill's basic tactic is to fire all lodges and slaughter fleeing inhabitants who die by the hundreds.

1644: The Indians, greatly reduced in numbers and starving, negotiate for peace. Pressure from traders and farmers prevents their total extermination.

1655: A Dutch farmer kills a Delaware woman for picking peaches in his orchard. Her family kills the Dutchman and the "**Peach War**" is underway. Several Dutch settlements are attacked, including New Amsterdam. Governor **Peter Stuyvesant** orders out the militia and destroys several Indian villages. The **Esophus** Indians continue the fight but **Gov. Stuyvesant** warns them to come in for a council or be exterminated. The Esophus chiefs come in to parley but Dutch soldiers murder them while they sleep. When the news gets out, eight captured soldiers are burned alive.

1660: Governor Stuyvesant comes up with a plan to insure the peace: take **Delaware** Indian **children** as hostages and if their tribe makes war, sell their children into slavery in the English West Indies.

1664: The **Esophus** Indians make peace when Stuyvesant calls in the Mohawks to exterminate them.
English troops capture New Netherland and rename it **New York.**

1639
CHURCH & STATE
Governor Rosas and **Fray Juan de Salas,** *Father Custos* for the Franciscans in N.M., are in the midst of a
long-standing quarrel. (Father Salas asserts the Indians are disheartened by these disputes.) The
Santa Fe **Cabildo** sides with Gov. Rosas. Each friar is "accused" of having 1,000 sheep while
ordinary citizens are doing well to own 500 or less. The Santa Fe Cabildo writes to the Viceroy,
charging that serious ecclesiastical abuses are occurring in N.M.: Despite the vow of poverty, the
friars are acquiring wealth at the expense of the colony as a whole; the friars use censure, interdic-

tion, excommunication, and prosecution by the Inquisition to achieve their ends; the friars don't respect the authority of the King, threatening to abandon Santa Fe completely, for *"...no other reason than their pleasure so that by keeping the land oppressed and afflicted they can control it with such a powerful and superior hand."*

January: Gov. **Rosas** banishes Fray **Juan de Góngora** from N.M.

MARTYRDOM
December 28: The Taos Indians kill Fray **Pedro de Miranda** (who replaced Fray Nicolás Hidalgo). A few days later the Jémez Indians kill Fray Diego de San Lucas *"clinging to a cross."*

1639-1640
APACHE RAIDS
Apache raids destroy an estimated 52,000 bushels of corn and trade relations at Taos, Picurís, and Pecos are disrupted.

CHURCH & STATE
Civil and religious authorities denounce each other constantly in reports to Mexico City.

1640
SOCIETY & LABOR
It is estimated that some 50 to 60 colonists hold around 100 *encomiendas* so the Viceroy decrees that no more than 35 may continue to be held.

CHURCH & STATE
Fray Juan de Salas closes the church in Santa Fe and orders all Franciscans in N.M. to meet at Santo Domingo, Franciscan headquarters, to consider what action to take against Gov. Rosas. Seventy three citizens join the group. The Franciscans remain at Santo Domingo for over a year.

1641
Juan Flores de Sierra y Valdés is Governor.
GOVERNMENT
Gov. Sierra y Valdés begins the customary *residencia* (mandatory review) of the Rosas administration but Valdés dies before it is completed. The Cabildo of Santa Fe has Rosas arrested and sequesters his property.

[W.A. Beck writes: *"Even the most competent administrators"* learned that bribery insured a favorable residencia more than *"the irresponsible justice of Spanish law."*]

SOCIETY & CUSTOM
Evolving N.M. traditions dictate that hair be worn long. Males form their hair into two braids, females into one and tied at the back of the head. These hairstyles symbolize personal honor and virtue. Short

hair is only for criminals and other unsavory elements of society, therefore cutting off somebody's hair is a very severe punishment.

Hispanic females often masque their faces with a coat of flour paste as protection against the sun and as a skin cleanser. *Alegría,* red cockscomb, is used for rouge.

Playing cards is a favorite pastime and the Crown has a monopoly on the sale of cards.

Pueblo Indians feel much the same about long hair, hairstyle even assuming some religious significance. Besides braids, Pueblos also use the *chongo* hairstyle.

1641-1642
Francisco Gómez is Governor.

1642
CRIME
January 25: Ex-Governor **Rosas is killed** by Nicolás Ortiz (who had been gone for most of Rosas administration, but when he returned he found his wife in the house where Rosas had been held under arrest.)

1642-1644
Alonso de Pacheco y Heredia is Governor.

1643
PUNISHMENT
Gov. Pacheco investigates Gov. Rosas death and concludes that eight men, Nicolás Ortiz, Diego Márquez, Juan de Arechuleta, Juan Ruiz de Hinojos, Francisco de Salazar, Juan de Archuleta, Diego Martín Barba, Cristóbal Enriquez, are guilty of his murder and of sedition.

July 21: The eight are beheaded

CHURCH & STATE
Relations between Church and State are calm.

1644-1647
Fernando de Argüello Carvajal is Governor.

1644
AMERIND DISCONTENT
More than **40 Indians** are hanged, whipped, or imprisoned for sedition.

CHURCH & STATE
All friars convene at Santo Domingo in order to plan a defense against the "lies" which have painted them

as traitors in the eyes of the King. They condemn the effect of Rosas on the Pueblos, *"...who are for certain the best Indians in the world .... it is truly a miracle that they have not killed us all."*

AMERIND CONSPIRACY

A plot to kill Hispanic settlers at the hands of **Apaches** and the **Jémez** is discovered and 29 Amerinds are executed by hanging.

1647-1649

Luis de Guzmán y Figueroa is Governor.

1649-1653

Hernando de Ugarte y la Concha is Governor.

1649
AMERIND CONSPIRACY

A plot by Apaches, Isleta, Alameda, San Felipe, Cochití, and Jémez is discovered; nine leaders are executed and others are sold into slavery.

Ca. 1650
TRADE FAIR

The **first N.M. trade fair** makes its appearance (probably in the Taos valley).

AMERIND CONSPIRACY

A **revolt** is planned by Native Americans but word leaks out and the leaders are hanged while accomplices are sold into slavery for 10 years.

1653-1656

Juan de Samaniego y Xaca is Governor.

AMERIND
Juan Zuñi, a 27-year-old Hopi, is charged with the sacrilegious impersonation of Fray Alonso de Posada by inviting Awatovi villagers to church where he mimics Posada saying mass and performing other rites. He is also charged with cohabiting with "fourteen Indian women" of the Pueblo. He is found guilty and ordered to render personal service in the convent in Santa Fe where he can receive instruction in the Faith.

1656-1659

Juan Manso de Contreras is Governor.

1657
FRANCISCANS

There are **70 friars in N.M.** They are the most educated and powerful segment of the population. Their most difficult tasks are to rid the natives of idol worship and to impose Christian monogamy, both of which are resisted strenuously by the Pueblos. The friars resort to whipping as a physical punishment (commonly used in the European legal system of the day) for failure to attend religious services, sexual immorality, idolatry, and participation in certain "pagan" dances.

1659
AMERINDS & LAW
Juan Zuñi is charged with stealing supplies from the convent storeroom in Santa Fe, stealing
    dental tools, linens, chocolate, sugar, etc., along with an accomplice by the name of **Cristóbal
    Meco.**

Captain **Diego Romero,** *Protector and Defender of the Christian Indians* for N.M., is assigned to appear on
    behalf of the two men. Romero's defense is based on the cultural differences between the native
    and European, saying that the Indians' forthwith confession signifies they don't realize what might
    be their punishment for European criminal behavior.

Governor Manso de Contreras isn't swayed: both men receive 200 lashes then must serve forced labor, 10
    years for Juan, five for Cristóbal.

[The office of *Protector of the Indians,* also known as *Capitán Protector, Protector Partidario,* etc., unknown in the English or French colonies in the new world, existed only in Hispanic lands. The Protector's most important duty was to aid and defend Native Americans, which expressed itself primarily in the courtroom. He was also charged with seeing to their spiritual welfare, upholding native rights to their lands and working to nullify lands Spaniards might have acquired contrary to the kings laws. He was to see to it that Hispanics, blacks, mulattos, mestizos, etc., didn't live inside Indian villages. He was to report any abusive working conditions suffered by the Indians under his care and the Protector couldn't trade with his charges. The Protector couldn't be removed from office except after an official investigation by the regional audiencia (for N.M. that was the **Audiencia of Guadalajara).** New Mexico Indians never paid any fees or expenses related to the office of Protector. While the Pueblo people usually worked through their Protector, they were also free to petition through their mission priest, the *alcalde,* or the Governor himself.

The Protector in N.M. was usually an upstanding Spanish individual from a prominent family. He had no formal legal training but relied on strength of character, a strong sense of justice, and experience. *"The Protectorship proved to be an effective way for the Pueblos to defend their land titles"* according to C.R. Cutter.]

1659-1661
Bernardo López de Mendizábal is Governor.

1659
SOCIETY
N.M. is in the throes of a severe famine.

MISSIONS
Friar García de San Francisco and Father **Francisco de Salazar** establish a mission and convent which they

name *Nuestra Señora de Guadalupe del Paso del Norte* (which becomes the Villa of **El Paso del Norte** after 1680).

1660
CHURCH & STATE
Ten new *carretas* are delivered to Governor Mendizábal which he uses to ship merchandise South. In less than a year Mendizábal dispatches two caravans of trade goods to Parral.

Gov. López de Mendizábal decrees that all Indian laborers, including mission employees, must be paid no less than one *real* per day. Clerics dismiss their Indian *pastores,* saying they can't afford such Wages.

Thousands of sheep are lost to Apache raiders. Gov. López de Mendizábal forbids exporting sheep out of N.M. but the friars ignore the decree, saying their sheep are the only commodity they have with which to buy sacramental and other church items.

Carretas (Carts)
Courtesy Museum of NM #11830

RELIGION
Fray **Salvador de Guerra from Isleta** finds his Puebloans doing a forbidden "pagan" dance and when his orders to stop are ignored he strips, whips himself in their midst then puts on a crown of thorns and shoulders an enormous cross which he drags several times from one end of the village to the other. The Isletans, greatly moved, beg him to stop and ask his forgiveness.

CHURCH & STATE
Gov. Mendizábal proves himself tolerant of Indian ritual, causing much bitter denunciation from the friars, even having some Tesuques dance for him at Santa Fe. He remarks: *"Look there, this dance contains nothing more than this hu-hu-hu and these thieving friars say it is superstitious."*

Mendizábal's efforts to win the Indians away from the friars give rise to the influence of native leaders. Divisions develop between Amerinds that are Christian/non-Christian and traditonalist/Hispanicized, in each Pueblo.

Mendizábal publicly charges the friars with failing to observe their own rules of chastity, poverty, and obedience. The friars coun5charge that Mendizábal is a crypto-Jew and is having sexual relations with slaves **(an offense punishable under Spanish law by a life sentence to a slave galley).** When the Governor investigates charges against the friars he is charged by the Inquisition for impinging on ecclesiastical privilege. He is shackled and taken to Mexico City to answer all charges.

[Mendizábal dies in prison, protesting his innocence to the end. The Inquisition exonerates him posthumously.]

1661-1664

Diego Dionisio de Peñalosa Briceño Berdugo is Governor.

1661
AMERIND CHARGES AGAINST GOVERNOR

Antonio González, Notary of the Santa Fe Municipal Council and *Protector of the Indians,* speaks on behalf of the hundreds of Indians who have grievances against ex-governor López de Mendizábal during his *residencia* (inquiry into someone's administration). Indians charge the governor didn't pay them for bringing in piñon, salt, firewood, etc., or for producing blankets, stockings, oxcarts, etc. They ask for compensation amounting to hundreds of pesos.

[No records survive regarding the disposition of these findings.]

1662
INQUISITION

Sergeant Major **Francisco Gómez Robledo** (and two other prominent New Mexicans), holder of the Pecos Pueblo encomienda, the richest in N.M., is arrested by the Inquisition. He is confined, chained, and even leg irons are placed on him. He would not learn what the charges are for more than a year. He is held at Santo Domingo for five months, with other prisoners of the Holy Office, his property embargoed except that which is sold off to pay the expenses of his imprisonment, until the southbound supply caravan leaves in October. All costs for the six-month journey to Mexico City are charged to his estate, as are expenses there during his imprisonment while awaiting trial.

All charges are read at trial, including the accusation of being a Jew, which is proved to be mere hearsay. A physical examination proves that don Francisco "has no little tail," and that scars on his penis do not indicate circumcision. He answers all questions forcefully and directly, and is acquitted of all charges.

September 17, 1665: Francisco Gómez Robledo is back in Santa Fe, the ordeal with the Inquisition costing him three years, four months, and 14 days of his life. In money it has cost several thousand pesos. He gets back the property that hasn't been sold, his house on the plaza, titles to lands, encomiendas and tribute. The tribute usurped by Governor Peñalosa he gives to the Inquisition for its chapel in Mexico City.

TIMELINE

1662: There are some **40,000 English** living in (what is now called) New England while there are perhaps half that number of Native Americans. Puritan authorities vigorously prosecute Indians for hunting and fishing on the Sabbath, for using native medicines, or for marrying outside the Church. It is an automatic death sentence for denying the Puritan religion.

1663
CHURCH & STATE

Governor Peñalosa gets into a serious dispute over livestock with **Pedro Durán y Chaves II,** whom the governor orders put under arrest. Chaves seeks sanctuary in church but Peñalosa has him dragged out and jailed. Friar Custos **Alonso de Posada** writes to the governor that the right of sanctuary must be observed, therefore Chaves should be released immediately. Peñalosa refuses and Posada finally threatens him with excommunication.

One night Governor Peñalosa gathers his men and surrounds Posada's convent in   Pecos. With orders not to let anyone out of the building (*"If St. Francis himself comes out, kill him!"*), Peñalosa confronts the Custos and finally forces Posada to accompany him to Santa Fe where he (Agent for the Inquisition as well as religious custodian for N.M.) is kept for nine days. Posada, knowing that the entire colony is watching the situation, instructs his friars to open their churches to Peñalosa, thus ending the impasse for the moment.

1664

Governor Peñalosa issues a decree which forbids *"...the masters of doctrine to employ Indian women in spinning, weaving mantas, stockings, or any other things without express license from me or him who may govern in my place."*

March: Governor Peñalosa leaves N.M. for Mexico City. Upon his arrival he is jailed by the Inquisition and charged with 237 counts of malfeasance.

[The trial takes two years and the verdict ruins him forever in all Spanish lands. He flees to England then France where, as the self-styled **Count of Santa Fe,** he offers plans for an invasion of Spanish America which are to result in the La Salle expedition.]

1664

Tomé Domínguez de Mendoza is interim Governor

1664-1665

Juan Durán de Miranda is Governor.

CHURCH & STATE

Fray **Juan de Paz** is Custos and Agent for the Inquisition. The Cabildo in Santa Fe protests to Mexico City that to the friars *everything* is a matter for the Inquisition, no matter how trivial. The Holy Office investigates then, wishing to disassociate the Inquisition from local politics, sides with the Cabildo and Paz is removed. (Paz is the last Franciscan in N.M. to hold both offices simultaneously.)

1665-1668
Fernando de Villanueva is Governor.

1666-1670
SOCIETY

N.M. is plagued by **drought** which results in **famine.**

1667: **Francisco Gómez Robledo,** member of a prominent N.M. family, is *Protector of the Indians.* As with most Protectors, Gómez Robledo is an active participant in community affairs and has a basic knowledge of Spanish legal procedure, though he has no formal legal training. (Common sense and good judgment are necessities for frontier living and therefore highly valued.)

1668
INQUISITION

Fray Juan Bernal, Agent for the Inquisition, has **Bernardo Gruber,** a Sonora-based German peddler, locked up for distributing, along with his wares, certain slips of paper which Gruber claims *"...will make you invulnerable for twenty-four hours."* Bernal sends an emissary for instructions from Mexico City.

1669: Inquisitors reply to Bernal that he has no authority to arrest Gruber without prior orders from the Inquisition. Further, matters like disrespect toward Franciscans is not a matter for the Inquisition, that an Agent must not meddle in affairs that are beyond his jurisdiction because it gives *"...rise to much prejudice and hatred against this Tribunal."*

Bernardo Gruber still isn't released however, so after some 27 months of incarceration he escapes with an Apache companion, fleeing into the perilous desert country south of Socorro. His remains, or those of his companion, are found later [along what is still referred to as *la Jornada del Muerto, Dead Man's Route*].

1668-1671
Juan de Medrano y Mesia is Governor.

1669
REPORT ON N.M.

Fray Juan Bernal reports that N.M. is in dire straits. **Apaches** *("...a brave and bold people-who hurl themselves at danger like people who know not God, nor that there is a hell...")* are at war with the province and all Christian Indians, whom they kill at every opportunity. Besides the ravages of constant warfare, crops haven't been harvested for three years because of the **drought.** There is such hunger that people are eating boiled cowhide.

1670s
APACHES RAID PUEBLOS

Apache warfare imperils the **Piro** pueblos of southern N.M. as well as commerce on the *Camino Real.* East of the Manzano Mountains the Apaches are attacking the **Salinas** pueblos.

[No fewer than six Piro and Salinas pueblos perish because of drought, famine, disease, and the fierce Apache.]

1670
SOCIETY

There are about 2,000 Hispanics living in the disintegrating, discontented colony of N.M. Civil and religious authorities can't stop feuding with each other; Pueblo Indians are being abused and efforts are made to suppress their native religion; the subsistence economy doesn't support the population during times of crisis; supply centers are far away and increasingly hostile Apaches impede the *Camino Real;* and worst of all, the terrible **drought** continues.

1671-1675
Juan Durán de Miranda is Governor.

TIMELINE

1671 : **Wampanoag** chieftain **Metacom**, known as **King Philip** in New England, has seen the English multiply tremendously [by 1662 there were some 40,000 English in New England alone] from the days when his father **Massasoit** took pity on them and gave them land on which to live. As more and more English arrive they make demands for more land and become harsh with his people. After Massasoit, the new sachem is **Wamsutta** (Alexander), Philip's brother, who is poisoned by English officials, thus making Philip sachem. He sends runners to various native nations asking that *all unite to throw out the tyrannical English oppressors.*

1672
RAIDS

Apaches and Navajos, also hard hit by drought, raid established settlements for food.

TIMELINE

The **British Royal African Company** is established and immediately dominates the African slave trade because of British naval superiority. Many of the foremost families of England and New England control much of the slave trade and grow richer off it.

1713: The **Asiento** agreement gives the British the right to supply Spanish colonies with slaves from Africa.

1673

Apaches sweep into **Zuñi** in a rampage of killing, burning, and looting. **Father Avila y Ayala** is among the dead. *("He fled into the church and embraced a cross and an image of Our Lady. They dragged him out and stripped off his habit. At the foot of a large cross in the patio they stoned him, shot arrows at the writhing nude figure, and finally smashed his head with a heavy church bell."*

1675
MARTYRDOM

The **Pueblo** people are openly discontented and talk about throwing out the Spanish, whom the medicine men blame for their ills. **Witchcraft** is blamed for the deaths of seven friars and various settlers.

Fray **Francisco de Ayeta** arrives in N.M. and finds the missions and the province in desperate straits. Upon returning to Mexico City he petitions the government to send additional soldiers with full equipment as well as supplies and a thousand horses.

1677: Ayeta returns to N.M. with 50 soldiers, equipment, and supplies in an effort to stop the ruination of N.M.
1678: Ayeta is in Mexico city preparing for the next mission supply service which he will take to N.M. in 1680.

OMEN

The **Virgin of Toledo** appears to a sickly New Mexican girl, curing her, and directs her to arise and *"...announce to this custody that it will soon be destroyed for the lack of reverence that it shows its priests"*.

Fray **Juan de Jesús** writes to his brother friar at Jémez to stop building on the church for they must *"unite ourselves with God and prepare to die for our Holy Faith..."* for soon all *"...will end in ashes and many of us in death."*

1675-1677
Juan Francisco de Treviño is Governor.

TIMELINE

June,1675 : When three **Wampanoags** are hung for the murder of a Praying Indian, thought to have been a spy, a skirmish with settlers escalates into attacks on settlements all over **New England** from the Atlantic Ocean to the Connecticut River. Fifty-two of the 90 English settlements are burned or seriously damaged. **Nipmuc** and **Narragansett** tribes join the Wampanoags, as do others from as far away as Maine, in an effort to end the brutal English tyranny.

The **New England Confederation** (Massachusetts, Plymouth, Rhode Island, Connecticut) launches several armies against the native patriots.

July: The first major encounter takes place in the **Pocasset Swamp** and other large battles follow in August and September along the Connecticut River.

December: The Narragansetts are destroyed.

May, 1676: Indian forces are routed at Deerfield.

August: Indians are routed at Bridgewater. Soon after King Philip is killed and his body dismembered for trophies. His wife and son are sold into slavery in the English West Indies colonies from whence they never return. Many tribes, including the Wampanoag, Nipmuc, and Narragansett nations are virtually wiped off the face of the earth.

RELIGIOUS INTOLERANCE

Governor Treviño launches a campaign against Amerind idolatry. Known sorcerers are hung and 47 medicine men who admit practicing witchcraft are arrested, flogged, and are to be sold into slavery. Armed **Tewas** descend on Santa Fe and demand the release of all prisoners or they threaten to kill Treviño and all Hispanics in N.M. Governor Treviño releases the prisoners.

One of those released is **Popé,** from **San Juan.** He moves to Taos and begins plans for a province-wide revolt. Popé confers with dissenters, *caciques* and war chiefs from various Pueblos, telling them their ancient gods will not return with happiness and prosperity until the Spanish and their Christian god are dead. He promises that *"who shall kill a Spaniard will get an Indian woman for a wife, and he who kills four will get our women, and he who kills 10 or more will have a like number of women."*

1677-1683

Antonio de Otermín is Governor.

1679
SOCIETY

Hispanic N.M. has a population of around 2,400 to 2,500 people who live in areas from Taos in the north to Socorro and Senecú in the south; from Pecos in the east to Jémez in the west. Basic administrative divisions are *Río Arriba* and *Río Abajo,* separated by *La Bajada.*

Pueblo population totals are estimated at 17,000.

1680
PUEBLO REVOLT

Popé enlists the caciques of Taos, Picurís, San Lorenzo, Santo Domingo, Jémez, and Pecos, as well as a number of well-known mixed-bloods like **Domingo Naranjo** of Santa Clara, **Nicolás Jonva** from San

Ildefonso, **Domingo Romero** from Tesuque, meeting secretly each time a village celebrates its feast day. The first night of the new moon, **August 13, 1680,** is selected as the date for revolt, before the supply caravan arrives in September from Mexico City.

August 9: Popé dispatches messengers to all Pueblos, knotted cords signifying that in four days all are to rise in revolt. By now all know that the god **Poheyemo** has appeared to Popé and appointed him as his representative, ordering him to kill all Christians and their missionaries and to destroy all vestiges of the Christian religion so that everyone can return to freedoms of the past. Any who disobey the representative of Poheyemo, *"who was very tall and black, with frightful eyes that are large and yellow,"* will be executed immediately. Further, three supernatural beings appear to Popé *"in the form of Indians, most horrifying in appearance, shooting flames of fire from all the senses and extremities of their bodies"* who instruct him as to how to carry out his plans.

Other leaders working with Popé include: Luis and Lorenzo **Tupatú** (from Picurís), Antonio Malacate (Cochití), Francisco **El Ollita** and **Nicolás Jonva** (San Ildefonso), Domingo **Romero** (Tesuque), Antonio **Bolsas** (Santa Fe), Cristóbal Yope (San Lázaro), Alonzo **Catiti** (Santo Domingo), El Jaca (or Saca, from Taos), Domingo **Naranjo** (Santa Clara)...

Two men from Tesuque, Nicolás Catua and Pedro Omtua, are arrested by Maese de Campo **Francisco Gómez Robledo** because they are found with knotted ropes in their possession.

Caciques at *la Ciénega,* Tanos, and San Marcos oppose the revolt and inform Gov. Otermín of Popé's plans. Popé learns he has been discovered so he puts out the word that **August 10 is the day for revolt.**

August 10: **Fray Juan Pío** walks to Tesuque from Santa Fe to say Mass but the Pueblo is virtually empty when he arrives. When he finds them the warriors are heavily armed and wearing warpaint. *"What is this,"* he asks, *"are you mad? Do not disturb yourselves. I will help you and die a thousand deaths for you."* He is rewarded with a deadly shower of arrows, his accompanying soldier, Pedro Hidalgo, escaping to Santa Fe only because he is on horseback.

Popé's instructions are carried out all over N.M.: **DEATH** to all Christian Hispanics and Christian *wethead Indians!*

Everyone found in outlying ranchos is killed immediately, whether man, woman, or child.

For example:
Petronila de Salas and her family of **ten sons and daughters** are murdered in their home.

At the hacienda of Tomé Dominguez **38** people are butchered in that one place.

The bodies of three missionaries are piled one on the other at the San Ildefonso church door.

Bands of heavily armed Indians comb through all farms and ranches and *everyone* found in **outlying areas** is killed immediately. All homes are pillaged then burned, the smoke casting a deadly pall throughout the countryside.

The **Spanish Archives** in Santa Fe are burned.

Horses and mules are taken or killed so Hispanics will be unable to communicate with New Spain.

All **friars** are killed immediately. The Pueblos take particular delight in destroying the churches and **torturing missionaries** who had forced them to destroy their own kivas and their own religious items. To add insult to injury, the enraged Indians urinate and defecate on church altars, they tear up priest's vestments, smash crosses and santos, rip apart altarscreens, benches, confessionals, etc., then set fires to the rubble. Within a short time all **churches** are razed to the ground, including the **massive   Pecos church,** the grandest in N.M.

Amerinds who refuse to give up their Christian doctrine are summarily killed.

THERE ARE TRAGIC ACCOUNTS of some of the missionaries' last moments on this New Mexican earth:

Fray **Juan de Jesús** at   **Jémez** is captured and informed he will be **knighted**. He is taken to the cemetery at night and **stripped naked** then, *amid many candles* as in a solemn Christian ceremony of knighthood, **he is forced to mount a pig** then beaten as he is challenged to have his stupid Christian God and his warrior St. James *"come and save you now."* Finally he is kicked off the pig and forced to get on all fours while **warriors** take turns mounting his back and *whipping his naked flank with a quirt*. Despite all this the **valiant Fray Juan** tells them ***"Do with me as you wish for this joy of yours will not last and in ten years you will consume each other."***
This infuriates his tormentors even more so they bludgeon him to death with war clubs until his face is unrecognizeable.

At **Oraibi**, one of the **Hopi** villages, the warriors were wearing **kachina masks** when they broke into the priests' house and murdered the two friars.

Fray **Lucas Maldonado** and Fray **Juan de Val** are seized at **Acoma**, along with an elderly Christian *mestiza*. All three are **stripped naked**, the woman is forced between the two friars and all are tied together with a rope. The trio is then led around the pueblo while they are beaten all the while. At the entrance of the convent the warriors invite everyone to finish them off with rocks and they are stoned by all who wish to do so. Then as they lay dying their bodies are pierced time and again with warriors' lances. Their bloody but now lifeless forms are then dragged around the pueblo and eventually thrown into the **garbage pit.**

In a few hours some 400 settlers and 21 friars lay dead. Aside from Santa Fe, **Los Cerrillos** villagers, led by Sargento Mayor **Bernabé Márquez** and other Márquez family members, are the only ones to hold their attackers at bay until they are rescued by a squadron of soldiers.

[It is estimated that there are about 170 colonists in N.M. who can bear arms against about 8,000 warriors, for an approximate ratio of 47 to 1.]

Hispanic survivors from the Río Arriba gather at Santa Fe while those from the Río Abajo congregate at Isleta (which is attacked) under the leadership of **Alonso García.**

August 13: **Santa Fe** is the only Hispanic settlement undestroyed but it is surrounded by mounted Pueblos and Apaches. Governor Otermín asks for peace *"...and you will be pardoned."* The Indians jeer at the offer and demand that all Native Americans held by the Spanish be given up to them, along with the hated secretary of war Francisco Javier *"...who is the reason we have risen...."* Governor Otermín refuses and the **battle for Santa Fe** rages for nine days until the water supply is cut off.

August 14: News reaches the congregated settlers at Isleta Pueblo that all Hispanics in the Río Arriba area have been killed. A vote is taken as to what to do after which Maese de Campo **Alonso García** leads the settlers south toward El Paso in accordance with their vote.

August 20: The Indians around Santa Fe are heard shouting: *Your god is dead, the god who was your father is dead and Mary who is your mother and your saints are pieces of rotten wood...*

August 21: Governor Otermín gathers his forces and sallies out to do battle, believing it is better to *"die fighting rather than of hunger and thirst..."* Amerinds lose about 350 warriors while others are sent scattering but thousands of fighters remain and time is on their side.

Governor Otermín leads all colonists in a retreat out of Santa Fe toward Isleta where he hopes to link up with the colonists from the Río Abajo and return to quell the rebellion. The warriors, who might have killed everyone with a mass attack from all sides, allow the hated Christians to leave without further bloodshed.

September 6: The **survivors from Santa Fe and Isleta** link up south of Socorro and continue to El Paso where they are saved by Fray **Francisco de Ayeta** who is leading the supply caravan to N.M. There are searches for family members or friends who might have made it through the unexpected attack. About 400 Hispanics, mostly noncombatants, are lost in the slaughter.

MARTYRS
The 21 Franciscan missionaries killed by their charges include: **Juan Bernal, José Espeleta, José Figueroa, Juan de Jesús María, Francisco Lorenzana, Lucas Maldonado, José Montes de Oca, Antonio Mora, Luis Morales, Juan Pedrosa, Juan Bautista Pío, Matías Rendón, Antonio Sánchez, Agustín de Santa María, Juan Talabán, Manuel Tinoco, José Trujillo, Tomás Torres, Juan del Val, Fernando Velasco, Domingo Vera.**

After defeat of the Christians, Popé and some of his captains like **El Jaca** of Taos, **Alonso Catiti** of Santo Domingo, and **Luis Tupatú** of Picurís, travel throughout the province, instructing all people to live according to their ancient customs in order to engender peace, harmony, and prosperity. At Santa Ana a large feast is prepared from the kitchens of the missionaries and served in the Hispanic manner. Popé sits at the head of the table, Catiti at the other end. Using chalices taken from churches they toast curses to the Christians and their hated religion. Popé toasts Catiti: *To your health Reverend Father*, and Catiti replies: *And to yours, Excellency*.

Churches are razed, including the massive   Pecos church, the grandest in N.M., crosses and images are hacked to pieces, vestments are torn up, chalices are fouled with human excrement.

The Spanish Archives in Santa Fe are thrown into the public square and burned.

Amerinds still guided by Christian doctrine are summarily killed.

Estufas, kivas, are to be rebuilt and masks for use in kachina dances are to be made. Couples married in church are permitted to leave their spouses and take whomever they wish. Christian names are abolished and only traditional ones are used. [Upon baptism, Native Americans were given Christian, i.e., Spanish, names.] Baptism is washed away with yucca-root soap. Anyone who speaks Spanish is punished with a severe whipping.

Hispanic   crops are outlawed and all Hispanic seeds are ordered destroyed.

TIMELINE

1680-1730: **The commerce of the proliferating English settlements in the Carolinas depends on trading hides, furs, rum, and slaves.** The English make slaves of *"countless thousands"* of Indian men, women, and children from dozens of coastal tribes and instigate stronger nations to bring them captives if they want English trade goods like guns and metal knives. Many nations like the **Cusabo, Wimbee, Edisto, Klawa, Stoono, Coosa, Isaw, Wanniah, Ashepoo, Sampa, Elaisie**, etc., virtually disappear from coastal regions. English slavers now have to raid further inland, all the while encouraging larger tribes to bring in captives to exchange for trade goods.

1704: Carolina governor and slave dealer **James Moore** sends his troops against the Spanish Franciscan missions in the Floridas . He ravages all missions, burns the Franciscan priests at the stake, virtually wipes out the populations of **Apalachee, Timucua**, and **Calusa** nations, and returns to South Carolina with more than 6,000 Christian Indians, taken from the Spanish missions, for the thriving English slave trade.

slaves are an *"insatiable demand"* in **New England, New York, Pennsylvania**, etc., and in other English colonies like **Bermuda, Jamaica, Barbados, the Bahamas**, etc. The slavery is so brutal few Indians survive their first year and therefore must be replaced, giving the slave trade great impetus.

1730: Indian populations have to be sought so far inland, reaching to the **French Louisiana Territory**, that it is very expensive for the English to finance slaving expeditions and to boot the

French adhere to a more protective policy toward Indians. English authorities finally decide it is **cheaper to import black Africans** so Africa is looked to for new slave populations.

[A.M. Josephy writes that the slave labor structure of the eastern seaboard and American South was founded *"on the backs of Indian people,"* that Indians were thus utilized until the English colonies ran out of Indian populations to enslave, thus exterminating nation after nation via a brutal system of slavery that saw most Indian slaves dead within a year. Then, says Josephy, the English took to importing black Africans for slave purposes.]

1681

November 5: **Gov. Otermín leads an expedition north to reconquer N.M.** It is learned that Popé has already been deposed because of his tyrannical rule. From Indians captured along the way he learns the **reasons for the Pueblo Revolt:** for more than 70 years the Indians resented the Christians because they had destroyed native religious objects, prohibited ceremonials, and humiliated and/or punished the Elders; constables had ill-treated and punished them; their kivas were destroyed; forced labor was so burdensome the Amerinds didn't have time to work for themselves; Church duties came to be a tiresome burden...

December 5: **Isleta Pueblo** is recaptured easily. Fray **Francisco de Ayeta** arrives the next day and is greeted cordially. Gov. Otermín sends emissaries to other Pueblos, asking for peace. But the villages are deserted. A few individuals are captured, among them one **Bartolomé de Ojeda,** a ladino from Zía Pueblo.

TIMELINE

By late 1681 **anarchy is reported in Pueblo land**: the drought continues; civil war erupts when food shortages causes inter-Pueblo thefts; internecine battles take place because caciques, medicine men, and warriors all demand to be acknowledged as leaders; mounted Apaches raid what little food the Pueblo nations possesses; Popé is deposed (and replaced by Luis Tupatú) because of his excessive demands for grain, livestock, and women; the alliance that had thrown out the Spanish is now shattered beyond repair; the drought lasts for nine years while hunger and pestilence rules the land.

1683-1686
Domingo Jironza Petriz Cruzate is Governor.

1684
AMERIND LAND GRANTS

Governor Jironza Cruzate is given permission to make land grants to Pueblo people: each Pueblo is documented as owning a parcel of land containing four square leagues (17,712 acres) around its village.

1685

1685: The French attempt to establish a colony in Texas under the leadership of **La Salle**. Diego de Peñalosa, ex-governor of N.M., is credited with supplying information for the expedition.

1686-1689

Pedro Reneros de Posada is Governor.

1689-1691

Domingo Jironza Petriz Cruzate is Governor.

PUEBLO LAND GRANTS

In an effort to conciliate the Pueblo people, Governor Cruzate reaffirms official land grants awarded to the Pueblos who swear allegiance to Spain. **Bartolomé de Ojeda** from Zía Pueblo advises Governor Cruzate as to conditions in various Pueblos [and it is thought he returned to Pueblo-land with written documentation that the various Pueblos would legally continue to exist and be respected in perpetuity].

September: Land grant documents are issued for Acoma, Jémez, San Felipe, Santo Domingo, Zía, Cochití, Pecos, Picurís, San Juan, Zuñi.

Ca. 1691-92
PUEBLO DIPLOMACY

According to Pueblo traditions, a group of men from Jémez, Zía, Santa Ana, San Felipe, Pecos, etc., journey to El Paso to confer with the Spaniards and ask them to return to Pueblo-land. The group is guided and guaranteed safe passage by **Bartolomé de Ojeda.**

Diego de Vargas

NEW MEXICO'S KNIGHT VALIANT

November 8, 1643: **Diego José de Vargas Zapata y Luján Ponce de León y Contreras** is baptized. His parents are **Alonso Vargas** and **M. Margarita Contreras y Arráiz** of Madrid, Spain. [Diego's ancestors had been written about for six centuries because they were *"warrior knights, bishops, advisors to kings, and friends of the saints."* Four generations of Vargas men, including Diego's father, were knights in the military Order of Santiago.]

1646(?): Margarita and her children are living with her parents while Alonso is away on campaign.

1647: Capt. Alonso de Vargas moves his family to the ancestral Vargas residence an Almendro Street in Madrid. They are part of the middle-ranking nobility in the Spanish capital.

April 17, 1649: Margarita, five-year-old Diego's mother, dies. She is 26 years old.

1650: Alonso de Vargas is appointed as Alcalde Mayor of Chiapa (then in **Guatemala)** and sails for the New World. His family stays in Madrid where Diego spends his growing years.

1659: Alonso is **Maese de Campo** in Santiago de Guate-mala. He marries Jerónima de Guinea y Murga, daughter of a prominent family, and they have three children.

1660: Diego requests that Lic. José de Castro Castillo be named his legal guardian to manage the allowance that Alonso Vargas had provided for his son. Diego owns various books, studies Latin, has a manservant who earns 100 reales a month. Diego has a tailor who makes him suits for the various seasons, he wears fancy hats, silk stockings, gloves, etc., and owns 22 pairs of shoes. He takes dancing lessons.

1662: Diego petitions the Crown for permission to act legally for himself.

November, 1662: Vargas goes to the University of Valladolid for advanced studies.

May 5, 1664: Diego marries **Beatriz Pimentel de Prado Vélez de Olazábal.** They reside mostly in Torrelaguna and their five children are all born there. Diego is active in managing all family affairs.

Diego de Vargas
Courtesy Museum of NM, #11409

1666: Alonso Vargas dies in Guatemala.

1667: Money is scarce and Diego borrows 4,000 ducados against the revenues of the Vargas estate.

1670: Diego asks the Crown for an appoint-ment to a post in the New World.

Calligraphy by Jimmy Ning

1672: Vargas gets his appointment.

1673: After exasperating and expensive delays Diego finally sails to Guatemala *"to settle affairs and his share of the inheritance resulting from his father's death."* He is described as of average stature, straight hair, broad face. He talks with a lisp.

Once in Guatemala he is appointed to an interim post in the mining district of Teutila. He has to borrow 2,200 pesos from a friend.

1674: Diego is Alcalde Mayor of Teutila with a salary of 250 pesos a year.

July 10, 1674: Vargas receives the news that his wife has died back in Spain.

1676: A fire breaks out in the parish church and Diego leads the effort to save the statues in it. Vargas is lauded for his bravery.

1679: Diego de Vargas is transferred to the major silver- and gold-mining area of Tlalpujahua. He owns a residence in Mexico City and around this time he is living with a woman (thought to be) named **Nicolasa Rincón**. They have three children but never marry.

1684: The Viceroy reports that Vargas has tripled Crown revenue from its silver mines in Tlalpujahua and recommends that Diego be considered for higher office.

1687: Vargas is appointed to the governorship of New Mexico after a payment of 2,500 pesos. Due to bureaucratic delays and errors Diego is reappointed to Tlalpujahua.

September, 1692: Vargas is finally permitted to journey north to New Mexico.

1692-1697

Diego de Vargas Zapata Luján Ponce de León is Governor.

1692

February: Governor Vargas finds the New Mexican refugees living in El Paso in terrible condition. He reports that soldiers of the garrison have neither leather jackets nor swords and only 132 horses. There are scarcely 100 heads of families who own maybe 200 horses and mules, no cattle, perhaps 600 sheep, most of them belonging to the missionaries. He requests modern muskets and makes immediate plans to lead a reconnaissance expedition to Santa Fe, assuring the Viceroy that he will restore the Pueblo Indians to Spain and Christianity *"without treachery, even though it might cost him his life."*

AMERIND CULTURE

The **Spanish horse** has proliferated among Native American nations and changes their lives like few other facets of European culture.

1692

T I M E L I N E

"Witches" are being put to death in the Massachusetts Bay Colony at Salem.

1611 : **Father Alonso de Salazar**, a judge for the **Spanish Inquisition**, issues a report containing *"decisive and devastating objections to witch trials"* after investigating a "witch panic" which had come in from France to the Basque country of Spain. He orders his investigators to take all confessed "witches," many of whom were children, to the scene of the supposed **sabbat** and have them each relate what had transpired. All accounts contradict each other and Father Salazar concludes that there isn't *"to be found a single proof nor even the slightest indication from which to infer that one act of witchcraft has actually taken place."*

[No one in Spain is executed for witchcraft after 1611 due to the empirical methods used by the **Spanish Inquisition**. This is a stark contrast to proceedings in other European countries and the English colonies.]

1647-1691 : At least **83 witchcraft trials** have been heard in court from **Massachusetts to Virginia** during this period. Twenty-two have resulted in executions.

1662: The post of **Witch Finder General** is in effect in English lands but up to this date only two people have been executed for "witchcraft" in the English colonies.

1692: **Puritan divines** control the legal and political apparatus of the **Massachusetts Bay Colony**. They are convinced that *"Satan is loose in our midst"* so they lend all support to prosecution of witches. Hundreds are charged with causing the *"demonic possession"* of a number of adolescent girls and various other members of the community. The accused, mostly women, are interrogated while standing for hours on end, their naked bodies are *"inspected"* for any marks *"of the devil,"* etc., and they could be thrown into deep water to see if they would float, which was a sign of guilt. There are 20 executions, 19 of which are women, including:
Rebecca Nurse, age 71, is sentenced to die by hanging for afflicting (biting, pinching, bruising, tormenting their breasts) various persons of the community, who also saw her *"riding behind the Black Man;"*
the beautiful **Susanna Martín** is condemned to death because she has *"appeared"* to so many men of the community in their dreams, etc.;
Giles Cory refuses to speak at his trial so his property can't be confiscated but the automatic sentence for refusing to testify is to be *pressed to death*. Cory dies lying naked on the bare ground, his arms and legs pulled apart with ropes, covered with *"as much iron and stone as he can bear and more...untill hee dye."*

[The witchcraft craze begins to die down only when members of the upper classes are accused of "witchery."]

1693 : The eminent Puritan divine **Cotton Mather** (the most prolific author of the English colonial period) publishes *The Wonders of the Invisible World* as a defense of the Salem witch trials and executions.

1700: Boston merchant **Robert Calef** writes *More Wonders of the Invisible World* in answer to the "ridiculous" work of Cotton Mather. **Increase Mather**, Cotton's father, orders the public burning of all copies of Calef's work in the yard of **Harvard College**.

1702: Witch hunter **John Hale** writes in his account of the Salem trials that *"at last it was evidently seen that there must be a stop put or the Generation of Children of God would fall under condemnation for witchcraft."*

1750: **The "witch craze" is ended in the Western world.**

[**Joseph Klaits** writes that *"witch trials were symptomatic of a dramatic rise in fear and hatred of women during the era of the Reformation."* **W.A. Beck** postulates that *"Ample evidence exists that especially Spanish women"* took on *"basic beliefs and superstitions"* of the Indians, which is what happens when *"Europeans"* blended their blood and culture with the *"natives."* He doesn't give reasons as to why "witches" appeared in Europe or from Massachusetts to Virginia.]

1692 (con't)
RECONQUEST

August 16: The official effort to recover N.M. is launched from El Paso with an expedition led by Capt. **Roque de Madrid.** Camp is made at Robledo where Vargas arrives with the main expeditionary force. **Bartolomé de Ojeda,** from Zía Pueblo, is invaluable for his abilities in warfare and because he is an excellent interpreter who can speak, read, and write Spanish.

Ojeda reports to Vargas that N.M. is being destroyed by anarchy, civil war, and Apache attacks. The Zuñis and Hopis are at war with the Keres Pueblos, who fear the Tewa groups will also attack them; the Apaches are attacking all of them.

August 17: Vargas crosses the Río Grande river and rides north with 50 presidial soldiers from El Paso along with their officers, 10 armed citizens, 100 Pueblo Indians, 3 Franciscan friars, pack animals, live-stock, wagons full of provisions, one small cannon and a mortar. While the expedition is small for the task of reconquering and resettling N.M., Vargas is considered an effective leader who can deal with the hardships of travel, service in isolated outposts, and dangers of military campaigns.

Even more important, he is able to lead, effectively manage, and relate to Hispanics, Indians, blacks, etc., within the strictures of colonial society.

September 11: Vargas enters Santa Fe unopposed. With him comes *Nuestra Señora del Rosario,* Our Lady of the Rosary, **La Conquistadora** [now referred to as *Our Lady of Peace*].

September 16: The **Tupatú brothers** of Picurís Pueblo, **Luis and Lorenzo** (Luis being one of the principal leaders in the 1680 Revolt) confer with Vargas and the missionary fathers over cups of chocolate. The Tupatús become allies of Vargas and are given full pardon for their role in the great rebellion.

September 21: An expedition against the large **Pecos Pueblo** begins and includes 300 well-armed warriors from Picurís, led by the Tupatús. The   Pecos people led by **Juan de Ye** welcome Vargas peacefully.

October 7: Vargas enters an abandoned **Taos Pueblo** but two men later come down from the mountains to confer with him: Governor Francisco Pacheco and a *ladino* boy named Josefillo (Little Joe). Vargas likes this youngster, **José López Naranjo,** who leaves with the Spanish force, casting his lot with the Spaniards.

October 30: A western expedition begins, targeting Cochití, Santo Domingo, San Felipe, then Acoma, Jémez, Zuñi, and the Hopis. There are only 89 soldiers and 30 Native American allies in the expeditionary force. There are scouting reports of conspiracies but not one single battle has to be fought.

Several persons believed to have perished in the Revolt are found alive: Francisco Márquez finds the wife and daughter of his uncle, Pedro Márquez; Martín Hurtado finds his sister and their mother Juana; José Domínguez de Mendoza finds his sister and her five children; etc.

The first *entrada* is a complete success and within four months 23 Pueblos of 10 different nations are again allies instead of enemies. Vargas writes that the province now has to have Hispanic colonists *("five hundred families")* and at least 100 soldiers in order to secure the bloodless Reconquest.

1693

T I M E L I N E

The *Mercurio Volante,* **written by Professor Carlos de Sigüenza, a tribute to** Diego de Vargas **for the reconquest of New Mexico, is published in Spain.**

PIONEERS

October 4: **The recolonization of N.M.** begins with some 800 persons [who didn't all arrive at the same time] which includes families, various soldiers, and a number of Indian allies led by **Bartolomé de Ojeda** from Zía-Picurís Pueblos, along with 900 cattle, 2,000 horses, 1,000 mules. **Carlos Lopopolo** provides the following general list of colonists:

[Names may and usually do have variant spellings; carrying the mother's surname, generally written after the father's surname, must also be kept in mind; an "M" abbreviates *María,* a "J" for *José*]:

A:

Abalos: Antonio; Abrego: Francisco; Francisca; Acosta: María; Aguila: Miguel Gerónimo;

Aguilar: (Capt.) Alonso;

Aguilera: Pedro, M. Luisa;

Agular: J. Benito Isari; Antonio Isari;

Aguliar: Miguel Gerónimo;
Alamais: Manuela Antonia;
Alatia: María;
Alcalá: J. de Atienza;
Alemán: M. de la Cruz;
Almazán: Ana;
Anaya: Antonio de; Ana de; Juana; Francisco de Anaya; J. Salvador de Anaya; M. Josepha de;
Altamirino: Felipa Lechuga; Juan Tafoya; Anaya: Ynes; (Capt.) Francisco; Nicolasa; Luis; Ancizo: Juana;
Angel: Miguel Angeles: Catalina de los; Antonio: Juan;
Anzures: Bartolomé; Gabriel, Juana; Teresa; Apodaca: Cristóbal; Francisco; J. Gonzáles; Aragón: Juan de
Pedrasa; Antonio; Catalina Varela; Cristóbal; Félix; Francisco; Ignacio; Josefa Gonzáles; Juan; Juan Antonio; Juana; María;
Aranda: Mateo; Archuleta: Juan; Juana; Pablo; Pasquala; Juan; Andrés; Leonora; Juan; Cristóbal;
Aretia: (Capt.) Francisco;
Argüello: Juana;
Aris: Phelipa; Diego; J. Mateo; Joseph; Juana; Martín; Armijo: Antonio;
Arratia: Antonia; Juan Antonio; Mathais; Phelipa;
Arroyo: Diego; Arteaga: Felipe; M. López, Miguel;
Arvizu: Felipe; Tomás;
Aspeltia: Inés;
Atencia: Calstano; Francisco; Ignacio; Juan; María;
Atienza: José; Juan;
Avalos: Antonio; Juana; Pedro; Avila: María; Pedro Ayala: Diego Márquez; Antonio; Miguel; Azate: Juan;
B:
Baca: Cristóbal; Felipe; Ignacio; Lenora; Manuel,
Bachiniva;
Balanegra: Simón;
Barba: Domingo Martín;
Barbosa: Simón;
Bejarano: Tomás;
Belásquez: Miguel;
Bernal: Francisco;
Betanzos: Andrés; Diego;
Brito: Agustín; Francisco; Joseph; Juan
          León;
Brixida: María;
Brusales: Juan;
Bustillos;
Busto: Juan de la Paz;
C:
Cabrera: Josefa; M. de Medina;
Cáceres: (Sgt.) Juan Ríos;
Caldana: Mateo; Camarillo: Diego;

Stephen Gallegos, Illustrator
Atlanta, Georgia

Candelaria: Blas de la; Feliciano de la;

Carabajal: María;

Caras: Juana de Aras;

Cárdenas: Petronia;

Careres: Juan Ruiz;

Carrera: Tomás Gutiérrez de la;

Carrillo: M. Nicolasa;

Cásares: Juan Ruiz;

Casitias: Joseph;

Castillo: Isabel López del; José Cortez; Lucía del; (Sgt. Mayor) Diego del; Pedro López del; Castro: María; María Rodarte de; Cervantes: Juan Manuel Martínez; Manuel; María Zuniga y; Chávez: (Capt.) Fernando Durán y; Joseph Durán y; María; Pedro Durán y; Christina: Juana; Cisneros: María;

Coca: Miguel de la Vega y;

Concepción: Pascuala de la; San Juan de: María de la;

Contrertas: Joseph; Cordero: Juan Ruiz;

Córdoba: Antonio Coronanda: María;

Cortés: Juan;

Cortez: José;

Cortinas: Pedro;

Crisostomo: Juana;

Cruz: Tomás de la; Ana de la; Cecilia de la; María de la; Miguel de la;

Cruzate: (Capt. Gen.) Domingo Jironza Petriz de;

Cuellar: Cristóbal;

Cueva: Petronila de la;

Cuitar: Alonso Rodríguez de la;

D:

Dios: Juan de;

Dominíguez: Antonio; Francisco; José; Juan; Juana; Petrona; Petrolina; Joseph; Antonia; Durán: Antonia; Antonia Ursala; Antonio; Bartolomé; Catallina; Cristóbal; Diego; Francisco; Felipe; Josepha; Juana; Lázaro; Luis; María; Miguel; Salvador; Ysabel;

E:

Encarnación: María de la;

Escalante: Antonio Gonzáles;

Esperaza: Catallina Montoya;

Esparza: María;

Espindola: Catalina; Francisco;

Espinosa: Nicolás;

Esquibel: Juan Antonio; Esteban: Juan;

Estrada: Juan;

F:

Farfán: Fray;

Félix: Antonio;

Fernández: Diego Manuel de la Santísima Trinidad de;

Florida: Geronima Días;

Fontes: Cristóbal; Francisco; Josepha;

Foranco: Ygnacio de Santa María;

Fragua: Pedro;

Francisco: Matías;

Fresque, Ambrosio;

Fresqui: Mariana;

G

Gaitán: Isabel; Joseph;

Gallegos: Joseph;

Gamboa: Antonio;

Ramírez; Manuel; Miguel; Juan; Phelipa;

Garas: Juana;

García: Ana María; Alonso; (Ensign) Alonso; Antonia; Antonio; Casilda; Cristóbal; Diego; Elvira; Esteban López de; Felipe; Francisca; Francisco Jurado de; Ignacio López de; Juan; Juan de Noriega; Juan Esteban López de: Juan Jurado; Juana; Lucía; Luis; María; María Francisca; Miguel; Nicolás; Ramón; Theoria; Vicente;

Geuterero: Juana;

Gilteme: Joseph;

Girón: Rafaél Tellez;

Godines: Antonio; M. Luisa de Villaviecencio y; M. Luisa;

Godo: (Sgt. Mayor) Juan Lucero;

Godoy: Juan de Dios; Juan Lucero; María Luzero; Francisco Luzero; Nicolás Lucero;

Gómez: Antonio; Catalina; Diego; Domingo; Francisco; Josepha; Juan; Laureano; Manuel; Marcial; Margarita; M. de la Rosa; María; Thomana; Ursala;

Góngora: Cristóbal; Francisca; Gregoria; Juan de; Juana de; Juan Joseph; M. Gertrudis;

Gonzáles: Andrés; Antonia Blas; Catalina; Cristóbal; Damiana; Diego; María; Estefana; Francisco; Francisco de la Rosa; José; Josepha; Juana; Juan; Melchora de Los Reyes; Pedro; Petronia; (Councilman) Sebastián; Sevastián; Ysabel;

Granillo: Domingo; Josepha; Juan; Luis; María; (Sgt. Mayor) Luis; Gregoria: Antonia; Juan;

Greimaldos: Diego Sánchez;

Griego: Ana Martín; (Ensign) Blas; Agustín; Catalina; Francisco; Juan; Lenor; María;

Grola (Gurule): Santiago;

Guadalajara: Jacinta;

Guatamala: Juana;

Guebara: Pedro;

Guerrero: Felipa,

Guerro: Juana;

Guevara: Juan de Fernández de Atienza Ladrón de; Miguel Ladrón de;

Guido: Juan;

Gutiérrez: Ana; Antonia; Juan Rogue (Roque); Miguel; Phelipe; Rogue;

H:

Heras: María de las;

Hernández: Francisco; Gertrudis;
Herrera: Antonio; Domingo; Gertrudis de la Candelaria; Josepha; Juan; Juana; Luisa; M. Tapia; Miguel;
Sebastián; Ynes;
Hidalgo: (Ensign) Diego; Pedro;
Hinojos: Diego; Fernando; Josepha; Nicolás Ruiz;
Hita: Tomás;
Holguín: Cristóbal; (Capt.) Salvador; Juan; Juan López; Tomás;
Hurtado: Andrés; Catalina; Diego; Juan Páez; María; Mariana;
I:
Iñigo: Francisca Sánchez y; Jacinto Sánchez de; Pedro Sánchez;
Isasi: Antonio de Aguilera;
J:
Jaramillo: Cristóbal Varela; Lucía; Lucía Varela; Juan Varela; María; Yumar Varela;
Jirón: Diego; Isabel; Joseph Telles; Nicolás; Tomás; Jorge: Antonio; Jurado: J. García; Francisco;
K:
L:
Lara: Ana Morena de;
Larea: Isabela;
Layba: Pedro; Juana;
Lechuga: Pedro;
León: Cristóbal;
Leyba: Francisco; Juana;
Linares: Miguel;
Lobato: Bartolomé;
López: (Ensign) Pedro; Angelo; (Capt.) Francisco; Carlos; Cristóbal; Francisco; Jacinto; José; Joseph;
        María; Nicolás; Pedro; (Sgt. Mayor) Diego;
Lorenzo: Francisco;
Losada: Juan Cristóbal; Lucía Varela; María Varela; Magdalena Varela; Pedro Varela;
Lucero: Antonio; Catalina; Francisco; Juan de Dios; Nicolás; (Sgt. Mayor) Diego;
        Luis: (Capt.) Juan;
Luján: Agustín; (Capt.) Juan Luis; Cristóbal; Diego; Domingo; Isabel; Josefa Juana; Juan; Matis (Matías?);
        Miguel; Pedro;
Luna: (Capt.) Diego; Diego; Juan;
Lusana: Clara,
Luxan: Agustine; Francisco; Luis, María;
M:
Machuca: Juan de Vargas;
Madrid: Francisco; (Capt.) Juan; Jacinto; José; Joseph; Juan, Juana; Lorenzo; Pedro; Rogue; (Sgt. Mayor)
        Lorenzo;
Maes: Luis;
Maese: Alonso; Alonso López; Luis; Miguel;
Magdalena: María;
Mandragón: Sebastián Monroy de;
Mantaño: José;

Manzanares: Ana de Sandoval y; Juan Mateo Sadoval y; María Sandoval; Sevastiana de Sandoval y; Marcelino; Cristóbal;

Marcos: Lucas;

Marín: Francisco;

Márquez: (Capt.) Antonio; Bernabé; Diego; Francisco; Juan; Juana Jaramillo y Zamora; Pedro;

Martín: (Ensign) Pedro; Antonio; Apoliar; Cristóbal; Diego; Domingo; Francisco; Hernando; Juan; Juana; Lucía; Luis; María; Pasquala; Pedro; Sevastián;

Martínez: Gerónimo; Juan de Dios Sandoval;

Mascareñas: J. Bernardo;

Mederos: (Capt.) Pedro López;

Medina: Alonso; Juan; Micaela; Manuela;

Méndez: Thomas;

Mendoza: Antonia; Antonio Dominíguez de; Francisco Dominíguez de; Juan Domingo; María; Tomé Dominíguez;

Mestas: Tomás;

Miguel: José;

Miranda; Miguel;

Mizquia: Lázaro;

Molina: Sebastián; Simón;

Montalvo: Rogue;

Montaño: Antonio; Catalina-, Lucas; María;

Montero: Pedro;

Montesuma: Ysabel Caso;

Montiel: José;

Montoya: Ana María Griego; Antonio; Diego; Felipe; Francisca; Josepha; María; Onafre; Phelipe;

Mora: Francisco de la; María;

Moraga: Ana; Antonia; Felipe; Lázaro; María;

Morales: Francisca;

Moreles: Juan;

Morán: Agueda; Miguel;

Moriello: Cristóbal;

Moya: Antonio;

Munier: Pedro;

N:

Naranjo: Pasqual;

Negrette: Manuela; José Jaramillo; Mateo;

Nevares: (Capt.) Joseph; José;

Nicolás: María de San;

Nieto: Cristóbal;

Noriega: Juan García de; Juana García de;

Nuñez: José;

Stephen Gallegos, Illustrator
Atlanta, Georgia

0:

Ocanto: María;

Ochoa: Juan;

Ojeda: Antonio; Juana;

Olivas: Isabel; Juan de la Cruz y;

Olives: Juan Bautista;

Ontiveros: Francisco;

Organo: Magdalena;

Orozco: Mariana Salas;

Ortega: Andrés; Dionisio; Josepha; María; Nicolás; Nicolás de; Pablo; Simón; Tiburcio;

Ortíz: Juana; María; Nicolás de; Nicolasa; Sebastiana;

Osuna: María;

Oton: Nicolás; Margarita;

P:

Pacheco: Acencio; Juan; Silvestre; Padilla: Joseph de; Páez: Agustine;

Palocios (Palacios): María de Encarnación; María de; Palomino: Tomás; Papigochu; Parades: Ganzalo de;

Parra: Gregorio Cobos de la; Pasqual Covos de la; Paz: Juan de la; Manuela de;

Pedraza: Miguel; Francisco Romero;

Pedroza: Lázaro de Artiaga y;

Pelaez: Jacinto;

Peralta: Juan Bautista Anzaldo de;

Perca: Agustine; Antonia Varela; Isabel; Juan; Juana; Phelipe;

Porras: Francisco; Posada: (Capt.) Pedro Romero;

Q:

Quebara: Pedro;

Quintana: Miguel;

Quiros: Diego Aris de; José; Juana;

R:

Ramiréz: Gregorio; Nicolás; Petrona;

Ramos: Marcos; Miguel; Juan;

Reina: Juan;

Reinoso: Ana;

Rey: Nicolás Rodríguez;

Reyes: Agustine de los; Inés de los; María de los; Sebastián de los;

Ribera: Ana; Juan; Salvador Matías;

Rincón: Antonio Francisco;

Río: Alonso del; (Capt.) Alonso del; (Capt.) Juan del;

Ríos: Juana de los;

Riva: Miguel García de;

Rivera: Francisco; Josefa; Teresa;

Robledo: Ana María; Bartolomé Gómez; Francisco Gómez;

Rodon: Francisco Palamino;

Rodríguez: Agustín; Alonso; Francisca; José; Juan Severino; Manuel; Nicolás; Sebastián;

Rojas: Phelipa Rica de;

Romero: Baltazar; Bartolomé; Catalina; Diego; Felipe; Francisca; Francisco; Juan; Juan Antonio Juan
        Francisco; María; Phelipe; Salbador; Salvador;

Rosa: Antonia de la; María de la;

Roxas: Josepha Rico de; Ysabel Rico de;

Rueda: Juana;

Ruiz: Gregoria; Elena;

S:

Salas: Sebastián;

Salazar: Agustine; Baltazar Romero; Miguel; Francisca Ramiréz; Francisco; Isabela; Lucía; María; Pedro;
        Martín Serrano;

Samano: María; San Juan de Concepción;

San Nicolás: María;

Sánchez: Felipe; Juan; José; Pedro;

Sandoval: Phelipa; Tomás de Herrera y;

Santiago: Francisco; José; Julián;

Santos: Juan de los;

Sayagoa: Antonia;

Sedana: Antonia; Josefa;

Sedillo: Felipa Rico de Rojas; Joachin Rico de Roxas; Juan Rico de Rixas; María de Nava; Pedro; Pedro de;

Senorga: María Luisa de;

Serna: Antonia de la; Cristóbal de la; Felipa de la;

Serrano: Fernando Martín; Sevastián Martín;

Sevillana: Gertrudis;

Sierra: Nicolás;

Silva: Antonia;

Sisneros: Antonio

Solís (Ensign); Sonora;

Soria: Felipe;

Soto: Diego; Pasquala;

Sotomayor: María;

Suazo: Juan;

Susana: Clara,

T:

Tapia: Ana; Angela; Cristóbal; Lusía; María;

Tenorio: Miguel; Todos Santos San Bartolomé;

Torreón: Valle de;

Torres: Cristóbal: Francisco; Juana;

Toscano: Juan;

Trinadad: María;

Trujillo: Cristóbal; Cristóbal de (Elder); Cristóbal de (Younger); Damián; Diego; Bernadina de Salas y;
        Estafana; Gertrudis; Gregoria; Joseph Joaquín; Juan; Nicolás; Pasqual;

U:

Ulibarrí: Gertrudis Bautista de;

V.

Vaca: (Sgt. Mayor) Ygnacio; Valdés: J. Luis;

Valencia: Francisco, Juan; Juana; Juana de;

Valenzuela: Antonia;

Valle: José del;

Vallejo: Manuel;

Vendura: Francisco;

Varela: Cristoval; Diego; Teresa; Francisco; José; Petrona; Polonia; Rogue;

Vargas: Diego; Eusebio; Manuel; Vicente;

Vega; Francisca de la; Juana de la; María de la; Miguel de la;

Velasco: Cristóbal; (Capt.) Cristóbal de; Francisca; José; Micaela; Miguel García;

Velásquez: José;

Vera: Ana Jorge; Antonio; Isabel Jorge de; Melchor de; Vigil: Francisco Montes;

Villapando: Carlos; Juan;

Villasur: Pedro;

W:

X:

Xaramillo: Pedro Varela; Xavier: (Capt.) Francisco;

Ximénez: Phelipa;

Xirón: (Capt.) Joseph Telles; Rafaél Telles;

Y.

Yñigo (Iñigo): Jacinto Sánchez; Pedro Sánchez; Ysabel: Bernardina;

Z:

Zambrano: Josepha; Zamora: Juan; María de Mora

Zarate: Miguel;

Zepidia: María de;

Zevin: Diego.

[Hispano surnames that now become distinctively New Mexican include:
Abeyta, Acuña, Anaya, Apodaca, Aragón, Archuleta, Armijo, Baca, Barela, Benavídez, Bustos, Chávez, Córdova, Durán, García, Gallegos, Griego, Herrera, Jaramillo, Lucero, Luján, Madrid, Maestas, Mares, Montaño, Montoya, Ortiz, Pacheco, Padilla, Quintana, Romero, Saavedra, Salas, Salazar, Sánchez, Sandoval, Serna, Tafoya, Tapia, Trujillo, Valdez, Vigil, etc.

Among distinctive given names are **Esquipula, Secundino, Onofre, Belarmino, Miterio, Ologia, Abrelio.**]

1693 (con't)
SOCIETY
Bernardino Sena, nine years old, is among the many colonists with the Vargas groups. Brought to N.M. by his foster parents, **José del Valle and Ana de Ribera,** Sena begins a family tradition as a blacksmith and service to the Church [which survives into the 20th century; the Santa Fe *Sena Plaza* bears his name].

AMERIND
Pueblo population totals are estimated at 14,000 (an 18% drop from 1679).

REVOLT
Scouting reports indicate various Pueblos have changed their views and are contemplating resistance. **Santa Ana** and **San Felipe** remain loyal, along with **Pecos,** led by the valiant **Juan de Ye.** The resisting Pueblos are suspicious they will be punished for the Revolt of 1680. Vargas decides to send missionaries to the Pueblos but all 18 missionaries sign a petition saying that, while martyrdom is an acceptable price for conversion, **suicide is not.** They refuse to throw their lives away in a mere gesture.

December 29: After the rebellious Tanos refuse to surrender, Santa Fe is taken by force of arms in two days of bloody fighting. Nine Tanos die in battle, two commit suicide, and 70 are executed. The 400 who surrender are allotted to various Spaniards for 10 years of servitude.

1694
DIPLOMACY
January: **Juan de Ye** of Pecos reports to Governor Vargas that a large force of Tewas, Tanos, Picurís, and Apaches are massing for an attack on **Pecos Pueblo.** Vargas can't leave Santa Fe but he sends his second-in-command, **Roque de Madrid,** with 30 soldiers to defend the village, as he promised he would do if the Pecos ever needed help, and if the situation demands it, he will come himself if called. The attack doesn't materialize but the Pecos are *"...grateful for the sending of these soldiers to protect us..."* who were *"...welcomed warmly, and having the Spaniards so firmly on their side, they feel secure."* When the opportunity arises a trading holiday is proclaimed, and it is to be held at Pecos.

MILITARY
March: Vargas and native allies attack **San Ildefonso Pueblo,** without success.

SOCIETY
Food shortages are imperiling the newly arrived Hispanic colonists.

PUEBLO ALLIANCE
Juan de Ye, Governor of Pecos, confers with Vargas and offers to assist him in the pacification of N.M. These services, thought to have been prompted by Vargas' refusal to destroy Pecos in 1692, are to prove invaluable. Vargas often expresses the affection he feels for the Pecos people, *"...because they are loyal to the king our lord, are Christians, and friends of the Spaniards."*

[The aid provided by "don Juan" and his people secure them a permanent place in New Mexico's multi-cultural history.]

MILITARY
April 17: Warriors from **Cochití and Santo Domingo** are surprised at La Cieneguilla by the

Spanish and their loyal Pueblo auxiliaries led by **Bartolomé de Qjeda.** Christian forces
win the day.

PIONEERS

June 23: Fray **Francisco Farfán** and Capt. **Crist6hal de Velasco** lead slightly over **200 more colonists,**
which includes 67 families, into N.M. Formerly from the city and valley of Mexico, this new group
comes to be known as the *Españoles Mexicanos*. In this group are three survivors from the La
Salle colony. A list of these colonists [names may have variant spellings] includes:

A:

Aguila, Miguel Gerónimo del (with spouse Gerónima Días Florida, one child);

Aguilera, Pedro de (with spouse Juana de Torres, four children);

Aguilera Isasi, Antonio (with spouse Gertrudis Hernández, one child);

Anzures, Gabriel (with spouse Felipa Lechuga de Altamirino, one or two children);

Aragón, Ignacio (with spouse Sebastiana Ortiz, three children);

Atienza, Juan (widower, two children);

Atienza, José (with spouse Estafana de Trujillo and her two brothers, Damián and Joseph Joaquín Trujillo);

Atienza Alcalá, José (with spouse Gertrudis Sevillana);

B:

Betanzos, Andrés (widower, with two sons);

Betanzos, Diego (with spouse María Luisa de Senorga);

Busto, Juan de La Paz (with spouse Manuela Antonia de Alamias, two children);

C:

Cárdenas, Andre (with spouse Juana de Avalos, two children);

Castellanos, José (with spouse Manuela de Paz and their five children);

Cervantes, Manuel de (with spouse Francisca Rodríguez);

Cortés, Juan (spouse Juana de Aras [Caras?] with one, Perhaps three children);

Cortés del Castillo, José (with spouse María de Carbajal, two children);

D:

Dios, Juan de (with spouse and son);

E:

Esquibel, Juan Antonio (with spouse María de San Nicolás, two children);

F:

Fernández de Atienza Ladrón de Guevara (with spouse Teresa de Rivera, one child);

G:

Gamboa, Juan (with spouse María de Zepidia, three children);

Gamboa, Manuel (with spouse Ysabel Caso Montesuma);

Gamboa, Miguel (with spouse);

García Jurado, José (with spouse Josepha, de Herrera, and their two sons);

García de Riva, Miguel (with spouse Micaela Velasco and their five children);

Godines, Antonio (widower, with daughter);

Góngora, Cristóbal (with spouse Inés de Aspeitia);

Góngora, Juan (with spouse Petronila de la Cueva, five children);

H:

Herrera y Sandoval, Tomás de (with spouse Pascuala de la Concepción, two children);

J:

Jaramillo Negrete, José (with spouse María Sotomayor, three children);

Jirón, Diego (with spouse María de Mendoza, two children);

Jirón, Nicolás (with spouse Josefa Sedano);

Jirón, Tomás (with spouse Josefa Gonzáles de Aragón, two children);

L:

Ladrón de Guevara, Miguel (with spouse Felipa Guerrero, one child);

Leyba, Francisco;

Lorenzo, Francisco (with spouse and one child);

Luján, Juan (with spouse Petrona Ramiréz, one child);

M:

Marcelino, Cristóbal (with spouse Juana de Góngora);

Márquez de Ayala, Diego (with spouse María de Palacios, two children);

Martínez de Cervantes, Juan Manuel (with spouse Catalina de los Angeles and a maid Cecilia de la Cruz);

Mascareñas, José Bernardo (with spouse María de Acosta, two children);

Medina, Juan (with spouse Juana Jaramillo y Zamora Márquez);

Medina, Juan de (with spouse Antonia Sedana, a sister of Josefa Sedana above married to Nicolás Jirón);

Molina, Simón (with spouse Micaela de Medina);

Moya, Antonio (with spouse Francisca Morales);

Nuñez, José (with spouse Gertrudis de la Candelaria Herrera);

O:

Ortiz, Nicolás (with spouse María Coronada, six children);

P:

Palomino, Tomás (with spouse Gertrudis Bautista de Ulibarrí, two children);

Porras, Francisco de (with spouse Damiana Gonzáles, one child);

Q:

Quintana, Miguel (with spouse Gertrudis de Trujillo, sister of Estafana Trujillo above);

R:

Rodríguez, José (with spouse María de Sarnano, three children);

Rodríguez, Manuel (with spouse María de la Encarnaci6n Palacios, one child);

Rincón, Antonio Francisco (with spouse Antonia de Valenzuela, three children);

Romero, Juan Francisco (with spouse María de Avila);

Rosa Gonzáles, Francisco de la (with spouse Antonia de la Serna);

Ruiz Cordero, Juan (with spouse María Nicolassa. Carrillo);

S:

Salas, Sebastián (with spouse María García);

Sánchez de Hita, Tomás Fulano (with spouse Antonia Gutiérrez, one child; Tomás died in Zacatecas and Antonia continued to N.M. where she married Juan de Archibeque in 1697);

Sánchez, José (with spouse Josefa Gómez de Rivera, with father-in-law José Cortez);

Sayago, Antonio (with spouse María de Mora Zamora, two children);

Silva, Antonio (with spouse Gregoria Ruiz, one child);
T:
Trujillo, Nicolás (with spouse María Luisa de Aguilera, four children; returned to Mexico City in 1705);
V:
Valdés, José Luis (with spouse María de Medina Cabrera, two children);
Valle, José del (with spouse Ana de Ribera, with adopted child Bernardino Sena);
Vallejo, Manuel (widower, one child);
Velasco, Francisca (widow, with nephew Miguel García Velasco and niece Manuela);
Velasco, José (with spouse María de Tapia Herrera, one child);
Vega y Coca, Manuel de la (spouse Manuela Medina and mother-in-law Josefa de Cabrera).

[Three Frenchmen had been captured before the Pueblo Revolt and now returned to N.M. with stripes on their faces: Pedro Munier, Santiago Grola, and Juan de Archibeque.]

1694 (con't)
SOCIETY
Santiago Roybal is born.

MILITARY
June 30: Vargas leads a foraging expedition north. He finds Taos Pueblo deserted and is unable to get the people to return from their mountain strongholds. Governor **Francisco Pacheco** suddenly appears with heavily armed warriors, including Apaches. **Juan de Ye** translates for Pacheco and Vargas. No agreement is reached, but Pacheco invites don Juan to spend the night at the Taos camp for further discussion. The offer is accepted because of the friendship between Pacheco and Juan de Ye.

Neither shows up the next morning. Vargas sends messengers to inform the Taos to meet by noon or their pueblo will be sacked. Nothing happens so Vargas gives the order to break into the pueblo and a wealth of corn is uncovered. He confiscates the corn and delivers it to his colonists.

Juan de Ye is never seen or heard from again. It is believed he was imprisoned then executed by the Taos somewhere in their mountain stronghold. Vargas mourns the loss of his friend and ally.

July 21: A western campaign opens against the   Jémez, Acoma, Hopi, and various bands of Apaches. **Bartolomé de Ojeda** informs Vargas that those villagers have vowed to expel the Spanish or fight to the death.

July 24: **Jémez** falls after a bloody, 10-hour battle. Over 300 women and children are taken prisoners. Jémez emissaries plead with Vargas for the restoration of their women and children. He tells them that if they make peace and help conquer **San Ildefonso** he will grant their requests.

September 4: The **last major campaign of the Reconquest** begins when Vargas and his allies, now including Jémez warriors, march on **Tesuque Pueblo.** The Spanish attack fails but siege is laid on the rebel Pueblo stronghold, the peñol north of San Ildefonso. Rebel food supplies run out and they sue for peace whereupon they are ordered to reoccupy their pueblos within eight days.

September 11: All Jémez women and children are released unharmed to their families as Vargas promised.
September-December: Governor Vargas visits every Pueblo in N.M.

[Vargas has been described by W.A. Beck as possessing *"unbelievable energy and strength of character,"* with *"courage verging on the foolhardy."* He was also *"capable of implacable cruelty toward the Indians ... which was to prove harmful to the Spaniards in the long run."* English language writers in the KGD cycle don't mention that the Pueblo people were not exterminated as punishment for the carnage of the Pueblo Revolt. A desire for extermination, which can readily be seen when various non-Hispanic Europeans are dealing with Indians (Amherst, Custer, Sheridan, etc.), was not what returned Hispanics to New Mexico.]

RELIGIOUS
November: Fray **Francisco de Vargas,** new Franciscan custos, arrives in Santa Fe, bringing some 500 sheep and cattle. Within a few months he goes to El Paso and buys another thousand sheep for use in the missions.

1695
PACIFICATION
January 10: **The Reconquest of N.M. is considered complete,** though frontier difficulties will continue. The year is spent in consolidation of military victories, establishment of government, continuous inspections for security, agrarian efforts, missionizing, repopulating of Pueblos, and replenishing the food supply. Pueblo land ownership is guaranteed, along with native rituals necessary to their culture, so long as there is no open conflict with Christianity. Spanish sovereignty is accepted and a firm alliance is established between the European Hispanic and the Native American Pueblos in central N.M.

PIONEERS
May 9: Capt. **Juan Páez Hurtado** arrives in Santa Fe with more livestock and some 45 new families. The new colonists are from the **Zacatecas-Sombrerete** area of Mexico and include:

Aranda, Mateo (with Teresa de la Cruz and María Rodríguez);
Arellano, Cristóbal (with his sister and niece); Armijo, Antonio (with spouse Manuela Negrete and Antonio's brother Marcos);
Camarillo, Diego (with spouse Antonia García);
Cortinas, Pedro (with spouse María Ortiz and a son);
Crisóstomo, Juana (with Toribio Nicolás and Juana Nicolasa);
Durán, Catalina (widow with three children);
Espinosa, Nicolás (with a sister and brother);
Félix, Antonio (with spouse Francisca Valencia, one son and two nephews);
López, José (with spouse María Osuna, one daughter);
Marcos, Lucas (with Juana de Guadalupe and Juan Nicolás);

Gómez, Laureano (with spouse Josefa Cruz and a nephew);

González, Francisco (with two cousins, Baltazar Rodarte and Terese de Jesús Rodarte); Guerro, Juana (with a son and daughter);

Guido, Juan (with spouse Isabel de los Reyes Ribera and a son);

Hernández, Francisco (with spouse Juana García and one son);

Lobato, Bartolomé (with spouse Luisana Negrete and one son);

López, Angela (and her two brothers Juan and Antonio Ortiz);

Martínez, Jerónimo (with spouse Antonia de la Rosa and a daughter);

Méndez, Tomás (with spouse María de la Cruz and one daughter);

Montalve, Roque Pantoja (with two other people, Miguel Gutiérrez and his sister Natiana);

Montes Vigil, Francisco (with spouse María Jiménez Armijo);

Montes Vigil, Juan;

Morillo, Cristóbal (with Sebastián Canseco and María Gutiérrez);

Miranda, Miguel (with a daughter and son);

Negrete, Mateo (with spouse Simona Bejar and one daughter);

Olivas, Isabel (with daughter and her brother José Rodríguez);

Olives, Juan Bautista (with spouse Magdalena Juárez and daughter);

Quiros, José (with a daughter and a nephew);

Quiros, Juana (with a son and nephew);

Ramos, Marcos (with spouse Isabela Larea);

Ramos, Miguel (with sister Antonia and a servant Josefa de la Rosa);

Reina, Juan (with spouse María Encarnaci6n and a nephew);

Reinoso, Ana (with daughter and son);

Reyes, Inés de los (with a daughter and son);

Reyes, María de los (with daughter María Canseco and nephew Nicolás Ararmujes);

Ribera, Salvador Matías (with spouse Juana Rosa and one son);

Rodríguez, Agustín (with spouse Nicolasa Ortiz);

Rodríguez, Sebastiana (widow with three children);

Romero, Juan Antonio (with two nieces and one nephew);

San Nicolás, María de (with a son and daughter);

Santos, Juan de los (with spouse Josefa Cristina Durán and a nephew);

Soria, Felipe (with spouse María Castro and one son);

Tenorio, Miguel (with a daughter and Cristóbal Rodríguez);

Trinadad, María de la (widow with two sons);

Zarate, Miguel (with spouse María de la Rosa and a son).

DEMOGRAPHY

New Mexicans during this era have been described by Angélico Chávez as members of **five distinct groups**:

"**Native New Mexicans**" who came with Oñate or shortly thereafter, with names like Archuleta, Baca, Chávez, Lucero, Montoya, etc., and whose families had increased during their 13 year stay in El Paso;

The "**hundred gentlemen soldiers from Spain**" who came with Vargas, with names like Páez Hurtado. Fernández de la Pedrera, Roybal, etc.;

The *"**Españoles Mexicanos**,"* some 67 families living in the Valley and City of Mexico, selected by the
Viceroy himself, with names like Aragón, Medina, Ortiz, Quintana, etc.;
The **families from Zacatecas and the mines of Sombrerete**, with names like Armijo, Vigil, Vargas, etc;

Many New Mexicans at Guadalupe del Paso, like the Padillas, Pereas, etc., returned to N.M. but some chose
to stay there while their relatives went north. They still considered themselves New Mexicans, even
after the Crown decided to align El Paso with the Province of Nueva Vizcaya for administrative
purposes. In the future they would provide trading contacts for their relatives from up north.

During the 17th and 18th centuries the New Mexicans became "**one big family**" through intermarriage,
referring to virtually everyone as *"primo"* or *"prima."*

SETTLEMENT
Santa Cruz de la Cañada is reestablished north of Santa Fe with the settlement of some 44 families from
Santa Fe. Santa Cruz becomes a fountainhead for northern expansion of Hispanic settlement into
the **Española Valley** and beyond.

AGRICULTURE
Crop failures cause great hunger during the winter of 1695-1696.

1696
REVOLT
June 4: **There is a second Pueblo revolt.** Taos, Picurís, Cochití, Santo Domingo, Jémez, and the Tewa
Pueblos rise in rebellion, killing 21 soldier-settlers. Five missionaries are murdered: Friars Francisco
Corbera, José Arbizu, Antonio Carbonel, Francisco de Jesús María, and Antonio Moreno.

Pecos, Tesuque, San Felipe, Santa Ana, and Zía remain loyal, refusing to join the uprising.

[**N.M. Loomis** finds it *"sometimes astonishing"* that the Spanish didn't send out forces against the Indians
"and wipe them out and get rid" of them. *"Spaniards were slow to take a hint."* Extermination of Indians
was not Hispanic policy, which is why the Pueblos are in existence to this day, and perhaps due to cultural
bias, it appears some people don't/can't/won't understand that.]

Bartolomé de Ojeda from Picurís writes to Vargas, asking for *"firearms, powder, and bullets..."* to help
combat the rebels, who are also in league with the *"indios bárbaros,"* both of whom are targeting
"indios cristianos." Ojeda informs Santa Cruz alcalde **Roque de Madrid** that combined Indian
forces from Hopi, Zuñi, Acoma, possibly with Ute confederates, are massing to annihilate the
Spaniards of N.M. **Lucas Naranjo** of Cochití is leading the rebels.

Vargas instructs all settlers and Christian Indians to withdraw to fortified communities like Santa Fe. He
decides to wait before taking action. Knowing that the rebels have abandoned their food supplies
when they fled into their mountain strongholds, they will have to surrender or face starvation.

July: Battles against the Jémez, Acomas, and Zuñis result in Spanish and Pueblo-allies victories. Rebel leader **Lucas Naranjo** is killed at the battle of El Embudo where he made a determined effort to kill Fray **Juan Alpunte,** chaplain of the expedition.

August 14-15: The attack on Acoma isn't successful but food supplies are confiscated or destroyed. Vargas returns to Santa Fe.

September 21: The northern campaign is reopened. Warriors from **Pecos and Tesuque** join with presidial soldiers from Santa Fe at Santa Cruz in order to combat the rebels.

September 26: Rebel food stores are captured and the rebel warriors surrender. There is a mass flight from Picurís Pueblo toward the northeast, including **Lorenzo Tupatú,** where the Picurís join the **Apaches** (or are captured by them).

December: Once again there is peace in Pueblo land, though **Acoma, Zuñi, and Hopi** villages aren't subdued militarily. There are also those individuals who join various Apache and Navajo bands.

[Once again the Pueblo people are not exterminated and henceforth the **Hispanic and Pueblo** people become staunch allies.]

Contrary to Spanish policy, Vargas sees to it that the Pueblos have access to horses and firearms.

WOMEN & LAND

Antonia Moraga petitions Governor Vargas and is granted farming lands in the *ciénega* immediately northeast of the Palace of the Governors. The ciénega contains a number of crucial springs. She successfully petitions for the ancestral Moraga hacienda and lands in Chimayó, but Vargas rules she must give up the ciénega property

BOOKS

Governor Vargas owns the (reputedly) largest private collection of books in N.M., 33 volumes.

T I M E L I N E

From the 100 or so friars who served in N.M. during the I600s, 49 were martyred by the Native Americans. Between 1700 and 1849 hostile Indians killed 820 whites; 3,294 descendants of hostile nations were baptized.

1697-1703

Pedro Rodríguez Cubero is Governor.

1697
POLITICS

Upon his arrival in Santa Fe, **Cubero imprisons Vargas** on charges of cruelty to the Indians, blaming him for the revolt of 1696. (Vargas is later exonerated but he serves three years under house arrest in the meantime). Vargas and Cubero are now bitter enemies.

SOCIETY

Spring: Food, clothing, and other much needed supplies arrive in Santa Fe, promoting economic recovery of the province. Goods and livestock are distributed according to family size. The distribution provides for a partial census of Hispanic N.M., beginning with families then followed by an assortment of bachelors and **single women.** According to J.O. Baxter about 1,000 New Mexicans receive approximately 4,000 ewes, 170 goats, 500 cows, and 150 bulls.

On the average, families receive 10 to 25 ewes and two or three cows. Widows and orphans are amply provided for.

Frenchman **Jacques Grolet,** who had been with the ill-fated La Salle, is listed as *Santiago Grolle.* [He took up residence in Bernalillo and became the progenitor of the N.M. **Gurulé** families.]

Miguel de la Vega y Coca, a young widower, takes his ewes and in time becomes owner of the (now famous) *El Rancho de las Golondrinas* south of Santa Fe.

CENSUS
According to figures collected by the *Cabildo,* Hispanic New Mexico has under 1,500 persons (excluding higher officials and their families, and the missionaries). These include:

approximately 96 New Mexican Spanish families, about 404 persons;

17 Mexican families who had been in N.M. before the Pueblo Revolt and returned to N.M. from El Paso in 1693 (some 71 persons);

124 families from the Zacatecas/Sombrete area, plus 25 orphans (totaling 449 people);

83 persons listed as bachelors, orphans, single women, mixed-bloods, etc.

1698
DIPLOMACY
June: Cubero persuades refugees from different Pueblos, still rebellious atop Acoma, to make peace and join in society by establishing their own pueblo.

July 12: The former refugees join the new pueblo north of Acoma, San José de Laguna.
1700
AMERINDS
Apaches are now the most dangerous threat to the existence of Pueblo and Hispanic N.M.

José Naranjo is alcalde mayor of Zuñi. He petitions the viceroy to appoint him *Capitán de la guerra* for all Native American troops fighting as allies of the Spanish.

May: **Hopis** (Moquis) send their war captains to sue for peace, asking for missionaries. They change their minds, however, and Cubero leads an unsuccessful expedition against their villages (in present northeastern Arizona). They remain independent throughout the 18th century.

LAND GRANT
The first land grant in the Española Basin, the Mesilla of San Ildefonso, is made to **José Trujillo** for land at the junction of Pojoaque Creek and the Río Grande. The land is so desirable the area realizes its full growth by 1780.

1702
LAND GRANTS
Ignacio Roybal requests the remainder of **Jacona** Pueblo as a land grant. Governor Cubero grants the petition.

José Domínguez receives land in the **Taos valley** but the viking tribes of Indians are an ever-present danger so the area develops slowly.

1703-1704
Diego de Vargas is Governor.

[Diego de Vargas now has the title of *Marqués de la Nava Braziñas.*]

1703
LAND
Land grants are made to Hispanics by Gov. Vargas.

Grants generally fall into two categories:

PRIVATE, which is made to one individual who owns the entire grant and can sell it after possession requirements are met;

COMMUNITY grants which are made to a group of people who each receive a *solar de casa* (plot of land for a house), *suerte* (an irrigable plot), and rights to use the common lands (unassigned grant land) for pasture, watering, logging, collecting firewood, hunting, fishing, rock quarrying, etc. According to M. Ebright, **common lands** in N.M. referred to variously as *ejidos, montes, pastos, abrevaderos, leña, árboles frutales, caza, pesca,* etc., **were owned by the community and couldn't be sold under Hispanic law since they belonged to everyone.**

AMERINDS & LAW
Six **Teguas** protest their false imprisonment and ask that **Ramón García Jurado** be named as their *Protector of the Indians* to represent them in court.

[Disposition of this case hasn't been located in the archives but it demonstrates that New Mexico's Native Americans knew how to utilize the Hispanic legal system.]

SETTLEMENT
Atrisco (*Atlixco*, Aztec for "upon the water") is founded south of present Albuquerque.

PLOT
March 7: A **Zuñi** effort to kill alcalde mayor **José Naranjo** is discovered and foiled.

1704
AMERIND LAND
Alonso Rael de Aguilar is *Protector of the Indians*. He represents **San Felipe Pueblo** when two *vecinos* (Hispanic colonists) petition for land outside the San Felipe pueblo league. Rael testifies that the Pueblo had always owned this tract and used it agriculturally, that if Hispanic livestock are permitted in the vicinity the animals will surely damage Indian crops, etc., and to boot the San Felipes have always been "loyal vassals," not joining the rebellions of 1693 and 1696. Governor Vargas rejects the vecinos' petition and San Felipe Pueblo retains the land.

MILITARY & APACHES
March-April: Vargas leads an expedition into the Sandía Mountains against the **Faraón Apaches.** Hispanic and Pueblo forces are united against the viking Apaches, as they would be henceforth in defense of their N.M. homeland. **José Naranjo** of Zuñi is captain of Indian Scouts.

April 2: **Vargas is stricken with a serious illness.**

April 8: **Diego de Vargas dies in the Bernalillo home of Fernando Durán y Chaves.**

AMERIND LAND & LAW
San **Ildefonso Pueblo** leaders relate to Rael de Aguilar that Capt. **Ignacio de Roybal** has acquired a tract of pueblo land. Interim Governor Juan Páez Hurtado orders an investigation and the disposition is that Roybal's grant won't be confirmed.

1704-1705
Juan Páez Hurtado is Acting Governor

REVOLT & RUMORS
Rumors abound concerning conspiracies of more Pueblo uprisings. They center around San Juan and it appears an alliance is being formed between the Jémez, Utes, Jicarilla Apaches, and Navajos. But there is no rebellion.

DEFENSE & ARCHITECTURE
Watchtowers, *torreones*, are built for defensive purposes, especially in small villages as the population spreads out, usually unattached to other buildings. These circular, two-story structures have walls three feet thick with slits toward the top from which a defense can be made. The interior has a

diameter of around 15 feet, sometimes a fireplace for winter heating or cooking, a trapdoor leading to the roof. During times of peace the torreones are used for crop storage, sometimes as jails.

1705-1707

Francisco Cuervo y Valdés is ad int. Governor

1705
NAVAJO/APACHE & MILITARY

April 16: Cuervo convenes a war council to organize a campaign against the **Navajos** but he soon realizes the viking tribes far outnumber New Mexican Hispanics and Pueblos.

June-September: There are extensive campaigns against the **Gila Apaches.** Under the command of Maese del Campo **Roque de Madrid,** Jémez and various Navajo bands are attacked, with some success, resulting in a period of peace the following year. (Madrid writes a journal on his campaign.)

NEW AMERINDS

Comanches begin to move into the southern plains in large numbers. This warrior nation soon appears in eastern N.M. where they displace various Apache bands who in turn relocate to areas south of the New Mexican settlements.

1706
SETTLEMENTS

Bernalillo is founded and contributes some of its families to the founding of Alburquerque.

PIONEERS

Alburquerque, which had been referred to as *Bosque Grande de Doña Luisa*, is founded by **pioneer families**, about 252 persons, 12 of which live in the [present] Old Town area, the others along the river in settlements called "*Ranchos*" such as "Ranchos de Alburquerque," Los Varelas, Los Duránes, Los Poblanos, Los Griegos, Los Candelarias, etc., and on the west side of the river and downstream were Los Corrales, Atrisco, Armijo, etc. Into the Sandía Mts. were Carnué and San Antonio.

A list of **heads of Albuquerque families** includes: Juan Barela; Cristóbal Barela; Xavier Benavides; Francisco Candelario; Sebastián Canseco; Pedro Durán y Chávez; Francisco García; Tomás García; Antonio Gutiérrez; Martín Hurtado; Cristóbal Jaramillo; Pedro López y Castillo; Juana López y Castillo; Nicolás Lucero; Andrés Montoya; Juan Pineda; Baltazar Romero; Bernardina Salas y Trujillo (widow); J. Sebastián Salas; Joaquín Sedillo; Antonio Silva...

GOVERNMENT

January: **Alfonso Rael de Aguilar** is appointed to the office of **Protector General of the Indians.**

SETTLEMENT & GENÍZAROS

April: Cuervo recognizes the need to establish new settlements so he resettles the (present) vicinity of

Galisteo with 150 families, about 630 persons, many of whom are Christianized Tano Indians and *genízaros*. A new church is built and various   crops are planted.

[**Genízaros** (Jenizaro, Janizary) are usually plains Indians, with a scattering of Navajos, Utes, Apaches, who have lost their tribal identity and reside in or about the Spanish settlements. T. Chávez and G. Espinosa tell us they are displaced Native Americans who aren't Hispanic and aren't accepted by the Pueblos, and who wish to have settlements of their own so they are awarded lands on the outskirts of those held by Hispanics and Pueblos, where they function as excellent Frontiersmen due to their warrior proclivities and where they have land enough to be self-supporting. For example, Abiquiú and Belén started as genízaro settlements.]

Torreón
Courtesy Museum of NM, #59243

AMERIND REFUGEES

July: People from **Picurís Pueblo** who had fled during the 1696 revolt have often asked for help of the Spanish because they have been enslaved by the Apaches after their flight. Cuervo decides to fight the **Apaches** (who live around present Pueblo, Colorado) and rescue the Picurís. **Juan de Ulibarrí** is put in command of the expedition to this tierra incognita where **Lorenzo Tupatú,** son of Luis Tupatú, is chief of the Picurís. Using his main scouts, **José Naranjo,** famous Pueblo leader from Zuñi, and **Juan de l'Archebeque,** a Frenchman from the La Salle expedition, the Picurís are located in scattered rancherías (encampments), destitute and without horses. The people, between 62 to 74 in number, are returned to their pueblo.

[This humanitarian campaign is the highlight of the Cuervo administration.]

Ulibarrí claims the area (Colorado) for Spain and the large peak *El Capitán* (now **Pike's Peak**) is identified.

PUEBLO-HISPANIC ALLIANCE

Hispanic garrisons are withdrawn from Santa Clara, Cochití, Jémez, and Laguna because Cuervo believes they aren't necessary and the Viceroy has so ordered. **The alliance between Hispanics and Pueblos is strengthened by the bonds of Christianity and self-preservation.**

ARTS & CRAFTS

Navajo weavers supply their people with textiles and during times of peace they trade surpluses with Hispanics.

TIMELINE

1706: **Chihuahua** is founded by silver miners and the new town soon eclipses Parral as the mining and commercial center of Nueva Vizcaya. Chihuahua becomes a trading center for New Mexicans.
[The commercial trail from *Santa Fe to Chihuahua* is referred to as the *Camino Real* and traverses the towns/villages of Santo Domingo, Algodones, Bernalillo, Alameda, Albuquerque, Isleta, Peralta, Tomé,

Belén, La Joya, Socorro, San Marcial, Fray Cristóbal, Laguna del Muerto, Ojo del Perrillo, Robledo, Doña Ana, Las Cruces, El Paso del Norte, Isleta del Sur, Socorro del Sur, San Elizario, Ojo de Lucero, Jesús María, Ojo de Gallego, Encinillas, El Sauz, Chihuahua, etc.]

LADINO
José Naranjo, famous scout and interpreter, is living at Santa Cruz.

GOVERNMENT
January 7: Cuervo holds a council for all Indians in which he informs them that his replacement will soon arrive in N.M. Pueblo leaders, including **Domingo Romero** from Tesuque, commend Cuervo for pacifying the land and ask him to stay. The Governor states he would like to continue serving them.

Domingo Romero is acknowledged as a renowned warrior and *Capitán mayor de la guerra* for all Christian Indian auxiliary forces. He is fluent in Spanish and various native languages. **Felipe Chistoe** of Pecos is also famous for his warrior abilities.

1707-1712
José Chacón Medina Salazar y Villaseñor is Governor.

The new governor, also known as *Marques de la Peñuela,* continues and extends the policies of Cuervo.

1708
APACHE & NAVAJO RAIDS
Apaches raid Spanish and Pueblo settlements, killing many people, stealing livestock and horses. Governor Chacón attacks them vigorously and an unstable peace is achieved by November.

Navajos have been at peace for over two years but now begin raiding again.

Gov. Chacón denounces Pueblo ritual associated with the **Scalp Dance.**

AMERIND GOVERNMENT OFFICIALS
November: Governor Chacón recognizes all Pueblo governors elected by their constituents and endorses their authority. **José Naranjo** is interpreter for the ceremonial affair.

1709
NAVAJO RAIDS
Five **separate campaigns are directed against the Navajos,** who have been raiding Santa Clara and especially Jémez, where they sack not only houses but the church itself, taking sacred vessels and ornaments.

CHRISTIANIZATION
Governor Chacón works for three years to further Christianize the Indians. He wants them to stop doing

scalp dances because they are unchristian, and stop holding "heathen" rituals in their kivas. It appears he achieves some success or the Indians go underground with their religious practices.

AMERIND LEADERS
The Viceroy orders that **Domingo Romero of Tesuque** be assigned the title of *Native Governor* and *Captain General* of the Tewas, Taos, Picurís, Keres, Jémez, Acomas, Zuñis. **Felipe Chistoe of Pecos** is elevated to the same rank over the Pecos, Tanos, and Southern Tiwas.

SOCIETY
N.M. is relatively peaceful by the end of Chacón's term in office and Pueblo populations are on the increase.

1710
TRADE FAIRS
Trade **fairs** begin to pop up all over N.M. In time the most popular is the October gathering at Taos because of its size, noise, color, pageantry, and the wide variety of people and nations that it attracts. French merchandise appears at these fairs because the Pawnees trade it to the Comanches who bring it to N.M.

CHURCH & STATE
Civil and religious authorities feud with each other constantly. Both assert that the Pueblo people are oppressed, *by the other side.*

[It is difficult to ascertain the extent of oppression. Leaders like **Felipe Chistoe and Juan Tindé** of Pecos enjoyed Spanish titles, Spanish ceremonial dress, governmental privileges. They had great influence over native troops and native trade, both of which were prized by Hispanic New Mexicans. Their lives *...were not all that miserable. Nor were the Pueblos slow to take advantage of a fight between Spaniards, to play one set of 'protectors' off against the other.*]

CARPENTRY
Diego Velasco of Santa Fe is a certified master carpenter.

1712-1715
Juan Ignacio Flores Mogollón is Governor.

1712
SETTLEMENT
Hispanic colonists found Soledad (Los Luceros).

SOCIETY
Times being peaceful, Hispanics and Pueblos begin an unregulated trade with **Apaches** and other viking nations. Governor Flores Mogollón declares the trade illegal.

GOVERNMENT
Nicolás Ortiz Ladrón de Guevara is *Protector of the Indians.* **Juan de Tafoya,** a Spaniard, passes himself off

as an agent of the Crown and dupes several natives from San Juan Pueblo into giving him 15 *gamuzas,* tanned skins. The Protector exposes Tafoya and returns the skins to San Juan.

SANTA FE FIESTA

September 16: The Santa Fe Cabildo meets and decides to establish a fiesta in order to honor the reestablishment of Christianity in N.M. A fiesta is to be held annually with an elevation of a holy cross, that a sermon be recited followed by vespers, Mass, and a procession. Funding for all activities will come from *"we, those present obligate ourselves, and obligate those who may succeed us."*

1713
UTE RAIDS

Utes raid **Taos** and **San Juan**, causing an expedition to be sent against them.

NAVAJO RAIDS

October: An expedition is sent against the Navajos for raiding at **San Ildefonso**.

SOCIETY

Juan de Atienza Alcalá is *Protector General* of the Indians. When **Jerónimo Dirucaca,** ex-governor of Picurís Pueblo, is charged with witchcraft, Atienza Alcalá promises to represent him in the matter according to his best knowledge and ability. Dirucaca then lets it be known, from his jail cell in Santa Fe, that he knows where a rich silver mine is located. A pardon is promised if the claim is true and Dirucaca leads four government officials to a hill where four veins of silver ore are discovered. Atienza Alcalá is informed about the pardon of Jerónimo Dirucaca.

1714
WOMEN & LAND

Juana Luján buys land near San Ildefonso Pueblo and builds the family home that comes to be known as *Rancho de San Antonio*. Juana, and later her sons, encroach on the lands of San Ildefonso. She builds an important trade business with El Paso and Chihuahua merchants. She becomes a livestock owner of significant importance according to M. Weigle.

NAVAJO RAIDS

March: **Navajos raid Jémez,** killing the Governor. **Roque de Madrid** leads a force against them which kills 30 Navajos, captures 7, and confiscates 316 bushels of corn, 11 cattle, and 110 sheep, which are distributed in Jémez.

SOCIETY

July 5: A *junta* is called by Gov. Flores to discuss critical issues like arming the Christian Indians, the use of paint during war activities, and trading with enemy nations. Military representatives are in favor of denying the above.

Religious representatives led by Fray **Juan de Tagle** oppose the military, stating that firearms are necessary for defense against the viking tribes; that painting themselves is an age-old practice that the new Christians aren't yet ready to let go, etc.

The council deadlocks and the entire matter is referred to the Viceroy (Duke of Linares) for a final decision. The Viceroy sides with the friars and reverses Flores' decision.

Government policy now has a decidedly tolerant thrust which fosters mutual Hispanic-Amerind self-preservation.

1715
WOMEN & LAND
Francisca Gigosa [also written Guijosa, Aguijosa, Equijosa] *petitions* Governor Flores Mogollón for a grant of land in the Taos valley where she can pasture her sheep and goats. The petition is granted.

1716: Francisca buys property in **Santa Cruz** where she lives for several years. She hires construction workers from Taos Pueblo to work for her (a practice of dubious legality).

1725: Francisca sells her Taos valley grant to Baltazar Trujillo.

MILITARY
The Santa Fe adobe fortress, which has always been manned by colonists, is partially restored. Soldiers in the province now receive a salary of 450 pesos per year (some of which is paid in goods charged to them at highly inflated prices).

APACHE RAIDS
July: Apaches attack Albuquerque and Isleta then take refuge in the Ladrón Mts. **Alonso García** of Albuquerque leads an expedition against them.

August: An expedition is sent east against the **Faraón Apaches,** the force going as far as [present] Amarillo, Texas. Pueblo auxiliaries are led by the famous bicultural warrior/leader **José Naranjo.** Pueblo warriors use firearms and leather jackets as do Hispanics. For the first time in history, other **Apaches,** 31 in number, are part of the expeditionary force.

1715-1717
Félix Martínez is Governor.

1716
SETTLEMENT
Los Lunas is founded.

MILITARY & HOPIS
Governor Martínez endeavors to establish peace with the **Hopis** (Moquis) and get them to return to their former pueblo along the Río Grande. The Hopis say they welcome peace but will not return. Martínez attacks, destroys their crops, to no avail. The Hopis remain independent.

UTE & COMANCHE RAIDS

October: Ute and Comanche attacks in the Taos area causes Governor Martínez to send a force against the raiders.

GOVERNMENT

During the *residencia* (official inquiry into someone's administration) of Félix Martínez, various residents of **Pecos Pueblo** charge ex-Governor Martínez with not paying them for cutting, dressing, and hauling more than 2,000 wooden planks to be used for construction purposes. **Antonio Becerra Nieto,** the judge conducting the *residencia* investigation, orders Martínez to pay the Pecos for all materials and labor.

1717

Juan Páez Hurtado is Governor.

1717

HISPANIC-PUEBLO MILITARY ALLIANCE VS. COMANCHES

Juan de Padilla leads 500 men, Hispanic and Pueblo as is the tradition by now, eastward and engage the surprised **Comanches** on the **llano estacado,** ["stockaded" or "palisaded" plains, often referred to inaccurately as the *"staked plains"* according to H.E. Bolton]. Nearly 700 Comanches are taken prisoners.

POLITICS

There is much **internal conflict and rivalry** between Martínez, Hurtado, and Valverde over the governorship of N.M.

ORGANIZATIONS

La Cofradía de Nuestra Señora del Rosario,   La Conquistadora, a lay brotherhood, owns 308 sheep which they entrust to **Juan Gonzáles Bas** from the Albuquerque area.

EDUCATIONS

Fray **Antonio Camargo** of Santo Domingo sends out a circular wherein he states the King of Spain has mandated that Indians be taught the Castilian language so that they may be instructed properly in the Catholic faith. Schools are to be established ... the first at Santa Fe and four children are to be selected from each Indian pueblo to attend it. Pueblo authorities are to be informed of the plan and parents or family are to provide assistance for the maintenance of the students, who shall be charges of the secular priest. Schools are to be established in the other two villas, Santa Cruz and Albuquerque, when possible.

1717-1722

Antonio Valverde y Cossio is Governor.

1718

PUEBLO EXPERTISE IN GOVERNMENT

Amerinds from Santo Domingo, San Felipe, and Cochití go to Governor Valverde y Cossio and charge that Alcalde Mayor **Manuel Baca** has *"bothered and mistreated"* them by making them work on his acequia and whipping the Governor of Cochití, *"contrary to His Majesty commands."* An investigation is conducted; Baca is stripped of his office and ordered to serve in two military campaigns against enemy Indians.

1719
MILITARY ALLIANCE

August 13: A council is held to discuss **Ute and Comanche** attacks on northern Pueblos.

September: Governor Valverde leads a force of 600 soldiers, settlers, and Pueblos against the viking tribes. The Pueblos, 465 strong, are led by Capt. **Luis García.** Twelve **Apaches** from the Cimarrón area enlist for service as do 69 Sierra Blanca Apaches from the Trinidad area. The large expedition fails to find Utes or Comanches, who flee the area in advance of the army.

1720
INVESTIGATION

Alcalde Mayor **Juan de Ulibarrí** is called to Laguna where a resident named **Juanchillo** has killed one **Lavrián.** It turns out that Juanchillo's sister caught Lavrián stealing melons from her garden and when she tried to stop him he beat her. Juanchillo learned about it, shot Lavrián with an arrow then killed him with a large rock to the head. Ulibarrí explains the situation to Lavrián's family members who vow no vengeance.

Comanche Chieftain
Courtesy Museum of NM, #54166

LITERACY

Vicente Armijo of Santa Fe enters into a contract with master tailor **Joseph García** from El Paso to teach Armijo's son the trade. Vicente declares that his son is already able to read and write, therefore ready for the four-year apprenticeship with García.

[Literacy was a prerequisite for entering into an apprenticeship contract.]

VILLASUR EXPEDITION

September: The Viceroy orders Gov. Valverde to investigate rumors of French incursions into Spanish territory. **Pedro de Villasur** commands the expedition into the northeast which is ambushed on the banks of the Platte River in central Nebraska by *indios bárbaros,* probably Oto, Optata, and Pawnee. Forty-five persons are killed, including Villasur, redoubtable scout **José Naranjo,** inter-

Villasur Expedition (Segesser Hide Painting)
Courtesy Museum of NM, #149804

preter **Juan de l'Archeveque, and Fray Juan Mínguez.** French threats are more imagined than real but
    campaigns against the viking Indians continue.

HIDE PAINTINGS
[A painting depicting the defeat of Villasur is thought to be the **earliest extant painting** drawn in N.M. (and
therefore the USA). An unknown Franciscan friar and a shoemaker named **Francisco Xavier Romero** are
thought to have done most of the religious paintings on hide, buffalo or elk, that decorated the churches/
chapels of this period.]

1721
AMERIND EDUCATION
A convention is held in Santa Fe to discuss possibilities for establishing schools in the Indian Pueblos and
    Hispanic villages.

1722-1731

Juan Domingo de Bustamante is Governor.

1723
TRADE

The **Taos Fair** is formally established as the chief trading event for all the plains and mountain tribes. Because of the universally recognized truce of God, all participants are accorded "safe conduct" so that business can be conducted without fear of being attacked. Pueblos, Comanches, Utes, Navajos, Apaches, etc., as well as Hispanics love the trading atmosphere with its constant bartering, horse races, drinking bouts, cooking of different foods, shopping around for a desired item, and amorous encounters. From the Native American side, **Comanches** are acknowledged as the most important participants, and the most volatile. During one fair the Comanches put a group of women up for sale and when no one buys them they are butchered on the market ground. When the Spanish King hears of the incident he orders the creation of a mercy fund to ransom such captives and give them Christian guidance afterward.

[Knowing that captives would be ransomed, Comanches took more captives for eventual sale in Taos.]

1724
MONEY

New Mexicans make annual trading trips to Chihuahua for items like chocolate, ironware, etc., which they can't grow or manufacture themselves according to M.L. Moorhead. The **monetary unit** is the *peso* but in actual use it has four sliding concepts of value:

peso de plata: a silver coin with the value of *eight reales* [**which standard was later adopted by the United States for silver dollars**];
peso of six *reales;*
peso of four *reales;*
peso de la tierra of two *reales.*

[Chihuahua merchants pay New Mexicans with the *two real peso* and require that they buy in *pesos de plata* (**eight** *reales).*]

1725
SETTLEMENT

Hispanic settlers found **Embudo** when three men, Juan Márquez, Francisco Martín, and Lásaro de Córdova, petition for a grant of land for themselves and various families [who settle at San Antonio del Embudo, now called Dixon].

MESTIZAJE (RACIAL/ETHNIC MIXING)

Carlos Lopopolo reports there were some 51 designations used for signifying **racial or ethnic mixing** in Spanish colonies.

In N.M. the most common designations are terms like *Español, Indio, Mestizo, Genízaro*, etc. These are
used mostly by churchmen, sometimes government officials, but by and large ordinary New
Mexicans use *mestizaje* terms *(mulato, cuarterón, zambo*, etc.) mostly when they are teasing or
angry at someone. The New Mexican frontier environment didn't concern itself much with race or
ethnicity while living under the threat of enemy attacks or in situations like needing help from one's
neighbors during periods of prolonged heavy labor.

[Spaniards have been described as the best record keepers in the world and the designations
might verify a "melting pot" society based on the goal of assimilation. It can be observed that anti-Hispanic
prejudice of some English language writers often use these designations to maintain there was a rigid caste
system in Hispanic societies, thereby overlooking the equality fostered by the Church. It might be interesting to compare these societies to the situation in N.M. where so many people from so many different
countries in the world refer to themselves as "Anglo" though very few ever came from England.]

SOCIETY
Felipe Chistoe, famous Pecos leader, dies (Ca. 1725).

1725-1743
LAND GRANT
The **Pueblo Quemado** (Córdova) land grant is made and settled during this period.

1746: Records show that plots of land are under private ownership.

1748: Indian raids force the settlers to move into more populous villages for protection but they return in
time, fighting bands of Utes,   Comanches, or Apaches from *torreones*, houses, and rooftops.
Women also join the defense by stoning the attackers from rooftops. Many individuals become
famous for their heroics in defense of the land.
1776: Fray Francisco **Atanasio Domínguez** is visiting the missions of N.M. and remarks that Quemado's 52
families (220 people) have good sites of farmland but no church.

1832: A chapel is constructed and dedicated to St. Anthony, Córdova's patrón.

1840s: **Pedro Córdova** becomes the wealthiest patrón in the area.

Use of commons land is crucial for sheep and goats which are basic to the Córdovans' subsistence
economy.

1892: The Pecos River Forest Reserve takes over the upland commons land used for grazing livestock and
restrictions are imposed but not enforced so the Córdovans go about their lives as they always
have without realizing what is happening.

1893: The "notorious" **T.B. Catron** and his partner **Charles Coons** petition the Court of Private Land Claims
for confirmation of the grant but it is denied and not appealed.

1895: Quemado valley lands are included in the survey of the adjoining Nuestra Señora del Rosario, San Fernando y Santiago grant, Córdovans thus gaining title to their lands but this did not include the uplands which were used for grazing sheep and goats.

1915: The uplands grazing lands are incorporated into the newly created **Santa Fe National Forest** and grazing regulations severely restrict Hispanic access to the former commons land. The people have to give up their livestock and are thus forced to seek wage labor wherever they can find it in order to survive.

1726
GOVERNMENT

The chain of authority from Spain to N.M. is as follows: King, who has direct dealings with the Council of the Indies, Viceroy, Audiencia of Guadalajara; Council of the Indies deals directly with the Viceroy; Viceroy and Audiencia of Guadalajara deal directly with the Commandant General; Commandant General deals directly with the Commandant Inspector; Audiencia of Guadalajara and Commandant Inspector deal directly with the **Governor** of New Mexico.

The Governors' documentation to superiors has to be in duplicate or triplicate;

Governor deals directly with the **Alcalde Mayor;**

Alcalde Mayor deals directly with the **Teniente Alcalde** in handling minor local matters.

Duties of the alcalde include military and police activities when necessary; examining applications for land grants and placing grantees in possession of a grant if approved by the Governor; recording of cattle brands; judicial responsibilities regarding minor matters; initiating and preparing the paperwork relating to serious incidents (called the *sumaria*, which includes statement of charges, preliminary testimony by witnesses, declaration by the accused, all of which are passed on to the governor); summoning residents of each Hispanic and Indian town to the central plaza and proclaiming all royal edicts, laws, or decrees; seeing to Indian welfare; etc.

GOVERNMENT INSPECTION TOUR

May: Brigadier **Pedro de Rivera,** Visitador General, arrives as part of the tour to inspect the entire northern frontier system of defense. Rivera states that Gov. Valverde should have been the one to lead the Villasur expedition. The **Santa Fe presidio** remains at 80 soldiers, though Rivera doesn't approve of soldiers dabbling into business matters. He tours the 24 Indian Pueblos and states there are about 10,000 friendly Native Americans in N.M. [a figure which has been judged too low, according to some contemporary writers]. He is very impressed with the **Pueblo people,** whom he terms exemplary in many categories.

TRADE RIGHTS

August: A fight breaks out during the **Pecos fair** when traders refuse to abide by the authority of the

Alcalde Mayor **Manuel Tenorio.** Santa Fe trader **Diego Manuel Baca** is the leader, yelling that trading is for the people, not government officials.

1729
LAW
Rivera's inspection tour leads to the *Reglamento de 1729* which in N.M. provides that **80 soldiers** garrison the   presidio, which includes one lieutenant, one *alférez,* one sergeant, and 77 soldiers. Governors and commandants can't assign soldiers to private duties related to business interests. No war can be waged against friendly or neutral Indian nations, or against hostile groups until all peaceful overtures have failed. No Christian Indian nation can be made to wage war against another Christian nation unless it specifically asks for help, though the use of native auxiliary forces is permitted, along with their use of horses and firearms. The Governor of N.M. is required to visit all Pueblos twice each year and *alcaldes mayores* are enjoined from any form of mistreatment of Christian Indians, disregard of which will bring a fine of 1,000 ducats, to be paid to the treasury and the aggrieved Indian community. Soldiers are prohibited from causing disorders in Indian communities. Prisoners of war can be taken during hostile campaigns but *family units are never to be broken up.*

[The Reglamento of 1729 is the beginning of the era which officially recognizes that Christian Native American communities are an integral part of Spanish N.M.]

MILITARY
Campaigns are still necessary against **Apaches,   Comanches, and Utes.**

WEAVING
Nicolás Gabriel Ortega [the first known weaver of the Ortega family of Chimayó] is born.

1730
EPISCOPAL VISITATIONS
Three Bishops from Durango make **visitations to N.M.** during the 18th century:

1730: **Benito Crespo, the first bishop to set foot in N.M.,** charges that missionaries don't learn native languages therefore they really can't missionize, making them aliens in their own missions. The friars respond that when they learn a language they are transferred to another mission where natives speak a totally different tongue.
[Bishop Crespo is described as *"...strongly pro-Jesuit"*]

1737: **Martín de Elizacoechea.**
1760: **Pedro Tamarón** charges that missionaries must make more effort to learn native languages.

CHURCH & STATE
Fray **Pedro Antonio Esquer** of Pecos Pueblo condemns Gov. Bustamante.

SOCIETY
Juan Tindé, Pecos leader, dies.

RELIGIOUS
Padre **Santiago Roybal,** *New Mexico's first native priest,* returns to his native land after many years of study in Mexico City. He is now Vicar for Bishop Benito Crespo of Durango.

1731-1736
Gervasio Cruzat y Góngora is Governor.

1731
WOMEN
Elena Gallegos, owner of the **Elena Gallegos land grant** east of Albuquerque, a *"poor* widow," makes her last will and testament.

PUEBLO RIGHTS & LAW
Taos **Pueblo** officials go to Gov. Cruzat y Góngora with complaints against Sebastián Martín, Baltasar Romero, and others who let their animals wander into Pueblo fields. The governor orders all concerned to *"place as many herders as necessary"* in charge of the animals, to keep them at least one league from Pueblo agricultural fields, under penalty of a fine of 100 pesos.

1732
SLAVERY
Governor Cruzat orders that **Apaches** captured in war may no longer be sold into slavery.

SOCIETY
Fray **Diego de Arias of Zía Pueblo** accuses Alcalde Mayor **Ramón García Jurado** of misusing his authority by not paying Zía laborers for commissioned work. Governor Cruzat forces García Jurado to pay and removes him from Zía.

Due to frequent raids by the viking nations, **Hispanics and Pueblos** are required to be able to present themselves for service at any time. Military obligations are equal.

CHRISTIANIZATION
Padre Techungi goes to the **Hopi** country in an effort to convert the Hopis to Christianity. He isn't successful but he persuades five runaway Tiwas to return to their Río Grande homeland. [Refugees returned from Hopi lands are referred to as *Moquinos.*] They settle at Isleta.

MILITARY & UTES
April: Lt. Gov. **Juan P. Hurtado** leads an expeditionary force of 36 presidial soldiers, 50 settlers, and 70 Pueblos against the Utes.

LITERACY & APPRENTICESHIP

Francisco Mascareñas of Santa Fe asks blacksmith **Bernardino de Sena** to take on a Mascareñas nephew
as an apprentice. Sena replies that first the nephew must learn to read and write, that **Tomás de
Sena** could instruct him.

1732-1820
LITERACY

[Using the accepted practice of the **signature** as an indicator of literacy it is estimated that about one-third
of New Mexican males were literate. No study has as yet been done for the women. Of the 424 New Mexican
soldiers studied by **Bernardo P. Gallegos** during this period the most popular occupations were artisanry
and husbandry with the agricultural workers being more literate than the artisans. Literacy rates of soldiers
grouped by locale are as follows:

Chihuahua (from outside of N.M.): 78.9% literate;
Santa Fe: 36.4% literate;
Río Arriba: 16.7% literate;
Río Abajo: 13.2% literate;
Overall literacy rate of enlistees: 32.3%.]

1733
SOCIETY

Francisco de Jesús y Espejo of Albuquerque, thought to have been a seller of *libritos* (little books,
booklets) often found in New Mexican households, dies.

1734
INQUISITION

Miguel de Quintana from Santa Cruz is recognized for his writing abilities as a notary public and practical
lawyer, public scribe, and as a playwright for religious and community productions.

Two Franciscans, Fray **Manuel de Sopeña and Fray Joseph Irigoyen,** denounce him to the Inquisition as a
hypocrite and a heretic according to E. Gonzáles-Berry.

Quintana maintains that the Franciscans are motivated by jealousy and personal differences which have
nothing to do with religion. For example, in 1726 Sopeña ordered him not to write any more
Christmas plays, an order which he ignored because inner voices urged him to continue with his
work. Apart from his plays he writes poems which he testifies are dictated to him in verse form by
the voices.

[Quintana's prose is powerful, employing abstractions, contrasts, antitheses, parallelisms, plays on words,
etc., according to Gonzáles Berry.]

The Inquisition's investigation lasts five years. A lengthy file of evidence is accumulated, weighed and
considered by the Holy Office in Mexico City which finds (in 1735) the accused to be suffering

from some sort of damage to the imaginative faculty, thus negating the heresy charge. Quintana is instructed to stop talking about his supposed revelations and to stop believing in such nonsense or he will be subject to the full force of canonical law.

Miguel de Quintana accepts the decision, which reaches him in 1737, and appears to be contrite but he produces a new barrage of poetry and prose in his final defense.

[The record closes without further notation and he dies around 1748, a New Mexican symbol for freedom of expression and a writer's courage to combat powerful authority.]

LAND GRANT

Bartolomé Trujillo receives land in the **Chama River Valley** near the confluence of the Rito Colorado and the Chama River. Settlement growth is slow but steady.

1736-1739

Enrique de Olavide y Michelena is Governor.

AMERIND

During this period **Comanches** armed with French firearms displace the **Apaches** living in areas north and east of the Río Grande settlements, which are encircled when the Apaches move southward. **Comanches** devastate eastern frontier settlements of N.M., including Pecos Pueblo.

1739-1743

Gaspar Domingo de Mendoza is Governor.

1739
SETTLEMENT

Tomé is founded.

HUMANE WARFARE

Comanche prisoners of war are being mistreated so Gov. Mendoza issues an order that Hispanics will be fined 300 pesos for any such mistreatment and Pueblos will be subject to 100 lashes.

LAND GRANT

The **Nicolás Durán y Chávez** land grant is made [in the area of the present Los Chávez].

FRENCH TRADERS

The **Mallet** brothers, **Pierre and Paul,** lead a party of Frenchmen to Santa Fe, hoping to establish trade relations. Two of the Frenchmen, **Juan Bautista Alari** [Alaríd] and **Luis María Moreau** [Mora] remain permanently when the others leave.

1740
RELIGIOUS

There are 40 **Franciscans** in N.M. They are not as demanding (as before the Pueblo Revolt) when missionizing the Indians, concentrating more on the Hispanic population. Pueblo populations begin to decline. There is much ill feeling between the friars and civil authorities.

LAND GRANT
The **Belén** land grant is made to Captain Diego de Torres, his brother-in-law Antonio Salazar, and 31 other heads of families.

1742
Belén is refounded.

AMERIND SETTLEMENT
Father **Carlos Delgado** is unable to convert the Hopis to Christianity but he convinces 441 Tiwas to return to the Río Grande area. They are settled at Jémez temporarily, then at **Isleta.** Some years later an additional 350 Tiwas return and settle at **Sandía Pueblo.**

1743-1749
Joaquín Codallos y Rabal is Governor.

1743
TAOS& COMANCHES
Taos Pueblo is reported to be trading with the Comanches and informing them as to military activities. Gov. Codallos orders this to stop, on penalty of death.

1744
APACHE RAIDS
Settlers from the **Río Abajo** (Albuquerque, Bernalillo, Belén, Socorro, etc.) report that Faraón **Apaches** are stealing livestock then taking refuge in the Magdalena and Ladrón Mts. Lt. **Manuel Saenz de Garbuzu** leads an expedition against them.

PUEBLO EDUCATION
Fray **Miguel de Menchero** reports that the religious are carrying on educational activities in most of the Pueblo missions.

COMMERCE
Albuquerque residents petition the Governor to be allowed to sell wool to a buyer from Mexico City. The sale is permitted because there *is "...no local market."*

NAVAJO CHRISTIANIZATION
Fray **Carlos Delgado** and **Fray José Yrigoyen** journey to *Dinétah,* Navajo land, in western N.M., in order to evangelize the Navajos. Some Navajos are willing to have their children baptized in exchange for clothing, livestock, etc.

1744: A mission site is chosen at **Cebolleta** with a second one at **Encinal.** Progress is reported for five months until, the missionaries assert, the governor sends forced labor from Laguna and Acoma to work in his fields and also to build churches.

1750: The Pueblos express dissatisfaction with their forced labor and the Navajos henceforth refuse to cooperate with their missionaries. Governor Vélez Cachupín holds councils with the *Diné* who declare they oppose colonization and refuse to live in pueblos, that they never asked for missionaries nor could they live in one place because they were raised to be free like the deer. Soon after the missions at Cebolleta and Enicinal are abandoned.

AMERIND LITIGATION
Agustín, a Pecos carpenter, files a complaint against the heirs of the governor of Cochití Pueblo for nonpayment of his work.

1746
COMANCHE RAIDS
June 23: **Comanches** descend on **Pecos Pueblo,** evidently intent on rubbing it off the face of the earth. They fight as if possessed, trying even to burn the church, but the Pecos defenders throw them back. A dozen Pecos are killed.

1747
GOVERNMENT
Cristóbal Martínez is appointed to the position of *Protector of the Indians* (though he doesn't arrive in N.M. for two years).

1748
SETTLEMENT
Córdova is founded.

HOPIS TO SANDÍA
Hopis who had been living at Jémez are awarded a tract of land around the abandoned site of **Sandía Pueblo.**

COMANCHES & UTES
For reasons unknown, **Utes and Comanches become enemies.** The Utes seek Spanish aid against the Comanches, as do various small Apache bands.

MILITARY & COMANCHES AT PECOS
January 21: More than 100 mounted **Comanches** swoop down on **Pecos Pueblo.** Defenders led by Governor Codallos himself march out to meet them. The Comanche cavalry advances *"...with such an outcry and screaming to strike fear that only the presence of mind and energy of Gov. Joaquín Codallos, aided by God, could have overcome such boldness."* When the Comanches are a pistol shot away Gov. Codallos orders his men to march into the cavalry charge, maintaining their square formation. Several volleys are fired at point blank range then lancers and bowmen decimate the attackers, who withdraw a short distance, out of range.

A group of older men from the pueblo go a short distance to view the action. They are spied by another of two approaching groups of Comanche horsemen and 11 of the Pecos are slaughtered.

The two new columns of horsemen unite with the group fighting Codallos, giving the Comanches about 300 warriors, horses prancing just out of musket range, preparing for the final charge.

Gov. Codallos orders everyone to fall back to the Pueblo, little by little, Indians first. Just then additional troops from Santa Fe appear on thc road, extra horses in tow, the column thus appearing to be larger than it really is. The Comanches depart the same way they had come.

Father **Estremera** later writes that *"...the generalship, courage, and discipline of the lord governor were the reasons the enemy barbarians did not finish off the entire pueblo by killing and capturing its natives, for this was their avowed intention. All the Indians thanked the Governor a thousand times and embraced him for having delivered them from their enemies."*

1749-1754
Tomás Vélez Cachupín is Governor.

1749
POPULATION
Hispanics in N.M. number around 4,353.

SOCIETY
Pedro Antonio Fresquis is born in the Chimayó area, a part of the Santa Cruz parish.

[Fresquis will become the santero referred to as the Calligraphic Santero and the Truchas Master.]

GOVERNMENT
Cristóbal Martínez presents his credentials (*"amidst a particularly strident period in CHURCH & STATE relations"*) as Protector of the Indians to the governor, who informs him that all activities will be confined to Santa Fe or he will be considered a personal enemy. Martínez doesn't assume the duties of office.

Felipe Tafoya is employed in a role similar to *Protector of the Indians.*

PROFESSIONS
Arrieros (mule packers, muleteers) are the highly respected **transporters of goods** in N.M. via the packing of mules, burros, and sometimes horses according to C. McWilliams. Arrieros are famous for their honesty and dependability, their feelings of brotherhood for one another, their skill in packing and transporting all kinds of goods, their knowledge of and care for the animals they work, and the courage with which they face all dangers on desert and mountain trails.

Recuas (**packtrains,** which often consist of hundreds of animals, usually divided into atajos, **strings)** are under the direction of the patrón or mayordomo (pack master) who is responsible for the men, animals, and cargo. The cargador (head loader) is the mayordomo's second-in-command who supervises the loading and unloading of mules.

Arrieros work in pairs when loading or unloading. The animal to be loaded is blindfolded with tapojos (cloth of wool or even silk, with the mule's name embroidered on it). The jerga (a square saddle blanket) is placed on the animal, then a pad of sheepskin upon which a packsaddle is secured, to which is tied the pack of goods being transported, which is protected with a petate (cover) against the elements. Loading an animal is accomplished within three to five minutes. Animals are unloaded at the end of every day, packs and packsaddles arranged so that the same animal receives the same load the next day.

If there is no professional cook each arriero takes his turn at cooking the evening meal for the group after which the men socialize around the campfire with singing, somebody playing the guitar, harmonica, or accordion, and relating stories of various adventures, animals, personalities, etc.

Arriero holiday outfits include high-heeled top boots with tiny spurs, a silken sash wrapped around the waist two or three times, an embroidered shirt, a cone-shaped hat with a silver snake around the crown, the brim trimmed with silver braid. Equipment is decorated with carved figures of birds and animals. Pack saddles are beautifully stamped and carved while bridles are inlaid with gold and silver.

Arrieros earn reputations as **men who never turn their backs on friend or foe,** who care for their animals, and never rob or cheat anyone.

1750
SETTLEMENT
Hispanic settlers found **Velarde** (La Joya), named in honor of **Juan Matías Velarde.**

RANCHING
Sheep ranching is becoming New Mexico's most important industry. The *partido* system is widely used and the **churro** breed thrives everywhere. **Sheepherders,** known as *pastores* or *borregueros,* who live mostly in isolation and depend mostly on their own resources, are masters of sheep husbandry.

Highly trained **sheep dogs** are indispensable to the industry because they can do the work of three men on horseback in rough country.

Goats, used as *marcaderos,* markers, are always mixed in with flocks of sheep, usually on a ratio of 1 to 100, to facilitate counting the sheep. Because of their intelligence, goats are good leaders as well as lookouts for predatory animals. Goats also supply **milk** for orphan lambs and herders.

PUEBLO CANINES

Pueblo dogs are described as being able to climb up and down Pueblo access ladders.

WEALTH

Rico families increasingly dominate the economic life of N.M., along with political and religious affairs. Prominent *ricos* include Clemente Gutiérrez, Juan Miguel Alvarez de Castillo, Joseph de Reano II, Mateo J. Pino.

OCCUPATIONS

Local industries include weaving, carpentry and hat-making as well as the basic farming and ranching.

CHURCH & STATE

Fray **Carlos Delgado** inveighs against alcalde abuses directed at Pueblo Indians.

RELIGIOUS ART

[Some art historians refer to 1750 as the beginning of the *santero* period in N.M. folk art.

WEAVING

The **Río Grande blanket** is a recognized item of New Mexican manufacture. This utilitarian blanket is coarsely woven and usually designed with simple stripes. Variation in decorative design is width of the stripes. Harness looms, about 15 of them, are in use.

1750-1805
SANTERO

18th Century Novice is creating religious art during this period. The *Novice* paints *retablos* with built-up lighter areas over a dark red underpainting in an effort to model faces, limbs, and pedestals. He may have apprenticed with **Miera y Pacheco.**

1751
LAND GRANT

Twelve families from Santa Fe are granted land at **Las Trampas.** The settlement is intended as a buffer against hostile Indian raids. The petitioners are from the Analco district of Santa Fe. **Juan de Argüello** is leader of the **"Trampas 12."**

Comanche Chieftain
Courtesy Museum of NM, #56166

COMANCHE RAIDS

Summer: Three hundred **Comanches** *"...hurl themselves at the pueblo of Galisteo in an attempt to enter and sack it."* Defenders repulse the attack, killing six Comanches and wounding others.

PROFILE

Clemente Gutiérrez

KING OF THE CHIHUAHUA TRADERS

Clemente Gutiérrez, one of New Mexico's most successful entrepreneurs, arrives in the Río Abajo around 1750 and begins a 30-year business career.

1755: Clemente marries Josefa Apolonia Baca, daughter of the Pajarito sheepman Antonio Baca. Clemente purchases land whenever possible.

1762: Ana María Ortiz de Reaño files suit against Gutiérrez in a dispute over financial accounts.

1777: Clemente is very active in ecclesiastical affairs, serving as syndic for the Franciscans and thus making him responsible for management of church lands and livestock. Along with his Baca relatives he donates vestments to the Franciscans at Isleta and maintains close ties with the socially important *Conquistadora cofradía*. He also represents the Bishop of Durango as official collector of tithes in N.M.

1785: Clemente Gutiérrez dies. At the time of his death he owns three ranches in prime sheep country: Pajarito, San Clemente on the Río Grande, and the huge *Virtientes de Navajo* on the Río Puerco. Some 13,600 sheep are ready for fall delivery.

MILITARY

September 4: Gov. Vélez Cachupín leads an expeditionary force against the **Comanches.** A major battle is fought, over 100 Comanches are killed; women and children are allowed to surrender. Comanche weapons, horses and saddles are awarded to the Pueblos. The Governor now learns that only some Comanche leaders, not all, *share a grudge against Pecos and Galisteo.*

Comanches sue for peace and are dealt with leniently by Vélez Cachupín. They keep the peace for the remainder of his administration.

DIPLOMACY & ALLIANCE

Gov. Vélez Cachupín forms an alliance between Hispanics, Pueblos, Faraón Apaches and the Utes. **Indian raids cease in the Río Abajo area.** Governor Vélez Cachupín is credited with grasping the key to peace with the viking raiders of N.W: active personal diplomacy backed by warrior force when necessary; and a large supply of gifts with plenty of opportunities for trade.

1752
SOCIETY

Juan Bautista Pino is born in Tomé. His grandfather and father are merchants from Mexico City. His mother, **Teresa Sánchez** of Tomé, is a native New Mexican.

POPULATION

Pueblos outnumber Hispanics in N.M. almost two to one.

CHURCH & STATE

Civil and religious authorities begin to have serious quarrels as in the previous century.

1753
GOVERNMENT PROTECTION FOR TAOS

The Governor orders that Hispanics around Taos Pueblo must fence in their property so that stock may not roam into Pueblo fields. (This was a most extreme measure taken to preserve Pueblo property rights.)

SOCIETY

N.M. enjoys relative peace. Gov. Vélez Cachupín establishes an extensive **early warning system** [probably the first in all of North America]. The Pueblos ask that Vélez Cachupín remain as Governor. He petitions the Viceroy to allow him to serve another term but is denied.

PUEBLO WARRIORS

Father **Manuel de San Juan Nepomuceno y Trigo** writes that the **Pueblo warriors are excellent fighters** in defense of their homeland, even the women helping when attacked by   Comanches.

1754-1760

Francisco Antonio Marín del Valle is Governor.

1754
SETTLEMENT

Truchas is founded.

SOCIETY

Bernardo Miera y Pacheco, military officer, cartographer, and *santero,* arrives in N.M. (Unlike many other N.M. santeros who use vegetal pigments, don Bernardo also works with oil paints.)

RAIDS

(For reasons that are still unclear) **Comanche raids resume.**

ARMAMENT & COMANCHES

The Governor orders that no one is permitted to sell **firearms** to the   Comanches, which had been done during trade fairs, and that no traders of any kind can visit them at their *rancherías* (encampments), on pain of 50 lashes.

1757
LIVESTOCK ACCOUNTING
Gov. Marín del Valle makes an inspection tour which includes the most famous cartographer of the day, **Bernardo Miera y Pacheco**, who produces a map of N.M. with the following information in the margins:

There are 5,170 Spaniards residing in N.M.; they own 2,543 horses, 7,832 cattle, and 47,621 sheep and goats. The Pueblo and Hopi Indians number around 9,000; they own 4,813 horses, 8,325 cattle, and 64,561 sheep and goats.

1760
Mateo Antonio de Mendoza is Acting Governor.

MILITARY NEEDS
Visiting **Bishop Pedro Tamarón y Romeral** is alarmed by the lack of defenses in N.M. He suggests that **3,000 soldiers** need to be recruited for service in this frontier.

IRRIGATION & AGRICULTURE
[**Acequias,** irrigation ditches, are the lifeblood of N.M. and each settlement by a water source has a system of ditches put into operation after church and housing are erected. The *acequia madre* (main ditch) carries water directly from the water source then secondary ditches channel it to individual farms. The mayordomo (ditch boss) is the elected official who settles disputes over water, supervises the annual cleaning of ditches, and sees to it that all receive their fair share of water. Silt, rich in nutrients like phosphate, potash, and nitrogen, carried by irrigation waters, enriches irrigated land so that fertilizer isn't needed. Silt also coats the ditches, thus working to prevent loss of water through seepage.]

Pueblo farmers are expert in the art of irrigation.

1760-1762
Manuel Portillo Urrisola is Acting Governor.

1761
SOCIETY
Wages are about 10 pesos a month, with perhaps some rations of corn and beans.

RELIGIOUS PATRONS
Ex-Governor **Antonio Marín del Valle** and his wife **María Ignacia Martínez de Ugarte** donate the altar screen to the chapel of *Nuestra Señora de la Luz* later called the *Castrense* [which altar screen is now at **Cristo Rey Church** in Santa Fe].

MILITARY & COMANCHES
December 22: Governor Portillo makes a surprise attack on a **Comanche** encampment near Taos.

1762-1767

Tomás Vélez Cachupín is Governor.

1762
MINING

Tomás Antonio Sena, a blacksmith and armorer by profession (son of the renowned **Bernardino Sena** who came to N.M. as an orphan with the Vargas colonists in 1693), and two others register the Nuestra Señora de los Dolores gold mine.

DIPLOMACY & COMANCHES

Governor Vélez Cachupín restores peace with the   Comanches and other plains nations. The peace holds for the rest of his administration.

1763
TIMELINE

1763: An Ottawa chieftain by the name of **Pontiac** forms an alliance among Great Lakes and Ohio country Indian nations in order to stop the theft of their lands. **Chippewa, Ottawa, Potawatomi, Menominee, Huron, Delaware, Shawnee, Seneca, Fox, Mingo, Kickapoo, Mascouten, Wea, Sauk, Miami,** etc., unite to destroy the British tyranny, laying siege and capturing most of the British forts from Michigan to Indiana. Forts Detroit, Pitt, and Niagara don't fall and **Sir Jeffrey Amherst,** Commander of British forces in North America, orders a war of extermination:

"Could it not be contrived to send the smallpox among the disaffected tribes of Indians? We must on this occasion use every stratagem in our power to reduce them... you will do well to try to inoculate the Indians by means of blankets, as well as to try every other method that can serve to extirpate this execrable race... the vilest race of beings that ever infested the earth, and whom riddance from it must be esteemed a meritorious act for the good of mankind."

A peace delegation is invited into Fort Pitt and given the infected blankets. The scourge quickly rages through the Indian villages, killing men, women and children in such numbers that the will to resist the British is eventually broken.

1765: Pontiac's War is finally ended and the chief is assassinated in the Illinois country. In the meantime, the British Crown had realized what the English were doing to aboriginal populations so it enacted a royal proclamation that decreed all country west of the Appalachian Mountains would forever be Indian land. British settlers were forever prohibited from crossing the Appalachians and those now living there were ordered to withdraw. Britishers, especially those who had long speculated in western (Indian) lands, vowed to ignore the decree [and the issue became a potent factor in favor of the American Revolution].

GOVERNMENT & AMERIND PROTECTION

Two genízaras (Indian women of plains nations living in a Hispanic community) seek and get an audience with **Governor Vélez Cachupín** to air grievances against their Spanish master. The Governor conducts an investigation which brings out that the women were forced to herd sheep, a man's job, and while out in the fields one of them was raped. The Governor rules the women have not been properly cared for nor have they been instructed in Christianity so he removes them from the offending household and places them in better homes *"where they will be fed and clothed in return for household chores and instructed in Christian doctrine and customs."*

TIMELINE

1763: Spain acquires the Louisiana Territory from France, Frenchmen and "Germanic-Americans" already living there.

[It is a popular misconception that European nations could acquire title to Native American territory from each other. The fact is that France and Spain were merely transferring "first rights to treat with the Indians" for their land because international law as articulated by jurists like Vitoria recognized that Indians possessed and therefore owned their native lands. Some European nations disregarded international law in land dealings with the Indians.]

1766-1768: The **Marqués de Rubí** is on an inspection tour of all frontier presidios, including Santa Fe.

1788: Spain invites foreigners to settle in Louisiana if they become Catholics and vassals of the king. **Thomas Jefferson** remarks: *"I wish a hundred thousand of our inhabitants would accept the invitation. It may be the means of delivering to us peaceably what may otherwise cost us a war."*

1765
SOCIETY

Bernardino de Sena dies. As syndic for the Franciscans and one of Santa Fe's most respected citizens [he owned the Santa Fe Sena plaza and part of the world-famous center of Santa Fe carries his name to this day as *Sena Plaza*] he is buried in St. Michael's Chapel, vested in a Franciscan habit. His only son, **Tomás Antonio,** who is married to **María Luisa García de Noriega,** accedes to his father's reputation and property.

Tomás Antonio later holds the posts of *Alcalde Mayor* in Galisteo and Pecos. Governor Vélez Cachupín tells his successor that Tomás A. Sena *"... is greatly loved by the Indians because of his kindness ... you could not find anyone who would wish to serve in that office if he should be separated from them..."*

POPULATION

There are some 20,104 (non-aboriginal) persons in 4,196 families (nearly 5 persons in each family) living in N.M.

WEAVING

Diego de Trujillo arrives in the Chimayó area and begins the Trujillo family weaving tradition by starting a weaving business that utilizes six looms.

1766
SOCIETY
Domingo Labadia (Labadie) is married in Santa Fe.

LAND   GRANT
Juan Pablo Martín is awarded the **Polvadera** grant. Martín relates that the tract is unappropriated and
unsettled, suitable for some cultivation and the rest pastureland. Governor Vélez Cachupín sets the
condition that the grant is for Martín, his children and heirs, that the land must be settled and
occupied for at least four years to acquire legal title. The *alcalde* of Santa Cruz places Martín in
possession later the same year. (See **1876.**)

1767-1778
Pedro Fermín de Mendinueta is Governor.

[Mendinueta's administration is one of the most tumultuous in the history of N.M. because of Indian
raiding. **Christian settlements are surrounded** by   Utes to the north,   Comanches to the east, Apaches to
the south, and Navajos to the west. Defenders against these viking nations are 80 presidial soldiers, citizen
militia, and Pueblo auxiliaries. **N.M. is virtually an island colony in danger of extinction at any time.**]

1768
COMANCHES & ARMAMENT
A Pueblo man from Taos informs Governor Mendinueta that   **Comanches** are receiving firearms from the
Jumanos (Wichitas) who get them from English traders to the east.

PROFILE

Narbona

W A R R I O R   F O R   P E A C E

Narbona is born in the *Tachii'nii* clan. At the age of six he is given his first pony.

1773: Utes make fearsome raids on Navajo camps.

1774: Laguna and Acoma raiders capture some 50 women and children. They are enslaved at
the pueblos and forced to become Christians. Narbona's father and other Navajo warriors make
raids on Spanish settlers along the Río Puerco and Río Grande.

1789: At the age of 16 Narbona takes up the raiding trail. He is taller than most Navajos and his
bow matches his height.

Ca.1795: Narbona marries *Bikee'dijoolf.* Later, during a raid on Zuñi, he captures a woman and makes her his second wife.

1800: Narbona is made leader of his band. Spanish settlers move into the Cebolleta country and councils with Governor Chacón do not result in withdrawing the colonization of Navajo land in the area of the sacred Turquoise Mountain (Mt. San Mateo to the Spanish).

1804: At least a thousand Navajos attack Cebolleta but are unable to wipe out the Hispanic settlement.

1805: The Spanish campaign against the Navajos all the way to Canyon de Chelly.

1816: Narbona and his people have enemies coming at them from all directions. He decides the road of peace is the only way to survival.

1818: Warriors from various Navajo bands unite to war against their enemies.

1819: Narbona is instrumental in making a peace treaty with the Spanish New Mexicans. But there are other pressing problems: a drought is killing all crops so Narbona finally leads his people away, winding up at the Hopi mesas, where they live in peace.

Ca.1828: The drought finally breaks and Narbona returns his people to their homeland on the eastern side of Dinétah.

1829-1833: Narbona makes various trips to Santa Fe to help keep the peace with New Mexican officials. There are Spanish raiders coming out of Aibquiú, Cubero, Cebolleta, Sandía, Jémez, and Cochití but his band isn't attacked.

1835: General war breaks out and the New Mexicans are defeated at Copper Pass. Raid and counteraid continues as a way of life.

1846: Narbona is invited to come in and talk peace with a new people, soldiers from a country called the United States, who say they now own all the land. Eighty-year-old Narbona says he will sign a peace treaty but emissaries must come to Navajo land for the signing.

November 22, 1846: Col. **Alexander Doniphan** meets Narbona and headmen **Zarcillos Largos, Pedro José, Caballado Mucho, Cayetano, José Largo, Archuleta, Cebolla Sandoval, Manuelito,** etc., at Bear Springs. The occasion is festive and a treaty is signed (but never ratified by Congress).
August 31, 1849: Narbona and a few headmen council successfully with Lt. Col. **John M. Washington,** military governor of N.M. When the affair is over a dispute breaks out, a soldier saying that a Navajo is riding a stolen horse. As the Navajos ride away Washington orders his soldiers to open fire, including the cannon. Narbona is *killed.*

BOOKS

Juachín José Pino of Tomé declares in his last will and testament that he owns 10 volumes written by Padre Murillo, three volumes entitled *Monarquía Indiana* by Padre Torquemada, a book on medicine by Tresainese, and another one by Juan Paride Montalbán.

MILITARY

May: A temporary military post is established by the **Cerro de San Antonio,** north of Ojo Caliente [thought to be the first in present-day Colorado].

COMANCHE LEADER

October: **Comanche** chieftain **Cuerno Verde** is identified for the first time in Spanish chronicles. He wears a green horn on his forehead and is the undisputed "kingly" leader of his group of Comanches.

[Cuerno Verde will become one of the most implacable enemies New Mexicans are ever to face according to C.L. Kenner.]

1769
WOMEN & WEALTH

Josefa Bustamante is the wealthiest woman n N.M. She becomes instrumental in reestablishing the Confraternity of *Nuestra Señora del Rosario* (Our Lady of the Rosary,   *La Conquistadora)* and the annual fiesta in her honor.

1769-1775
CASUALTIES

Some 50 people have been killed by **Comanches in Pecos Pueblo.**

1770s
Comanches capture **M. Rita Peralta** during a raid in Tomé.

WEAPONRY

It is reported that about 250 persons in N.M. possess **firearms,** the outdated flintlock muskets called *escopetas.* Some Pueblos also have escopetas but they defend their homeland chiefly with bows, arrows, and lances.

SETTLEMENT

Sabinal is founded (the southernmost frontier outpost at the end of the century).

1770-1780
SANTERO

Bernardo Miera y Pacheco is creating religious art during this period. A cartographer by profession, Miera y Pacheco is also a sculptor and painter who begins the N.M. tradition of painting on wood covered with *yeso,* gesso (gypsum and glue). He uses homemade water-based paints (that become the staple of 19th century santeros).

1771
COMANCHE RAIDS
A raid by 500 **Comanches** on **El Valle** (on the Las Trampas land grant) takes the lives of many settlers.

1772
GOVERNMENT
The **Marqués de Rubí's** suggestions are put into effect as the *Reglamento de 1772.*

TIMELINE

It is estimated that in the previous 25 years about 4,000 people have been killed and more than 12,000,000 pesos have been spent in efforts to pacify the frontier north of Chihuahua.

1773
REPORT
Governor Mendinueta writes his *Report of Missions* directed to **Viceroy Bucareli.**

WOMEN & CAPITAL PUNISHMENT
A mother and daughter from Cochití, María Josepha and María Francisca, confess to the murder of the daughter's husband. A *curador* (defender for minors) is assigned to the case but both women are found guilty of premeditated murder and, *"in a rare example of capital punishment,"* are executed by hanging.

AGRICULTURE
A colonist remarks on how the **Río Grande Valley** is fertilized by silt-laden irrigation and/or flood waters, functioning much like the **Nile River.**

1774
MILITARY & NAVAJOS
Several expeditions are sent against the **Navajos.**

COMANCHE RAIDS
Comanche raiders are put to flight at **Santa Clara.**

Comanches raid Sandía Pueblo in the heart of the Christian Río Grande settlements.

MILITARY & COMANCHES
September: Governor Mendinueta commissions veteran Indian fighter don **Carlos Fernández** to raise an expeditionary force and retaliate against the Comanches. He gathers some 600 poorly equipped soldiers, citizen militia, and Native American allies. East of Santa Fe the force encounters a Comanche ranchería and launches a surprise attack which routs the raiders, killing and capturing

some 400 people. Despite this impressive victory, Comanche raids intensify.

1775
DEFENSE

Torreones (five) are in use at **Taos Pueblo** for protection against **Comanche raiders.**

GOVERNMENT

October: **Viceroy Bucareli** says he will send 1,500 horses to N.M. upon the request of Governor Mendinueta, but the horses don't arrive. **New Mexico is once more on the brink of extinction.**

1775-1776

Hugo O'Conor tours the northern provinces to implement the *Reglamento de 1772.*

1776
ORGANIZATIONS

Six **confraternities** exist in N.M.: St. Michael (at Santa Cruz), Our Lady of the Rosary (Santa Fe), Blessed Sacrament (Santa Fe and Santa Cruz", Carmel, Poor Souls, Our Lady of Light.

TIMELINE

July 4,1776: **Thirteen colonies on the eastern seaboard of North America** [sources say the English had 30 colonies in the Americas] **declare their independence from England and in a unanimous declaration they affirm:**
"We declare these truths to be self evident, that all men are created equal, that they are endowed by their Creator with certain unalienable Rights, that among these are Life, Liberty, and the pursuit of Happiness. That to secure these rights, Governments are instituted among Men, deriving their lawful powers from the consent of the governed..."

1776: **Silas Dean, Benjamin Franklin,** and **Arthur Lee** go to Paris, seeking military and economic aid from the French, who inform them Spain must be in on the effort. The Spanish Prime Minister, the **Count of Floridablanca**, and the ambassador to Paris, the **Count of Aranda,** provide secret aid to the Americans for the next three years.

June 9, 1776: **Carlos III** of Spain opens an account of a million pounds (some $5,000,000) for the Colonies, which buys 216 cannons, 209 gun cartridges, 27 mortars, 12,826 bomb shells, 51,134 bullets, 300,000 pounds of gunpowder, 30,000 rifles with bayonets, 30,000 army uniforms, 4,000 camp tents, and a large quantity of lead for bullets, for **George Washington's** army.

1777: Arthur Lee meets with Floridablanca in Burgos (away from Madrid, where the English were scrutinizing all activities); Lee is informed that help will come from Spain and various ports in the Americas; he is also briefed on the negotiations between **Bernardo Gálvez,** Governor of Louisiana, and **Charles Lee,** representative of the colonies.

Governor Bernardo Gálvez [for whom *Gálvez town,* **Galveston, Texas,** is named] sends similar munitions up the Mississippi, a vital supply line, since the colonial seacoast is blockaded, with Charles Lee. Gálvez also supplies general **George Rogers Clark,** who is fighting in (what is now) Indiana, to the tune of $7,730,000.

September, 1777: Benjamin Franklin asks Spanish representatives for large amounts of arms and munitions, plus a loan of two million sterling pounds. Aid is rendered through Paris, Cuba, New Orleans, and Spanish agents (**Juan de Miralles, Diego de Gardoqui, Francisco Rendón**) in Philadelphia and New York.

1778: The English protest the presence of "American" ships in Spanish ports like New Orleans and Havana, which works against the English blockade of colonial ports on the Atlantic coast. Spain replies they are merely English ships in Spanish ports and there is no reason to deny them entry. If they are "revolutionary" that is a matter for England to attend to, not Spain.

[But in reality, American ships often sail under the Spanish flag to fool the English, and the Spanish Navy often "captures" American ships on the high seas and "forces" them to port in New Orleans, whereupon they are allowed to enter the Mississippi and disgorge their cargo at various points along the river.]

1779: Carlos III now has ample proof that the American colonials will settle for nothing less than independence. He asks England to call for a cease-fire and seek a political solution. England rejects the petition and warns the king not to interfere, adding that if Spain will remain neutral England will return Gibraltar and Florida, and grant fishing rights off New-foundland.
J u n e 22, 1779: Spain declares war on England. Gibraltar is blockaded and English bases in the Bahamas are attacked while Spanish warships patrol the Atlantic seacoast. England now has to fight on several fronts.

September, 1779: Governor Bernardo Gálvez marches on and conquers the English forts which control the English side of the Mississippi. The lifeline is now open to the interior of the American continent.

February 12, 1780: Bernardo Gálvez enters the **Bay of Mobile** and conquers a strong Fort Charlotte.
March 9, 1781 : Gálvez launches a surprise attack through **Pensacola Bay** which is defended by two strong English forts garrisoned by 10,000 soldiers and several thousand Indians. After two and a half months of ferocious fighting on land and sea, **General John Campbell** surrenders to Gálvez. (Fourteen thousand British soldiers are now out of the fighting during the rest of the American Revolution.)

1781 : Minister **John Jay** goes to Madrid because the American bid for independence is bankrupt. A $100,000 total is sent to Philadelphia through Diego Gardoqui. Despite this infusion, by spring the army of **General Rochambeau** is out of resources and unable to continue the war.

Rochambeau sends an urgent petition to Cuba where the Governor, **Miguel Cajigal,** takes up a collection which totals 1.2 million pounds, plus 12 ships loaded with arms, munitions, clothes, medicines, etc. This aid finances the **Battle of Yorktown** (October 17,1781) which successfully ends the American War for Independence.

1776 (con't.)
POPULATIONS
Hispanics in N.M. number about 9,742.

COMANCHE RAIDS
Comanches attack Tomé. Some 23 persons are killed.

MISSION REPORTS
Fray **Francisco Atanasio Domínguez** writes a comprehensive inventory and description of the N.M. missions *(The Missions of New Mexico, 1776)* and states that **sheep** are the medium of exchange in the province. He also remarks on the lively **commerce** carried on from Abiquiú and Taos with the **Comanches and Utes** during times of peace.
The religious headquarters at Santo Domingo houses a **library** of more than 256 volumes.

Domínguez describes the pedagogy of Fr. **Joaquín Ruiz** of Jémez Pueblo: during the week the bell is rung in the morning and in the evening people come to recite and intone hymns in praise of the Sacrament and the Salutation, singing the response while the minister intones the verses and prayers...little ones are placed in the first row, then the girls with their faces uncovered so they won't chew on their toasted maize, then the older youths in the same order. Two choirboys stand with the catechism in their hands, reciting aloud, and all make responses, *in Latin.*

DOCTRINARIOS & PUEBLO EDUCATION
Native American youngsters being educated by missionaries and living in the religious convent are referred to as *doctrinarios* because they help to disseminate Christian doctrine among their people.

EXPLORATION-OLD SPANISH TRAIL
July 29: The **Domínguez-Escalante Expedition** begins out of Santa Fe when two Franciscan friars, **Francisco A. Domínguez** and **Silvestre de Escalante** lead a party of nine explorers, one of whom is the famous **Bernardo Miera y Pacheco,** in an effort to chart a trail to Monterey, California. They explore parts of New Mexico, Colorado, Utah (where the eastern edge of the Great Basin is discovered), and Arizona before returning to Santa Fe some five months later, without reaching Monterey, but opening up part of what comes to be known as the **Old Spanish Trail** (from Santa Fe through western Colorado or northern Arizona/southern Utah, Nevada, and California).

GOVERNMENT
August 22: **A crash program** of frontier organization begins with the appointment of **Teodoro de Croix** as Commandant General of the Interior Provinces (Texas, Coahuila, Nueva Vizcaya, Sonora, Sinaloa, New Mexico, and the Californias). New Mexican conditions are the worst in the whole Spanish

Empire because it has been involved in more continuous warfare over the previous decade than any other portion of the Empire. Croix studies the situation exhaustively for two years. New Mexico defenses are crucial because they are a buffer for the other provinces under his jurisdiction.

1776-1786
SANTERO

Fray **Andrés García** is creating religious art during this period. García is a painter and sculptor much like **Miera y Pacheco.**

[Both artists knew something about lineal and aerial perspective; both patterned their work after Renaissance art.]

1777

SHEEP & MANUFACTURERS

Governor Mendinueta complains that from the **exportation of sheep** *"...results in the lack also of mutton and wool, because by exporting of this species both in sheep and uncarded wool, the looms on which it is being utilized are idle."*

1778

Francisco Trebol Navarro is Acting Governor.

REPORT ON N.M.

Fray Juan Agustín de Morfi writes *Account of Disorders in New Mexico, 1778.* **Pueblo Indians** build their well-ordered towns around a circular plaza, with the buildings three to seven stories high, using ladders to get to upper stories. The courageous Pueblos have been able to defend themselves against Apaches, Navajos, Utes, and Comanches. Pueblo people are responsible and maintain a well-ordered economy. They attend Mass and partake of the Sacraments regularly. They aren't prone to thievery or drunkenness. They live in pleasant abundance because of their harvests. Spanish towns can take a lesson from the Pueblos, for Christian settlements are strung out, usually along a water source, as if to flee from the company of their brothers.

Albuquerque stretches more than 12 leagues along the banks of the Río Grande. This makes protection impossible since neighbors aren't near at hand. Isolation also destroys their inhibitions and lewdness holds destructive sway here.

Trade is hindered in N.M. by the evil juggling of prices and the illusory moneys that are used to swindle innocent people. A farmer is forced to sell cheaply and buy at a rate five times higher, thus putting him into debt which never ends. Chihuahua merchants must be regulated and one monetary system must prevail in order to cure this disorder. N.M. must reduce its dependence on Chihuahua. New Mexicans are industrious and they have raw materials like wool and cotton in abundance but they need craftsmen to manufacture their own necessities instead of depending on importation from Chihuahua.

Laws prohibit Spaniards, Mulattos, Mestizos, and Negroes from taking up residence in Indian Pueblos but
said laws aren't enforced. While this has caused much good it has also its adverse effects: natives
are encouraged to go into debt in order to win control over them. All outsiders should be expelled
immediately from Pueblo lands. Government officials, who should be enforcing royal laws, are
among the worst offenders, especially the *alcaldes mayores*. Among the worst are men like
Clemente Gutiérrez, Francisco Trebol, Baltasar Baca, Pedro Pino, Nerio Montoya, Manuel Vigil, and
José Miguel de la Peña. In Spanish towns there exists a class of Indians called *genízaros,* who are
Comanches, Apaches, Navajos, etc, taken when they were children and now living in Christian
towns. They are excellent soldiers, very warlike, and formidable fighters against our enemies, so
they are invaluable to N.M. Pueblos will have nothing to do with them, being from enemy tribes.
Belén and Tomé were started by genízaros and they wish to form another village at El Sabinal, a
most dangerous frontier. Their requests for land should be honored and encouraged with the same
privileges and exemptions enjoyed by Pueblo Indians.

1778-1780
DROUGHT & SOCIETY

N.M. is in the grips of **drought.** Some parents have to place themselves or their offspring of working age in
domestic service in order to pay debts [there being no process of "bankruptcy" in that society].

1778-1788

Juan Bautista de Anza is Governor.

[Anza already owns an heroic reputation when he arrives in N.M. at the age of 42. He is American born and
reared on the Sonora frontier. He is a frontiersman who can negotiate diplomatically or fight hand-to-hand as
the situation demands, embrace a Comanche or smoke with a Navajo. Unlike some of his predecessors, he
can tell the difference between a Pueblo and an Apache just by meeting them.]

1778
MILITARY & COMANCHES

Governor Anza decides to campaign vigorously against the viking nations then strives to make them allies.
He instructs people living in isolated ranchos to move into more protected settlements. Chief
Cuerno Verde is referred to as *"the scourge of New Mexico."* Anza believes that Cuerno Verde
hates N.M. because his father was killed in the province. Anza keeps a diary on the campaign
against Cuerno Verde.

[W.A. Beck writes that Comanches are reported *as "boasting"* that the only reason they didn't wipe out
N.M. was that they wanted the *"Spanish and Mexicans ... to raise horses for them."* He doesn't explain how
Comanches could be referring to Hispanics as "Mexicans" in 1778.]

1779
RANCHING
Sheep numbers are 40% less than they were when reported by **Miera y Pacheco.**

MILITARY & COMANCHES
Anza leads a force of 600 men against the **Comanches** under Chief **Cuerno Verde** [for whom Green Horn
  Mt. is named in Colorado]. Anza's expedition goes through the **San Luis Valley,** augmenting his
  army with **Utes and Jicarillas.** Near (present) Colorado Springs, Anza goes east and surprises
  Comanche camps until he gets to (present) Pueblo where Cuerno Verde's village is captured
  because the warriors are raiding in Taos. As they are returning, a bloody battle is fought at the
  Green Horn Mt. Cuerno Verde and his warriors, completely outnumbered, fight heroically to the
  last man.
Various **Comanche** bands conduct horrible raids in Texas but attacks in N.M. are repulsed with such heavy
  Comanche casualties that they come into Taos and ask for peace. Anza tells the chiefs that all
  bands must come in and sign a treaty or there will be none with anybody. **Chief Toroblanco** insists
  on making war while **Chief Ecueracapa** wants peace.

Campaigns against the **Apaches** are also beginning to be successful.

1780s
GOVERNMENT
Carlos Fernández is employed in a role similar to *Protector of the Indians.*

1780
WOMEN
Antonio Gil Ibaro finds **M. Rita Peralta** at a Comanche slave auction in Texas, purchases and returns her to
  her parents in Tomé.[M. Rita had been enslaved by the Comanches for nearly 10 years.]

NAVAJOS
Teodoro de Croix, Commander-General of the Interior Provinces of New Spain, writes to José Gálvez that
  *"The Navajos, who, although of Apache, kinship, have a fixed home, sow, raise herds, and weave
  their blankets and clothes of wool."*

1781
HEALTH
A smallpox epidemic has devastated N.M., killing around 5,025 people, a quarter of the entire population.

1782
GOVERNMENT
N.M. is still divided into eight alcaldías: Santa Fe, Santa Cruz de la Cañada, Taos, Keres (Jémez), Sandía,
  Albuquerque, Laguna, and Zuñi.

Each Pueblo within each unit is governed by a native of that Pueblo, with the alcalde as local magistrate for
  minor cases.

TIMELINE

1782: King of Spain Carlos III decrees that all free subjects in Spanish colonies should contribute to the war (American Revolution) against England. Each Indian and mixed-blood will give one peso, each Spaniard two pesos. Those in poverty are exempted.

SOCIETY

Spanish-born friars, sometimes called *gachupines*, charge blatant discrimination under (American-born) Gov. Anza, citing nine specific cases.

[Tension is building between American-born friars and those from Spain.]

MAIL

Regular mail delivery is begun from Santa Fe to El Paso and points south. (Heretofore mail had been carried by caravans or travelers on the Camino Real.) Taos, Santa Fe, and Albuquerque are now linked to the rest of northern Mexico though delivery is possible only four times a year with departure scheduled for the first day in April, July, September, and November. Postage costs half a peso.

REPORT

Father **Juan Agustín de Morfi** reports that several northeastern Pueblos have to be abandoned due to constant Comanche raids, Pecos being a prime example.

1785
COMANCHES

Chief **Toroblanco** is murdered by members of the **Comanche** Peace faction. Toroblanco's followers then join with those of Chief **Ecueracapa**. José Manuel Roxo, probably a trader, goes to the Comanche camps and urges them to ask Anza to make peace. Ecueracapa is chosen as spokesman for the various bands.

BOOKS & LITERACY

Francisco Trébol Navarro of Santa Fe lists his books in his will: three books of Ordinances, the History of Gibraltar, a complete volume on all the sciences, Castilian Orthography, Swiss Philosophy, A Guide for Foreigners, Regulations for Presidios, Christian Catechism, Complete History of Religion (in two volumes, one of which is on loan).

WEALTH & SOCIETY

Clemente Gutiérrez dies. His estate includes 7,000 yearlings and two-year-old wethers, plus another 6,600 recently purchased from other ranchers. He owns 13,000 ewes being held in partido by 24 Río Abajo citizens. He owns three ranches: Pajarito and San Clemente on the Río Grande, and the huge Virtientes de Navajo along the Río Puerco.

1786
LAND GRANT
Official documents of the **Embudo grant** have become torn and frayed (since 1725) so heirs of **Francisco Martín,** one of the original grantees, take them to the alcalde of Santa Cruz, José Campo Redondo, who makes a certified copy of the original documents.

COMANCHE PEACE
February: Comanche chieftain **Ecueracapa** leads his people to   Pecos and orders that they set up their tipis in peace. The chief is then escorted to Santa Fe where he is received by Governor Anza amid festivities and honors due any chief of state: a military escort, the town council in attendance, and the assembled crowd applauding at every turn.

Ecueracapa is enchanted and his greeting of Gov. Anza takes at least 10 minutes. Then they go indoors where a Ute delegation (their "mortal enemies; *'Comanche'* is a Ute word for *'enemy'* and *'wants to fight me all the time' "*) accepts peace *"if Ecueracapa does."* He does and there are three days of conferencing and festivities. Then everyone adjourns to   Pecos to sign the peace document.

February 28: New Mexican Hispanics, led by Gov. **Anza,** and Comanches, led by Chief **Ecueracapa,** hold a peace conference at   Pecos where the following terms are agreed upon:

Comanches may move closer to the N.M. settlements; they will keep the peace with all nations friendly to N.M.;   Comanches may come into Santa Fe and free trade fairs will be established at Pecos;   Comanches will help fight the Apaches; the Governor of N.M. will endorse whomever the Comanches select as chiefs. Anza gives his own sword and banner to Ecueracapa for display to leaders of other bands not in attendance.

The   Comanches at   Pecos crowd around Anza at every opportunity. *"All, one by one, come up to embrace him with such excessive expressions of affection and respect ... and rub their faces against his."* Governor Anza is at his best and he has lunch with the Comanche captains in their camp.

The next day being Ash Wednesday, Anza receives ashes at service, along with all the Comanche and Ute captains in attendance. Then a trade fair is declared with the Governor proclaiming set rules to prevent cheating the Indians.

April, 1787: All three branches of the Comanche nation have signed peace treaties with Governor Anza.

[Despite the replacement of Anza, the death of Ecueracapa, hostilities of other Native Americans, etc., **the peace forged at   Pecos stands unbroken for generations** and the alliance is second in importance only to that with the Pueblo people.]

Comanches are described as robust, good-looking, and very happy people. Their faces display their martial, honest, and generous character. Their clothes are fashioned from buffalo skins and they paint their faces with red ochre and other colors, their eyelids with vermilion. They love to adorn themselves with anything that shines brilliantly, intertwining beads, ribbons, gold trinkets, etc., in their hair, which they often wear braided.

The **Comanche Peace (from 1786 to 1846** and continuing somewhat into the beginning of the U.S. period of domination) enables New Mexicans to survive then prosper. The Comanches become stalwart allies, much like the Pueblo, and a deep bond forms between Hispanics and the warrior Comanches, who are scrutinized by other warlike nations of the Plains.

[Bolton writes that **Anza's historical record** shows him to be *"...a man of heroic qualities, tough as oak, silent as the desert from which he sprang."* According to Bolton, the great achievement of Lewis and Clark would compare to Anza's if they had returned to Missouri, raised and equipped a colony of 240 people, then led them successfully back to the mouth of the Columbia River. Bolton writes that there is no one in *"Anglo-American annals with whom to compare"* Anza.]

COMMERCE

Comanchero trade becomes big business. Standard Comanchero **trade items** include Comanche bread, cornmeal, wheat flour, sugar, dried pumpkins, onions, tobacco, barley meal, saddlery, dry goods, lances and tomahawks, liquor making its appearance later. Comanches trade buffalo meat and hides, horses, mules, and guns at a later date. Contests of all kinds (shooting, horse racing, wrestling, foot races) are part of the festivities. Ransoming of captives also becomes part of the action.

Comancheros, Hispanic and Native American traders who go out onto the plains to barter with Plains nations, become an important part of New Mexican history and the economy of the day. They are a courageous lot of *llaneros,* master plainsmen, for their enterprise takes them out into the lands of warrior tribes.

PROFESSIONS

1810: A small party of armed **Americans** is captured east of Pecos. Governor Manrique, seriously lacking in professional troops, encourages traders, who come to be known as Comancheros, to go out onto the plains and relate any intelligence acquired. The **Comanchero trade** increases dramatically.

Comancheros are described by C. L. Kenner as *"striking, picturesque, daring New Mexicans who traveled the Plains to trade with the Comanches"* and other Indians like the Kiowas, Cheyenne, Utes, etc. The trade between New Mexicans and plains Indians was made possible because of the Comanche Peace established by Anza and Ecueracapa in 1786. The traders are Hispanic and Pueblo Indian, They were described by **Josiah Gregg** as *"the indigent and rude classes of the frontier villages"* (but this flies in the face of reason because they had to have substantial amounts of goods to trade in order to be in the business).

Comanchero trade becomes big business at least by 1820 and bridle paths are full-fledged cart roads by the 1840s.

August and September are the most popular months for trading. Standard Comanchero **trade items** include Comanche bread, cornmeal, wheat flour, sugar, dried pumpkins, onions, tobacco, barley meal, saddlery, dry goods, lances and tomahawks, liquor making its appearance later. New Mexican lances and tomahawk were *"more slender and graceful in design than those supplied by English or American traders."* They also traded *"ready made iron or steel arrow spikes"* to replace traditional flint points.

Comanche bread is an especially popular item. The bread was baked in hornos until it was dark, dry, crisp to the point that it was imperishable. **Josiah Gregg** described the loaves as *"exceedingly hard and insipid while dry ... but soft and very palatable when soaked in coffee or even water."* **Lewis Garrard** was really taken by it and proclaimed it to be *"light, porous, and sweet-a perfect luxury with a cup of coffee by a mountain-pine fire."*) The Comanches enjoyed it so much they would trade a good horse for a sackful.

Pueblo traders specialized in bread, flour, and cornmeal as Trade items. The following testimony was recorded about the trade: When the men were going to the plains to trade with the Comanches,

---

PROFILE

Juan Bautista de Anza

KNIGHT OF THE SOUTHWEST

1735: **Juan Bautista de Anza** is born at Fronteras in Sonora, Mexico, into a military family. His grandfather had been a presidio Captain at Janos and his father had served for 30 years at Fronteras.

1753: Following the family tradition, Juan enlists in the army at the age of 18.

1755: Anza is promoted to Captain. He petitions the government to lead an exploration party overland to California but is refused due to Indian uprisings.

1760: Juan is assigned as Commander of the Tubac presidio. Soldiers are required to take part of their pay in government supplies and one of the first of Anza's orders is to lower the exorbitant prices existing upon his arrival.

Other settlers arrive to live at Tubac, including a sister of the post chaplain, **Ana de Serrano,** whom Anza marries. In time he comes to know and admire **Father Garcés.**

Juan leads expeditions against the warlike Apaches and Seris. He defeats the chief of the Pápagos in hand-to-hand combat, thus winning their fealty. He is recognized for his personal courage, his ability to fight Indians and/or deal with them diplomatically.

1773: After riding a 1,000 miles a soldier named Juan Valdez brings orders that Anza is granted permission to find an overland route to California. (Viceroy Bucareli, whose task it was to carry out the policies of Charles III, was instrumental in helping Anza realize his expeditions.)

January, 1774: With Fr. Garcés in the group, Anza leads an expedition out of Tubac, California being some 600 miles away across burning desert country. Fr. Garcés and Fr. Juan Díaz record all events in their diaries. Juan Valdez is also in the group as is **Sebastián Tarabal**, an Indian from Mission San Gabriel, serving as guide.

March: The expedition reaches San Gabriel Mission, Monterey, in May and is back in Tubac the same month. In October Juan is promoted to Lieutenant Colonel.

September, 1775: Anza leads a second expedition, this time with 240 colonists, to California. Second in command is the stalwart **Joaquín Moraga.** On the first day out a mother dies in childbirth but there are no other deaths and three infants are born during the trek so the expedition ends with more people than when it began. **Fr. Pedro Font** serves as chaplain, diarist, and astronomer. The powerful **Chief Palma** of the Yuma nation lends his aid to Anza and his people.

January, 1776: The expedition arrives safely at **San Gabriel** mission.

March: Anza's settlers are now at **Monterey** and Captain Moraga leads them on to San Francisco where sites are selected for the presidio and Mission Dolores.

1777: Anza is appointed Governor of New Mexico but he must stay in Sonora until he quells an Indian uprising.

Juan Bautista de Anza (Painting by Fray Orci)
Courtesy Museum of NM, # 50828

1778: He assumes his duties as Governor of New Mexico. (See **1778-1788.**)

1781: The Yumas rise in rebellion and Anza is unjustly accused of causing it by making promises that weren't kept.

December, 1788: Upon the arrival of his replacement Juan Bautista de Anza leaves for Mexico City but he dies en route and is buried in the little village of Arizpe.

the women would grind whole loads of meal for them to carry. Several women would grind together at night; they ground the corn successively on three or four *metates* ranging from rough to smooth. On the first one they broke up the corn and reduced it to fine flour by the fourth, toasting it after each grinding. Meanwhile the men sang the grinding song or beat a rhythm on the drum and the women kept time to the music with slow, regular strokes.

Comanches' trade items include buffalo meat and hides, horses, mules, and **guns** at a later date.

Contests of all kinds (shooting, horse racing, wrestling, foot races) are part of the festivities.

Ransoming of captives also becomes part of the action.

1837: A Mrs. **Sarah Ann Horn** is being held captive by the Comanches when a Comanchero from San Miguel barters for her freedom by giving "a horse, four bridles, two looking glasses, two knives, some tobacco and some powder and balls." The woman is released to the generous Comanchero and later Horn relates that she could have been released sooner but an "Anglo trader" to whom she had first been offered had been willing to give "only a poor old horse that looked like an aged rack of bones." Mrs. Horn reported that the New Mexican Hispanos *"of whom I was so much afraid ... were very kind ... and they brought me enough of the food and drink"* which the distraught woman so desperately needed.

Description:
1845: Lt. **Abert** meets some Comanchero traders who are dressed in *"conical-crowned sombreros, jackets with the stripes running transversely, large bag breeches extending to the knee; long stockings and moccasins."* Abert describes the Pueblo traders as characterized by their *"jet black hair which is tied up in stumpy queues with some light-colored ribbon."* **Whipple** describes some Comancheros from Santo Domingo as being *"wrapped in blankets and wearing headbands around their hair."*

Abert also describes the **carretas** used by the Comancheros: *"Two eccentric wheels, not exactly circular formed by sawing off the ends of large logs, and rimming them with pieces of timber to increase their diameter ... They were perforated in the neighborhood of the center to receive an axletree of cottonwood. A suitable pole and a little square box of wicker wood completed the laughable machine."*

Traders ranged over an extensive area: to the east as far as the Wichita Mountains (Sierra Jumanos) of Oklahoma; to the southeast as far as the Davis Mountains; to the north **Manuel Lisa** reported that Comancheros were trading with the Arapahoes around the South Platte River. A very old trader from San Juan Pueblo once recalled that as a youth he had gone far to the north to trade with the Sioux, Cheyenne, Arapaho, Crow, Utes, and Shoshones.

Comancheros become an important part of New Mexican history and the economy of the day. They are a courageous lot of *llaneros,* master plainsmen who can move skillfully and at will over the feature-less landscapes of the plains. Their enterprise takes them out into the lands of warrior tribes and this was always dangerous. There were instances when the Comanches reclaimed the horses they had traded to the Comancheros; Lt. **Whipple** wrote about encountering five Comancheros who were fleeing from some Indians who had robbed them of nearly all their goods. It is believed these incidents stemmed more from personal grudges than general antipathy toward the traders.

Comanches, acknowledged masters of the southern plains, sometimes intervened on behalf of the Comancheros: **Adolph Bandelier** relates that some Pueblo Comancheros on their way to trade with Comanches were stopped by Kiowas who asked them to trade, which they did. After the bartering was completed the Kiowas demanded the return of their goods, which the Comancheros refused. The Kiowas were getting ready to attack when a Comanche war party rode in, ascertained the cause of the problem, and ran the Kiowas out.

According to **Kenner** there is no record of thc Comanches having killed any of the traders but the Kiowas were *"notorious for their treachery and viciousness"* and they attacked Mexican and Pueblo Comancheros alike. **Navajo** war parties also went out onto the plains and presented a serious menace to the Comancheros whether Mexican or Pueblo. And in areas where Americans had influence with the Indians like the Cheyenne, the American traders greatly resented what they referred to as the *"GREASER"* Comancheros.

1861: The **Civil War** comes to N.M. and the *despised* Comancheros are now recruited as "knowledgeable" **Scouts** for the Army.

1786 (con't)
GOVERNMENT
Viceroy **Bernardo de Gálvez** issues guidelines on how to maintain the peace with Native Americans:

Allied Indians will be allowed to barter for horses, guns, and ammunition;

Comanches who break the law will be given over to Comanche chiefs for punishment; Comanches are to be entertained liberally during visits to Hispanic settlements.
[In 1789 the sum of 5,906 pesos is spent on gifts for the various nations. When the Comanches try to return gift for gift, as is the Indian custom, they are told it is unnecessary, further bonding the alliance.]

Specially trained **Indian Agents** are based at **Taos, Santa Fe,** and **Pecos** in order to deal with Indian affairs.
Symbols of authority, silver handled canes, silver medals, scarlet cloaks, shall be given to all native leaders recognized as chiefs.

SOCIETY & COMANCHE PEACE

Hispanics from N.M. can now travel the plains in relative safety. **Governor Juan B. de Anza** is mainly
responsible for the Comanche Peace. Chief **Ecueracapa** sends his son to Anza to be educated in
Santa Fe. Anza now adds **Utes, Navajos,** and **Jicarilla Apaches** as allies, all of whom target hostile
Apache bands.

ARMAMENT

April: Anza receives a shipment of 200 *carabinas,* which are an improvement over the old *escopetas.* Close
Native American allies like the Pueblos get some of the new weapons, as well as a few Comanches
and Utes.

PROFESSIONS

Ciboleros, *"Rugged, daring, and picturesque..."* **Hispanic buffalo hunters** are in the habit of organizing
hunting parties to the buffalo plains east of N.M. Buffalo hunting becomes a basic part of the
economy. After the fall harvest is in, hunters from various settlements band together for expeditions to the plains to secure a winter's supply of meat. (Ciboleros' departure is often celebrated
with a dance for the entire village.)

Favorite cibolero rendezvous are Lucero *(Placita de los Ciboleros* in the Mora country), Taos, Santa Cruz,
San Miguel del Vado, Manzano, and El Paso. Each group of Ciboleros, sometimes more than 150
men, elects a **comandante** (mayordomo) whose word is law and must be obeyed for the success
of the expedition. Ciboleros wear buckskin clothes: leather shirt, leather pants that reach just
below the knees; teguas (hard-soled moccasins, common footwear in N.M.); and a leather hat,
pointed on top and adorned with a curved feather.

Cibolero **horses** are the best in the villages, highly trained and courageous enough to charge into a herd of
stampeding buffalo, guided only by knee pressure. They are never used for farm labors.

The **lance,** with a shaft 6 to 8 feet long with a double-edged blade of 12 to sixteen inches affixed to the end,
is the ciboleros' favorite hunting tool.

A **campsite** is selected and riders go out to find the herds. When a herd is sighted the hunters charge into it,
lancing as many buffalo as possible until the horses are tired.

A good horse and hunter can down 20 to 25 buffalo in a run of about three miles. Helpers, *los siguidores,*
come behind the hunters and bleed the downed buffalo, after which the carts arrive with the
butchers who cut up the carcasses and haul them back to camp. Everyone in camp works on
processing the meat, which is cut into long, thin strips to dry as tasajo (**charqui,** jerky) on rope
stretched between carts, salting the hides, preserving the tongues, which could be sold in Chihuahua for a peso each, rendering tallow for use in greasing cart wheels and the making of soap and
candles, the latter being an important export item in the N.M. economy, making chicharones, and
selecting choice marrow bones used in stews back home. Horns are sawed off and buffalo hair is
gathered for use in mattresses. Virtually every part of the buffalo is used.

After a successful buffalo hunt the journey home is a high-spirited affair, the men from different villages
visiting and playing the guitar, harmonica, accordion, often singing in chorus around campfires,
many songs composed spontaneously, telling of their adventures and those of famous hunters.

There are still dangers: sudden blizzards or other storms can be dangerous and hostile Indian war parties
will cause the men to form a circle with their carts. Villagers celebrate the return of their Ciboleros
with a dance, the most popular of New Mexican celebrations.

1787
TRAILS & EXPLORATION
Pedro Vial blazes a trail from San Antonio, Texas, to Santa Fe. During the last leg of this history-making
journey, Vial is escorted as far as   Pecos Pueblo by Comanche warriors.

José Mares, long-time soldier and scout, duplicates Vial's feat, only in reverse, from Santa Fe to San
Antonio. He is accompanied by **Cristóbal de los Santos,** who had been with Vial, and interpreter
Alejandro Martín.

1788-1794
Fernando de la Concha is Governor.

COMMERCE
Commandant **Jacobo Ugarte y Loyola** reports that New Mexico's principal exports are skins, coarse textiles,
and livestock. There is a lack of circulating currency. New industries and old ones like weaving
need to be encouraged.

SOCIETY
The **Gila Apaches** in southwestern N.M. give occasional trouble but *the province enjoys relative peace.*

Ranchers and farmers report that numbers of cattle, mules, and horses are increasing; bumper   crops are
harvested.

Efforts are made to prevent native allies from fighting each other.

N.M. populations begin to increase.

Cultural interchanges between Hispanics and Native Americans, especially the Pueblos, with the
Comanches some distance behind, are accepted as a way of life.

1788-1789
TRAILBLAZER
Pedro Vial maps a trail from Santa Fe to Natchitoches, to San Antonio, then back to Santa Fe.
1789
MILITARY & APACHES
Apaches suffer serious defeats in battles so they sue for peace. Governor Concha is wary of their sincerity

so he puts them on probation for six months to test them.

CARPENTRY

Lorenzo Ortega creates and signs a nativity cradle [making it one of the earliest dated and signed pieces of woodwork in N.M.].

COMMERCE

Governor De La Concha suggests that European manufactures can be imported at New Orleans then shipped to St. Louis or Natchitoches by riverboat, then delivered by mule train to N.M. at a savings of 40% over the cost of transporting from Veracruz-Mexico City then up the *Camino Real*. **He is given permission to blaze a route to St. Louis.**

1790
SOCIETY

N.M. is an isolated, remote frontier outpost with no mineral wealth to speak of. **Missionary activity is strong and paid for by the Spanish government**. Hispanics and their Pueblo allies are a buffer against hostile Amerind nations. Like the Pueblo people before them, Hispanic men and women have carved a home out of the wilderness, against all odds, and survived.

[According to R. Gutiérrez **modern statistical analysis shows that 93% of all N.M. households held no servants or slaves in 1790.**]

FURNITURE

Homes are furnished with distinctive New Mexican style chests (*cajas*), chairs (*sillas*), benches (*bancos*), and tables (*mesas*). Wealthy people also enjoy free-standing cabinets (*armarios*), writing desks (*escritorios*), and beds with headboards (*camas altas*). Rawhide-covered boxes called *petacas* (imported from Mexico) are also in use.
Much of the furniture is decorated with carving.

[When flour mills become more accessible during the beginning of the next century most houses include a kitchen cupboard (*trastero*, with an aerated upper cupboard in which to store baked goods or other such foods) and the rodent-proof chest (*harinero*) to store flour or grain.]

POPULATION

There are 16,358 Hispanos living in N.M. according to the Census of 1790.

The population of Pecos Pueblo is 154 (down from 449 in 1750).

There are 44 carpenters in N.M.

SANTERO

The **Laguna Santero** may have arrived in N.M. by 1790. He completes various works before returning to Mexico in 1808.

COMANCHE - KIOWA PEACE

Groups of **Comanche and Kiowa,** traditional enemies, chance to visit in (an unnamed) N.M. village on the
same day. Nervous hosts ask them to negotiate their differences in order to avoid trouble. A few
days later an alliance is forged between the two nations, never to be broken. (Comanches are now
at peace with the Kiowas and the Utes.)

BUSINESS

Manuel Delgado leaves the military service and becomes a prominent businessman in Santa Fe. His wife,
Josefa García de Noriega from El Paso is a member of a family with important business ties in
Chihuahua and N.M. While Delgado deals with local products, he also becomes a dealer in El Paso
wine and brandy.

SOCIETY

Manuel Armijo [to be three-time Governor of N.M.] is born at Plaza de San Antonio.

Laguna Pueblo Church, altar detail.
Courtesy Museum of NM, #14481

Ca. 1790-1810
SANTERO

The **Laguna Santero** is creating religious art during this period. [It is possible he was an artist from Mexico.]
His best known work and "masterpiece" is the altar screen at the Laguna Pueblo Church (described by L. Frank as the most *monumental* item created by a New Mexican santero) though altar
screens in Santa Fe, Pojoaque, Acoma, Santa Ana, and Zía are thought to have been created by

him. It is believed he had some formal training though he painted with tempera instead of oils. His early work seems to strive after a third-dimension and his production is characterized by styles of Mexican baroque paintings in their dark, rich colors, and by a three-quarter view of faces, three-quarter-length portraits, the use of white paint for decorations and details on clothing, and a distinctive representation of hands. It is believed he trained other New Mexican santeros, referred to as the **School of the Laguna Santero,** in a fairly popular studio workshop.

1790-1830
SANTERO

Pedro Antonio Fresquis is creating religious art during this period. Fresquis is (thought to be) the first native-born santero (and referred to by later investigators as the *Truchas Master* and the *Calligraphic Santero.)* His considerable number of retablos (some of which can be found at Nambé Pueblo church, at the Chapel of San Pedro y San Pablo at Chamisa, at Truchas, etc.) are two-dimensional and have no empty spaces. His style includes figures in frontal view and faces with almond-shaped eyes. He provides different interpretations for his subjects, a personal spontaneity, as well as a mystical quality.

[While Fresquis is known principally for his retablos it is now thought that he also created bultos. It is possible he is the *Santero of the Delicate Crucifixes.* It is believed he trained various (unknown) students.]

APACHE PEACE

Summer: **Apache chiefs make peace with Gov. Concha in Santa Fe.** The Apaches promise not to raid El Paso [part of N.M.], Chihuahua, or Sonora. They will settle down and take up farming so Gov. Concha settles them at **Sabinal** between Belén and Socorro. Albuquerque and Bernalillo residents are required to help their most implacable enemies with money and livestock, *with which they comply.* The Sabinal Apache experiment lasts for three years, while Concha is governor.

1791
MILITARY

The **Santa Fe presidio** is completed, containing barracks for 100 soldiers.
SOCIETY

Toribio García Jurado and some of his Belén neighbors are ordered to take their oxen to Isleta where some will be chosen to help build a bridge across the Río Grande at San Felipe. There is no mention of pay and **Apaches** are raiding so the men from the **Gabaldón Plaza** say they can't comply with the order while Santiago Trujillo and 15 other men from the vicinity accede to the demands.

Manuel Arteaga, the magistrate at Isleta, refuses to accept the "excuses" of the men from Gabaldón Plaza and orders that they be placed in jail because they are required to contribute to the general welfare of N.M.

T. García Jurado is ordered to appear in Santa Fe and many men wish to accompany him because he is representing the group, not just himself, but only García and his three sons are allowed to go because of the danger from raiding Apaches.

In Santa Fe the men are interrogated separately as to who led the opposition to obeying the order. Each declares he doesn't know of any leader, that all parties acted together because their oxen were worn out from previous work details, that they indeed believe they are obligated to contribute to the common good, that they always have in the past, that their oxen were not up to the requirements of the job at hand.

Governor Concha makes the final determination: it would be excessive punishment to handle this matter according to the law therefore a fine of three silver pesos will be paid by each offending citizen, said fines to be applied toward costs of this action and the remainder to help finance the Apache mission in the Belén jurisdiction. If anyone violates the law in the future maximum penalties will be applied. All persons are now at liberty subject to the above conditions.

PROFILE

Pedro Vial

M O S T   F A M O U S   O F   T R A I L   B L A Z E R S

1770s: **Pedro Vial** (b. *Pierre Vial* in Lyons, France) is in the Illinois country.

1779: Vial is living in the Taovaya villages on the Red River, practicing the trade of gunsmith.

1786: Pedro is in **Bexar** (San Antonio) and is sent by authorities there to open a trail to Santa Fe. He travels only with **Cristóbal de los Santos.** During the trail blazing journey he becomes ill and spends weeks recuperating in a Tawakoni (Wichita) village. When he recovers his health he follows the Red River to the Comanche village of Chief **Zoquiné** where he also stays for a while. Then he goes to Santa Fe and reports to the Governor, giving him two maps of his route [one of which still exists].

1787-1802: Vial's knowledge of the upper Missouri River country is [now] known to be the most accurate.

1788-89: Vial leaves Santa Fe heading eastward across the Texas Panhandle, down the Red River to **Natchitoches** (in a route that eventually goes from Santa Fe to New Orleans) and on to San Antonio where he spends the winter, then back to Santa Fe (a journey of some 2,377 miles in one year and two months). He is accompanied by several men, two of whom, **Santiago Fernandez** and **Francisco Xavier Fragoso,** keep a journal.

1789: While spending the winter in San Antonio, Pedro is sent to take presents to various Comanche encampments.

1791: Vial is working out of Santa Fe as an interpreter for 6 *reales* per day.

1792-93: Vial blazes the **Santa Fe Trail** [a round trip of 2,279 miles] from Santa Fe to San Luis (now St. Louis). On the way east he and his men are captured by Kansas Indians, threatened with death for six weeks, and held naked to prevent their escape but they are finally released and complete the first transit in history of the Santa Fe Trail. After his return to Santa Fe, Vial continues to explore and take trips into Indian country for the authorities in Santa Fe. As an interpreter he earns six *reales* a day while working with the Taovaya (Wichita), Comanche, Jicarilla Apache, Pawnee, Osage, Kansas, etc.

1795: (There is an indication that Vial might have some children.)

1796: Vial is referred to as *Manitou* (a Chippewa word that can mean *devil* or *great spirit*).

1797: Pedro is living with the   Comanches.

1799: Vial is living at Portage des Sioux (north of San Luis).

1803: Pedro returns to Santa Fe.

[The famous town attracts other interpreters and personalities like Alejandro Martín, interpreter for the Comanche and Kiowa; José Chalvert; Juan Lucero, Jean Baptiste Lalande, Laurenzo Durocher, etc.]

1804: Pedro is awarded back pay.

1805: Vial leads an expedition to the Indian country, perhaps as a counteraction to the **Lewis and Clark** expedition that appears to incite the Indians against the Spanish because Vial's group is attacked.

1806: Pedro leads another expedition, this time to the Pawnee, but many of his men desert so he returns to Santa Fe. He continues working as an interpreter.

1808: Vial is issued a license to trap on the Missouri River by **William Clark** (of *Lewis and Clark* fame), U.S. Indian Agent.

1814: Pedro Vial dies in Santa Fe and is buried there. Though never married, his will identifies **M. Manuela Martín** as his beneficiary.

APACHE RAIDS

August: **Apaches** attack Tomé. Some 33 Hispanics die in defense of their village while the survivors barricade themselves in the church and are saved by warriors from **Isleta** led by **Captain Taschelnate.**

1792
TRAILS & EXPLORATION

May 21: **Pedro Vial,** with companions Vicente Villanueva and Vicente Espinosa, leave Santa Fe for the purpose of mapping a trail to **San Luis** in order to open a trade route between the two Spanish provinces. After many harrowing adventures, the trio arrives in San Luis (now **St. Louis**) on October 6, 1792. The famous trail blazer is back in Santa Fe the following year.

[*The Pedro Vial route later becomes famous as the* **Santa Fe Trail**.]

1793
SOCIETY

January 16: **Antonio José Martínez,** later to be known as **Father Martínez,** is born in Abiquiú.

1794-1805

Fernando Chacón is Governor.

1794
SETTLEMENTS

Because of security provided by the Comanche Peace, **San Miguel del Bado** is founded on a grant of land east of Pecos Pueblo, down the Pecos valley by **Lorenzo Márquez** and 51 other families. Thirteen *genízaros* are in the group. [Genízaros, excellent Frontiersmen, often form the nucleus for eastern expansion.]

Early in the next century **San José del Vado, La Cuesta,** and around 1822, **Anton Chico,** are founded.

RELIGION

Baptismal books show that large numbers of Comanches and Plains Indians are baptized at San Juan and Taos during the waning years of the century.

MISSIONS REPORT

Fray **Cayetano José Ignacio Bernal** writes a follow-up survey of the N.M. missions in which he says **sheep and textiles** are basic exports. Fifteen to twenty thousand *carneros* are driven south to Chihuahua each year.

WEAVING

Governor Chacón remarks that Navajo weavers *"...work their wool with more delicacy and taste than the Spaniards."*

SOCIETY

Pedro Córdova is born in Córdova.

1796
LAND GRANT
The **Don Fernando de Taos** land grant is made.

WOMEN & SOCIETY
By the end of the 18th century, **women in N.M. outnumber men** by a ratio of 10 to 8. (Defending the land has taken its toll on the male population and New Mexican society.)

NAVAJO RAIDS
Some bands of Navajos raid sporadically in western and northwestern N.M,

REPORT ON NEW MEXICO
Governor Chacón reports that N.M. has a wonderful climate, high mountains, plains, and deserts. The population numbers about 35,751, most of them farmers and/or rancheros living in the Río Grande valley, where they grow various crops. Being so isolated, few crops are exported so there is seldom a surplus. The **Pueblo people** make up about a third of the population, hard workers who are expert in agriculture and often enjoy surpluses. At least 25,000 sheep are driven to Chihuahua markets each year. Hogs are scarce and the shortage of lard limits soap production. Hostile Indian **raids** limit horse and mule breeding. External commerce depends wholly on the caravans going and returning from the south in which more than 500 men usually participate, going to El Paso, Sonora, Coahuila, Chihuahua, Durango, etc.

COMMERCE
New Mexicans **export** livestock, coarse cloth, furs, piñon, etc., and **import** textiles of all kinds, hats, iron-work, hardware, dyes, drugs, paper, chocolate, sugar, rice, ink (homemade varieties are created when supplies run out), etc. Records are kept and writing is done with **quill pens** cut with a "penknife."

SOCIETY
Santero **José Rafaél Aragón** is born in Santa Fe.
1799
RANCHING
Juan Candelaria, pioneer rancher in N.M. and Arizona, imports sheep from Vera Cruz which include four purebred **Merinos,** three ewes and a black ram.

POPULATION
Census figures show that there are 23,648 Hispanics in N.M., which includes El Paso, and 10,557 Indians, presumably Pueblos.

PUEBLOS & GOVERNMENT PROTECTION
Alcalde Mayor **Manuel García de la Mora** and his assistant are removed from their jurisdiction and barred from holding any public office for a period of eight years for having failed to provide justice for **Juan Domingo Carache** of San Ildefonso Pueblo when accused of witchcraft by Fray **Antonio Barreras** (who had conducted an investigation which resulted in Carache's death).

PROFILE

Pedro Córdova

THE IDEAL OF EL PATRON

1749: Pablo Córdova, Pedro's grandfather, is one of the original petitioners of the Pueblo Quemado land grant.

1756: **Santiago Celedonio Córdova,** Pedro's father, is baptized.

1783: Santiago Celedonio marries **Juliana Martín.** Both are financially solid if not wealthy.

1794: Pedro is born to Celedonio and Juliana.

1806: Pedro is a member of the local militia but has no horse, firearms, or lance. His equipment consists of a bow and 25 arrows.

1817: Pedro marries **Ramona Mondragón,** also of Córdova, and they have 10 children.

1838, 1844, 1845: Pedro receives permits for transporting goods to and from provinces of Chihuahua, Durango, Zacatecas, and Lagos. His trade wagons, 8 to 10 of them, are loaded primarily with wool and woven goods like blankets, serapes, pants, linen, and cloth.

By this time Pedro Córdova is a wealthy pillar of the community. He owns large amounts of agricultural land in Córdova, Las Truchas, Cundiyó, Río de an Medio, Chimayó, Santa Cruz, as well as in the plain east of Córdova. His home has 13 rooms, he owns a second house in Córdova, seven in Truchas, one each in Río de en Medio and Chimayó, and two in Cundiyó. He has many pieces of furniture, many santos, and firearms in abundance. He owns storehouses for his grain, a mill, and a *mielero* for making molasses which are also used by others in the community (without a fee being charged). He owns 40 teams of oxen as well as cattle, mules, donkeys, horses, goats, and pigs.

1858: Pedro Córdova dies. His estate is valued a, $9,243 and he owns 5,480 varas of land in six communities. (By contrast, other wealthy people of the day would include José Antonio Córdova of Truchas who owned an estate worth $375 when he died in 1853; Hilario Trujillo from Chimayó, $263 in 1860; José Antonio Vigil from Cundiyó $1,682 in 1861.)

Commandant General **Pedro de Nava** punishes the two officials for ignoring the laws governing a prosecution for witchcraft and for *"abandoning the defense"* of Carache. Fray Antonio Barreras, not subject to civil law because of the *fuero eclesiástico* (ecclesiastical privilege), is removed from San Ildefonso, and henceforth serves only in the Río Abajo jurisdiction.

1800
COPPER MINING

Col. **José Manuel Carrasco** discovers a fabulous deposit of copper which comes to be known as the **Santa Rita Mine**.

1804*:* The mining of copper begins (making Santa Rita one of the oldest copper mines in the USA).

LAND GRANT

The Cebolleta (Seboyeta) land grant of about 200,000 acres is awarded to *30* families from the Albuquerque-Atrisco area. The settlement is intended as a buffer to forestall Navajo raids on the Río Grande communities. Navajos living in the immediate area are forced out [to the present Cañoncito area]. (See **1804.**)

EDUCATION

Gerónimo Becerra establishes a school in Abiquiú.

SETTLEMENT

Alamillo and **Socorro** are founded around this time.

RELIGIOUS ART

Santero **art** *[one of the rare, truly indigenous art forms to be found in the U.S.]* has become an important aspect of N.M. culture and day-to-day living, the product of a unique New Mexican environment which includes:

Isolation from the rest of the Americas. N.M. is the northern-most outpost of Spanish civilization for more than two centuries, the deepest penetration of a European society into North America, cut off from other communities by mountains, deserts, and hostile Indians. Distances are multiplied by primitive transportation and a lack of navigable rivers.

Loss of Renaissance artistic influences: Renaissance art embraced a visual realism and linear perspective that glorified life. N.M. realities are as harsh as the landscape and the problems of making a living on it. These are reflected in Santero art, along with medieval religiosity as represented by the Franciscans. N. M. **Hispanics** are basically one large, **extended family** and religion is a familial celebration that centers around Christ, Mary, and the saints. N.M. Catholicism requires a large number of images, which are unavailable from outside sources so they must be produced locally.

Rural traditions: most New Mexicans live in small villages where they farm and tend stock. There is a dearth of artistic training, tools, materials.

Santero art is created almost exclusively from home-crafted native materials and is of three kinds:

Retablo, a painting made on a pine wood panel, sawed at the top and bottom, the surface hand-azed then covered with gesso, mixture of gypsum and glue, and painted with watercolors. (Small retablos are often taken along on journeys or for use while in camp.)

Bulto, a statue carved from cottonwood root then covered with gesso and painted, sometimes clothed ornately, especially the *Virgin Mary.*

Reredo, altar screen, a large structure of panels, finished like retablos, placed behind and above a church altar.

Although they take stylistic liberties, New Mexican saint makers draw on traditional Christian iconography from illustrated missals, bibles, devotional cards, etc., as well as paintings and sculptures brought up from Mexico.

Main subjects favored in *Santero* art (which represents New Mexican endurance, suffering, and survival in an often hostile world surrounded by palpable dangers that can be combated only by family effort and Christianity) are:
The **Trinity:** God the Father, Christ *(Nuestro Padre Jesús),* the Holy Spirit;

The **Holy Family:** Joseph is the strongest of human father figures; the Christ Child appears often with Mary and also alone as the *Santo Niño, Santo Niño de Atocha, el Niño de Praga, el Niño Perdido;*

Mary with various titles: *Nuestra Señora de los Angeles, de las Candelarias, de la Purísima Concepción, del Socorro, del Rosario, de los Dolores, de la Soledad,* etc.
Angels: (often "elder brother protectors") Gabriel, Michael, Raphael, and the Guardian Angel;

Saints (patrons and protectors, male and female): Joseph, Francis, Isidore, John Nepomucene, Raymond Nonnatus, Rita, Rosalia, Veronica, Jerome, John the Baptist, Agnes, Anthony, Ann, Rosalie, Stanislaus, Aloysius Gonzaga, Lucy, Apolonia, Lawrence, Bárbara, Ignatius, etc.

[These figures are familial intermediaries and if they don't "deliver" what is prayed for they can be "disciplined" by turning them to the wall or putting them in a trunk.]

Allegorical: *doña Sebastiana,* Death, utilized as a reminder of human mortality.

A santero artist is considered something of a **holy man,** a person dedicated to portraying higher beings *and their power,* a humble servant who rarely even signs his name to his creations. He works according to tradition and doesn't innovate. He generally gathers his own materials from around the area where his village is located. A *santero* is highly respected in a community (and there are precious few in the province).

Santero art is not aesthetic in the sense of creating something beautiful but rather intended for a religious purpose. New Mexican life is difficult so a *santo* has to have powerful holiness to enable people to

149

survive, endure, and prevail. Frontier life demands more than the luxury of gazing at beauty. Santos help to validate the lives of New Mexico's Hispanic men, women, and children for their struggles are thereby linked to everlasting life, which they believe is the primary reason for living.

Santos are often considered to be virtual family members by New Mexican Hispanics. Many homes have their own private chapels with an altar and santos. Those in churches are cared for by members of the community who watch over their safety and attend to proper dress according to the religious calendar. Small *retablos* are taken by sheepherders while they are tending their flocks and popular santos and/or retablos are integral parts of religious processions. They are often carried into people's homes for use in praying for help and they are also taken into the fields during times of harvest or drought.

When a certain santo is prayed to and the prayer is answered a *velorio,* wake or prayer meeting, is celebrated. A *Resador,* prayer leader, is hired to lead the prayers and sing *alabados,* Penitente Brotherhood hymns. Friends, relatives, and their families, especially los *Viejitos,* the Elders in the family, are invited to participate and when all are present the praying and singing goes on until midnight when supper is served after which the singing continues until dawn when the *Alba* is sung, ending the gathering.

Courtesy of J. and J. Márquez family.

1800-1845
SANTERO

(Antonio?) **Molleno** is creating religious art during this period. Molleno is the most prolific and experimental of N.M. santeros, developing three distinctive styles of painting during his long career. [Some critics say he is the best.] He signs his name to a painting only once and his first name comes down by oral tradition only. He lives somewhere between Chimayó and Taos. It is possible that he apprenticed with the **Laguna Santero.** His later creations are rendered mostly in reds, blues, and blacks, sometimes on a white background, with feathery brush strokes, and a consistent and systematic design style. Decorative red wedges characterize his early work, for which he is dubbed "The Chile Painter." His style for drawing beards on male figures is distinctive. Realism is portrayed through attention to detail, colored to dark backgrounds, garment detail, and the human face. A versatile artist, Molleno paints on deer and buffalo hides as well as hand-azed panels.

1801
SOCIETY

April 27: **Estefana Delgado**, Manuel Delgado's daughter, marries **Juan Rafaél Ortiz.**

1802
Rafaél Luna of Taos is born.
[He is the first of the five-generation Luna family tradition of filigree jewelers.]

1803
REPORT
Governor Chacón reports that farming methods in N.M. are backward, that up-to-date manuals are needed. Books are needed for everything pertaining to agriculture and animal husbandry. The province being so isolated, export of foodstuffs is ignored by most farmers, motivating mere subsistence farming, which is very dangerous if crops fail. **Pueblo farmers** utilize better techniques that result in surpluses, which they sell to the presidial quartermaster.

With respect to *arts and trades,* it may be said with propriety that there are none in this Province, there being no apprenticeship, official examination for master workmen, any formality of trade unions, or other things customary in all parts, "*but necessity and the natural industry of these inhabitants has led them to exercise some, for example weaving in wool, shoemaker, carpenter, tailor, blacksmith, and mason in which nearly all are skilled.*"
Tobacco is a popular crop because it yields a good profit. Most of the clergy smokes it or dips it as snuff.

New Mexicans are much given to **dealing and bartering** with each other and the tribes of nomadic Indians, which is conducted in **sign language.**

New Mexico isn't poor as it is generally represented to be and its decadence and backwardness is traceable to the lack of development and want of formal knowledge in agriculture, commerce, and the manual arts.

Further proof that the Province isn't poor can be found in excessive display of **luxuries** as compared to the rest of the Internal Provinces. New Mexicans don't experience total famines, even though outside relief aid is never forthcoming, because they are able to augment their diet with **meat** during scarcity of grains and vegetables. In New Mexico there is never seen nakedness or begging. The people shouldn't be overburdened with taxes and exempting the Province from the *alcabala* [sales tax] for 10 years is wisdom on the part of the King.

EDUCATION
Nemesio Salcedo of Chihuahua mandates the establishment and maintenance of **schools**. Instruction is to occur in the morning and afternoon; the teacher is required to teach Christian doctrine, reading, writing, and counting. Paper must be provided if children are too poor to provide for themselves.

TIMELINE

1803: The United States purchases the Louisiana Territory [which meant purchasing "first rights" to treat with the native owners of the soil if international law was recognized] from France in order "to secure it for the spread of democracy and its government where citizen have

the power." But the people of New Orleans let it be known they don't want American government, preferring Spanish sovereignty and its civilization, according to A.K. Weinberg. The Louisianans cite Jefferson's own "consent of the governed" to prevent the American takeover. As the time draws near to take possession of New Orleans, President Jefferson sends in American troops to prevent "disorder and install the blessings of American democracy."
[The people of Louisiana were not permitted to form a state or territorial government on the grounds that they had no experience in self-government. A government was formed in which they had no representation.]

1805: *James Wilkinson*, commander of American forces in Louisiana, writes to H. Dearborn that the Comanches "*...have it in their power to facilitate or impede our march into New Mexico should ever such movement become necessary.*"

1804
PIONEERS

Among the families living in Cebolleta (Seboyeta) are those of: Francisco Aragón; Domingo Baca; Josefa Baca; Marsial Baca; Antonio Chaves; Bicente Chaves; Juan Antonio Chaves; Juan Bautista Chaves; José Chaves; J. Santos Chaves; Salvador Chaves; Francisco García; Anastacio Gallego; Felipe Gallego; Juan Cristóbal Gallego; J. Gregorio Gallego; Manuel Gallego; Pablo Gallego; Román Gallego; Miguel Herrera (?); Juan Domingo Herrera; Gregorio Jaramillo; Javier Jaramillo; Diego Antonio Márquez; Bentura Peralta; Santiago Peralta; Juan J. Perea (?); Lorenzo Romero; Manuel Romero; Judás Satillanes...

August: **A thousand Navajo warriors attack Cebolleta** with the intention of wiping it off the face of the earth. Villagers and their terrified domestic stock gather in the fortified plaza and defend themselves from arrows and burning pitch-pine knots. The town is besieged for several days and there are heroic feats of valor on both sides. Individual warriors try to open the gate to the plaza in order to overwhelm the defenders by sheer numbers.

Antonia Romero, who like the other women is helping with making bandages, taking water to the men, and trying to calm the terrified livestock, suddenly sees that a Navajo has made it over the wall during a furious assault and is about to remove the bar from the gate. She picks up a heavy *metate* [grinding stone basin], arrows whizzing all about her, and hurls it at the foe, crushing the warrior's skull and saving the village from certain death, for the moment.

Domingo Baca and a group sally out and in a hand-to-hand encounter his abdomen is sliced open by a Navajo lance. The Cebolletanos retreat to the plaza, Baca's entrails hanging but for his hands that keep them from falling out. His fellow defenders believe he is a goner but once in safety he puts a pillow to his belly and lashes it in place, returning to help throw back the assault by firing his musket. When the assault abates, he removes the pillow and *sews up his abdomen himself.* [Baca made a complete recovery and lived for many years thereafter.]
The Navajos finally call off the attack. It is reported they lose 22 men killed and about 50 wounded.

Virtually all of the Cebolletanos are wounded and their military corporal is dead. They know it is just a matter

of time before the Navajos return for another assault on the tiny village. After a town meeting they
decide to give up the settlement so they pack up their *carretas* and move to Laguna for temporary
security.

Governor Chacón sympathizes with their plight but he knows it is illegal to abandon frontier outposts once
they have been claimed. He refers the matter to the military commandant in Chihuahua. The
commandant also sympathizes but the law must be obeyed so he orders the settlers back to
Cebolleta, to be escorted by a troop of 30 well-armed soldiers from Chihuahua to help protect them.
Cebolletanos return to their village.

1805: Navajos attack Seboyeta once again but with the Chihuahua reinforcements they are driven off. **Raids
and counter-raids** become integral parts of the history of Cebolleta for the next half century or so.

Frontiersmen like **Chato Aragón and Redondo Gallegos** become famous for their heroics as they, and several
other Cebolletanos, become part of New Mexican folklore and legend, Navajos finally claiming
their lives.

REPORT

Governor Chacón issues a report critical of the N.M. missions: missionaries gouge the citizenry with
exorbitant fees because they have a monopoly on dispensing the sacraments. If someone can't
pay the fees they must work it off. If a colonist dies, the friar suddenly becomes the deceased's
sole heir. Indians are made to pay to celebrate their mission's patron feast day or it is canceled. On
All Souls day the Indians are required to bring part of their harvest to church for the friars. If an
Indian dies his family must pay burial expenses in livestock or personal service. The friars don't
know native languages and don't try to learn them...

TRADE & FOREIGNERS

Jean Batiste Lalande, working for William Morrison of Kaskaskia, arrives in Santa Fe with trade goods. He
is arrested and sent off to Chihuahua but allowed back the following year. He doesn't return to the
U.S.

1805-1808

Joaquín del Real Alencaster is Governor.

1805
GOVERNMENT

Governor Real Alencaster wants to curtail trading between New Mexicans and the plains nations. **Felipe
Sandoval** leads a protest movement and is jailed by the governor, along with **José García de la
Mora,** *"defender of the people of the Río Arriba."* Outraged citizens descend on Santa Fe and
refuse to disband until they are certain the two are released from jail.

HEALTH

Vaccination against smallpox is introduced in N.M.

TRADE & FOREIGNERS

James Purcell, a Kentuckian who has been living with the plains Indians, arrives in Santa Fe with some trade goods. He is arrested immediately.

1806
LAND GRANT
Francisco Salazar and 30-some settlers petition for a grant of land, the *Cañon del Río de Chama*, which is awarded and comes to be known as the **San Joaquín land grant.**

EDUCATION
Efforts are made in Santa Fe to recruit students for the **Royal Cantábrico Seminary** where "an eminent faculty" teaches Religion, Physical Education, Political Education, Literary Education with emphasis on classic authors... "and for primary education the methodology of Pestalozzi."

[University level education was unavailable in N.M.]

AMERICAN EXPEDITION
It is learned that an American spying expedition is being sent into Spanish territory. **Facundo Melgares** leads a troop of soldiers to intercept it. Due to a delay in the start of the **Zebulon M. Pike** expedition, the two groups don't meet.

1807
Z. M. PIKE
The **Pike Expedition** is encountered, marched to Santa Fe and then Chihuahua. Pike maintains that he was lost but throughout his experience he records what people from all walks of life tell him concerning the economy, the extent of their patriotism, how they feel about foreign trade markets, etc.

[Pike's journal provides the first information available to the American public on the area that would be called the Southwest. Because of Pike's information, traders realize there is a significant imbalance in New Mexico's trade because of requirements imposed by Chihuahua merchants. They want to take over the lucrative trade because their prices are lower.]

WEAVING
March 3: The **Bazán** brothers, **Juan and Ignacio Ricardo,** master **weavers** from Mexico City, arrive in Santa Fe through a government-sponsored program to instruct N.M. weavers in the fine points of their craft.

1808
Alberto Maynez is Acting Governor.

SOUTHERN TRADE CARAVAN
N.M. businessmen usually gather their trade goods and livestock during August and November at the traditional rendezvous site of **La Joya de Sevilleta,** the starting point for the trade **caravans** going south to Chihuahua. All participants are well armed and the large force precludes attacks from hostile Indians.

PROFILE

Cebolla, Antonio Sandoval

N A V A J O   L E A D E R   I N   T H R E E   W O R L D S

1807: **Cebolla, Antonio Sandoval,** is born in the *Tótsohnii* clan. As a child he learns some of the Spanish language from New Mexican captives.

1816: Comanche raiders drive Cebolla's band into hiding.
1818: Navajo warriors ride against Cebolleta, Cochití, Sandía, etc.

1819: A peace treaty is signed and Cebolla's people settle on the Turquoise Mountain [Mt. San Mateo, now Mt. Taylor] area not far from Cebolleta.

1821: The Spanish government is overthrown and a peace treaty is signed in 1822 but life seems to be endless raids and counter-raids. Because of their proximity to Cebolleta, Cebolla's people are often the first in danger, even when they are guilty of nothing.

1829-1830: Because of his knowledge of the Spanish and Navajo languages, Cebolla Sandoval acts as interpreter when Narbona counsels with Governor Viscarra.

1834: Cebolla takes part in a raid against San Fernández de Taos.

1839: Governor Armijo signs a peace treaty with the Navajos. Cebolla Antonio Sandoval is a successful rancher and designated *Capitán* by Armijo. He is recognized as a Navajo leader by Hispanos from Cebolleta, Santa Fe, Albuquerque, and Socorro. He applies for and receives official land grant papers which verify their land holdings legally belong to his people.

1840: Because of attacks from western Navajos, Juan Ramírez of Cebolleta attacks Sandoval's *ranchería*. At the next Navajo Naachid council, Cebolla counsels peace. But the war faction considers him something of a traitor and threatens him personally. He realizes he is walking a tightrope of diplomacy.

1846: Western Navajos refuse to stop raiding so Cebolla enlists 60 New Mexicans and leads a successful counter-raid against them.

November, 1846: Sandoval explains what Americans are saying at the Bear Springs meeting.

1846-1849: Sandoval alerts western bands when American soldiers are entering their domain. Capt. Croghan Kerr accuses Cebolla of treachery.

1850: Raiders attack ranches along the Río Puerco and Cebolla volunteers to lead a counter-strike against the renegades. He takes Navajo captives and sells them. Now he is at war with some Navajo bands.

1853: Sandoval is paid $120 by the U.S. Government for his services as guide and interpreter.

1856: Sandoval's band is attacked by Apaches then Utes. Members of Cebolla's band now ride as guides for the U.S. Army.

1858: A war breaks out but the Army doesn't attack Sandoval's band. His people are deeded land some 30 miles west of Albuquerque, an area called **Cañoncito,** and many warriors serve as scouts for the Army.

1859: Cebolla is riding a half-broken horse during a mustang chase when his mount goes wild and throws him. Cebolla Antonio Sandoval dies from his injuries a few days later.

1863-1865: Sandoval's loyal band is forced from its Cañoncito land and imprisoned at the **Bosque Redondo** concentration camp along with all other Navajos (until 1868).

1808-1814

José Manrique is Governor.

1808
CIBOLEROS
June: **Francisco Amangual** reports meeting a party of 120 *ciboleros* hunting near the Canadian River.

EDUCATION
There are 140 children in the Santa Fe school associated with the presidio: 20 can write, 108 can read, and 12 can recite prayers.

PROFESSIONS
Mesteñeros (mustangers: men who make a living from capturing wild horses on the plains) are an important factor in New Mexico's economy as well as its ranching history.

Mustangers often **work in large groups** of 100 or 200 men under the direction of a captain whose leadership is unquestioned since capturing wild horses necessitates cooperation.

Expeditions to the plains are challenging due to lack of firearms and ammunition, sudden changes in the weather, hostile Indians, etc.

Mustangers have to be **self-sufficient:** they make their own lariats of rawhide, weave their girths, bridle reins, and hackamores from roached horsehair; rope wild cattle and javelinas for meat. Coffee and sugar (*piloncillos*) are luxuries on the plains.

Early in June mustangers build or repair **circular corrals** at known watering places on the plains east of
N.M. Each corral is located in a **strategic place** like the bank of a creek used by mustangs as a
crossing, at brushy hollows, or in canyons. No corral is considered complete until it is **named** (*Las
Comas, Las Animas*, etc.), often dedicated to a saint, and a cross is put at the entrance.

Mustangs are driven into the corral by using tried and tested techniques developed by Hispanic
mustangers. The horses are then trained to the saddle by mustangers working in pairs. When the
horses are ready they are sold to ranchers for use in their work.

Tradition decrees that two out of every hundred mustangs sold will go to pay for masses for dead
mustangers, a duty called *El Lazo de las Animas* (**Lariat Bond of Souls**) and shouldered by the
captain of the group.

The **Trujillo** brothers, **Pedro and Celedón,** from Las Vegas are among the most famous mustangers on the
Great Plains. The Trujillos specialize in capturing **colts.** Their summer expeditions to the plains
often include women and children, many burros, milk cows, dogs, etc. and wagons loaded with
equipment.

Teodoro Gonzáles was also a renowned mesteñero who was so accomplished he made capturing mustangs
appear to be a simple frontier sport.

Mustangers become real-life **folkheroes of N.M.** and the Southwest according to **J.E Dobie.** The mustanging
era ends when the open range is fenced off by large cattle owners who slaughter most of the wild
mustangs to make way for their cattle.

T I M E L I N E

1808: Napoleon installs his brother Joseph as king in Spain. Spanish colonies in the Americas reject the new king and begin to govern themselves.

Ca. 1810
SHRINE - SANTUARIO DE CHIMAYO

Legend has it that **Bernardo Abeyta,** a member of the *Hermandad de Nuestro Padre Jesús,* discovers a
crucifix while performing customary penitential penances in the hills of El Potrero. Abeyta suddenly
sees a light emanating from one of the slopes and he goes to investigate. The light is coming from
the ground so he digs the spot with his hands until he finds a Crucifix of Our Lord of Esquipulas.
Not knowing what to think, he goes to the village and tells his neighbors of the find and someone
is sent to inform Father **Sebastián Alvarez** at Santa Cruz. Father Sebastián quickly goes to the spot,
picks up the Crucifix and in a joyous procession takes it to the church where he places it on the
main altar.

But the next morning the Crucifix is missing and can't be found until someone finds it where it was originally discovered. It is returned to Santa Cruz, disappears again and returned and again disappears to be found in the hills for the fourth time. It is decided that the Crucifix of Esquipulas definitely wants to remain in Chimayó.

1813: Father Sebastián Alvarez writes about people arriving in pilgrimage to the place where the Crucifix was found. Some even claim to have been cured of their ailments.

1814-1816: A chapel is built in Chimayó to house the Crucifix of Esquipulas. It is privately owned by the Abeyta family but community people help with construction of the Santuario. It has five *reredos* (series of sacred paintings). The one behind the main altar was painted by Molleno, while the other four are (probably) by José Aragón of Córdova, Miguel Aragón, and Molleno.

[The **Santuario de Chimayó** comes to be called the *Lourdes of America*.]

1920s: The Santuario has fallen into disrepair and many community people, including Mary Austin, Frank Applegate, John Gaw Meem, etc., gather funds for its restoration.

1929: The property is deeded to the Archdiocese of Santa Fe.

1970: The Santuario de Chimayó is designated a *National Historic Landmark* by the U.S. Department of the Interior.

[Many thousands of people visit the Santuario each year, coming to fulfill a promise, seeking inner peace, searching for hope and redemption.]

SANTEROS

Two (unidentified) santeros are creating powerful and masterful bultos around this period:

The **Master of the Lattice-Work Cross** creates [under a dozen extant] crucifixes depicted with classical harmony and balance in the European sense. The artist's title is derived from a crucifix with a Jerusalem cross which consists of 12 crosses, symbolizing the Apostles, sculpted together [the only such creation in the history of New Mexican religious art].

The **Santero of the Mountain Village Crucifixes** works in the high mountain villages of Córdova, Truchas, Taos, and surrounding areas. His style is vigorous and original.

1810
MILITARY

A small party of armed **Americans** is captured east of Pecos. Governor Manrique, seriously lacking in professional troops, encourages traders to go out onto the plains and relate any intelligence acquired. The **Comanchero trade** increases dramatically.

Santuario de Chimayó (Interior Detail)
Courtesy Museum of NM, #91907

GOVERNMENT

Juan José Quintana of Cochití Pueblo travels to Chihuahua in order to ask that the office of *Protector of Indians* be resuscitated and filled by **Felipe Sandoval Fernández de la Pedrera,** a prominent citizen from the Río Arriba jurisdiction. Governor Manrique is contacted and endorses Quintana's nominee. Paperwork is forwarded to the Audiencia of Guadalajara and Felipe Sandoval, stepson of **Felipe Tafoya,** is vested in the office of *Protector Partidario,* protector for Quintana's district and the rest of the Pueblos of N.M.

MAIL

A **postal convoy** is in operation (separately from the regular autumn caravans) from Santa Fe to points south. It is escorted by two captains, a lieutenant, and 10 soldiers.

TIMELINE

September 16, 1810: **Padre Miguel Hidalgo** begins a rebellion against Napoleonic Spain in the small Guanajuato village of Dolores, Mexico.

159

1811
SETTLEMENT
La Joya is founded.

1812
REPORT ON NEW MEXICO
Pedro Bautista Pino, New Mexico's representative to the Spanish **Cortes,** writes his *Exposición sucinta y sencilla de la provincia del Nuevo México*. It is published in Cádiz and relates:
There are about 40,000 people in New Mexico, living in 3 villas, 102 plazas, and 26 Indian towns. There are public schools in Santa Fe, Albuquerque, Taos, Belén, San Miguel, and Santa Cruz. There are 22 friars in the province. No bishop has visited the province in over 50 years. There is only one physician in N.M. **Medicinal herbs** are widely used by Natives and Hispanos alike.

Agricultural products include the famous **El Paso wines.** Hostile Indians and great distances make it impossible to export fruits and vegetables.

Hunting is a profitable business. Buffalo are the most important because of their great abundance, superb meat, and utilitarian hides. There are a variety of deer, especially elk. There are many wild horses, rams and ewes.

Wool and cotton items are the basic manufactures in N.M., though bits and spurs are also made. The government should lift bans on free production of manufactures. Any exports are at the expense and risk of the merchants themselves.

Groups of at least 500 men gather at La Sevilleta (La Joya) during the month of November to **caravan** to southern markets. Such force and numbers are necessary to repel Indian attacks.

New Mexican spirit and loyalty have endured continuous warfare with 33 hostile tribes for 118 years and has not lost one span of land from its original boundaries. After acquisition of the Louisiana territory the **United States** has tried to win over the New Mexicans in order to own the land and invade the interior of Mexico. They have built forts on the New Mexican frontiers and given firearms to hostile tribes opposed to us in order to break us, to no avail.

A **voluntary militia** of about 1,500 men (three companies) defends the province, without salary and at their own expense, and there are only 121 professional soldiers paid by the Crown. Five presidios need to be established. Sons of the province are discriminated against when it comes to selecting officers in the Army.

Government monopolies on the manufacturing of tobacco, gunpowder, and Playing cards are counterproductive because more tax could be collected if these items were produced in N.M.

New Mexicans are basically on their own when it comes to education, health, commerce, manufacturing, and national defense. Some people can't even sign their own name.

New Mexicans are in dire need of the following: establishment of a bishopric in Santa Fe; a seminary college for secondary studies and public schools; uniformity in the military service and the additional presidios; establishment of a civil and criminal high court no further than Chihuahua.

*"Sire, I hope that Your Majesty will also become aware and be attentive to the fact that the **United States** having bought Louisiana has opened the door to the Americans as much for arming the wild Indians and inciting them against us, as for invading the province themselves. **Once lost it will be impossible to recover it**..."*

New Mexicans have **land,** which is probably the reason why there are no poverty-stricken vagrants and beggars as found in other territories.

Pueblo Indians live in multistoried housing much like the people of Cádiz. Pueblo people wear clothes, shoes; the women are endowed with natural grace and beauty, dressing much like the ladies of Cádiz.

Pagan nations that surround N.M.:

> **Apaches** are a numerous people with several different bands. They are generally a traitorous people, warlike, and cruel. But they fear the brave and honorable Comanches. **Comanches** are known for their robust and graceful presence, a frank martial air, modest dress, particularly the women, and other commendable qualities. They are the most powerful militarily, accepting no quarter but granting it to those they conquer. They have been friendly to New Mexicans since the Comanche Peace was established by Governor Juan Bautista de Anza.

[S. Noyes writes that George Catlin described the   Comanches as *unattractive and slovenly-looking* and when Pino gives a more positive description he is accused of being *prejudiced.*]

> **Navajos** are now given to farming and manufacturing since they fought Hispanos in the three-year war when don Fernando Chacón was governor. Their woolen goods are the most valuable in N.M., Sonora, and Chihuahua.

> **Utes** are very interested in material goods and they will steal if necessary.

Giving gifts to the Indians has been immensely successful diplomacy.

Indian women use certain herbs to abort unborn children, thus diminishing the native population.

1812 (con't)
Ca. 1812: **Mariano Medina** is born in Taos.

[Z. Gates states in the Preface of her book that Mariano Medina is just *"one of the most noteworthy"* of unsung heroes of the West, in which group she mentions Travis Omega, José de Mirabal, José (Osay)

Dolores, Sol Silver, Chato Quintas, Jesús Abrien, "Mexican John," Jesús (Suis) Luis, Miguel Alona, John Baptiste, Antoine Dubright, Rafaél Corafel, and "Loretto."]

PROFILE

Mariano Medina

M O U N T A I N   M A N

Ca. 1812: **Mariano Medina** is born in Taos to Antonio Medina (from Spain) and María Hurtado from N.M. (The town is a mecca for mountain men.)

1833: Mariano is visiting in St. Louis, Missouri, a fur trading center.

1843: Mariano is working as an interpreter, guide, and courier for the Freemont expedition.

1844: Medina is making his living by trapping along the Snake River in Utah Territory. One of his associates is **Louis E. Papin** ("Papa") who decides to return to the States but his Indian wife refuses to leave her homeland, despite the fact she is pregnant. Medina gives Papin some horses and the woman **Tacanecy** (Kansey) stays with Mariano. When the baby is born it is named Louis Papin.

Ca. 1847: Tacanecy and Mariano have a son, who is named Antonio. The family is now living at Fort Lewis at the head of the Missouri River in Montana.

1848: Mariano's camp at the head of the Columbia River is attacked by the Blackfeet. Mariano kills two of them and then pays reparations of many horses. He leaves the country because the fur trade is ending and he must find a new way to make a living.

1853: Medina is at Fort Bridger with **Jim Bridger, Louis Vásquez, Jack Robinson**, and other mountain men.

1856: Mariano is operating a ferry on the Sweetwater River in Wyoming where the Oregon Trail leaves the river and goes over South Pass.

1857: President James Buchanan decides to send troops against the Mormons in Utah. Mariano, referred to as *"Mary Anne"* in official reports, is one of the guides under Capt. **Randolph B. Marcy.** Toward the end of November the army is running short of supplies and Col. A.S. Johnston sends Marcy to New Mexico to replenish them. Winter warnings from Digger Utes are ignored and the expedition is caught in a ferocious blizzard. Marcy's $150-a-month guide, **Jim Baker,** makes a serious mistake and leads the group in the wrong direction for a whole day until **Miguel Alona** explains the situation to Marcy. Mariano Medina then tells Marcy that the peak some 100 miles away in the distance is the area of their destination (a place called *Massachusetts*) in N.M. Olona is then made the guide and threatened with hanging if he misleads the expedition, which would die from starvation or freezing anyway so Olona says he'll *"risk his neck on it."* The expedition has to retrace its steps and the men are on the verge of starvation so Marcy sends Olona and Medina on ahead to get help and return with a relief column. When they don't return within the week they are presumed lost but they return on the 11th day amid much jubilation. (Marcy later writes in his book, *Army Life on the Border,* that Mariano, *"a half-breed Frenchman and Indian, was famous for being able to speak French, Spanish, English, and several Indian languages."*)

1858: Gold is discovered at Cherry Creek (Denver) and Mariano Medina is living by the banks of the Big Thompson River by the middle of the year. He becomes associated with José de Mirabal (Merivel, for whom *Miraville* was named).

1860: Medina and his family settle in Miraville, later called "Big Thompson" and then "Mariano's Crossing" where he builds and operates a toll bridge. He becomes the first businessman and one of the wealthiest men in the area.

1868: Mariano is living in the Thompson Valley of Colorado where he entertains his friend **Kit Carson** for a week.

TIMELINE

1812: With the British occupied militarily against Napoleon, American "War Hawks" demand that the U.S. attack weakly garrisoned Canada in an effort to get more land. Toward the beginning of the war the only real obstacle to American forces overrunning Canada is principally **Tecumseh** and his warriors.

1813
PUEBLO VS. PUEBLO
Felipe Sandoval, *Protector of the Indians,* is called upon to settle a complicated land dispute between Santa Ana and San Felipe Pueblos.

EDUCATION
There are 201 children of the soldiers and citizens attending school associated with the presidio in Santa Fe. Of those in attendance 50 can write, 17 can count, 76 can read, and 50 can recite their prayers.

1814

Fernando VII is reinstated as king of Spain but his Empire is crumbling. **Father José M. Morelos** renews Padre Hidalgo's revolt in Mexico and the king decides to fight the rebels.

LAND GRANTS

The Los Trigos grant is made in the Pecos area, followed by the Cañon de Pecos grant in 1815.

1815-1816

Alberto Maynez is Governor.

1815

SETTLEMENTS

Arroyo Seco and **Arroyo Hondo** are founded.

BOOKS & LITERACY

Manuel Delgado lists the volumes in his personal **library**: The Works of Charles V, Flor Santuarón (3 vols.), Criminal Practice, Mexican Theater, The Light of Faith, Color de Escrivanos (2 vols.), The Conquest of Mexico, Cmaines [sic], Prior de Agricultura, Salomón Coronado, David Perseguido (3 vols.), Hebrew Monarchy (4 vols.), Ordenanzas Militares (3 vols.), Recopilación de Ordenanzas de Milicias, Holy Week, eight novels, Voz de Naturaleza (3 vols.), Life of Charles XII, Life of Estevancillo, Divertimiento del Hacer (9 vols.), Daily Exercise.

SOCIETY

(Padre) **José Manuel Gallegos** is born to Pedro Ignacio Gallegos and Ana María Gabaldón Gallegos in Abiquiú.

SOCIETY & WEALTH

Manuel Delgado dies. The inventory of his estate includes 2,240 breeding ewes and 9,000 pesos in cash, as well as the famous *Rancho de las Golondrinas.*

PUEBLO LAND & LITIGATION

Felipe Sandoval, *Protector of the Indians,* is called upon by **Cochití Pueblo** to help in a land dispute with **Luis María Cabeza de Baca** over tracts known as the Rancho de Peña Blanca and the Ojo de Santa Cruz. Cochití residents say the sale of land by some of their citizens was illegal then Indians from Santo Domingo Pueblo testify that some of their land got involved in the illegal sale. Finally, Governor Maynez orders Baca to vacate said lands, leaving all improvements for the pueblos since settlement was effected without authorization. But Baca doesn't leave.

Juan José Quintana of Cochití once more treks southward to seek justice at the higher court level at Durango. He confers with José Joaquín Reyes, Protector of the Indians, who sides with him.

Baca's defense attorney decries what he calls *privilege of the Indians* and emphasizes that urban legal documentation is rare on the frontier, the people having to rely on *known truth and good faith.*

The case is forwarded to Mexico City [though it should have gone to Guadalajara].

The quest of the Cochitís is carried on by **Antonio Quintana** [related to Juan José?] and four other native
sons in the metropolis of Mexico City. Antonio introduces himself as the *"retired captain of the
King's troops in the continual wars against the Apache nations"* when he introduces his case,
without the aid of an interpreter because of his knowledge of the Spanish language, before the
Juzgado General de Indios tribunal. Then he requests that the matter be carried on by an authorized legal representative and also requests funds to maintain the emissaries during litigation and
for the return trip home. Both requests are granted.

[The case is finally sent to the proper jurisdiction of Guadalajara where the Cochitís receive a favorable
judgment. Luis María Cabeza de Baca is ordered to vacate the land in question and pay court costs. Some
sort of accommodation is made back in N.M. because Cabeza de Baca remains in the general area.]

CONTRIBUTIONS FOR THE KING

March: Governor Maynez convenes a group of leading New Mexicans and informs them that the Viceroy
has called upon them for a **donativo voluntario** [voluntary gift] of 5,000 pesos to be prorated among
50 individuals from all over N.M. Santa Fe merchants and **Río Abajo sheepman** receive the biggest
allocations:

Francisco Xavier Chaves is put down for 1,000 *pesos.*
Manuel Delgado, Joaquín Alvarez del Castillo, and Juan **Rafaél Ortiz** are in the 100 to 200 peso range.
Pedro Bautista Pino declares that his 100 pesos are a *gift*, not a loan, to his king.

Governor Maynez raises the entire 5,000 pesos within a few short months. When the money is sent south it
is put in the *caja de tres llaves* (box with three keys) which is always used to bring the military
payroll into N.M. Ordinary citizens of N.M. oppose any new taxes to help suppress the **Morelos
revolution,** stating they are doing more than their share by paying church tithes and fighting Indian
wars. Maynez reminds them that the Crown has averaged 50,000 pesos annually to maintain N.M.

Ca. 1815-1862
SANTERO

Rafaél Aragón is creating religious art during this period and becomes the most popular and prolific of
santeros during his lifetime. A dynamic artist dedicated to his profession, he produces great
numbers of bultos and retablos, both of which are of high quality. Aragón doesn't sign most of his
work, though a few are signed and dated, thus documenting his career of more than 40 years. His
work is two-dimensional but his saints are devoutly beautiful, well proportioned, often with
almond-shaped eyes. Many communities commission him to do their church altar screens as well as
bultos and *retablos*. According to C.L. Briggs he is a highly respected *santero* in any number of
communities, creating most or all the religious imagery for the Córdova chapel, the altar screens at
Llano Quemado, Picurís, the Santuario in Chimayó, the Durán chapel at Talpa, San José de Chama,
San Miguel del Valle, Santa Cruz, the Carmen oratory at Llano de Talpa, etc.

1816-1818

Pedro María de Allande is Governor.

1816
SETTLEMENT
Manzano is founded by settlers (probably) from the Belén valley.

RELIGIOUS ARCHITECTURE
The *Santuario de Chimayó* is completed, its architecture reflecting the single nave mission churches built in the N.M. Pueblos during the 1700s.

PROFILE

José Rafaél Aragón

THE SANTEROS' SANTERO

1795: José Rafaél Aragón is born of New Mexican parents. He lives in Santa Fe.

July 19, 1815: Rafaél marries **María Josefa Lucero** in Santa Fe. He is a member of religious lay confraternities like Our Lady of the Rosary and the Blessed Sacrament.

1823: Rafaél and Josefa live in the San Francisco barrio (neighborhood) of Santa Fe where other woodcarvers have their studios. (In the 1823 Census he is listed as an escultor, sculptor.)

1825: Aragón creates an altarpiece for the San Lorenzo Church at Picurís Pueblo (his earliest known important work) and a number of fine bultos.

[It is estimated that Rafaél alone built and painted at least 12 altarpieces during his lifetime. This is prodigious production considering that between 1776-1797 and 1806-1826 some 40 reredos were created by all other New Mexican santeros combined.]

1832: Josefa dies and Rafaél moves his family to Pueblo Quemado (Córdova). In time he marries the widow **Josefa Córdova.** He is commissioned to do paintings and carvings for the San Antonio de Padua church [rated among his greatest creations].

1834-1838: Rafaél supervises work on the entire religious art of the San Antonio church and paints the central altarpiece which consists of 12 panels.

[Art scholars assert that this reredo ranks with that of Laguna in quality.]

1838: In honor of Father **Antonio J. Martínez** of Taos, Rafaél Aragón creates the altarpiece, bultos, etc., for the Chapel of Our Lady of the Rosary at Talpa. It is possible that Rafaél is now a member of the Brotherhood. He uses the title *maestro* so perhaps he is the master of a workshop and his tremendous production suggests he might have utilized apprentices or followers under his direction.

Father **Juan de Jesús Trujillo,** pastor at Santa Cruz de la Cañada from 1838-1869, is important in Aragón's career because the good priest commissions Rafaél for many projects.

1862: J. Rafaél Aragón dies. (The classic period of New Mexican Santero art is coming to an end.)

COMMERCE
Trade items going south along the Camino Real in the annual caravans include agricultural products, textiles, sheep, wool, hides, piñon, salt, El Paso brandy, blankets, etc. Coming north are ironware of all kinds, especially tools and firearms, along with cloth, boots, shoes, clothes, chocolate, sugar, coffee, tobacco, paper, ink, books, etc.

SOCIETY
Felipe Sandoval, famous *Protector of the Indians*, dies suddenly.

1817
AMERIND
Pawnees attack a group of ciboleros, killing seven and capturing a 10 year-old boy who is later ransomed by **Manuel Lisa,** the leading American fur trader in St. Louis.

HEALTH
Lt.. **José María de Arce,** commander of the trade caravan going south, is entrusted to procure additional **smallpox vaccine** which is needed to continue the immunization program for N.M. children.

SOCIETY
Luis María Cabeza de Baca, *"...one of the most notable men of his time..."* from **Peña Blanca,** is a major personality in the development of the **Las Vegas** land grant.

GOVERNMENT
Ignacio María Sánchez Vergara is selected for the post of *Protector of the Indians* upon the death of Felipe Sandoval.

[Sánchez Vergara is the only Protector known to have sent a report on the spiritual condition of his Indian charges.]

NATIVE RELIGIOUS
Five young New Mexicans leave for the seminary in Durango to study for the priesthood: Antonio José
Martínez from Taos, Juan Felipe Ortiz, the twin brothers Rafaél and Fernando Ortiz, and Ramón
Ortiz, all from Santa Fe. (Eventually Ramón became the pastor in El Paso, the others returned to
N.M.).

1818-1822
Facundo Melgares is Governor.

1818
COMANCHE VISIT
Soguara, a Comanche chieftain, arrives in Santa Fe with more than 1,000 of his people on a trading expedi-
tion. So many gifts are given out that the government warehouse is almost empty. Governor
Melgares writes his superiors to send more, as quickly as possible.

INVASION RUMORS
New Mexicans gird up for a rumored invasion of U.S. filibusters from the east and a flare-up of Navajo
warfare from the west. Rich and poor alike from Taos to Socorro make very generous contributions
of supplies, especially corn and sheep, for the troops.

SOCIETY
October 18: **Manuel Antonio Chaves** is born at Atrisco to Julián Chaves and María Luz García Chaves.

December 18: **Antonio Ortiz,** resident of Santa Fe, applies for a grant of land for his sheep east of the Río
Gallinas, southeast of present Las Vegas, because of **Navajo** hostilities to the west.

1819
DIPLOMACY
Manuel Antonio Rivera spends the summer with **Comanches** and reports to Santa Fe that Americans are
coming to attack N.M. but the Comanches will unite to fight the invaders because *"...they
[Americans] advance taking Comanche horse herds and captives and because the Spaniards of
New Mexico are their friends..."*

TIMELINE
The **Depression of 1819** in the USA causes dim financial conditions in places like **Missouri**
where there is a severe shortage of hard cash. Many Missourians hit the trail to trade with the
Indians in order to support themselves. Within a couple of years Indian traders like William
Becknell, John McKnight, Thomas James, and Hugh Glenn enter N.M. for trading purposes.

LAND GRANTS
Bartolomé Baca receives the Torreón grant in the Manzano Mountains, south of Chililí.

Antonio Ortiz receives the Gallinas grant, southeast of Las Vegas.

EDUCATION
Fray **Sebastián Alvarez** is conducting a school in Taos.

1820
TRADING TRAILS
Well-traveled trails along the Canadian River lead eastward toward the plains.

1820-1840
SANTERO
The artist known as "**A.J.**" is creating religious art during this period. A contemporary of other major
classical santeros, his work is distinguished by a palette of blues, purples, oranges, and browns.
No altarpieces are attributed to him but he creates (small) retablos for home and private chapels, as
well as bultos. He uses prints for models and the paints he utilizes seem to glow. He is familiar with
biblical themes and depicts subjects not usually portrayed in N.M. (the Visitation, the Annuncia-
tion, Our Lady of Querétaro). He gives his figures a frontal point of view rather than the often used
three-quarter perspective.

1820-1835
SANTERO
José Aragón is creating religious art during this period. Aragón might have been born in Spain but he
blends into N.M. traditions after arriving around 1820. He tends to work from engravings,
incorporating the engraver's technique of cross-hatching, to letter on retablos, and sign them more
than any other santero. He lives in the village of Arroyo Hondo and then at Chamisal. His work
indicates he reads the Bible. It is probable that he conducts a studio workshop, guiding other
artists. He produces many small retablos [but the only altar screens attributed to him are at
Santuario de Chimayó]. His human figures are usually well proportioned and set within a linear
border.

1835: It is belierved José Aragón moves to the area of El Paso, Texas, around this time.

T I M E L I N E
1820-1950: The United States encourages **immigration** from Europe. The larges numbers of
immigrants arrive from the following countries during this period:

Germany: 6,248,529;
Italy: 4,776,884;
Ireland: 4,617,485;
Austria/Hungary: 4,172,104;
Russia/U.S.S.R.: 3,343,895;
England: 2,753,443;

Sweden: 1,228,113;

Total immigration from **Europe** during this period: 33,246,339.
Total immigration from **Asia** during this period: 950,319.
Total immigration from the **Americas** during this period: 4,756,270.
Total immigration from **Africa** during this period: 33,427.

1821
FAIRS & COMMERCE

Trade fairs at Taos, Pecos, Jémez, and other outlying communities begin to decline. Because of commerce arriving over the Santa Fe Trail and heading toward **Chihuahua**, the main centers of commerce become **Santa Fe, Albuquerque, and El Paso**.

GOVERNMENT & AMERIND PROTECTION

January 11: The office of **Protector of the Indians** is abolished by royal decree.

February: **Ignacio Sánchez Vergara** states that *"Indians have emerged from their minority and have no need of a protector."*

FUNDING & DIPLOMACY

August: Due to the revolution against Spain there are no gifts for Comanches and other nations. As a group of disappointed Comanches ride through the El Vado district they kill livestock, steal whatever they fancy, sack several homes, and rape two women. Settlers are furious but they take no action in order to avoid a Comanche war. Citizens like Manuel Durán as Governor Melgares to solicit funds with which to buy gifts for Comanche visitors. The governor agrees and New Mexicans use their own resources to keep their allies.

CHANGE OF SOVEREIGNTY

Mexico wins its independence from Spain. As of September 27, 1821, **New Mexico is a part of Mexico.**

MEXICAN REPUBLIC

TIMELINE

1820: The U.S. has a population of around 9,600,000 and stretches through the Louisiana Territory.

1820s: Mexico has an estimated population of 6,200,000 and its domain extends from Guatemala to Oregon. It has lost about 10% of its population during the war for independence, mainly young men, or around half of its work force. In the tumultuous 16 years between 1821-1837 the presidency of Mexico changes hands 21 times [facilitating the "inevitable triumph of the Americans" according to W.A. Beck].

1820s
MOUNTAIN MEN

Fur trappers are described as "some of the most important men in American history" when they "captured the imagination" of the USA because of their exploits and "return to savagery." These men are said to include Kit Carson, James Ohio Pattie, Ewing Young, Jim Bridger, Jebediah Smith, and the groups of brothers Bent, Sublette, and Robidoux.

1821
AMERIND

The **Treaty of Córdova officially** recognizes all Native Americans as citizens of Mexico. The designation of *genízaro* is officially dropped.

LAND GRANT

The **Town of Las Vegas grant** is awarded to **María Luis Baca** and his *17 sons*.

1825: The N.M. Departmental Assembly ratifies the grant.

1835: Believing the land to be unclaimed, the Town of Las Vegas grant is made to **Juan de Dios Maese** and 27 others.

[When this situation later came up for adjudication by Surveyor General William Pelham, two Las Vegas grants comprising 496,447 acres, he decided he didn't have the authority to settle this kind of duplication so he recommended confirmation of both claims. Then the Baca heirs agreed to simplify matters by taking an equivalent amount of land in five lieu selections, which came to be known as **BACA LOCATIONS,** in N.M., Arizona, and Colorado, Baca #1 and Baca #2 being in N.M.]

1821-1846
SOCIETY & FOREIGNERS

Ninety **foreigners,** some of them from the U.S., are baptized in order to marry N.M. women. These individuals assimilate into Hispanic society and their children are hispanicized, all of them marrying Hispanics "...*with rare exceptions.*"

[Americans in N.M. hail from, in order of frequency, Missouri, Kentucky, Tennessee, Pennsylvania, Virginia, New York, Vermont, Ohio, Illinois, Maryland. Men like these are also described as "...*forming a veritable Fifth Column...*" for the American takeover of N.M. and the Southwest.]

1822

Francisco Xavier de Chávez is Governor.

F. X. Chávez, from Belén, **is the first native New Mexican** ever to serve as Governor. He is married to **Ana M. Castillo**, also from Belén, and they have nine children, all but one marrying into prominent Río Abajo families. (Two of their sons, Mariano and José, later serve as New Mexico governors and four grandsons are elected Delegate to the U.S. Congress.)

TRADE LAWS

Trade restrictions are lifted by the Mexican government and American traders are permitted into the country.

American trader **Thomas James** is captured by **Comanches** while en route to N.M. Word gets out that James and his party will be killed the next day but several Hispanics ride into camp and stop the execution, telling the Comanches that Americans are brothers now that Mexico is independent. (James later writes that the Comanches had nothing but contempt for New Mexicans.)

Commerce between N.M. and the U.S. utilizes the **Santa Fe Trail.** (The route is basically the one blazed by Pedro Vial in 1792.) **William Becknell**, an Indian trader of French extraction, is credited by some writers as "Father of the Santa Fe Trail" because he was one of the first merchants emanating from the States.

[Becknell was searching for Indians with whom to trade when he chanced to meet some New Mexicans who invited him to bring his goods to N.M. Some writers refer to him as "**Captain** Becknell" without explaining the *promotion* from "Indian trader" to "Captain."]

Becknell was the first to use wagons instead of pack animals and to utilize the Cimarron Cutoff, thus shortening the journey to Santa Fe by more than 100 miles.

January 6: New Mexicans celebrate Mexican independence. According to J. Kessell, *"wide-eyed, waspish"* **Thomas James** relates how he *"... was indispensable, erecting the seventy-foot liberty pole and running up the first flag."* But the joy scandalizes him: *"No Italian carnival ever exceeded this celebration in thoughtlessness, vice and licentiousness of every description."*

1822-1823

José Antonio Viscarra is Governor.

1823

SOCIETY

Juan Esteban Pino, son of the famous **Pedro Bautista Pino,** applies for a grant of land near the confluence of the Gallinas and Pecos rivers, where he had established an hacienda the year before and entertained American traders like William Becknell and Merriwether M. Marmaduke.

José Concepción Trujillo is born. (José is the first of the Trujillo family weavers from Chimayó.)

Carlos Beaubien, a French-Canadian, arrives in N.M. (by way of Missouri) where he and his companions are arrested and taken to Mexico City where authorities apologize and tell them they may remain in N.M. if they wish. The genial Beaubien returns to Taos where he opens a store that caters to traders and trappers.

1827: Beaubien marries **María Paula Lobato.**

1829: Carlos Beaubien becomes a Mexican citizen and in time is wealthy and influential.

SANTA FE TRADE

New Mexican merchants form their own trading companies and journey to Missouri to acquire American trade goods without utilizing American middlemen. Despite resentment from their American competitors, "many Mexicans succeeded."

Carlos Beaubien
Courtesy Museum of NM, #8799

BEAVER

Besides silver and mules, beaver pelts, called "hairy banknotes" by American mountain men, become another source of wealth in the Santa Fe trade. N.M. becomes a base for the fur trade.

1824: Areas close to the New Mexican settlements are quickly trapped out so trappers penetrate the Rockies in western Colorado and eastern Utah.

1831-1832: Beaver pelts worth $100,000 are carried over the Santa Fe Trail.

1835: Beaver is now scarce to nearly extinct in northern areas of Mexico.

1843: More than half of the commerce on the Santa Fe Trail is controlled by Mexican traders. *"The full story of involvement in the Santa Fe trade of Mexicans such as Manuel Simón de Escudero ... or Antonio José Chávez, of a politically powerful and affluent New Mexico family, has yet to be told."*

[Susan Calafate Boyle published her excellent book, *Los Capitalistas: Hispanos Merchants and the Santa Fe Trade* when this *Multi-History* was virtually completed.]

MILITARY & NAVAJOS

Governor Viscarra decides to force the Navajos to come to terms. He councils with various leaders and demands that all Mexican captives be surrendered and then Navajo captives will be given their liberty if they wish to leave. All stolen livestock must be released and missionaries will be sent if they settle in one place. Nothing is settled and both sides make plans for battle.

June: Navajos kill 16 New Mexicans in the **Río Abajo.**

June 18: Viscarra leads some 1,500 men into Navajo country. Assaulting the Diné from different directions the expeditionary force spends 74 days in the field, fighting its way to the Canyon de Chelly before it returns to Santa Fe.

SOCIETY & RELIGION

The **Penitente Brotherhood,** more correctly referred to as the **Brothers of Our Father Jesús** according to M. Weigle, is an important part of N.M. village life, especially in the more isolated hamlets, because of chronic and even desperate inadequacies of clerics which foster the emergence of this *"folk religion"* in the province. The Brotherhood fills a need for the *"devoutly Catholic and of necessity stoutly independent pioneer people..."* of Hispanic N.M. **Josiah Gregg** reports witnessing a Good Friday procession at Tomé (sometime between 1831 and 1840), the first non-Hispanic to do so.

[Clergyman **Ross Calvin** says that *"...popular ignorance, left without the guidance of the Church, relapsed naturally into fanaticism, and the Mexican zealot inheriting from the Spaniard a tragic interpretation of Christianity, and from his Indian forebears a recent and thinly covered savagery, evolved presently a cruel and schismatic cult of the scourge."*]

1833: **Bishop Zubiría** visits N.M. and notes that the Hermandad de Penitentes exists without authorization or knowledge of the bishops. He bans "immoderate corporal penances" and the use of large crosses.

1853: **Bishop Lamy** approves rules for the Brotherhood.

The **morada** is the lodge or meeting place for the Penitente Brotherhood. It contains (at least) two rooms, a capilla (chapel) and a meeting hall. (*"The immaculateness of the interior of the morada always is remarkable, with spotless whitewashed walls, packed earth floors clean enough to eat from, and white lace curtains..."*) It is decorated with santero religious art (and in time the Brotherhood is the chief patron of this folk art form).

The **Brotherhood** is natively referred to by **various names:** Brothers of Our Father Jesús, Brothers of Light, Fraternal Order (Pious Fraternity, etc.) of Our Father Jesus of Nazareth, Third Order of St. Francis, etc.

Duly elected **officers** conduct all matters relating to the Brotherhood: *Hermano Mayor* (Elder Brother), Warden (sergeant-at-arms), Agent (keeps members informed), Teacher of Novices, Treasurer, Clerk, Nurse, Reader of prayers, Flutist, etc.

Membership in the morada signifies separating oneself from the outside world, submitting to authority of the Elders (Brothers of Light), welcoming self-sacrifice that sustains the Brothers and their community.

There are three ranks in Brotherhood membership: Brothers of Blood (individuals engaged in active penances, like novitiates), Brothers emerging from Darkness, and Brothers of Light (officials of the morada). Serious transgressions of Brotherhood rules result in expulsion, lesser wrongdoings by penance.

Women are not members of the Brotherhood, though they can serve as *Auxiliadoras* (Auxiliaries) who help with various duties. They are also referred to as Verónicas, Carmelitas, or Terceras.
[Some writers have related that in the 19th century there were groups of female Penitentes.]

Purpose of the Brotherhood is to practice fraternity, community responsibility, and piety. Brothers must...attempt to emulate His life by living simply and morally and by performing unobtrusive good deeds... Throughout the year members are required to render "...*service to God through Christ's teachings; observance of the Ten Commandments; leading a humble life like Jesus; avoidance of discord; shunning worldly temptations such as saloons; and charity and mutual love toward Brothers by setting a good example, aiding in times of illness or anguish, pardoning, tolerating, and respecting one another.*"

Activities of the Brotherhoods include to conduct *velorios* (wakes) after seeing to the needs of the bereaved, preparing the body for burial, digging the grave, etc.; gather for group prayer for special (e.g., serious illness of a member) as well as religious occasions; own flocks of sheep with which to meet expenses; invite the community to the morada for certain ceremonies; hold (religious) processions in which the villagers may partake; commission santeros for the production of bultos, retablos, reredos, etc., with which to grace their moradas; serve community needs; enact spiritually beneficial rituals.

Brotherhood devotions are expressed through ritual, prayer, discipline, music, and humility **Lent** (*La Cuaresma*) and **Holy Week** (Semana Santa) are observed universally by the Brotherhoods but there are also **other devotional celebrations:** Corpus Christi (Thursday after Trinity Sunday), Assumption (August 15), All Saints Day (Nov. 1), All Souls Day (Nov. 2), the day of the morada's patrón saint, as well as traditional celebrations which vary from village to village (days of St. John, St. James, St. Anne, Holy Cross, La Porsiúncula, the Twelve Days of Christmas, etc.).

During **Holy Week** observances [described as *"...a folk equivalent of the Catholic Mass"* by Fr. T.J. Steele, S.J.] the Brothers retreat in their morada, from Palm Sunday through Holy Saturday, or more frequently, from Holy Tuesday to Good Friday. During retreat villagers are welcomed into the morada and time is spent praying and maintaining vigils. Public processions and Stations of the Cross are celebrated. Women from the community donate **meatless meals** for the Brothers, called *charolitas* (Lenten dishes), like *torta* and *panocha*.

Penance, or penitential exercises, includes walking on knees, carrying large crosses, self-flagellation with whips, called disciplinas, the most common form of penance, wrapping yourself in rope or chain, etc. All penances are under strict control at all times by the Hermano Mayor (Elder Brother). Individuals doing penance, wearing *vendas* (hoods) to insure humility, are accompanied by helpers and persons who pray, sing *alabados*, play the flute, or carry sacred images.

Major processions are held on Wednesday (Procession of Sorrows), Thursday (Procession of the Holy Cross), and Friday (Procession of the Blood of Christ).

Las Tinieblas ceremony, usually held at night on Holy Thursday or Good Friday and preceded by a rosary service in which villagers participate, involves a candelabrum of 13 to 17 candles, each candle or pair of candles being extinguished after the singing of an alabado. When the last single candle is extinguished there is utter darkness and then loud noises from chains, matracas, drums, screams, etc., fill the air. The tumult alternates with periods of silence during which *sudarios* (prayers for those departed, said while covered with a blanket) are recited. A single candle, representing Christ as the light of the world, is relighted then the other candles from it.

Good Friday is a day of mourning. Matracas, wooden clackers, are used in place of bells in all activities. The individual selected to reenact the symbolic crucifixion is bound to a cross for a short time, after which he is brought down and taken into the morada.

[According to M. Weigle there is no substantiated evidence that nails have ever been used in the crucifixion.]

1823-1825

Bartolomé Baca is Governor.

1823
SANTA FE TRADE

Caravans returning to Missouri bring back sorely needed coin, gold dust, and silver bars but also the invaluable commodity of **mules.**

[The mule was the preferred beast of burden and draft animal on the Santa Fe Trail and the Camino Real. It was cheaper to freight by muletrain than wagons because each mule could carry up to 400 pounds without protection for their hooves and travel 12 to 15 miles a day. Mules could traverse the roughest trails with a sure-footedness that no horse could equal. Mexican arrieros (mulepackers, muleteers) were experts at managing their animals and their "skill in roping, tiding, loading, and caring for their animals" impressed everybody, even those chroniclers who were critical of almost everything and everybody in New Mexico. **Caravans leaving Missouri** were mostly comprised of wagons. The mule came to be preferred over the horse but some traders still favored oxen. Wagons were of several makes but the favorite came to be the **Conestoga** (Pittsburgh wagon, Prairie Schooner) manufactured in Pittsburgh and patterned after the covered wagons of Lancaster County.]

Some 400 jacks, jennets, and mules arrive in Missouri, giving rise to the "*Missouri mule*" industry.

More than 600 mules are taken to Missouri. Some of these Mexican mules are sold in Missouri for breeding purposes, some are employed in the expanding caravan trade, and still others are sold in the southern states for work on plantations.

1832: More than 1,300 mules are taken to Missouri.

FIREARMS
American traders are furnishing guns and ammunition to the Navajos.

1824
SOCIETY
Pedro José Perea from Bernalillo receives a land grant in the Santa Rosa area to where he moves his flocks. Perea builds one of the greatest mercantile-livestock dynasties of the **Río Abajo.**

Antonio Sandoval, also from the Río Abajo, petitions for pastureland in eastern N.M.

SANTA FE TRADE
José Escudero, a Chihuahua merchant, leads a delegation of 25 Santa Fe businessmen to various points in the Mississippi Valley in an effort to encourage trade with New Mexico.
[This is the beginning of significant commerce on the Santa Fe Trail.]

Eighty merchants from Missouri bring in $35,000 worth of trade goods. (New Mexicans are now buying more from Missouri than Chihuahua.) The following year $65,000 worth is brought in and the market is glutted. Some trade goods are taken to **Chihuahua,** which is almost twice the size of Santa Fe, with rich mining operations and a mint that stamps out more than 500,000 pesos worth of coin each year, and in time it becomes the most important trading center.

GOVERNMENT
July 6, 1824: N.M. becomes a Mexican Territory.

1825-1827
Antonio Narbona is Governor.

1825
SOCIETY

Ceran de Hault de Lassus de St. Vrain arrives in Taos from Missouri. He is "a giant of a man," energetic, honest, and possessed of much natural charm. He works at trapping then supplying fur trappers.

1828: St. Vrain meets **Charles Bent**, a fellow Missourian, and in time the firm of Bent, St. Vrain and Co. is founded, which includes brothers of both, William and Marcellin, respectively, and both marry Hispanic women from Taos.

SANTA FE TRADE

Mexican troops protect merchants on the Santa Fe Trail but protection is needed on the American side so Governor Narbona sends a special envoy, **Manuel Simón Escudero,** to St. Louis to arrange it. Two Mexican merchants, and their pack train of 500 animals loaded with trade goods, accompany Escudero. The *Franklin Intelligencer* newspaper reports that the Escudero party expended large sums in the purchase of various trade goods and observed that the journey "*may be considered as a new era*" in trade between Mexico and the USA.

[William Becknell is often cited as the "Father of the Santa Fe Trail/trade" and there is no doubt he was one of its precursors from east-to-west but the *Intelligencer* appears to designate **Escudero** as the "new era" *Founding Father of the Santa Fe Trade*.]

Led by Senator **Thomas Hart Benton** of Missouri, provisions are made in Congress to protect and encourage the Santa Fe trade. American consuls are appointed to reside in Santa Fe and Chihuahua, peace is made with the Osage Nation, a road is surveyed to Santa Fe, but military protection isn't forthcoming for some years.

T I M E L I N E

1822: **Joel Roberts Poinsett** visits Mexican officials and presses for a boundary that will place Texas, N.M., Sonora, and the Californias within the United States. The proposal is rejected by Mexican officials who recognize the Transcontinental Treaty boundary set in the Treaty of 1819 between Spain and the U.S.

1825: Joel Poinsett is the first Minister to Mexico.

[When Poinsett returns to the U.S. he does so with a flower which Mexicans use in their Christmas Eve celebration. This *Flor de Noche Buena* is renamed "poinsettia" and becomes popular in the U.S. under his name.]

Secretary of State Henry Clay suggests that if Mexico will let the U.S. have its northern territories Mexico will be better off because Mexico City will then be in the center of the country (according to Dr. David Weber).

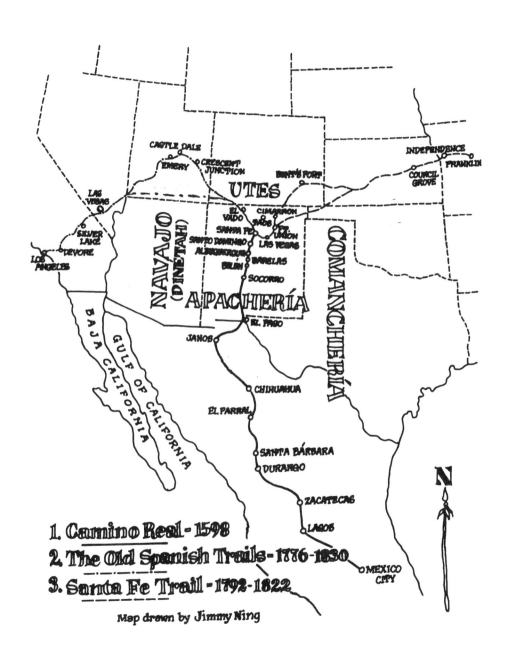

1. Camino Real - 1598
2. The Old Spanish Trails - 1776-1830
3. Santa Fe Trail - 1792-1822

Map drawn by Jimmy Ning

SOCIETY

Weddings are formal as well as festive affairs. Procedure is set by tradition and "proper" behavior is a mark of good breeding whether one is rich or poor. The ritual includes:

La pedida de la novia (Asking for the bride): The young man (*novio*) informs his parents that he wishes to marry. If the parents approve they speak (or write, depending on distance) to the parents of the young lady (*novia*) and if they are in favor of the marriage, items like the dowry and wedding arrangements (like the banns that have to be read for three Sundays) are discussed.

[Oral tradition has it that an Hispanic suitor is expected to give filigree jewelry to his fiancée.]

El prendorio: A *fiesta* (party) is sponsored by the bride's family, complete with food and dancing, in which the other party's relatives meet the bride and groom-to-be by attending and giving them presents. The novio gives jewelry to the novia.

La boda: The wedding is held in church and relatives and friends from near and far make special efforts to attend in order to celebrate. A wedding dance is held after the church ceremony and there is much good food to enjoy.

La entriega: The newly wedded couple is taken to both sets of parents and verses are sung or recited on the sacredness of their marriage, the responsibilities to each other, etc. Everyone dances far into the night, even if the newlyweds leave before the dance is over.

Ca.1825-1835
SANTERO

An individual known only as the **Arroyo Hondo Santero** is creating religious art during this period. Little is known about him but the Arroyo Hondo style is thought to have been heavily influenced by **José Aragón,** with whom this santero might have studied. Bultos appear to be his best work.

[L. Frank gives the working dates of 1830 to 1850 for the Arroyo Hondo Santero.]

1825-1844
RELIGION

Some 136 **Indian captives are baptized** in the community of San Juan alone during this period.

1826
BOOKS

J. 0. Pattie relates in his book *The Personal Narrative of James Ohio Pattie* that he and his companion mountain men arrive in Santa Fe to find that **Comanche** raiders have just terrorized the town and made off with several captives, including the daughter of a former governor. The *"cowardly New Mexicans"* cower in fear as Pattie and his friends pursue the Comanches, rescuing all captives.

[The **Comanche Peace** is in effect during this period. No raids take place in Santa Fe during 1826. Records show that Pattie was definitely in California, where he did jail time, and Arizona. Pattie's "adventure" is now known to have been created by his editor, **Timothy Flint,** who used the same incident in his novel, *Francis*

Berniam. Flint acknowledged in the foreword that he made contributions to Pattie's book.]

SOCIETY
Kit Carson, fleeing from his apprenticeship as a saddler in Missouri, arrives in N.M. and almost immediately takes up residence in Taos.

RELIGIOUS
July 23: **Padre Martínez** is installed as the Pastor of Taos.

November: Padre Martínez opens a school.

PROFILE

Christopher "Kit"   Carson

A M E R I C A N   H E R O

1809: **Christopher Carson** is born in Kentucky. The family later moves to Missouri.

1822: Kit is apprenticed to David Workman.

1826: Carson joins a caravan led by **Ceran St. Vrain** that is bound for Santa Fe. Upon arriving in the state he goes to Taos, using it as a headquarters between periods of travel.

1830: Kit lives the life of a mountain man and fur trapper.

1834-1842: Carson is employed by the Bent brothers as a hunter, supplying Bent's Fort with fresh game. During this time he marries an Indian woman who dies within a year.

1842: Kit returns to Missouri for a visit. In St. Louis he meets **John C. Fremont** who wants to hire him as a guide for a California expedition he is planning.

1843: Kit marries **Josefa Jaramillo** in a ceremony conducted by Fr. **Martínez** of Taos.

March 6, 1844: Carson is a guide for the Fremont Expedition which arrives at Sutter's Mill on this date. Kit is back at Bent's Fort in July.

1846: Kit is establishing a ranch when Fremont sends for him again for another journey to California where he participates in *"taking California from the Mexicans"* (according to R.E. Twitchell).
Carson is returning to N.M. when he meets General   **Kearny,** who orders him to attach himself to the Army as scout for its advance into California. The soldiers are stopped in the

---

vicinity of Los Angeles and Carson makes it through enemy lines to bring reinforcements from R.F. Stockton in San Diego.

1849-1854: Carson has many adventures with the Indians.

1854-1861: Kit works as Indian Agent for the Ute, Apache, and some Pueblo nations.

1861: Carson commands the First New Mexico Cavalry Volunteers during the Civil War.

Christopher "Kit" Carson
Courtesy Museum of NM, #166242

1863: Kit leads the military expedition that breaks the Navajo Nation of all power. The *Diné* are forced to **Bosque Redondo** where Carson works until he resigns in disgust with conditions in the concentration camp.

1864: Carson goes out to the plains and is later involved in the Battle of Adobe Walls against Comanche warriors.

1865: Carson is promoted to the rank of Brevet Brigadier General.

1866: Kit is the commander at Ft. Garland.

1867: Failing health forces Carson to resign from the Army.

January, 1868: He is appointed Superintendent of Indian Affairs for Colorado Territory.

May 23, 1868: One month after the death of his wife Josefa, Kit Carson dies at Ft. Lyon.

SANTA FE TRADE

New Mexicans are sending trade wagons full of goods to "eastern" markets in the U.S. The people in the Río Abajo are the most active in this overland trade.

1843: New Mexicans control more than half of the entire Santa Fe trade.

SOCIETY

Santiago Abreú observes that Americans seem to want *"to settle, buy land, and even marry"* in N.M. He says many of them are of benefit to the province but **New Mexicans have to take much care that their generous nature isn't abused** so only Americans who are honorable and have a useful trade should be permitted to stay.

FUR TRAPPERS

Governor **Narbona** states that despite the 1824 prohibition against trappers hunting the beaver to extinction the foreigners have continued to trap just as much as when they had the liberty to do so and that his poorly equipped troops couldn't defend the province against hostile Indians and chase unruly American trappers too. He tries to control trappers by requiring that they buy licenses and take New Mexicans along with them as apprentices.

1826-1850
SOCIETY

There are some **218 non-Hispanic names** listed in N.M. church records for this period:
French: 87 names, 77 of whom are living in Taos;
United States: 125 names, more than 75 in Taos;
German: 2 (in Taos);
English, Irish, Scotch: 1 from each country (all living in Taos);
and one Simon Levi, origin unknown.

1827-1829

Manuel Armijo is Governor.

Governor Manuel Armijo is 34 years old (this is the first of Armijo's three terms as governor). He confronts and arrests American smugglers among the traders from Missouri, who cause him to receive much bad publicity in the U.S.

[Three American writers are especially virulent in their condemnation of Governor Armijo:

George Kendall, editor of the *New Orleans Picayune* newspaper, was part of the invading Texas-Santa Fe expedition captured by Armijo, whom he accuses of *"assassinations, robberies, violent debauchery, extortions, and innumerable acts of broken faith"* in his writings which appear in the best-selling *Narrative of the Texan Santa Fe Expedition;*

Manuel Armijo
NEW MEXICO'S POPULAR GOVERNOR

1790: **Manuel Armijo** is born at Plaza de San Antonio, the son of Vicente Armijo and Bárbara C. Durán y Chávez. He is the youngest of 12 children (8 sons and 4 daughters).

[The Armijo and Durán de Chávez families are related to and are among the wealthiest and influential families of N.M. The Armijos are noted farmers, stockmen, businessmen, bankers, educators, and soldiers.]

1819: Manuel marries **Trinidad Gabaldón,** the *belle of New Mexico*. They have no children but they adopt three orphan girls: **María, Cleofas,** and **Ramona**.

1827: Armijo becomes Governor of N.M., the first of three terms in that post.

[Manuel Armijo and Bruce King share the record for number of times to serve as Governor of N.M.]

1837: Armijo leads a counter revolution against the insurgents of 1837.

1841: Armijo captures the **Texan-Santa Fe expedition** sent out by President Lamar of Texas.

August 8, 1846: Armijo issues a proclamation for all New Mexicans to defend their country against U.S. aggression. New Mexicans make preparations to meet the enemy at Apache Pass but **James Magoffin** bribes **Col. Archuleta** into withdrawing his regulars and Armijo orders the militiamen to disband in order to avoid a needless slaughter

1846: James Magoffin is jailed as a spy in Chihuahua (where he had gone to help Gen. Wool as he had Kearny in N.M.) then he is moved

Goveror Manuel Armijo
Courtesy Museum of NM, #50809

to Durango where he is to be shot as a spy. Manuel Armijo is in town on business so he goes to the authorities saying that Magoffin is an American citizen and his execution will result in bloody retaliation by the U.S. Army. Magoffin is released.

1847: Armijo sells his house in Albuquerque and in time it becomes the La Fonda Hotel.

December 9, 1853: Manuel Armijo dies in his home at Lemitar.

(On Dec. 13, the Legislative Assembly offers its *"most sincere condolences to the family and friends of General Armijo and to the Territory for the loss of one of its greatest benefactors; resolved that in respect to the memory and distinguished services of General Armijo this Council now adjourn until ten o'clock tomorrow."*)

Josiah Gregg, *Commerce of the Prairies,* portrays Armijo as an *"ambitious and turbulent demagogue..."* and other such things;

W.W.H. Davis in his book El *Gringo, or New Mexico and Her People,* is the third American writer to vilify Armijo by repeating some of the material he read in Gregg and Kendall, according to Janet LeCompte.

Among the few modern writers to contradict the Kendall-Gregg-Davis cycle is **Sytha Motto** who believes no one in *N.M. "has been more falsely maligned"* than Manuel Armijo, that an impartial investigation of the historical record depicts *"an entirely different picture of the man."*

Motto has written that American writers began the vilification by saying that Manuel's father once buried much gold in Lemitar then killed a faithful Indian servant and buried the two together. Records prove that Manuel Armijo's father never lived at Lemitar.

Manuel is accused of getting his start by stealing sheep but records show the Armijos were independently wealthy.

Armijo is accused of being a coward for, among other things, running from General   Kearny but an impartial investigation of the historical record shows even his handful of regulars informed him they would not fight. Militiamen armed mostly with antiquated weapons would be no match for the modern weaponry of the U.S. so to avoid the slaughter he disbanded the militia, telling them to go home.

Kendall vilified Armijo and vented his "bitter hatred" of Mexicans, excepting the women.

Gregg's bias is grossly apparent. **Susan Magoffin's** remarks are nonsense: that he "had 6,000 soldiers," that his parents were "persons of ill repute," etc. Historian **R. E. Twitchell** wrote *"everything derogatory he could about Armijo"* then said he couldn't verify the reliability of his sources.

1827
REPORT

Statistician and attorney (from Chihuahua) **José Agustín de Escudero** compiles a report for Gov. Narbona in
which he enumerates N.M. livestock:

Sheep and goats:

Santa Fe, 62,000;

Albuquerque, 155,000;

Santa Cruz de la Cañada, 23,000.

New Mexico's **Río Abajo** region dominates the sheep industry.

There are also 5,000 cattle, 2,150 mules, and 850 horses.

Escudero describes the **partido system** then being used in N.M.: the *partidario* (share-owning herder)
agrees to care for a flock of sheep that belong to someone else, usually a rico, in exchange for a
share (partido) of newborn animals. The partidario is usually paid a cash advance for his services
and in good times he builds up his own herd and prospers. If animals are lost, due to hostile
Indians, weather conditions, etc., the herder might not be able to pay off the cash advance,
remaining in debt until he does so.

[Various American observers often described this "debt" as "debt peonage slavery" and that American
slavery was the superior institution, *"but the peón was not legally a slave nor was peonage limited to one
race ... nor was it hereditary"* according to D. Weber.]

TIMELINE

1827-1831: Independence, Missouri, is settled and becomes the starting point for the Santa Fe
Trade from the American side.

1828
MINING

Gold mines which come to be known as the *Placer de Dolores* are discovered in the Ortiz Mountains
southeast of Santa Fe. The boomtown of **Dolores** springs up almost overnight.

1833-1840: Between 2,000 to 3,000 miners work the Placer de Dolores (and it is estimated that a million
dollars in gold is taken out).

1839: A **second gold strike** is made, called *Nuevo Placer*, the mining camp referred to as El Tuerto in the
nearby San Pedro Mountains. Water has to be hauled in to pan dry creek beds but nuggets
weighing as much as a pound-and-a-half are found. *"Nearly all the gold of New Mexico is bought
up by the American traders and smuggled out of the country to the United States."*

AMERIND

Manuel de Jesús Rada writes: Indians of N.M. are well supplied with firearms, powder and lead, lances and
other weapons, which they purchase at low prices from the United States of North America.

[Hostile nations are referred to as *indios bárbaros, salvajes, gentiles* or *naciones errantes.*With American armament the Indians hold the balance of power in N.M.]

1829

Juan Bautista Pino, son of the famous Pedro B. Pino, reports to the Mexican Congress that *norteamericanos* (Americans) are pushing Indian nations like the Kiowas toward the west and they in turn push on other tribes and *"in time we will probably have them on top of us."* Displaced Indian people are constantly pushed toward N.M. (northern Mexico).

TARIFF

Juan María Alaríd condemns the new tariff law that prohibits the importation of nails, locks, some types of woolen and cotton goods, etc., into N.M., which he says will burden the poor even more. If necessary items can't be bought from the Americans then New Mexicans will once again fall into the clutches of the Chihuahua and Durango merchants. Alaríd asks that factories be built in N.M or make it an exception to the law.

SANTA FE TRADE - U.S. CAVALRY

Various traders petition Washington officials to provide soldiers to protect against Indian attacks for caravans going to Santa Fe. They are successful: Major **Bennett Riley** and four companies of the **Sixth Infantry** escort the caravans until the New Mexico line where they wait until the return trip. But while they are waiting they are targeted by Indians on horseback and the soldiers can do little since *they are on foot.* Washington finally agrees that soldiers on the plains need to be issued horses and the **U.S. Cavalry is born.**

SOCIETY

April 19: **Pedro Bautista Pino**, author of *Exposition on the Province of New Mexico, 1812,* dies.

1829-1830
OLD SPANISH TRAIL

Antonio Armijo from Abiquiú leads a trading expedition of at least 30 people to **California.** He pioneers a westward route that skirts the north rim of the Grand Canyon. Everyone survives the harsh Mojave desert, though they have to eat horse and mule meat, but their trading goods, woven woolen goods like serapes, blankets, and quilts, are intact.

December 25, 1829: A reconnaissance party goes out and returns without (teenager) **Rafaél Rivera** who isn't reunited with the group until January 7 after having explored some 506 miles and discovered the **Las Vegas Valley** in Nevada (the first non-Indian to see Las Vegas).

The New Mexican's goods are traded for horses and mules from the California ranchos.

The venture is profitable so the two-month journey becomes a **yearly event**. Wives and children of the traders often accompany the caravan on what is called the *Old Spanish Trail.*

California stock is also taken to Missouri to sell.

Antonio Armijo decides to live permanently in Solano County, California. Other New Mexican Hispanos do likewise: **Hipólito Espinosa** (1840), **Manuel Baca** (for whom Vacaville is named) in 1841, **Julián Chaves** (1850), etc.

[When the 1850 census was taken, 213 N.M. Hispanos were recorded in California, 172 of them in Los Angeles County. And by 1900, in San Bernardino, Riverside, Los Angeles, and Orange counties there were hundreds of people noted to be California-born of New Mexico-born parents.]

1829-1832
José Antonio Chaves is Governor.

1830

TIMELINE

1823: Secretary of War John C. Calhoun leads the movement to **remove all Indians from east of the Mississippi** as had been "promised" by President Jefferson.

1825: **President Monroe** announces that removal of all Indians from east of the Mississippi is official American policy.

1830: **The Indian Removal Bill is passed by Congress.** The Supreme Court declares the Bill *unconstitutional* but **President Jackson ignores the Court** and utilizes military forces to expel all Native Americans from their ancestral homelands east of the Mississippi for lands west of that river, later to be called Indian Territory and Oklahoma, which is inhabited by other Native American nations. Native Americans are thus dispossessed of their land and all property which can't be transported in this death march across America.

DEFENSE CIRCLE

Twenty-five soldiers accompany some *cibolero* hunters to the plains for the fall buffalo harvest. If hostile Indians are encountered all ox carts are formed into a circle.

TIMELINE

April 8, 1830: **The Congress of Mexico abolishes all forms of slavery.**

1830s
LITERACY

Josiah Gregg estimates that about 25% of New Mexicans are literate, which *"compares favorably to the rest of Mexico...and to the American frontier."*

Ca. 1830-1850
SANTERO

A person known only as the **Quill Pen Santero** is creating religious art during this period. He uses some
sort of pointed instrument, a stylus or quill pen made from a feather to draw the finer lines of a
design on his retablos [which appear similar to Indian designs, causing some to suggest he might
have been Native American], switching to brushes when he adds color. The lines usually depict
halos, cross-hatching designs, as well as background objects and patterns. His style is characterized by oval faces for his subjects, elliptical eyes, and highly detailed intricacies on clothing and
the borders of his work. He might be a student of **Molleno.**

[There are fewer retablos by this santero or his school than any other New Mexican santero.]

Ca. 1830-1860
SANTERO

An individual known only as the **Santo Niño Santero** is creating religious art during this period. He is so
named because of his frequent depictions of the **Christ Child** *(El Niño Perdido, Santo Niño de
Atocha,* etc.). It appears that this artist doesn't do altar screens, concentrating on bultos and small
retablos, but his work is brilliant. His bultos are the *"crowning achievement of santo sculpture"* in
N.M.: the eyes are large and life-like, faces often narrow, eyebrows arched, nose prominent and
long, the mouth strong above a delicate chin.

[His work is found in villages between Santa Fe and Taos but it is unknown where he lived. It is possible he
trained with **J. Rafaél Aragón** or in the same workshop because of similar artistic characteristics.]

1831
EDUCATION

Wealthy Hispanos begin sending their sons to Missouri to be educated. **Nepomuceno Alario** of Santa Fe is
one of the first students to go to Missouri.

SOCIETY

Santero **Pedro Antonio Fresquis, the Truchas Master,** dies and is buried at the *Santuario de Chimayó.*

SANTA FE TRADE

A treaty of "amity and commerce" is signed between Mexico and the U.S. in which America is a "most
favored nation." Trade is valued at around $250,000, with about $80,000 of it going to Chihuahua.

[This action is taken because American merchants had been complaining that New Mexican authorities were
charging purely arbitrary duties and levying illegal taxes on their trade goods and commercial establish-
ments. But complaints continue.]

SOCIETY

May 1, 1831: One **George Antonio (Romero),** nine days old, is baptized in Taos, the "legitimate" child of
Antonio Martínez, son of Severino Martínez and María del Carmen Santisteban, and **Teodora
Romero,** daughter of José Romero and María de la Luz Trujillo. Godparents are Santiago Martínez

and his wife, María de la Luz Lucero.

May 9, 1933: **María de la Luz (Romero),** six days old, is baptized in Taos with the same parents and grand-parents as George Antonio. *"This child must have died..."*

September 4, 1935: **María de la Luz (Romero),** 11 days old, is baptized in Taos with the same parents and grandparents as above.

June 1, 1842: **María Soledad** (born of Teodora Romero; the father's name isn't recorded) is baptized.

April 20, 1844: **Vicente Ferrer** (born of Teodora Romero; the father's name isn't recorded) is baptized.

1850: The Territorial Census for Taos lists "Antonio José Martínez," clergyman, with no other members in his household. The next entry because she lived next door, is "Teodora Romero" with the following members of her family:

George Antonio Romero, 20; María de la Luz Romero, 15; María Soledad Romero, 9; María de la Luz Quintana, 18 (Perhaps an orphaned relative); J. Vicente Ferrer Romeo, 7; María de la Luz Trujillo (Teodora's mother).

COMMERCE
July 28: **Manuel Doroteo Pino** exports 12,000 wethers, 500 *varas* of *jerga,* and 20 sarapes for sale in the southern trading centers of Chihuahua, Durango, Mexico City.

1832-1833
Santiago Abreú is Governor.

1832
REPORT
Antonio Barreiro writes *Ojeada sobre Nuevo México,* **A Glimpse At New Mexico,** a detailed social and economic report in which he states: *"Whoever has a slight conception of the ignorance which reigns in this country, will not require other colors to paint vividly the deplorable and doleful state in which the administration of justice finds itself."*
[This meant N.M. was a society functioning without lawyers.]

Sheep have increased with incredible numbers and N.M. would enjoy prosperity if peace could be made with hostile tribes. A few families dominate the sheep industry.

Ciboleros, Hispanic buffalo lancers, are harvesting from 10,000 to 12,000 buffaloes annually. Favorite rendezvous sites for cibolero hunters include Taos, Santa Cruz, **Lucero** in the Mora country is nicknamed *La Placita de los Ciboleros* because it is such a popular gathering place for hunters, San Miguel del Vado, Manzano, etc., to as far south as El Paso.

Ramón Abreú, Secretary of the Legislature, buys a printing press and with the aid of Jesús María Baca, a printer from Durango, **Barreiro publishes the first newspaper in N.M,** *El Crepúsculo de la Libertad* (The Dawn of Liberty).

[The press is acquired in 1835 by Father Martínez of Taos who uses it to publish items used in his private school. Two other newspapers are later published on it, *La Verdad* and *El Payo de Nuevo México*.]

Schools are operating in Santa Fe, San Miguel del Bado, Santa Cruz de la Cañada, Taos, Albuquerque, and Belén, but he says *"The schools are in deplorable condition. No noticeable results are achieved by primary instruction, a condition which is due both to the neglect, carelessness, and ignorance of many of the teachers and to the lack of interest shown by the authorities."* He states no one is better paid than the teachers of the province.

Crafts *"are in the worst state imaginable."* There is very little iron and metal tools are difficult to come by. Nails are at a premium. There is no machinery with which to spin fine yarn or fine cloth. Foreign artisans are the only hope for development of the crafts and he identifies foreign "tailors, carpenters, blacksmiths, tinsmiths, gunsmiths, hatters, cobblers," etc., working in N.M.

LAND GRANT

1832: The **Tierra Amarilla** land grant is made to **Manuel Martínez** as "principal petitioner." He has six sons, J. Julián, J. Vicente, J. Eusebio, J. Sixto, J. Antonio, J. Francisco and two daughters, M. Dolores and María de Jesús. Francisco and Antonio accompany their father and settle on the grant, as do a number of other citizens not related to the Martínez by blood. The Ayuntamiento (Town Council) of Abiquiú expresses the stipulation that all Abiquiú residents retain use of the common lands *"according to the custom prevailing in all settlements,"* despite Martínez' protest.

1838: Settlement of the Tierra Amarilla is prevented by hostile Indians until about this date.

1850: More than 50 people are reported killed by Navajos, Utes, and Jicarilla Apaches on the T.A. grant.

1860: Francisco Martínez petitions Surveyor General W. Pelham to validate the T.A. as a private, not a community grant, which Pelham does and which Congress confirms.

[M. Ebright believes that "translator and clerk" **David J. Miller,** who later became a land grant speculator, translated all documents to make it appear that the grant had been private from the beginning. Further, he states unequivocally that the "prime culprit" in this situation is the system of adjudication *"devised by Congress for N.M."* because it was a *"one-sided administrative procedure totally lacking in due process."* Due process, guaranteed by the U.S. Constitution, was denied to New Mexican villagers of the T.A. grant and consequently their land was taken from them.]

1861: Francisco Martínez is giving deeds, *hijuelas*, which confirm individual holdings to the settlers in the seven communities of the T.A. grant. These deeds guarantee ownership of house and garden lands, as well as the right to use unalloted land for pasture, waters, firewood, and timber cutting, as well as access to all roads. All deeds are notarized and 113 of them are recorded in the Río Arriba County Court House.

1861-1865: There are some 132 heads of families, about 600 people, living in Tierra Amarilla villages known as Brazos, Barranco, Cañones, Ensenada, Nutritas, Los Ojos, La Puente, as well as a few outlying areas.

1874: **Thomas B. Catron** buys the Martínez family interests in the T.A. grant as well as 42 of the hijuela deeds which "purportedly" convey all grant interests to him.

1876: *Tameling v. U.S. Freehold and Emigration Co.*: **John G. Tameling** homesteads a 160-acre tract located on the T.A. grant and the Emigration Co. (owners of that section of the grant) files suit to eject him. Tameling argues that the original grant couldn't be more than 96,000 acres under the Mexican Colonization Law and the present acreage was 998,780 acres. The case goes all the way to the Supreme Court, which decrees that an Act of Congress signifies that title is coming from the United States and therefore not governed by the laws of Mexico. Grant title now rests with the U.S., whatever the acreage, and congressional action is *"not reviewable by any court."*

[The Tierra Amarilla, Sangre de Cristo, and Maxwell land grants were thus authorized by the U.S. and there were no avenues for appeal. With Francisco Martínez "owning" the 594,515 acres of the T.A. grant all residents of the other villages were occupying the land illegally, yet they had the hijuela deeds to vouch for the legality of their ownership.]

Thomas B. Catron is receiving royalties (as much as $50,000 a year) from the T.A. grant due to an arrangement with the Denver and Río Grande Railroad Co.

1883: Catron files a quiet title suit in order to be legally recognized as the owner of the T.A. grant, which he now wants to sell. Defendants named are the "**unknown heirs** of Manuel Martínez," not the settlers living in the seven villages, **who are not informed of the litigation,** and Catron's title becomes final in the legal sense.

1889: T.B. Catron is sued by 46 plaintiffs who contend that Catron's grazing and timber-cutting leases also belong to them since they are also owners of the common lands. The suit is dismissed.

1909: Catron sells the T.A. grant for an estimated $850,000. (Large-scale ranchers like Bill Mundy eventually acquire much of the land.)

Mundy files a legal action to eject José M. Martínez and five others from the "Mundy tract" of the T.A. grant. The N.M. Supreme Court rules that the Martínez hijuela deed is invalid because there is insufficient description of the common lands and it isn't worded according to Anglo American legal practice. The fact that it was legally recorded according to standard legal practice is of no significance.

1960: A case dealing with the hijuela deeds is rejected by the District Court, which maintains that "none of these documents grant any right to pasture and wood..."

[Ebright feels the only possible redress open to New Mexicans who were dispossessed of their lands is the establishment of a body along the lines of the Indian Claims Commission, which could be called the Hispanic Claims Commission, which must have the legal power to make reparations for lands that were "*taken unjustly.*"]

BENT'S FORT

A huge adobe structure known as **Bent's Fort is completed** on the north bank of the Arkansas River near the mouth of the Purgatory. The large structure is 137 by 178 feet surrounded by 14-foot walls 3 feet thick, surmounted by 18-foot corner bastions that fly the American flag, "a stronghold and hospice in one." Inside there are living quarters, trading rooms, warehouses, recreation center, stables, etc.

William Bent manages the fort, **Charles Bent** brings supplies from Missouri, and **Ceran St. Vrain** manages satellite stores in Taos, Santa Fe, and expands the business into Chihuahua and Sonora.

[New Mexicans charge that hostile Indians acquire firearms at Bent's Fort and then are encouraged to attack New Mexican villages. Authors like Rodolfo Acuña *(Occupied America)* and Genaro Padilla (*My History, Not Yours*) have written that Charles Bent was a leader of U.S. citizens operating around Taos who openly supported Texas claims to N.M. while they indulged in smuggling, theft, collusion with various Texans, and harboring known thieves.]

CUSTOMARY LAW

There are no lawyers in N.M. (except for the visiting **Antonio Barreiro** from 1831 to 1834).

[The **legal system** is based on Spanish *customary law* and its emphasis on conciliation. Litigants each appoint an *hombre bueno* (a good man) to recommend a fair solution to the *alcalde,* who renders a decision on the matter at hand if the *hombres buenos* can not agree on a settlement. If litigants accept the decision the matter is closed. If they don't then written testimony is taken, reviewed by the alcalde, then passed on to the *ayuntamiento* or finally the Governor himself for a decision.

By contrast, Anglo-Saxon common law is individualistic and adversarial in nature, which engenders decisive outcomes with clear winners and losers. Hispanic systems of justice during this period emphasize compromise and conciliation intended to promote healthy community living. These differing cultural values were to be crucial when N.M. and the Southwest were taken over by the United States.]

SHEEP RANCHING

Mariano Chaves y Castillo of **Los Padillas** makes marketing history by sending 30,000 head of sheep to Durango (the largest delivery sent south by a single individual during the Mexican period of N.M. history).

1833-1835

Francisco Sarracino is Governor.

1833
SOCIETY

J. Francisco Chaves is born in Los Padillas, the son of (Governor) **Mariano Chaves y Castillo**, the most
successful sheep trader during the Chihuahua/Durango-market years, and **Dolores Perea Chávez**,
daughter of Pedro José Perea. Francisco's grandfather is (Governor) **Francisco X. Chávez**.

SETTLEMENT

Sixty-one families from Albuquerque found **Cubero.**

RELIGION - BISHOP VISITATIONS

Bishop **José Antonio López de Zubiría** of Durango visits N.M.
during this year (as well as in 1845 and 1850).

July 5: The bishop remarks that many of the native *Santos* appear "de-
formed," that new ones should no longer be commissioned or
blessed by priests unless they are better done.

July 21: Bishop Zubiría decrees against penitential excesses and orders
that all instruments of flagellation be removed from church
property and that the Penitente Brotherhood is dissolved.
(Both bans are ignored.)

Bishop Zubiría
Courtesy Museum of NM, #13140

MILITARY & MILITIA

Governor Sarracino criticizes the rich people of N.M. for habitually leaving defense *"in the hands of the
impoverished class,"* a foolish policy which will bring ruin to all *"if we continue in this inaction
which offers dishonorable testimony to our indifference."* The lower class will fight, but without
enthusiasm, though Antonio Barreiro reports that nearly all militiamen *"own land or stock,"*
therefore having a vested interest in defense activities. In many expeditions, regular army troops
usually comprise no more than 10% of the fighting force. Most militiamen are armed with bows and
arrows while hostile Indians are acquiring guns.

SOCIETY

April 22: **Rafaél Chacón** is born in Santa Fe (according to his biographer J.D. Meketa).

PRINTING

Ramón Abreú of Santa Fe is the owner of a "little hand-press" which he brought from Mexico.

1834
NEWSPAPER

Antonio Barreiro, Santa Fe barrister and governmental deputy from Mexico City, publishes (four issues of)
the first newspaper in N.M., *El Crepúsculo de la Libertad.*

[It has been described as the first newspaper west of the Mississippi. Some writers maintain that Fr.
Martínez of Taos published the first newspaper but Fray Angélico Chávez says it was Barreiro.]

1835-1837

Albino Pérez is Governor.

GOVERNMENT

Pérez is the first outsider to hold the office of Governor since 1827. He has an outstanding record as a
soldier and is considered handsome and talented by some. He has a wife in Mexico City but he
fathers a son with his housekeeper. Adultery is frowned upon by New Mexicans and Pérez doesn't
understand local politics. New Mexicans don't like Pérez and his fancy city clothes. They resent
him even more when he brings better efficiency to collecting taxes.

1835

AMERICANS

Upon meeting some Comancheros in eastern Colorado, Capt. **Lemuel Ford** of the First Dragoons writes in
his diary: *"...these Spaniards are the meanest looking race of People I ever saw, don't appear
more civilized than our Indians generally. Dirty filthy looking creatures."*

LAND GRANTS

The Las Vegas land grant is made as a community grant but permanent settlement doesn't commence until
1835.

The Town of Mora grant is made to José Tapia and 25 others.

SOCIETY

Felipe Chávez is born at **Los Padillas.**

[His grandfather was Francisco X. Chávez, the first New Mexican native son to serve as Governor, his father
was José Chávez y Castillo, Governor of N.M. in 1845, his mother was Manuela Armijo, a cousin of Governor
Manuel Armijo.]

FRONTIERSMAN

Manuel Antonio Chaves, perhaps 16 years old, is part of a trading expedition led by his elder brother José
into Navajo country. There are some 15 young men from **Cebolleta** (which was also known for
slave-taking among the Navajos) but no Indians can be found until they approach Canyon de
Chelly where religious ceremonies are being held. The Navajos attack the small group, retreating
only when all the Cebolletans lay dead, or so they think. Manuel Chaves is wounded seven times
but he is alive, as is **Pahe,** an Indian raised in Cebolleta, though he too is seriously wounded.
Cebolleta is nearly 200 miles to the west but the two begin the journey, traveling by night at first to
avoid chance encounters with war parties. Pahe dies one night and Manuel continues alone until
he chances upon some shepherds from Cebolleta who carry him into the village.

SANTA FE TRADE & TAXES

American merchants are using various techniques to avoid paying duties and/or taxes on the goods they
import to New Mexico. Bribes are commonly employed. Since import duties are charged according
to the number of wagons entering the country, some wagons are emptied into others then dis-

carded after saving the iron parts, which are later sold in Santa Fe at good prices.

James Webb writes in his journal that his company of *"recognized and confessed contrabandists"* passed many prohibited items through customs after *"negotiations"* with the Governor. American merchants prefer to deal with Santa Fe customs officials because, as the American Consul observes, *"...we pay less than the tariff calls for."*

["Friction" between traders and New Mexican authorities is also attributed to the "capricious manner" in which the law is enforced, therefore it is "inevitable" that Americans "accustomed to the consistent operation of Anglo law," should object violently says W.A. Beck.]

PUBLISHING
November 27: **Padre Martínez** of Taos buys Ramón Abreú's printing press, takes it to Taos along with printer Jesús María Baca, donates it to the community then invites everyone to make literary contributions to be printed on it.

Cuaderno de Ortografía, a spelling primer, is published by Padre Martínez, the **first book ever produced in N.M.;** pre-nuptial interrogation forms called *Diligencias Matrimoniales* are also printed [which information is crucial to genealogical information so highly studied in the present day]. Then there are "many publications" over the years. The energetic Martínez is Pastor of Taos, running a school, publishing needed books and other materials, farming and stockraising, and soon he is to plunge into politics.

PROFILE

Manuelito

THE WARRIOR

Manuelito of the *Bit'ahni* clan goes into his first battle at the age of 17. Narbona, his father-in-law, leads his people to victory over the Hispanic and Pueblo New Mexicans at Copper Pass. In time he becomes known as an advocate for war to settle problems.

1846: Manuelito is 28 years old at the signing of the Bear Springs treaty.
1849: When American soldiers kill Narbona he considers them more villainous than the New Mexicans, who at least respected Narbona's efforts for peace. He leads many raids.

1853: **Zarcillos Largos, Ganado Mucho** and other peace leaders try to persuade Manuelito to stop raiding, to no avail.
1855: Zarcillos Largos resigns as "Captain" and Manuelito is appointed to take his place by Governor Meriwether. Later he is wounded in a skirmish with Comanches but he recovers.

1856: Manuelito protests the order to remove all Navajo stock from the grazing lands around Ft. Defiance.

186: Manuelito and his warriors attack Ft. Defiance. New Mexicans are attacked in the Chuska Valley.
1861: A peace treaty is finally signed by Manuelito. But Utes attack the Navajos and Manuelito fights back.

1863: General J. H. Carleton orders a general war against the Navajos and Apaches. They are to be rounded up and taken to Bosque Redondo. Kit Carson begins *"his campaign of legendary horror"* in which he *"burns down Navajoland"* and herds the people into exile.

1866: Tired of hiding, Manuelito surrenders and is taken to Bosque Redondo with the rest of the Diné where they suffer until 1868 when they are allowed to return to their homeland.
1876: Manuelito visits with President Ulysses S. Grant in Washington and is persuasive in showing how the Navajos are in dire need of more land (which the Nation gets in 1878, 1880, 1884, etc.).

1882: Convinced that education is the key to survival, Manuelito sends two of his sons to the Carlise, Pennsylvania Indian School. But when one of his sons dies he is violently angry with the school and becomes disheartened with life.

1893: Manuelito becomes gravely ill and in his delirium hears Zarcillos Largos saying, *"Come, the path of beauty will restore your strength"* and Manuelito closes his eyes forever.

1836

TIMELINE

18 3 6: President Santa Anna's forces suffer a devastating defeat at the hands of **Texans at San Jacinto**. The province of Texas is lost to Mexico though Mexican authorities refuse to acknowledge it.

GOVERNMENT

The *alcaldías* are abolished, along with the post of Alcalde Mayor, when N.M. is declared a Department with two subdivisions known as *Prefecturas*, Prefectures, each headed by a Prefect who is directly responsible to the Governor.

1844: A third Prefecture is added to administer northern N.M. The territorial *Diputación is* replaced by the *Junta Departamental* which then becomes the *Asamblea Departamental*, Departmental Assembly.

1837
DANGERS
The **Department of New Mexico is threatened on all sides.**

Across her northern boundary of the Arkansas River there are American trading posts, considered to be possible bases for a military invasion of N.M. by the U.S. The trading posts supply modern guns to Plains Indians and encourage them (unofficially) to raid throughout Mexico, though the Comanche nation helps to keep the peace in N.M.

To the east is the new slave **Republic of Texas,** officially recognized by the U.S., whose leaders claim N.M to the Río Grande, often declaring their intention to secure their claim, by invasion if necessary. (Slavery is illegal in N.M. and the rest of Mexico but in the Southern American states the brutal institution is a pillar of society.)

To the west are the Navajos who can be fierce raiders or trading partners during periods of truce.

To the south are warriors of the Gila and Mescalero **Apaches** who can wage war and block communication with Mexico at their will.

SOCIETY
Manuel A. Chaves of Cebolleta is visiting relatives in Atrisco (Ca. 1836-1837) and down the Río Grande when he chances upon German merchants on their way to New Orleans. Manuel hires on as an *arriero* and sees the big metropolis at the mouth of the Mississippi.

PONY EXPRESS
A system of mail carriers, the solitary horseman referred to as an *extraordinario violento*, is used to correspond with people and authorities in Mexico.

[This system is later referred to as the **Pony Express** when the U.S. enters the Southwest.]

TRADERS
American traders in Santa Fe are the most reliable source of revenue for the government. Some of these men are stable, *"cultivated or useful men,"* while others are *"...shameless smugglers, and their teamsters are rough and rowdy..."* frontier types, *"... always armed, often drunk, the source of trouble at dances and public gatherings"* according to J. Lecompte.

TAXES
Summer: Twelve of N.M.'s leading **sheep exporters** gather before alcalde **José Antonio Chaves** at Isleta to discuss government taxes. **Juan Estevan Pino** is selected to press their petitions with the Congress in Mexico City.

REVOLT OF 1837
August: Revolution breaks out in the Chimayó-Santa Cruz area. It is led by the *alcalde* **Juan José Esquibel** and supported by a 12 member council referred to as *El Cantón de la Cañada*. Their avowed purpose is to sustain God, the nation, the faith of Christ; to defend N.M. to the last; not to allow

the Departmental Plan or any tax associated with it; and to stop the excesses of those who try to carry them out. An army is gathered.

Governor Pérez decides to talk to the rebels until he learns how big the movement really is. Then he issues a call to arms but can collect only about 200 militiamen, many of them Pueblo warriors from the Río Abajo area. With two cannons, the little army marches north, but Pérez still has hopes of negotiating differences.

At La Mesilla government forces meet four groups of insurgents numbering from 1,500 to 2,000 men. Negotiations stop when the rebels open fire and disorder reigns. The two cannons are captured along with much of the Governor's force.

Governor Pérez doesn't have enough soldiers to quell the uprising so he flees south but is stopped on August 8th in the vicinity of Agua Fria road southwest of Santa Fe. Pérez puts up a heroic personal resistance and when his horse is shot from under him he fights on foot with his pistols. When he is out of ammunition he fights with his dagger, killing several of his assailants. Finally he is seriously wounded and killed.

Others of the Pérez party are hunted down and executed, including Santiago Abreú (who was brutally tortured before dying), and Jesús María Alaríd. In all, 17 men die, 6 of them soldiers.

José Gonzáles, a highly successful and therefore popular cibolero, is chosen as Governor of N.M. by the *Cantón*.

[Lecompte relates that José Gonzáles has been identified as an Hispano from Taos in contemporary accounts of the rebellion, an Indian from Taos Pueblo by writers like W.W.H. Davis, L.B. Prince, R.E. Twitchell, and W.E. Beck, a genízaro from Ranchos de Taos by "recent" historians. Rafaél Chacón writes that Gonzáles was a "creole" of Spanish blood, *"...a peaceful and worthy citizen who was made a tool for the ambition of others who were more worldly-wise than himself."* **Josiah Gregg** "testifies" in El Paso that Gonzáles is *"...an idiot neither worthy nor capable of keeping the position he usurped,"* later amending his view for his book *Commerce of the Prairies* that the new Governor was *"without civil virtues and so ignorant that he was unable even to sign his own name."*]

Governor Gonzáles is totally against the Departmental Plan so he suggests to **Elisha Stanley,** an American trader, that all American traders join the *Cantón* movement and ask the **United States to annex N.M. to the American Union.** Stanley refuses to become involved.

Rebel unity now begins to unravel as does support for the cause when the *Cantón* comes out against Gonzáles' moderate goals. Opponents are jailed and threatened with death. Now there are two rebel factions: those with Gonzáles and those with the *Cantón*.

September 8: The Curate of Tomé, **Francisco Ignacio de Madariaga,** invites influential men of the Río Abajo to meet with him and formulate a strategy to stop the revolution in the north. The **Plan de Tomé** manifesto is issued by **Manuel Armijo** and others, decrying the anarchy. Armijo is named to lead a liberating army.

September 11: Governor Gonzáles is informed of the Plan of Tomé and ordered to surrender, which he does with the *"greatest enthusiasm."* He is put in the Santa Fe jail.

September 14: Manuel Armijo arrives with his liberating army from the Río Abajo. Rumor has it that the Cantón army of 3,000 rebels would soon be descending on Santa Fe. Manuel Armijo states he is not a trained soldier, that he knows nothing of battle tactics, so he asks Colonel Juan Esteban Pino to take command of the Río Abajo army.

September 19: Col. Pino declines Armijo's request, pleading advanced age and illness. So Armijo must shoulder the responsibility.
[Lecompte writes that Armijo's *"disinclination to command troops in battle was obvious on several notorious future occasions, and for this he acquired the reputation of a coward."*]

September 21: Armijo lets it be known that he wants to negotiate with Cantón leaders like Pablo Montoya, former *alcalde* of Taos, because he feels innocent people have been duped into joining the rebellion out of ignorance or fear. An agreement is signed and the rebels disband, thus ending the conflict. Some leaders like José Gonzáles and Pablo Montoya are granted amnesty.

1837-1844

Manuel Armijo is Governor.

1837

New Mexicans resume their daily lives when Manuel Armijo assumes the governorship while waiting for instructions from Mexico City. Manuel Armijo is considered *"essentially a merchant and trader"* and a native son known to everyone, as well as an experienced administrator, so his leadership is reassuring.

[Manuel Armijo is the product of a *rico* family from Albuquerque. He grows up *"handsome, bright, and arrogant,"* according to J. Lecompte, and in 1819 he marries **Trinidad Gabaldón,** the belle of New Mexico.

Some writers in the KGD cycle assert that Manuel Armijo got his start *"by stealing sheep from his employer--supposedly once stealing the same animal thirteen times."* On another occasion he is reported by W.A. Beck to have disguised himself as an Apache in order to steal a flock of sheep.]

October 5: Armijo writes to all alcaldes that he expects to give up command of troops to a commander chosen by the military chief in Chihuahua.
October 17: Armijo is back in Albuquerque. The next day a message is received that rebels are massing at the village of Las Truchas and intending to invade Santa Fe.

GOVERNMENT
December 3: **N.M. is made a Department of Mexico.**

1838
January 9: Ninety-four dragoons arrive from El Paso. Manuel Armijo is now officially appointed as constitu-

tional Governor of N.M., Commandant of all troops, and Colonel of Militia.

January 24: Leaders of the rebellion are in jail in Santa Fe but when a rescue is threatened by other insurgents, Juan José Esquibel, Juan Vigil, Desiderio Montoya, Antonio Abad Montoya are executed by decapitation.

January 27: Governor Armijo marches his forces toward Santa Cruz for a final battle with the rebels, who are easily routed. **The rebellion of 1837 is at an end.**

September 27: **Padre Martínez** of Taos fills out the burial entry for **José Angel Gonzáles** after conducting services for the leader of the 1837 rebellion, whom he buries in the graveyard of the Taos Pueblo cemetery.

WATER
Tired of years of endless fighting over water from the Río Lucero, partisans from Arroyo Seco confront those from **El Prado/Taos Pueblo** to settle the matter in a trial by combat. Armed adversaries face each other on the designated day but a thunderstorm momentarily delays the battle. So much rain falls that the Río Lucero floods, providing enough water for all. The fight is canceled.

AMERIND
Pecos Pueblo, once the most populous pueblo in N.M., is abandoned. Some of the remaining Pecos take up residence at Jémez.

GOVERNMENT
April 27: The Mexican Congress exempts New Mexico from the *alcabala* (sales tax) for seven more years.

1839
SOCIETY
Manuel A. Chaves leaves N.M. for St. Louis after a horse racing incident involving Governor Armijo according to M. Simmons. He is away for almost a year and a half until Armijo asks him to return.

SANTA FE TRADE
José Cordero is among the New Mexicans who travel east in a caravan of more than 100 wagons to establish direct commercial ties with suppliers in the USA. Upon his return he pays more than 10,000 pesos in import taxes.

1840
COMMERCE
Hispanic New Mexicans travel to St. **Louis** and other U.S. cities to acquire merchandise for resale in Santa Fe and other markets along the *Camino Real*. A regular trading pattern becomes discernible: caravans depart from Santa Fe during April/May, reach the Missouri towns like Independence or St. Louis, then continue to large eastern centers like Pittsburgh, Baltimore, Philadelphia, New York. In June the Hispanos begin the return home, weather allowing, and arrive sometime in September/October.

ARTS & CRAFTS
Tinwork produced by native New Mexican craftsmen begins to appear on the market.

BOOKS
Matt Field travels to N.M. in 1839 and publishes articles about the land and its people in the *New Orleans Picayune:* His first view of the *"mud built city of Santa Fe"* appears to be *"...an assemblage of mole hills..."* but upon closer inspection of the housing he is impressed with the practicability of local architecture. He concludes that *"...a Santa Fe dwelling is even preferable to an American brick or frame residence. "*

N.M. **blankets** are *"...handsome (sometimes really beautiful ...) with their brilliant colors and weaving so fine they can hold water."*

The **dark-eyed Señoritas** looking at him are *"...more delightful than the exhilaration of the wine bowl..."* though he finds them *"...dark complexioned, some of them pretty, but many of them plain, and most of them Ugly-but slightly removed from the Indians-and they paint their faces like the Indians, with vermilion, by way of ornament."* [Field is unaware of the protective facial masque.]

Amusement in Santa Fe centers around dancing and the game of monte, a card game. Field is fascinated by the most famous monte dealer in town, "Señora Toulous." American *"Traders often lose the profits of a whole season in an hour's play...."* at monte with La Tules, who appears to despise *"...both her fools and the tools by which she ruled them."* He describes a richly attired *"cavallero ... a fine gentleman of Santa Fe-with an enormous sombrero corded with gold ... a jacket of black cloth covered with frogs and braid-pantaloons with the outside seam of each leg left open from the hip down, for the purpose of exposing the white drawers beneath ... silver espuelas-with saddle and other gear gorgeously decorated with silver, and little bells and ornaments jingling..."*

One of the drivers in Field's caravan wants to buy Santa Fe from three ladies walking out of a store: *"I'll give a heap of paysos for Santa Fe just for your sakes, though its a monstrous low place. Your houses are all in one story, like a pack of thieves; built of mud, too, so they ought to be dirt cheap. Madame, will you have a cigar? Miss, I beg pardon, I don't know your name-0, I remember-seenyora-Miss Seenyora ... Six months since I've seen a gal, so help me Cupid, and I'll marry are [sic] a one of you-I'll marry the whole bunch of you right off..."*

The arrival of a caravan in Santa Fe is always an event: *"...the drivers, reckless and insolent fellows, cracking whips and jokes simultaneously.... the pass whiskey began to operate, and groups of noisy American drivers were heard singing, shouting, and rioting in every street..."*

Field goes to a wedding dance where the bride is *"...smoking her chupar. She would pass for handsome among all who do not consider a fair skin absolutely indispensable to beauty...music is a guitar and violin...One waltz ... represents a battle ... exciting and delightful. Few Americans can partake in this dance, as it requires a rapidity of movement which they find by no means easy to acquire ... the people could not exist without the waltz ... With all this unrestrained freedom of manners they seldom quarrel, and the harmony of an evenings amusement is seldom broken unless by some imprudent conduct of the Americans themselves..."*

New Mexico's children *"are generally ugly and in fact really repulsive..."*

1840 (con't)
TEXTILES
New Mexican textile exports peak during 1840 when more than 20,000 items are shipped to Mexico. The
textiles are of three basic types: *sabanilla*, a plain-weave wool cloth used in clothing, mattresses,
and backing for colcha embroidery; *jerga*, a coarsely woven cloth used for saddle blankets, floor
coverings, etc.; **Río Grande blankets,** in a variety of patterns, used for bedding, seating, etc.

[As with other fields of endeavor, certain families in certain communities become well known for their
abilities in various arts and crafts, passing on their expertise to succeeding family members.]

T I M E L I N E

Texans invite a dozen **Comanche chiefs** to come to San Antonio and discuss peace and
exchange of prisoners.

March 19 , 1840: The chiefs arrive along with some warriors with their women and children
and go to the courthouse where the Texans are waiting with many soldiers. The Comanches are
told they will be held prisoners until all captives are delivered up. The chiefs immediately bolt
for the doors and windows whereupon the **Texans open fire**. Some Comanches make it outside
where more soldiers are firing volley after volley. Thirty-three Comanches are slain, many of
them chiefs, and 32 women and children are thrown into jail. The following day one woman is
released to inform her people that all captives must be surrendered or the women and children
will be executed. When she reaches her people all Comanches vow vengeance against the
treacherous Texans.

March 28 : **Chief Isananica** approaches **San Antonio** with 300 warriors. He and a single
warrior ride into town and challenge the Texans to come out of a bar and fight. Customers at
Black's Saloon tell them the soldiers are at Mission San José, to go fight them. At the mission a
Captain Redd tells them he is under orders to observe a truce for 12 days, to come back in 3
days when the truce period is over. The Comanches leave in disgust at what they consider to be
cowardice but for the next 35 years the Council House Massacre is to motivate Comanches to
wage incessant war against the duplicitous Texans.

1841
EDUCATION
Various teachers have schools in Santa Fe: Doña Mariquita ("Beginners School"), don Serafín Ramiréz,
Teacher Pacheco.

TEXAS INVASION
The **Texan-Santa Fe Expedition** begins in the spring when **President Lamar of Texas** wishes to bring the
rich Santa Fe trade into Texas. He claims the western boundary of Texas is the Río Grande River as

signed over to the Texans by General **Santa Anna** so he outfits an expedition of about 300 men under the command of brevet Brigadier-General **Hugh McLeod** to go to N.M. and invite the people to unite under the Texas flag of freedom or at least to trade. Cannon are part of the military equipment with the men in the expedition, who refer to themselves as the **"Texian Invincibles."**

Governor Armijo and New Mexico authorities have long heard rumors that Texans will invade N.M. because they demand the eastern half of N.M. for Texas. Ordinary New Mexicans believe Texans offer "freedom" as a way to make them slaves like the blacks whom they victimize in accordance with Texas law. Governor Armijo puts out word of the impending invasion and instructs anyone living in eastern N.M. to report all information on the invaders. The strategy works: three spies are taken, escorted into Santa Fe and instructed to stay in the capital, but after they escape and are recaptured they are executed.

Militia forces are called into service on the eastern frontier. Five men from the Texan expedition are captured, disarmed, and put in a Santa Fe jail. Another group of 94 Texans surrender at Antón Chico, their property is taken from them and they are marched under guard to Mexico City. The main body of Texans under McLeod, about 200 men, surrender to Armijo on the 5th of October and, as invaders, they too experience the cruel march to Mexico City.

[W.A. Beck considers the surrender *"one of the blackest marks upon Texas military prowess"* because after Goliad *"Texans were not supposed to be taken alive by Mexicans."* But then he accomodates: surrender was permissible because it was a trading expedition anyway and the Texans were without adequate food, horses, and ammunition. They believed *"one Texan was equal to ten Mexicans in a fight"* but even after a victory it would be impossible to manage the return trip home. So the *"Texan-Santa Fe pioneers"* succumbed to the treachery of one of their own and the *"false promises of Armijo."*]

George W. Kendall, editor for the *New Orleans Picayune* newspaper, is among the captured invaders. He relates his experiences in the newspaper (1842) then the sketches appear in the (1844) *Narrative of the Texan Santa Fe Expedition* which is widely read in the U.S. Kendall vilifies Governor Armijo, asserting that it was Manuel Armijo who secretly fomented the rebellion of 1837 for his own advantage. Kendall further states that Armijo went to the rebel camp to claim the governorship but they ignored him because he hadn't been active in the fighting. When Armijo routs the rebels at the battle at Pojoaque, Kendall writes that Armijo ordered the execution of the leaders *"...more to prevent disclosures than for any crime they had committed."*

[Kendall doesn't say how or when he arrived at this information. It is certain he had no archival resources at his disposal during the march to Mexico City.

Josiah Gregg *"repeats the story in many of Kendall's words"* in his *Commerce of the Prairies,* though he writes that he heard about the incident from **Armijo's brother.** *"Only Americans accused Armijo of promoting the rebellion, and not all of them at that"* according to J. Lecompte.

W.W.H. Davis relates the same story in his book, El *Gringo; or New Mexico and Her People,* adding that

Armijo sentenced to death *"...many of the persons who had aided him with money and arms...and caused many others to be privately assassinated."*

The story of Armijo's complicity in the rebellion of 1837 exists only in the writings of Kendall, Gregg, and Davis, who are the principal vilifiers of Governor Armijo. The vilification has been perpetuated by many American historiographers.

Other writers have provided their viewpoints:

"They were simply armed invaders, who might expect to be attacked, and if defeated, to be treated by the Mexicans as rebels, or at best-since Texan belligerency and independence had been recognized by several nations-as prisoners of war," writes H.H. Bancroft

"The evidence is overwhelming that the Texan-Santa Fe expedition was intended only as a trading venture" but that if the people of N.M. wanted to be a part of Texas as had been reported an attempt would be made to take over the area writes W.A. Beck. Governor Armijo used the situation to refortify his waning popularity.

Texans swear vengeance and plans are made to raise a force that will bring *"freedom"* to N.M. and Chihua hua to boot. Col. **Jacob Snively** is to raise 800 men, *"...the only difficulty being to keep the number down..."* to liberate the land under *"...the banner of freedom."* The grand scheme somehow fizzles out and the Texans content themselves with raiding on the Santa Fe Trail.

The **Santa Fe Trade** is made more difficult after the Texan-Santa Fe Expedition because some New Mexicans feel American traders are also working as spies for the United States until it can invade and take the country. Governor Armijo and other authorities demand observance of all laws. Some American merchants turn to smuggling and bribery in order to avoid taxes, practices for which they *"boastfully supply the details"* in their journals writes M.L. Moorhead.]

1841 (con't)
LAND GRANTS
Governor Armijo grants land in an effort to encourage private enterprise and to create barriers against
        Indians, Texans, and Americans.
1841: Beaubien-Miranda grant: **Guadalupe Miranda and Carlos Beaubien** receive lands east of the Sangre de
        Cristos along the Cimarron and Canadian rivers.

[Father Martínez of Taos argued that the Beaubien-Miranda grant was larger than the law permitted, that it included some of the land of Taos Pueblo, that Charles Bent was an illegal partner in the deal. Bent excoriated Martínez and became his political enemy.
Interim Governor Mariano Chávez annulled the grant but Beaubien appealed to the departmental assembly which restored it, only to have new Governor Mariano Martínez order it vacated. Then Interim Governor José Chávez reinstated it.]

1843: **Narciso Beaubien,** son of Carlos, and **Stephen Louis Lee,** whose wife is a sister of Carlos Beaubien's wife, receive the Sangre de Cristo land grant in the San Luis Valley which straddles the N.M.-Colorado border.

The Las Animas grant in eastern Colorado is made to **Cornelio Vigil and Ceran St. Vrain.**

The Río Don Carlos grant is made to **Gervacio Nolan,** a naturalized French Canadian.
1845: Two New Mexicans and a French-Canadian receive a grant on the Canadian River.

A group of Mexican and American partners receive land on the eastern plains northwest of Las Vegas.

[Armijo seems to have chosen foreigners "cautiously," favoring men who had been in N.M. for decades, married native women, and who had become naturalized Mexican citizens. To boot, he gave them land only in association with New Mexican partners. In his *Mercedes Reales,* **V. Westphall** declares*: "Few Native New Mexicans were willing to risk the isolation and dangers from Indian attacks even for the promise of vast expanses of land, but foreigners were more daring and ambitious."* Then in the chapter titled **Exploitation: Anglo Commercialism,** he relates that *"only 6 of the 42 grants"* awarded by Gov. Armijo *"included Anglos among the original claimants,"* by way of substantiating that *"Anglo entrepreneurs"* didn't take over for their personal gain.]

HEALTH
A **smallpox** epidemic breaks out.

SOCIETY
J. Francisco Chávez is sent to Missouri for schooling at St. Louis University, his father's parting counsel being: The heretics will soon be flooding our country. Go learn their language and come back prepared to defend your people.

1842
TIMELINE

October 19, 1842: **Commodore Thomas Catesby Jones** enters **Monterey** harbor with two warships and calls on the **California** garrison to *surrender because the country has been taken for the United States of America.* The totally surprised commandant complies immediately and the American flag is raised over the military fort. The next day Commodore Jones discovers that the *Mexican War hasn't broken out yet,* that he has made a mistake in "capturing" Monterey. He takes down the American flag, apologizes to the authorities and, joined by **Counsel Larkin,** sponsors a dance and banquet for the community after which he sheepishly sails away. D.M. Pletcher observes *"Authorized or not, Jones' attack on Monterey clearly showed American intentions toward California."*

SETTLEMENT
Cuesta (then referred to as *San Antonio*) is founded.

SOCIETY

Kit Carson is baptized, by Padre Martínez of Taos, into the Catholic faith so he can marry **Josefa Jaramillo.** Josefa is the 15-year-old sister of **Ignacia Jaramillo Bent,** wife of **Charles Bent.** The Carson-Jaramillo marriage takes place the following year, with Padre Martínez performing the ceremony.

Higinio V. Gonzáles is born.
[He is to become a noted tinsmith, *santero,* and musician.]
February 16: **Nicolás de Jesús Pino** marries **M. Juana Rascón.** Nicolás is the son of Pedro B. Pino. Juana is from Mexico.

1842-1843
SANTA FE TRADE BANDITS

Texans, *"three bands of marauders under leaders commissioned by Texas"* are preying on the caravans on the Santa Fe Trail:

Col. **Charles A. Warfield** and his band attack the village of Mora, killing five and stealing several horses.

Antonio J. Chávez, son of Francisco Chávez, leads some wagons, which contain $12,000 in gold, among other things, toward Independence, Missouri. Bandits under the leadership of **John M. McDaniel** attack the caravan, killing everybody. McDaniel and some of his cutthroats are later apprehended and executed by U.S. authorities.

Col. **Jacob Snively** attacks the advance guard of militiamen on the Cimarron Cutoff, killing 23, wounding several others and capturing most of the survivors. Later Snively is arrested and his whole group disarmed by Capt. **Philip St. George Cooke** on the American side of the trail.

[Gov. Armijo is reported to be on the plains with 500 men but when he hears that Snively's forces are some 140 miles away he *"flees in terror"* according to W.A. Beck.]

MILITARY

The **22nd Regiment** consisting of nine companies totaling 979 officers and men of the Mexican Army is stationed in Santa Fe to protect all of N.M. The troops are poorly equipped according to R.W. Frazer, an observation based on the writings of Maj. G.A. McCall.

1843
REPORT

Father Martínez of Taos directs a *Memorial* to President Antonio López de Santa Anna:

American traders are debauching Indians and encouraging their attacks on N.M. Indians steal livestock then exchange it for liquor at American posts like **Bent's Fort.** They are also killing buffalo in such great numbers, merely for the hide, that the species will soon become extinct and the *naciones bárbaras* will then have to *"rob and pillage"* in N.M.

WOMEN & COMMERCE

Gertrudis Barceló *(la Tules),* owner of the most popular gambling establishment in Santa Fe, invests the sum of $ 10,000 in the Santa Fe Trade.

SANTA FE TRADE

1843: Hispanic New Mexicans receive a total of 70 trading permits for commerce with USA markets. Non-Hispanics receive 21.

April: Forty-two wagons, 180 men, and some 1,200 mules leave Santa Fe for Independence, Missouri, where they arrive in the middle of May. In the wagons are many furs and between $250,000 and $300,000 in bullion. (Accompanying the caravan are the young J. Francisco Chávez and the Perea brothers, **Francisco and Joaquín,** on their way to college.)

1844

Mariano Chávez is Governor.

GOVERNMENT & SOCIETY

Governor Chávez writes: *'We are surrounded on all sides ... by many tribes of heartless barbarians, almost perishing; and our brothers in Mexico instead of helping us are at each other's throats in their festering civil wars."* New Mexicans are becoming alienated from the Mexican government to the degree that when Mexico City wants to shut down the Santa Fe Trail they insist on keeping it open.

1846: Donaciano Vigil writes: *"To wait for protection from the central government...would be to wait in vain."*

COMMERCE

Over 52,000 wethers are traded south along the *Camino Real.*

Governor Chávez maintains a store at **San Miguel del Vado,** gateway to the eastern plains and commercial center for Bernal, Antón Chico, Tecolote, and Las Vegas. He sends $26,474 worth of trade goods to Chihuahua and later in the year some 6,000 sheep.

MINING

Josiah Gregg estimates that more than half a million dollars' worth of gold has been mined at *Real de Dolores* (also known as *El Placer)* south of Santa Fe. The "crude" mining techniques disgust Gregg.

SANTA FE TRADE

1844: Goods taken over the Santa Fe Trail from are valued at $200,000. In the month of August alone some eight Mexican merchants buy $90,000 worth of imported goods for resale in Chihuahua, Durango, Aguascalientes, etc.
1845: Trade goods are valued at $342,000.

Most of the trade is now going to the interior of Mexico and trade goods are coming from New York, Philadelphia, etc.; Liverpool, England, and Hamburg, Germany. Some 32 wholesale houses in the eastern U.S. enter the trade directly, importing from Europe and using their own agents for selling to the caravans. Mexican merchants who trade directly with the U.S. do much business with the Spanish firm of **Peter Harmony, Nephews and Co.,** New York importers of English, French, German, and Venetian items.

Trade items include a "bewildering variety" of goods. Indians value bottles of all kinds and will trade their agricultural products for them.

1846: Trade is valued at $1,000,000 with a record 363 wagons crossing the plains, of which 315 continue to El Paso, Chihuahua, Durango, Zacatecas, Aguascalientes, etc., and eventually to Mexico City.

Many merchants become well known in the Santa Fe trade: Juan Otero of Peralta, Samuel C. Owens of Kentucky, James (Santiago) W. Magoffin of Kentucky, Albert Speyer of Prussia; David Waldo, Edward J. Glasgow, Henry Connelly, etc.

MILITARY ACADEMY
March 11: **Rafaél Chacón** and other prospective cadets leave N.M. for the Military Academy in Chihuahua, a branch of the Normal Military School of the Republic at Chapultepec in Mexico City.

1844 (con't)
Felipe Sena is Governor.

AMERINDS & FIREARMS
Utes increase their raids on N.M. settlements. American traders at Pueblo, Hardscrabble, Greenhorn, etc., openly exchange firearms for stolen N.M. livestock.

BOOKS
Commerce of the Prairies by **Josiah Gregg** is published in the U.S. and is widely read by Americans interested in the Southwest.
[Gregg's observations and impressions make him one of the most popular chroniclers of the Santa Fe Trail, according to some writers.]

Gregg describes a *cibolero* met on his caravan's approach to Santa Fe; a *fandango* (dance) is held to celebrate the arrival of a caravan;

Oñate, founder of N.M., is an example of "*...that sordid lust for gold and power, which so disgraced all the Spanish conquests in America; and that religious fanaticism, that crusading spirit, which martyrized so many thousands of aborigines of the New World under Spanish authority...*" The "*pacific and docile*" aborigines of N.M. "*had neither intelligence nor spirit to resist...*" Oñate's settlers.

New Mexicans prepare the best **chocolate** in the world; their horsemanship and ability with the **lazo** (rope) are remarkable; the **arrieros** are extremely skillful transporters of goods; **sheep raising** is the most important industry and Mexican sheepdogs are highly trained.

"...The New Mexicans appear to have inherited much of the cruelty and intolerance of their ancestors, and no small portion of their bigotry and fanaticism. Being of a highly imaginative temperament and of rather accommodating moral principles-cunning, loquacious, quick of perception and sycophantic, their conversation frequently exhibits a degree of tact-a false glare of talent, eminently calculated to mislead and impose. They have no stability except in artifice, no profundity except for intrigue: qualities for which they have acquired an unenviable celebrity. Systematically cringing and subservient while out of power, as soon as the august mantle of authority falls upon their shoulders, there are but little bounds to their arrogance and vindictiveness of spirit.."

Northern Mexicans*..."have often been branded with cowardice: a stigma ... of the wealthier classes... though the rancheros ... and yeomanry ... possess a much higher calibre of moral courage. Their want of firmness in the field, is partially the result of their want of confidence in their commanders... and inefficacy of their weapons..."* The *"Mexicans, like the French, are remarkable for their* **politeness** *and suavity of* **manners..."**

Gregg writes that *"Goldsmiths and silversmiths are perhaps better skilled in their respective trades than any other class of artisans whatever...."*

Mexicans harbor a variety of gross **superstitions** that are *"....fantastic and improbable in idolatrous worship..., the most popular being the apparition of the Virgin of Guadalupe. The superstitious blindness of the people causes them to believe in a legion of saints and this ...abject idolatry sometimes takes a still more humiliating aspect, and descends to the worship of men in the capacity of religious rulers..."* as on the occasion of Bishop Tamaron's visit to Santa Fe when *...the infatuated population hailed his arrival with as much devotion and enthusiasm as if it had been the second advent of the Messiah."* The padres lead the people in vice and get away with it because *"...the Romish faith is not only the religion established by law, but the only one tolerated by the constitution, a system of republican liberty wholly incomprehensible to the independent and tolerant spirits of the United States..."*

Josiah Gregg
Courtesy Museum of NM, #7226

Indians boast they *"would long before this have destroyed every sheep in the country, but they prefer leaving a few behind for breeding purposes, in order that their Mexican shepherds may raise them new supplies."*

SOCIETY

Tinsmith **José María Apodaca** is born.

Manuel *A.* **Chaves** marries **María Vicenta Labadie** of Tomé.

1844-1845
Mariano Martínez de Lejanza is Governor.

1844
SOCIETY
Luz Beaubien marries **Lucien B. Maxwell**. Luz is the daughter of Judge Carlos Beaubien who together with Guadalupe Miranda owns the huge Beaubien-Miranda land grant .

[With the addition of the Sangre de Cristo land grant the whole area later becomes publicized by various writers as the **Maxwell land grant** .]

SOCIETY & MONEY
In an era when a worker is paid three to six pesos a month, some New Mexican families deal with huge amounts of money: Mariano Chávez sends $26,474 worth of trade goods to Chihuahua; José and Juan Perea send $25,128 worth; Manuel and Ambrosio Armijo send $28,318.

TERRORISM
Donaciano Vigil y Alaríd is in his home when **Charles Bent** and a **Mr. Workman** enter the elderly man's domicile and demand to know why Vigil y Alaríd is accusing consul Bent of refusing to stop American smugglers on the Santa Fe Trail. Donaciano replies, *"Because it is true,"* whereupon Workman strikes him with his whip, knocking him down and striking him repeatedly with the whip then jumps on him and punches him with fists until Bent *"thought he had given him enough so I pulled Workman off."*

SOCIETY
Custom and tradition are basic guidelines for Hispanic life in N.M. Individualism is strong but it is exhibited in basically the same consistent fashion. Men are expected to be *muy hombre* and live by their *palabra de hombre*, which assures honesty and dependability. A man's word is his bond and written documentation is therefore unnecessary.
Males learn and refine the skills of planting, hunting (especially the buffalo), building, animal husbandry, harvesting, etc., and, above all else, **horsemanship**.

Females learn to be stable, responsible (*muy mujerota*) hearts of family and home life. They learn the home arts for the day that they will be wives and they help on the farm/ranch whenever necessary. Hispanic tradition enables them to own property separately from that of their husbands and utilize or dispose of it as they choose.

[Dr. D. Weber contrasts this with *"American or British women who lost control over their property as well as their legal identity upon marriage."*]

Husbands can make no claim to their spouse's property if it was owned before marriage and wives could not be held accountable for their husband's debts. Women can sue and be sued in court. A wife can own land within the law and her husband can't alienate it without her consent.

[This "Hispanic tradition" became the basis for the concept of community property in modern American law.]

Partly due to religious personalities like Mary and the female Saints, Hispanic women are heirs to a special status at home and in social circles which gives them certain freedoms and responsibilities in society.

Women outnumber men in settled, older communities like Santa Fe, Abiquiú, etc., but in most settlements the ratio is fairly equal. (It is estimated that during this period from 45% to 50% of New Mexicans are under sixteen years of age.)

CULTURE

Extemporaneous poets known as *trobadores*, men and women who can improvise rhymed verse, are popular throughout N.M. according to A.L. Campa, especially at social gatherings. These poets also compose:

adivinanzas (guessing word games);

alabados (religious hymns and chants especially popular with the Penitente Brotherhood and religious gatherings);

autos (short plays on religious themes);

canciones (songs, the most popular of all forms);

coplas (poetry in the form of a four-line stanza);

corridos (narrative ballads descended from romances);

cuandos (accounts of adventures like buffalo hunting, always starting with "when");

cuentos (short stories);

decimas (popular poetry structured in an introductory quatrain called a *planta*, then followed by four 10 line stanzas, each of which ends with a line from the planta, respectively);

dichos (sayings, proverbs);

folk theater;

inditas (witty and amusing variants of corrido forms, characterized by dancing between sung verses and the use of drums and Native American Indian rhythmic patterns; among others, sheepherders often composed inditas);

love poetry;

romances (narratives sung to a catchy melody; one of the oldest New Mexican romances is *La Aparición*, "The Apparition," which tells about a bereaved husband's encounter with his wife's ghost who counsels him that he must adjust, find a good wife and seek happiness).

Among the many **trobadores** are Tomás Quintana, Juan Bautista Vigil y Alaríd, Antonio Martínez, Juana Marchanta, Vicente Maestas, Jesús María Gonzáles, etc.

Famous trobador **J.B. Vigil y Alaríd was** once challenged that he couldn't create a verse that ended with the phase "*I say that there is no hell*" while not uttering anything offensive or blasphemous in the poetry. The good doctor considered the challenge then recited:

> Holy Virgin Mary,
> Mother of my good Jesus,
> Give me a ray of your light
> Since you are the dawn of the day;
> Mother and advocate of mine,
> Free me from the eternal fire,
> And as one who loves you faithfully
> *I can say that there is no hell.*

FAMILY

The extended family is part of Hispanic community living. Blood relations are the nucleus of family life but there is also the *compadrazgo*, which includes godparents (*padrinos*) as responsible kin in the event that something happens to the parents of one's godchild, parents and godparents referring to each other as *compadre* or *comadre*.

[*Primo/prima* is often used when addressing someone because most New Mexicans are related by blood.]

LABOR

The mutual assistance tradition known as *peonada* (from *peón*, worker) is common among farmers and rancheros in N.M. For example, when the harvest time demands intensive labor a farmer will alert his neighbors who send *peones* (workers) to help until the harvest is in. The farmer then provides workers when his neighbors need them.

[Some writers have depicted this working mutual assistance as *peonage slavery*.]

RECREATION

The **dance** is the most popular of social gatherings and the happiest way to celebrate an event. *"During the entertainment no one had quarrels or fights, all had respect for their betters and consideration for their equals. Before the arrival of the Americans...the people lived simply and very contentedly,"* according to Rafaél Chacón.

Professional troops of *maromeros* (rope walkers, acrobats, actors, etc.) travel north from Mexico to entertain the people. They also introduce new dances such as the quadrille, the *contradanza*, the waltz.

Horse racing, bullfighting and cockfighting are popular.

[Santa Fe has a bullring in 1845.]

PROFILE

Padre José Manuel Gallegos

DELEGATE TO CONGRESS

October 30, 1815: José Manuel is born to **Pedro Ignacio Gallegos and Ana María Gabaldón Gallegos** in Abiquiú.

1830: José Manuel is studying in the school of **Padre Martínez** of Taos. The "spirited and handsome" youth declares he wants to study for the priesthood.

1840: Gallegos is ordained into the priesthood and upon his return to N.M. He works as assistant to Vicar **Juan Felipe Ortiz.**

December, 1840: Governor Armijo banishes Padre Gallegos from Santa Fe due to a false accusation made by some militiamen.

January, 1841: Vicar Ortiz challenges Governor Armijo
to indict Gallegos formally or drop the matter, which
soon blows over.

1845: Father Gallegos is assigned as pastor in Alburquerque where he has many relatives in his Río Abajo homeland. For a period of about seven years (1845-1852) he works in his parish and with his parishioners, even using his own patrimony as finances to restore and enlarge the dilapidated Franciscan friary of old, making it a comfortable residence.
August 18, 1846: General Kearny and his Army take New Mexico in the name of the USA. Padre Gallegos and most of the clergy accept and even welcome union with the USA.

October, 1846: Lt. J.W. Abert reports an incident in which Gallegos performs a clownish trick in which the punchline is portraying Abert as an "astronomer and mathematician" because he could differentiate a square from a triangle.

[A. Chávez states this incident has been used by some writers to "prove" what a dullard Gallegos really was.]
1847: After a revolt in Taos rumors circulate that the uprising was masterminded by Padre Martínez of Taos, Vicar Ortiz of Santa Fe, Padre Gallegos of Albuquerque, etc.

[Chávez believes these false rumors were created by the more bigoted element of the American population and writers like W.W.H. Davis, the U.S. Attorney and later author of the "classic" *El Gringo or New Mexico and Her People,* which continues to be read to the present day.]

1850: The Census lists Padre Gallegos as a 35-year-old priest with assets worth $8,000 with a household consisting of four males and seven females [which include orphans or homeless persons given a home by Gallegos, typical behavior for Hispanic clergy in N.M.]. His housekeeper is Jesusita, **María de Jesús Trujillo do Hinojos** [whom Lt. Abert described as "a very handsome lady" four years earlier and whom Machebeuf termed a "slut" six years later], a partner in the Gallegos store,

1851: Bishop **Jean-Marie Odin** of Galveston (who had never set foot in N.M.) warns **Jean Baptiste Lamy** and his close aide **Joseph P. Machebeuf,** who are traveling to take custody of N.M., that the New Mexican clergy and people are immoral and dissolute. But the people and clergy greet the French clergymen, who are traveling with two other priests and two lay youths, as heroes in every town all the way to Santa Fe. In Albuquerque Gallegos feasts them with a banquet.

José Manuel Gallegos
Courtesy Museum of NM, #9882

1852: Machebeuf instigates and promotes a struggle between "superior" French clergy and "immoral" Hispanic priests. While Lamy is away in Baltimore, Machebeuf suspends two priests, though he doesn't have canonical authority to do so. Parishioners accuse him of revealing secrets of the confessional but Machebeuf ignores the charges and decides to address the rumors concerning Padre Gallegos of Albuquerque. When Gallegos goes south to Durango, Machebeuf takes over the parish and suspends the absent pastor. Machebeuf appropriates Gallegos' comfortable lodgings.

1853: Bishop Lamy writes that the troubles in N.M. are being caused in reality by native priests who are resisting his reforms as listed in his Christmas *Pastoral.*
[Chávez writes this was merely a red herring to cover up the true danger, that Vicar Machebeuf had violated the sacrosanct seal of the confessional, for which there were very real disciplinary actions to anyone found guilty of such abuse.]

José Manuel Gallegos devotes himself to commerce while the Franco-Hispano struggle rages. In time he decides to run for Delegate to Congress, defeating W.C. Lane in the September election. While Gallegos is in Washington, Lamy and Machebeuf move to take the house and land which Gallegos maintains belongs to him personally, not the Church.

1855: Gallegos defeats **Miguel A. Otero (I)** by the very slim margin of 99 votes for a second term as Delegate.

1856: Both Houses of the New Mexico Territorial Legislature issue a formal address to the Pope, attacking Bishop Lamy for malfeasance in office and his unjust treatment of certain native priests. Gallegos is the leader of the movement and a parcel of documents is sent to the Pope.

Vicar Machebeuf goes to Rome and answers all charges: the native clergy, addicted to drunkenness, adultery, and cupidity, are rebelling against the reforms of the Christmas Pastoral; the people of **New Mexico are most Ignorant and vicious,** their legislators are "dishonest and immoral." José Manuel Gallegos is especially excoriated by Machebeuf as *beaucoup d'esprit at d'Exterieur* but vain and pretentious, doing business in his store on Sunday, living with a married woman who has an assortment of illegitimate children, etc.

[Chávez titles Machebeuf's defense **"The Big Roman Lie,"** asserting that Lamy and Machebeuf did little but lie about New Mexico, its people and realities, to cover their own conduct.]

The Propaganda Fide finds in favor of Bishop Lamy and Vicar Machebeuf.
February, 1856: M. A. Otero contests the Delegate election and manages to unseat Gallegos. (New Mexico's Hispanic population is polarizing: the land- owning ricos are being drawn to the Republican groups interested in business and high finance while the Democrats champion the common people as a whole.)

1857: J.M. Gallegos moves to Santa Fe.

1860-1862: Gallegos is Speaker of the Territorial House of Representatives.

1862: The Confederate Army takes Santa Fe without firing a shot. José Manuel Gallegos and Facundo Pino, heads of the two legislative Houses, are jailed on charges of being "Union sympathizers."
1865-66: Gallegos serves as Territorial Treasurer.

1868: J.M. Gallegos, aged 53, marries Candelaria Montoya, 31, in the Episcopal Church. (They have no children.)

April 21, 1875: José Manuel Gallegos dies.

FRONTIER COMBAT

August: **Governor Martínez** receives word from Abiquiú that a large war party of Utes have come in to complain that militiamen had attacked them and killed 10 of their men and taken four children captive. They demand compensation and Martínez orders they be paid only to learn that the Utes are already on their way to Santa Fe, led by their war chief **Panasiyave**.

August 5: Governor Martínez receives the Utes (6 chiefs and 102 warriors, all heavily armed) in the Palace of the Governors. He tries to placate them with presents, food, and lodgings but the next morning Panasiyave and his warriors throw all food and gifts into the street. Martínez tries to calm them but insults turn to blows and the Governor defends himself by leveling Panasiyave with a chair. Mrs. Martínez brings her husband a sword and soldiers are called whereupon the chiefs crash through a window to reach their warriors. Soldiers pour our of their barracks and citizens come out of their shops to join the melee. The Utes retreat westward down San Francisco street, killing several woodcutters who chance to be coming into town. When the encounter is over, Martínez, sword still in hand, views the numerous corpses scattered in the plaza, one of them Panasiyave.

1845
José Chávez y Castillo is Governor.

EMIGRES
Lorenzo Trujillo leads some 30 New Mexican families to California where they settle in Los Angeles and San Bernardino. California rancheros need help to protect their livestock so the New Mexicans are welcomed because of their reputation as Indian fighters.

AMERIND LITIGATION
Isleta Pueblo files a petition objecting to the **Ojo de la Cabra** land grant made to **Juan Otero.** The Isletans argue that it is fully accepted custom to use the land as common pasture but it should not be privatized by Juan Otero. After lengthy litigation that goes all the way to Chihuahua the land grant is annulled and the New Mexican official who made it is suspended from office for stating the land had not belonged to anyone.

FRANCISCANS
Fray Mariano de Jesús López arrives to work with various Pueblos. His accidental death in 1848 marks the end of Hispanic Franciscanism in N.M.

NATIVE HISPANIC PRIESTS
According to A. Chávez there are **"eighteen native padres"** of N.M. ordained by Bishop Zubiría of Durango between 1833 and 1845: Tomás Abeyta, José de J. Baca, (?) Bustos, Rafaél Chávez, José Manuel Gallegos, (?) Gallegos, Mariano de J. Lucero, José de J. Luján, José Vicente Montaño, Vicente Saturnino Montaño, José Antonio Otero, José Antonio de J. Salazar, Ramón Salazar, Juan de J. Trujillo, Eulogio Valdés, (?) Valencia, (?) Varela, José- de la Cruz Vigil. Some of these men studied in the school of Padre Martínez.

[Chávez relates that J.A. Otero, (?) Varela, (?) Gallegos, and Bustos remained in Durango.]

1845: Padre José Manuel Gallegos is assigned as pastor in Albuquerque.

GOVERNMENT
New Mexico is financially bankrupt though import duties collected amount to $105,757 on $342,530 worth of goods entering over the Santa Fe Trail.

NEWSPAPERS

La Verdad newspaper is published in Santa Fe for a short time.

T I M E L I N E

1845: **John L. O'Sullivan**, editor of the *Democratic Review,* writes that Texas should be admitted Into the Union because it is America's *"...manifest destiny* to overspread the continent allotted by Providence for the free development of our yearly multiplying millions!" [The famous phrase is thus created.]

TAXES

February 14: The Departmental Assembly enacts a law authorizing taxation of property in proportion to
wealth. Large land owners become very discontented.

SOCIETY

May 16: **Mariano Chávez,** New Mexico's biggest sheep trader, dies suddenly. His passing marks the end of
an era that saw the sheep industry become the basic strength of the New Mexican economy.

T I M E L I N E

December 20, 1845: Presidential Envoy **John Slidell** goes to Mexico to discuss the purchase of northern Mexico but Mexican officials refuse to discuss anything except the annexation of Texas by the U.S., which they believe to be illegal under international law. In an effort to start a war, **President Polk** sends a force under **General Zachary Taylor** to the Río Grande River where Taylor blockades the river to prevent supplies from reaching Matamoros .
[**Ulysses S. Grant** is quoted as saying: *"We were sent to provoke a fight but it was essential that Mexico should commence it,"* according to R. Griswold del Castillo.]
Mexico doesn't respond to the provocation and war is averted.

May, 1846: Weary of waiting, President Polk informs his cabinet of his decision to request Congress to **declare war against Mexico** on the basis of her refusal to meet her international obligations (according to M.M. Quaife).

1845-1846

Manuel Armijo is Governor.

1846
POPULATION

There are some 65,000 people in N.M. The average rate of population growth is 2.1 percent (double the rate of
Mexico as a whole).

LAND

Aside from the people's private and community land grants there are also some 6,000 **small-holding claims** which haven't been conveyed formally as a land grant and indicate that perhaps 3,000 persons, or 1 out of every 26 New Mexicans are small farmers, *"independent tillers of the soil"* who don't live on grant lands. The overwhelming majority of the remaining citizens reside on community grants (private grants were used more for grazing than residential purposes), own their private residential and agricultural lands and share the common lands *"so it is evident that the majority of the populace was in no way dominated by any owner-tenant relationship."*

[**Westphall** doesn't believe **debt peonage** was a basic institution in N.M. though many writers have so described it and compared it to American slavery of Africans.]

SOCIETY

Donaciano Vigil criticizes the central government for harassing foreign businessmen and hounding them out of N.M. He denounces the government's prohibition of arms importation and its monopoly on the production of gunpowder. He believes N.M. can't exist without proper weapons but the government won't supply them or allow their import, which he describes as a "calamity."

TIMELINE

April 25, 1846: Mexican forces attack a small contingent of Taylor's dragoons who are on Mexican territory.

May 11: **President James K. Polk** had prepared a speech asking Congress to declare war on Mexico because she had refused to honor international obligations but now he informs Congress that *"American blood has been shed an American soil...War exists, and notwithstanding all our efforts to avoid it, exists by the act of Mexico herself."*

May 13: **Congress declares war on Mexico.** The Northeast views the declaration of war as a conspiracy of slave-holding states to gain more slave territory. **Abraham Lincoln** introduces his **"Spot Resolutions,"** challenging Polk to name the spot where American blood was shed on American soil. Congress calls for 50,000 volunteers but men from the Northeast virtually refuse to enlist.
[Other writers on the Mexican War hold contrasting opinions:
O.B. Faulk writes that *"The origins of this conflict can be traced"* to different cultures, debts owed to American citizens which Mexico refused to pay, the desire for California, the Texas issue, and Mexico's unwillingness to seek a peaceful way out, since the French had said Mexico could win a war against the U.S. President Polk *"sought every honorable avenue of settlement"* and didn't ask for a declaration of war until Mexican troops attacked American soldiers north of the Río Grande. *"Congress responded on May 12 [sic] with a declaration of war."*

B. DeVoto relates how it was felt that *"Polk's bound to take no sass from Johnny Bull, nor the Greasers neither. Or Polk's set to make us fight a war if he can't get slave territory noways else."*

R.E. Twitchell assures us that *"The policy of our government toward Mexico was one of kindness, consideration and forbearance...it was plainly the duty of the U.S. to extend American protection over her* citizens and soil...the Missouri Volunteers who invaded N.M. were men of good reputation and character *"as found in the ranks of few armies which ever went into battle...the citizen soldier of our country finds no parallel anywhere in the world."*]

AMERICAN INVASION

July 11: Governor Armijo causes a meeting of important persons to be held to discuss the American invasion and how to combat it. Blas Trujillo, Juan Vigil, Cornelio Vigil, Buenventura Martínez, Carlos Beaubien, and Curates José María Valdez, Mariano Lucero, and Eulogio Valdez attend the meeting. Padre Martínez of Taos is invited but [for some unknown reason] doesn't attend we are told by W.A. Keleher. **Diego Archuleta,** professional soldier and leader of the professional dragoons, **favors an all out military defense.**

July 26: Col. Kearny and his staff reach Bent's Fort. His official orders are to take New Mexico and California.

[Kearny was already a "legendary" leader known so far and wide that "men fought to enlist in the invading army" reports W.A. Beck.]

He meets with **James W. Magoffin** because the latter is on a mission directed by President Polk, Sec. of War Marcy, and Senator Benton of Missouri. Magoffin, accompanied by Capt. St. **George Cooke** and 12 dragoons with a flag of truce, is sent ahead to confer with Governor Armijo. Kearny's letter to Governor Armijo, delivered by Magoffin, states that the American government is **taking possession of all lands cast of the Río Grande River as the designated boundary of Texas.** The American Army is too strong for any resistance. Submit to fate and avoid needless bloodshed.

July 31: Kearny issues a proclamation from Bent's Fort: the American Army comes to N.M. to better the condition of New Mexicans; remain peaceful and you will be protected in your property and religion; take up arms and you will be treated accordingly.

August 1: The advance guard of the **Army of the West** is on New Mexican soil.

August 8: Armijo issues a proclamation to all New Mexicans: We are invaded and all citizens must defend the most just and holiest of causes...for if we are not able to preserve the integrity of our territory, all that country would very soon be the prey of the greed and enterprising spirit of our neighbors of the north...Let us be ready for war since we are provoked to it. We can expect help from no one but ourselves...

August 10: The Departmental Assembly is asked to appropriate $1,000 to maintain the dragoons, which is done, but the appropriation is revoked the next day.

August 12: James Magoffin has secret talks with Governor Armijo and other leading men of N.M., including Col. Diego Archuleta and Henry Connelly. **Magoffin bribes Col. Archuleta into not resisting American forces.**

[This was attested to by Henry Connelly in his statement of Sept. 29, 1848. It is unknown what, if anything, was offered to or accepted by Armijo, though many writers promote the idea that it was Armijo who was bribed.]

August 15: **General   Kearny address the people of Las Vegas** from atop an adobe building: Mr.. Alcalde and People of New Mexico: I have come amongst you by orders of my government to take possession of your country and extend over it the laws of the United States. We consider it, and have done so for some time, a part of the territory of the United States. We come amongst you as friends, not as enemies, as protectors, not conquerors. We come among you for your benefit, not for your injury. General Armijo is no longer your governor. I am your governor ... remain peaceably in your homes attending to your crops and livestock and you shall be protected by me in your property, persons, and religion. *Not a pepper, not an onion* shall be disturbed or taken by my troops without pay ... But Listen! He who promises to be quiet and is found in arms against me, I will hang!

Governor Armijo deploys his citizen militia, estimated at about 3,000, in the mountains through which the Army of the West must pass to get to Santa Fe.

[It was thought "the militia" would "run at the first sign" of battle, reports W.A. Beck.]

Col. **Archuleta and his professional soldiers inform Armijo that they will not fight. Archuleta orders his professional dragoons to proceed south, abandoning New Mexican defenses.** Deprived of professional armament, Armijo decides to avoid useless carnage and directs all citizens to return to their homes. He travels south to avoid capture.

August 19: General   Kearny addresses Santa Feans in the Plaza:

New Mexicans: We come among you to take possession in the name of the United States. We come with peaceable intentions and kind feelings toward you, as friends to better your condition and make you part of the republic of the United States. We mean not to murder you or rob you of your property. Your families shall be free from molestation; your women secure from violence. My soldiers shall take nothing from you but what they pay for ... Manuel Armijo is no longer your governor, his power is departed but he will return and be as one of you. When he returns you are not to molest him. You are no longer Mexican subjects but now American citizens subject only to the laws of the United States ... I am your governor, henceforth look to me for your protection.

Acting Governor Juan Bautista Vigil y Alaríd, representing the people of N.M., makes a response:

General: The address you have just given us gives us some idea of the wonderful future that awaits us ... the inhabitants of this department humbly and honorably present their loyalty and allegiance to the government of North America ... Today we belong to a great and powerful nation. Its flag, with its stars and stripes, covers the horizon of New Mexico, and its brilliant light shall grow like good seed well cultivated. We are aware of your kindness and of your courtesy and that of your accommodating officers and of the strict discipline of your troops. We know that we belong to the republic that owes its origin to the immortal Washington, whom all civilized nations admire and respect. How different would it be at the hands of other European nations for we are aware of the unfortunate condition of the Poles ... In the name then, of the entire Department, I swear obedience to the Northern Republic and I render my respect to its laws and authority.

August 22: **General Kearny** issues a proclamation in Santa Fe: *All of New Mexico with its original boundaries is now a part of the United States.* All property and freedom of religion will be respected. Protection will be given against the wild Indians. Anyone who takes up arms will be considered an enemy and a traitor, and his property shall be confiscated. **All persons are hereby considered citizens of the United States.**

September 22: General Kearny issues the **Organic Law** of the Territory of N.M., popularly known as the **Kearny Code.**

Charles Bent is appointed Governor, **Donaciano Vigil** is Secretary.

Donaciano Vigil
Courtesy Museum of NM, #11405

TIMELINE

Later, when trying to collect his bribe money from the American Congress, Magoffin was to write: "Col. *Archuleta would have fought. I quieted him. It was he who afterwards made the revolt which was put down with much bloodshed by Gen' Price. Fight was in him, and it would have come out at first, carrying Armijo with him if it had not been for my exertions ... I could state exactly how I drew off Archuleta from his intention to fight..."*

Feb. 21, 1849 : **Capt. St. George Cooke writes a corroborating letter to the Congress, specifying Magoffin's role in the bloodless conquest of N.M.:** "*... particularly in neutralizing the contrary influence of the young Col. Archuleta, by suggesting to his ambition the part in bringing about a pronunciamento of western N.M. ... Gen' Kearny's first proclamation claiming only to the Río Grande ... your services ... at the expense of a large bribe ...*"

[Magoffin finally collects less money than he had put out and later sides with the **Confederacy** during the Civil War.]

SETTLEMENTS

The **Las Vegas** land grant contains the communities of Las Vegas, San Antonio (Upper Town), Agua Sarca, Valles de Tecolote (San Gerónimo), Plaza del Burrito (Santa Ana), Plaza del Torreón (Tecolote), Plaza de los Garcías (Lagunas), Valles de San Agustín (San Agustín), Ojitos Fríos, Cañada del Salitre, and Los Ojos (Hot Springs).

COMMERCE

Trade with cities in Mexico comes to an abrupt halt.

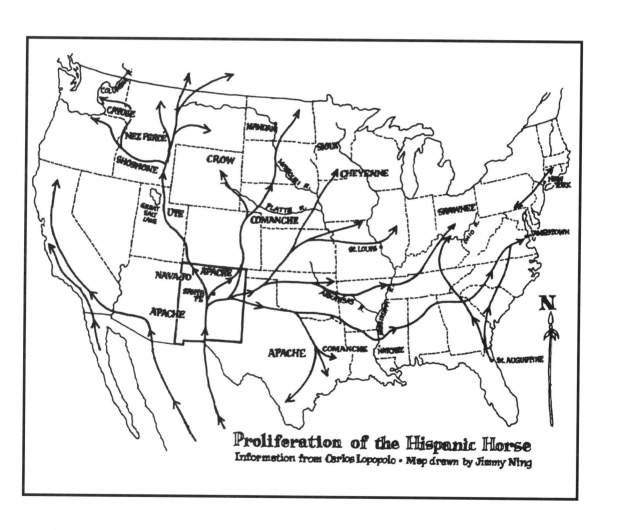

Proliferation of the Hispanic Horse
Information from Carlos Lopopolo • Map drawn by Jimmy Ning

American Occupation

1846 (Aug.-Sept.)

Brig. Gen. Stephen W. Kearny is Military Governor.

SOCIETY

Charles Bent writes about New Mexicans, stating: *..There is no stability in these people, they have no opinion of thare* [sic] *own, ...entirely governed by the powers that be ... the most servile people that can be imagined... they are not fit to be a free people, they should be ruled by others than themselves..."* [according to A. Sunseri].

KEARNY CODE

Francis Preston Blair, a professional lawyer and therefore assigned to the post of attorney general, is directed to draw up a code of laws for the territory, referred to as the **Kearny Code.** (Kearny "commandeers" the press of Fr. Martínez of Taos in order to print the Code and other items as well as controlling the flow of information to prevent a revolt.)

BOOKS

Eighteen-year-old **Susan Magoffin,** wife of Samuel Magoffin, arrives in N.M., the first American female to do so. She keeps a diary in which she records her impressions *"with a tolerance rare for most Americans, who consistently deprecated Spanish culture and religion:"*

Husband Samuel is referred to as *"mi alma"* (my soul).

The **Mora** settlements are *"a fit match for some of the genteel pig stys in the States..."*

The **women** smoke *"little cigarritas."*

To eat the *"chilly* [sic] *verde"* she has to double a piece of tortilla and use it as a scoop, native style.

She arrives believing the *"...Mexicans are as void of refinement and judgement as the dumb animals..."* but she changes her opinion, now seeing them as a *"...very quick and intelligent people ... decidedly polite, easy in their manners, perfectly free...how very happy and contented I am, how I am delighted with this new country, its people, my new house..."*

The **women** cover their faces with a flour paste beauty masque. They don't wear bustles as is the custom in the States.

Susan Magoffin doesn't **dance** but she reports on one, remarking that Mexicans are extremely talented dancers and the women dress in "silks, satins, ginghams."

S.M. is overwhelmed with the manners and maturity of "a little market girl" who would put ....many a mother in the U.S. to the blush.

At church the priest repeated some Latin "...neither understood by himself or his hearers..." The tunes she heard at church were "the same" heard at the dance.

Mexicans are a "strange people." They are brave when they have numbers with them if lead properly. "Take them one by one and they will not flinch from danger."

MEXICAN WAR BATTLE

December 25, 1846: Col. **Alexander W. Doniphan** is on his way to reinforce American forces fighting in Chihuahua when he engages and defeats Mexican troops at **Brazitos** in the Las Cruces-El Paso area [the only battle of the Mexican War to be fought on New Mexican soil, according to some sources].

1846-1847

Charles Bent is Governor.

1846
FORTS

Fort Marcy is established on a hill overlooking Sena Plaza in Santa Fe. [Named for Secretary of War William L. Marcy, it is the **first U.S. military post in the Southwest.** Twenty other forts are established in time: Ft. Lowell, Cantonment Burgwin, Ft. Union, Ft. Wingate I, Ft. Wingate II, Ft. Bascom, Ft. Sumner, Ft. Tularosa, Ft. Conrad, Ft. Craig, Camp Ojo Caliente, Ft. Stanton, Ft. West, Ft. McRae, Ft. Webster, Ft. Bayard, Ft. McLane, Ft. Thorn, Ft. Cummings, Ft. Selden, Ft. Fillmore.

FAMILY

Solomon Jacob Spiegelberg, one of the first Jews in N.M., sets up a business in Santa Fe along with his two brothers, **Levi** and **Elias**. Within a few years other Jews (**Staab, Seligman, Ilfeld**) and their family members are businessmen in N.M.

Charles Bent
Courtesy Museum of NM, #7004

CIVIL RIGHTS

October 9: **Governor Bent** writes to Col. Doniphan protesting the treatment meted out to New Mexicans by American soldiers: ***"...offensive and abusive conduct of the ... troops** of our command, my duty compels me to call on you to interpose your authority and compel the soldiers to respect the rights of the inhabitants. These outrages are becoming so frequent that I apprehend consequences may result sooner or later if measures are not taken to prevent them."*

[The Americans "lost no opportunity" to show New Mexicans what they thought about "greasers" according to W.A. Beck.]

REVOLT

Winter: Mounting discontent is brought to a head by **Diego Archuleta** and **Tomás Ortiz,** among others. A revolt is planned for December 19, then moved to the 25th. Plans are leaked and many arrests are made, stopping the rebellion. Archuleta and Ortiz flee to the south.

CONSPIRACY CHARGES

One day **Manuel Antonio Chaves** and the **Pino** brothers, Nicolás and Miguel, are sitting under the portal of the Exchange Hotel [now called the **La Fonda**] when they are arrested on a conspiracy charge. "*Certain persons of influence*" recommend to **Col. Sterling Price** that Chaves be "*shot immediately*" as an example to others and because he is the most dangerous fighter of the three but Price chooses to do things by legal procedure because he "*wished to demonstrate the equability of the American system of justice*" [according to W.A. Beck]. The Pinos are released and **Chaves is charged with treason against the United States.**

January, 1847: Captain **Angney** is assigned to defend Manuel Chaves. During the trial he points out that Manuel is still a citizen of Mexico, that the war is still raging, and it is patriotism, not treason, that causes Chaves to behave as he does, deserving "*the admiration of all brave men,*" that the United States would be forever disgraced "*if it undertook under any pretext to shoot a man for endeavoring to defend his country in time of need.*" Manuel Chaves is acquitted and released.

T I M E L I N E

1846: **Senator Lewis Cass** (Michigan) declares in Congress: "... *We do not want the people of Mexico, either as citizens or subjects. All we want is a portion of territory ... with a population which would recede, or identify itself with ours...*"

1847
REVOLT

January 19: **Governor Bent** believes the rebellion has been squelched. He is at his home in Taos when insurgents, Hispanos and Native Americans led by **Tomásito Romero** from Taos Pueblo, break into Bent's home and assassinate the Governor. Several others are killed, including **Cornelio Vigil** and **Narciso Beaubién.**

Padre Martínez is on his way to church when one **Elliot Lee** is being pursued by a mob bent on killing him. Martínez yells at the mob to find out what is going on and they tell him. He berates them as murderers and takes Lee into his own house, the mob not daring to follow. He warns them that American soldiers will soon arrive to mete out justice.

[N.M. historian **R.E. Twitchell** was later to write that Padre Martínez was the mastermind of the revolt because "*His power over his parishioners was absolute and his hatred of the Americans and American institutions was recognized by all.*" As proof he cites Bent, St. Vrain, and even Kit Carson. Angélico Chávez declares that the "*logic of politics*" must be investigated for "*bigotry no less ethnic than religious.*"]
"Anglos" are attacked in Mora and Arroyo Hondo.

January 24: Col. **Sterling Price** arrives in **Taos** and deploys cannon and other arms of overwhelming force against bows and arrows, destroying the insurgents led by **Pablo Montoya.** Some 150 rebels are slaughtered.

January 25: Captain **I.R. Hendley** leads some 80 men to **Mora** where an estimated 150 "insurrectionists" defend the town. Hendley is killed and since the contingent of **Missouri Volunteers** has no artillery they retreat to Las Vegas.

February 1: Captain **J.B. Morin** leads 200 men and artillery against **Mora**. The village is virtually destroyed with only a few buildings left standing according to H. Bryan.

May 20: Major **B.B. Edmonson** arrives in Las Vegas and dispatches two companies of Missouri Volunteers against raiders while he leads 75-80 soldiers to **Wagon Mound** where a small wagon train has been attacked.

May 26: Edmonson's troops are attacked at Red River Canyon [now called Canadian River Canyon] by "400 to 600" men, as reported by Edmonson. The attackers flee during the night.

Remembering General Kearny's *"not a pepper, not an onion"* promises, Mexican farmers complain that soldiers are allowing their horses, mules, and oxen to enter corn and wheat fields, thus destroying their crops. The complaints are ignored.

June 27: Raiders drive off military horse herds near Las Vegas. Four men sent to investigate never return.

July 5: Three Mexicans are apprehended and taken to Edmonson. They refuse to answer questions so a noose is placed around the neck of one of them and pulled into the air three times before he decides to tell what he knows: the four men were killed at Los Valles. Edmonson takes some 60 men and a 12 pound howitzer to Los Valles, destroys the village then sets fire to the rubble.

Las Vegas mayor **Juan de Dios Maese** is accused of complicity with the raiders and soldiers burn down his Gallinas River mill. (Maese is later exonerated and released.)

Edmonson sends 40 Mexicans to Santa Fe to face military court martial on **charges of treason**.

August 3: Mexicans convicted of treason against the United States are **executed by hanging**.

Lewis Garrard (an eye-witness who wrote about these events in *Wah-To-Yah and the Taos Trail*) is part of an expedition out of Bent's Fort which heads to N.M., the object of which is *"to travel as far as we could toward Taos; kill and scalp every Mexican to be found, and collect all the animals belonging to the Company and the U.S."*

By the time the group makes it to Taos the country has been pacified by Col. Price and many New Mexicans are put on trial.

While waiting for court the 17-year-old Garrard writes that smoking, while repugnant in ladies, *"certainly does enhance the charms of the Mexican señoritas ... How dulcet-toned are their voices, which, siren-like, irresistibly draw the willing victim within the giddy vortex of dissipation!"* But, in the final analysis, *"From the depraved moral education of the New Mexicans, there can be no intellectual enjoyment. The only attractions are of the baser sort."*

Judges for the court are **Carlos Beaubien** and **Joab Houghton.**

[Beaubien's son was killed by the rebels and Houghton was a close friend of the murdered Charles Bent. Foreman of the grand jury was one of Bent's brothers.]

A jury is empanelled.

[The edition omits Garrard's depiction of the jury so we must go to R.E. Twitchell for the following report.]

One of the jurors, a Frenchman named Baptiste, *with not two ideas above eating and drinking, goes to 'Monsieur Chad-week'* [Chadwick] and asks *"Vot shall I say?"*

Chad replies, *"Keep still, man, until we talk awhile to the rest about it."*

"Vot shall we do?"

"Baptiste man, keep still! Why hang them, of course. What did you come in here for? Wait till I'm done with these Mexicans [part of the jury] *and I will tell you what to do."*

Baptiste understands: *"Hang 'em, sacre enfants des garces...hang 'em, hang 'em, sacree!"*

[Garrard is now quoted by Twitchell: I

"It certainly did appear to be a great assumption on the part of the Americans to conquer a country, and then arraign the revolting inhabitants for treason ... Treason indeed! The poor wretches ... Men remanded to jail till the day of execution, they drew their serapes more closely around them and accompanied the armed guard."

[Now Twitchell omits the rest of Garrard's paragraph, which states:

"I left the room, sick at heart. Justice! Out upon the word, when its distorted meaning is the warrant for murdering those who defend to the last their country and their homes."
Mexican patriots are executed by hanging at Santa Fe and Taos for treason against the U.S.

[These events have been depicted by W.A. Beck as being *"in accordance with the traditions of Anglo-Saxon justice"* because the rebels were given *"a fair trial."* The composition of the court and jury couldn't be helped due to the nature of the *"closely-knit"* community.

Considering the situation, *"that a trial was even held"* established a *"valuable introduction to the U.S. legal system."*

It is often written that "one" individual was executed for treason because prosecuting attorney **Francis Preston Blair,** a lawyer by profession, *"believed"* General Kearny had granted citizenship and *"did not understand"* that a general wasn't empowered to do so.

New Mexico author Howard Bryan reports that while President James Polk stated that he *"agreed with the punishment,"* military officials in N.M. were in error in *"designating and describing the crimes of conquered Mexican inhabitants as treason against the United States."* President Polk then appears to have dismissed the matter as unimportant but the fallacy that New Mexicans were immediate citizens of the U.S. has been perpetuated: R.E Dickey writes that *"Since hardly a skirmish occurred in the taking of N.M., and both the Spanish residents and the Pueblos were peaceful and cooperative, there was no excuse to overwhelm the region with Yankee strength.* ***The Spanish villagers were given automatic citizenship in the United States."***

These heinous events transpired in 1846 and citizenship wasn't granted until 1912.]

1847 (con't)
NEWSPAPER REPORT
April 29: The [unnamed writer] *Missouri Republican* states: *"A country with but few exceptions is inhabited by ignorant, dishonest, treacherous men; and women who are believed scarcely what virtue
is beyond the name, is now part of the American Union! Are they worthy of a protection from the
Indians?"*

The following month it declares: *"Verily, annexation of such a horde of barbarians and slaves, is a
novelty in our history. I say slave for a large number of the Mexican population are actually
slaves, though not in the same sense in which we use the term in the United States."*

SOCIETY
Some "Anglos" in N.M. refer to the **Army** as a military mob.

LAW
Fernando Aragón of Taos writes to **Donaciano Vigil**: "It is my bad luck to have been appointed Sheriff
because I do not understand these new laws. Please teach me to understand this new code."

LITERACY
Lieutenant Abert writes: *"I have been much surprised by the many men and children of the lower class
that I have met with who both **read and write;** in fact, all that we questioned seemed to be
educated."*

TIMELINE

August 22, 1847. The U.S. army is poised on the outskirts of Mexico City when Generals **Santa Anna** and **Scott** agree to an armistice then enter into negotiations. Four Mexican representatives meet with North American envoy **Nicholas Trist**. [Griswold del Castillo writes: *"Had it not been for Trist, all of Mexico might have been made part of the United States.*]

September 1: Negotiations begin in earnest and a tentative agreement is reached after several days: the U.S. will annex Alta California, New Mexico, and pay $30,000,000; Mexico will retain the Nueces River as a boundary which will continue in a line that permits Mexico to retain San Diego. But Presidents **Polk** and **Santa Anna** reject the agreement: if the U.S. accepts the Nueces River as a boundary it will be tacit admission that the U.S. is guilty of aggressive warfare because the first battles were south of the Nueces. Santa Anna wanted to retain Monterey Bay and refused to consider the annexation of N.M. Negotiations are broken off and Scott's army fights the bloodiest battle of the war at **Molino del Rey**.

September 13 : **Chapultepec Castle** is captured and the American army enters Mexico City. Santa Anna resigns and the City surrenders the next day. Trist contacts the new Mexican president in an effort to reopen negotiations.

November 16 : **Polk now realizes that all of Mexico is his for the taking.** Trist is ordered to return to Washington.

Trist informs Mexican officials that he will take their latest offer to Washington but some individuals want him to stay despite his recall.

December 4: **Trist decides to ignore his recall and forge an agreement, if possible, to end the war.**

December 6: Trist writes to **Secretary of State Buchanan** to explain his actions. Trist *"assumed that Polk did not truly want peace"* and the infuriated president *"made Trist an outlaw within his administration,"* writing in his personal diary that Trist's letter is *"arrogant, imprudent, and very insulting to his government, and even personally offensive to the President."* But Polk takes no action.

January 2, 1848: Final negotiations begin and continue until a treaty is agreed to by negotiators.

February 2, 1848: The treaty is signed and sent for ratification. There is much deliberation over articles in the treaty on both sides of the projected border. American officials demand that **Article 10 be deleted**, saying there was ample security for **land titles** in the eighth and ninth articles. Buchanan assures that Mexican property, religion, and liberty will be protected by the Constitution, saying: *"These invaluable blessings, under our form of government, do not result from treaty stipulations, but from the very nature and character of our institutions."* However, Buchanan and Secretary of the Treasury Walker openly oppose the treaty because it doesn't giveenough land to the U.S.

[Sam Houston wanted to take land as far south as Vera Cruz and Jefferson Davis wanted all of the northern Mexican states.]

The **Whig Party** opposes it because it would gain too much territory which would only be used to increase the slavocracy's power in Congress. Mexicans declare that the U.S. doesn't want to protect bona fide land titles and that Mexicans in the ceded territories would be victimized by American racism.

May 3 0, 1848: Ratifications of the **Treaty of Guadalupe Hidalgo** are exchanged and entered into force, **with Article 10 deleted**.

[Westphall quotes Malcolm Ebright as considering the deletion *"a cunning stratagem employed by the Polk administration to evade a clear-cut statement of a standard that will be used to adjudicate land grants in the newly acquired territories."* American authorities could now do as they wished with regard to land titles.]

LEGISLATIVE

December 6: Acting Governor **Donaciano Vigil** addresses the first **General Assembly,** initiated by Vigil himself, by asking it to formulate laws for N.M. Everyone understands that **Col. Price** can accept or reject any laws.

SOCIETY

December 17: **Padre Martínez** of Taos and other leading Hispanos sign a petition of loyalty to the U.S., rejecting rebellion or violence.

1847-1848

Col. Sterling Price is Military Governor.
Donaciano Vigil is Civil Governor.

LAW & MILITARY

Justice of the Peace **Desiderio Baca** decides a case that military authorities review and reverse. Baca resigns in protest.

Col. **Price has the real authority in N.M.** Price can imprison anyone, deny a jury trial, and prevent the use of *habeas corpus* according to R.W. Larson. The **Kearny Code** is observed or ignored as Col. Price wishes.

Sterling Price
Courtesy Museum of NM, #10350

1848-1849

Col. John M. Washington is Military Governor.

1848

T I M E L I N E

1848: **Senator J.C. Calhoun** (S.C.) declares in Congress: ... *To incorporate Mexico would be the first departure of the kind, for more than half of its population are pure Indians and by far the larger portion of the residue are mixed. Ours is the government of the white man. The great misfortune of what was formerly Spanish America, is to be traced to the fatal error of placing the colored race on an equality with the white. That error destroyed the social arrangement which formed the basis of their society. This error we have wholly escaped ... Are we to associate with ourselves as equals, companions, and fellow citizens, the Indians and mixed races of Mexico? I would consider such association as degrading to ourselves and fatal to our institutions.*

AGRICULTURE

The **Río Puerco** area is a garden spot of N.M. Hispanic ranchers graze thousands of sheep on the *(Ojo del Espíritu Santo* Grant) land. The community of **Cabezón** is established by settlers from **Peña Blanca** and extensive irrigation systems are constructed, diverting water from the Río Puerco.

MILITARY

Secretary of Defense **William L. Marcy** issues instructions that *"The important duty of the military force will be to protect the inhabitants of the Territory of New Mexico in the full enjoyment of life, liberty and property."*

SOCIETY

The family of **Rafaél Chacón** moves to the Mora area in an effort to escape the severities of the American occupation. The family is impoverished by the change of sovereignty.

LEGISLATIVE

January 11: On the opening of **New Mexico's first legislative session** under the Kearny Code an [unnamed] observer writing for the *Missouri Republican* states that he is *"...really **disappointed in finding so intelligent looking an assembly of Mexicans.** I am certain they are not just representatives of their constituents, for a more ignorant and degraded lot never set up pretensions to civilization than a large majority of the population of this Territory...proceedings in both houses conducted in dignity and decorum and in a manner highly creditable to men unaccustomed to any system of legislature. All that is wanted is a little time and a little labor to make New Mexico a worthy and respectable portion of the United States... "*

[Pre-Territorial legislatures operate despite interference from military commanders. For example, when the legislature attempted to pass a land registry law, Sterling Price vetoed it.]

MILITARY

March: Additional regular troops are assigned to N.M. but they don't arrive so Major Washington authorizes the raising of five **volunteer companies** *"....for the protection of the property and lives of the inhabitants of the territory of New Mexico against the depredations of the marauding bands of Indians which infest it."*

[Despite the change in sovereignty and promises of protection, New Mexicans are thus responsible for defending themselves as they had been for centuries. The Treaty of Guadalupe Hidalgo stipulated that the U.S. would be responsible for controlling Indian raiders, including those going into Mexico. General **Thomas S. Jesup** stated that raiders should be allowed to pillage in Mexico to prevent them from doing so in the U.S., that if the Indian treaties didn't guarantee their subsistence the Indians would raid or starve, so the U.S. must either feed them as guaranteed by treaties or exterminate them altogether.]

EDUCATION
May: **Francisco Ortiz** announces the availability of **textbooks and a classroom** for anyone wishing to start a school in Santa Fe.

TIMELINE

May 30, 1848: **Treaty of Guadalupe Hidalgo** is ratified only after Article 10 (which provided *"a fair standard for adjudicating land grants"*) is deleted from the Treaty. Mexican commissioners insert the **Protocol of Querétaro** that states the U.S. isn't trying to annul legitimate land grants by deleting Article 10 and is accepted by American commissioners. The **U.S. State Department later refuses to recognize the validity of the Protocol**, thus enabling American authorities to have a free hand at adjudicating land titles.

TRAIL RECORD
Francis X. Aubry traverses the Santa Fe Trail from Santa Fe to Independence, Missouri, about 800 miles, in five days and 16 hours [a record that was never broken].

SOCIETY
August 2: Two-hundred weary gold seekers known as the "Peoria Company" and guided by the infamous Apache scalp hunter **James Kirker,** arrive at Galisteo. One of the group, "Old Roberts," purchases 500 sheep for $250. Upon reaching California he sells his sheep in the gold camps for more than $8,000.

MILITARY & NAVAJOS
Col. Washington leads an expedition into Navajo country. A peace treaty is signed, then as everyone prepares to leave there is a dispute over a horse. As the Navajos ride away Col. Washington orders his troops to fire on them, including cannons, killing several among whom is **Narbona,** the most important peace chief of the Navajo people.
[Lt. **James H. Simpson** keeps a journal of the expedition in which he names the highest peak of the Cebolleta Mts., *Mt. San Mateo* to Hispanics, as **Mount Taylor.** When the new name is used on a map it becomes permanent.]
STATEHOOD
October 10: Influential citizens in Santa Fe convene to decide on New Mexico's status within the Union.

There is so much discord that some members withdraw. After four days a Memorial is drafted asking Congress for *"the speedy organization by law of a Territorial Civil Government..."* which will unequivocally **exclude Negro slavery and absolute rejection of Texas boundary claims.**

1849-1851
Col. John Munroe is Military Governor.

1849
SETTLEMENT
Costilla is settled by **Carlos Beaubién,** who owns the **Sangre de Cristo** land grant.

PROFILE

PROTESTANTISM IN N.M.

1849: Baptist missionary **Hiram W. Reed** arrives in Santa Fe. Three fellow ministers follow and all work to establish congregations and day schools.

1850s: Methodist and Presbyterian ministers are now in N.M.

1854: Baptists build a chapel in Santa Fe. It is used by missionaries of other groups until 1866 when the Presbyterians purchase the building and land.

1863: Rt. Rev. Josiah C. Talbot, Bishop of the Northwest, makes a visitation to N.M,

1866: Presbyterians are active in establishing churches and day schools.

1870s: Mormon families from Utah are established in villages like Ramah.

1871: Methodist minister **Thomas Harwood** arrives in Watrous and is active in New Mexican society for a quarter of a century.

1880: The Congregational Church is formally organized in N.M.

1900: The major Protestant denominations are established throughout N.M.(In time impressive conference centers like Ghost Ranch and Glorieta Assebly are established.)

1990s: It is said the Southern Baptists dominate the state's Protestant community, claiming more members than all other Protestant groups combined.

MILITARY & APACHES

August: **Jicarilla Apache** chieftain **Francisco Chacón** leads a contingent toward Las Vegas to sign a peace treaty. Army troops attack and kill fourteen of his group. The daughter of Chief **Lobo Blanco** (White Wolf) is captured and jailed in Las Vegas.

Capt. **H.R. Judd** later reports that the Apaches intended to "commit depredations" so he ordered their seizure which resulted in hand-to-hand "conflict" and a routing of the enemy.

According to a newspaper report, the captured female is later taken to Wagon Mound by soldiers and ordered to point out the Apache camp. At the top of the mound she seizes a knife and attacks the 20 soldiers and is shot to death by *"a Sgt. Martínez."*

Indian Agent **John Greiner** reports the incident differently: that 20 soldiers under the command of Sgt. H. Swartwond go in pursuit of Indians and take the Apache daughter along as a guide and hostage to be exchanged for a captured white woman. The detachment camps for the night at Wagon Mound where the young Apache woman asks to go to the top of the mound where she begins to weep, causing the soldiers to believe she is trying to warn her people. In the morning when the soldiers are *"trying to load the woman into a wagon"* she seizes a butcher knife and tries to stab them, causing her to be shot dead.

GOVERNMENT AT PUEBLOS

Supt. of Indian Affairs **James S. Calhoun** remarks on how Pueblo Indians seek legal channels for redress to grievances from *"Mexican oppressions."* At a later date he is *"excessively annoyed, for the last fifteen days, by complaints from these Indians."*

[C.R. Cutter observes that Pueblo petitions to American officials weren't *"miraculous overnight adaptation to Anglo law but rather the product of their long experience with Hispanic legal procedures."* Few English language writers of history seem to be aware of historical realities mentioned by Dr. Cutter.]

COMANCHERO TRADE

Calhoun is astonished that Mexicans and Pueblos go out on the plains and trade with Comanches, especially during the months of August and September. He wants to put a diplomatic stop to it so he makes rules to govern the trade:

Pueblos are given a trading permit upon request, without fee.

Mexicans must supply testimonials of good character, post a bond of up to $5,000, pledge not to trade in war materiel, state the specific tribes with whom they are going to trade, and pay $10 for a license.

Three licenses are issued to Mexicans during Calhoun's first year but he learns that unlicensed Mexican traders "club" with others possessing a license. Since regulations are made very difficult to comply with, many traders, Pueblo and Hispanic, merely go out and trade as they always have.

Calhoun also reports: *"The wild Indians of this country have been so much more successful in their robberies since General Kearney* [sic] *took possession of the country, they do not believe we have the power to chastise them."*

RAIDS

October: Traders discover a number of dead bodies, victims of an Indian attack, at the Point of Rocks area on the Cimarron branch of the Santa Fe Trail. One of the victims is **J.M. White** who was traveling with his wife Ann, daughter Virginia, and a black female slave, all of whom are missing. (It is later learned the attackers were Apaches led by **Lobo Blanco,** whose daughter was taken earlier by soldiers who had attacked the group of Jicarillas led by Francisco Chacón.) A $ 1,000 reward is offered for the return of Ann and Virginia White and a company of dragoons goes out to rescue them and is later joined by Kit Carson.

November: The Apache camp is discovered but the element of surprise is lost and Ann White is riddled with arrows.

[Nothing is ever learned about the daughter or black slave.]

EMIGRATION

Padre Ramón Ortiz is the envoy of the Mexican government to help people emigrate to Chihuahua if so desired. Major Washington assures him of American cooperation as stipulated in the peace treaty. Ortiz begins at **El Vado** where it was believed there was the smallest number of persons wishing to return to the republic of Mexico. Of the less than 1,000 or so families living in the settlements more than 900 enlisted to leave *"..a country whose government gave them fewer guarantees than our own and in which they were treated with more disdain than members of the African race...,"* even with the understanding that all their lands would be forfeited to the U.S. government. Ortiz writes that *"...those who didn't enlist failed to do so because the heads of families were absent."* Upon seeing the enthusiastic response to Padre Ortiz and some 3,000 New Mexicans fleeing American aggression, the authorities refuse to allow Ortiz to visit other parts of N.M. and the migration effort is terminated.

SOCIETY

Juan Bautista Vigil y Alaríd, who delivered the proclamation of welcome that asserted *a wonderful future* awaited New Mexicans upon becoming Americans, is among those who flee their homeland to rid themselves of American oppression, selling his properties in Santa Fe and settling in a village near Chihuahua. He opens a drug store and works there for three years then moves to **Mesilla,** a Mexican town just south of the American border established by New Mexicans who couldn't tolerate American injustice in their native land.

[The area came under American domination in 1854 with the **Gadsden Purchase.**]

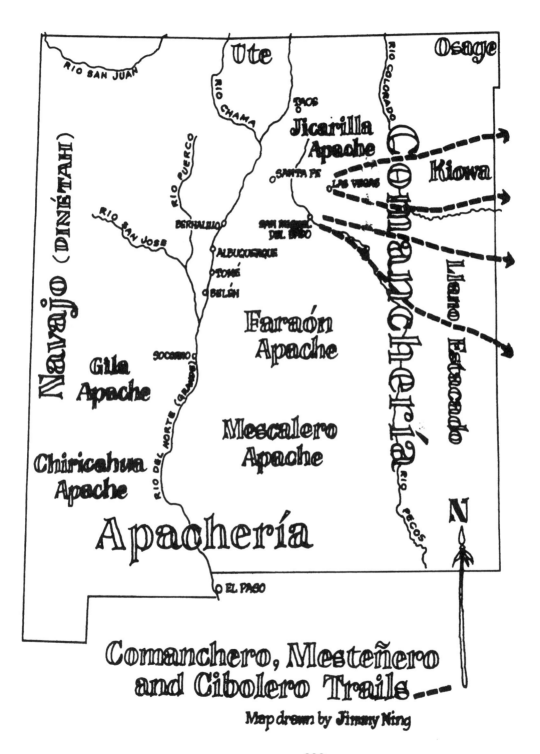

Comanchero, Mesteñero
and Cibolero Trails ---

Map drawn by Jimmy Ning

PROFILE

Padre Ramón Ortiz

H E R O   I N   T W O   W O R L D S

1813: Ramón Ortiz is born in Santa Fe. Teresa, Ramón's mother, dies a few months later but she instructs her eldest daughter, Ana María, that Ramón is to be raised for the priesthood. The daughter vows it will be so.

Ana María marries Colonel **Antonio Vizcarra,** the noted Indian fighter who defeated the Navajo in western New Mexico and who also served as Governor. Vizcarra becomes Ramón's idol and the boy decides for a career in the military instead of the priesthood.

1822: Ana María holds true to her mother's wishes and sends Ramón to a seminary in Durango, Mexico. The boy studies hard but he is miserable and writes many letters to Vizcarra asking him to help him get into a military academy. Vizcarra becomes so concerned over Ramón that he travels south to see him. The two spend long hours talking and it is decided Vizcarra will send Ramón to a military academy in France. But a cholera epidemic breaks out in Durango and Vizcarra dies. Ana María writes that Ramón must stay and fulfill his mother's dying wish. He remains at the seminary until he is ordained a priest.

Padre Ramón serves as a missionary in northern Mexico then he is assigned to the parish of **Guadalupe de El Paso** (where he would remain for the next 50 years).

1841: **Governor Armijo** captures the invading Texans of the Texas-Santa Fe expedition and sends the prisoners off to Mexico City. The ragged, starving Texans make it to El Paso where the military commandant General J. Elías y González asks Padre Ortiz to clothe and feed the suffering prisoners. The padre's sisters and many townspeople help to sew clothes, cook meals, donate medicine, bandages, shaving items, etc. for the men. One of the prisoners, a journalist named **George W. Kendall** [who later wrote a book in which he criticized almost everything pertaining to Southwestern Hispanics] commends Padre Ortiz and the charitable people of El Paso.

1846: Col. **Alexander Doniphan** seizes El Paso for the United States and immediately arrests Padre Ortiz because he has been alerting Mexican forces in Chihuahua as to the U.S. advance. Doniphan marches toward Chihuahua and takes Ortiz along as his prisoner though Padre Ramón is allowed to travel in his own coach. When army provisions give out on the road Ortiz shares his with the hungry, thirsty soldiers.

1848: Believing the Treaty of Guadalupe Hidalgo to be unfair and much too harsh, Padre Ortiz works against its ratification but his efforts fail. With his beloved New Mexico in U.S. hands he leads the effort to enable Hispanics to move across the new border but American authorities put a stop to his efforts when they see how many people want to get away from the severities of USA domination.

From Juárez he continues to minister to needs on either side of the border. He becomes famous as a mediator, a friend of the poor, and he raises dozens of orphans in his home. The people truly love him.

1896: Padre Ramón Ortiz dies of cancer. The *El Paso Times* writes: His *great heart was full of kindness, his nature was gentleness itself, and he did good for the love of doing it.*

MAIL

New Mexico's first **Post Office** is established, in Santa Fe.

1850: The second Post Office is opened, in Las Vegas. Custom has it that the receiver, not the sender, pays for postage.

1851: Six more post offices are opened, including Albuquerque and Socorro. When word gets out that mail has arrived it is necessary to drop by the post office and ask if mail has been received for so-and-so. (If mail remained unclaimed the post office would publish a list of those people's names in the newspaper.)

1878: Some 145 post offices have been authorized in N.M. (though some had closed down by this date).

LEGISLATIVE

September 24: **Delegates convene to establish some sort of government for N.M. Fray Martínez** of Taos is elected to preside over the group. A committee is selected to create a constitution. **Hugh N. Smith** is designated envoy to Washington to watch over issues crucial to New Mexico. Indian hostilities delay Smith's arrival in Washington.

1849-1950
NEWSPAPERS

The New Mexican newspaper is in publication throughout these years. The publication is in English with Spanish translations. News is dominant but poetry and literary prose are also included.

1850s
CARPENTRY

"Anglo-American" cabinetmakers introduce the frame saw and molding plane, with which New Mexican craftsmen create a rich variety of decorative patterns and continue the unique style of New Mexican furniture.

Gabriel Jeantet, the son of a French fur trapper who married a Taos woman, is recognized as a master cabinetmaker and blacksmith. He works in Taos all his life and his sons **Filiberto and Plácido** also become cabinet makers.

1850

RELIGIOUS

There are 16 Catholic clergymen in N.M., all of them native born.

RETALIATION RAID

Chief **Lobo Blanco** strikes again at the very place where his daughter was killed the year before. **Lt. Ambrose Burnside** [of later Civil War fame and for whom his style of facial hair was named "burnsides" which became *sideburns*] reports on the deaths of the mail carriers and others who accompanied them.

MAIL

July 1: The U.S. Post Office inaugurates mail service between Independence and Santa Fe. The mail is guarded by eight men armed with repeating rifles who can fire a total of 136 shots without stopping to reload.

MILITARY

The American military in N.M. numbers 1,019 officers and men: five companies of the First Dragoons, four companies of the Second Dragoons, 10 companies of the Third Infantry, and two companies of the Second Artillery.

Military posts are increased to 11 with the addition of Abiquiú, Las Vegas, Rayado, San Elizario, and Cebolleta.

PROFILE

Jesús Arviso

NAVAJO STATESMAN

Jesús Arviso, age 13, is captured in Sonora, Mexico, by a band of Apaches led by **Mangas Coloradas.** He is taken north and traded to Navajos led by *Bi'éélizhinii,* Black Shirt, who adopts him as a member of his family with the name Sóós.

1860: While camping in the Ft. Defiance area Arviso's family is approached by Cavalry soldiers. Jesús rides out to let them know the camp is friendly and talks to the soldiers led by Capt. McLaws, who winds up offering Arviso a job as interpreter for the Army. Jesús accepts the offer and in time becomes one of the Army's best interpreters and guides.

1861: Arviso interprets at a peace treaty for the first time. He is very impressed with **Ganado**

Mucho when he speaks.
1863: Kit Carson leads the Army's rampage into **Dinétah, Navajoland**.

[General Carleton ordered the removal of the Navajos because he believed there might be gold in their country.]

Arviso advises **Barboncito, Delgadito**, and **Sarracino** to come to Ft. Wingate and discuss matters with Commanding Officer **J. Francisco Chávez.**
March, 1864: Arviso decides to go to **Bosque Redondo** in the Ft. Sumner area along with his Navajo people. The march is one of inhumane cruelty, those who can't keep up being shot on the spot, as are those who try to help the fallen. Raiders and soldiers take what they want from the people, including women. Upon arriving at Bosque Redondo conditions go from bad to worse and 1,500 Navajos die during their imprisonment.

1865: Jesús gives positive information on the Navajos when questioned by military authorities.

1868: Arviso accompanies Barboncito for an interview with President Johnson. Jesús translates Barboncito's Navajo commentary into Spanish then James Sutherland puts it into English for the President, then the process is reversed. Johnson decides the Navajo people should be allowed to return to their homeland.
[American officials had since learned there was no gold in Dinétah.]

The walk back home is more joyful than the one to the concentration camp but still very difficult. Once on their native soil the Diné are given two or three sheep for every Navajo (a great contrast to the thousands they owned before).

Arviso settles his family east of **Tohatchi** and his services as interpreter are still needed by the government.

1872: Arviso goes to the Shiprock area with Agent J.H. Miller and T.V. Kearn in search of a good locale for a new agency office in the San Juan Valley. They are attacked by Utes and Miller is killed.
Chee Dodge is hired as interpreter. Chee translates directly from Navajo into English.

1880s: Jesús Arviso meets **Dr. Washington Matthews**, army surgeon at Ft. Defiance, who wants to write down Navajo legends and stories. Jesús helps him and suggests he also write about sandpainting. Chee Dodge helps with the work.

1884: Nearly 50, Arviso wants only to return to his family at Tohatchi and live out his remaining years.

1932: Jesús Arviso dies.

STATEHOOD

June 20: New Mexicans approve a State constitution and **"...urge upon Congress the admission of this Territory into the Union as a State."**

Slavery is rejected as are Texas land claims to N.M. territory east of the Río Grande.

Dr. **Henry Connelly** is elected Governor, Manuel Alvarez is Lt. Governor, and William Messervy is Delegate to Congress.

The **Statehood party** is in control of the legislature.

Col. Munroe is still the authority in power. He declares the newly elected government will *"...remain inoperative until New Mexico be admitted as a State..."* and warns of the *"...unstable elements of the Mexican character, the general ignorance of the people, their manifest dislike, although latent to [sic] Americans, and the strong sympathies a large number entertain for Mexican institutions and its government as opposed to that of the United States..."* He denies the authority of the selected state officials and continues to act as civil and military governor.

[This is a sharp contrast to Brig. Gen. Bennett Riley who is overseeing similar circumstances in **California** where efforts toward State government and statehood are encouraged.]

Richard Weightman, elected Senator, warns that the opposition plans to report about revolution or to foment violent disturbances by oppressing the people then have the military called out and argue the unfitness of New Mexico for self-government and thus defeat the Statehood movement.

September 9: Congress decrees that N.M. will be a Territory, so all previous elections for office are nullified.

TIMELINE

1850: **California and Utah become States in the Union.**

LEGISLATIVE

The **Organic Act of 1850** provides a bicameral legislature for N.M., a House numbering 23 members and a Council of 13, empowered to debate and pass bills, the Governor (appointed by the President of the U.S.) being able to veto any bill.

The national Congress has to approve all legislation [which was never done with any other territory of the U.S.].

The majority of legislators are Hispanic, not fluent in English, causing all proceedings to be published in English and Spanish, since American authorities are not fluent in Spanish.

The Organic Act acknowledges commitment to the Treaty of Guadalupe Hidalgo but, according to J.E. Holmes, also provides the territorial legislature with an option to restrict voting rights:

> *Every free white male inhabitant, above the age of twenty-one years, who shall have been a resident of said territory at the time of the passage of this act, shall be entitled to vote at the first election, and shall be eligible to any office within the said territory, **but the qualifications of voters and of holding office at all subsequent elections, shall be such as prescribed by the legislative assembly...***

[Therefore members of the "legislative assembly" can pass a law to deny people the right to hold office or even vote, but because of numbers Hispanics who don't hold to such views get into the assembly. But New Mexicans do not have full civil rights: they aren't allowed to vote for their governor or the president of the U.S.; the decisions of their elected representatives are subject to federal approval and the judiciary isn't independent; New Mexico's Pueblo Indians, voting citizens under Mexico, are disenfranchised under American rule. In 1849, Indian Agent James S. Calhoun visits all Pueblos and convinces them to accept ward status, which they do in 1851.]

Some "Anglo" observers like **W.W.H. Davis** believe native New Mexicans are incompetent when it comes to the workings of democracy.

[This is the same charge leveled at the inhabitants of Louisiana when it was taken over by the USA.]

Territorial and Statehood factions are now identifiable:

Territorial proponents include judge Houghton, judge Carlos Beaubién, and Thomas Johnson, known as the **Houghton faction.**

Among Statehood proponents are Richard Weightman, J.S. Calhoun, and Manuel Alvarez, the **Alvarez faction.** (See **1872.**)

PROFILE

Pat Garrett

THE PEOPLE'S SHERIFF

Pat Garrett is born in Alabama. The family moves to Louisiana where his father runs a small plantation that is ravaged during the Civil War.

1869: Pat works as a cowboy in Dallas County, Texas.

1875-77: Garrett is a buffalo-hide hunter on the southern Texas plains.

1878: Pat Garrett settles in the Pecos Valley at Fort Sumner where he frequents saloons, dance halls, and meets people like Pete Maxwell, John Chisum, William Bonney, etc. Sociable, easy-going and enjoying a good conversation, he is popular with Hispanic people, who call him *Juan Largo* because he is six-feet-four-inches tall and slim.

1879: Garrett moves to Roswell and is appointed Deputy Sheriff by George Kimball.

1880: Garrett marries Apolinaria Gutiérrez of Fort Sumner.

November: He is elected Sheriff over George Kimball, who has been unable to capture cattle thieves, especially Billy the Kid. (See **1878.**)

Pat Garrett
Courtesy Museum of NM, #46217

BOOKS

Col. **G. A. McCall** writes his *Report on Conditions in New Mexico*:

Pueblo people are *"intelligent, moral, sober, and industrious ... better off than the lower class of Mexicans."* Many of them speak Spanish and officials can write it well enough to function in business.

Mexicans are like those found elsewhere but *"the effect of intercourse with our people, have begun to show themselves."* There is less filth in Santa Fe streets *"...and the improved dress and personal cleanliness of the people, together with the cloaking of immorality...."* are due to American example.

People of **Spanish blood** are few, that of the Indian predominates. Native people have an *"...extreme aversion to continued labour."* They love the cigarrito, the fandango [dance], and the monte table. The lower class is as ignorant as it is idle and education is *"woefully neglected"* amongst all classes.

Manufacturing is at the lowest possible level. Mining is neglected because of *"an inherent fear of los Indios."*

"Nabajoes" and Apaches are a menace to stock raising. *"The Nabajoes said on a recent occasion their only reason for not exterminating the New Mexicans long ago was that it was in their interest to keep them as their shepherds."*

The status of agriculture is the worst of all.

"Cibolletta" [Cebolleta] is an important military post because Navajo trails pass through the vicinity.

About 83 people have been killed by Indians during the year and some 13 have been taken captive. Stolen stock numbers about 114,050.

POPULATION
The Census of 1850 [not considered very accurate] states that there are 56, 984 non-Indians residing in N.M., about 550 of these being classified as "Anglos."

WEAVING
Río Grande blankets are very aesthetic because they are made with "designs that were vastly more complex in structure than any of the previous weavings." The old striped design persists in the coarser weaves.
[Navajo technique and design are not incorporated into Río Grande blankets.]

ARCHITECTURE
Pitched roofs begin to appear in Santa Fe.

SHEEP COMMERCE
William Z. Angney, of French extraction, and his group of "Anglo" businessmen buy 6,000 sheep to sell in California. He finally manages to sell his stock the following year.

SHEEP RANCHING
N.M. sheepmen are cut off from traditional business contacts and because the land is now U.S. territory new arrangements must be made *"...in a world of strangers where shady business practices were the rule"* according to J.0. Baxter.

The rich sheep industry of N.M. burgeons eastward. **Comanches** are peaceful but it is estimated that **Apaches** steal around 450,000 sheep between 1846-1850.

AGRICULTURE

The **Río Abajo** (land "down river," south of La Bajada) is highly cultivated and considered the most productive ranching section of N.M.

HISPANO MERCHANTS

Among the most prominent New Mexican families involved in commercial capitalism are the Otero, Perea, Yrizarri, Armijo, Chávez, Luna, Baca, González, Barela, etc., clans:

Vicente Otero and his sons Antonio José, Manuel Antonio, and Miguel Antonio I have important roles in the history of N.M., family members being involved in commerce, ranching, and politics.

Juan and **José Leandro Perea** are heavily involved in the Santa Fe Trade at least by 1844 when they bring in more than $40,000 worth of goods. By 1870 José Leandro Perea is the wealthiest man in the territory with assets listed at $408,000.

Mariano Yrizarri owns several stores (one located in Ranchos de Albuquerque) and runs wagon trains to bring in merchandise from the East. In July of 1859 Yrizarri ships in 63 tons of goods. By the 1870s his assets are worth about $500,000 and he owns 100,000 sheep.

The **Armijo family** produces several traders who ply the Santa Fe Trail: Cristóbal, Rafaél (cousin to Governor Manuel Armijo), Manuel, Nestor, and Juan own about five percent of all wagons traveling through Council Grove in 1859. Salvador Armijo, cousin to Rafaél and Manuel, is another successful businessman and astute politician who owns a major store on the Albuquerque plaza.

The above rico families are followed by others of considerable means like the Delgado, Vigil, Ortiz, Gallegos, Sandoval, Gutiérrez, Sánchez, etc., clans. Other merchants like Miguel Córdova, Manuel García, Prudencio López, Pablo Pino, Antonio Ribera, etc., are also well-to-do. (More than half of the wealthiest New Mexicans reside in the Río Abajo.)

New Mexicans involved in the Santa Fe Trade have a reach that extends to California in the west, Mexico City in the south, New Orleans, Pittsburgh, Baltimore, and New York to the east, as well as England, France, Italy, Spain, and Portugal.

LEGISLATURE & BLACK SLAVERY

Despite American pressure, the legislative convention rejects the legal introduction of black slavery into N.M.

SOCIETY

Moses Sachs, a 28-year-old single Jewish merchant born in Germany, is the only non-Hispanic living in Los Lunas.

1850-1860

Cebolleteños, a band of men from Cebolleta on the Navajo frontier, can be hired to kidnap young Navajo boys and girls. (It is a custom for wealthy Hispanics to give one or two of these young Navajos as a bridal gift to a newly wedded couple.)

PIONEERS

Hispanic settlers found La Placita [later to be renamed **Lincoln**] and are farming in the Hondo River Valley.

1840-1863: *El Torreón*, Lincoln's lookout tower and place for protection from Indian attacks, is built sometime during this period by **Andricus Trujillo,** who might have emigrated from Manzano, along with other colonists.

1850: Hispanics are engaged in placer gold mining in the Jicarilla Mountains [near the later site of **White Oaks**].

TIMELINE

Between 1850 and 1865 the U.S. federal government spends **$15,000 to keep the peace with the Pueblo people** of the Southwest but it has to spend **$30,000,000 to fight the Plains Indians.**

Territorial Government

1851-1852

James S. Calhoun is Governor.

1851
SETTLEMENT
San Luis [the oldest settlement in present-day Colorado] is founded
    by families from Taos and Mora.

RELIGION
Reverend **W.J. Kephardt** is the first Presbyterian (Protestant) mission-
    ary in N.M., to be followed by Reverends **David E.**
    McFarland (Santa Fe, 1866), **J.A. Annin** (Las Vegas), **James**
    M. Roberts (Taos), Sheldon Jackson and **Alexander M.**
    Darley (Colorado). They *"came under attack from the*
    Catholic press."

BISHOP LAMY & VICAR MACHEBEUF
July: **Vicar Juan Felipe Ortiz** learns of the impending arrival of New
    Mexico's new bishop. Ortiz sends out circulars containing
    the news and informing parishioners, military commanders,
    civil authorities, etc., to prepare a grand reception for the
    new prelate. He prepares his own house for the bishop's
    residence then rushes the hundred or so miles south to greet
    his superior then returns to finalize the celebration, the likes of which have never been seen in
    Santa Fe.

James S. Calhoun
Courtesy Museum of NM, #9835

August 9: French-born **Jean Baptiste Lamy** arrives in Santa Fe as Vicar Apostolic of N.M., with his fellow
    Frenchman **Joseph Projectus Machebeuf.** They are very impressed with the joyful civic and military
    reception accorded them.

[There are two diametrically opposed interpretations of historical fact concerning Lamy/Machebeuf and
New Mexico's native clergymen, one represented by **Paul Horgan** (author of *Lamy of Santa Fe*), the other
by **Angélico Chávez** (author of books on Padre Martinez and Padre Gallegos). Both views are provided.]

Horgan: After the jubilant reception, ex-Vicar **Ortiz** (**Machebeuf** is now in that post, though Ortiz remains as
    pastor of Santa Fe) informs Lamy that he isn't recognized as the bishop for Santa Fe.

Chávez: After the reception Lamy and Machebeuf write to their friends abroad (both were inveterate letter
    writers) concerning *"the gravest suspicions"* they have regarding the native clergy. Machebeuf
    says they are *"horrible lechers" who* don't want to reform their sexual morals.

[Chávez says neither Lamy nor Machebeuf had as yet been out of Santa Fe. Lamy is quiet and dignified but subject to spells of depression in times of stress. Machebeuf has suffered from a "spiritual malady called scrupulosity," an irrational fear of certain damnation which ultimately emanates from "a sexual basis." Further, Chávez points out that there was an *amicitia particularis or amitié particuliere*, a **particular friendship** between the two, a relationship "frowned upon in the ascetical manuals." There is no mention of these perspectives in Horgan's biography.]

Horgan: Lamy acquaints himself with New Mexican society.

[Horgan uses quotes from writers like W.W.H. Davis, J. Gregg, H.S. Turner, etc., to illustrate what Lamy might have been encountering. For example, he quotes **Davis:** *"The priests of New Mexico"* were noted for corruption and profligacy, as notorious for their *"lascivious pleasures as their priestly duties, leading the populace in vice and immorality, with most having a family of illegitimate children."*

Turner is quoted as saying that *"of the devout women who attended Mass ... not one was supposed to be virtuous,"* that some traders and soldiers *"concluded that the native women were for the most part prostitutes"* because "a certain class of females" was there for use by the newcomers who had money to spend in a society so lacking in money because of its aversion to work.]

Machebeuf writes to Rome about ex-Vicar Ortiz, Fr. Luján and his succession of mistresses, the "scandal" of Gallegos in Albuquerque.

September, 1851.
Horgan: Lamy sets out, with one "lay attendant," to "confront" **Bishop Zubiría** regarding the **native clergy's defiance.**

Chávez: Lamy and ex-vicar Ortiz travel to Durango to confer with Bishop Zubiría regarding diocesan matters like including the El Paso settlements in his N.M. vicariate. Lamy's "worshipful biographers" have "deliberately" ignored telling how Lamy acquired an organ, how Ortiz traveled south to greet Lamy upon his arrival, and that Ortiz went with him to Durango, etc., because it makes for a better story to declare the native clergy in defiance of Lamy, despite the fact that the good bishop makes no mention whatsoever of native contrariness in his correspondence of this period. Neither does Machebeuf mention any such defiance. When Lamy and Ortiz return to N.M. they continue in friendship for many months ahead.

The story of defiance was construed from Archbishop Salpointe's general comment, some 50 years later, that New Mexican people and priests were suspicious of strangers, therefore Lamy had to go see Zubiría. Further,

Archbishop Jean B. Lamy
Courtesy Museum of NM, #9970

Rev. Joseph P. Machebeuf
Courtesy Museum of NM, #88590

Machebeuf's "gross lie" to the Roman Curia gave writers "substantiation" for the defiance spin.

January, 1852: Lamy returns to Santa Fe. Machebeuf has news of disrespect and scandal from the native clergy. Lamy suspends the pastor of Pecos. In time Lamy orders the expulsion of all Santos from New Mexican churches because of their "ugliness." Chávez: Bishop Lamy "was a fair-minded" individual when beyond the influence of "his bosom friend" Machebeuf. Lamy and Padre Martínez of Taos become mutually respected friends.

April, 1852: Lamy leaves for Baltimore. Vicar Machebeuf is now in charge of N.M., preaching here and there. He is absent from his Albuquerque parish so much that parishioners complain. In time he suspends four priests, including Father Gallegos of Albuquerque (while Gallegos is away) and Father Salazar of Abiquiú.

Chávez: Machebeuf glorifies his own "heroicity" in his letters which are exaggerations "peppered with lies" and which "admiring biographers" have taken as gospel.

December, 1852: Bishop Lamy issues his **Christmas Pastoral Letter.**

Horgan: The school for boys and the convent school for girls are not yet expensive but will be. Education is a necessity. Costs for church services are reduced as are the pastors' share. Voluntary tithes will be instituted and ignoring them will prevent the sacraments from being administered to such as choose to be "outside the fold." As for society, divorce, dancing, and gambling are scandalous occasions for sin. He also quotes I Corinthians 6:9--*Be not deceived, neither fornicators,* **"then adjusted the text to his hearers"** [an observation made by writer Horgan] *nor adulterers, nor highwaymen, nor those given to drinking, nor blasphemers, nor thieves, shall inherit the kingdom of God... therefore glorify God in your body.*"

There is an immediate explosion of defiance from the native clergy.

Chávez: Lamy's **Christmas Pastoral** is addressed to the faithful in general, not the native clergy. "*If later detractors*" of New Mexican priests construe I Corinthians 6.9-10 to be directed at the native clergy, "*which it most certainly was not,*" one could use "*the same unfair reasoning*" to ask why Lamy had omitted the part of the quotation stating "*nor the effeminates, nor sodomites...*" which would be "*reprehensible to say the least,*" but biographers have done that for Lamy and Machebeuf at the expense of the New Mexican clergy.
[Horgan doesn't call attention to the omission of "*nor the effeminates, nor sodomites*" anywhere in *Lamy of Santa Fe.*]

Padre **Martínez** writes to Lamy concerning Machebeuf's illegal suspensions of priests on the grounds that a vicar isn't so authorized under canon law, that Machebeuf appropriated parish funds then sermonized principally on the payment of tithes and threatened to withhold sacraments, that he was inimical to native priests and, worst of all, that **he was violating secrets of the confessional.** The letter is signed by Martínez and other padres, having nothing to do with Lamy's authority but rather with the behavior of Vicar Machebeuf. Lamy understood that revealing confessional secrets entailed a summons before the Roman Curia and then, if guilty, defrockment and consignment to a strict monastery for life. Lamy demands proof and in time Martínez is mollified.

January 1853: **Francisco Tomás C. de Baca** of Peña Blanca writes to Lamy complaining that Machebeuf is neglecting the parish and further, revealing secrets of the confessional.

Horgan: Lamy replies that proof is necessary or he will consider the charges as "a calumny of the most malicious kind-and it shall be my duty to punish....for such accusations."

February 24, 1853: Padre **Martínez** writes to Bishop Lamy that Machebeuf's reply to charges of disclosing confessional secrets *"can be accepted as proof, provided your Lordship considers this sufficient at this time."* But Francisco C. de Baca will not back off.

Horgan: W.W.H. **Davis** is quoted to depict New Mexicans: Spain and Mexico kept their people ignorant and they were very successful in N.M. where "half the population" couldn't read their catechisms or write their own names. But there is a slight change for the better since the country has been taken over by the U.S. and Bishop Lamy will *"produce a good effect."*

February-March: Padre **J.M. Gallegos** returns to Albuquerque from Durango only to learn he has been suspended *in absentia* and his parish taken over by Machebeuf.

March, 1853: Probate Judge **Ambrosio Armijo** of Albuquerque writes to Bishop Lamy, protesting the behavior of Vicar Machebeuf and demanding his suspension, especially for disclosing the secrets of the confessional. **His letter includes the signatures of 950 heads of families.**

Padre Antonio José Martínez
Courtesy Museum of NM, #174508

Chávez: Lamy writes letters in which the native clergy are described as in rebellion against him and his authority, *"which was a lie,"* because the actual problem was the accusation of Machebeuf and the confessional, which Lamy never mentions.

April, 1853: Padre **Martínez** writes to Lamy concerning the suspensions of native clergy, all effected illegally under canon law, a matter which will be appealed "to higher authority." The letter is signed by three other priests.

Chávez: Lamy writes to Bishop Purcell of Cincinnati, declaring *"in a deliberate obfuscation of the facts"* that the native clergy were in defiance of him because he was trying to reform abuses. Certain laymen like C. de Baca, Armijo, etc., were also excoriated as leading *"scandalous lives."* There is no mention of the charges against Machebeuf.

December, 1853: Padre Martínez informs Bishop Lamy of the accusation that is being carried to Rome. (Was this the *"beginning of a serious breakdown in the personality of Padre Martínez?"*)

Horgan: VI. **Scandal At Taos, 1852-1861. i. Martínez Rampant.** Lamy writes to an official in Rome that *"two or three Mexican priests"* might send negative information because they refuse to abide by the rules.

March, 1856: **Machebeuf** goes to Rome to answer charges,

April, 1856: Padre **Gallegos** writes to **Pope Pius IX,** asking for the removal of Lamy and Machebeuf and making 10 distinct accusations, including Machebeuf's violation of the sacramental seal of confession.

Horgan: Machebeuf makes a written refutation to all charges. His handwriting scramble indicates that *"his pen could not keep pace with his thoughts."*

Chávez: Machebeuf is in the "wildest panic" of his life, his *"contestation covers page after page of hurried scribblings, mostly unpunctuated or else replete with dashes."*

Horgan: Machebeuf rebuts that the people of N.M. are deprived of schooling and little accustomed to governing themselves. Most can't read and if you can sign your name you're considered educated. The legislature is *"composed of ignorant men, corrupt, dishonest,"* feared by the people who are related to each other and therefore against a foreign bishop who wants to reform their morals. Several legislators signed the complaint *"without knowing what it meant."* The accusations against himself are *"absurd,"* the people and Padre Martínez of Taos himself so stating in the attached document.

The suspended native clergymen were known to be notorious, mentioning Fathers J.F. Ortiz, Salazar, Luján, Gallegos, and **Martínez,** the latter's "character is so false and deceptive, so hidden, so flattering" that he tries to appear as a friend while he works to destroy Bishop Lamy, *duplicity* being his strongest characteristic.

Chávez: In what he labels **Remarques**, Machebeuf dismisses legislators' charges against Lamy *"simply by* *running down the native people of New Mexico.*" He also "lies" about Padre Gallegos, depicting "*his housekeeper as a prostitute,*" and stating that Padre Luján was the "*paramour of doña Gertrudis Barceló*" merely because Luján wept at her funeral.

The verdict is returned and titled: *Reclami dedotti al S. Padre contro Mons. Lamy Vescovo di S. Fe e contro il suo Vicario Machebeuf:*
Signore Machebeuf has satisfactorily answered all charges against himself and his bishop. Disorders resulted because of Lamy's Christmas Pastoral. Some native clergy lead certain followers from "a people so ignorant and vicious," especially Gallegos who was living with a prostitute. The accusations regarding the sacramental seal of confession are false, testified to even by "Priest Martínez who is purely one of the adversaries of the Bishop" and therefore credible.

"*The red herring of the Christmas Pastoral had worked!*" as had the vicious lies against Hispanic New Mexicans and their legislators. **And Padre Martínez' letter had been the clincher.**

1875: Upon Bishop Lamy becoming the first Archbishop of Santa Fe, Machebeuf boasts that the ecclesiastical Province of Santa Fe is *une petite Auvergne* with Lamy as Archbishop of Santa Fe, Salpointe as Bishop of Tucson, and himself as Bishop of Denver, along with three-fourths of all priests being Frenchmen, or, as he put it, *Auvergnats.*

1851 (con't)
MILITARY
Fort Defiance is established in the Navajo country.

ELECTIONS
The **election for legislative officers** is marred by violence and corruption, unregistered soldiers and teamsters voting "three or four times;" in Bernalillo County men are killed and wounded in ethnic clashes.

Richard H. Weightman is elected **Delegate to Congress.** Weightman's opponent contests the election and political feuding often results in bloodshed. Weightman states that violence during elections and other public functions were rare in N.M. until "Anglos" appeared on the scene.

June 3: The first ever N.M. Territorial Legislature convenes.

Governor Calhoun includes the following in his **first address to the Legislature:**
"*The relations between* **masters** *and* peons *should be distinctly defined, and each should understand their respective obligations and appropriate remedies for the violation of them upon the part of either, should be provided.*"
Governor Calhoun doesn't know what do with "*...our* **Pueblo** *friends...who own portions of the richest valley lands in this Territory--why exempt them from taxes ... and are you prepared to elevate them to full fellowship? I cannot recommend such a union. But it is inevitable,* **they must be slaves (dependents),** *equals,* **or removal** *to a better location for them and our people must occur...*"

Governor Calhoun [described by C. Horn as the "vanguard of democracy"] asks the Legislature to **bar free Blacks from N.M.,** saying that *"...Free negroes are regarded as nuisances in every State and Territory in the Union, and where they are tolerated, society is most degraded. I trust the legislature will pass a law that will prevent their entry into this territory. The disgusting degradation to which society is subjected by their presence, is obvious to all, and demands a prohibitory act of the severest character..."* But the Legislature refuses to pass such a law.

SOCIETY
Governor Calhoun appoints **Hispanos to public office,** which becomes *"...a source of resentment among many Anglos who feel deprived of political and financial opportunity."*

A **Memorial** is sent to President M. Fillmore (by the **Houghton faction**) saying that Governor Calhoun needs to be removed from office because he protects the Mexican population in the perpetuation of *"murder,"* that *"...there is no hope for the improvement of our Territory unless Americans rule it, and that the spirit of Mexican rule must be corrupt, ignorant, and disgraceful in a Territory of the United States..."*

(The *Gazette* newspaper publishes these perspectives and is controlled by the Houghton faction. New Mexican journalism now develops along partisan lines.)

Richard Weightman accuses the Houghton faction of creating rumors that a rebellion is about to break out in Taos, that the St. Vrain mills have been burned, etc.

[Troops were sent to investigate and found the rumors to be false but the negative publicity damaged the image of N.M. and its people.]

W.C. Anderson pummels a young Hispanic boy in Santa Fe then shoots him in the head, execution style. The authorities take no action against Anderson.

The **Masons'** Montezuma Lodge is chartered.

EDUCATION
Baptist minister Rev. **M. Reid** opens the **Santa Fe Academy** where subjects taught include "ABCology, *Farley's Geography, with the sublime mysteries of simple subtraction."* The school is not open for long due to lack of funding.

USA - MEXICO BOUNDARY
American and Mexican negotiators set the New Mexico-Chihuahua border at 32 degrees, 22 minutes north latitude.

EDUCATION
Bishop **Lamy** founds an English language school in Santa Fe.

MILITARY
July 26: **Fort Union** is established 25 miles northeast of Las Vegas. It becomes the principal supply depot for the area and the junction point for the Cimarron and Mountain branches of the Santa Fe Trail. [The fort was abandoned in 1891.]

1852
SOCIETY
May: **Governor Calhoun** dies while crossing the Kansas plains. His body is taken to Independence, Missouri, for burial.

1852

John Greiner is interim Governor.

COMMERCE
Richens Lacy Wootton (later known as **Uncle Dick Wootton**) drives sheep to California and realizes a good profit.

Francois X. Aubry drives sheep to California, with another flock the following year.

MINING
Serafín Ramiréz and **Antonio Sandoval** develop a silver mine south of Santa Fe.

SOCIETY
Zuñi people complain that **Navajos** continue as nuisances along with **American** immigrants to California who steal sheep, mules, horses, and grain while posing as purchasing agents for the U.S. government.

Francisco Chávez returns from schooling in St. Louis and New York and launches a phenomenal career that includes ranching, military achievement, law, and politics.

BUSINESS
The brothers **Manuel** [not the former governor] and **Rafaél Armijo** own the largest commercial house in Albuquerque.

MILITARY
Military expenditures in N.M. average about $3,000,000. Military commander **E.X. Sumner** describes N.M. as an economic wasteland. He believes that all troops should be withdrawn from the Territory. **C. Conrad,** Secretary of War, considers the proposal.
The *Santa Fe Gazette* denounces the suggestion and declares N.M. is being treated like a step child. It is pointed out that:

Minnesota, with a population of 16,192, received $10,000 for geological surveys (nothing for N.M. with its population of 61,000);

Minnesota was given two townships of federal territory for the support of education (nothing for N.M.);
Minnesota received $40,000 for roads, $80,000 for public buildings, $160,000 for legislative needs, $60,000 for its Indian agency (while N.M. received nothing except $20,000 for a much more severe Indian situation).

It concludes that no one is fighting for N.M. in Congress.

EDUCATION
Samuel Gorman establishes a school at **Laguna Pueblo.**

The **Sisters of Loretto** found a school for girls, *La Academia de Nuestra Señora de la Luz,* which would become **Loretto Academy** [which serves New Mexicans until 1969.] The Sisters are **Catherine Mahoney, Magdalen Hayden, Rosanna Dant, Monica Daily, Roberta Brown,** and all teach. Over the next two decades the Sisters establish schools at Taos (1863), Mora (1864), Las Vegas (1869), Las Cruces (1870), Bernalillo (1875).

1852-1853
William Carr Lane is Governor.

1852
CIVIL VS. MILITARY
Military commander Col. **Sumner** resents **Governor Lane** and a strong enmity develops between the two. Lane finally challenges Sumner to a **duel,** which the latter declines. Col. Sumner later writes that all troops and civil authorities should be withdrawn from N.M., allowing natives to sink or swim on their own. Secretary of State **Daniel Webster** and Secretary of War Conrad side with Sumner.

Indian Agent **John Greiner** writes concerning the hostile Indian situation and the American military :
> *"There are some 92,000 Indians in this Territory. Many of them are at war. We have not 1,000 troops here under Col. Sumner to manage them.* **Our troops are of no earthly account. They cannot catch a single Indian** *... although several expeditions have started after them, not a single Indian has been caught!"*

SOCIETY
Solomon Jacob Spiegelberg advances the territorial legislature the sum of $4,000 with which to pay its members. (The loan is repaid the following year.)

GOVERNOR'S SPEECH
December 7: Governor Lane addresses the Legislature: Protection against hostile Indians is totally inadequate; red and white **thieves** overrun the Territory; official use of the **Spanish** language or of both languages is counter to U.S. practice, though Spanish is "beautiful" in daily life; N.M. is one of the healthiest spots on the globe...

1852-53
SETTLEMENTS
San Pedro, San Pablo, and San Acacio are founded.

1853
GADSEN TREATY
The **Gadsden Treaty** establishes the present boundaries of N.M/Arizona by paying Mexico $10,000,000 for an additional 29,142,000 acres of Mexican land. **Article 6** of the treaty states that *"...only land grants whose boundaries are located on the ground and whose documents are recorded in the archives will be recognized by the U.S."*

[New Mexicans who fled south to areas like La Mesilla to escape United States aggression are once again under American jurisdiction.]

REPORT
Col. **Joseph K.E. Mansfield** writes that there are *"not more than two schools in the whole Territory"* of N.M.

SHEEP RANCHING
Antonio J. Luna, Rafaél Luna, Ambrosio Armijo, and **Miguel A. Otero I,** among others, drive a flock of 25,000 sheep, the largest of the season, to California. When they return to N.M. they bring back $70,000 in coin and gold dust.

[Anglo sheepmen thought this was ridiculously low. Tradition has it that **Ambrosio Armijo** received his payment in octagonal $50 gold pieces which were being minted in San Francisco at the time.]

POLITICS
Padre José Manuel Gallegos is elected Delegate to Congress over W.C. Lane when Congress refuses to accept votes cast by **Pueblo Indians.** (It is charged that Padre Gallegos doesn't speak English.)

REPORT
Col. E.V. **Sumner** describes **Hispanic New Mexicans** as being *"...thoroughly debased and totally incapable of self government..."* that nothing *"... can ever make them respectable. They have more Indian blood than Spanish, and in some respect are below the Pueblo Indians; for they are not as honest or as industrious."*

COMANCHEROS
September: Lt. **A.W. Whipple** reports encountering five Mexican Comancheros on the 8th, six Comancheros from Santo Domingo on the 12th, other traders on the 15th, 15 on the 18th, and 22 on the 22nd. He is amazed that defenseless traders mingle *"...with the savage and treacherous tribes on their own soil."*

SOCIETY
Fall: The **Cibolero War** pits cibolero hunters against the **Cheyennes.** Col. **John Garland,** commander of

troops in N.M., supports the Cheyennes because the buffalo are the lifeline of the Indians.

1853

W.S. Messersvy is interim Governor.

BOOKS

W.W.H. Davis, the first U.S. Attorney in N.M., encounters a group of *ciboleros* on the plains and writes that they look like a *"band of Gypsies."* He can't drink the *aguardiente* which they offer him. Davis writes a book (*El Gringo, or New Mexico and her People)* in which he describes N.M. and its people:

The modern town of **Santa Fe,** like its great namesake and prototype, Timbuctoo [sic], is built of mud...

Except for beans, the cultivation of vegetables in N.M. has only been attempted to any extent and variety *since the U.S. acquired the territory.*

The *abrazo* (embrace) is the most common form of greeting between friends *"and even filthy beggars in the streets meet and embrace each other with an affection truly laughable."*

Smoking is habitual with all classes, not excepting the most lovely and refined females, some of whom even smoke in bed.

Burial expenses are exorbitant.

Recreation includes el coleo (tailing) and catching a greased pig, *"...both of which are reckoned intellectual performances."*

In **dress** New Mexicans like bright colors *"...but display little or no taste in the adornment of their persons.*

W.W.H. Davis
Courtesy Museum of NM, #9862
((Fredrick Gutenbunst photo)

Illiteracy is greater in N.M. than in any other state of the Union because *"it was always the policy of Spain and Mexico to keep her people in ignorance..."*

The native plow is the same implement as used in the time of Moses.

Sheep dogs *"...exhibit an intelligence and sagacity truly astonishing.*
New Mexicans are fine **horsemen** and remarkably skillful with the *lazo.*

With regard to **race,** *"New Mexicans are of Eastern origin, and in general possess all the vices..."* of Mediterranean people. The **Moors** intermarried with the Spanish and formed a mixed race, many of which found their way to N.M., where they mixed with Indians for a *"...second blending of blood"* which produced a *"...dark and swarthy"* people, and *"...there is no present hope of the people improving in color."*

New Mexicans possess *"the cunning and deceit of the Indian, the politeness and spirit of revenge of the Spaniard, and the imaginative temperament and fiery impulses of the Moor. They have a great deal of what the world calls smartness and quickness of perception, but lack the stability of character and soundness of intellect that give such* **vast superiority to the Anglo-Saxon race over every other people."**

The New Mexicans have been unjustly accused of cowardice.

Vice is prevalent among all classes of society and *"...female chastity is deplorably low, and the virtuous are far outnumbered by the vicious."*

Prostitution is carried *"to a fearful extent; and it is quite common for parents to sell their own daughters for money to gratify the lust of the purchaser..."*

It is *"almost a universal practice for men and women to live together as husband and wife, and rear a family of children, without having been married."* Married men have mistresses *"...and but too frequently the wife also has her male friend."*

New Mexicans are extremely superstitious, with *"...an abiding faith in* **saints and images,** *and with the mass of the inhabitants their worship appears no more than a blind adoration of these insensible objects."*

New Mexican **peonage** is *"worse"* than black slavery: *"...the difference is in favor of the negro. The average of intelligence among the peones is lower than that among the slaves of the Southern States; they are not so well cared for nor do they enjoy so many of the blessings and comforts of domestic life..."*

Priests are *"...leaders in vice"* for the people, and the New Mexicans *"should be compassionated rather than shunned because of their degraded condition, and an efficient effort should be made to raise them to the standard of enlightenment ... that is found in our land ... with the virtues and wisdom possessed by our own people, who have been reared under a purer code of morals and a wiser system of laws ... let us endeavor to work out the regeneration of the people of New Mexico, morally, socially, and religiously..."*

[In the preface to the 1938 edition, **Harvey Fergusson** states: *"...Had he been consciously working as the agent of posterity, Mr.. Davis could hardly have done better--because he was critical rather than imaginative--his book is one of the best books about nineteenth century New Mexico..."*]

AMERIND

Capt. John Pope reports that **Comanches** are so peaceful they are hardly ever seen or heard of in N.M.

RACISM

A **visitor to N.M.** writes that *"...the truth is that the whole country is not worth a good regiment of soldiers. It is fit for nothing but black Mexicans--white people can't live there as white people."*

1853-1856

David Meriwether is Governor.

1854
LAND LAW

The **Donation Act** becomes law: Any **white male citizen** (or who declares his intent to become a citizen) may acquire 160 acres of land by continuous residence and cultivation of that land for a period of not less than four years; the claim has to be filed on surveyed land. There are exclusions: **claimants of Spanish/Mexican land grants may not file for donation claims;** donation land holders may not file for Homestead or Preemption land.

1858: **Pinckney R. Tulley** is the first donation claim on record. The first donation certificate of title is issued to **James T. Johnson.**

1858: The Donation Act is already becoming a potent instrument for land fraud and Secretary of the Interior Jacob Thompson asks that it be abolished.

1880-1881: The cattle industry begins to boom and donation entries increase dramatically.

1884: Land Inspector **Frank D. Hobbs** declares that not over two percent of the 457 donation applications on file are valid claims.

SURVEYOR GENERAL

William Pelham is selected as Surveyor General. (Six years have passed since the end of the Mexican War.) Pelham is to *"ascertain the origin, nature, character and extent of all claims"* filed in his office, and he has the authority to summon witnesses.

[Congress provides no comprehensive system for adjudication of land titles and insufficient funds are allocated for staff and expenses, thus making his office *"...a passive agent of the government..."* with a procedure that *"...was not really an adjudication at all. It lacked the essential element of all true adjudication: due process of law."* And the Treaty of Guadalupe Hidalgo "guaranteed" all New Mexicans equal treatment under the law. Pelham is considered conscientious, honest and intelligent but ill-prepared for the task at hand because he was not versed in the law, couldn't read, write, or speak Spanish, wasn't familiar with Spanish or Mexican law, legal history, or cultural traditions relating to land and there were no books from which to study these things and no one who cared to find or send him some. The designs that saw to it that Article X of the Treaty of Guadalupe Hidalgo was deleted and that the Protocol was ignored were continued through the Surveyor General's office.]

Government attitudes don't help as when Pelham requests authority to ask for military protection when necessary due to dangers posed by hostile Indians. He is informed there is no law to permit such a procedure, but if attacks are made on survey crews he can petition the President of the U.S. to order military protection, according to V. Westphall.

LAND SPECULATORS

The office of Surveyor General is held by nine different men and continues for almost four decades during which **land speculators** are able to enrich themselves, usually at the expense of settlers living on the land grants, with three of the Surveyor Generals themselves described as "*...blatant land speculators*: T. Rush **Spencer** (1869-1874), James K. **Proudfit** (1872-1876), and Henry M. **Atkinson** (1876-1884)." The office of the SG is used "*to further the interests of land speculators*" at the expense of settlers.

Speculators employ two principal **strategies to acquire land grants**: purchasing a settler's interest in a community grant (interests which could not be sold under Hispanic law) and the partition suit in a government court. Congress proves itself susceptible to influence from speculators and their lands are confirmed and patented. With the speculators taken care of, "*Congress exhibited a startling lack of concern*" for other claimants, virtually ignoring the rest of New Mexicans, Treaty of Guadalupe Hidalgo notwithstanding.

RAIDS

Cheyennes attack N.M. settlements, harming no Americans as they had promised but killing or capturing Mexicans wherever possible. The Army does nothing, to the consternation of Gov. Meriwether.

SHEEP COMMERCE

Sheep prices plummet in California, ending the first phase of trade with New Mexicans. "Anglo" sheepmen lose much interest in the industry so Hispanos regain "*...ascendancy as their Anglo competitors faded away.*"

[During the previous four years, over 100,000 sheep had been driven to California. Sheep owners received payment in gold or U.S. currency, providing New Mexicans with circulating money.]

AMERIND

Jicarilla Apaches are believed responsible for the theft of some cattle and **Lt. David Bell** leads a detachment of soldiers to recover them. **Lobo Blanco** and some of his warriors are encountered on the plains but they deny stealing any cattle. Lt. Bell declares he will hold the chief until the cattle thieves are given up. A fight ensues and Lobo Blanco is killed.

REPORT

June 8: Indian Agent **E.A. Graves** reports on the **Indians of N.M.:**

The **Jicarilla Apaches** are indigent, lazy, and indolent; a cowardly band, they are nevertheless cruel and vengeful;

Utes roam about in six bands, hardy and muscular; they are brave, impudent, and warlike, reputedly the best warriors in the Territory; they use rifles with ease and shoot with accuracy; they raise good horses and are excellent horsemen; *they claim some of the best land* in the area;

Navajos are fierce, intelligent, and warlike; they are rich in livestock and manufacture superb blankets; they have warred on the New Mexicans extensively;

Apaches excel all Indians in savage cruelty and hostility toward N.M.; they make their living through robbery and plunder and they take many captives; they are brave, daring, warlike, and cruel;

Comanches (on the eastern and southern borders of N.M.) are fierce, powerful, and warlike;

Graves estimates there are from 24,000 to 28,000 uncivilized Indians in N.M., excluding the Comanches (10,000 to 15,000). He admits that setting government policy regarding these tribes will be no simple matter but he concludes *"...That this race, the **aborigines of America,** are destined to a speedy and final **extinction,** according to the laws now in force, either civil or divine, or both, seems to admit of no doubt, and is equally beyond the control or management of any human agency. All that can be expected from an **enlightened and Christian government,** such as ours, is to graduate and **smooth the passway for their final exit from the stage of human existence..."** according to WA. Keleher.

AMERIND SUFFRAGE
The Legislature passes a **law prohibiting the Pueblo nations from voting** except in elections for local water officials.

[But their citizenship is confirmed in a number of territorial cases: 1869, *Lucero;* 1874, *Santistevan;* 1876, *Joseph;* 1904, *Delinquent Taxpayers;* 1907, *Mares.*]

EDUCATION
Congress grants the N.M. Territory 46,080 acres of land on which to establish universities. [But there will be no public college or high school until 35 years later in 1889.]

SOCIETY
Ex-Governor **Manuel Armijo** dies at his home in Lemitar.

August 18: **Richard Weightman** kills famous trail-blazer **Francois X. Aubry** in a gunfight.

AMERIND
November: **Cheyennes** ambush 25 hunters from **Taos Pueblo,** killing 12.

1854-1855
SETTLEMENTS
Chama and San Francisco **(Lavalley)** are founded.

1855
POLITICS
Miguel A. Otero (I) is elected Delegate to Congress.

SANTA FE TRADE
Commerce over the Santa Fe Trail is valued at $5,000,000. Substantial profits are being realized by traders like Leitensdorfer, Hough, Glasgow, Magoffin, Branham, Conelly Clark, Waldo, McCoy, Aubrey, Spayer, Morris, Folourney, Courtney, McKnight, Ferguson, and Colburn.

MILITARY
Fort Stanton is established 10 miles west of *La Placita* [later renamed **Lincoln**], on the eastern slope of the White Mountains *(Sierra Blanca)*. This military protection marks the beginning of "Anglo" settlement along the Río Ruidoso and Río Bonito that join to form the Hondo River flowing through the Hondo Valley.

SOCIETY
Construction of a **penitentiary** is begun and lucrative contracts for building materials are awarded to merchants like Ceran St. Vrain, Joab Houghton, and Theodore Wheaton. Due to a shortage of bricklayers, Governor Merriwether orders Chairman of Construction Joab Houghton to use stone rather than brick, which Houghton does, since he controls all stone quarries in the area.

Ranchers like **Lucien Maxwell, Samuel Watrous, Alexander Hatch**, **James Giddings**, and **Preston Beck** establish large spreads along the eastern borders of N.M. Comanches and Kiowas seethe with resentment against these intruders on their lands. Simultaneously, Comanches are being driven westward by other warlike nations, like the Osages, and they declare they wish to live in N.M. Gov. Meriwether orders them to return to Texas. Ranchers soon report "depredations" and demand protection from the Army.

AMERINDS
A punitive expedition is sent against the **Utes and Jicarillas** for attacking the trading post at Fort Pueblo. (The Utes later state they attacked the post because **smallpox-infested blankets** had been given to their people by the territorial Superintendent of Indian Affairs.) The **Mexican Volunteers** in the expedition are described as *"...a more daring and expert band of horsemen has seldom been collected..."* Commander of Company D is **Manuel Chaves** and his half-brother **Román Baca** is a second-lieutenant.

February: **James H. Quinn** sets out for California with a flock of 15,000 sheep. Rampaging **Arapahoes,** incensed because the Government hasn't kept treaty obligations, kill thousands of sheep and force

Quinn's return to Taos. He drives another herd the following year but prices are so low the effort is a failure.

GOVERNMENT & LAND SURVEYS

March 9: **Surveyor General Pelham** lets his first contract. After surveying 108 miles it is learned that the wrong length of chain has been used and the work must be redone (at the expense of another $2,160). The most serious problem to surveying N.M. continues to be hostile Indians. Government payments by draft are difficult to convert into cash. *"Currency was principally in Mexican silver dollars, which bore a premium over gold of six per cent, and which in disbursements by public officials counted only at par..."*

MILITARY

November: A post referred to as **Hatch's Ranch** is established 33 miles southeast of Las Vegas. Hatch serves as sutler for the garrison and makes large profits.

1856-1857

W.W.H. Davis is interim Governor.

1856

BLACKS & SOCIAL LEGISLATION

After constant pressure by American authorities the Legislature passes a bill **restricting the movement of free blacks in N.M.:** Blacks living in N.M. must post the sum of $200 to insure good behavior and the ability to support themselves; A free black may not remain in N.M. for more than 30 days; Intermarriage with blacks is now against the law; Newly freed blacks must leave N.M. within 30 days of manumission.

RELIGIOUS

Escorted by the Right Reverend Joseph Machebeuf, **Thomas A. Hayes** comes to N.M., recruited by Archbishop Lamy, and is soon ordained into the priesthood. After ordination he is assigned to Santa Clara Pueblo, then later to Bernalillo.

DAVIS & FRAUD

Interim Governor **W.W.H. Davis,** the first U.S. Attorney in N.M. and author of the widely read *El Gringo; or New* Mexico *and Her People,* is **charged with embezzlement** and removed from office.

[There is no record of his return to N.M. but his book is considered by some as a basic source of information to this day.]

1857-1861

Abraham Rencher is Governor.

1857
SETTLEMENT
Paraje is founded.

SHEEP RANCHING
Sydney A. Hubbel, married to **M. Ignacia Perea,** goes into the sheep business with his brother-in-law
Joaquín Perea; he drives a flock to California and makes good profits. **Joaquín Perea, José
Jaramillo** and other sheepmen prepare for the biggest drive ever to California.

EXCOMMUNICATION
Padre **Martínez** of Taos and Padre **Lucero** of Arroyo Hondo are excommunicated by Bishop Lamy.

LEGISLATURE
Governor Rencher states that the N.M. legislature is superior to those of Kansas and Oregon. Like his
predecessors, he is unable to get the legislature to pass a bill for property taxes.

MILITARY & APACHES
June: The **Gila Expedition** is mounted against fierce bands of Mogollón, Gila, and Coyotero **Apaches.** Col.
B.L.E. **Bonneville** asks **Manuel Chaves** to be *Chief of Scouts* and he accepts (at three dollars and
one ration per day) the job, bringing Román Baca, Lorenzo Labadie (his brother-in-law), and Jesús
Chaves with him.

The Scouts set the pace necessary to encounter the Apaches but the troopers become so exhausted they
begin failing asleep in their saddles. But the hostiles are discovered in a steep-walled canyon and
strategy is laid for the assault: split the command and attack from both sides. But Chaves objects,
saying only a quick dash down the slopes will capture the Apaches. One of the younger officers
remarks it is ridiculous to unhorse cavalry soldiers and send them down to fight man-to-man
without even knowing how many Indians there are. Chaves answers: *"Well this is how we New
Mexicans fight, and for those who have the stomach for it, it is the best way."*

Col. W.W. Loring, commander of the column, effects a compromise but he is with Chaves during the charge
down the canyon. The Apaches are engulfed and eight are slain, including the chief **Cuchillo
Negro.** A flock of 1,500 sheep is recovered along with skin tents, field equipage, much packed
meat, and 10 captives.

Col. Loring gives credit to Manuel Chaves for his tracking aptitude, perceptive advice, and absolute
coolness in battle.

SOCIETY
March 29: **Félix Martínez** is born in Peñasco.
November 25: **J. Francisco Chávez** marries **Mary Bowie** of Montreal, Canada. They honeymoon in Panama,

Havana, New Orleans, and New York before returning to N.M.

GOVERNMENT & LAND TITLES

November 30: Surveyor General **Pelham** is so ignored in the General Land Office and the Congress that he writes a long letter to **Miguel A. Otero,** territorial Delegate to Congress, in which he charges that *Congress refuses to take any action on land titles.*

T I M E L I N E

1857: **Dred Scott, a Negro slave from Missouri,** is taken into free territory and sues to have his freedom recognized by the courts. The Dred Scott case makes its way to the **Supreme Court** (*"probably the most famous in the history of the Court"* according to H.S. Commager) and it decrees that Scott is neither a citizen of the U.S. nor of Missouri so he isn't entitled to sue in the first place. **Justice C.L. Taney** renders the opinion of the Court that Negroes *"weren't intended to be included under the word citizens"* as used by the framers of the Constitution, that they were *"considered as a subordinate and inferior class of beings subjugated by the dominant race."* Whether emancipated or not, Negroes are subject to the authority of the *"dominant race"* and have no rights or privileges except those which authorities in power might wish to grant them. The U.S. Constitution recognized *"every person and every class and description of persons as citizens if they were so recognized by the States, but none other... it was formed by them, and for them and their posterity, but for no one else."* Neither the **Declaration of Independence** nor the **Constitution** applied to *"the class of persons who had been imported as slaves, nor their descendants, whether they had become free or not, and could not be included in the general words employed in that memorable instrument."* By custom Negroes have been *"regarded as beings of an inferior order, altogether unfit to associate with the white race, either in social or political relations, they have no rights that the white man is bound to respect, the negro might justly and lawfully be reduced to **slavery for his benefit**. This opinion is universal among civilized white people ..."*

1858
EDUCATION

The **Joseph Institute** is opened in **Taos** by Mr.. and Mrs. **J.H. Holmes.** Boys are taught reading, geography, arithmetic, and etiquette. Girls study needlework, embroidery, and guitar.

COMANCHE RAID

Samuel Watrous establishes a ranch 130 miles below Fort Union. **Comanches** warn his foreman to abandon the ranch. Their warning ignored, they kill all ranch hands, except the Mexicans, and burn all buildings. Col. Garland reports that Watrous had been advised against ranching so far away from established settlements and Army protection.

[*"More than likely,"* they were directed *"by a group of treacherous Spanish-Americans known as Comancheros"* who went about trading in *"hostile Indian country,"* trafficking in stolen livestock, according to W.A. Beck.]

RESCUE ATTEMPT

Manuel Chaves and **Jesús Armijo** are in Mesilla when they learn that the group of **E.J. White,** his wife and
child, have been attacked by Apaches. **S.W Cozzens** (who recorded the story in his *The Marvelous Country*) gathers some men and, guided by Chaves and Armijo, all ride out in pursuit. Within a
couple of hours the bodies of White and a servant are found but Mrs. White and her child are still
with the Apaches. At a watering hole that evening the body of the child is found, lanced through
with a spear.

The Apache camp is sighted and Cozzens wants to attack immediately. Chaves forbids it, saying the woman
will be killed at the first sign of trouble: they must be surprised if Mrs. White is to be rescued alive.
After the Indians bed down for the night a signal is given and 20 rifles boom out in unison then the
men charge into the encampment, cutting down all who oppose them by not fleeing. Mrs. White is
found still warm but bleeding from perhaps a dozen stab wounds inflicted at the first sound of
gunfire. Her remains are buried by the grieving rescuers in the shadow of the Florida Mountains.

SOCIETY

Santero **José Benito Ortega** is born.

Col. J.X. Reeve writes that the Mexicans are "*...villainous vagabonds*" who are aiding the Indians.

The Army purchases 2,000 head of cattle in Santa Fe.

April: **Rafaél Chacón** marries **Juanita Páez.**

1859
RELIGIOUS

There are **20 Catholic clergymen** in N.M.; four reside in Pueblo villages.

ORGANIZATIONS

The **Historical Society of New Mexico** is founded.

BLACKS & GOVERNMENT

The Legislature enacts the **Slave Code Act** [described as "indicative" of Miguel A. Otero's influence; after
he married a *"southern belle"* it was a move to *"win favor with southern congressmen"* as told by
WA Beck].

[Black slavery in N.M. is debated in Congress: **Daniel Webster** and John Bell assert that the climate and soil
of N.M. will not support the expenses of slavery; **William H. Seward** and others maintain that Black slaves
may be used profitably in mining and industrial activities.]

GOVERNMENT APPROPRIATIONS

Congressional delegate **Miguel Otero (I)** convinces Congress to fund a much needed geological survey and
the resumption of renovation work on the state capitol.

Congress appropriates enough money to restore the **Palace of the Governors,** ensuring its preservation as an historical treasure.

SETTLEMENT
La Plaza de los Leónes [modern-day **Walsenburg**] is founded.

EDUCATION
El Colegio de San Miguel, later known as **St. Michael's College** [the oldest chartered secondary school in N.M.] is founded by the Christian Brothers of St. John the Baptist de La Salle. It quickly becomes the leader of Catholic education in N.M. In its first year it has 250 day students and 30 boarders.

1866: Some classes are provided free of charge for needy but promising students,

1894: The curriculum includes courses in elementary and business English; French, Spanish, German phonology and writing; chemistry; the study of minerals; instrumental music.

COMANCHES
July: **R.E. Clements** and his group of government surveyors are captured by **Comanches** while working in the Canadian Valley. Clements promises to abandon the survey and his Mexican employees ask that Clements be spared. All are released.

Autumn: **Comanches** launch attacks along the eastern frontier, this time also targeting Hispanics like Feliciano Guterous [Gutiérrez?] and E. Chávez.

BUFFALO HUNTING
Rafaél Chacón writes about going *"...to* **hunt buffalo** *in the winter. There were millions of them. I killed them for beef. There were from ten to twenty persons in my party. We had no wagons. We used pack animals, mules. We took only the best of the carcass; sometimes we saved the hides. I was able to sell the best buffalo meat in Taos and Santa Fe for twenty-five cents per pound...Later I made trips to the Comanche Indians to trade, and my profits were four to one and even more ... I bought fifteen wild horses, paying one piloncillo [a cone of brown sugar weighing about one pound] for each wild horse..."*

CHURCH & SOCIETY
Manuel Chaves fences off the east boundary of his property in Santa Fe [sometime during the late 1850s] in order to separate it from the Guadalupe Chapel owned by the Church. **Bishop Lamy** orders Chaves to remove the fence because it encroaches on church land but the latter maintains it is his land and refuses. Lamy threatens him with excommunication and Chaves answers his wife could not live with it so *"you will not excommunicate me."*

Bishop Lamy draws up the document, which has to be read in church in order to be official. The Sunday designated for the reading finds a packed church, only one bench vacant close to the altar. Chaves, his half-brother Román Baca and another friend walk into church, armed with rifles, and take the bench. When the priest ascends the pulpit for the sermon and announcements he pulls out the order of excommunication. The three men sitting on the front bench cock their rifles, the sounds perceptible throughout the church. Without another word, the priest descends from the pulpit and continues mass.

[The order of excommunication was never read.]

1860s
SETTLEMENTS

Many villages are founded: Ruidoso, San Patricio, Hondo, Analla (Tinnie), Picacho, Arabela, Agua Azul (Bluewater), La Luz (north of modern Alamogordo), Puerto de Luna; and San José, Pueblo Viejo (into present Arizona).

POTTERY

Nampeyo is born at Hano, First Mesa, Arizona, and begins creating pottery at an early age.

1895: While a crew member of the Fewkes Archaeological Expedition, Nampeyo's husband **Lesou** uncovers prehistoric pottery designs and together with those of the **Hopi** the two inspire the great revival of Hopi pottery.

Ca. 1910: The Fred Harvey Company promotes Nampeyo's work at the Grand Canyon.

1942: Nampeyo dies. Her daughters **Annie Healing, Frannie Polacca, Nellie Douma, and Cecilia Lesso, and Lynette Lesso,** continue working in the Nampeyo style, as do her succeeding generations:

Annie's: Rachel Namingha, Beatrice Naha, Daisy Hooee, Juanita Healing;

Fannie's: Elva Tewaguna, Neva Choyou, Harold Polacca, Tom Polacca, Tonita Hamilton, Iris Youvella, Leah García;

Nellie's: Marie Koopee, Augusta Poocha, Zella Kooyquattewa;

Rachel Namingha's: Eleanor Lucas (and her Karen, Stephen), Lillian Gonzáles, Ruth James (and her Darlene Vigil, Dextra Quotskuyva (her Hisi Quotskuyva), Priscilla Namingha; (from Emerson) Les Mamingha;
Daisy's: Shirley Berm;

Marie's: Emma Lou;
Elva's: Miriam, Adelle, David Lalo, Elton, Neva:

Leah's: Melda, James García, Fawn Mavasie, Rayvin García;

Harold's: Clinton, Vernida, Reva;

PROFILE

Henry McCarty

B I L L Y   T H E   K I D

Henry McCarty, later to be known as **William H. Bonney** and **Billy the Kid,** is born around this time, probably in New York state. His widowed mother, **Catherine McCarty**, moves to Wichita, Kansas, to raise Henry and his younger brother Joseph, then they move to Denver.

March 1, 1873: Catherine McCarty marries **William H. Antrim** in Santa Fe then the family moves to Silver City. The boys attend school there and Henry is described as loving to read books, sing, and dance.

September 16, 1874: Catherine dies of tuberculosis. Shortly after Henry leaves Silver City and is now on his own. He uses the name *Billy Antrim* and his boyish appearance prompts some people to refer to him as "the Kid." He spends much time practicing with the gun, horse, and rope, working as a drifter-cowboy in Arizona.

1877: Billy the Kid is described as very skillful with the rope, horse, and gun. He is fluent in the Spanish language.

August: A blacksmith named Francis Cahill (with a reputation as a bully) taunts and assaults Billy, who shoots him, Cahill dying the following day. Billy flees to N.M.

October: Billy is riding with the notorious **Jesse Evans** gang ("The Boys") of horse and cattle rustlers in the Mesilla Valley. In the Seven Rivers area [below Roswell], Billy is boarded with Heiskel Jones and his family and he develops much respect and affection for "Ma Jones." He says his name is "**William Bonney**," though he is commonly referred to as "the Kid."

November: Billy moves to the Lincoln area, builds a reputation as a hard worker who loves good times and dancing. He isn't

Billy the Kid
Courtesy Museum of
NM,#30769

much of a drinker and doesn't use tobacco. He enjoys poker and monte. He loves his guns and horses. He gets along well with Hispanic people. He has a good head on his shoulders and physically is very agile. He also has a quick temper that can turn lethal at the slightest provocation.

1878: Eighteen-year-old Billy the Kid signs on at the **Tunstall** ranch on the Río Felíz. He becomes good friends with **Fred Waite** who is part Choctaw Indian. Serious troubles begin when Sheriff Brady attaches merchandise at the Tunstall store. (See **1875, 1878**.)

Tonita's: Eugene, Loren Hamilton;

Tom's: Gary, Carla, Elvira, Marty Naha;

Iris': Wallace Charlene, Nolan, Doran;

Priscilla Namingha's: Nyla Sahmie (her Michael Collateta), Rachel Sahmie, jean Sahmie (her Donella Tom), Randy Sahmie, Ida Sahmie; Bonnie Chapella;

Dextra Quotskuyva's: Camille.

1860
SOCIETY & GOVERNMENT

New Mexicans are so outraged at the passage of the Slave Code Act of 1859 that a movement is begun to force the Legislature to repeal it. Elected officials hold firm and the law stands, the will of the people notwithstanding.

TIMELINE

1860: **The USA has by far the largest slave population, almost 4,000,000, of any country in the Western Hemisphere. Almost all are American-born.**

SANTERO

José de Gracia Gonzáles (from Chihuahua) arrives in N.M. He works at restoring and/or creating altar screens and devotional images throughout northern N.M. He uses oils to paint five altarpieces for the church of San José de Gracias in Las Trampas and he does an altar screen in Arroyo Seco. He produces a small number of retablos; facial expressions are influenced by Mexican art. In the 1870s José moves to Trinidad, Colorado, where he dies around 1891.

BUREAUCRACY & SURVEYOR GENERAL

Surveyor General William **Pelham** resigns in disgust over bureaucratic policies. The Government owes Pelham $463.35 in back pay (which he receives 14 years later).

SETTLEMENT
Felipe Baca from Guadalupita begins a settlement that comes to be known as **Trinidad.**

SANTA FE TRAIL
It is estimated that 3,033 wagons, 9,084 men, 6,147 mules, and 27,920 oxen pass over the Santa Fe Trail.

SOCIETY
The first **Yom Kippur** in N.M. is held in the Santa Fe home of **Levi Spiegelberg,** most of the Jewish popula-
tion attending, a list of which includes the entire
Spiegelberg clan, the two Staab brothers, the two
Dittenhoffers, Louis Gold and his son, Joseph Hersch,
Louis Felsenthal, Aaron Zeckendorf, Herman Ilfeld,
Philip Schwartzkopf, and one Solomon Spiegelberg
[not the famous Solomon Jacob Spiegelberg, it
appears].

EDUCATION
The Legislature passes a bill for **compulsory public education.**
Teachers receive 50 cents per pupil per month.

Levi Spiegelberg
Courtesy Museum of NM, #90171

LAND TITLES
Juan Batista Vigil charges that Surveyor General **W. Wilbar**
is guilty of dereliction of duty under the Treaty of Guadalupe
Hidalgo, referring specifically to the property guarantees
which stipulate that bona fide land titles are to be acknowledged by American authorities. Vigil's charges are ignored and
all land titles are considered to be in jeopardy when being
reviewed by the government.

Three circumstances prevent granting of official title to lands (before 1891):
1. Farming lands are structured as relatively narrow strips that front along a water course, which is not
   compatible with the basic rectanguar pattern survey used by the U.S.
2. Hispanic New Mexicans generally live around a plaza as protection against attacks by hostile Indians
   while U.S. land laws require residence on land to which title is sought.
3. Communal ownership of land is not traditional in the U.S. *"The situation was allowed to drift in the old
   manner of possessory rights..."* which is *"...poor policy because technically the land was public
   domain and was so designated on official maps"* according to V. Westphall.

[American historiography being what it is, no author has explored the idea that the government never
intended to lose control of land ownership in New Mexico. A war was fought to acquire land, not to deed it
over to possessors of the soil, but such observations would be considered "controversial."]

AGRICULTURE

Governor Rencher writes that the corn crop is a partial failure because of **drought.** "Anglos" are contemptuous of N.M. subsistence farming, agricultural management, and implements.

[W.A. Beck relates that *"Several factors"* are blamed for *"agricultural backwardness"* of New Mexico's Hispanics: the attitude that labor was for slaves and peóns, not gentlemen; methods were obsolete, as were farming implements; unfenced lands; Indian raids; lack of outside markets.

"Anglos" brought in things like *"iron plows but more important, a new attitude toward farming"* as an honorable activity instead of *"work for slaves,"* which in time wore down the *"traditional Hispanic resentment"* toward farm work.

But the same author stated earlier in the same book that during the colonial period of New Mexican history *"most of the people"* made their living by farming the soil, the *self-sufficient economy* structured around raising crops through irrigation.]

ANGLO DOMINATION & SOCIETY

In **Santa Fe** [during this year] *"...Anglos ... 18.5 percent of the gainful workers ... dominate the occupational structure, owned most of the wealth, and held most of the positions of authority"* according to R. Nostrand.

LAND GRANT

The **Las Vegas land grant** survey shows it to contain 496,446 acres.

[Some 40 years later the grant is resurveyed and reduced in size by about 65,000 acres.]

1870s: Attorney for the grant is **Joab Houghton,** who urges the Government to issue a patent of ownership.

1878: The Land Office directs the Surveyor General to determine the proper western boundary of the grant, and then the same for the southern boundary.

1885: **George W. Julian** becomes SG. He tells the General Land Office that he can save 4,000,000 acres of claimed land grant land for the **public domain** if he receives sufficient funds from Congress. Julian recommends that the Las Vegas grant be resurveyed to include only allotted private tracts, arguing that legal title to pasture lands remained with the Mexican government, therefore it must remain with the U.S.

1887: The General Land Office approves Julian's recommendation.

Julián appoints **Will Tipton** to conduct the survey (though Tipton is not a surveyor). Problems arise because private allotments, instead of being in a solid body, are scattered in various settlements along the Gallinas River. While the Government authorities work to reduce the size of the grant, other conflicts are raging between Julian, who states common lands now belong to the public domain, **speculators** who have bought into the grant, and **settlers** who believe they have perpetual use of the common lands as their birthright under Hispanic law and guaranteed by the Treaty of Guadalupe Hidalgo.

1887: **Milhiser v. Padilla:** Three Padilla brothers (José, Francisco, Pablo) fence off pasture lands at La Monilla. **Judge E.X. Long** appoints **M. Johnson** to act as Referee and take evidence for recommendations. Judge Longs decision is that common lands aren't owned exclusively by the original grantees (this infuriates speculators like **T.B. Catron and S.B. Elkins** who have brought grants from original grantees) and that Las Vegas common lands are owned by the town of Las Vegas and therefore not public domain, i.e., Government owned, as desired by Julian.

A protest group called the *Gorras Blancas* (White Caps) is formed to combat the ideas that common lands belong to the Government or to the original grantees as private property. Gorras Blancas believe occupants of the land own it and should receive its benefits. They are accused of cutting barbed-wire fences that enclose common lands, burning timbers that are going to be sold to the railroad by the wealthy **Romero** family (Eugenio, Cleofas, Margarito, etc.).

1889: The house of Surveyor General **E.E Hobart** is burned; fences, crops, and farm equipment of **J. Ignacio Luján** are destroyed. **S.G. Hobart** recommends that a patent be issued for the entire Las Vegas grant and claims he is part owner of the common lands.

1902: A group led by **Ezequiel C. de Baca** proposes to incorporate the town of Las Vegas and request delivery of the land patent. Businessmen from **East Las Vegas,** led by banker **Jefferson Raynolds,** call instead for the court to appoint a board of trustees to take charge of the grant.

Judge **William J. Mills** (son-in-law to land speculator **Wilson Waddingham**) appoints a board of trustees: Jefferson Raynolds, Charles Ilfeld (who had earlier been indicted for land fraud), Elisha V. Long, Eugenio Romero (who had taken much timber from the common lands to sell to the railroad), F.H. Pierce, Félix Esquibel (a prominent rancher) and Isidoro Gallegos (a wealthy land and livestock dealer).

1931: More than 300,000 acres of the Las Vegas grant have been sold.

1942: Common lands in the Las Vegas grant number about *29,000* acres.

1990: Common lands in the Las Vegas grant number about *2,400* acres. Monies derived from sale of common lands go for attorney's fees, surveyor's fees, taxes, expenses, salaries for board members (which don't include "substantial" amounts of land deeded to board members in compensation for services rendered). Residents of the grant get very little.

PROFILE

Huning Brothers

LIVING THE AMERICAN DREAM

The Huning brothers, Franz, Charles, and Louis, all from Hanover, Germany, arrive in N.M. around this period (1860s). In time they buy out the Jules Fruendenthal store in Belén.
[It is said that Louis had $45 in his pocket when he got to Los Lunas. The brothers found a store in Los Lunas and devote their energies to building up a mercantile business. The Hunings are part of New Mexico's "German colony" of the day, which would include **Fredrick Scholle, Fredrick and John Becker, Oscar Goebel, Moses Sachs,** etc. These citizens of Germany had to learn *both English and Spanish* in order to be successful in their business ventures.]

1871: The Huning brothers have six branch stores and they handle hundreds of thousands of dollars in merchandise. They have a highly successful livestock business, owning some 60,000 sheep from which they harvest 200,000 pounds of wool, and 8,000 cattle.

1873: Louis Huning marries Emma Gehrling (from Missouri) but Emma dies.

1876: Louis Huning marries Henry Bush (from Germany) and they have four children.

1860 (con't.)
EL MILLIONARIO

Felipe Chávez moves from Los Padillas to Belén and begins a phenomenal business career. First he starts a general merchandise store on the *Camino Real* [today Belén's Main Street] where all traffic stops for supplies. He begins acquiring sheep and cattle and in time his herds are the largest in the rich Río Abajo area. He sends and receives merchandise over the Santa Fe Trail as well as south to and from Mexico.

Items freighted in from the States include sugar, coffee, rolls of cloth like calico, gingham, velvet, poplin, bleached white cloth referred to as manta used for making clothes, cosmetics, jewelry, candles, plows, hand tools, nails, etc.

Tradition has it that twice a year Felipe Chávez would bring out all his **gold and silver** to sun it in the patio of his Belén mansion in order to prevent rust from setting in. Many "old-timers" recall seeing these piles of gold and silver in the Chávez patio.

Chávez' business interests stretch from California, where he sells sheep, to New York City, where he has an agent on the Stock Exchange.

[It is said that Felipe Chávez was born with a silver spoon in his mouth and during his lifetime he changed it to gold.]

MILITARY & COMANCHES
March: A campaign is planned to seek and destroy all **Comanches.**

SHEEP RANCHING
Summer: **Francisco Perea, Jesús Luna,** and other sheepmen drive 50,000 sheep to California, the last (because of the Civil War) of the big drives.

HISPANO MERCHANTS
The following Hispanic New Mexican merchants, many of whom are involved in the Santa Fe Trade, are listed in the 1860 Census along with their (rounded) total assets:

$200,000 or more: José Leandro Perea, Mariano Yrizarri;

$100,00 or more: Manuel A. Otero, Juan Cristóbal Armijo;

$82,000: Cristóbal Armijo;
$74,000: Manuel Armijo, Rafaél Armijo;
$67,000: Felipe Chávez, Antonio José Luna;
$66,000: Navarro González
$65,000: Antonio J. Otero, Anastasio Barela;
$55,000: José Jaramillo;
$46,000: Luis Baca;
$42,000: Manuel Vigil;
$30,000-$39,000: José M. Gallegos, Anastasio Sandoval, Ramón Luna, Gaspar Ortiz y Alaríd;
$20,000-$29,000: Juan Montoya, Rafaél Gutiérrez, Ambrosio Armijo, Simón Delgado, José Salazar, Nestor Armijo, Agustín Torres, Juan J. Sánchez, Salvador Armijo;

José Leandro Perea
Courtesy Museum of NM, #50560
(C. Batchelor ink wash)

$16,000-$19,000: Pedro Baca, Antonio Lerma, Nestor Montoya, Miguel Romero, Toribio Romero, Manuel Yrizarri, Wensilao Luján;

$10,000-$15,000: Antonio Ribera, Pablo Meléndez, Miguel A. Córdova, Francisco Armijo, Juan Armijo, Saturnino Barrientos, Stanislao Montoya, José Armijo, José Miguel Baca, Nepomuceno Ancheta, Felipe Delgado, José Miguel Romero;

$5,000-$9,900: José María Romero, Prudencio López, Ignacio González, Manuel García, Pablo Pino, Tomás González, Antonio María Baca, Nestor Barela, Benito Larragoiti, Mariano Silva, Manuel Abeita, Francisco Ortiz y Delgado, Rumaldo Chávez, Fernando Delgado, Vicente García, Dionisio Jaramillo, Antonio Abeita, Miguel Sena y Quintana, Gregorio, Baca, José Guadalupe Gallegos, Jesús María Barela, Pablo Delgado, Clemente Sarracino;

$3,000-$4,500: Vidal Romero, Antonio Constante, Francisco Baca, José Francisco Armijo, Félix Ulibarrí, José Martín, Manuel Saenz, Manuel Salazar, Pablo Chávez, Celso Cuellar Medina, Severo Trujillo, Ambrosio Chávez, Leandro Martínez, Miguel Ortiz, Manuel Sandoval;

$2,000-$2,800: Guadalupe Miranda, Pedro Sánchez, Lorenzo Montoya, Reyes Armijo, Candelario García, Bernardo Baca, Juan Montoya, José Gutiérrez, José Armijo, Francisco Montoya, Juan López, Antonio Ortiz, Vicente Trujillo;

$1,900 or less: Manuel González, José Jaramillo, Desiderio Naranjo, Antonio Herrera, Bonifacio Romero, José Tomás Griego, Francisco Abreú, Jesús María Chávez, Reyes Contreras, Ramón Nevares, Dolores Gallegos, Antonio Abeita, Ramón Baca, Antonio Robles, Desiderio Sánchez, Agapito Vigil, Manuel Sánchez, Verislao Luna, Jesús Ochoa, Cecilio Robles, Tomás Baca, Segundo Oceáno, José Sena, Higinio Salas, José Trujillo Salazar, Marcos Apodaca, José Crespín, Pablo Armijo, Rosalia Colomo, Jesús Sánchez, Bautista Silva, Leonardo Márquez, Juan Luis Ortiz, Teodoro Ortiz, J.D. González de Rueda, Miguel López, Lupes Mes, David Ariscón, Albino Roybal, Simón Segura, Basilio Leyvas, Gemelo Dena, Victoriano Baca, Nicolás Armijo, Carlos Barela, jog Estrada, Felipe García, Jesús María Luna, Eleuterio Mayagoitia, José Pablo Montoya, Vicente Otero, Jesús María Salazar, Juan Salazar, Pablo Valdez, José M. Velásquez.

LAND TITLES
June 2: Congress confirms the **Las Trampas land grant** to the Town of Las Trampas.

MILITARY & COMANCHES
June: Comanches with their families and pack animals loaded for trading at the Pecos settlements are attacked by an Army detachment. Indian Agent Levi Keithly later verifies that the Comanches were a peaceful trading party.

July: Major Ruff leads his detachment in search of **Comanches** and when he doesn't encounter any he blames "*...lying Mexicans who never tell the truth, if a falsehood can possibly be made to answer the purpose.*" Lt. **J.X. Dubois** writes in his diary: "*Alas for those who put their trust in Mexicans... There is no truth in them. Their evident intention was to take us away from the Indians and they have succeeded.*" The campaign is called off because Comanches can't be located.

SOCIETY & INTERSECTIONAL LOYALTY
July 4: At a celebration in Taos, New Mexicans of the area proclaim loyalty toward the Union.

MILITARY & AMERINDS
September 23: **Manuel Chaves** is in command of an expedition of about 450 volunteers who serve at their own expense, furnishing their own weapons, horses, food, and clothing, to fight the Navajos. A number of skirmishes are fought and much livestock is recovered. Captives, mostly women and children, are taken.

November: An Army detachment discovers a **Comanche** trading party asleep in the courtyard at the house of don **E. Ulibarrí** at **Chaparito.** The soldiers open fire, killing and wounding some of the sleeping Comanches. The survivors take refuge in Ulibarrí's house whereupon the soldiers take their horses and mules which they sell in Las Vegas the next day.

TINSMITHS

Tinwork is now a New Mexican craft practiced by about 25 persons [between 1840 to 1940 according to L. Coulter and M. Dixon; the number seems a low estimate]. New Mexican tinsmiths produce from 5,000 to 10,000 pieces for homes, family chapels, moradas, and village churches. Tinsmiths travel from village to village to sell their creations, much like *santeros*. Early New Mexican tinwork, primarily frames, *"...exhibits meticulous craftsmanship and inventive design-with extensive stamping, diagonally scored engaged columns, and square corner bosses..."*

CARPENTRY

Furniture in the distinctive New Mexican style is being produced in large quantities now that water-powered sawmills are in the Territory.

1860: Four cabinet shops in Santa Fe turn out some 1,500 pieces of furniture. But eastern styles begin to make their appearance.

1860s-1870S
Roque Candelaria, originally from Tomé, operates a highly successful cabinet shop in Manzano.

1860-1890
SANTEROS

José García Gonzáles and **Juan Miguel Herrera** are creating religious art during this period. García Gonzáles works in oil paints; in the early 1880's he moves to Trinidad, Colorado, takes a railroad job and creates santero art only intermittently.

1861-1866

Henry Connelly is Governor.

1861
LAND GRANT CHICANERY

The office of the Surveyor General is working very slowly with only 17 Pueblo land claims and 19 private and town land claims approved, causing native New Mexicans to think that the government authorities want to swindle them out of their lands.

For example:

Heirs of the **San Joaquín land grant,** numbering around 400, petition the SG for confirmation of their grant, which is estimated to contain about 184,000 acres, in 1861. *The petition is ignored for 17 years.* When a survey is done in 1878 the acreage is at 473,000 acres and speculators own most of the common lands.

[The grant had already been recommended for confirmation by Surveyor General Proudfit in 1872, before a survey, and would be again after its enlargement, in 1880.]

Henry Connelly
Courtesy Museum of NM, #9846

Seventeen individuals protest the 1878 survey of the San Joaquín grant, saying that their **private lands** have been included in the survey and confirmation of the grant will rob them of their land.

[**Will M. Tipton**, a key assistant to the U.S. Attorney, was a member of the survey crew.]

While the San Joaquín is being contested in N.M., **William Blackmore** is trying to sell it in England. T.B. Catron is attorney for some of the speculators who claim ownership of San Joaquín.

The Supreme Court finally rules in 1896 that since common lands were owned by Spain/Mexico, the U.S. is now owner of said lands.

[**Daniel Tyler,** cited by **M. Ebright** as studying all community land grants in N.M., writes that "*...the ejido (common lands) belonged to the community to which it was appurtenant.*" Ebright concludes that "*...it is somewhat appalling to contemplate the injustice that resulted from the United States Supreme Court's blanket acceptance of what Mr. Reynolds and Mr. Hall* (attorneys working for the Government) *told them about the Hispanic land law of New Mexico.*"]

SOCIETY
Military spending is recognized as basic to the economy of N.M., "*with the Anglos and ricos realizing almost all of the financial benefits.*"

John V. Watts is chosen to replace **Miguel A. Otero** (I) as Delegate to Congress.

MILITARY & COMANCHES
January 4: The N.M. military destroys a **Comanche** encampment on the Cimarron River, killing 10 Comanches and wounding many more. Forty horses and 150 lodges are burned along with a quantity of buffalo robes. Comanches ask for peace via several Comanchero parties but the Army ignores the offers until a Mescalero Apache uprising.

WOMEN & LAW
April 26: Judge Benedict finds **Paula Angel** guilty of murder and she is executed by hanging, the first white woman to be hanged on the Western frontier.

TIMELINE
April 12, 1861: **Southern forces fire an Fort Sumter, commencing the Civil War.**

MILITARY PERSONNEL
Spring: Officers and enlisted men in N.M. talk and argue over things like slavery, the right to secede from the Union, allegiance to the State of one's birth, duty to a country or to one's section, etc. Hispanic New Mexicans vow to repel any Confederate invasion coming from Texas.

May 1: It is rumored that Capt. **J.R. Baylor** *"...a fast stepping and energetic Texan if there ever was one.."* has recruited 1,000 *"...rough, tough and determined Texas riflemen..."* for the invasion of N.M.

May 7: Capt. **R.S. Ewell** resigns his commission in N.M. and goes over to the Confederates where he eventually achieves the rank of Lt. General.

BLACKS & LAW
The Slave Code Act of 1859 is repealed immediately upon the outbreak of the Civil War.

MILITARY & COMANCHES
May 10-11: A peace conference is held by the Pecos River at Alamo Gordo Creek: **Comanches** will stop all raids, ignore wagon trains on the Santa Fe Trail and all settlements in eastern N.M., and trade only at Fort Union or other places designated by the military. They are warned not to listen . . ..to any other people" or they will be in trouble. A few days after the signing, **Chief Esaquipa** leads a trading party to Chaparito and is attacked by a military detachment from Hatch's Ranch. Rancher **Levi Steck** writes that soldiers are provoking hostilities by firing on peaceful Comanches. (When troops are withdrawn from the area because of the Civil War, hostilities come to an end as Comanches and Comancheros resume their trading relationship.)

MILITARY PERSONNEL & CIVIL WAR
May 13: Officers **T.T. Fauntleroy, W.W. Loring, H.H. Sibley** [inventor of the *Sibley tent* and later the *Sibley stove*] resign their Union commissions and go over to the **Confederacy.**

June: Officers **W.J. Longstreet** and **G.B. Crittenden** resign their commissions and go over to the Confederacy.

June 16: Col. Canby orders Major **L. Lynde** to remove all government property and his Union command to Fort Fillmore, abandoning **Fort McLane** (situated near the Santa Rita copper mines).

June 23: **E.R.S. Canby** is appointed to head all military troops in N.M. Troops are disorganized and confused as to loyalties so his first task is to bolster morale because he feels the Confederacy will attack N.M. first in order to win the Southwest which has rich gold fields in California and Colorado.

[As fate would have it, the general of the Confederate army would be **H.H. Sibley,** Canby's brother-in-law.]

Gen. Henry Siblley
Courtesy Museum of NM, #50541

July 1: Capt. **Baylor** and 400 men, the Second Texas Mounted Rifles, reach Fort Bliss and are welcomed to **El Paso** by, among others, **James Magoffin.**

July 5: Major Lynde's command readies **Fort Fillmore** and is augmented by three more companies. Because the fort is surrounded by hills he writes to Canby saying the area can't be defended against cannon so he asks for permission to abandon it.

July 25: Capt. Baylor enters **Mesilla** with 250 men and prepares to fight the 700-man Union force at Fort Fillmore, which Canby has supplied with additional weaponry.

Lynde takes 380 men and marches to the outskirts of Mesilla where he demands an unconditional surrender. There is a skirmish and Lynde orders a retreat to **Fort Fillmore** but he is convinced the fort can't be defended against Baylor's artillery so he decides to abandon it and retreat to **Fort Stanton** some 154 miles to the northeast. Wagons are quickly loaded with supplies, ammunition, women and children. The men hear that kegs of hospital **brandy** and medicinal **whiskey** are to be left behind so many partake of the liquor on the spot and most **empty their water canteens and fill them with liquor.**

July 26: Fort Fillmore is evacuated and everyone is on the road toward Fort Stanton. Heavy dust clouds inform Baylor of the evacuation so he sends a detachment to take over the abandoned Fillmore while the main body of his troops speed to intercept the retreating Union forces at San Augustín Pass. **Union soldiers** [described officially as *"...well disciplined and drilled troops..."*] are literally dying of thirst in the heat because they have had **nothing but liquor to drink** and they surrender in exchange for water. Less than 200 Confederates capture nearly 700 Federal soldiers without firing a shot.

Upon hearing of Lynde's surrender to Baylor, troops at Fort Stanton set fire to all government stores and abandon it. A sudden rainstorm puts out the fire and people living in the area help themselves to supplies.

August 2: Capt. Baylor issues a proclamation: All of N.M. south of the 34th parallel is now the **Confederate Territory of Arizona.** Mesilla is designated the capital and Baylor appoints himself Governor.

August 8: Gen. Canby suspends the **writ of habeas corpus** throughout N.M. and issues *"an order to enable every commander to guard against the treasonable designs of persons disloyal to the government of the United States..."*

August 8: **Manuel Chaves** is assigned command of **Fort Fauntleroy** [at Bear Springs, where years ago as a teenager he had bathed wounds inflicted on him by Navajos] which is garrisoned by **New Mexican Mounted Volunteers.** His orders are to prevent an outbreak of hostilities with the Navajo.

August 13: **Rafaél Chacón** and his company of men report to Fort Union where he is commissioned a Captain in the **New Mexico Volunteers.**

TREASON

August 17, 1861: The Grand Jury of the United States District Court at Santa Fe issues 26 indictments for treason against the Union. One person in the group, **Manuel Barelas,** is Hispanic. *Twenty-five indictments are dismissed* but **Manuel Barelas** is found guilty and all his property is confiscated.

MILITARY

Summer/Fall: The Territory of N.M. raises five regiments of volunteers, a regiment of militia, a battalion of militia, three independent companies of militia which enlist for three months, as well as four independent cavalry companies enlisted for three months to fight in the Civil War.

November: **Governor Connelly** calls for volunteers to fight the Confederacy.

[During the Civil War 3,500 New Mexicans fought for the Union, out of a total population of 50,000, motivating Connelly to pay tribute to a people *"so patriotic in nature"* because they had been with the USA only since 1846 and as yet hadn't even been granted the status of regular citizens.]

Rafael Chacón
Courtesy Museum of NM, #148455

November 18: Gen. **Canby** writes to the Paymaster General in Washington that regular troops haven't been paid in 12 months and volunteers not at all. He must have money if he is to meet the Confederate threat and hostile Indians who, especially the **Navajos,** are causing much suffering with their depredations. *"Extermination by the sword or by starvation is our only remedy for the evils which they have caused and will continue to cause our people so long as there is one in existence..."*

December 20: Confederate Gen. **H.H. Sibley** addresses a proclamation to the people of N.M.: An army under my command enters New Mexico to take possession of it in the name and for the benefit of the Confederate States ... we come as friends ... to liberate ... from the yoke of military despotism erected by usurpers upon the ruins of the former free institutions of the United States. Your persons, your families, and your property shall be secure and safe. All taxes are hereby abolished ... To my old comrades in arms ... drop at once the arms which degrade you into the tools of tyrants, renounce their service, and array yourselves under the colors of justice and freedom... (See **Feb. 21, 1862.**)

RECRUITMENT

The "despised" **Comancheros** are recruited for service by Union officers.

1862
LAND LAW & FRAUD

The **Homestead Act** becomes law.

A citizen may file for 160 acres of land. **Water sources** are sought for privatization because whoever controls the water controls all the land around it.

1890: Large cattle ranchers become adept at using land laws to their advantage and they are not timid when the *"...alternative was fraud."* There are 2,940 persons in N.M. eligible by law to take out a homestead [in the decade of the '80s] but there are filed 5,740 original homestead entries which require five years of residence and 6,937 preemption (six months of residence) declarations. During the same decade there are 1,547 Timber Culture and 1,207 Desert Land applications.

TREATY BREAKING

A law is passed by Congress that requires **land grant claimants** to pay for all surveys necessary to adjudicate their land titles. Further, the government retains *"the power of appointing the surveyor to do the work and of fixing his compensation."*

[The law is contrary to the Treaty of Guadalupe Hidalgo and is a strong factor in destabilizing land titles in N.M.]

SETTLEMENT

San Mateo is founded by families from Cebolleta,

COMMERCE

New Mexicans export one million pounds of **wool** (worth 12 to 15 cents per pound in Kansas City) and a new industry is born in N.M. Sheepmen cross *Merino* rams with the native churros, accelerating the change from mutton to wool production.

SOCIETY

Santero **José Rafaél Aragón** dies in Córdova.

INDIAN SLAVERY

It is estimated [by R.E. **Twitchell,** quoted by V. **Westphall**] that there are **600 Indian slaves** in all of N.M.

CIVIL WAR BATTLES

February 21: The **Battle of Valverde** begins soon after dawn, continuing throughout the day and into the next. Union troops from Fort Craig march out to engage the Confederates, along with a full regiment of **New Mexico Volunteers** under Kit Carson, as well as two companies of Colorado troops, the **Pike's Peakers.** The Río Grande River separates the two armies and Union forces charge across the river as the Confederates open fire. Many Federal soldiers are killed or wounded but Company K makes it across with two 24 pounders and they fire on the Confederate position. The Southerners attack and counter-attack until Canby orders a retreat to Fort Craig, leaving the Confederates victorious in the field. Union officers, especially Gen. Canby, **blame the New Mexico Volunteers for the defeat:** *"...the battle was fought ... with no assistance from the militia and but little from the volunteers, who would not obey orders or obeyed them too late to be of any service..."*

[**A.A. Hayes** later wrote that Valverde was lost by mismanagement at the command level. **J.W Ellis,** a member of K Company in the battle, wrote that Canby had lost the battle by ordering a retreat. **W.W. Mills** also verified later that the fight went well for the Union until General Canby appeared on the scene. The "Mexicans" were branded as cowards or deserters despite their high casualty rates "*...always from Anglo pens-while conveniently overlooking any shortcomings exhibited by the Anglo soldiers...*" according to J. Meketa, author of the R. Chacón biography.]

Confederate General **Sibley** stops in **Belén** and demands of **Felipe Chávez** $5,000 and "considerable" numbers of sheep and cattle for his troops. In return Chávez is given Sibley's IOU.

March 2: **Confederate forces occupy Albuquerque** but Canby has ordered that all government property be put to the torch and only smoking ruins remain when the town is taken without a fight.

[Sibley's troops have lived off the country in their march from Valverde through Socorro, Peralta, etc., to Albuquerque, taking whatever they wish.]

March 5: Governor Connelly and all Federal troops abandon Santa Fe, fleeing to Fort Union. Col. **Manuel Chaves** is ordered to gather militiamen and join the retreat.

[M. Simmons writes that from the beginning of the Confederate invasion, the mass of New Mexicans had shown themselves apathetic toward the issues of the war, and "*coupled with their inborn fear of Texans,*" most did not render dedicated service. This historical interpretation is in direct contrast to Governor Connelly's tribute to New Mexicans who, out of a population of some 50,000, a full 3,500 served with Union forces, motivating Connelly to praise New Mexican loyalty. New Mexicans knew the Confederates were in reality a Texas army and resolved to war against them. Hispanics had captured other Texas invaders in 1841 which might have something to do with the *fear* charge.]

March 23: The **Confederates hoist their flag in the Santa Fe plaza** without having to fire a shot. Two days later they march eastward intending to attack Fort Union.

March 27: A number of skirmishes take place:
    at a watering place known as **Pigeon's Ranch;**
    at **Apache Canyon;**
    at **Johnson's Ranch;**
    at **Kozlowski's Ranch,** amid beautiful mountain country or grassy meadows.

March 28: Scout **Manuel Antonio Chaves** guides Colorado troops led by Preacher **J.M. Chivington** and **J.P. Slough** to the Confederate army's supply and ammunition train. The "Pike's Peakers" are taken down the mountain to the rear of the train, Chaves telling Chivington: "*You are right on top of them, Major.*" In the distance opposing armies are engaged in the **Battle of Glorieta Pass** but the surprise move captures the entire supply column which turns out being a death blow to Confederate plans in the Southwest.

[M. Simmons reports that "*Strangely...*" Chaves' role "*found little to no mention*" in Chivington's official report.]

A rumor gets started in Confederate ranks that Gen. Canby's army has captured their supply train and will soon attack the main Confederate army, which is now without sufficient ammunition.

April 15: Sibley's forces withdraw to Texas, **ending the Civil War in N.M.**

Conditions in N.M. are severe because of the destructive fighting during the Civil War. Confederate and Union forces alike have confiscated, pillaged, stolen, or burned whatever they wished. Territorial officials have no money with which to pay soldiers or volunteers. There is open antagonism between Union and Confederate sympathizers. Hostile Indians prey on ranches and small villages. Men want to get home and plant crops to avoid hunger during the winter.

PROPERTY CONFISCATION

July: Congress passes an act for confiscation of property of Rebel sympathizers.

August 16, 1862: U.S. Marshall **Abraham Cutler** (and "perhaps" Gen. **J.H. Carleton**) see an opportunity *"to confiscate tempting properties" so* they work with **Joab Houghton** and Judge **Benedict Kirby** to enable the Military to move against certain people like Rafaél Armijo, E.H. Cavenaugh, S.M. Baird, José María Chávez, Manuel Barela, Julián Tenerio [sic], Blas Lucero, etc. The confiscations target goods and/or cash and Cutler collects some $52,065.

1866: With **John Pratt** now serving as U.S Marshall, **Abraham Cutler is indicted for embezzlement** and ordered to submit a record of his proceedings while serving as Marshall. His account maintains that after collecting more than $52,000 the federal government owes him $571.29.

FRONTIERSMAN

Manuel Antonio Chaves is honorably discharged from military duties. He returns to his ranch to learn that the Navajo have taken virtually all his stock, including 30,000 sheep. [In 1862 he files a claim against the government; a relief bill is introduced in Congress by 1876 but it isn't approved until after Manuel's death.] He decides to move his operation eastward toward the Pecos River country but before he moves he receives an appeal for help from settlers living by Socorro: more than 100 Navajos are raiding ranches in the vicinity, killing shepherds and taking huge numbers of stock. **Matías Contreras,** one of the most distinguished residents of the area, is going after the raiding war party because it has made off with his young son. Manuel takes eight men with him, confers with Contreras at his hacienda and with another six men the 14 ride in pursuit immediately after sending a messenger to Fort Craig asking for assistance.

The trail is followed to the foothills of the San Mateo mountains and as the 14 approach *Ojo de la Mónica* (Monica Spring) they see signs that the Navajos are very near. But the war party's rear guard discovers their pursuers and all warriors are signaled to come join the battle. The warriors form a battle line, confident that the small group of *Nakai* can be taken on the first charge.

Manuel Chaves directs his men to take cover among the junipers and the battle is joined by all combatants, Manuel wearing a conspicuous red kerchief around his neck and firing his single-shot Hawkins throughout the afternoon and early evening until only he, **Matías Contreras,** and **Tomás Baca** who is suffering from a serious wound in the leg, are alive.

At dawn the next morning Manuel finds three bullets left for his Hawkins, which he had fired eighty times during the fight, and he realizes one more charge will be the end. But the Navajos are not to be found as sun rays flood the land and junipers, having abandoned the battlefield. The seriously wounded Tomás Baca is carried on a litter back toward the Río Grande. The rescue detail of Román Baca and soldiers from Ft. Craig are met on the trail.

[Tomás Baca lost his leg but lived for many years in Socorro County. Matías Contreras, who later served in the territorial legislature, found and ransomed his son within a few months. Manuel Chaves, who admired courage, later said the *Ojo de la Mónica* fight was his greatest because the Navajos, though well armed with rifles, had shown tremendous courage in their attacks and had the Hispanics possessed any less, none would have lived to tell about it.]

PROFILE

Manuel Antonio Chaves

M R .   S O U T H W E S T

October 18, 1818: **Manuel Antonio Chaves** is born to Julián Chaves and María Luz García (de Noriega) Chaves at Atrisco.

1827: The Chaves family relocates to the village of Cebolleta (Seboyeta) on the Navajo frontier. Manuel grows up helping the family in small-scale farming and stockraising. He also works at mastering the use of weapons like the knife, rifle, bow and arrows, etc., and especially horsemanship (at which New Mexicans are described as masters).

1832(?): Julián Chaves dies. The following year María de la Luz marries José Antonio Baca. In time a son, **Román Antonio Baca,** Manuel's half-brother, is born.

1835(?): Manuel joins a trading expedition into Navajo country. The Navajos attack the expedition in the area of Canyon de Chelly. Manuel is wounded seven times and the rest of the Cebolletanos are wiped out. Miraculously, Manuel makes his way back to Cebolleta which is nearly 200 miles away.

1837(?): Manuel goes to visit his grandmother in Atrisco. He hires on as an arriero with a group of German merchants who are going to New Orleans. After a few months in New Orleans Manuel returns to Atrisco.

1839: Chaves enters his prized horse, *Malcreado,* in a contest against a racer owned by Governor Armijo. Malcreado is winning easily when he suddenly drops dead. Rumor has it that Malcreado was poisoned and Manuel resolves to make Armijo pay. But the Governor puts a price on Manuel's head and Chaves escapes to Missouri, settling in St. Louis.

1840: Manuel forms a partnership with a young Cuban named Alfonso Fernández in the operation of a fruit store. The enterprise does well until Fernández absconds with all the money. Chaves pursues him to New York and then to Cuba but can't catch up with him so he returns to St. Louis. Manuel is now completely literate in English as well as Spanish.

1841: Governor Armijo sends word to Manuel that he has been "pardoned" and asks him to return to New Mexico. Uncle Mariano Chávez guarantees his safety so Manuel returns to Santa Fe.

June 19, 1841: President Lamar of Texas sends an armed force of 321 men, known as the Texan-Santa Fe Expedition, to New Mexico. The hapless Texans are easily captured by Governor Armijo and his New Mexican militiamen. Manuel serves as secretary and interpreter for the New Mexican forces.

Manuel Antonio Chaves
Courtesy Museum of NM, #9833

1843(?): Chaves builds a large home in Santa Fe. Manuel is soft-spoken, has chestnut colored hair, fair complexion, grey eyes, is five-foot-seven-inches tall and weighs around 140 pounds.

1844: Manuel Chaves marries **M. Vicenta Labadie** of Tomé.

August 18, 1846: The Army of the West enters Santa Fe and takes New Mexico (which also includes Arizona) for the USA.

December 1846: Manuel Chaves is jailed on a charge of treason against the United States. The matter is taken before a military tribunal. Captain Angney, a lawyer from Missouri, is assigned to defend Manuel. Angney orates that Chaves is still a citizen of Mexico and if he took part in defending his country he should be commended as a patriot, that the United States would be forever disgraced if it executed a man for defending his country in a time of need. Chaves is acquitted and released. He makes a formal oath of allegiance to the United States.

May, 1848: Manuel works at building a livestock business. He forms a partnership with his brother-in-law Lorenzo Labadie. They are involved in the Indian trade as well as commerce to Chihuahua.

1849: Daughter **Perfilia** is born. In time **Amado** and **Irineo** are born.

1851: Manuel begins to take part in military campaigns against hostile Indians. As his reputation grows more and more American army commanders as well as N.M. citizens seek him out for help against raiders because of his coolness under fire, familiarity with Indian warfare and its tactics, and his knowledge of trails and terrain.
Spring, 1851: Manuel leads an expedition against the Navajos.

1852: Chaves drives sheep to California.

1854: Manuel and Lorenzo borrow $6,200 from Miguel Pino.

1855: Manuel is commissioned a Captain to lead one of the six companies during the Ute-Jicarilla War. Twenty-one-year old **Román Baca,** Manuel's half-brother, is a second lieutenant in the same company.
1857: Manuel is *Chief of Scouts* for the Gila Expedition against the Mogollón, Gila, and Coyotero Apaches. With him are Román Baca, Lorenzo Labadie, and Jesús Chaves. (Military troopers under Colonel Loring become so fatigued they start failing asleep in their saddles in an effort to keep up with the New Mexican scouts.)

1858(?): Chaves clashes with **Bishop Lamy** over the boundary that separates his Santa Fe land from that of Guadalupe Chapel. When Manuel fences "his" land, Lamy threatens him with excommunication. Chaves denounces any attempted excommunication on the grounds that it would *"break my wife's heart."*

The writ of excommunication is scheduled to be read the following Sunday at Guadalupe Chapel. The church is packed with only one bench remaining at the front where Manuel, Román, and a close friend go to sit, all heavily armed with rifles. When the priest [Machebeuf?] mounts the pulpit and pulls out a roll of parchment from his sleeve the three men seated on the bench cock their rifles as if wafting for the reading. The priest descends from the pulpit and continues the service without any readings.

Summer, 1858: Manuel Chaves is in Mesilla when citizens ask him to lead the rescue mission of E.J. White, his wife and little baby. With Manuel is also the celebrated guide Jesús Armijo when the group hits the trail in pursuit of the raiders and their captives. At dusk the rescuers enter an oasis of a valley where they find the baby lanced through and through by spears. The enemy camp is discovered but Manuel forbids an immediate attack because he knows all captives will be killed at the first sound of battle. The rescuers get close enough for a sudden attack but Mrs. White is killed instantly upon the sound of gunfire.

1859(?): Manuel moves his family to the **Ojuelos Ranch** on the eastern edge of the Tomé land grant. On one occasion an Apache warrior is thundering out of the yard with little Irineo under his arm. Manuel shoots the warrior dead and Irineo drops to the ground. He is unconscious from the fall but otherwise all right.

1860: Manuel is in a fight against the Apaches at Salada, one of his lambing camps. His son Amado witnesses the battle.

Summer, 1860: Juan Cristóbal Armijo sends word to Manuel at Ojuelos that a war party of some 20 Apaches is headed his way with 200 stolen mules. At a timbered ridge south of the ranch Manuel confronts the warriors and "by waving his men to come join him in battle" he bluffs them into thinking he has many men in the forest. The warriors retreat.

September, 1860: Manuel holds the rank of Lt.-Col. but actually functions as field commander of an expedition against the Navajos which goes as far west as the Hopi pueblos.

August 8, 1861: Chaves is placed in command of Fort Fauntleroy. A contested horse race between Dr. Kavenuagh's thoroughbred and a Navajo sorrel pony results in almost ending Manuel's military career.
The Civil War comes to New Mexico. A militia regiment is led by Col. Miguel Pino and Lt.-Col. Manuel Chaves.

March 28, 1862: Manuel leads Chivington's Colorado troops, known as "Pike's Peakers," behind Confederate lines. All Confederate supplies are destroyed, causing the Texan army to hightail it back to Texas.

Manuel receives notice that Navajo raiders have driven off 11,000 of his sheep from his Ojuelos ranch.

1863(?): Manuel is in the *Ojo de la Mónica* fight against the Navajos. (Chaves was later to say this was his finest hour because if the warriors had attacked the following morning they would have found him with only three bullets left for his single-shot Hawkins.)

1864(?): Román Baca and scores of *Cebolletanos* found the village of San Mateo on the other side of the mountain from Cebolleta.

1865-1875: Manuel's life is relatively free of combat.

1874: Chaves sells his Santa Fe house situated behind the Guadalupe Chapel.

1876: Manuel relocates to San Mateo and builds an hacienda.

1882: Amado Chaves travels to Washington, D.C. on behalf of the claimants of the Cebolleta land grant.

1888: **Charles F. Lummis** visits Manuel in San Mateo. The old knight is suffering intensely from his many wounds, his vision is no longer clear, and he weighs less than 100 pounds. But all is borne stoically and he enjoys his extended family.

While on a journey to Tucson, Archbishop Lamy stops at the Chaves hacienda long enough to bless the chapel.

January, 1889: Manuel Antonio Chaves, *El Leoncito*, dies. He is laid to rest beneath the altar of his chapel. His wife, Vicenta, follows him six years later and is buried beside him.

[Perhaps the description by Charles F. Lummis best describes New Mexico's valiant Hispanic knight: "*a courtly Spanish gentleman, brave as a lion, tender as a woman, spotless of honor, and modest as heroic.*"]

LAND LAW

May 3: The **special deposit system** is instituted by an Act of Congress: surveys of townships will henceforth be paid for by settlers in said townships.

1871: Deposits by settlers can be used as part payment for lands in townships and these deposits can be used for surveying expenses.

1879: Certificates of deposit are negotiable and can be used in payment for public land under the terms of the Preemption and Homestead laws. **Cattlemen posing as "settlers"** in certain townships use the certificates to acquire valuable land.

TIMELINE

May 5, 1862: A poorly equipped Mexican army composed mostly of citizen patriots led by **General Ignacio Zaragosa** meets the highly touted professional French army of Napoleon III outside of **Puebla, Mexico**. Mexican forces win the day [and in time *Cinco de Mayo* becomes a symbol throughout the hemisphere for all who would be free as well as for rejoicing via parades, community gatherings, concerts, and street fiestas].

MILITARY

August 7: **General James Carleton** arrives with the **California Column** (nearly 2,400 men) with orders to preserve N.M. for the Union. Carleton assumes command of all military forces in N.M. by September 18.

[C. Larson writes that Gen. Carleton believes in the **Manifest Destiny** of the American nation, that Americans can make treaties with the Indian tribes then break them when convenient, that Americans have the right to make Indians change their culture, economy, religion, and to remove them from ancestral homelands. Negotiating is mere courtesy, not requirement, and displays of humanity are largesse rather than human rights owed Native Americans.]

[W.A. Beck writes the Indians believed the U.S. Cavalry couldn't punish them for "depredations" so they became convinced that *"neither the white man nor his treaties"* were of any particular importance. But the Navajos *"were careful not to destroy things"* because they wanted the Pueblos and Spanish to continue farming so Navajos could harvest the crops.]

Gen. James Carleton
Courtesy Museum of NM, #22938

BOSQUE REDONDO

Carleton selects a site known as **Bosque Redondo,** a 40 square-mile area on the Pecos River 165 miles southeast of Santa Fe, on which to locate all **Navajos** and all **Mescalero Apaches** (who were traditional enemies).

Work is begun building **Fort Sumner** but Dr. **Michael Steck,** Supt. of Indian Affairs, warns that the area is not fertile enough to support the Indians and that it is most dangerous to place enemy tribes on the same land.

Kit Carson is given orders to relocate all Mescaleros to Bosque Redondo and to kill all men resisting the relocation. When a party of Mescaleros travel to Santa Fe to meet with Carleton, 10 are shot down by troops, including a female, **Manuelito** and **José Largo,** two leading chiefs. Carleton tells the Mescaleros they must submit or be exterminated so around 800 finally report at Bosque Redondo. But small groups continually escape from the reservation and return to their native haunts.

CIVIL WAR & COMANCHES

November 3: Comanche **Chief Mowway** arid his warriors help to capture Confederate sympathizers that are trying to escape through the Canadian Valley. Mowway and Little Buffalo offer their help if Union forces will come down and fight the Texans but it is decided Union forces are too small to be split.

1863
LAND TITLES

The **Embudo grant** is filed for confirmation with Surveyor General John Clark. [The request is ignored for thirty (30) years.]

MILITARY

General Carleton assigns Lt. Col. **J. Francisco Chaves** to oversee the construction of Fort Wingate on the eastern border of Navajo country.

TIMELINE

February 24,1863: **The Territory of Arizona is created from western New Mexico.**

NAVAJO CAMPAIGN

Summer: Kit Carson leads American soldiers against the widely dispersed Navajo, *Diné,* The People. The strategy is one of scorched earth, skirmishes, and relentless pursuit but General Carleton's orders to the troops are also to *"Kill every male Navajo and Apache you can find"* according to J. Kutz.

[Kit Carson didn't instigate the campaign but he is described as being *"Carleton's tool."* Furthermore, while Carleton wanted to educate the Navajos into the ways of civilization and Christianity in the experiment that has been referred to as *Fair Carletonia,* he also believed there might be rich mineral deposits of gold and silver in *Dinétah,* Navajo land, so he wanted them out of the way.]

January 10, 1964: Carson and his troops corner a large group of starving, freezing Navajos in Canyon de Chelly. There is a brief skirmish of bows and arrows against rifles and the Navajos surrender.

Many Navajos are now gathered at Fort Wingate and forced into the death march known as the *Long Walk* to **Bosque Redondo**, a distance of over 300 miles. The long lines of Navajos are under Army guard and soldiers shoot stragglers who can't keep up or fall by the wayside.

The Long Walk is also forced on the **Cañoncito Navajos,** who had aligned themselves with the Americans (and been labeled *Diné Anaaii,* Enemy Navajos, by the rest of The People), served as scouts in the U.S. Army, and whose famous leader, **Cebolla Antonio Sandoval,** had gotten them title papers to their Cañoncito lands west of Albuquerque.

1864: There are some 9,000 Indians at Bosque Redondo. (It is estimated that some 5,000 additional Navajos, now labeled "hostiles" by the *Bilagáana,* were still out.) The basic problems are hunger, disease, shortages of every kind, bureaucratic fraud, raiders, and crop failure. About 2,321 Indians die from smallpox. *"Thousands of Indians die of starvation."* Kit Carson resigns in disgust.

Bishop Lamy is appalled at the poverty, degradation, disease, and starvation of Bosque Redondo when he visits the reservation concentration camp.

Throughout the years the Dine petition to be allowed to return to their native lands.

[No gold or silver is discovered in Dinétah.]

1868: Finally, the Navajos are permitted to return to their ancestral homelands and they begin the Long Walk once more, but this time toward home.

MILITARY
August: Camp Easton is elevated to a permanent post and renamed Fort Bascom.

CIVIL vs. MILITARY
Cordial relations with the **Comanches** are jeopardized by a feud between the military and the Indian Department: the Military will not give the Indians rations if the Indian Dept. doesn't reimburse costs. When Chief Esaquipa reports Confederate movements at Fort Bascom he is turned away without presents.

MILITARY DISCRIMINATION

October 1: **Rafaél Chacón** tenders his resignation from the Army, citing discrimination against Hispanics when it comes to promotions. **General Carleton** promises him the deserved promotion to Major and Chacón stays in the military.

THE HERMIT

Giovanni María Agostini joins a wagon train owned by **Manuel Romero** in Kansas and walks all the way to Las Vegas, black cape over his shoulders, a long staff, to which was fastened a small tinkling bell, in hand. (Romero offers a seat in a wagon but Agostini prefers to walk.) It is learned that this Italian in his early sixties is of noble birth, well educated and much traveled on three continents.

Once in Las Vegas word gets out that Manuel Romero is hosting a holy man and in time crowds are constantly after him for advice and prayer so he walks out of town to live in the wild. But villagers follow him and soon he climbs *Cerro del Tecolote* [Owl Peak which then becomes known as Hermit's Peak] in the *Sangre de Cristos* to find peace and solitude. Even there friends come to see *El Hermitaño,* The Hermit, from time to time, taking simple food like cornmeal and repairing his shelter. He lives there for a period of four years.

1867: Agostini goes into Las Vegas to announce he is heading south toward Mexico. He turns up in the Mesilla/El Paso area where he is befriended by many people, including Col. Albert J. Fountain.

April, 1869: The Hermit decides to climb the highest peak in the Organ Mountains to establish a shelter. Fountain warns him that the Apaches are masters there and very dangerous. Agostini says he will light a signal fire to let everyone know he is safe. But the fire is never seen so a search party goes after him.

May 10: The Santa Fe *New Mexican* reports the remains "*of the Italian recluse*" have been found in the Organ Mts., killed by Indians.

The Hermit
Courtesy Museum of NM, #110764

SOCIETY & PUEBLOS

November: Continuing on the Hispanic tradition, **President Lincoln bestows silver crowned canes** on each N.M. Pueblo governor via Michael Steck, Superintendent of the Territorial Indian Service. Each cane is inscribed with the name of the Pueblo, the year "1863," and the signature "A. Lincoln."

SOCIETY
Stephen Benton Elkins arrives in N.M. (from his native
    Missouri).

1864
SETTLEMENT
San Marcial is founded

COMANCHERO TRADE
José Tafoya, known as the "Prince of Comancheros" because
    of the magnitude of his trading ventures with Indians
    on the plains, testifies that Captain **Bergmann,**
    commander at Fort Bascom, had personally furnished
    him with goods and supplies to trade for Comanche
    cattle.

AMERINDS
April: Physician H.T. Ketcham reports that **Kiowas** and
    Comanches are in possession of large herds of Texas
    cattle. **Robert North** accuses Mexicans of helping them
    to drive stolen livestock to N.M.

Stephen B. Elkins
Courtesy Museum of NM, #105381

August: **Cheyennes** go on the warpath with some Comanches and Kiowas joining them to attack a small
    wagontrain on the Santa Fe Trail. Five Americans are killed and scalped while the New Mexican
    teamsters are unharmed. On hearing the news, **General Carleton** rages that a vile alliance is afoot,
    that the American government and its people have been grievously insulted; the tribes are
    declared hostile.

Comanche and Kiowa chieftains go to Fort Bascom and declare for peace. Gen. Carleton rejects their offers
    as insincere, telling them that ... *their hearts are bad and they talk with forked tongues.* Indian
    Supt. **Michael Steck** tries to convince Carleton that the Comanches have been at peace for several
    years, that the Kiowas are the instigators. Gen. Carleton picks Kit Carson to lead the campaign
    against the Comanches but there are few soldiers available for war.

November 25: Comanches attack at **Adobe Walls,** the warriors having an overwhelming majority over
    Carson's 335-man cavalry. Only excellent management of two mountain howitzers saves the
    cavalry from annihilation, although Carson reports that he *"...taught these Indians a severe
    lesson."* Carson blames **Comancheros** Jesús Amalla and José Castillo for not winning a more
    decisive victory, believing they informed the Comanches about his campaign while trading with
    passes authorized by Supt. Steck.

TIMELINE

November 29, 1864: A group known as the **Colorado Volunteers** under the command of **Reverend J.M. Chivington** stage a dawn attack on a peaceful camp of sleeping Cheyenne and Arapahoes at **Sand Creek** in **Colorado**. Chief Black Kettle raises an American flag then a white flag from a pole but the soldiers fire cannon into the village then ride through it, shooting everybody in sight. Black Kettle's wife is shot seven times. Women and children aren't allowed to surrender; all are slaughtered. **George Bent** later states that he counted 163 Indian dead, 110 being women and children; some of the women had their privates cut out ... Chivington's report states that *"All did nobly"* and the men are *"received as heroes and saviors of the frontier"* according to R.L. Andrist.

[Kit Carson refers to the Coloradoans as *"cowards and dogs."* Native Americans are incensed, directing some of their hatred toward N.M.]

SOCIETY
November 30: Gen. **Carleton** orders the arrest of anyone trying to contact the Comanches.

1865
Comanches start gathering stray cattle on the frontier and selling them to New Mexicans.

Sisters of Charity arrive in N.M. They are Vincent O'Keefe, Catherine Mallon, Theodosia Farn, Pauline Leo.

SETTLEMENTS
Hispanic settlers found **Missouri Plaza** on the Río Hondo southwest of Roswell and **El Berrendo** in north Roswell around this time.

COMANCHES
January 2 1: Chief **Skeerkeenakwaugh** of the Comanches visits Fort Bascom and speaks for peace.

SOCIETY
February 27: **Elfego Baca** is born in Socorro.

AMERIND
May 1: **M. Steck** is forced to resign and is replaced by **Felipe Delgado.** Word is received that **Comanches and Kiowas** are ready for war because of Carson's campaign. New Mexicans are also targeted because they comprised part of Carson's force. An alliance is sought with Texans but with the defeat of the Confederacy the Indians are left without support.

COMANCHERO TRADE
August 25: Mrs. **Marian Russell,** wife of a lieutenant at Fort Bascom, writes that most of the **army personnel at Bascom supply Comancheros** with items to trade the Comanches for Texas cattle. She personally sends a copper kettle and a small Navajo blanket for which she receives a dozen cattle.

October: Gen. Carleton sends **José Ulibarrí** to parley with the Comanches and a treaty is signed, restoring the peace.

SOCIETY

December: **Felipe** (The Millionaire) **Chávez,** a Democrat, supports his famous Republican cousin, **J. Francisco Chávez,** in his successful bid for Delegate to Congress. From Washington D.C. he writes to Felipe that *"The evil forces are at work and all points to doing great harm to President Lincoln."*

1865-1866

Rafaél Chacón is elected to the Territorial Legislature as senator from Taos County

1866

W.F.M. Arny is interim Governor.

PIONEER

Rancher **Juan Candelaria** from **Cubero** (near Laguna) relocates his 700 sheep to the headwaters of the Little Colorado River in Arizona.

SETTLEMENT

Río Palomas **(Las Palomas)** is founded.

SOCIETY

Heiskell Jones and his family are the first "Anglos" in Chaves County, settling at a site some six miles above the confluence of the Hondo and the Pecos.

MILITARY

Fort Bayard is established.

Congress creates six **Black regiments,** to be commanded by white officers, in the U.S. Army.

[Nearly 4,000 Black soldiers will see action in N.M. during the Indian wars. Native Americans refer to them as the "Black White Men," or the "Buffalo Soldiers" because they think their hair resembles that of the buffalo. See **1880.**]

CATTLE TRAIL

Motivated by a need for beef at Fort Sumner, **Charles Goodnight and Oliver Loving** blaze a new cattle trail across the lower Pecos area of N.M. Called the *Goodnight-Loving Trail,* it becomes the standard route for cattle drives from N.M. and Texas to markets in Colorado and Wyoming.

Fellow Texan **John Chisum** shows up at Fort Sumner with 600 steers.

COMANCHERO TRADE

Army officers **CJ. Jennings, H.H. Healy, R.C. Vose,** and **E.W Wood** conceive a plan to corner the

Comanchero trade. The quartet is able to deceive the Commissioner of Indian Affairs, the N.M. Supt. of Indian Affairs, and the agent for the Comanches on the basis that they are "...*honest, loyal American citizens...*" They are given trading permits and the Army bans trade by anybody else by order of Gen. W. S. Hancock himself. The Pueblo agent issues trading permits and Comancheros club with them, thus destroying the monopoly while the quartet incurs heavy losses.

BEEF
Merchants are buying a cow for about two dollars and selling dressed beef at 10 cents a pound.

RAIDS
Comanches take herds of Texas cattle with apparent ease and even the Comanches admit the Texans are being *"robbed poor."*

February: **Manuel Olona** of Valencia County is returning from the Comanche country when his party is attacked by **Navajos** at Pintadea. The attack is repulsed.

June 11: Col. **J. Francisco Chávez** writes to his cousin **Felipe** *(El Millionario)* Chávez about an Indian attack on his wagon train on the Santa Fe Trail: The battle rages for three hours though the Army escort provided for protection refuses to fight, defense thus falling to the few Hispanic *arrieros* who struggle valiantly until they succumb to superior numbers and the Indians rob the wagon train.

SOCIETY
July 27: **Thomas Benton Catron** arrives in Santa Fe (from Missouri).

PROFILE

Thomas B. Catron

TERRITORIAL POWERHOUSE

October 6, 1840: Thomas B. Catron is born.

July 4, 1860: Thomas graduates from the University of Missouri.

1865: Catron is paroled from the Confederate army.

1866: T.B. arrives in Santa Fe.

December 14: He moves to Mesilla as District Attorney for the Third Judicial District.

1867: Catron is admitted to the bar.

1868: Serves in the Territorial House of Representatives.

1869: Becomes Attorney General.

1872: Commissioned as United States Attorney.

1878: Marries **Julia Walz.** Resigns as U.S. Attorney on October 10.

1882: Catron is defeated in the election for Territorial Council.

1884: Elected to the Territorial Council, defeated in 1886, elected in 1888, 1890.

February 8, 1891: An assassination attempt is made on T.B.'s life.

Thomas B. Catron
Courtesy Museum of NM, #50616

1892: Catron is defeated as Delegate to Congress.

11894: Elected as Delegate to Congress.

1[895: Catron is acquitted in disbarment proceedings.

1896: Defeated as Delegate to Congress.

1898: Elected to Territorial Council, defeated in 1900, elected in 1904, defeated in 1906, elected in 1908.

1906: T.B. is the Mayor of Santa Fe.

1910: Catron is a member of the constitutional convention.

1912: TB. is appointed to the United States Senate, defeated in 1918.

May 15, 1921: Thomas B. Catron dies.

ALLIANCE REPORT

September: J.R. Mead reports that the **Kwahadi Comanches** are strongly allied to the New Mexicans because of the Comanchero trade.

1866-1869

Robert B. Mitchell is Governor.

1867

T I M E L I N E

Congress abolishes all forms of indentured servitude in the USA (including "peonage").

[W.A. Beck **writes** that there were an *"estimated"* 1,500 to 3,000 Indian slaves in N.M. There were some *"500 to 700 wealthy families"* with the rest of the population, according to Beck from 50,000 to 70,000, *"most of them"* held in the *"bondage"* of debt peonage. He remarks that *"travelers"* often agreed that *"Negro slavery"* was much more humane than New Mexican peonage. Other writers like D. Weber, S. Motto, R. Nostrand, etc., report that *peones* were merely workers, not slaves.]

SOCIETY

April 14, 1867: Governor Mitchell *"frees the peons of New Mexico."* In order to enforce the new laws some 300 witnesses are subpoenaed to testify before a Grand Jury. There are no violations and therefore no indictments.

[S. Motto writes that peonage was little more than getting into debt because it was never limited to one race or class, never involved any loss of civil rights, there was never any sale or transfer of services, and no legal obligation on the part of children to take on a parent's debt. *Peones* could be acculturated Indians or Hispanics, including relatives. It wasn't slavery any more than getting into debt in the modern day.]

RAIDS

Beef contractor for the military **A.M. Adams** is robbed of three different herds while on the Pecos Trail.

SOCIETY

1867: **Nathan Bibo** arrives in Santa Fe (one of seven in this German family who eventually come to N.M.) to join his brother Simón.

1868: **Willie Spiegelberg** hires Nathan to manage his Ft. Wingate business with the Navajos. In time Nathan and Simon locate in Cebolleta, thus becoming part of the history of west-central N.M.

1872: Nathan establishes a store in Bernalillo after being prompted to do so by **Francisco Perea,** Bernalillo's leading citizen and one of the territory's richest men.

CIBOLEROS

General **James Carleton** decides to put a stop to the **cibolero hunting** because he believes they are really trafficking in stolen livestock. But Hispanics claim that hunting is their right and ancient tradition, just like Americans fishing from the Newfoundland banks. Hunting doesn't cease but it becomes more difficult to do so without bothersome interference from the military.

CATTLE BARON

John Chisum arrives in N.M., driving his herd of cattle up the Goodnight-Loving Trail (and is on his way to becoming one of the legendary cattle barons of the West).

PROFILE

John Chisum

C A T T L E   K I N G   O F   T H E   P E C O S

1824: **John Chisum** is born on his grandfather's plantation in Tennessee.

1837: The Chisum family moves to Pads, Texas.

1852: John is the county clerk of Lamar County.

1854: With partner Stephen Fowler, Chisum goes into the cattle business.

1855, 1857: Daughters are born to Chisum and a mulatto slave girl named **Jensie**. (Though he never married the girls' mother, Chisum never denied his paternity and always provided for family needs. As the record would show, he never married and there are no other known children.)

1861-1865: Chisum is a beef contractor for the Confederacy.

1872: Chisum buys the Bosque Grande ranch site and is a permanent resident of N.M. By the end of the year he has 20,000 cattle branded with his long rail line from hip to shoulder and marked with the famous "jinglebob" slit ear.

1875: John Chisum is the largest cattle man in southeastern N.M. with 80,000 head of cattle grazing on a hundred-mile stretch of public domain. newspapers begin to refer to him as the "Cattle King of the Pecos." The route to Arizona used by his trail drivers becomes known as the **Chisum Trail.**

John Chisum
Courtesy Museum of NM, #9843

Chisum relocates to South Spring and begins to experiment with different crops to see what grows best in the soil of the Pecos Valley.

1876: Chisum takes action against the rustlers known as the Seven Rivers Gang.

1877: Chisum men open fire on an unsuspecting party of *ciboleros,* killing all of them and stealing their cattle.

Chisum aligns himself openly with new residents A.A. McSween and J. Tunstall against the Murphy-Dolan faction, perhaps because his bids for government beef contracts had been thwarted by Murphy's Santa Fe Ring allies like **Thomas B. Catron,** who *"used every opportunity to damage Chisum either legally or financially."*

[Hostilities between Chisum and small stockmen and rustlers were a contributing factor to the Lincoln County War.]

FIREARMS

Traders based in Kansas are supplying western Indians with large quantities of liquor and guns. Charlie Rath operates out of Fort Zarah.

COMANCHERO TRADE

John Watts (appointed to the Territorial Supreme Court the following year) receives a license to trade with the Comanches.

While **José Tafoya** is the most famous of the **Comancheros,** many New Mexicans like Julián Baca, Manuel Gonzáles, Vicente Romero, José Medina, Polonio Ortiz, Manuel Chávez, José Antonio Vigil, etc., are involved in the Comanchero trade. Comancheros prove themselves masters of the trackless expanses of plains while pursuing Army personnel get lost on the *Llano Estacado* [**Palisaded Plains**, not "**Staked Plains**" as has been erroneously translated].

RELIGIOUS

Jesuits are brought into N.M. from Naples, Italy. Reverend **Donato M. Gaspari** leads the Jesuit missions and in time organizes what comes to be known as the New Mexico-Colorado Mission. Gaspari establishes the Catholic Press in N.M. and becomes the first editor of *La Revista Católica.*

July 27: **Fr. Martínez of Taos dies, in schism.**

COMACHERO TRADE

August: A **Comanchero** party is arrested and taken to Fort Bascom where their trade goods are inventoried: 200 pounds of commeal--500 loaves of Mex. hard bread--35 to 40 butcher knives--9 files--vermilion--many shirts--red and white flannel--one vest--iron hoops--Ducking and Calico--shelled corn--tea--sugar--flour--letter paper--candy--one regalia--one box of army caps (100), 400 percussion caps--several pounds of lead--five pounds of powder--16 elongated balls calab.58. The Comancheros are released but their **goods are kept by military personnel**.

COMANCHE RAIDS

August 23: **Comanches** tell **Lorenzo Labadi,** a veteran Indian agent, that various Union officers encourage
them to raid in Texas.

1868

SOCIETY

The **Navajo Reservation** [ultimately about 15,000,000 acres] is
established in parts of N.M., Arizona, Utah.

The **Roswell** area is surveyed.

Santero **José Dolores López** is born.

SANTA FE TRADE

Hispanic sheep ranchers from northeastern N.M. band together to
haul their wool to eastern markets. **Rumaldo Baca** of Las
Vegas and **José Manuel Gonzáles** are the biggest shippers
though sheep king families like that of **Francisco Perea** are
still strong. There are 200 ox-drawn wagons in the train
which includes at least 3,200 oxen, more than 500 mules and
horses, and some 500 men. About 100 men guide the
caravan and watch for hostile Indians. In Kansas the
flooding Arkansas River takes six days to cross but the
wool shipping venture is a financial success.

Francisco Perea
Courtesy Museum of NM, #105371

EDUCATION

Father Truchard, a priest at San Felipe de Neri in Albuquerque, wants to start a school in Old Town so he
asks the **Sisters of Charity** if they would teach in the projected boarding school. Sisters
Mary Joseph Dennis, Teresa Alaríd, and Mary Jerome Murphy come to teach and the school
opens with 10 students.

When **Father Gasparri** takes over duties at San Felipe de Neri he pays Truchard what it cost him to start the
school by borrowing $ 1,000 from **José Leandro Perea** and $500 from **Antonio Larma.**

COMANCHEROS

1868: Major General **Philip Sheridan** begins a major military offensive against the Comanche and Kiowa
nations. The Army believes Comancheros are in league with the hostiles.

Vicente Romero of Córdova goes on a Comanchero trading expedition for the first time at the age of 18. The
group spends three months on the plains during this expedition.

[Romero was to return many times to trading with the Comanches on the plains, often as comandante. **Lorin
Brown** interviewed don Vicente for the WPA and recorded valuable history and reminiscences. For example,
Romero told the story of **José Antonio Vigil** of Cundiyó and his deadly fight with the Comanche chieftain

Capitán Corona. Vigil became such a famous frontiersmen that in northern New Mexico he was referred to as *Capitán Vigil* by those who knew of his exploits. According to Brown, when Romero talked about the "old days" on the plains he would exclaim *"Those were the times!"*]

RAIDS

January 13: **Anirecha López** straggles into **Fort Bascom** and relates how his entire party of hunters, 47 in number, were massacred while hunting 200 miles east of the fort.

February: **Kiowas** open fire on a New Mexican trading party in the area of the Oklahoma panhandle, killing three and forcing the others to flee, abandoning their trade goods.

SOCIETY

April 23: **Josefa Carson**, 41 years of age, dies 15 days after giving birth to Kit Carson's eighth child.

May 23: **Kit Carson** dies at Fort Lyon. (Kit and Josefa are buried in the Taos Cemetery, also the final resting place of the renowned Father Martínez who had married them.)

COMANCHE RAIDS

July: A party of Comanches takes 4,100 Texas cattle within one week.

1868-1869
MILITARY & COMANCHES

General R. Sheridan leads a winter campaign against the **Comanches.** He encounters parties of *ciboleros* but no Comanche.

1869-1871

William A. Pile is Governor.

The most infamous historical incident in Gov. Pile's administration is his **attempt to destroy the archival records** (which date back to 1681) of N.M. A Methodist preacher, Pile went into the Army, thus winding up in N.M.

[*"He was a very weak man intellectually and every other way-He was up to all sorts of chicanery, was not honest, and if it had been any other country he would have been driven out of the country."*]

William A. Pile
Courtesy Museum of NM, #10341

Some of the ancient archives are sold to merchants and grocers for wrapping paper while many bundles of records are dumped in the street. A wood hauler named **Eluterio Barela** sees the bundles of archives, empties his wagon of wood and fills it with the archives, preserving most of them. Irate citizens form a committee that pressures Gov. Pile to demand the return of all documents, most of which are retrieved, though some are lost forever. (See **1892.**)

[The destruction of the archives would have wiped out records of every kind, including those related to land ownership, and all documents would have had to be sought in Mexico or Spain. The attempt to destroy New Mexican records was an assault on the area's long recorded history.]

1869
LAW & PUEBLOS
In the case of *United States v. Lucero,* the N.M. Supreme Court rules that the **Nonintercourse Act,** which protects native tribes against trespass and prohibits settlers from entering or settling on Indian land, doesn't apply to the Pueblos. Disputes over Indian land can now be settled in State courts [personnel from which have been targeting rich Indian farmlands since the American occupation began].

MEDAL OF HONOR - FRANCIS OLIVER
For bravery in action at the Chiricahua Mountains in Arizona on October 20, 1869, **Francis Oliver** [enlisted in N.M.] receives the Medal of Honor. Date of issue: February 14, 1870.

NEWSPAPERS
A.X. Aoy (born in Spain) launches Las Vegas' first newspaper, *The Acorn,* a weekly published in both English and Spanish.

1871: **S.H. Newman and W.N. Bollinger** start the *Las Vegas Mail.* Newman is convicted of publishing "libelous statements" about U.S. Attorney **T.B. Catron** and, unable to pay the fine, he edits from his jail cell.
Louis Hommel (German born) buys the *Mail* plant and launches his Las Vegas *Gazette.*

1875: **J.H. Koogler** takes over the *Gazette* and makes it one of New Mexico's leading newspapers.

1879: **Russell A. Kistler** begins publication of the *Las Vegas Optic* in East Las Vegas.

T I M E L I N E

Lt. General Philip Sheridan is at Fort Cobb during the Washita campaign when a Comanche named Turtle Dove introduces himself to Sheridan, finishing with "Me good Indian." Sheridan replies *"The only good Indians I know are dead,"* thus giving rise to the infamous motto of **Manifest Destiny:** *The only good Indian is a dead Indian.*

COMANCHE RESERVATION
Comanches are being forced to Oklahoma but the **Kwahadis** and part of the **Kotsotekas** go to Fort Bascom and advise Commander **Getty** that they want a reservation in N.M. Getty tells them they must live in Oklahoma but **Mow-way** and other chiefs are adamant so they are sent to Santa Fe to confer with Indian Supt. North. Rumors abound that the Comanches will be murdered, as happened in the

Texas council house murders, so the chiefs flee at night but Col. Getty captures them and sends them to Oklahoma.

SANTERO ART

The **Italian Jesuits** in charge of **San Felipe de Neri Church** in Albuquerque inform their parishioners that money is being collected to buy plaster statues from Mexico City. They **rid the church of all New Mexican santero art,** giving away bultos to donors who want them.

SOCIETY

La Placita in southeastern N.M. is renamed **Lincoln** and made the county seat.

May 15: Dr. **T. Rush Spencer** is appointed Surveyor General. He becomes aligned with dominant Republican territorial leaders.

July 14: The cornerstone is laid for the **Cathedral of Santa Fe.**

1870
LAND GRANT BUSINESS

Surveyor General **Spencer** is in the land grant business with **T.B. Catron** and **S. B. Elkins.** He is also an official in the **Maxwell Land Grant and Railroad Company** with Governor William A. Pile, John S. Watts, John Pratt, and Miguel A. Otero.

T.B. Catron and S.B. Elkins have acquired 16 "undivided shares" of the Mora land grant.

MORA LAND GRANT

1835: Settlers, some 76 families, from Río Arriba and Taos counties are awarded a community land grant in the Mora and San Antonio valleys. (Various other families had been living in these areas since the early 1800s.) Within a few years little placitas, villages, spring up wherever there is enough water and arable land to sustain new settlers. Various villages become rendezvous sites for groups of ciboleros and comancheros going out to the eastern plains to hunt the buffalo and trade with Comanches. Some villages in the Mora country are located close to the **Santa Fe Trail** and villagers sell grain, flour, hay, vegetables, livestock, etc., to travelers. (By the end of the century there are thousands of people living on the Mora grant, farming the arable land and raising livestock, especially sheep.)

1843: **Bandits from Texas** attack the community of Mora, stealing livestock and killing five people. A village posse pursues them, recovers the livestock and captures the Texans' horse herd, leaving the Texans to walk back to Texas.

1846: The U.S. invades the country and takes New Mexico.

January 24, 1847: Some New Mexicans can no long tolerate American brutality so they revolt. Mora is attacked by an American unit but repulsed by the inhabitants. Reinforcements with cannon return on February 1 and Mora is destroyed.

185 1: The construction of **Fort Union** is begun (on grant land). The Army thus becomes an important market for hay, grain, fruits and vegetables, livestock, etc.

People from the States as well as from Europe settle in the area because of the fort, the Hispanic communities absorbing these Irish, German, etc., newcomers as they had the French earlier.

1854: The post of **Surveyor General** of N.M. is established. Through their attorneys, **José María Valdez** and **Vicente Romero** submit a petition to the SG to confirm the Mora community land grant to them and all settlers living on the grant.

July 1, 1859: The SG holds the required hearing then recommends to Congress that the Mora grant be confirmed to the Mora communities.

1860s: **Stephen B. Elkins** "acquires an undivided share" of the Mora commons land as payment for legal service.
[**Clark S. Knowlton** believes this might have been the beginning of the rationale that commons "shares" could be bought and sold. Such trafficking was illegal under Hispanic (Spanish or Mexican) law: common lands were strictly for use by residents and couldn't be alienated from the rest of the land grant. This was ignored by American officials in order to get control of the land, Treaty of Guadalupe Hidalgo notwithstanding.]

June 21, 1860: Congress confirms the Mora grant to its residents. Boundaries are the *Río de Ocate* on the north, *Aguaje de la Yegua* to the east, the confluence of the Sapello stream and Mora river to the south and the *Estillero* to the west.

1861: **Thomas Means** is contracted to survey and mark the outboundaries of the Mora grant, which turns out containing 827,621 acres.

1862: Commissioner of the General Land Office **J.M. Edmunds** rejects the Means' survey on the grounds that the grant is larger than what Mexican law allowed at the time it was made. Means is directed to resurvey the grant and a new commissioner, Willis Drummond, accepts the new survey.

1870: S.B. Elkins and Thomas B. Catron have bought up 16 undivided shares in the Mora land grant. They form a group of investors which includes speculator Col. S.S. Smoot, government surveyor Cap. E.N. Darling, Surveyor General T. Rush Spencer.

1871: Without knowledge of his partners, Smoot sells an English investor, William Blackmore, his one-fifth share, purportedly some 138,000 acres, of the Mora grant for $5,000. (At this date all shares were in Elkins' name and the entire group together didn't own 138,000 acres. Blackmore committed suicide in 1878 and his heirs never got the land or the $5,000.)

Surveyor General **Spencer** recommends to Congress that a patent be issued to **Catron** and **Elkins** for the Mora Community Land Grant. Residents on the land stage serious protests.

June 20, 1876: Commissioner of the General Land Office issues a patent to Catron and Elkins despite serious protests from inhabitants of the grant.

1877: Catron and Elkins petition the Court of New Mexico's First judicial District to partition the Mora common lands. Residents denounce the proceedings as a fraud and a swindle. The Court orders that common lands be sold as quickly as the western boundary line can be properly identified. The original investment pool disintegrates and other investors enter the complicated proceedings. Eventually Catron receives 250,000 acres. Years are spent in boundary investigations.

1909: Catron deeds his interest in the Mora land grant to his son, Charles C. Catron.
1911: The western boundary of the Mora grant is definitely set at the Pecos National Forest (a line established years earlier by the rejected Means Survey).
C.C. Catron's agent and representative, Robert Sammon, is found murdered.

1913: Catron's Mora land is sold for non-payment of taxes. **Frank Roy** from Las Vegas is the buyer.

Ca. 1915: The Elkins- Catron partition suit of 1877 is revived (now 38 years later and accepted by the Court as still valid) in the District Court.
[Clark S. Knowlton has written that the "Anglo" court and "Anglo" land interests might have enjoyed "a quiet arrangement" on this matter. Such "arrangements" haven't been investigated by historians.]

The entire legal action is kept a secret so those residents living on the land never know their lands are being adjudicated away by the court when it decrees that all common lands must be sold.

February 22, 1916: Common lands of the Mora land grant are sold (to G.A. Flemming, W. Shllinglaw, and R. Eagle, the State Investment Company) at the courthouse door in Mora. Residents may no longer legally use the grazing lands for their stock or wood cutting but they aren't informed immediately in order to avoid confrontation. In time they are deprived of their ranching base and the people have to look for outside work, laboring on farms, in mines, or the railroads.

1930s: The drought and Great Depression added to the swindle of their land brings Mora County residents to near destitution. Government programs like the WPA and the PWA help a little but many families relocate to cities in search of work.

1940-1980: The population of Mora County falls from 10,981 to 4,205, the largest decrease for all N.M. counties.
1980: The median family income for the State of New Mexico is $16,928. The median in Mora County is $6,819.

COMANCHEROS
The *Daily New Mexican* charges that **Comanche traders** are responsible for the bloodshed and misery being inflicted on Texans by the plains Indians.
FAMILY

José Julián Espinosa moves his family, which is ultimately to include **fourteen (14) children,** to El Carnero, Colorado, following his military service with the New Mexico Volunteers during the Civil War.

1898: José's son **Aurelio Espinosa** graduates from high school then enrolls at the University of Colorado where he graduates (the first college graduate of a family that is to be described as *"the most educated family in New Mexico."*)

SOCIETY
John Becker (from Hanover, Germany) arrives in N.M. at around this time. His uncle, Louis Huning, well established in the mercantile business in Belén and Los Lunas, gives him a job with the starting salary of $30 a month. At the end of four months his salary is increased to $50 and he is put in charge of the Belén store.

BUSINESS
Martín Amador is managing the family business in **Las Cruces,** providing goods and supplies to the military. He begins a freighting service from Santa Fe to Chihuahua that proves to be highly successful (until the advent of the railroad, when he uses the railroad to do his shipping), and builds Amador Hall, a rooming house for travelers of all sorts. He later expands into the **Amador Hotel,** which becomes a center of Las Cruces social life. He also invents the Amador combination plow that revolutionizes the use of animal teams in farming.

LAND & T.B. CATRON
Lawyer **Thomas B. Catron** begins trafficking in land grants.
[During his career he owns or has an interest in at least 34 land grants totaling some 6,000,000 acres. At one time or another he owns at least 2-to-3,000,000 acres, *"undoubtedly the largest individual landholder in the history of the US."* He is the attorney in at least 63 land grant suits in N.M. with others in Colorado and Arizona.]

BANKING
Lucien B. Maxwell opens the First National Bank of New Mexico (the first bank in the territory).

1871: T.B. Catron, S.B. Elkins and other associates take over the bank.

1872: The Spiegelberg brothers found the **Second National Bank of New Mexico** with Solomon, Levi (in New York), Lehman, and Willi (in Santa Fe) as principal stockholders.

TEXAN RAID
July: Texans trail a stolen herd of cattle to a Comanche camp and gun down everyone except one lone escapee.

COMANCHEROS
July 17: The *Santa Fe Weekly Post* states that Comancheros should be shot down like dogs because they are worse than the savages whom they help.

September: Gov. Pile issues a proclamation against Comanchero traffickers.

TIMELINE

September 20, 1870 : **The various Italian states are finally unified into the country of Italy.**
January 18, 1871: **The various German kingdoms are unified into the country of Germany.**

MILITARY

October: Fort Bascom is to be closed in a governmental economy move but it remains as an outpost for the next four years.

1870-1890
TINSMITHS

The **Mora Octagonal Tinsmith** is producing works during this period. Operating in **Mora County**, this tinsmith produces a variety of items, including massive *nichos* and octagonal frames. Characteristics in his work include extensive surface stamping and embossing, scalloped borders, and the use of wallpaper panels.

The **Fan Lunette Tinsmith** is producing tinwork during this period. The work of this unknown artist [not even his working locale has been discovered] is characterized by a crest in the form of a partially open fan.

Ca. 1870-1895

Northern New Mexico tinsmiths (referred to as the *Río Arriba Workshop*) are producing a large number of frames, *nichos,* and other items during this period. These craftsmen live in or near the **Española Valley.** Characteristics of these artists include extensive use of the circular serrated stamp and reverse single-dot punch, a serrated U stamp combined with an embossed single-dot punch, multipointed stars, and bird designs. Their *nichos* are creative and superbly styled. The best of these creations rank with the best in N.M.

Ca. 1870-1900

The **Valencia Red and Green Tinsmith** is producing tinwork during this period. Much of his work is collected from villages around the **Belén and Los Lunas** area of Valencia County. He is *"talented and prolific..."* producing easily identifiable work because it combines dark scarlet and forest green paint on the tin surface, as well as extensive single-dot punching and embossing which are also filled with red and green coloring. He decorates his pieces with stylized floral and leaf designs, as well as complementary colors like blue, yellow, and a lighter green. He is a master of *"...variety, skill, creative imagination ... and unusual forms."*

Ca.1870-1905

The **Taos Serrate Tinsmith** is producing tinwork during this period. This artist (or artists) is distinguished by consistent use of serrated borders on lunettes and the side end panels of his frames and nichos. He also ornaments with multiple chevrons and simple rosettes.

1871-1875
Marsh Giddings is Governor.

1871
COMANCHERO TRADE
Comancheros flock to the plains and commerce is as great as ever.

RANCHING
Wilson Waddingham buys [in 1871-'72] about 12,000 acres of land from the Government along the Canadian River and Ute Creek water sources. The land comes to be known as the **Bell Ranch.** Settlers living on unregistered land in this area are evicted.

SOCIETY
February 10: **Pablo Abeita** is born at **Isleta Pueblo.**

COMANCHEROS
May: **Comancheros from Isleta Pueblo** fight off an Army detachment until they are overpowered. Their cattle herd of 700 is shot until ammunition becomes scarce. Other trading parties are arrested and, along with their cattle, taken to Fort Bascom. Cattle cramp the fort and in time the Isletans are put in charge of the herd, which winds up at Isleta Pueblo.

August: **W.F.M. Arny** reports that **Army** personnel are stopping Comanchero traders and appropriating Comanchero trade goods for themselves.

September: Governor **Vicente Garron of Isleta Pueblo** writes to N.M. authorities on why buffalo hunting is crucial for the survival of his people.

POLITICS--MESILLA RIOT
August: Colonel **J. Francisco Chaves,** Republican candidate for Territorial Delegate to the U.S. Congress, and his opponent, Democrat **José Manuel Gallegos,** happen to make campaign appearances in Mesilla on the same day. Partisans for each hold lively rallies which include parades. Marchers are heavily armed and when they meet in the plaza gunfire breaks out. Some 50 people are wounded.

1872
RANCHING
It is reported that 90,000 cattle have moved up the Goodnight-Loving Trail during this year.

TINSMITH
January 28: *Tinsmith* **H.V. Gonzáles** delivers an inscribed (which is a rarity) commissioned *nicho* which reads:

> "At the request and expense of Faustín Vigil, a devoted servant of the most blessed Virgin. Dedicated to the honor of our most blessed Guadalupe of Mexico, today the 28th day of January of 1872 by H.V. Gonzáles, San Ildefonso, New Mexico."

[It is possible that Gonzáles, considered to be quite active, creative, and accomplished, works in the **Española Valley.**]

MILITARY
February: A detachment of the **Fourth Cavalry** stumbles across a Comanchero party and a *"brisk little fight"* ensues.

MAGAZINE
March 1: Reverend **Sheldon Jackson** starts the *Rocky Mountain Presbyterian* as a monthly magazine, later a weekly, then renamed (1881) the *Presbyterian Home Missionary* when taken over by the Board of Missions. (*"Evangelistic work among the Hispanic communities was much slower and less readily accepted."*)

GOVERNMENT
March 13: **José M. Gallegos,** Delegate to Congress, writes to President Grant: *"My people are extremely anxious to have Gov. Giddings removed as Governor, he's offensive, meddling, disagreeable man to my people."*

Governor Giddings appears to be a proponent of Statehood, though he describes **Santa Fe Mexicans** as *"...the lowest class on God's earth..."* Later Governor Giddings is beaten senseless on a Santa Fe street.

COMANCHE REQUEST
April: **Kwahadi Comanches** meet with former Indian Agent **Lorenzo Labadi,** asking for peace and a reservation in N.M. The Army refuses both requests.

PUEBLO BUFFALO HUNTERS
May 26: A group of **Pueblo buffalo hunters** are attacked by 300 Kiowas but the Pueblos take refuge in a natural cave on the side of a cliff and beat off their attackers.

STATEHOOD
June: In a very light voter turn out, **New Mexicans reject the proposed constitution and Statehood.** No official count of the vote is announced to the public, giving both pro- and anti-statehood factions an opportunity to complain. (See **1873**.)

TEXANS
July: Texas rancher **John Hittson** and a force of 90 men enter N.M. in an effort to recover stolen Texas cattle.

[They roam for three months, appropriating some 6,000 cattle.]

Military officials supply the Texans with ammunition and other necessities. A delegation from Las Vegas asks **Miguel Otero** (I) to stop the Texans from stealing cattle. Otero visits the Hittson camp and is told: *"These goddamn greasers have been stealing our horses and cattle for the past fifty years, and we got together and thought we would come up this way and have a grand roundup, and that is why we are here. What is more we intend to take all the horses and cattle we come across and drive them back to Texas where they belong. My advice to you fellows is don't attempt to interfere with what we are doing unless you are looking for trouble."*

A rancher named **Simpson** is gunned down at his corral when he tries to prevent Hittson's men from taking his cattle.

Citizens of **Loma Parda,** led by police chief **Edward Seaman,** get in a gunfight with Hittson's men. Seaman is killed and all cattle are taken by the Texans.

New Mexicans demand that Hittson's activities be stopped by the courts or the Army if necessary.

GOVERNMENT
September 30: **James K. Proudfit** becomes **Surveyor General.**

SOCIETY
October 19: **J.K. Proudfit** is an incorporator of the Consolidated Land, Cattle Raising and Wool Growing Company, along with S.B. **Elkins,** Marsh **Giddings,** T.B. **Catron,** and William W. **Griffin.**

TEXANS
December: **John Hittson leaves N.M.** with his men in possession of about 6,000 cattle.
[He later states that expenses were about what the animals were worth.]

COMMERCE
The **Comanchero trade** is diminishing. **Utes** ask for more traders to visit them.

COMANCHE REQUEST
Cohepa, a leading Comanche chieftain, asks military authorities for a treaty that will permit a reservation on the Canadian or Pecos rivers so Comanches can continue their ties with New Mexicans. The request is ignored.

1873
TIMBER LAW
The **Timber Culture Law** is enacted to encourage the planting and culture of trees. The law is manipulated for immediate use of the land without incurring expense, **fraudulent entries** being the handiest method to operate.

Ute Chiefs (Ouray sitting front center.)
Courtesy Museum of NM, #58629
(W.H. Jackson photo)

During prosecutions, *"...not a single person knew of any timber being planted..."* (Of the **64 persons prosecuted** for violation of timber laws one was Hispanic.)

COMANCHEROS

Venturesome New Mexicans continue to seek out **Comanches, Utes, Kiowas,** etc, for trading on the plains. Comanchero **Juan Pieda** challenges Army troops to catch him.

COMANCHE RAIDS

Texan **John Hittson** states that Comanche raiders are being accompanied by Mexicans who are *"...more savage and expert than the Indians themselves."*

FLOOD

The Río Grande overflows its banks and floods Albuquerque.

Father Gasparri of San Felipe de Neri in Old Town dismantles his printing press for fear that another flood will damage it Citizens and priests from Las Vegas ask him to send the press there, which he does.

STATEHOOD

May 2 1: **Stephen B. Elkins,** Delegate to Congress, delivers a speech as to why N.M. should be admitted to STATEHOOD: more than sufficient population as required by American law; duties of the U.S. as stipulated by the Treaty of Guadalupe Hidalgo; New Mexican Hispano's unfailing loyalty during the Civil War public education is vastly improved; tremendous resource potential and salubrious climate ... (See **1875.**)

SPIRAL STAIRCASE

July: A chapel is begun for the **Sisters of Loretto.** Plans for the chapel are drawn up by an architect named **Mouly** (who designed Bishop Lamy's cathedral) and the edifice is to be Gothic and similar to Lamy's "beloved" Sainte Chapelle in Paris. **Mother Magdalen** records that the building of the chapel is commended to *St. Joseph,* who is prayed to for divine help every Wednesday evening. The chapel is large: 25 by 75 feet and a towering 85 feet high. French and Italian masons dedicate themselves to building the stone structure. When the beautiful chapel is nearing completion it is discovered that no stairway has been provided to get to the exceptionally high choir loft Mother Magdalen brings in several carpenters to build a stairway but they all say ordinary stairs will take up much room in the chapel proper. It appears a ladder will have to be used to get to the loft or it will have to be torn down and rebuilt.

Neither alternative is acceptable to Mother Magdalen and the Sisters of Loretto so they decide to make a novena to St. Joseph in hopes that he may provide a solution.
On the last day of the novena an elderly, gray-haired man arrives at the Loretto Chapel, leading a donkey that carries basic carpentry tools. The man asks Mother Magdalen if he can help the Sisters by building the stairway. She gives her consent and the man sets to work with hammer, saw, and T-square. He is observed by the Sisters as he works for more than half a year, without much in the line of blueprints or helpers. But the staircase slowly takes shape in the form of *two complete 360 degree turns* which connect the chapel floor to the choir loft. No nails are utilized, only wooden

pegs. The curved wood which forms the turns is beautiful.

Mother Magdalen and the Sisters are overjoyed with the beauty and strength of their spiral staircase.

(A young 13 year-old who later joined the Sisters of Loretto, **Sister Mary,** related how she and a friend were among the first to use the stairway. They walked up without a problem but coming down was so frightening that they did it on all fours. There was no banister at that time.)

Mother Magdalen draws the money with which to pay the carpenter but he doesn't show up at the chapel. When he doesn't appear within a week they ask about him in town but no one has seen him. The carpenter has disappeared without a trace. Mother Magdalen can't understand what has happened but she goes to the lumber yard to pay at least for the wood that was used. Wood, what wood? asks the yard manager, for no one has bought any wood for Loretto Chapel.

[It has been written that there is no record that the labor or materials used in constructing the Spiral Staircase have ever been paid for.]

Sisters of Loretto
Courtesy Museum of NM, #8150
(H.H. Dorman photo)

April 25, 1878: The Loretto Chapel of Our Lady of Light is dedicated.

1952: The Sisters of Loretto celebrate the centennial of their arrival in Santa Fe. The Spiral Staircase has been in use throughout the years and now has a strong banister.

1960: **Sister Januarius** reports that people have come from all over the world to gaze at the Spiral Staircase. Among the many visitors are professional architects who declare, without exception, that they don't understand how the staircase, not having a center pole, didn't crash to the floor the first time someone used it or how it remains so sturdy after so many years.

Urban C. Weidner, a Santa Fe architect and wood expert, is permitted to inspect the staircase. He reports that the way the wood is spliced and curved is a herculean feat, especially considering that it was accomplished by one carpenter working with primitive tools in the 19th century in an isolated place like Santa Fe. The wood used in construction of the staircase has been identified as "edge grained fir" or "long leaf yellow pine." Weidner states emphatically that these *woods are not native to New Mexico.*

1873 (con't)
SOCIETY
Felipe Maximiliano Chacón is born in Santa Fe, son of Lucia Ward and Urbano Chacón. Urbano is superintendent of Santa Fe schools and a widely respected and successful newspaper publisher in northern N.M. and southern Colorado.

MEDAL OF HONOR - EBEN STANLEY
Eben Stanley [enlisted in N.M.] received the Medal of Honor for gallantry in action near Turret Mountain Arizona, on March 25-27, 1873. Date of issue: April 12, 1875.

COMACHERO TRADE
August: Juan Lucero is arrested for trading with Comanches.

August 28: Capt. **Young** leads a reconnaissance in force to apprehend **Comancheros** on the plains. They trail a large group which turns out being Texan surveyors working for the Great Northern railroad. He continues his search for a total of 58 days, marching more than 1,000, and not encountering a single Comanchero. Young finds the Texas Panhandle full of buffalo **hide hunters,** slaughtering the animals at such a rate that he informs his superiors there will be an Indian war if the hide hunters aren't stopped.

HORRELL WAR
December: **Ben Horrell** (Harrell?) and four other men ride into Lincoln *"...for a spree"* according to J.R Wilson. They drink then begin shooting their guns, causing constable **Juan Martínez** to demand they surrender their guns, which they do. Later, at a brothel, the rearmed men start shooting again while they threaten authorities, including a judge. Martínez is called to the scene and while talking he is shot dead by *"...a Texan named Dave Warner."* Warner is killed by return fire, as are Ben Horrell and another of his companions after they flee the scene.

Major J.S. Mason in command at **Fort Stanton** reports that Horrell and his Texan companions were murdered in cold blood while trying to surrender.

["The post commander's bias against Hispanic settlers was all too evident in his other remarks, and typical of officers at that time. However, this paled beside the murderous antagonism shown by the Horrell clan" according to J.R Wilson.]

Three days later **Seferino Trujillo** *"and another local man"* are found murdered at the Horrell ranch.

Sheriff Mills organizes a posse of about 25 armed citizens and sets off to arrest the Horrells, who refuse to surrender. The sheriff withdraws to avoid a bloody shooting.

December 20: A **wedding dance** is in progress at Chapman's Saloon. The Horrells and their compatriots pour a **volley of deadly fire** through the windows at the dancing celebrants.

[Motivated by revenge, the Horells *"attacked a group of Mexicans at a wedding"* reports W.A. Beck.]

Three men are killed on the dance floor and three others, which include two women, are seriously wounded. The Horrells later deny any involvement.

Civil authorities petition for military protection but they are told the Army will not intervene in civil affairs, Governor **Marsh Giddings** does proclaim a $500 reward for the capture of the three Horrell brothers and two other Texans.

January, 1874: Guerrilla warfare breaks out, each group shooting at the other when encountered.

January 20: Sheriff Mills sets out with 60 men to arrest the Horrells but they have abandoned their ranch and moved down the Hondo, out of reach of the posse, where they *"...have the support of the cattlemen on the Pecos River They are perfectly lawless and visiting their revenge on the Mexicans as a race..."*

The Horrell group numbers from 50 to 70 men, some of whom want to destroy the entire town of Lincoln, but the Horrells maintain they only want to get the 12 or so individuals (Mills, Murphey [sic.], Juan Patrón, Juan Gonzáles, Dolan, Stanley, Haskins, Joe Warnock, Montanya [sic.], and one or two other Mexicans) responsible for their brothers death, that they will kill them sooner or later.

Joe Haskins is taken out of his bed one night and murdered by the Texans after which they quit the country, stealing horses and mules along their return route to Texas.
[*"The Horrell War left an evil heritage in addition to the ill feelings between ethnic groups in Lincoln County."*]

1874
GOVERNMENT BROKEN PROMISES
The Government doesn't comply with its promises of annuities for the **Kiowas and Comanches.** A young mystic by the name of **Ishatai** speaks for war.

SOCIETY
About 50 families are living on the **Jacona land grant** in the area known as **Jacona** (or Los Roybales).

COMMERCE
Charles Ilfeld buys out his partner Adolph Letcher and the **Charles lifeld Co.** eventually becomes the largest mercantile firm in N.M.

AMERIND WAR
June 27: **Comanches, Kiowas, and Cheyenne** strike a hide hunters' camp at **Adobe Walls.** They are repulsed but their fellow tribesmen come off their reservations and ravage the frontier along a 600-mile arc from the Arkansas to the Pecos rivers. Isolated ranches in eastern N.M. are the

Charles Ilfeld
Courtesy Museum of NM, #70674
(Nicholas Brown photo)

hardest hit.

July: The Army is petitioned for protection and all out war is declared on hostiles.

August: Seven **Comancheros** returning from the Indian country are killed by **Texans.**

September: **Mackenzie** routs a force of hostiles, captures **1,424 horses and has all of them slaughtered** so they may never be used again.

1875

William G. Ritch is interim Governor.

STATEHOOD

Newspapers express their views on whether or not to admit **N.M. and Colorado** into the Union:

New York Times: N.M. is "...thinly populated, the towns scattered over its vast area are few and ill-regulated, and a large part of the people is ignorant and utterly destitute of enterprise and public spirit."

Chicago Tribune: Neither should be made a State but if a choice has to be made let it be Colorado.

Cincinnati Commercial: Most New Mexicans are of "Mexican descent" and almost "wholly ignorant of English, ... aliens to us in blood and language .. popular ignorance prevails like a pall throughout the whole Territory, with few and insignificant exceptions..." and that out of 158 churches, **152 are Román Catholic.** Besides, the two territories have decidedly Republican leanings. (See **1889.**)

1875-1878

Samuel B. Axtell is Governor.

1875
RELIGIOUS

J.B. Lamy is consecrated **Archbishop** amid much ceremony and jubilation.

BUFFALO

Hide hunters are slaughtering the buffalo herds in such numbers that *ciboleros* declare that within a few short years they will have nothing to hunt with their lances if the carnage isn't curtailed.

TINSMITH

José María Apodaca, sometimes called the *"Small Scallop Tinsmith,"* begins producing tinwork, a craft which he practices until 1915. Apodaca comes to N.M. as a teenager from Juárez , Mexico, homesteading in **Ojo de la Vaca,** a village outside of Santa Fe. He is very prolific in production of his *nichos,* frames, boxes, sconces, etc., then he goes on horseback to sell them in Santa Fe and villages along the Pecos River. Apodaca's workshop is the family kitchen, using the table as a workbench and heating his soldering irons in the cast iron cooking stove. His work is of high quality, combining sophisticated design, highly developed craftsmanship, and superb color. His most distinctive characteristic is the scallop-like surface decoration on the edges of his pieces.

SOCIETY

Flora Langermann Spiegelberg, born in New York and educated in Germany, arrives in Santa Fe. As the wife of **Willie Spiegelberg** she makes her home a social center for personalities from politics, business, the military, religious, and visiting dignitaries. She is a product of European culture and visitors appreciate her cuisine, wines, collection of fine paintings, and her classical piano music.

Benjamin Read (1853-1927) is teaching at St. Michael's in Santa Fe.

PRINTING

Manuel Romero of Las Vegas converts a house into a shop for Father **Gasparri's** printing press. Under the direction of Gasparri, **Fray Ferri** prints textbooks for school as well as those for religious instruction.

NEWSPAPER

1875: The *Revista Católica Newspaper* is issued from Las Vegas under Father Gasparri's direction.

1916: The printing of the *Revista Católica* is moved to El Paso and publication is continued from there.

COMANCHES

June: **Kwahadi Comanches** are the last to surrender. Many chiefs are sent to **prison in Florida** and their people are put on reservations outside N.M. though they asked to be allowed to live in the state.

[There are nineteen Pueblo villages thriving in present day N.M. and one can only wonder what the State would be like if there were a number of Comanche towns in eastern portions of N.M. It is quite possible the Comanches could have been preserved as a distinct culture. From the commercial point of view, the Pueblos have become an integral factor in the state's economy and it is logical to assume that Comanches and their culture would be another tremendous attraction for people from all over the nation.]

SOCIETY

September 14: **Reverend F.J. Tolby**, a Methodist-Episcopal minister, is murdered. Popular sentiment around **Colfax county** blames the **Santa Fe Ring,** which is working to acquire title to Maxwell Co. land.

[Reverend **Thomas Harwood** later says the vile deed was committed by **Penitentes.**]

November 10: Citizens of Colfax County stage a **mass protest** in which the **Santa Fe Ring** is charged with the murder of Reverend Tolby.

Benjamin Read

NEW MEXICAN HISTORIAN

September 20, 1853: Benjamin Read is born to **Benjamin F. Read** (from the Read family of Baltimore and direct line descendant of George Read, a signer of the *Declaration of Independence*) and **Ignacia Cano** Read.

1856: B. F. Read dies, leaving three sons for Ignacia to raise. In time she marries **Mateo Ortiz** and they also have three sons: Modesto, Luis, and Juan. (All receive excellent educations and in time the Read brothers become lawyers.) At one point Bishop Lamy notices much intellectual ability in Benjamin and provides him with schoolbooks.

Ca. 1870: Benjamin works for the Kansas Pacific Railroad in Colorado as a section hand.

1870s: He begins to do historical research because he won't accept the "slanted and biased" writings of some authors who falsify Hispanic history.

1873: Read is working for Governor Giddings as a translator.

1875-1878: Benjamin is teaching at St. Michael's, his alma mater.

1876: He marries **Asensión Silva,** who dies two years later.

1878: Benjamin marries **Magdalena Silva** (Asensión's sister) and they have seven children.

1878-1880: Benjamin Read is superintendent of the Santa Fe schools.

1885: Read is admitted to the Bar and becomes asuccessful attorney in Santa Fe. He goes into politics as a Republican and is highly respected, even by opponents and their newspapers. He is a devout Catholic and not anti -Protestant. He despises bigotry in any form, is proud of his homeland's anti-slavery stance during the Civil War. He supports women's rights. Though he is bilingual, he uses Spanish most in his personal and professional life.

1893: Magdalena Read dies and in time Benjamin marries **Onofre Ortiz.** (They have no children.)
1901: Read serves as Speaker of the House in the Territorial Legislature.

1904: Onofre Read dies, leaving Benjamin with three daughters (from Magdalena) to raise.

Henceforth Benjamin dedicates himself to the study and writing of New Mexican history. He writes in Spanish but advocates that everyone learn both languages well.

Benjamin Read's passion is history and he understands that if *"the increasingly influential Anglo historians"* are allowed to control the historical record then Hispanic New Mexicans will be relegated for all time to the lower strata of society. His historiography has to be based on historical documents in order to be considered, he realizes, so he uses primary historical records from the archives of Spain, Mexico, and the Territory itself, which costs him much time, energy, and money.

1910: Benjamin publishes *The Mexican American War (La Guerra Mexico-Americana),* in Spanish, and dedicates it to his three daughters. He is proud to be the first *hijo del país* to publish a history of his homeland, proud to be descended of the Latin and Anglo-Saxon groups of N.M. He states that his goal is to expose the ignorance with which some "Anglo" historians have written New Mexican history. In parts of his work he disputes aspects of the histories written by **Ralph E. Twitchell** and **H.H. Bancroft**

1911: Benjamin Read publishes *The Illustrated History of New Mexico (Historia Ilustrada de Nuevo México).* The work is divided into four parts and is 616 pages long, utilizing extensive footnotes and photos of territorial personalities. It contains 146 profile biographies of well-known New Mexican men and women.

Benjamin Read
Courtesy Museum of NM, #111958

(R. E. Twitchell's monumental *Leading Facts of New Mexican History* also begins publication during the year 1911.)

1912: Read hires a professional translator to put his *Illustrated History* into English, thereby attempting to portray New Mexican history from an Hispanic point of view for English readers so as not to lose it

1919: Benjamin publishes A *Treatise on the Disputed Points of the History of New Mexico.*

[Two additional book-length manuscripts, *Hernán Cortes and his Conquest of Mexico,* in English, and *New Mexico in the Wars of the American Union, 1855-1919,* in Spanish, remain unpublished to this day.]

LINCOLN COUNTY

Lawrence G. **Murphy,** James J. **Dolan,** and John H. **Riley** own the commercial enterprise known as "the Store" or "the House" that serves everyone (Hispanics, "Anglos," the military, Indians) around the vicinity of Lincoln in a virtual monopoly. The three are *"audacious and ambitious,"* determined to maintain themselves in this frontier society. They buy stolen cattle at $5 a head when regular stockmen are selling at $15. In time **J. "Billy" Mathews** is made a "silent" partner.

James Dolan, Emil Fritz, W.J. Martin, L.G. Murphy
Courtesy Museum of NM, #104912

1875: **Alexander A. McSween,** a lawyer who had considered the ministry as a career, decides to open a business to rival "the House." A young Englishman by the name of **John H. Tunstall** joins him the following year.

1876: **William Brady,** a former military officer who had served with Murphy, is elected to the post of Sheriff for a second term. Governor **Axtell** accepts a loan of $1,800 from the firm.

1877: Murphy sells his interest in the firm, which is now called J.J. **Dolan and Co.** Santa Fe attorney **Thomas T. B. Catron** holds the mortgage on the business.

The House has enough political clout to install its cohorts as county sheriff, judge, and prosecutor. It has influence at the state level: **William L Rynerson,** district attorney for southern N.M., is an ally; **T.B. Catron,** U.S. Attorney and Territorial Attorney General, has a financial stake in it because he supplied the money with which to buy out Murphy; Governor **Axtell** is a personal friend who owes it money.

August: The McSween-Tunstall store is open for business.

McSween is hired by the brother and sister of **Emil Fritz** to collect the proceeds of Emil's life insurance policy. McSween collects, takes out his fees and expenses, then places the remaining sum in his bank account in St. Louis.

Dolan demands that the account of Emil Fritz be paid off from the insurance money, claiming Fritz owed the firm some $51,000 at the time of his death. McSween obtains a court order to inspect the firm's books but Dolan refuses to comply and McSween ignores Dolan's demand. Dolan gets sister Emilie Fritz to press a charge that McSween has absconded with Fritz money when McSween and John Chisum travel to St. Louis. McSween is jailed but is quickly out on bond with the charge still pending.

Judge **Warren Bristol** signs a writ for Sheriff Brady to attach property belonging to McSween up to a value of $8,000.

[The action taken to execute this order is what leads to the first shots of the **Lincoln County War.** See **1878**.]

1878: Tunstall writes a letter to the *Mesilla Independent* charging that Sheriff **William Brady** has allowed Dolan and Co. to use tax money to buy cattle. (When the tax funds don't arrive in Santa Fe by the specified time, Catron covers the amount.)

McSween and Tunstall form a bank.

Frank W. Angel (from New York) is sent by the government to investigate the troubled conditions in Colfax and Lincoln counties. He reports that Dolan and Co. have been lying about how many Indians are being supplied by padding their numbers and consistently overcharging the government for salt, grain, and beef. He also says that when buying from citizens, Dolan and Co. pay below-wholesale prices but when selling to them they charge above-retail prices. [See **1878**.]

Ca.1875-1900
TINSMITHS

Río Abajo Tinsmiths from the **Belén-Los Lunas** area villages are producing tin art during this period. Río Abajo tinwork is among the most elaborate produced in N.M. It is characterized by closely placed stamping, smooth and notched crescent shapes, notched bar stamps, single-dot punches, toothed circular stamps, which combine to form highly complex patterns.

1876
SETTLEMENT

Farmington is founded by **William and Simeon Hendrickson,** two gold prospectors from Colorado. [**Durango,** Co., is started five years later.]

SOCIETY

The first *bar mitzvah* takes place in Santa Fe when young **Alfred Grunsfeld,** a nephew of the Spiegelbergs and son of **Albert Grunsfeld** [for whom **Congregation Albert** is later named in Albuquerque] is inducted into manhood.

STATEHOOD - ELKINS' HANDSHAKE

Delegate to Congress **Stephen B. Elkins** walks in on the end of (Michigan's) Rep. J.C. Burrows' passionate oration denouncing attacks by Southerners on the civil rights of Blacks. Elkins is the first to shake Burrows' hand, in full view of the Southerners. Southerners vote *against* New Mexico statehood.

[Elkins is a controversial figure in New Mexican history and the "handshake" preventing statehood is more fantasy than fact. For example, the story began to be circulated more than two decades *after it actually happened*. The " Elkins factor" is more related to getting Congress to confirm land grants owned by speculators but he failed in getting confirmation for some 51 additional claims. **Oscar D. Lambert,** his biographer, has stated that he encountered no valid accusations of unfair practices used by Elkins. **Harold H. Dunham** openly accuses Elkins of fraud in being elected Delegate and serving monopolistic interests while in office. **H.R. Lamar** agrees with Dunham. **R.W Larson** censures Elkins for allegedly securing confirmation of the **Mora** Grant when he knew many residents on the land would be evicted and were protesting as unjust the confirmation to speculators.]

TIMELINE

August 1, 1876: **Colorado becomes the 38th state in the Union.**

LAW

United States vs. Joseph: the N.M. Supreme Court decrees that State rather than federal law has jurisdiction over N.M. Pueblos.

LAND GRANT

1876: The **Polvadera** grant is filed with Surveyor General Atkinson,

[Beginning in 1766 when the Polvadera was awarded to Juan Pablo Martín, numerous people established residency on the grant, farming the arable land and using the commons *(ejidos)* for grazing, etc., thus establishing usufruct rights.]

March 17: Lawyer **Samuel Ellison** files a claim with the SG for (it is supposed) Manuel García, Donaciano Gallegos, and Francisco Manzanares as owners of the 35,924 acres. It is stated that *"no known individuals hold adverse possession"* to Polvadera lands (meaning that all the people living on the land are *"unknown"* and the courts are accepting the assertion).

1882: The grant is approved by the SG and recommended for patenting by Congress (though it is never acted upon by Congress; it is therefore without legal title because Congress refuses to legalize it). But the acreage is "sold" [by whom?] to **Frank Perew** of Buffalo, N.Y. **and Willis J. Currier** (Perew's brother-in-law) who is establishing a cattle ranch in the upper Polvadera.

1892: Frank Perew applies for confirmation of the grant to the Court of Private Land Claims. It appears that **residents of the grant are never informed** that the Polvadera is being sold to Perew or anybody else but the Court seeks no *"disinterested testimony"* (which means no one living on the land is recognized by the Court as an owner of the land he uses or lives on).

1893: The Court confirms the grant to the *"heirs, legal representatives, and assigns* of **Juan Pablo Martín**" who are now recognized by the courts as Perew and Currier.

[Perew and Currier *"bought it"* and all others can be evicted from their homes, their land, and their way of making a living, evicted by officers of the law up to and including the Army if need be.]

1897: Survey of the grant is assigned to **Clayton G. Coleman** who encounters legitimate adverse possessors of Polvadera grant land, noting the situation in his field notes but these are unheeded by his superiors in Santa Fe or Washington.

1900: A patent is issued to **Alice R. Perew,** widow of Frank Perew, for the Polvadera Grant.

[**V. Westphall** wonders why "*adverse possessors of the land*" (i.e., land owners who were being evicted from their land) didn't challenge the Perews then he supplies possible answers:

First: The "ordinary Hispano land owner" was unacquainted with the office of the SG or the Court of Private Land Claims, and neither sought out the Hispano land owner; besides, attorneys had to be present and Hispanos didn't trust them or have money to hire them.

Second: It is "quite probable" that residents on the grant weren't even aware that the land they were living on was under litigation, that public notices were required to be "duly published" in territorial newspapers but "few Hispanos could read them" and it was not pointed out to them.

Third: Claimants who were taking the land "*were as secretive as possible about their actions.*" **Secrecy was their most effective strategy**.]

LAND LAW

The Territorial Legislature enacts the **Partition Statute:** a court can require a jointly owned land grant to be divided among its owners or sold in order to pay attorneys and other legal fees, when requested by *one* of the owners. The **instigator of a partition suit is often the attorney** who secures confirmation of the grant, who is usually working on a contingency fee: the attorney isn't paid unless he wins confirmation of the grant. Standard fee for confirmation is one-fourth to one-third of the commons land. **Lawyers usually want cash** for their efforts, not group ownership in land. So the Partition Statute enables attorneys to force the sale of commons land [**which had been illegal under Spanish/Mexican law but this is ignored by the American legal system even though the Treaty of Guadalupe Hidalgo stipulated that property rights would be protected**].

GOVERNMENT

Surveyor General James K. Proudfit is asked to resign.

March 3 1: **Henry M. Atkinson** becomes Surveyor General. "*By far the greatest amount of surveying in New Mexico was done under his supervision, and irregular practices were common during his tenure…Irregularities in surveys under Atkinson were prolific and brought repercussions while he was still in office.*"

LAND GRANT

The **Las Trampas** land grant is surveyed and found to contain more than 46,000 acres. Commissioner N.C. McFarland of the General Land Office says the eastern boundary is overlapping into the Santa Bárbara grant.

1885: **William Sparks** sets aside the first survey and orders a new one which finds that the grant contains around 28,000 acres.

[A patent is issued for this (greatly reduced) acreage in 1903.]

1900: Las Trampas heir **David Martínez** Jr. files a suit (along with four other heirs) to be paid for individual shares of the Las Trampas Grant. **Alonzo B. McMillan** is their attorney in the action. The suit names **five individual defendants** (instead of all the living heirs of the original **"Trampas Twelve,"** the hundreds of people living in the Trampas grant villages of Ojo Sarco, Cañada de los Alamos, Las Trampas, El Valle, Chamisal, and El Llano who were the "*heirs*") and a legal notice is "published" in the (English language) Taos *Cresset* newspaper informing "*unknown heirs*" about the action.

The Court appoints **Ernest A. Johnson** as referee to determine who are owners of the grant, how much of the grant is common land, and each owner's fractional interest in the common lands. **Referee Johnson** finds that 650 acres are private land and the rest is commons subject to partition. Citizens living on the land are not informed about what the Court says is the extent (650 acres out of the 28,000) of their private holdings.

Judge **Daniel H. McMillan,** substituting for judge **John R. McFie** enters an order for partition and appoints a board of commissioners to divide the common lands. Commissioners report that due to the nature of the land and large number of heirs a partition is impossible. People living on the land therefore will not get their "individual percentage share" of land from the grant.

Judge McFie returns to the bench and orders the **sale of common lands**. The only bid at sale is $5,000 by **H.F. Raynolds** and the lands are sold. Attorney Alonzo B. McMillan is awarded one-fourth of the net proceeds. McMillan has been buying interests in the common lands from various heirs and now he owns 10.6% of the grant, for which he must be paid.

A suit is filed by **Alois B. Renehan** to set aside the sale of the Trampas grant because the **buyer,** H.E Raynolds, turns out to be **Alonzo McMillan's law partner.** McMillan, Raynolds, and Referee Johnson's assistant **Amado Chávez** are accused of conspiring to buy the land for about 18 cents per acre because they could then sell it at $1.50 per acre, and that Referee Johnson has accepted a **bribe** to go along with the scheme.

Judge McFie sets the sale aside and orders a new one which is scheduled for February of 1903. Española merchant and sheepman **Frank Bond** bids $17,000 and is given title to the land. Attorney **Alonzo McMillan** gets his fee of around $4,200. David Martínez Jr. nets about $200. Villagers average about $25 for their "sale share" but the *fact that it is for sale of their common lands is hidden from them by allowing them to use the lands temporarily.*

1907: **Frank Bond** sells the grant to the Las Trampas Lumber Company owned by four Albuquerque businessmen. Villagers now realize their lands have been sold. They hire **Charles Catron,** son of T.B. Catron, to get their land back, beginning a new round of litigation.

1908: Las Trampas Lumber Company files a quiet title suit to clear title for the land bought from Frank Bond. **Alois B. Rcnehan** is attorney for the Lumber Co. *as well as for some of the villagers, who are defendants in the suit.*

1911: Charles Catron files an answer to the quiet title suit.

1913: The suit is **settled out of court** between Catron and Renehan: Villagers receive deeds to their private tracts of land and easement for all irrigation ditches; they retain **"use rights"** for grazing and wood gathering; they sign quitclaim deeds to the Lumber Co. for what had been common lands; La Trampas Lumber Co. receives the villagers' quitclaim deeds which make no mention of "use-rights," which the Co. grants to all villagers via an individual agreement with each one; Attorney Renehan now inserts a stipulation into the final settlement agreement: **"...neither this contract nor any contract delivered pursuant hereto by said company is to be acknowledged or recorded."**

[Under American law a document that is not notarized cannot be recorded and an unrecorded document is not binding. Therefore, Renehan guaranteed that villager "use rights" were nonexistent before the law while all villagers possessed written documentation from the Lumber Co. that "guaranteed" their traditional use-rights.]

Catron and Renehan have settled the quiet-title suit by documenting villagers **with perpetual "use rights"** to their common lands while supplying the Lumber Co. with official court documents that showed the land to be unencumbered by **"use rights,"** enabling a sale whenever desirable.

1914: **Judge Thomas Lieb** [it is unknown if he was aware of what had transpired] signs a decree quieting the title to the Las Trampas grant. Charles Catron is awarded a fee of $5,500.

1926: Las Trampas Lumber Co. declares **bankruptcy.**

The **United States purchases the Trampas lands** and villagers file their "use-rights" documents with the Government, which are turned over to the **Forest Service** in Albuquerque for advice.

The **Forest Service** questions attorney **Alois B. Renehan** who informs it that no "use rights" agreement exists.

When **Charles Catron** is questioned he states that the **"use rights" documentation** is in the court file but the Forest Service **can't locate it.** Since the use right agreements are not recorded nor referred to in the court decree, the Forest Service concludes *"...they are without any effect."* But villagers are lulled with the subterfuge that matters can be *"worked out."*

Traditional practices are permitted until 1915-1930 when the Forest Service restricts villager use rights. Grazing fees are charged, herds are limited and permits required. Unable to graze stock without paying onerous fees, villagers look to others ways to make a living.

The **Great Depression** breaks out and wage labor is more difficult to come by. Stock animals don't exist in sufficient numbers to make a living for most village families. There is hunger in the land.

1967: The **Tierra Amarilla Courthouse raid** causes the Forest Service to be a little more conciliatory in the needs of Trampas villages but little changes in substance.

1971: At a meeting held in Peñasco local residents demand that their use right agreements be honored. The Forest Service replies that the documents aren't legal therefore there is no obligation on its part.

1981: Ben E. Domínguez, José Paz López, and Ron Maestas are cited for gathering firewood without a permit in the **Carson National Forest.** They claim the right to take wood under their use-right agreements, which are introduced at the trial.

["...No court has yet recognized these agreements and the Forest Service still denies their efficacy" according to M. Ebright.]

TIMELINE

June 25-26, 1876: Lieutenant Colonel **George A. Custer** leads his **Seventh Cavalry** Regiment against a very large force of "hostile" Sioux and Cheyenne Indians. He splits his forces: some 264 under his command, perhaps 140 under Major Reno, with a total of some 255 soldiers and men under Captain Benteen. Overwhelming numbers of warriors attack Reno and destroy half his command, the other half are saved by the arrival of Benteen. Neither knew where Custer was until they heard heavy gunfire to the north of their position. Then most of the Indian resistance disappears because the Native Americans ride north to join the battle there.

Custer had promised to support Reno's forces but he turned and went north instead when word came the Indians weren't fleeing but attacking. With Reno under attack Custer saw that a very big village lay across the Little Bighorn River for perhaps three miles. Custer got his battalion on a ridge and informed his men that the hostiles were ripe for plucking. Then a great number of warriors led by **Gall**, a Hunkpapa Sioux chieftain, struck from the southwest. From the northwest came hundreds of warriors under **Crazy Horse** (Oglala Sioux) and **Two Moon** (Cheyenne). Before the actual battle Custer is shot while crossing a stream and then his men are wiped out on the Little Bighorn.

[**The Custer fight has become legendary in the popular mind.** The image is often one of Custer fighting to the last, saber in one hand and blazing revolver in the other, his blond hair streaming defiantly in the wind. There is no doubt that Custer possessed as much physical courage as anyone but it is historical fact that the land in question belonged to the Indians according to treaties made with the government of the U.S. so Custer was in effect leading a military invasion of sovereign territory. Custer had cut his hair off before the expedition and he never held a saber because the Cavalry didn't carry them in 1876. Indians were later to say that Custer was known among them as "woman killer" because he had fought only against friendly villages before the Little Bighorn which was the first time he actually fought warriors.

President Grant stated that Custer had "sacrificed his men." General Terry wrote in a confidential report that all died because Custer disobeyed orders when he refused to wait for the rest of the Army. The media and the nation, celebrating the centennial of 1876, portrayed the disaster as *Custer's Massacre,* ignoring the fact that it was a battle in which Army troops invaded foreign territory, were outnumbered and wiped out by Native Americans who believed they had a right to their lives, culture, and property. But the USA seethed with resentment and the Army targeted for extermination any free Indians who refused to come into assigned agencies.]

1877
SOCIETY
Sotero Ortiz is born at San Juan Pueblo.

CIBOLERO HUNT

Manuel Jesús Vásquez from **Peñasco** is sent by patrón don **Juan Policarpio Romero** to hunt buffalo on the plains. Manuel, who is 21 years old, married to **Rosario Frésquez,** and works in carpentry, leaves Peñasco with a Navajo Indian named Juan J. Romero, a member of Romero's household. They gather with men from **El Llano** like Albino Ortega, Jesús María Ortega, etc., totaling around 30 in number. Thus far there are 15 ox-drawn carts in the expedition.

November 15, 1877: More men and carts join the group in **Mora** and **Ocate.**

Election: The expedition travels east and in the area of Chico (in present Colfax County) the men halt to elect a Comandante. **Albino Ortega** is elected and all pledge to cooperate with their commander in order to have a successful hunt. When the time is right he gives orders to make or break camp, when the oxen are to be yoked, which route to follow, etc.

Scouts: Ortega selects scouts to ride ahead and reconnoiter for things like water holes, the best route across the prairie, and signs of Indian war parties. The scouts leave the group each morning and return by evening.

Route: The ciboleros pass by *El Ojo del Cíbolo* (Buffalo Spring, by modern Clayton) and continue across Texas into Oklahoma at a place called *Punta de Agua* (Waterhole). At a spot called Pilares they kill a buffalo bull which furnishes them with meat for a few days. They continue to search for the buffalo herds and arrive at the *Río de las Nutrias* (Beaver River) where they make camp and prepare to hunt. (They have been on the plains for a month now.)

Hunt: When the herd is sighted the hunters are ordered to get into line, the fastest horses on each end. Comandante Ortega leads a prayer for strength and a successful hunt. When the prayer is finished Ortega says *"Ave María Purísima"* and all hunters move forward as if they are one, quickly at a walk, trot, and finally at full speed, the fastest horses on the end encircling the group of buffalo to be brought down by the ciboleros' lances. Comandante Ortega decides when there is sufficient meat to fill all the ox carts and he gives the order to halt the lancing of buffaloes. Enough animals are killed to fill 50 carts with meat.

Processing: Skinners now come up to the downed buffaloes and skin them. Carts arrive and pack hides, meat, etc., into camp. Ortega sees to it that all parties divide the meat equitably, from the most desirable to the least. The meat is cut into working pieces then sliced thin and hung out to dry. When dry the meat is stacked like cordwood in order to be loaded into the carts for the return home. The group is in camp for around a month.

Indians: A party of 10 Kiowas suddenly appear and rides into camp. They ask for meat to eat and Ortega orders that they be given whatever they need. The Kiowas don't leave after they eat and some of the men wonder if the Indians should be killed before they go get large numbers of their brethren and return to slaughter the ciboleros and take all the meat. Manuel J. Vásquez opposes the plan and the Kiowas are ordered out of camp. They leave but stay within sight of the cibolero caravan for several days.

Return: Comandante Ortega gives the order to start the long trek home. The return journey takes another month. The three-month expedition turns out free of any dispute or fighting of any kind.

EDUCATION

The **Jesuit College** opens its doors in Las Vegas. The building, donated by **Francisco López**, is a house in "Old Town." All students are welcome, regardless of religious affiliation. Boarders pay $200 a year while day scholars pay from one to three dollars per month. By the end of the first term there are 132 students.

1882-1885: The Jesuit College is at its height of popularity and its training in the classics is compared favorably to schools in the East.

1884: Day scholars at the College include "all the Jewish boys in Las Vegas."

1888: The Jesuit College closes its doors due to lack of funds.

[The College provided a magnificent legacy because many prominent New Mexican literati like Eleuterio Baca, Eusebio Chacón, Ezequiel C. de Baca, Antonio Lucero, Camilo Padilla, etc., who were students there.]

MEDAL OF HONOR - ROBERT MCDONALD

Robert McDonald, b. New York, entered service at Fort Sumner. Citation: On January 8, 1877, Robert McDonald led his command in a successful charge against superior numbers of hostile Indians, strongly posted, at Wolf Mountain, Montana. Medal of Honor awarded on November 17, 1884.

REPORT

La Revista Católica editorializes on the approaching railroad era: *"...now that the trains come as far as the frontiers of New Mexico, there will be great dishonor to the religion which they [Penitentes] profess if they are seen naked and bloody on plains and mountains. Men who only seek pretexts for mobilizing public opinion against the Catholic Church come here in order to observe these places and then to report to newspapers in the States-attributing to the entire Catholic population in this land that which is only the effect of a few..."*

LAND LAW

The **Desert Land Act** becomes law. A citizen can acquire 640 acres of land at 25 cents an acre if the land is reclaimed (brought under irrigation) within three years whereupon an additional one dollar per acre is paid. **The law is used to acquire water sources** with which thousands of acres are converted to personal use by big ranchers. **Fraud is rampant.**

IRRIGATION

Many New Mexicans declare the Territory is as deserving of national **aid for irrigation** as other sections are needful of **aid for rivers and harbors.**

SOCIETY

George W. Armijo is born.

Frank Springer, Colfax County lawyer, charges that the 1876 annexation of Colfax to Taos County will result in Colfax cases being tried by Taos juries largely composed of Penitentes *"unfit"* for such service.

November 2: **John Becker** marries **Ann Vielstitch,** a native of Germany like himself, and in time they have six children.

1878-1881

Lew Wallace is Governor.

1878
LAND GRANT

The **Jacona land grant** of about 40,000 acres (as approved by the Surveyor General) is surveyed.

WEAVING

Río Grande blankets incorporate a mixture of decorative designs: striped, Mexican, and Navajo.

SOUTHEAST N.M.

Lincoln County is enlarged, becoming the largest county unit in the U.S. (slightly smaller than the state of New York).

Roswell is a growing settlement of "Anglos" from Texas and the Old South. Southern views hold sway regarding race and ethnic relations, **separatism** marking social ties between "Anglos" and Hispanics, the latter being regarded in the same vein as blacks.

When a traveling show of "Uncle Tom's Cabin" approaches the town a delegation of citizens meets them on the road and tells them to "keep moving," which they do.

Whiskey and modern guns are readily available and are "key elements in the violence."

Southeastern N.M. is now an area where "Anglos" and Hispanics have serious differences with each other, where large cattlemen want to get rid of sheepmen, small ranchers, and farmers; where large cattle companies battle each other through hired gunmen; where cattle rustlers prey on all ranchers; and where land grabbing is for anyone strong enough to defend himself.

REPORT

Susan Wallace, wife of the Governor, describes N.M. as "*the land of sagebrush and cactus...*" with villages that look "*like nothing so much as a collection of brick kilns.*" Lincoln County is an "*asylum for cut throats.*" If Statehood is achieved "*...the Americans would bear the taxes and the Mexicans hold all the offices--it is not in the interest of the white men to bring that about.*"

BUSINESS

With the help of his friend Felipe Chávez, **John Becker** opens his own store in **Belén.** In time Becker puts in a modern roller-process flour mill that can process more than 100 barrels a day.

TURMOIL

The **Lincoln County War** is about to break out when Sheriff **Brady** enters the McSween-Tunstall store with a court order and removes large quantities of goods, despite Tunstall's protests that McSween doesn't own any merchandise. Furniture from McSween's home is also taken then Brady and his men head for McSween's ranch to attach his cattle.
Tunstall's bodyguards, **Billy the Kid** and Fred Waite, watch as tension rises.

February 18: Tunstall and some of his cowboys are met by a posse of Brady-Dolan men. The cowboys seek cover in the pine trees but Tunstall stops to wait for the posse and is gunned down by **Billy Morton.** With Tunstall face down on the ground, **Jesse Evans** takes Tunstall's revolver and fires into the back of Tunstall's head.

McSween writes his last will and testament then arranges for a life insurance policy. He seeks and obtains arrest warrants for posse members from justice of the Peace **John B. Wilson,** who appoints **Dick Brewer** as constable. Brewer then deputizes Billy the Kid, Fred Waite, Frank Macnab, Doc Scurlock, Charles Bowdre, Henry Brown, and Sam Smith (which group comes to be known as the **Regulators**). A number of Chisum cowboys also sign on with Brewer's Regulators.

Alexander McSween
Courtesy Museum of NM, #46205

March 8: Governor Axtell visits Fort Stanton and Lincoln then returns to Santa Fe without inquiring into Tunstall's death.

March 9: Regulators ambush then arrest **Frank Baker and Billy Morton,** who were with the posse that killed Tunstall. When the group arrives at Lincoln, Baker and Morton are dead because they had "attempted to escape."
Governor Axtell declares that J.B. Wilson's appointment as justice of the Peace is illegal and that Brewer's deputizations are invalid. U.S. Attorney T.B. Catron does little to investigate Tunstall's death.

April 1: Sheriff **Brady** and deputies Billy Mathews, John Long, George Hindman, and George Pippin are walking in front of the Tunstall store when rifle shots are fired by Regulators (one of whom is **Billy the Kid**) hidden behind the gates of the Tunstall corral. Brady dies immediately, Hindman moments later while the others run for cover.

Billy the Kid comes out into the street and retrieves the rifle Brady had taken from him at an earlier date but a shot wounds him in a leg. Billy gets some medical care and all the Regulators ride out of town.

Deputy Sheriff **George Peppin** calls in soldiers from Fort Stanton. McSween and Brewer condemn the killings, declaring it was an isolated group of Regulators who perpetrated the violent deed.

April 4: A gunfight takes place at **Blazer's Mill** between Andrew "Buckshot" Roberts and a group of Regulators. Roberts is mortally wounded but before he dies he shoots Brewer between the eyes.

Newspapers throughout the territory report on the events in Lincoln County. The *Santa Fe New Mexican* favors the Dolan faction while the *Cimarron News and Press* of Colfax County are for McSween-Tunstall.

April 14: **Judge Bristol** [described as a member of the Santa Fe Ring] opens the annual court session. The grand jury clears McSween of embezzlement charges in the Fritz case; Jesse Evans and four others are indicted for the murder of Tunstall, with Dolan and Murphy named as accessories; Billy the Kid, Middleton, Wait, and Brown are indicted for the murders of Brady and Hindman; etc.

Rumor has it that Dolan is hiring gunmen at top pay. All are deputized and the Peppin-Dolan forces number around 40 men.

June: Three Chisum cowboys are killed while working cattle.

July: McSween is at Chisum's ranch when a large force of Dolan-Peppin men attack for some 24 hours.

July 16: McSween forces, numbering about 40, about 25 of which are Hispanic, shoot it out with the Peppin-Dolan faction in the otherwise empty town of Lincoln. (McSween men are described as being better marksmen and more courageous but the Peppin-Dolan faction has superior weaponry. In time the only group left is in the McSween house.

July 19: Col. Dudley marches into Lincoln with 35 troopers from Fort Stanton. The McSween house is set on fire. Susan McSween goes out to Col. Dudley and asks that he help stop the fire; he tells her it appears as if McSween himself started the blaze. Inside the house McSween is shell-shocked and Billy the Kid provides the leadership needed in such desperate circumstances: at dark everyone must dash out toward the Río Bonito; the Kid's

Susan McSween
Courtesy Museum of NM, #105449

group will divert enemy gunfire while McSween escapes.The plan is put into effect under the cover of darkness: Billy the Kid and others make it to safety. Several fall wounded or dead. McSween hesitates and is hit by five bullets and falls in his back doorway as his house burns.

The fighting over, the Peppin-Dolan forces celebrate through the night by looting the Tunstall store.

The federal government begins to take notice of the situation in N.M. The British Embassy presses for an investigation of Tunstall's death, Governor Axtell is openly accused of chicanery regarding the Maxwell Land Grant, and civil war is raging in Lincoln County.

September 30: **Lew Wallace** arrives in N.M. as Governor, replacing Samuel B. Axtell. Wallace is an accomplished man, having served in the Mexican and Civil wars, having published a novel and working on *Ben Hur*. His mandate is to end corruption and establish law and order, especially in Lincoln County. While the Dolan and McSween factions seek revenge upon each other there are new gangs of outlaws from Texas to contend with, led by "*notorious gunmen*" like John Selman and John Kinney who terrorize the area with "*murders, rapes, and thefts of livestock.*"

Governor Wallace obtains an executive order enabling him to use the military to enforce the law. Then he offers amnesty to all participants charged with crimes between February 1 and November 13 (but not for those already under indictment). However, the animosities don't abate.

1879: **Susan McSween** vows to recover her dead husband's property so she hires an aggressive attorney named **Huston Chapman** to sue Col. Dudley.

February 18: Chapman is shot dead on the street (one year to the day of Tunstall's death).

March 15: Governor Wallace arrives in Lincoln with Col. Edward Hatch, commander of military forces in N.M. Col. Dudley is removed from command at Fort Stanton and 36 arrest warrants are issued for people involved in the feuding. **Juan B. Patrón** is empowered to form a citizens' militia, the **Lincoln County Rifles.**

Wallace meets everyone, including Billy the Kid and Pat Garrett. The Kid had witnessed Chapman's murder so he arranges to meet with the Governor on the 17th when he offers to testify in return for a full pardon for any crimes he might be convicted of in the upcoming court session. He agrees to be placed under arrest as a protective measure.

April: Billy the Kid pleads not guilty to the Brady murder charge with no attorney representing him.

He testifies in Judge Bristol's court and helps secure indictments against the Chapman murderers.
District Attorney W.L. **Rynerson** obtains a change of venue to Doña Ana County because there is too much sentiment in favor of Billy the Kid in Lincoln. He also states that Billy won't be allowed to testify against Dolan and that Governor Wallace has no authority to pardon the Kid.
May 17: Billy is in jail but some friends help him escape. Now he is determined to remain free and perhaps realizes Governor Wallace isn't going to come through with his promise. He turns to rustling cattle

from people he doesn't like. Pecos Valley cattlemen demand his capture.

1880: Billy the Kid is now considered a tough cowboy gone over to the lawless element of society.

Pat Garrett, tough and incorruptible, is elected to be the new Sheriff of Lincoln County. He hires **Ash Upson** to handle the office work while he devotes himself to the capture of Billy the Kid.

December 12: The Kid writes to Governor Wallace: Sheriff Garrett is after me because of John Chisum. Chisum has benefited by all this and is working to get me.

The governor offers a $500 reward for the capture of Billy the Kid.

December 19: Billy and some of his friends are riding toward Fort Sumner when a posse led by Garrett intercepts them and demands their surrender. Tom O'Folliard is shot but the Kid gets away, holing up at Stinking Springs until all are captured by the posse.

December 28: Billy the Kid is taken to Santa Fe and Pat Garrett gets his $500 reward money. The capture is publicized all over the territory and the Las Vegas Gazette interviews the Kid in jail. Billy maintains he is being punished unfairly for the Lincoln County War and that he is no ringleader of cattle thieves.

1881: The Kid writes to Governor Wallace repeatedly, asking that he come through with some kind of protection as promised. The governor ignores him, being occupied with the release of *Ben Hur* and various of his mining ventures.

March 4: Finally the Kid writes to Wallace: "I guess they mean to send me up without giving me any show."

Under heavy guard, Billy is transferred to Las Cruces to be tried in Judge Bristol's court for the murder of Sheriff Brady. **A.J. Fountain** and **J.D. Bail** are appointed to defend the Kid but aren't given time to find witnesses for the defense. He is found guilty.

April 13: Judge Bristol sentences Billy the Kid to be hanged at Lincoln on May 13.

April 2 1: The Kid is imprisoned at Lincoln. Deputies **J.W. Bell and R. Olinger** provide round-the-clock security.

April 28: Bell escorts the Kid, handcuffed and shackled, to the outhouse and on the way back Billy slips off a handcuff, strikes Bell, gets his gun and shoots the deputy. Olinger hears the shot from outside the building and races up to help when Billy shoots him with a shotgun. Billy escapes without further incident. (His many friends help him to stay free.)

April 29: Pat Garrett learns that his two deputies are dead and Billy has escaped.

April 30: Governor Wallace, who still doesn't know about the escape, signs the death warrant for the execution of William Bonney, alias Billy the Kid.

July 14: Pat Garrett and some of his friends are at the home of Pete Maxwell at Fort Sumner where the Kid had been seen. Inside the house Garrett hears a knock at the door and Billy's voice asking in Spanish, *"Who is it?"* Billy the Kid enters then, sensing something wrong, he moves to leave when Garrett opens fire, the first bullet killing him instantly.

July 15: Billy the Kid's body is identified and later buried in the military cemetery at Fort Sumner.

1878 (con't)
RAILROAD
December 7, 1878: **"Uncle Avery" Turner** pilots the first steam train into N.M. at a point 15.7 miles south of Trinidad, Colorado, as related by D.F. Myrick.

1878-1880
COMANCHEROS
Hide hunters kill 12 Comancheros on the Pease River.

1879
SOCIETY
Comanches stage their last buffalo hunt. Promised annuities don't arrive and starvation is imminent but hunting as in olden times avails them nothing for the buffalo can't be found. A battalion of Texans attacks them unexpectedly, killing and scalping one, but further disaster is averted by the timely arrival of a detachment of **Negro Cavalry.**

The **buffalo** have been slaughtered by hide hunters, **Comanches** and other plains nations are concentrated in reservations, the **Comanchero trade** is dead, and the alliance between New Mexicans and Comanches is broken for all time.

RAILROAD
The **Atchison Topeka and the Santa Fe** railroad reaches **Las Vegas.**

"Anglos" are hired by the railroads as superintendents, yard masters, road masters, station agents, car inspectors, telegraph operators, office clerks, dispatchers, call men, switchmen, engineers, conductors, firemen, brakemen, porters, pumpers, machinists, boiler makers, carpenters, painters, or section foremen. **Hispanos** *"...were employed only as laborers or section hands."*

[The railroad brings in many business and professional people but also *"a large assortment of frontier riffraff, robbers, gamblers, swindlers* (called bunko men), *gunmen... murderers, thieves, and just plain tramps, along with dance-hall girls"* and/or prostitutes. These were known by an assortment of names: Hoodoo Brown, Rattlesnake Sam, Dummy the Fox, Johnny Behind-the-Rocks, Handsome Harry the Dance Hall Rustler, etc. It is said that no town harbored a more disreputable gang of gamblers, desperadoes and outlaws than did Las Vegas. In one month there were 29 men killed in or around the Vegas area. Billy the Kid, Wyatt Earp, Doc Holliday, Jesse James, etc., frequented the town though East Las Vegas, the railroad part of town, was run by the Dodge City Gang lead by Hoodoo Brown, whose real name was Hyman G. Neill, the first justice of the peace in East Las Vegas. He and his henchmen come to be known as the **Dodge City Gang.** Hoodoo Brown served as coroner, acting mayor and town council. He organized the police force, which consisted mostly of Kansas gunfighters and gamblers.]

July 26-29: **Jesse James** is lodged at the Las Vegas Hot Springs hotel. (It is said he met **Billy the Kid** and invited him to *"join forces and hit the trail together,"* but the Kid declined.)

John H. "Doc" Holliday operates a saloon and gambling hall on Centre Street with his partner. **Wyatt Earp** and his brother James join Holliday in Las Vegas in the fall, becoming part of the operation.

September: **Monte Verde** (usually referred to in newspaper accounts as **Monte Holman),** *"a beautiful, dark-eyed brunette,"* arrives in East Las Vegas and in time opens The Parlor, a *"palace of pleasure."* She dealt faro and entertained at the Globe Theater.

[When her history is published it is said that Monte Verde was really **Belle Siddons**, a Missouri socialite who had been a notorious Confederate spy during the Civil War.]

LAND GRANT
Father T. A. Hayes buys the Pedro Sánchez/Ramón Vigil grant from Ramón Vigil for $4,000 then sells it in a month for $16,000. Two years later Father Hayes buys it back, for the same price.

1881: Father Hayes is arrested in Albuquerque on a warrant issued in La Junta, Colorado, but the Albuquerque Jesuits take him in to avoid prosecution.

1884: Father Hayes sells the Ramón Vigil grant for $ 100,000 [a **profit** of $96,000, not counting interim expenses, which might be a record for successful N.M. land grant speculation].

NEWSPAPERS
Severino Trujillo (who was born in the mountain village of Guadalupita in Mora county) founds *La Estrella de Mora* newspaper.

1879-1883
APACHE RAIDS
Apache chieftain **Victorio** is raiding during this period, killing 200 New Mexicans, more than 100 U.S. soldiers, and 200 Mexicans.

1879-1891
EDUCATION

More than 60 **Protestant schools** are started in various towns and rural areas during this period.

RELIGION

The **Revista Católica** charges that the *"..Spanish Mission* [Protestant] *Schools went all out under the guise of education to take away the Faith of the poor and ignorant by offering them an education which the Church at the time could not afford. Their procedure was to blacken Catholicism in the eyes of the simple folk. The old canards about the evil secret lives of priests and nuns, the adoration of images, and other such lies were broadcast in print and by word of mouth in rural settlements ... What these sects did effect all too well was to confuse souls; they took away the Faith of many and left them, not Protestants, but infidels and scoffers."*

PROFILE

Severino Trujillo

A NEW MEXICAN INTELLECTUAL

1854: **Father John B. Guerín** is ordained and assigned to Mora. Severino Trujillo comes under the tutelage of Padre Guerín and even assists the priest in his duties and visits to outlying missions of the Mora parish. Severino is encouraged to study Greek and Latin in preparation for the priesthood.

1872: Severino travels to Paris to enter the Seminary of St. Suplice, remaining there until he completes his studies in 1876.

1877: Trujillo decides not to take Holy Orders and returns to Mora. He is appointed to political office.

1879: Severino founds *La Estrella de Mora.*

1884: While maintaining his residence in Mora, Trujillo moves to Trinidad, Colorado, to assist his friend Casimiro Barela. Severino helps to found the *Asociación de Mutuo Adelantamiento* to assist in advancing southern Colorado's Hispanic community.

1889: Severino is elected to represent Mora in the Constitutional Convention.
1892: When Archbishop Chapelle visits Guadalupita, Severino Trujillo delivers a famous speech in which he voices allegiance to the Catholic clergy who were so indispensable to his education. He attacks Protestant bigotry that is targeting Catholic New Mexicans by accusing them of being *"... victims of their own heritage--their Catholicism, their environment and their*

own leaders." (The speech is later published in *La Revista Católica.)*

1897: Trujillo is living in Mora County where he establishes a private school in Wagon Mound.

1911: Severino continues teaching in his private school in Wagon Mound.

1879-1900
NEWSPAPERS

Newspaper publication makes a resurgence in N.M. During this 21 year period 283 newspapers (most in English but many in Spanish) are launched. Las Vegas alone sees 44 newspapers during these years.

1880s: There are 16 bilingual and 13 Spanish-language newspapers being published;

1890s: There are 35 Spanish-language newspapers and 11 bilingual publications.

Most newspapers dedicate much space to **creative writing** as well as events of the day. Among the many Hispanics who contribute regularly to newspapers are Higinio V. Gonzáles, José Manuel Arellano, Jesús María H. Alaríd, Manuel M. Salazar, Eleuterio Baca, Urbano Chacón, Florencio Trujillo, Ezequiel Cabeza de Baca, Jesús Gonzáles, Antonio Lucero, Enrique H. Salazar, Severino Trujillo, Antonio B. Trujillo, etc.

Antonio Lucero
Courtesy Museum of NM, #87630

1880
RAILROAD

The railroad is completed to Albuquerque.

1880-1886
BANDELIER & FRIJOLES CANYON

Adolph E. Bandelier (born August 6, 1840 in Bern, Switzerland) is working in the Frijoles Canyon ruins area west of Santa Fe during this period, living in one of the kivas. He is the first to survey the area in scientific fashion and the first to study the ethnology and mythology of its Native American groups. He becomes a friend and associate of **Charles F. Lummis**. At the end of his sojourn he writes *The Delight Makers,* an ethno-historical novel portraying life of the early Keres people. (He goes on to become world renowned as ethnologist, archaeologist, and writer. (See *The Southwestern Journal of Adolph E. Bandelier, 1889-1892,* by Charles Lange.)

1740: Andrés Montoya is awarded a land grant on the *Rito de los Frijoles*. His descendants farm the area until around 1811 and during the period of American litigation of land titles the Montoya grant is declared invalid by government authorities.

1916: Bandelier National Monument is founded.

1932: Much of the area is made a part of the National Park Service.

1880-1914
PROSTITUTION

With the arrival of the railroad in Albuquerque there comes organized prostitution which is characterized by "soiled doves" and their "madams" who inhabit the "red-light district." ("No *red-light district existed in Old Albuquerque before the arrival of the railroad in 1880*" according to B.A. Johnson and S.P. Johnson.)

AGRICULTURE - VINEYARDS

There are some 3,150 acres of vineyards under cultivation in N.M. Around 905,000 barrels of wine are produced each year, ranking N.M. fifth in the U.S. and territories.

1914: Due to disastrous floods and then Prohibition, the Río Grande Valley now has about eight acres planted in vineyards.

1970s-1980s: European vintners buy land in N.M. and plant new vineyards, especially around the Elephant Butte area.

1990: N.M. is producing some 700,000 gallons of wine per year.

1996: Around 5,000 acres are under the cultivation of vineyards and there are 19 wineries around the state. N.M. wines win national and international recognition.

SANTA FE RING

The Santa Fe Ring is at the height of its power according to V. Westphall. *"Lawyers, judges, politicians, businessmen, and a sympathetic press were ... a network established for mutual gain..."* Besides the surveyors general mentioned earlier, virtually every governor of N.M. from the late 1860's to 1885 is a member of the Santa Fe Ring. Other members ... are T.B. Catron, S.B. Elkins, and H.L. Waldo; federal judges J.G. Palen, S.B. Axtell, L.B. Prince, and probate judge R.H. Longwill ... Many "Anglo" speculators work through Hispanic middlemen like ... Nicolás Pino...Antonio Joseph...

[No book or in-depth study of the Santa Fe Ring has been published as of the date of publication of this *Multi-History*, despite the fact that most writers acknowledge the Ring controlled the Territory.]

APACHE RAIDS

Chief Victorio and his band of Apaches attack **Tularosa.** A small detachment of Ninth Cavalry defends the town and although the famous "Buffalo Soldiers" are outnumbered four to one they win the battle. Sergeant **George Jordon** is later awarded the **Medal of Honor.** (See **1900.**)

RANCHING

There are some 500,000 cattle in all of N.M. and 300,000 of them are grazing in Lincoln County [which at that time comprised almost all of southeastern N.M.].

SOCIETY

Aurelio Espinosa is born in El Carnero, Colorado.

LITERATURE

Frederick Rudulph, a member of Pat Garrett's posse that took Billy the Kid prisoner, writes (around this time) *Los Bilitos,* a narrative poem in ballad meter which recounts the story of **Billy the Kid.**

Victorio
Courtesy Museum of NM, #2109
(Clarence Batchelor ink wash)

Ca. 1880-1907
SANTERO

José Benito Ortega (b.1858; before being accurately identified he was referred to as the *Mora Santero* and the *Flat Figure Santero)* is creating religious art during this period. *Retablos* are not much in demand (because, among other reasons, Currier and Ives prints are less expensive) so Ortega, from the **Mora** area, produces many *bultos.* He works with such limitless energy and dedication that his bultos can be found throughout northern N.M. and southern Colorado. His figures are very expressive and often brightly colored. Those intended for moradas are less colorful. He concentrates on faces depicting exalted saintliness.

Ortega ceases making santos when his wife dies in 1907 and he moves to Ratón with his children. With his death (and that of Rafaél Aragón, whose work was as widely circulated) the classic period of New Mexican santeros is at an end.

PENITENTE SANTEROS

There are a number of prominent but unnamed santeros who produce santos mainly for use by the Penitente Brotherhood:

Carver of the Muscular-Torso Crucifixes: This early santero (ca. 1840-1850) might have created bultos for the Brotherhood but his pieces also have an impressionistic, almost cubist sense about them. Very little is known about this artist.

Master of the Penitente Cristos: Thought to be the earliest known Penitente santero, this artist works in the **Ojo Caliente** area and is a very talented craftsmen with a highly developed power of expression which gives his bultos a surrealistic quality.

The **Abiquiú Morada Santero** is producing bultos from 1860 to the 1890s. His early pieces are delicately carved and painted with tempera while the later ones are more expressionistic and often painted with oils.

Juan Ramón Velásquez (1830-1902) lives in **Canjilón** after it is founded in the late 1850s or early 1860s. It is believed he is producing bultos by the 1860s or 1870s, painting first with tempera and later with oils. His creations, usually large figures, are principally for the Penitente Brotherhoods and their moradas. Velásquez is noted for the raw power of the suffering Christ, since they are made especially for moradas. At times he uses real hair and teeth as well as porcelain eyes.

Juan Miguel Herrera (1835-1905) from **Arroyo Hondo** creates bold, powerful bultos for moradas and chapels like the Medina Chapel, from the 1870s to the 1890s. He often asks villagers to model for him. (He also played the violin.)

TINSMITHS

A group of [unknown] *tinsmiths,* referred to as the **Río Abajo Workshop,** are producing the most elaborate tinwork made in N.M. during the 19th century. These artists are working in **Los Lunas, Belén,** etc., and as far south as **Socorro,** producing *nichos,* frames, crosses, chandeliers. Their work is characterized by a *"...consistent use of closely placed, tightly controlled stamping ... smooth and notched crescent shapes, notched bar stamps, single-dot punches, and toothed circular stamps..."* which combine to form beautifully complex patterns.

1880s-1890s
SOCIETY

Southeastern N.M. grows rapidly and flourishes because of *"an unmistakably American brand of rugged individualism,"* attracting the ambitious, wanderers, outcasts, outlaws, or those searching for a new beginning. The southeast thus becomes a convergent crossroads for different kinds of people.

Hispanos, the first to settle in the area by establishing *placitas* (towns), sheep ranches and farms, along the valleys of the Río Hondo, North Spring, and Berrendo rivers, at Roswell, and at the Río Felíz, came in from central N.M. as well as from Texas and Mexico.

"Anglos" came principally from Texas and the Old South *"where negative stereotypes of the Mexican people had gained wide currency over preceding decades."*

These stereotypes were reinforced by the writings of individuals like Gregg, Kendall, Davis, etc., which appealed to Americans. Further, books, magazine articles, letters, reports, etc., written to educate Americans as to N.M. and the Southwest, portrayed Hispanics as *"less moral, less hard-working, less frugal, and less enterprising"* than American "Anglos."

"Anglo" settlement at Roswell attracts a *"few hundred **courageous souls** who came to pioneer in a remote treeless place two hundred miles from the nearest rail depot and lacking access to many essential goods..."* as they enjoyed in Texas and the Old South according to C. Larson.
[Ft. Stanton, where these "courageous souls" could get military protection and help when necessary, had been in the area since 1855.]

The first **big cattle companies** in southeastern N.M. are the Chisum, the Lea, and the Littlefield Cattle companies. Among the other large cattle enterprises organized during these decades are the El Capitán, Cass, Cox and Peacock, Carrizozo, Bloom, Anderson, Dolan Fritz, C.A. Bar, Kirby and Cree, Milne-Bush, etc. *"These large enterprises, not content with the sizable acreage they owned, were continually in search of water rights and exercised great political and economic power in the county."* These enterprises all made claim on the public domain as much as possible, overstocked it, thereby deteriorating the rangeland.

TIMELINE

Between 1880 and 1935 more than 190 Spanish-language newspapers are founded in more than 30 Hispanic communities in N.M., Colorado, Arizona, and Texas. They often protest and combat the **"effects of internal colonialism, social antagonism, and historical erasure"** which target the Hispanic people of the Southwest.

1881-1885

Lionel A. Sheldon is Governor.

1881
RANCHING

John P. Casey of Albuquerque brings cattle into the valley of the Largo, south of Quemado. He names it the "American Valley," arranges to have the land surveyed and enters into an agreement with Surveyor General Atkinson. Lands on both sides of Largo Creek are obtained by homestead and preemption entries under various names though ownership goes to Casey. Settlers Alexis Grosset and Robert Elsinger homestead on land wanted by the company and they are murdered.
[These American Valley murders receive much notoriety but they are never solved. The Santa Fe Ring is said to be much interested in the case.]

LITERATURE

Manuel Salazar [thought to be one of New Mexico's first novelists, if not the first] writes a novel titled *La historia de un caminante, o sea, Gervacio y Aurora* (History of a Traveler, or Gervacio and Aurora).

RANGE DISPUTE

Cattleman **John Chisum** and two of his cowboys drive off a flock of sheep (owned by Judge Edmund Stone) headed toward a privately owned lambing ground because the sheep are on public land claimed by Chisum.

EDUCATION
Father Gasparri of Albuquerque Old Town invites the **Sisters of Charity** in Santa Fe to open a school for girls.

September 4, 1882: Sisters Blandina, Pauline, and Gertrude open the school called "Our Lady of Angels."

1883: Wayfarer's House for orphans, the sick, or maimed, is opened by the Sisters of Charity.

1884: The Armijo brothers donate six acres of land on which to build the New Town Our Lady of Angels, a boarding school for girls.

1885: A four-room building is added for a boys' school. Sister Isadora is the Superior of the Old Town school and convent.

1886: The name of Our Lady of Angels New Town School is changed to Saint Vincent's Academy.

TIMELINE

October 25, 1881 : Tombstone , Arizona, is the scene for a gunfight between three Earp brothers (Wyatt, Virgil, Morgan) and their friend Doc Holliday against the brothers Clanton (Ike, Billy) and McLaury (Tom, Frank).

[While the "gunfight at the O.K. Corral" lasted a matter of perhaps 15 seconds it has been portrayed as the "most famous in the West." Historical investigation shows the violent dispute took place on Lot 2, Block 17, which fronts on Fremont Street while the O.K. Corral fronted on Allen Street and extended to the rear edges of Fremont Lots 5 and 6. Historians have yet to decide if the confrontation was over mutual involvement in stage robberies, control of the prostitution industry in Tombstone, systematic terrorism in a raw frontier, etc.]

RAILROAD
March 8, 1881: A second transcontinental railroad is born when a silver spike is driven at Deming, connecting the Southern Pacific and the Santa Fe.

SOCIETY
October 23: **Nina** (María Adelina Isabel Emilia) **Otero** is born at Los Lunas.

1882
PIONEERS
Extended families of **García and Landavazo** (originally from **Seboyeta**) relocate from Cubero to Jaraloso Canyon and Atarque in **Arizona.**

ETHNOLOGY
Adolph Bandelier begins his work at Cochití and other middle Río Grande Pueblos. He is assisted by Fr.

José Rómulo Ribera, the parish priest at Peña Blanca.

[Ribera later leaves the priesthood, marries and raises a family, then publishes much sophisticated poetry in *El Boletín Popular.*]

REPORT

The *New Mexican Review* states that **cultural backwardness** prevents Mexicans from competing with outsiders, the former being content with satisfying their needs with few surpluses left over for selling. "Anglos" believe themselves products of *"civilization"* while Mexicans represent *"barbarism,"* an *"alien and inferior people."*

CORPORATIONS

The **Boston and New Mexico Cattle Company** is incorporated by T.B. Catron, John H. Thomson, and Surveyor General Henry M. Atkinson.

LITERATURE

Pat Garrett publishes his story concerning **Billy the Kid** in the *Santa Fe New Mexican.* The work, *The Authentic Life of Billy the Kid,* ghosted by **Ash Upson,** is to have a strong influence in the enduring legend of Billy the Kid. (The later chapters are described as an accurate record of historical events.)

CEBOLLETA LAND GRANT

President Chester A. Arthur awards a patent of ownership to the **Cebolleta** (Seboyeta) people for legal title to their land grant. Common lands are confirmed as belonging to citizens of the village. **Non-villagers** have homesteads on the far corners of the grant but Cebolleta villagers allow them to graze their stock on grant lands and take no action to throw them off the unfenced land.

1902: Various lawsuits are filed to **partition the land grant:** *"...by adjudicating its ownership as tenancy in common, and adjudicating the interest in common of each heir or assign of the thirty original owners, the ownership of each to be established in fractional parts of 1130th of the whole, with the exception of private lands where the little town was originally built, this not to exceed 16,000 acres..."*
Some 120 defendants are represented by **E.W. Clancy** and another 114 are represented by B.S. Rodey. L. **Bradford Prince** files an affidavit for services by publication upon **unknown heirs** of deceased persons.

1903: An Order is made and entered to the effect that *"...the said complaint and the matters therein contained be taken as true and confessed against all the defendants who have not appeared, answered or demurred*
*in the action ... naming unknown heirs of some 250 deceased owners of interests as established in the prior action No. 4710, and in that Order the court appoints **Harry E. Lee as Referee** to take proof as to the allegations in the Complaint and the matters in issue ... and to report the same with his findings of fact..."*
1904: There are more pleadings, amended pleadings, motions, etc., and the report of the Referee is approved,

as well as a list of **costs and charges.** Commissioners are selected to decide how the Cebolleta 200,000 acres will be divided.

Judge Crumpacker approves the Special Master's Report and the land is partitioned as follows:

> A.L. Richardson, et. al.: 51,518 acres;
>
> Raynolds and McMillen, et. al.: 51,116 acres;
> B.S. Rodey: 3,714 acres;
> E.W. Clancy, et. al.: 23,064 acres;
> L.B. Prince, et. al.: 20,201 acres;
> land to be sold for court costs: 15,000 acres;
> Cebolleta people and township: 20,533 acres.

Manuel and Felíz (Sena) García
(Residents of Cebolleta)

1941: **Lee Evans** files a Quiet Title suit for his ranch, most of which is situated in the "Unassigned Owners" section of the partition, where he had been allowed to live and work by the Cebolleta people. **Judge Johnson** decrees that since Evans has been paying taxes on the land the law declares he is the owner and therefore conveys a quiet title for the land. Evans fences off his land and will not permit Cebolletanos to graze their stock on it, shooting any such animals that stray onto "his" land.

1883
LAND OWNERSHIP
Thomas B. Catron is reputed to be one of America's biggest land owners, if not *the* biggest.

CORPORATIONS
The **New Mexico Land and Livestock Company** is formed by Surveyor General H.M. Atkinson, William H. McBroom, and Joseph H. Bonham.

ORGANIZATION
Lodge No. 336 of the **Independent Order of B'nai B'rith** (Sons of the Covenant) is formed, the first public Jewish organization in N.M. All American Jewish males are eligible for membership and the goals are fraternity, mutual aid, and acculturation.

LAND GRANT

The **Antón Chico** land grant is in the process of adjudication with the problem being deciding if it is a community or individual land grant.

Surveyor General **Atkinson** decides that Antón Chico was awarded as an individual grant to **Manuel Rivera** and thirty-six others and the patent is so issued. (Atkinson had "purchased" all interests from the heirs of Manuel Rivera, thus making himself the owner of the Antón Chico land grant; he deeds it over to the New Mexico Land Livestock Company, of which he is president.)

[After much legal hassle, the town of Antón Chico is declared the owner of the land grant and a patent is issued to the town.]

LAND FRAUD

More than 150 Spanish-surnamed **settlers along the Río Pecos** send a petition to the Secretary of the Interior requesting an investigation because they are **being fraudulently dispossessed** of their lands. "*...We settled the land ... many years ago ... when the Indians were bad...and had to defend our homes with the rifle...*" our land documentation was "*sent ... to the register in Santa Fe...*" and "*...returned by him with statements that the land upon which we had been living on for ten and twelve years had been taken up by parties which we know have never been on the land ... investigate the claims of homesteads made by one W.H. McBroom...in names of fictitious parties...*"

Special Agent Eddy investigates 200 homesteads and finds that 32.5% meet with homestead regulations. He concludes: "*An honest investigation would result in the cancellation of hundreds of fraudulent entries, and many thousand acres of land would be thrown open to entry by actual settlers ... the office should send at least six agents into this Territory without delay...*"

[The Santa Fe Ring and the enormous extent of land fraud have not seemed to interest many historians who write about so many aspects of New Mexico's long history. It would take much intestinal fortitude to bring out documented history on these matters because of the reaction people would probably experience.]

APACHE RESERVATION

The **Mescalero Apache Indian Reservation** is finally established with 474,240 acres in the Ruidoso area.

SANTA FE FIESTA

July: A festival named the **Tertio-Millenial Exposition** (anniversary of a third of a thousand years) is celebrated for 45 days in Santa Fe. Special trains bring in some 10,000 to 12,000 tourists from across the country.
Pageants, Indian dances, and markets are held in Sena Plaza.

A race track is constructed on Federal Place.

Civil War hero Maj. **José D. Sena** leads an elaborate historical parade. Sena is dressed as a Spanish knight and followed by the U.S. Infantry band, Apaches, Zuñis, and Pueblos from San Juan and Picurís.

Felipe Delgado plays the role of Coronado, leading a host of warriors, priests, wagons, etc. When the parade arrives at Federal Place the cannons at Fort Marcy give a 33-gun salute then the Spanish and Indians hold a mock cavalry battle.

1919: The Chamber of Commerce and the School of American Research revive the pageantry of the fiesta. A fee is now charged to see the Entrada and Fiesta programs.

September 13-15, 1920: The Fiesta now includes erection of the *Cross of the Martyrs*.

September 4-6, 1922: The First Annual Southwest Indian Fair and Arts and Crafts Exhibition is added to the Fiesta.

1926: The art colony, led by **Will Schuster** and **Jacques Cartier,** create Zozobra, "Old Man Gloom," which is burned to begin festivities.

1927: The Fiesta is incorporated and Hispanics select the first "Fiesta Queen."

1928: **Witter Bynner** writes that "*this new Fiesta*" includes Hispanics because "*their imagination, their sense of beauty, and their willingness to make monkeys of themselves are qualities more Latin than Anglo Saxon.*"

SOCIETY
July 1: **Miguel Archibeque** is born in San Miguel.

LAND DISPUTE
August 17: **Manuel Otero** of Los Lunas goes to Antelope Springs to investigate claims that **James** and **Joel Whitney** have made on the Otero Estancia ranchland. James meets Manuel with rifle in hand, but the two then go into the house to discuss the matter. The conversation soon becomes heated and Whitney pulls out "*...his pistol and fired point-blank at Otero, who was less than four feet away*" according to C. Whaley. Partisans join the gun battle on each side and Manuel Otero is one of the two who die in the fray.

The seriously wounded James Whitney is taken to St. Vincent's Sanatorium for treatment but his brother Joel whisks him away to a train going to Las Vegas for safety. But Otero family members intercept the train and demand that Whitney be taken to Los Lunas for trial. While stopped at Albuquerque a Judge Bell boards the train and releases Whitney on a $25,000 bond, thus permitting him to leave for California.

April 29: 1884: James Whitney is tried for the murder of Manuel Otero but is acquitted on the grounds of self-defense.

[**Miguel Otero II,** Manuel's cousin and Territorial Governor-to-be, later charges that Whitney had hired two expensive attorneys and bribed Judge Axtell who was prejudiced in Whitney's favor.]
August 18: The *Sunday Gazette* prints that Manuel Otero was "*...one of New Mexico's promising young men,*

cultured, kind, and noble. He died manfully contending for his rights, and his death is chargeable to the perpetrators and perpetuators of the **system of land grant swindles** *that have for years crushed out the progressive industries of New Mexico and are now striking at the lives of her best and truest citizens."*

1884
BUFFALO HUNT
Hunters from **Taos Pueblo go out** on their last (ever) buffalo hunt and return with 54 carcasses.

SOCIETY
Albert Eisemann marries **Sallie Grunsfeld** in what the newspaper reports to be *"The Most Brilliant Affair New Mexico Ever Saw."* Eisemann is a leading wool merchant and Grunsfeld is part of the **"house of Spiegelberg"** clan.

Sons of Levi Spiegelberg: (L to R) Albert, William, Sidney, Charles, Eugene, James
Courtesy Museum of NM, #11021

CORPORATIONS
The **New Mexico and Kentucky Land and Stock Company** is formed by Surveyor General H.M. Atkinson, Max Frost, WH. McBroom, and three men from Kentucky.

LAND FRAUD
N.M. leads the nation [with California second] in reported numbers of land fraud cases with 827. At least seven **Special Agents** for the General Land Office (R.J. Hinton, H.H. Eddy, J.M. Dunn, E.D. Hobbs, J.G. Evans, A.R. Greene, and C.A. Walker) have conducted investigations into charges of fraud in the Territory.

To 1883: there are **four cases** prosecuted for land fraud;
Through 1891: there are **641 cases** prosecuted for land fraud.

[The crux of the struggle over land was really control of water sources: if a group controlled the water then the land in every direction could be utilized. Since land without water was relatively worthless, ranchers fought other ranchers as much as agrarian interests for the control of water sources. Under Hispanic law a water source couldn't be "owned" by anyone but in the wide open society of the West at this time the situation encouraged *"the strong and the firstcomers"* according to V. Westphall. *"There were the greedy and the lawless but the widespread breakdown in morality..."* might have been impeded if larger parcels of land had been available legally.]

Most prosecutions aren't successful: a jury verdict of **guilty** occurs in 15 cases; the U.S. Marshall is **unable to find the defendant** (82 cases), often because the **person never existed** in the first place or is no longer in the country; cases have to be dismissed (209) because **court records/files have been lost (or stolen);** in 28 cases the **verdict is unrecorded** neither in the docket nor the transcript of the case.

Hispanic New Mexicans are blamed (in Washington) for *"...being unreliable witnesses who would swear to anything, and native juries were charged with never returning a verdict of guilty regardless of the evidence..."*

A partial list of persons/corporations indicted for fraud include:

Max Frost, Charles Ilfeld, Pedro Sánchez, Dubuque Cattle Co., Wm. H. McBroom, Luciano Baca, Red River Cattle Co., Lake Cattle Co., Palo Blanco Cattle Co., Prairie Cattle Co., Portsmouth Cattle Co., Stephen W. Dorsey, Miguel Martín, Cimarron Cattle Co., Wm. F. Purmont, George H. Purmont, Theo. Maxwell, Charles Blanchard, M.A. Upson, etc.

Max Frost, register of the Land Office in Santa Fe is *"...singled out over all the others"* because he is **indicted nine times.**

[Five cases against Frost are dismissed because **all records, files,** etc., *"... are missing from the office of the Clerk..."* It is obvious that defendants had access to the court's inner workings or that court personnel or officials could be bribed with relative ease. The *New Mexican* newspaper, of which Frost is president, manager, and editor, vilifies Governor Ross and Surveyor General Julian for *"persecuting"* Frost.]

Max Frost
Courtesy Museum of NM, #8876

GREATEST GUNFIGHT IN THE WEST

October 29-31: **Elfego Baca** is in a gunfight at Frisco [west of
Socorro, now Reserve] against 80 to 84 cowboys.

[W.A. Beck appears to have his own perspectives on Elfego
Baca for he writes that many communities produced *"legendary
gunmen"* and some are remembered as folk heroes instead of
the violent ruthless killers that they were; in this situation
"must be placed Elfego Baca." Baca *"resented"* the treatment
of Spanish-Americans at the hands of incoming Texans; the
Texas cattlemen also targeted (unarmed?) Mexican sheepherders *"who were powerless before the Texans' six-shooters."*]

Elfego Baca (at 19)
Courtesy Museum of NM, #128955

Nineteen-year-old Elfego, a Deputy Sheriff, comes into
Frisco on an electioneering trip and finds a cowboy,
Charlie McCarty (McCarthy?), employed at the **John
B. Slaughter ranch,** shooting up the small plaza.
Elfego arrests McCarty and decides to take him to
Socorro for trial when the local justice of the
peacestates the Slaughter cowboys will retaliate if
McCarty is tried in Frisco.

Cowboys from Slaughter's ranch, led by foreman **Young Parham** [Peraltam, Purham, Perryman, etc.] ride into
town and demand McCarty's immediate release. Elfego says he will give everyone to the count of
three to be out of town whereupon gunshots are exchanged, Parham dying from injuries when his
horse is hit and falls on him.

("In the tradition of Paul Revere, cowboy couriers" ride to cattle ranches spreading the word that *Mexicans are in revolt!!!--threatening to kill all Americans!!!)*

Some 80 to 84 cowboys converge on Frisco to find that one19-year-old Elfego Baca is the "Mexican War"
and "threat " to Americans. The cowboys gather at the local bar, McCarty pays $5 for his "drunk
and disorderly" charge and is released, but the cowboys are getting angrier by the minute.

Elfego seeks refuge in the *jacal* (shack) of Gerónimo Armijo, which happens to have a floor about 18 inches
below ground level. One of the **cowboys, William B. "Bert" Hearne [Hern, Herne, Heron)**
declares he has judicial authority to arrest Baca for the shootings of the previous day so he and
many others make their way to the Armijo jacal. Hearne orders Baca to come out then starts kicking
at the door, saying *"I'll get that little Mexican out of there!"* Elfego fires two shots and Hearne
falls dead.

Hearing gunshots, all cowboys converge on the Armijo shack and let loose a fusillade on the building.
Elfego returns the gunfire by shooting through cracks in the walls, protected because he is below
ground level. The cowboys try to burn down the shack (even sending for dynamite) without

success but continue to **shoot into the shack,** knowing their bullets will get him sooner or later. The next morning Elfego is very much alive, warming up coffee and tortillas for breakfast. The infuriated cowboys resume their fusillade, Elfego returning their fire.

Frank Rose, Socorro Deputy Sheriff, arrives in the afternoon and through intermediaries convinces Elfego to surrender and stand trial in Socorro. **Elfego accepts, on the condition that he retains his guns.** Cowboys keep their rifles trained on Elfego and want to lynch him immediately but he is taken to Socorro where he is found not guilty of all charges.

[More than **4,000 bullet holes** were later counted in the shack, 367 in the half-sized door alone, 8 bullet holes in a broomstick standing in a corner. The 33-hour siege had splintered everything inside the shack but no bullet touched Elfego or a statue of *Nuestra Señora Santa Ana*, which Elfego came to regard as his Guardian Angel.

W.A. Beck quotes Harvey Fergusson as saying that Baca's heroics deserve to be remembered but then states "*there are those who feel the facts have grown with the telling.*"]

SOCIETY
December 22: After traveling to Kansas for surgery described as successful, **John Chisum,** dies in Las Vegas and is later buried in the family plot in Paris, Texas.

1885-1889
Edmund G. Ross is Governor.

1885

TIMELINE

Due to the Government not keeping its promises and threats of assassination, **Gerónimo** bolts out of his Arizona reservation, accompanied by **42 men and 96 women.**

[Apache raids are well publicized in national newspapers, bolstering the image of N.M. and the Southwest as a wild, primitive land.]

In time there are only 33 people in the "renegade" band, 13 are woman, and **General Nelson Miles** is chasing them with **5,000 soldiers**, with perhaps as many on the Mexican side of the border. After more than five months of futile chase Miles sends two **Apache Scouts** into the mountains to negotiate Gerónimo's surrender. The chief is promised that after a couple of years of imprisonment he will be released to live in his homeland so Gerónimo surrenders. With Gerónimo and his men in shackles the Government orders that the entire Chiricahua band, some 498 men, woman, and children, be

Geronimo
Courtesy Museum of NM,
#2115 (C.S. Ely photo)

rounded upand sent into captivity in Florida dungeons. Into the forlorn condemned group are ordered the loyal **Apache Scouts**, including the two who risked their lives by making personal contact with Gerónimo in the mountains. The Apache Scouts were forced into life imprisonment alongside the "hostiles" they had helped catch because *"an Apache is always an Apache."*

[Many of the Chiricahuas sickened and died in Florida's lowland climate. Gerónimo was never released and no Chiricahua was ever permitted to return to Arizona. In 1894 the Chiricahuas were sent to Oklahoma Territory. Gerónimo often said he wished he had died fighting for his freedom instead of believing the forked-tongue American promises made to him to get him to surrender. He finally passed away in 1909, still a captive.]

PROFILE

Elfego Baca

H E R O
IN THE WEST'S MOST INCREDIBLE GUN FIGHT

February 15, 1865: **Elfego Baca** is baptized in the Socorro Catholic Church.

1866: The Baca family relocates to Topeka, Kansas. Elfego hears Spanish at home but is reared in the English-speaking environment of the Kansas frontier.

1872: Elfego's mother, sister, and brother die within a month of each other.
[No cause is given. Elfego returns to Socorro to live with his Uncle Abdenago but the return date is uncertain.]

1880: Elfego is living in Socorro.

1881: Baca meets Billy the Kid.
Elfego helps his father escape from a Los Lunas jail.

October 29-31, 1884: Elfego single-handedly defends himself against 80 to 84 armed cowboys in Frisco (Reserve).

1885: Baca is charged with murder because of the Frisco fight. He is acquitted of all charges.

August 13, 1885: Elfego marries **Francisquita Pohmer.** They live in Albuquerque.

1890s: The Baca family is living in Socorro.
1893: Baca is elected County Clerk of Socorro County and serves to 1896. (He let it be known that during the months of December and January there would be no charge for recording of

deeds, bills of sale, etc., thus helping the poor people of the community.) He studies law in a private law office (as was customary in those days).

1894: Elfego Baca is admitted to the bar and in two months becomes a junior partner in the Socorro law firm of Freeman and Baca.

1896-1898: Elfego is Mayor of Socorro.

1899(?): Baca tells some friends about entering a restaurant in Roswell. He is told *We don't serve Mexicans here.* He draws his gun and is quickly served the meal of his choice.

1900-1901: Baca is School Superintendent of Socorro County.

1904: Elfego is practicing law in El Paso, Texas.

Elfego Baca
Courtesy Museum of NM, #87489

1905-1906: Elfego is District Attorney for Socorro and Sierra counties.

1907: Baca moves to Albuquerque, lives at 401 North 6th Street, with legal offices in the N.T. Armijo Building on the corner of Central Avenue and 2nd Street. The following year he forms a partnership with Lowell Loughary. Baca is still interested in the prospecting and mining of gold, silver, and copper in N.M.

1911: The Republican Party nominates Baca for the House of Representatives. He loses to Democrat Harvey B. Fergusson.

1913: Baca runs but again loses for the House of Representatives. He establishes a printing plant and publishes *La Opinión Pública,* a weekly political newspaper. He organizes an independent political group, The Bolt and Nut Club, and later publishes a small paper called *La Tuerca* (The Nut). Subscription prices are "$2 a year to good citizens, $5 a year to bootleggers, $5 a month to Prohibition agents."

While he continues to work as a lawyer he also heads a private detective agency.

January 31, 1915: Elfego Baca shoots Celestino Otero in El Paso. Otero dies but in court the jury rules that Baca acted in self-defense.

April 10, 1915: Elfego and five others are indicted on a charge of conspiring to remove a federal prisoner from the custody of the U.S. Marshall. All are acquitted.

1919-1920: Baca is elected Sheriff of Socorro County. He often relies on his reputation to enforce the law. One of his strategies is to send out letters like the following:
Dear Sir: I *have a warrant for your arrest. Please turn yourself in no later than (date) or I will know that* you *intend to resist arrest in which case I will shoot you on sight when I come after* you.   *Elfego Baca, Sheriff.*
[Baca is supposed to have said that no person who got such a letter ever failed to turn himself in.]

1922: Elfego moves back to Albuquerque from Socorro. (For the next 25 years he runs for this office and that but is never elected.)

August 27, 1945: Elfego Baca dies peacefully at home. (In the story about Baca's death, the *Albuquerque Journal* quotes Elfego as having said he had killed nine men and wounded eight others during his lifetime.)

1959: **Walt Disney Studios** films a television series titled "The Nine Lives of Elfego Baca" which is televised nationally.

[The gunfight is never mentioned in the series.]

PENOLOGY

A penitentiary is completed south of Santa Fe.

1892: The prison is enlarged.

1903: Prisoners are used to build highways (the first program of its kind in the West).

1912: Increased numbers of prisoners work on road building. The State Highway Department pays the prison one dollar per day for each prisoner who works eight hours.

1914: A prison school is opened for the first time.

1917: Prisoners earn 15 cents per day and 40 days of "good time" for every 30 days of work.

SOCIETY & LAND FRAUD

Governor Ross declares: "*The curse of this territory is rings ... Many years ago a few sharp shrewd Americans came here-discovered a number of small Mexican and Spanish grants-- purchased them at nominal prices-learned the Spanish language-ingratiated themselves into favor with the Mexican people, and proceeded to enlarge the Grants they had purchased, and to manufacture at will, titles to still others, and to secure therefore Congressional recognition...*"

Gov. Ross feels **N.M. is in the hands of the Santa Fe Ring.** Ring members, Republicans and Democrats, fight his every action, constantly demanding his removal by President Cleveland.

Special Agents estimate that from 75% to 90% of all **Preemption claims** in N.M. are fraudulent.

George Julian is appointed Surveyor General and his primary goal is to break up the **Santa Fe Ring** because *"the public domain was being harvested by fraud at an unprecedented rate."* Julian orders a reexamination of 35 claims, confirmed by his predecessors, now pending before Congress. He recommends rejection of 22 of the 35 claims and for the remainder he recommends a much smaller acreage than was accepted by his predecessors.

Confirmation of a land grant is made much more difficult for the claimant (whether speculator or person living on the land).For example, Julian maintains the Mexican government retained common lands ownership, not the community.

William A.J. Sparks is appointed commissioner of the General Land Office and, like Julián, is intent on combating land fraud. He suspends final action on all land entries.

REPORT

Journalist **Birge Harrison** writes that *"...there are twenty thousand Penitentes, and as they are mutually sworn to assist and protect one another, even to the extent of perjury, it will readily be seen what a formidable hydra the New Mexican judges have to deal with."*

WEAVING

Río Grande Blankets are now distinguished by *"... an eight-pointed, star-like motif in the design, which though always present, varies in number and location on the field of decoration."* Blankets of this class are locally known as **Valleros** [... said to have once constituted a preferred style peculiar to some of the mountain valleys in southern Taos County]. Demand for these blankets is diminishing slowly because of those brought in by railroad.

NEWSPAPERS

José Segura founds *El Boletín Popular* (1885-1910) in Santa Fe. The newspaper provides readers with local, regional, national and international news as well as items related to literature and the arts. Items are authored by New Mexicans like J.M. Hilario Alaríd, Benjamin Read, Eleuterio Baca, Camilo Padilla, etc., as well as Adolph Bandelier and renowned authors from Mexico, Latin America, and Spain. Segura takes great care in editing all contributions and his attention to detail reflects the quality of Spanish-language publishing in N.M.

José Segura [described by G. Meléndez in his classic *So All is Not Lost* as the embodiment *"of a generation intent on leaving a cultural legacy to its descendants"*] is a member of *La Sociedad Literaria y de Debates de la Ciudad de Santa Fe*, a literary arts group that meets regularly to discuss literary topics, participate in debates, and in general promote culture in Santa Fe. José travels extensively in

Mexico and the eastern U.S. Coupled with his Jesuit education this gives him much knowledge of world literature, from which his readers benefit. For example:

July, 1886: Mexican writer and diplomat **Vicente Riva Palacio** visits Santa Fe and speaks to an assembled group. Segura publishes much of his poetry in future editions of *El Boletín.*

1892: Two novellas by Eusebio Chacón, *El hijo de la tempestad* and *Tras la tormenta, la calma*, are issued by *El Boletín.*

May, 1894: Segura informs his readers of the arrival of the Mexican modernist journal, *La Revista Azul*, which is edited by celebrated Mexican literati; readers of fine literature in the Territory "*should take advantage of the opportunity to subscribe to such an interesting publication.*"

Ca.1885-1910
TINSMITH
Valencia Red and Green II Workshop tinsmiths are producing works during this period. There are thought to be at least two craftsmen producing works that are "*...simple in concept and crude in construction...*" but with "*...a strong visual imagery that imbues the work with naive charm.*" They produce works in imitation of the **Valencia Red and Green Tinsmith.**

Ca.1885-1920
The **Isleta Tinsmith** is producing (the most easily recognizable) tinwork in N.M. during this period. It is unknown if he is Native American or Hispanic, or even where he works. He produces frames which contain oleographs, chromolithographs, Victorian greeting cards, Holy Cards, and photographs, a large number of painted glass items, as well as a few other pieces like nichos.

1886
LAND TITLES
Surveyor General **George Julian** recommends that the common lands of the San Joaquín land grant be rejected because the "*...boundaries were too indefinite.*" The following year Julian assigns experts to research and prove that common lands ownership remained with Spain/Mexico, therefore they must remain with the U.S.

RELIGION
Temple Montefiore in Las Vegas is the first synagogue in New Mexico

SOCIETY
Eloisa Luna Otero (widow of Manuel Otero) marries **Alfred Bergere.**

[According to C. Whaley "*Cross-cultural marriages between Anglo men* [Bergere is French] *and Hispanic women were not uncommon in New Mexico at the time, and such unions helped contribute to the Americanization of the Spanish Southwest. Many Hispanic women enhance their opportunity for social and economic mobility through marriage to Anglo men, but this was not true in the case of Alfred Bergere and*

Eloisa Luna Otero..." because she was the one with the wealth.]

CORPORATIONS
The **American Valley Company** is incorporated by H.M. Atkinson, Thomas B. Catron, W.B. Slaughter, and H.L. Warren.

PROFILE

Albert B. Fall

" T H E   F A L L   G U Y "

November 21, 1861: **Albert Bacon Fall** is born in Frankfort, Kentucky.
His boyhood is spent in Kentucky and his father, a school teacher named William R. Fall, serves in the Confederate army throughout the Civil War. Albert receives tutoring from his father and at one time he thinks he might enter the ministry but after reading law in the office of Judge William Lindsley, Albert decides to become a lawyer. But when his health fails he decides to go West. He works on cattle and sheep ranches in Indian Territory then West Texas. While working as a cowboy and chuckwagon cook Albert meets Emma Morgan, a school teacher.

1883: Fall marries **Emma Morgan** and the couple moves to Kingston, New Mexico, a thriving mining camp. While at Kingston, Albert meets individuals like Edward L. Doheny and Frank W. Parker.

1887: Fall moves to Las Cruces and practices Law, becoming known as a "fighting advocate." Albert founds *The Independent Democrat* newspaper which he uses to combat the Republicans. He begins to organize for the Democratic Party and in time is recognized as an outstanding political leader from southern N.M. and a political enemy of Col. Albert J. Fountain.

1889: Albert meets **Oliver Lee.** The two form a close working association because, among other things, they resent the workings of Republicans in general and the Santa Fe Ring led by Tom Catron in particular. Fall becomes the recognized attorney for Lee and his cowboys while they become his defenders and bodyguards.

Albert B. Fall
Courtesy Museum of NM, #102044

[W. **Keleher** describes Lee as *"a fine-looking young man, of good personality ... who spent his spare time on the range studying Greek and Latin ... and was a dead shot with his pistol and rifle."* A.M. Gibson, biographer of A. Fountain, writes that Lee and his followers were *"all lusty young gunmen ... Fall's leading partisans"* ... who were used to *"bully and intimidate local citizens in Las Cruces on Fall's behalf ... and he got them off in court when charged with homicide and rustling..."* Gibson doesn't write that Lee was a student of Greek and Latin and Keleher doesn't describe Lee as a gunslinger or enforcer.]

1892: Fall's Democrats win over Fountain's Republicans.

March 2l, 1893: President Grover Cleveland appoints Fall as associate justice for the Third Judicial District of N.M.

February 1, 1895: Fall resigns from the bench (after being accused of many "advocate" improprieties).

September 15, 1895: Deputy Ben Williams is in a shootout against Albert Fall and his brother-in-law Joseph Morgan. The campaign of 1895 is a bitter one but Democratic candidates are again victorious.

January, 1896: Col. A.J. Fountain and his eight-year-old son Henry don't return from Lincoln where Fountain was prosecuting **Oliver Lee** for *larceny of cattle and defacing cattle brands.*

(The bodies are never found. Fall's *Independent Democrat prints* stories that Fountain had been seen in St. Louis, San Francisco, Chicago, New York, Mexico City, etc., that he had run off with a younger woman, etc.)

When Oliver Lee is one of those indicted for the Fountain murders, Fall represents the defendants in court and after a sensationalistic trial all are adjudged "not guilty."

1897: Albert is Attorney General.

1900: Albert Fall resigns from the Democratic Party and becomes a Republican.

1903: Fall is elected to the Territorial Council.

1907: Fall is Attorney General once again. He acquires a ranch in the Three Rivers country.

October 15, 1909: During a banquet held in the Alvarado Hotel in Albuquerque to honor President Taft, Fall criticizes Taft for not leading a more vigorous fight for New Mexican statehood. President Taft answers the charges as untrue.

1911: Fall is elected to the N.M. constitutional convention.

March 28, 1912: Albert Bacon Fall and Thomas Benton Catron are chosen by the first New Mexico State Legislature to represent New Mexicans as Senators for the U.S. Senate.

1918: Fall is elected to the Senate by the people of N.M.

1921: President Harding picks A.B. Fall to be his Secretary of the Interior. (Fall is thus the first man from N.M. to be in the Cabinet of a President of the U.S.) In time there is a "Teapot Dome scandal" over oil leases and bribery charges that rock the entire country. Fall runs the gauntlet of Senate investigations, grand jury indictments, and court trials.

March 4, 1923: Fall resigns as Secretary of the Interior and Harding accepts the resignation.

July 21, 1931: Fall is enrolled as a federal prisoner in the State Penitentiary at Santa Fe, N.M.

[Albert B. Fall had served in the Territorial Legislature, in the Territorial Supreme Court, twice as Attorney General of the Territory, had been a part of the Constitutional Convention, been elected to the Legislature which selected him to serve in the U.S. Senate, been a member of the Harding cabinet, and now he was a convicted federal prisoner in the State Penitentiary. He protested his innocence to the end, saying he had been punished for others' actions, that history would vindicate him. The expression *"the fall guy,"* is said to be referring to A.B. Fall because he maintained to the end he had been *"set up to take the fall"* for everybody else. But history hasn't exonerated him.]

November 30, 1944: Albert Bacon Fall dies in El Paso, Texas.

AMERIND
The **Jicarilla Apache Indian Reservation** is permanently established (750,000 acres) by President Cleveland in Río Arriba and Sandoval counties.

SOCIETY
"Penitente hunters" are encouraged in their amusement by articles like the following in the *Albuquerque Morning Journal*, April 23:

"The Penitentes will hold their orgies at Los Griegos, a village three miles north of Albuquerque, today. Their rites consist of flagellations, carrying crosses, and other horrid rites which should be suppressed. W.L. Trimble & Co. will run hacks to Los Griegos this afternoon, leaving the San Felipe hotel at noon. nose who have not seen the penitentes ought to go. The sight is similar to drawing back the curtain from the 14th century." St. Francis is referred to as **"Big Frank."**

PROFILE

Félix Martínez

STATESMAN, ORATOR, NEWSPAPER MAN

Félix Martínez is elected to the territorial legislative assembly as a Democrat, helping to change the political climate of N.M. He becomes known for his oratorical abilities, in both English and Spanish.

1890: Martínez buys the controlling interest to *La Voz del Pueblo,* a leading Hispanic newspaper and moves it to **Las Vegas** where it voices the interests *of* the common man and the Democratic party.

With the help of his partners, **Ezequiel C. de Baca** and **Antonio Lucero,** Félix organizes *El Partido del Pueblo Unido,* a coalition party with populist ideals.

1892: Martínez is elected to the Territorial Council where, among other things, he introduces the legislation that creates **New Mexico Highlands University** and the State mental hospital.

1897: Martínez moves to El Paso, Texas, where he publishes the *El Paso Daily News.* He plays a critical role in the development of irrigation for the Mesilla Valley and El Paso by promoting the construction of Elephant Butte Dam.

1916: Félix Martínez dies.

Félix Martínez
Courtesy Museum of NM, #10292
(Frederick J. Feldman photo)

1887

TIMELINE

1 8 8 7 : The **Dawes Allotment Act** is passed, *"... which had as its purpose the breaking up of Indian tribal groups,* especially affecting New Mexico's Native Americans. The Bureau of Indian Commissioners proclaimed February 8 as "Indian Emancipation Day" because the avowed intention was to help Indians conform to American land-holding patterns of private ownership. Each Native American would be deeded 160 acres of land on which to work for himself.

Furthermore, Indians who chose allotment would be granted American citizenship. But the real thrust of the Dawes Act is to acquire tribal land for settlers arriving from the East, land which would be sold by the Government. Indian tribes owned some 135 million acres communally and if each individual held only 160 acres the surplus land would revert to the Government which would then sell to white "settlers."

LAND GRANTS

Surveyor General **George Julian** writes an article for the *North American Review*, [the now famous] *Land Stealing in New Mexico* because Congress will take no action to alleviate the status of land titles in N.M.

Stephen W. Dorsey writes a response to Julian's article, also published in the *North American Review*.

PROFILE

Nestor Montoya

FROM JOURNALIST TO STATESMAN

1858: **Nestor Montoya** is born in Albuquerque.

1874: Montoya graduates from St. Michael's College. He works for six years as assistant postmaster in Santa Fe.

1884: He is appointed court interpreter.

1888: *La Voz del Pueblo is* founded by Montoya and Salazar.

1890: Montoya sells his share of *La Voz del Pueblo* but continues as editor under **Félix Martínez.**

1893: He marries **Florence Maes** and they have five children.

1894: Nestor moves to Albuquerque where he works as deputy assessor and court interpreter.

1901: He founds *La Bandera Americana* newspaper in Albuquerque and through the years he is a member of the Alianza Hispano-Americana, the Knights of Columbus, and the Mutual Protective Association of Old Albuquerque.

1920: Montoya is elected to the U.S. Congress on the Republican ticket.

HOSPITAL

St. Joseph Hospital is started under the direction of Sister Catherine Mellon and Sister Emerentiana Corby in Albuquerque.

[The hospital had also been one of the goals of Sister Blandina Segale. It is the beginning of today's St. Joseph Medical Center.]

SOCIETY

Albert Bacon Fall (1861-1944) arrives in New Mexico.

December 25, 1887: **Conrad Hilton** is born in San Antonio, Socorro County.

1888
VINTER

Adolf Didier (born in Gap, France) establishes a winery in Belén. In time his fine wines are selling from Colorado to Mexico.

GOVERNMENT

Solomon Bibo (born in Germany, he is married to Juana Valle, daughter of former governor Martín Valle) is selected by the people of **Acoma Pueblo** to be their governor (a position he holds a number of times subsequently).

Sister Blandina Segale
Courtesy Museum of NM, #67735

RELIGIOUS

Father Juan B. Railliere arrives in Tomé around this period. The young French priest, who keeps a diary written in French and Spanish, likes the villagers, finding them friendly and rich in culture but in need of formal education. He establishes a convent where young people are trained in formal music education, learn to read music, sing hymns, and play musical instruments, especially the organ. His choir becomes the best in the Río Abajo.

Father Railliere encourages the founding of an elementary school which is funded through *La Capitación*, a per-capita fee of $1 per household per year to pay the teacher. One of the first teachers in Tomé is **José Silva,** who is paid $22 per month from the *La Capitación*. Students are required to contribute firewood for the stove during the winter and the school term is two or three months long.

Father Railliere establishes one of the largest **vineyards** in the Río Abajo. His more than *2,000* vines produce some fine wines. (Tradition has it that when his choir did exceptionally well on a Sunday he would reward them with a drink of *vino.*) He also promotes agriculture with new plants and methods which help Tomé villagers and others in the Río Abajo and N.M., since he ministers at Valencia and Peralta.

The beloved French priest makes note in his diary of the floods that have plagued the Tomé area, especially the particularly destructive ones of 1884 and those toward the end of the decade when Tomé was virtually destroyed and villagers left destitute. Fray Railliere sends to Belén for help and merchant **John Becker** responds with much needed food and other supplies while **Felipe** *"El Millionario"* Chávez sends much advice.

SOCIETY
Vicente Bernal is born in Costilla.

April 8: **Dennis Chávez** is born in Los Chávez.

NEWSPAPERS
Nestor Montoya *(1858-1923)* founds the newspaper *La Voz del Pueblo* (in partnership with E.H. Salazar).

November: The *Pecos Valley Register* becomes the first newspaper in southeastern N.M.

1891: The *Roswell Record* newspaper is established; two years later the name is changed to the *Roswell Daily Record.*

1889-1893
L. Bradford Prince is Governor.

1889
GOVERNMENT & LAND TITLES
The complete ineptitude of the Surveyor General system is apparent to everyone. There is a backlog of 116 land grants awaiting Congressional action. Congress hasn't confirmed any grants since early in *1879.*

[The *"dereliction of Congress"* is described by V. Westphall as neglecting to provide a system by which to adjudicate land titles with justice and the refusal to supply funds with which to manage the enormous task. Once the speculator grants were confirmed by Congress to people who had influence with congressional members, the issue of adjudication of titles was permitted to drift, playing into the hands of more speculators, mostly lawyers, who would help claimants at the expense of exorbitant fees. The various surveyors general repeatedly urged reform, to no avail, because Congress took no action until the Court of Private Land Claims was enacted by statute in 1891, half a century after N.M. had been taken by the U.S. And when Congress ended its neglect, all burdens of proof were on the claimants, usually ordinary farm and ranch people with few resources to combat the acquisitiveness of government officials bent on enlarging the public

L. Bradford Prince
Courtesy Museum of NM, #50445
(Torres photo)

domain at the expense of New Mexicans. *"The shortsightedness evinced by this neglect is a pathetic example of man's whimsical choice of values."*]

SOCIETY
January: **Manuel Antonio Chaves,** the incomparable frontiersmen known as *El Leoncito*, dies.

TIMELINE

April 1, 18 89: In the **Botiller et al. v. Domínguez** case, the U.S. Supreme Court reverses a California Supreme Court decision that Domínguez property is protected under provisions of the Treaty al Guadalupe Hidalgo, stating, *"This court has no power to set itself up as the instrumentality for enforcing provisions of a treaty with a foreign nation,"* that if international treaties are violated there must be international negotiation and more treaties. The Court thereby asserts that U.S. law takes precedence over international treaties, contradicting the Constitution (Article III, Section 2, and Article III, Section 2, Clause 1) which gives treaties the same status as the Constitution itself.

"In this case the protection of private property guaranteed by the Treaty of Guadalupe Hidalgo was essentially invalidated." **In California, Texas, and New Mexico,** *"Within a generation the Mexican Americans who had been under the ostensible protection of the treaty became a disenfranchised, poverty-stricken minority"* because *"Anglo-American land corporations and the state and federal governments were the primary beneficiaries of the legal interpretation of the Treaty of Guadalupe Hidalgo"* according to Griswold del Castillo.

NEWSPAPERS
Enrique Salazar (1858-1915) and **Nestor Montoya** take over ownership and management of *La Voz del Pueblo* in Santa Fe.

1890: Nestor Montoya resigns and Salazar moves the newspaper to Las Vegas, the largest city in N.M. but beset by pervasive political and ethnic conflict. The *Gorras Blancas* movement is born in San Miguel and Mora counties and the new political party known as the *Partido del Pueblo Unido is* created.

1893: Enrique sells the newspaper to Félix Martínez.

1894: Salazar launches a new paper, *El Independiente,* and edits it for the next 34 years.

Enrique is especially powerful in his editorials where he denounces the erosion of Hispanic civic and social power which is contrary to the guarantees of the Treaty of Guadalupe Hidalgo. He writes about history education, literacy, maintenance of Spanish language and culture, land grants, etc.

STATEHOOD
March 13: Rep. W.M. **Springier** (Dem., Ill.) introduces an omnibus bill which includes N.M., among others,

for statehood. (N.M. is Democratic in affiliation.) Eastern and Midwestern newspapers criticize N.M.:

Chicago Tribune: New Mexicans are *"...not American but **Greaser**, persons ignorant of our laws, manners, customs, language, and institutions ... lazy, shiftless, grossly illiterate and superstitious... at the mercy of unscrupulous rings of politicians."* Wyoming is worthy of statehood.

Indianapolis News*: "Partisan impudence..."*

The omnibus bill proposes to change New Mexico's name to **Montezuma** in order to avoid confusion with Mexico. New Mexicans reject any name change.

The **Struble Report** cites El *Gringo, or New Mexico and her People* by **W.W.H. Davis** as proof that New Mexicans are largely illiterate, superstitious, and morally decadent. Governor **L. Bradford Prince** writes a letter to the New York Tribune to dispel the information in the Struble Report.

A number of prominent businessmen from Albuquerque, about half of whom are (reported to be) Jewish, sign a **"Protest of Citizens of New Mexico Against the Admission of that Territory into the Union of States."** Counter petitions are sent to Congress, declaring that the "Protest" petition doesn't represent 1% of the residents of Albuquerque.

Rep. E.B. **Spinola** (N.Y.) and others criticize Republicans for **opposing N.M. statehood because it is Catholic** and from a Spanish background: *"Spanish Americans of New Mexico are Americans by birth, sympathy, and education...*they furnished more troops *"during the Civil War than some of the new states."*

"Anglo" New Mexicans fear that **"Mexicans"** will dominate a state government so they oppose statehood unless restrictions can be written into the constitution to curb **"native"** power.

New Mexico's bid for statehood is rejected when N.M. is dropped from the omnibus bill. The Constitution of 1889 is rejected at the polls. (See **1894.**)

LAND GRANT ACTIVISM

April: **Juan Herrera** and his younger brothers **Pablo and Nicanor,** organize the *Gorras Blancas* (White Caps, so called because they covered their heads with white cowled masks) to combat the encroachment upon and theft of community land in the **Las Vegas** area. Ordinary working people from El Salitre, El Burro, Ojitos Fríos, San Gerónimo, etc., whose primary concerns are property rights and land titles, quickly align themselves with the brothers and the Gorras Blancas become one of *"the most secretive and closely-knit association of men ever to exist in the Territory of N.M"* according to A.F. Arellano.

April 26: Gorras Blancas destroy four miles of fence line on a ranch belonging to two Englishmen.

June-July: They attack the farm and sawmill of José Ignacio Luján three different times, destroying his crops, fences, and equipment.

November: A few members of the Gorras Blancas are jailed and when the trial is scheduled to be heard some 63 men ride into Las Vegas and surround the courthouse. They ride in force to the home of District Attorney **Miguel Salazar** then to the jail where their friends are being held. Sheriff

Lorenzo López telegrams Governor **Bradford Prince** requesting 50 rifles with which to defend the expected onslaught.

Winter, 1889-1890: Activities include destroying fences, railroad bridges, buildings, crops, and haystacks.

March, 1890: Some 300 Gorras Blancas post Spanish-language leaflets explaining their ideas. They also post a notice advising people not to cut or sell lumber or railroad ties unless it is for a fair price nor to work for starvation wages.

July: Enemies of the Gorras Blancas charge the group with some 25 acts of violence and destruction, including murder.

[*No one was ever convicted of any alleged crimes committed by Gorras Blancas.*]

Juan José Herrera and his compatriots join ranks with the **Knights of Labor,** a populist political movement becoming the *Caballeros de Labor.* They stage a parade through town on the fourth of July, chanting: *"The community is king and public officials are its humble servants who must obey its mandates."* The newspaper owned by Félix Martínez, *La Voz del Pueblo* (The Voice of the People), becomes aligned with *El Movimiento del Pueblo* (Peoples' Movement) as the grassroots movement is called.

Adversaries assert that the Caballeros de Labor and the Gorras Blancas are one and the same.

August: Governor Prince visits Las Vegas to observe the situation for himself. Nestor Montoya of *La Voz del Pueblo* heads a committee that assures the governor the Caballeros de Labor are not the Gorras Blancas. Prince finally proclaims that lawless "white capism" won't be tolerated but ordinary working people maintain that lawless land grabbers and speculators, whom they consider to be the cause of difficulties, must be corrected also.

A new political party is formed: *El Partido del Pueblo Unido,* (the United Peoples' Party) with philosophy and objectives in harmony with the Gorras Blancas and Caballeros de Labor. It calls on everyone to work for the common good, regardless of party affiliation.

November: El Partido del Pueblo Unido scores resounding victories in San Miguel County. Some 500 men hold a torchlight victory parade through Las Vegas.

1891: Membership in the Gorras Blancas begins to diminish by the end of the year, believing that the **Court of Private Land Claims** (begun in March) will address the injustices of the past.

EDUCATION LAW

Enabling legislation provides for the founding of a university in Albuquerque, a school of mines at Socorro and an agricultural college at Las Cruces.

1890s
POTTERY

Ta-Key-Sane designs and creates pottery at **Santa Clara Pueblo.** His son and grandson continue the family tradition. They begin to sell outside the pueblo.

1890s: Lela Gutiérrez is recognized for her pottery. In time Severa Gutiérrez Tafoya becomes well known for her pottery, as do many members of her family:
Angela Baca and her Alvin, Leona, Daryl, David;
Tonita Tafoya's Paul (and his Adam), Kenneth, Ray (and his Jennifer, Leslie);
María Tafoya and her Stephanie, Alita, Wanda (and her Eric), Kathy, Gwen;
Lydia Tafoya's: Virginia, Greg, Tina;
Epimenia's: Roberto Cleto Nichols.

1905: Lela and Van Gutiérrez continue to develop the craft, creating polychrome styles.
    1960s: The children of Lela and Van, Margaret and Luther Gutiérrez of Santa Clara Pueblo continue the style of pottery created by Ta-Key-Sane, their great-great-grandfather. Luther's children Pauline (and her Stephanie) and Dorothy (and her Paul and Gary) do pottery.

PROFILE

J. M. Hilario Alaríd

NEW MEXICO'S POET-BALLADEER

1834: **Jesús María Hilario Alaríd** is born at Galisteo.

1837: Alaríd's father dies during the Chimayó Rebellion.

1840s: It is unknown how Hilario acquires his formal education. It is possible he was self-taught.

1841: The nefarious Texas-Santa Fe Expedition takes place.

1850s: Alaríd begins to teach and in time practices law in alcalde courts. He studies formally but he also develops oratorical and performative skills. He is often invited to speak at social affairs and is often asked to deliver eulogies.

1860s: Hilario writes and publishes various items in newspapers of the day.

1870s: It is possible that Alaríd is a staff member of *El Anunciador de Nuevo México* newspaper.
1880s: Hilario is considered a *bardo*, a New Mexican poet-balladeer.

1888: He writes a piece on New Mexican statehood, disputing the idea that New Mexicans aren't ready to govern themselves, that for Territorial officials Hispanos will be "ready" only when easterners are the majority. (The work endures and it is published again seven years later.)

1890s: Alaríd writes about his experiences while traveling to outlying communities where his orchestra performs for baptisms, weddings, and various celebrations. His writings are published in different newspapers around the state.
He founds the *Banda Lírica*, a twenty-five piece band/orchestra.

1895: Hilario lives in Trinidad but he continues writing for New Mexican newspapers.

Ca. 1915: Hilario lives in Galisteo. He loses his eyesight in old age.

1917: After his death his obituary reads in part: *"Professor Alaríd was prominent throughout his life in New Mexico and Colorado as an educator, public speaker, and musician. He served as a principal also and was a magnetic orator and a real artist in the musical arts."*

1890
TOURISM
Governor Prince coins the phrase *"Sunshine State"* in reference to N.M.

LANGUAGE
The **Public Education Law of 1890** makes English the language of instruction in all public schools.

MUSIC
J.M. Hilario Alaríd (1834-1917) founds *La Banda Lírica*, a 25 piece band/orchestra that becomes well known by playing regularly at community and civic events in the Las Vegas area.

Ca. **1890-1920**
TINSMITH
The **Mesilla Combed Paint Tinsmith** is producing works during this period [the only identified tinwork to have originated in southern New Mexico]. His work is characterized by reverse-painted and combed glass panels, colored paper or metallic foil placed behind the painted glass, scored fans, embossed rosettes, and ornamental scrolls on the sides of his frames and nichos.

TIMELINE

December 28, 1890 : **Big Foot,** a Sioux chieftain, is leading his people to an assigned agency when he is intercepted by Major S.M. Whitside and four troops of the **Seventh Cavalry**. Whitside demands unconditional surrender and Big Foot, ill with pneumonia and his group having only around 100 cold and hungry warriors, accedes to all demands.
December 29, 1890: With Col. G.A. Forsyth of the Seventh Cavalry now in command, the Sioux

band is conducted to a placed called **Wounded Knee**. The Army troops, 470 men, are deployed on all sides of the 340 Indians, 106 of whom are warriors, and on a little hill is placed a battery of (newly invented **machine guns** known as) *Hotchkiss* guns, four in number.

The Sioux are ordered to give up their weapons but when only a couple of pieces are handed over the soldiers are ordered to go into the teepees and take all weapons. They shove the Indian women out of their way, the latter protesting loudly, but some 40 guns are found, mostly worn-out, antiquated firearms. But one young brave pulls out a gun from under his blanket and shoots a soldier dead. The troops immediately reply with a volley at point-blank range, instantly killing perhaps half the warriors. The other braves pull out their knives or war clubs and engage the soldiers in hand-to-hand combat. The Hotchkiss guns open up on the entire camp, spewing out their two-inch explosive shells at nearly 50 a minute, the women and children who had been separated from the warriors being their first targets. The outer cordon of troops, who surrounded the entire camp, open fire and shoot down anyone trying to escape the carnage. Within a few minutes there are dead some 200 Indians and around 60 soldiers, the latter being victims of "friendly fire" from their own comrades. Fleeing women and children are pursued and slaughtered on the spot (their bodies afterward found to extend for more than two miles from the camp). The few survivors, mostly children, are coaxed out of their hiding places by the Indian scouts and then butchered by the soldiers. At the end there are some 300 dead Sioux, about 200 of them women and children.

January, 1891: A long pit is dug and the frozen bodies of the Sioux are unceremoniously tossed into it, most of them naked because souvenir hunters wanted their clothing, especially the Ghost Shirts.

[With Indians penned up on reservations, the buffalo nearly extinct, railroads beginning to crisscross the nation, etc., **the**West **is a bygone era.**]

1891
EDUCATION
Compulsory public education is permanently established in N.M.

New Mexico Military Institute is founded in Roswell.

NEWSPAPERS
Camilo Padilla (1864-1933) founds the *El Mosquito* newspaper in Mora.

[Padilla is one of the many *periodiqueros* (newspaper journalists) of the Territorial period of N.M. For a number of reasons political and cultural, the period isn't well known by many people.]

PROFILE

Camilo Padilla

MAGAZINE FOUNDER AND EDITOR

1889: **Camilo Padilla** is in Washington D.C. when he sends news and information *to El Boletín Popular,* edited by José Segura, Camilo's first cousin. In time Padilla becomes the newspaper's official correspondent in Washington. He writes many short stories as well.

1890: Camilo travels to Washington D.C. as secretary to Delegate Antonio Joseph. When Congress is not in session he works on newspapers in Mora County. He co-edits *La Gaceta de Mora* with his cousin, Nepomuceno Segura.

1891: He founds the *El Mosquito* newspaper.

1892: Writing from D.C., Camilo asserts it is self-defeating to sell New Mexican land to people who don't appreciate it .

1894: Padilla writes the essay *Nuestra Unica Salvación* in which he states a lack of unity will destroy Hispanic New Mexican well-being.

1898-901: Camilo resides in D.C., works in the Government Printing Office.

1907: Padilla moves to El Paso and founds the *Revista Ilustrada* (which he will publish until shortly before his death in 1933 according to G. Meléndez).

1912: Camilo is living in Santa Fe and issues the *Revista Ilustrada* from there, back to El Paso around 1918, then once again to Santa Fe in 1925.

BOOKS

Charles Fletcher Lummis publishes *A New Mexico David and Other Stories*, which include

A New Mexico David: Lucario Montoya fights a gigantic Ute chieftain in single combat;
The Enchanted Mesa: about Acoma;
Pablo Apodaca's Bear: *"Pablo lived in Cebolleta ... of a heroic history..."*
The Comanche's Revenge: *"If the true story of New Mexico could be written in complete detail, from the time when the brave Spanish conquistadores planted there the first European civilization in all the vast area now embraced by the United States, it would stand unparalleled in all the history of the world. No other commonwealth on the globe has met and conquered such incredible hardships, dangers, and sufferings for so long a time..."*

Little Lolita: about a three-year old Acoma girl;
How to Throw a Lasso;
The Gallo Race;
The Miracle of San Felipe: "I *hope some day to see a real history of the United States; a history not written in a closet, from other one-sided affairs, but based on a knowledge of the breadth of our history, and a disposition to do it justice, a book which will realize that the early history of this wonderful country is not limited to a narrow strip on the Atlantic seaboard, but that it began in the great Southwest; and that before the oldest of the Pilgrim Fathers had been born, swarthy Spanish heroes were colonizing much of what is now the United States; in their little corner of which they suffered for three hundred and fifty years such awful dangers and hardships as our Saxon forefathers did not dream of. I hope to see such a history, which will do justice to Perhaps the most wonderful pioneers the world has ever produced, but it has not come yet ... When that history is written you will find thrilling matter in the story of New Mexico..."*

A New Mexican Hero: about Col. Manuel A. Chaves, "*a courtly Spanish gentleman, brave as a lion, tender as a woman, spotless of honor, modest as heroic...who for over fifty years fought the Apaches, Navajos, Comanches, Utes. Two hundred of his relatives were killed by Indians and he participated in perhaps a hundred battles and carried a scar for most of them....*"

PROFILE

José Escobar

JOURNALIST IN EXILE

José Escobar, a journalist as well as creative writer, arrives in N.M., a political exile from the Díaz regime in Mexico. He allies himself with various New Mexican causes during his eight years in the Territory, editing at least 8 to possibly 14 different Spanish language newspapers during this time.

1891: Escobar attends the organizational meeting of *La Prensa Asociada* in Las Vegas. He is editor of *El Progreso* in Trinidad, Colorado.

1892: José writes for *El Defensor del Pueblo*, the Albuquerque newspaper owned by **Juan José Marrero** [leader of the *Caballeros de Labor* in Las Vegas; he came to Albuquerque after being accused of complicity with the *Gorras Blancas*], using the pen name **Zig-Zag.** His column is titled "Around the World: Chronicles in Literature, Science, and Fashion," and is addressed to female readers. The column is "*chatty,*" transporting readers to Mexico, Spain, Italy, France, Canada, etc., with information about authors, books, scientific discoveries, popular exhibitions, interesting locales for tourism, etc.

July, 1892: Escobar starts his own newspaper, *El Combate*. He edits and writes prose and poetry for this Populist, Democratic publication. He authors many essays and his short stories are based in history or legend. His poetry, which also appears in other newspapers of the day, is often dedicated to *"lovely, literate ladies."* Journalism and politics are passions with bachelor Escobar, poetry being an outlet for his creative nature. His beloved Mexican homeland and lost love are recurring themes in his poetry.

1896: Escobar edits *Las Dos Repúblicas*, a newspaper funded by **Casimiro Barela** in Denver. It is said the paper is among *"...the top publications in the West of this great North American Republic ... a useful and interesting sheet for all social classes with columns about the arts, science, literature, and other novelties..."* José also writes editorials, essays, and poems for the newspaper. For example: "New Mexico's Literary Progress" is a refutation to charges from the eastern press that New Mexicans are backward and lazy.

1897: José is editing *El Nuevo Mundo* in Albuquerque's Old Town. He publishes four short stories which have to do with miracles of the Virgin Mary performed in various parts of the Hispanic world:

The Fishermen: Deep religious faith of villagers saves two fishermen lost in a violent storm at sea;
A Mother's Rosary: has to do with faith lost then regained;
The Mariner: the Bishop of Panama is returning to Spain when a gigantic wave threatens to destroy the ship and all its passengers;
The Miracle of the Virgin: is based on one of Escobar's personal experiences in Zacatecas.

The themes of José's numerous **essays** include that:
1.) the U.S. Congress has ignored the Treaty of Guadalupe Hidalgo and the justice which it purportedly guarantees;
2.) N.M. has changed drastically because of the U.S. takeover and New Mexicans are now worse off than their ancestors;
3.) "material progress" brought in by "Anglos" has not benefited New Mexicans because they haven't been accepted as part of this "progress" but rather are considered servants to it;
4.) party politics have been used to keep New Mexicans divided, therefore relatively powerless considering their numerical superiority;
5.) Hispanic newspapers must share in the blame because all too often they are the pawns of self-serving politicians and political parties;
6.) subscribers to newspapers all too often don't pay their subscriptions, thus forcing newspapers to seek partisan patronage in order to pay the bills;
7.) parents are neglecting their children's after school activities, dangerous now that they are exposed to the negative aspects of a foreign culture;
8.) both male and female New Mexicans are quick to adopt "Anglo" fashions and lifestyle

only to be ridiculed by "Anglos" and some New Mexicans;
9.) the racist eastern press insults New Mexicans for no good reason other than its own feelings of being the master race;
10.) newspapers could be a much more powerful tool in education due to the scarcity of books;
11.) immediate statehood should be sought to end the colonial status of the Territory in which New Mexicans are second-class citizens.

SOCIETIES

Sociedades (societies) are formed by Hispanics to channel intellectual goals into social action. Various organizations come to life, including:

1891: *Sociedad Dramática Hispano-Americana;*
1891: *Casino Hispano-Americano;*
1892: *Sociedad Filantrópica Latino-Americana,*
1892: *Sociedad Literaria y de Ayuda Mutua de Las Vegas,*
1898: *La Sociedad Social, Literaria y de Devates de Agua Negra, Nuevo México.*

NEWSPAPERS

Manuel C. de Baca, an attorney, founds *El Sol de Mayo* in Las Vegas. His goal is to combat widespread corruption and lawlessness as well as the defense of New Mexicans and their homeland. But he has no sympathy for the populist Gorras Blancas and their illegal tactics, organizing *La Orden de Caballeros de Protección Mutua* (The Order of Knights for Mutual Aid) to counter them.

1892: Manuel authors and publishes *Noches tenebrosas del Condado de San Miguel* (Dark Nights in San Miguel County), a critical narrative of the Gorras Blancas.
May: C. de Baca installs Victor L. Ochoa as editor of *El Sol*.

1894: Manuel Salazar y Otero takes over the newspaper and in one of his first articles praises Félix Martínez, C. de Baca's foremost enemy.

TERRORISM

February (5?) 8: An assassination attempt is made on **Thomas B. Catron** while he is standing behind a desk in his Santa Fe office. The would-be assassins escape in the darkness.

PROFILE

Victor L. Ochoa

A CULTURAL HERO

Victor Ochoa, an exile against the Díaz regime of Mexico, founds the *Hispano Americano* newspaper in **Socorro.**

1892: Victor moves his newspaper to Las Vegas. He promotes the formation of an **Hispanic American Press Association** and is elected its first president. Under his leadership the Associated Press pursues a proactive agenda in favor of full participation in government for the state's Spanish-speaking.

For example:

the Legislature is petitioned to publish all legal and judicial documents in Spanish as well as English, a right guaranteed by the American Constitution under freedom of speech as well as in the Treaty of Guadalupe Hidalgo [Article *IX: "...maintained and protected in the free enjoyment of their liberty and property ...*]

1893: Ochoa is arrested in El Paso on charges of supplying arms for the freedom fighters combating Díaz in Mexico. He is acquitted but secretly put under surveillance.

1894: Texas Rangers arrest Ochoa on charges of organizing an armed invasionary force on American territory. He is sentenced to three years in prison for violating neutrality laws.

1891-1904

COURT OF PRIVATE LAND CLAIMS

The Court of Private Land Claims is operating during these years in an effort to settle disputed land titles in N.M. [and Colo., Wyo., Nev., Ariz., Utah, the largest jurisdiction of any court in history].

Justices are Joseph R. **Reed** (Chief, from Iowa), Thomas C. **Fuller** (S.C., died in 1901, replaced by Frank R. **Osborn** from N.C.), Henry C. **Sluss** (Kansas), William W. **Murray** (Tennessee), and Wilbur F **Stone** (Colorado). In keeping with the congressional act, no justice from a territory could serve in the Court. Why? In order *"to make sure that none would have experience with the problems involved"* according to V. Westphall.

Custom is not specifically mentioned as a factor to be considered by the Court.

Proof is required that all conditions imposed by Spain and Mexico had been met, within the time allowed. *"A stricter, more technical approach"* is followed in N.M. (compared to California) and the burden of proof resides with the plaintiff though all records are controlled by the government. Now the Court requires the claimant to prove the existence of a bona fide grant document, that the granting official had the authority to award said grant (further, if a worn or torn document had been recopied, it had to be proved that the person doing the copying had the authority to do so), that all necessary steps and procedures for validation of the grant had been fulfilled, etc.

Presumption is eliminated as a factor. (Previously the presumption of the existence of a grant document was aided by the existence of a settlement on said grant, that the settlement wouldn't have been there if the granting official didn't have the legal right to authorize it, etc.)

Technicalities are considered crucial by government attorneys and/or authorities who strive to lengthen the legal process as much as possible in order to create greater expense for the claimant. **Technical**

requirements include that the grant document has to be recorded in the Spanish/Mexican archives [the Archives that **Governor Pile** tried to destroy in 1870 and that were nearly burned in a "mysterious" fire in 1892], that the grant had to be approved by the territorial deputation if made during the Mexican period, and that absolute compliance has been made regarding the procedural process of petition, grant, and act of possession. And if a decision is in favor of the claimant the U.S. Attorney merely appeals it to the Supreme Court which usually sides with the government against the claimant. Many cases are won by appeal in the Supreme Court and claimants are ruined financially.

The Supreme Court is disposed to accept whatever government attorneys tell it. (For example, the Court is told that Spain/Mexico retained possession of title for all common lands in a land grant, which was patently untrue but accepted by the Court because present title would therefore reside with the United States.)

"Experts" like **Will Tipton and Henry Flipper** work for the government in order to add land to the public domain, which means Government ownership of the land. Claimants have to rely on their lawyers who have to be paid.

[It is Will Tipton who testifies to the Court that documents by which Governor Cruzate awarded grants to the Pueblos are *forgeries,* saying that the signatures of Cruzate and his secretary are in the same handwriting, that Cruzate's secretary was named Pedro Ortiz Nino de Guevara and not Pedro Ladrón de Guitara as written in the documents, etc.]

> *"The ... grants most deserving of confirmation were caught in the middle* [from a liberal to a conservative approach to land grant adjudication] *since many of the large speculative grants had already been confirmed. The **procedure** in the Court of Private Land Claims heavily **favored the government,** resulting in numerous unjust decisions"* according to M. Ebright.

[In California the confirmation rate for adjudicated land was 73%; in Florida, 90%; in Louisiana, 100% (according to some sources). **In New Mexico the Court of Private Land Claims confirmed 6%.** "A *soundly based estimate has been made that some 70% of the Court's rejections--even considering the relatively stringent guidelines provided by Congress--are subject to serious question."*]

Major reasons cited for rejection or reduction of acreage include:

1. alleged lack of authority of the granting official;

2. insufficiency of the grant document(s);

3. the belief that common lands were not granted to individuals or community, thereby remaining public domain, which accounts for the largest amounts of land rejected by the Court, thus making it property of the U.S.;

Adolph Bandelier (Ca.1882-84)
Courtesy Museum of NM, #9138

4. refusal to accept testimony of grant residents;

5. survey errors.

[M. Ebright sums up: *"One thing is clear: Hispanic people have not been treated fairly in relation to the land grant issue."* **C. Larson** is in agreement: *"Land grabbing"* was facilitated by legislation that required land grant heirs *"to pay for their own surveys and to undertake long, expensive litigation to protect their titles."* Many lawyers and judges were able to *"cheat"* heirs out of their grant lands, *"many of whom managed to obtain portions of the land in question even when Hispanic land-grant residents lost their cases in court."*] (See **1904.**)

1892
REPORT

Ethnologist/historian **Adolph Bandelier** writes: *"...The Spanish government recognized at an early date not merely that the Indian was a human being, but that he was, after all, the chief resource which the New World presented to its newcomers. The tendency of Spanish legislation is therefore marked towards insuring the preservation and progress of the natives..."*

PROFILE

Eusebio Chacón

NEW MEXICAN NOVELIST

December 16, 1869: **Eusebio Chacón** is born in Peñasco. His father, **Major Rafaél Chacón** of the U.S. Cavalry, takes his family and homesteads in the Ojo Verde vicinity some 25 miles from Trinidad, Colorado, when Eusebio is less than a year old. As Eusebio grows up he attends primary schools in Trinidad then later attends the Jesuit College in Las Vegas.

1884: Eusebio addresses a *mutualista* chapter from Las Animas County. The speech is noted in a Santa Fe newspaper.

1887: Eusebio and younger brother **Ladislao** enroll at Notre Dame University. Eusebio excels as a student and is recognized as an eloquent speaker.

1889: Eusebio graduates from Notre Dame. He accepts a position as English teacher at Colegio Guadalupano in Durango, Mexico.

1889: Chacón is graduated with a law degree from Notre Dame. Returning to N.M. he gains a reputation as an orator, writer, spokesman for the community, and promoter of literature, especially the novel.

1891: He returns to Trinidad, in poor health, but when he regains his vigor he becomes a member of the Colorado state bar and sets up law practice in his home town. He marries **Sofía Barela,** daughter of **Casimiro Barela.**

1892: Chacón's two novels appear in print:
El hijo de la tempestad (Son of the Tempest) which manifests tension and conflict due to varying forms of banditry;
Tres la tormenta la calma (Calm After the Storm) examines the concept of honor.

Eusebio Chacón
Courtesy Museum of NM, #50356
(George Pagan photo)

[G. Meléndez asserts this work is the first published narrative by an Hispanic author in the Southwest, *"una literatura nacional,"* and the first to be edited and published by a New Mexican newspaper business. Other critics state that the two works establish the writing of novels in the area and serve to disclose political, cultural and behavioral problems experienced by the people of N.M.]

He publishes poetry then is appointed Interpreter for the U.S. Court of Private Land Claims so for the next several years (1892-1899) the Chacón family alternates their residence between Santa Fe and Trinidad.

1894: Eusebio is admitted to the New Mexico state bar. He practices law in N.M. and Colorado.
1895: He publishes *Ocotlón,* a tribute to the beauty of Mexico, and later *A la patria,* a poem of homage and tribute to Mexico.

1896: Eusebio publishes a six-part history of N.M. in the *Dos Repúblicas* newspaper.

1899: Chacón is residing in Las Vegas.
1900: Chacón returns permanently to Trinidad.

1901: **Nellie Snider,** missionary for one of the Protestant denominations, launches an *"inflammatory campaign" against Hispanic Catholics in Las Vegas, referring to them as "ignorant, dirty, degraded people of mixed Indian and Iberian blood ... known for squalor, immorality and indigestible tortillas and fiery chili..."* Chacón refutes her racist arguments in *La Voz del Pueblo,* exposing her ignorance and calming the situation. In a famous speech delivered at a meeting known as the "Rally of Indignation" Chacón refutes her bigoted arguments ('a la Clarence Darrow') and sums up:...*We are not as abandoned by God around these parts as some writers portray us, passing among us like apocalyptic gentlemen with the cup of bile in one hand and the scythe of hate in the other. Are we to understand that our hope will not suffice to have our petition heard, and that we should continue in our precious state as national pariahs? People of New Mexico, if your destiny is to be only a beast of burden, if you are to remain in the sad government tutelage that you have had up to now, if you are not to participate in the public matters of this nation, which is as much yours, it is now time that you pick up your household goods and take them, along with the remains of your ancestors, to another more hospitable nation...*

1930s: Chacón contributes many items to (the leading magazine of the Territorial period) Camilo Padilla's *Revista Ilustrada.*

1948: Eusebio Chacón dies.

EXPOSE

Beginning on February 18, 1892, *El Sol de Mayo* of Las Vegas publishes a detailed, four-part narrative called "Dark Nights" accompanied by photographs of white-hooded night riders. (The series is thought to have been written by **Manuel C. de Baca.**) "Dark Nights" chronicles the lawlessness of the *Gorras Blancas* (whom C. de Baca opposed).

LITERATURE

Eusebio Chacón writes two short novels, *El hijo de la Tempestad* (Son *of* the Storm) and *Tras la tormenta la calma* (Calmness After the Storm).

RANCHERO LIFESTYLE

The lifestyle of New Mexico's *ranchero* (rancher/farmer) class is based on utilization of farming and grazing lands. A man's reputation and that of his family are based on how well he works the resources available from the land. *Not having to work for anyone else,* to be an independent ranchero, to work your own land and your own stock, is a cultural ideal.

LAND

January 11, 1892: Common lands in the **Quemado Valley** and beyond are taken away from the people of Córdova and become part of the "public domain" referred to as the Pecos River Forest Reserve. As a subterfuge the Córdovans are allowed to graze their livestock, principally goats and sheep, in the uplands surrounding the village and as far as the Truchas Peaks.

April 6, 1915: The Pecos and Jémez National Forests are merged into the unit known as the **Santa Fe National Forest** and livestock grazing is restricted to the point that Córdovans can't graze their sheep and goats because of the *"erosive dangers of overgrazing"* according to C.L. Briggs, though permits are granted to commercial operators for cattle production. Córdovans in particular and Hispanos in general are thus deprived of grazing rights by Forest Service officials while "Anglo" stockmen reap the benefit. Deprived of stock raising due to loss of land rights, Hispanos cannot live as independent rancheros and now must seek wage labor outside their villages.

ARCHIVES FIRE

May 13: A *"mysterious"* **fire breaks out at the State Capitol** where state archives are being housed. Frantic efforts are made by the citizenry to save the archives but many are puzzled by the event because there is insufficient water pressure with which to battle the blaze and the flames are described as resembling those of burning coal oil. A seemingly unconcerned American wearing a brown derby hat, light coat, with a heavily bearded face, is described as being at the scene by several witnesses during the investigation into the matter.

[It has been written that another "mysterious" fire also broke out at the same time in the archives in Mexico City.]

GANGSTERS

October: The body of **Patricio Maes** is found hanging by the neck from under a Las Vegas bridge. Only much later is it learned that Maes had been executed by the *Sociedad de Bandidos de Nuevo México* (Society of Bandits of New Mexico) led by **Vicente Silva.**

Vicente Silva (Ca.1896)
Courtesy Museum of NM, #143691

[It is said that Silva was born in Bernalillo County in 1845. As a young man he did some bartending in Albuquerque where he married **Telesfora Sandoval.** The couple moved to Las Vegas in 1875 where they opened a saloon, **The Imperial**, and in time expanded for gambling and meeting rooms. They adopted a foundling, naming her Emma, and Telesfora's brother Gabriel Sandoval was hired as Silva's business manager. Silva always gave the appearance of a neatly dressed businessman with a pleasant nature but The Imperial attracted men and women of the lowest character and reputation. Secretly, Silva organized them into the Society of Bandits which included three members of the Vegas police force. They rustled livestock and committed murders,rapes, thefts, etc., in the Las Vegas area. Silva managed to maintain an air of respectability in the community and his henchmen were known by their descriptive nicknames (Hawk, Owl, Romo, etc.). Everything came to light only after Silva murdered his wife and then was murdered in turn by some of his own men. In Las Vegas there are many stories of "Vicente Silva and His 40 Thieves." For example, gang member and policeman **José Chávez y Chávez,** a superlative marksmen even into old age, recounted his friendship with Billy the Kid and maintained that it was he, *not Billy,* who shot down Sheriff Brady and Deputy Hindman during the Lincoln County War.]

NEWSPAPER ORGANIZATION

March: The **Hispano-American Press Association** is formed with **Victor L. Ochoa** as its first president.

One of the first acts of the new organization is a resolution to censure Governor **L. Bradford Prince** for the negative, racist remarks he made to the *Chicago Tribune* and for his subsequent attempt to bribe the local press into not reporting it to the general public. The resolution denounces the hypocrisy of Governor Prince, *who* pretends to be the best friend of Hispanic New Mexicans then behind their backs *"treats them as disdainful greasers."* Everyone in the Territory and beyond should be warned that Prince merits neither trust nor favor.

HIGHER EDUCATION

June 15, 1892: The **University of New Mexico** opens its doors.

1892: Courses are offered for the first time at the **New Mexico Institute of Mining & Technology**.

PROFILE

Charles F.Lummis

E N A M O R E D   O F   T H E   S O U T H W E S T

1859: Charles FletcherLummis is born in Massachusetts.

1881: As a student at Harvard, he publishes a short volume of poetry titled *Birch Bark Poems* after walking throughout New England.

1882: Charles decides to go west. For a time he works for an Ohio newspaper.

1884: Starting from Cincinnati he walks across the continent, reaching Los Angeles in 143 days.

1885: Lummis and others start a newspaper, the Los *Angeles Times,* for which he works as city editor for three years.

1888: Due mostly to overwork, Charles suffers a stroke which paralyzes his left side, impeding his speech and rendering his left arm useless. He resigns from the newspaper and resolves to regain his health in New Mexico where in time he becomes enamored of Hispanic and Pueblo people. His career is now one of adventure as he regains his health and writes the short, autobiographical *My Friend Will*. He also writes many feature articles and poems for various magazines and newspapers, the articles becoming the basis for some of his 14 books on the Hispanic and Indian Southwest.

During this period he meets **Adolph F. Bandelier** and under his tutelage Lummis becomes an accomplished archaeologist. They explore western New Mexico, Charles taking thousands of pictures. The two then travel as far as Peru and Bolivia.

In time Lummis is one of the incorporators of the School of American Research and for his work on Spanish history he is knighted by the King of Spain.
His final years are spent in California and blindness strikes him but he compiles his poems of earlier years and publishes them as *The Bronco Pegasus.*

1928: Charles Fletcher Lummis dies.

Charles F. Lummis
Courtesy Museum of NM,
#7702 (Siefer photo)

1893
LAND GRANT

Antonio Griego and others file suit in the **Court of Private Land Claims** for title to their lands in the **Embudo grant.** *The case comes to trial five years later.*

Attorney **N.B. Laughlin** submits the Embudo documentation to the Court.

Government attorney **W. Pope** objects because the documentation is a copy, not the original, and therefore can't be confirmed by the Court. The Embudo grant is **rejected** in its entirety, making the land part of the public domain. Small holding claims like land with homes, churches, cemeteries, etc., as well as gardens or other improved plots, are permitted to remain with the people. The rest is now federal property (See **1974.**)

PROFILE

Luis Tafoya

O F   T H E   N E W   M E X I C A N   I N T E L I G E N T S I A

Luis Tafoya (1851-1922) is identified by Doris Meyer as the real name of the New Mexican writer known as X.X.X. Tafoya's parents are José Dolores Tafoya and Refugio Durán (who later marries prominent political and civic Santa Fe personality Antonio Ortiz y Salazar, thus making Luis a stepson to Antonio).

1860s: Luis Tafoya is educated at St. Michael's College.
1903-1910: Tafoya publishes many poems in *El Independiente* which is known for its defense of

New Mexican culture. They are of high literary quality in the romantic or modernist styles (as developed as those of his contemporaries José Escobar and Felipe M. Chacón).

1911: Luis creates a formal poem (in alexandrine quatrains) titled "To New Mexico" on the eve of being granted statehood. He stresses the importance of Hispanic ethnic unity and cultural affirmation. Tafoya's prose and poetry, written for the most part under pseudonyms, emphasize the importance of educating young New Mexicans, the need to learn English but preserve the Spanish language, the injustice perpetrated on New Mexicans by denying them statehood, the need to document New Mexican history. He interprets realities of the time for his readers, especially the communal spirit of New Mexican ancestors. He understands that New Mexico's rich history will be denigrated in order to devalue it, thus enabling "Anglo" society to dominate New Mexicans in all endeavors.

1917: While living in Taos, an assassination attempt is made on 67 year-old Luis Tafoya in an effort to silence him forever. (He lives alone, his time spent in the study of authors and their books, keeping informed through the contemporary press.)

Three months later another attempt is made on his life, this time with someone using chloroform in an effort to drug and kidnap him. Somehow, Tafoya foils his attackers once more.

March 8, 1918: Tafoya (probably) writes an editorial for *La Revista de Taos* in which he tells New Mexicans that *they* must be their own knowledgeable historians if they are to be rewarded with the honor and fame which New Mexican history has recorded.

[Doris Meyer states that Luis Tafoya was one of the *"individuals of powerful intellect and literary presence"* in the New Mexico of his day.]

SOCIETY
Aurora Lucero is born.

BOOKS
Reverend **Alexander M. Darley** publishes his *"controversial"* book *The Passionists of the Southwest,* in which he uses the Penitente Brotherhood to attack the Catholic Church in Colorado and *"...still priest-ridden New Mexico."* Darley states the Penitentes are political: *"...pull Padre pull Penitente is a very simple political penance to get Office."* Penitente *"...hysteria seems to have been generated by the press in endless verbal battles."*

The Land of Poco Tiempo is published by **Charles E. Lummis,** the *"...first of a number of writers to describe his fascination with the land and the native cultures..."* of N.M. as related by S. Forrest.

POLITICS
Lincoln County small ranchers and farmers are deeply angry over the "cabal" of land, cattle, and railroad interests that are working hand in glove with the **Santa Fe Ring.** Together they can dictate

anything from water rights, railroad hauling charges, access to land in the public domain, land prices, etc.

The **Republican Party** is accused of passing laws to protect use by the big cattle associations of the public domain, utterly disregarding the rights of settlers; absolving railroads from taxation; keeping Texas cattle out of N.M. in order to squeeze the small rancher out of business, etc.

NEWSPAPER ORGANIZATION MEETING

July, 1893: La Prensa Asociada Hispano-Americana (The Hispanic American Associated Press) meets in Santa Fe to install officers and draft a preamble and policy resolutions for this Association that draws prominent journalists from New Mexico, Colorado, and West Texas. President and Vice President are **Victor L. Ochoa** and **Camilo Padilla,** respectively. Others in attendance are José Escobar (*El Combate,* Albuquerque), Teófilo Ocaña Caballero *(La Lucha,* El Paso), Marcial Valdés (*El Tiempo,* Las Cruces), Pedro G. de la Lama (*La Opinión Pública,* Albuquerque), M. Lerma (*La Flor del Valle,* Las Cruces), *José* Segura (*El Boletín Popular,* Santa Fe), Manuel Salazar y Otero *(La Crónica de Valencia,* Socorro). Memberships are approved for newspapers from Eagle Pass and Laredo in Texas as well as for *El Estandarde de Springer* in N.M. The network by which to exchange articles and other information is enhanced.

[These *canjes* are described by G. Meléndez as reaching into the entire Southwest as well as into Mexico and Latin America, and vice versa, thereby providing cosmopolitan perspectives for New Mexicans.]

NEWSPAPER READING

La Opinión Pública of Albuquerque announces it is sponsoring a beauty contest open to all female residents of N.M., Arizona, and Texas between the ages of 14 to 35. Votes are cast by buying a subscription to the newspaper. (The contest would be from October, 1893, to April of 1894; by mid-January, señorita Flora Santisteban of San Antonio, Texas, was leading all contestants with 1,600 votes.)

1893-1900
LITERATURE

A writer known only as "X.X.X." is producing "sophisticated" poetry and other writings during this period. A poet and translator who worked for *El Nuevo Mexicano* newspaper in Santa Fe, X.X.X. wrote anonymously about international, national, New Mexican and local affairs, enjoying his role as *"the people's bard."* His poems are inspired by Washington politics, the Spanish-American War, the Boer War, etc., in *décima* form (the traditional structure of Spanish balladry), as well as the environment, events like the death of Col. Albert Fountain and the refusal of Congress to grant statehood to New Mexico. X.X.X. thus personifies a global as well as a New Mexican outlook.

[**Doris Meyer** asserts that *"literary and cultural histories"* of N.M. and indeed the entire Southwest have ignored the literature of N.M. and have given the mistaken impression that it didn't exist. Not only was there a very strong literary expression in N.M. but the fact that it was expressed in newspapers indicates that reading and literature were not only for elite circles but also for the typical New Mexican ranchero, home-maker, craftsman, etc.]

1893-1897

William T. Thornton is Governor.

1894
STATEHOOD

Thomas B. Catron is Delegate to Congress and committed to statehood. Catron is aided by **S.B. Elkins** so Elkins' political enemies fight Catron also. Both are *"...charged with being land robbers. Catron especially was slandered, being called a 'political freebooter' seeking to achieve his own selfish ends...Catron's controversial past had caught up with him, and at a most inopportune time."* (See **1902.**)

The Borrego Murder Case in which Catron's political enemy **J. Francisco Chaves** was murdered, gives Catron much bad publicity when he defends the accused in court.

MOTHER'S DEFENSE

Juliana V. Chaves, mother of the assassinated Mayor of Santa Fe, **J. Francisco Chaves,** writes a letter that is published in *La Opinión Pública* in which she defends her son's reputation when **T.B. Catron** attacks it. She believes political boss Catron is behind her son's murder and she challenges Catron to bring forth any evidence that Chaves ever did anything to injure the people he served.

HISPANIC BIOGRAPHY

April: **José Escobar** begins publishing a biweekly series entitled **New Mexico and Its Illustrious Men** for *La Opinión Pública* in Albuquerque. The series is sold separately from the newspaper and provides biographical portraits of famous New Mexicans. The work continues through the end of the year.

[Copies don't appear to have survived, according to D. Meyer. Works like "New Mexico and Its Illustrious Men" are unknown to the ordinary contemporary New Mexican.]

LABOR & DISCRIMINATION

The **Pecos Valley Railroad** is laying rail from Carlsbad to Roswell.

"Anglo" workers are paid $1.50 per day and charged $3.00 per week to eat at the company mess. Hispanics doing the same work are paid $1.25 and charged $3.50, respectively.

RAILROAD

October 6, 1894: Two trains are the first to arrive in **Roswell,** on the same day, a construction train with a private car at the end and a three-car passenger special which is allowed the honor of coming into Roswell first.

NEWSPAPERS

Jesús Enrique Sosa (1856-1918) founds the *El Gato* newspaper in Santa Fe.

Enrique H. Salazar founds the *El Independiente* newspaper in Las Vegas.

PROFILE

Enrique H. Salazar

STATESMAN, NEWSPAPERMAN AND CULTURAL CHAMPION

Ca. 1870: Enrique is born in Santa Fe, the son of **Josefina Salazar** (who later marries William H. Manderfield). He is educated at St. Michael's College.

1888: Along with **Nestor Montoya,** Enrique founds *La Voz del Pueblo* in Santa Fe.

1894: Enrique begins *El Independiente* and in time is considered a political force in San Miguel County and throughout the Territory.

1898: Salazar is appointed Postmaster by President McKinley and reappointed by President Roosevelt in 1902.

1901: He marries **Agueda López,** daughter of **Lorenzo López** of Las Vegas.

1910: President Taft appoints Enrique as receiver of the federal Office of Land Management at Fort Sumner. He has jurisdiction over 2,000,000 acres of land.

Enrique H. Salazar
Courtesy Museum of NM, #147745

Historiography: Enrique writes from Las Vegas that New Mexico's children need native history written through native eyes *"so all is not lost and relegated to darkness..."* which will happen if newly arrived individuals are allowed to monopolize the field of history.

[G. Meléndez states that New Mexicans were aware that local history was being distorted or ignored by citizens new to the Territory, that eastern journalists were promoting *"satirical allusions and biting falsehoods..."*]

Culture: Salazar declares that products of Hispanic culture, conquerors, settlers, and missionaries find no equal in the
"Pikes, Clarks, Fremonts ... whose travels have been given over to fame but which in reality are child's play..."
in comparison to actions recorded by Hispanics centuries before. He asserts that "heroic"Kit Carson was created by the eastern press, not historical fact, which merely verifies he was a local scout, guide, and Indian fighter whose basic claim to fame was leading the expedition which destroyed the Navajo people as an independent society.

He charges **W.W.H. Davis,** author of *El Gringo, or New Mexico and her People* with *"errors and inventions ... and such partiality against the native settlers of the land and their forebears..."* that the work has no historical value at all.

1914: Enrique H. Salazar dies.

1895
LAND LAW COMPILED
A compilation of Spanish and Mexican land laws is published. **Henry O. Flipper** [one of the few African Americans in N.M.] does most of the research and writing for this book which is then published under the name of **M.G. Reynolds,** the U.S. Attorney.

LITERACY
New Mexico has a *"vigorous oral tradition"* in poetry and prose as well as a *"learned literary tradition"* that is expressed through newspapers, according to G. Meléndez [whose book was released when this *Multi-History* was virtually complete]. Hispanic New Mexico has an intellectual community possessing higher education, the benefits of travel, and contacts with literary circles outside the Territory. Groups of literary circles "occasionally include female members." Some writers are able to translate stories and poems from the original English, French, German, etc., into Spanish for New Mexican readers.

PROFILE

J. Enrique Sosa

P R O F E S S I O N A L   J O U R N A L I S T

1856: **J. Enrique Sosa** is born in Guadalajara, Mexico. He receives a good education in Jalisco but he is orphaned at the age of ten.

1871: Enrique joins the Army at the age of fifteen. By the time of the war against France he has the rank of Captain. When he leaves the military he studies at the Academia de San Carlos in Mexico City, the premier institution for the study of Fine Arts. Sosa trains to be a painter (which he does the rest of his life).

1884: Sosa goes to Mexico City and studies to become a civil engineer. He works for various railroad companies.

1888: Enrique moves to El Paso and shortly applies for legal immigration status, deciding to become a professional journalist in the U.S.

1894: Sosa moves to Las Cruces and then to Santa Fe where he founds *El Gato*. He marries **Luz Alderete** of Las Cruces and in time they have ten children. He becomes a naturalized American citizen.

1896: Enrique founds a second newspaper, *La Estrella de Nuevo México,* in Santa Fe then moves it to Socorro. He also founds *La Hormiga de* Oro newspaper in Albuquerque.

1898: Sosa moves his printing plant to Mora where he founds and operates the Sosa Theater as well as *El Eco del Norte* newspaper.

LAND GRANT

United States v. Chaves is one of the land grant cases that *"...stands out as a beacon of fairness, showing how all these cases should have been handled..."*

1833: **Cubero** is begun by a community grant to various families. Original granting documents are lost but the Court of **Private Land Claims** confirms the grant because people living on the land are proof that the grant was made; other legal documents show that the settlement has been in continuous existence since 1833.

Government attorneys maintain that the granting document isn't extant so the claim must be rejected according to the 1891 Act. They **appeal the verdict** to the Supreme Court.

Justice Shiras voices the opinion of the Supreme Court by referring to international law, the Treaty of Guadalupe Hidalgo, and the fact that several residents had seen the actual grant document, and most importantly that Cubero had been inhabited continuously since 1833. The Supreme Court affirms granting the Cubero people a patent for their land.

1896

SOCIETY

Martín Vigil is born at Tesuque Pueblo.

POLITICS

Harvey B. Fergusson is elected Delegate to Congress. It is said power is slipping away from the Santa Fe Ring.

LITERATURE

Manuel C. de Baca writes the historical narrative *Historia de Vicente Silva y sus cuarenta bandidos, sus crímines y retribuciones* (The Story of Vicente Silva and his Forty Bandits, their Crimes and Retributions).

[**Silva** was born around 1845 in Bernalillo. He grows up to be intelligent, though he doesn't attend school, good looking, prosperous, apparently respectable. Around 1885 he opens a saloon and gambling hall in Las Vegas. He and his wife adopt an abandoned little girl.

Around 1892 Silva organized a society of outlaws and terrorized Las Vegas with a series of crimes until his death at the hands of one of his own gang members in 1893.]

SOCIETY

Pat Garrett returns to N.M. and is elected Sheriff of Doña Ana County.

ASSASSINATION

January, 1896: **Albert Fountain,** special prosecutor against cattle rustlers and other troublesome outlaws, is notified that death threats are being made against him.

January 31: Fountain and his nine-year-old son Henry leave Lincoln for Las Cruces. Neither are ever seen again and their bodies are never found.

Pat Garrett believes a cattleman named **Oliver M. Lee** (close associate of A.B. Fall) is involved in the Fountains' disappearance because Fountain had obtained indictments against Lee and some of his friends. In time the Sheriff obtains arrest warrants for Lee and **Jim Gilliland,** who say that Garrett is merely out to get them.

1899: Otero County is created (by Albert B. Fall, a political ally of Lee), thus removing jurisdiction for the Fountain case from Doña Ana County. Lee agrees to surrender to the new sheriff, George Curry, and stand trial.

There is media coverage from all over the nation for the trial.

TIMELINE

1896: **Plessy v. Ferguson:** *the Supreme Court upholds "separate but equal" racial segregation in American public life.*

HISTORY IN NEWSPAPERS

January 8, 1896: *El Amigo del Pueblo* newspaper in Ratón publishes part of a series called "Popular History of New Mexico, Its People, Its Traditions and Customs," by **José Escobar**. [Only one issue has been uncovered by Doris Meyer.]

March: *La Voz del Pueblo* of Las Vegas publishes lengthy historical articles under the title "America Before the Discovery." (The author is anonymous.)

Eusebio Chacón is collecting historical documents from which to write the history of N.M. He authors historical articles which appear in various newspapers.

PROFILE

Albert Fountain

CHAMPION LAWYER AGAINST VILLAINY

1838: **Albert Jennings (Fontaine)** is born on Staten Island, New York (it is believed), to Solomon Jennings, a sea captain, and (?) Fontaine. It is believed he was educated in local schools and colleges (but there are no extant records to that effect according to his biographer A.M. Gibson).

1857: It is believed that **Albert J. Fountain** is in California. He has worked in the gold fields and as a reporter for the Sacramento *Union* newspaper. He studies Law in the office of N. Greene Curtis.

1861: Albert is preparing for the State Bar but in August he enlists in the First California Infantry Volunteers (Company E) which will soon be fighting the Confederate Army. In training camp he wins honors as a marksman and is soon promoted to corporal.

August, 1862: Fountain and the California Column are in New Mexico and learn that General Sibley and his Confederate forces have fled back to Texas. Albert meets **Tomás Pérez** from Mesilla and the two form a strong friendship. Tomás introduces his 16-year old sister, **Mariana Pérez,** to his friend and Albert is soon in love with the beautiful young woman. They become engaged before he is reassigned to duty in El Paso.

October 11, 1862: General Carleton sends his army against the **Mescalero Apaches.** Colonel **Kit Carson** and his five companies of **New Mexico Volunteers** are ordered to campaign to the south of Fort Stanton. Carleton's orders are that "*... no council will be held with the Indians ... men are to be slain wherever and whenever they are found. Their women are to be taken prisoners...*" Fountain is assigned to the Mescalero campaign.

October 26, 1862: Albert marries Mariana at Mesilla before he leaves for the Apache war.

January 1, 1863: The Army returns from their unsuccessful war (no Apaches could be found) but the return is through Mesilla so Albert is reunited with Mariana.

Albert J. Fountain
Courtesy Museum of NM, #9873

May, 1863: Fountain is promoted to Lieutenant.

August 31, 1864: Albert is honorably discharged from the Army and returns to civilian life. He wants to continue his Law career but the prospects aren't promising and there are few other available business opportunities so he signs up with the Army as a scout and guide (over Mariana's objections) at five dollars a day.

1865: Fountain is commissioned a Captain in the New Mexico Volunteers. He works at recruiting New Mexicans and by April has around 75 men, described as "*a bastard company of differing ethnicities ... undisciplined ... wicked fighters who had no equals for enduring hunger, thirst, heat, cold, and fatigue without complaint.*"

Fountain is seriously wounded in an Indian encounter and after a lengthy convalescence he retires from the Army. He and his family live in El Paso where Albert pursues a career in Law but he also becomes interested in the rough-and-tumble world of politics. Because he can speak well in English or Spanish he is much in demand as a keynote speaker for Republican gatherings and conventions.

1866: Albert J. Fountain is elected as County Surveyor on the Republican ticket. Republican leader W.W. Mills offers Fountain an appointment as Customs Inspector and Chief Assistant to the collector (at an annual salary of $1,800) and he accepts because his law practice is still struggling. The post also brings him into contact with influential men from throughout the Southwest.

1867: Albert withdraws from a group that seeks to get private title to the Guadalupe salt beds because the people are accustomed to taking salt from them for their own personal use.

1868: The **Radical** (Republican) **Reconstruction Plan** is set in motion in Texas. (The tenets of the plan included a tutelage period of military rule, general disqualification of Confederates who couldn't take an iron-clad oath, drastic revisions in State constitutions, adoption of the 13th, 14th, and 15th amendments, all civil and political rights for former slaves, and a sort of de facto exclusion to the secession-tainted Democratic Party.) Fountain is a leading El Paso Republican but **W.W. Mills** becomes his rival and suspends Albert from his job as Customs Inspector.

1869: Fountain is elected vice-chairman of the convention for selection of candidates and developing the Radical platform. Fountain is nominated to the State Senate and elected in November because of his stand on the salt beds issue.

1870: Fountain is president of the Texas Senate. He is described as the *"dashing young Senator from El Paso"* and is lauded for his quick and resourceful mind. He is around five-feet-nine-inches tall and weighs some 165 pounds.

1871: Prominent Texas Democrats, including W.W. Mills, hold a convention in Austin to plan strategy for the fall elections.

1873: Democrats have a majority of 18 to 12 in the House. The Republican leadership is indicted on various charges and Fountain must answer against 17 felony indictments. Albert proves he is innocent of all charges but is nearly ruined financially and politically.

The Fountain family relocates to Mesilla, New Mexico, by December and Christmas is celebrated with Mariana's blood family and the Fountain children: **Albert, Thomas, Edward, Maggie, Marianita, John, Fannie, Catarina** (and in time **Henry** was the last to be born to Albert and Mariana).

1874: Fountain arranges a Mesilla reunion of the **California Column** veterans. He becomes a member of the Las Cruces Aztec Lodge chapter of the Masonic Order. He organizes the Mesilla Dramatic Association and produces the first play.

August, 1875: Republican delegates elect Fountain as president of the Doña Ana County Republican Convention.

1876: Albert founds the Mesilla Valley Publishing Company and during the next year he and two others are publishing the *Mesilla Valley Independent* newspaper. One of his motives is to publish articles to combat attitudes of in-coming Texas immigrants who believed that *"Mexicans are greasers."*

1878: Fountain interviews **Chief Victorio** of the Mimbreño Apaches who says the American government has forced the Mimbreño off their land twice in order to give it to miners and if they try to do it again he will die fighting *"on the warpath and leave a trail of blood and fire everywhere."*

Fountain writes many anti-Jesuit editorials because they *"wanted control of the schools"* and for trying to unite *Mexicans* to combat *"Anglos."* Many Catholics were alienated and in time the newspaper folded but not before he went on a crusade against the *"gunmen, horse thieves, and cattle rustlers, most of them imported from Texas"* for the Lincoln County war. After these articles his life is threatened in notes from anonymous writers.

1879: Victorio leads a band of warriors on the warpath after the government takes away their lands at Ojo Caliente for the third time and sends them to the San Carlos Reservation in Arizona. He skirmishes and defeats Army forces because of his mobility and shrewd generalship. By the end of the summer of 1880 it is said that some 300 people had been killed by Victorio's warriors.

Albert Fountain organizes the **Mesilla Scouts,** almost all of whom are Hispanic, to protect the Mesilla Valley against Victorio. Colonel **Edward Hatch** brings in 1,000 troops to fight Victorio. The troops "trap" the warriors in Hembrillo Canyon but Victorio easily cuts through them and escapes with his victorious warriors. Victorio eludes Hatch's Army, seemingly at will, until he and his warriors are killed by Mexican troops in northern Chihuahua. The old Chief Nana continues the struggle for a few months but he is soon captured.

1882: As the Apache menace subsides there begins an influx of *"Texas underworld fugitives ... highwaymen, rustlers, and professional gunmen"* into southern New Mexico where cattle are stolen and murders become common. When the R.S. Mason ranch is raided, Fountain is wired to muster his company and take whatever action necessary. Later he is selected to lead the Second Cavalry Battalion of the **New Mexico Volunteer Militia** as Major. He gets his men ready, describing them as "brave as lions," singling out Captain **Francisco Salazar** as especially impressive.

February, 1883: Governor Sheldon orders Major Fountain to be ready to attack the *"thirty to forty gunmen, many of them fugitives from Texas"* who are headquartered at Lake Valley and supposedly led by one **John Kinney.** Fountain's men capture a number of the gang but none of its leaders. Fountain receives a message from Kinney that *"Fountain and his greaser militia"* are afraid of an open fight, that no one would ever take him alive. But Kinney is captured without a fight just into the Arizona Territory and returned to Las Cruces where he is held by Fountain, Salazar, and six other of his troopers, pending trial. Major Fountain and his cavalry are the toast of New Mexico Territory and Kinney later is sentenced to seven years at Leavenworth.

1883: **Las Cruces** replaces Mesilla as the District Court center. It is described as a *"ripsnorting Anglo town ... as ugly as El Paso... wild, wicked, capable of indulging the most ribald tastes..."*

1884: Fountain begins to clash with Republicans in the Santa Fe Ring, charging it with *"party frauds"* and *"fixed nominations."*

1885: **Gerónimo,** some 45 warriors and close to 100 women and children break out of their San Carlos concentration camp and a massive manhunt begins throughout the Southwest. The

Army is described as *useless* when it comes to fighting Indians *"but we have high hopes that our militia boys will do some good work."* Fountain and his cavalry are reactivated with headquarters at Lake Valley.

Between campaigns against raiders and outlaws, Albert Fountain builds his law practice and by 1885 the top lawyers in the Territory are considered to be **Fountain** of Mesilla / Las Cruces, **Tom Catron** and **W.T. Thornton** of Santa Fe.

1887: **Albert Bacon Fall** arrives in Las Cruces, founds a newspaper, the *Independent Democrat*, and begins organizing the Democrats.

[He and Fountain are to become the bitterest of political enemies.]

1888: Fountain wins a seat in the Territorial Legislature by defeating A.B. Fall.

1890: The proposed State constitution, supported by Fountain and rejected by Fall, goes down to defeat. In November Fall defeats Fountain, by 45 votes, for the seat in the Legislature and defeats him again in 1892. Fountain writes that Fall is not an honest man, that his power base is various gunmen led by individuals like Oliver Lee, Jim Gilliland, Billy McNew, whom Judge Fall gets appointed as Deputy U.S. Marshals.

Fountain often finds himself as prosecutor while Fall is for the defense.

January, 1896: Albert Fountain and his eight-year-old son Henry go to Lincoln for the indictments of Oliver Lee and William McNew. During the recess of the final day of the hearings, Fountain receives an anonymous note: *"If you drop this we will be your friends. If you go on with it you will never reach home alive."*

January 30, 1896: Albert and Henry start their buckboard ride back to Las Cruces. Fountain notices that he is being followed by two men, sometimes three. He meets people on the road: one Santos Alvarado, a stage driver, tells Fountain he had seen three riders down the road. Saturnino Barela, another stage driver, is met and reports on three riders, suggesting to Fountain that he spend the night in the safety of the stage station. But Albert declines the offer and continues toward home. Neither Fountain is ever seen again, dead or alive.

February 22, 1896: The reward for the Fountain killers is $20,000.

Fall's *Independent Democrat* publishes stories that Albert J. Fountain has been seen in a number of cities in various parts of the country, in Cuba, in Mexico City, etc., that he has run off with a younger woman, etc. Oliver Lee is quoted as saying he doesn't care if Fountain is ever found. Gilliland hears someone say that the killing of a child like Henry is *horrible* to which Gilliland allegedly replies that Henry Fountain was *"a half-breed, no better than a dog."*

March 13, 1899: Lee and Gilliland surrender themselves and stand trial. They are to be defended by Fall, Harry Daugherty, and Harvey B. Fergusson. Prosecutors are Tom Catron and R.P. Barnes. A change of venue is made to Hillsboro. Media from all over the country is in attendance as the defense hammers away at the fact that no bodies have been found (a requisite to prove murder in Texas).

Lee and Gilliland are found NOT GUILTY.

HISTORY IN NEWSPAPERS (con't)

Francisco de Thoma publishes *Popular History of New Mexico from Its Discovery to the Present* (New York: American Book Company) in Spanish. He states that his desire in writing the book is to remind New Mexicans of the glories and suffering of their heroic ancestors, to nourish pride in those ancestors, to rescue the gallant and holy missionaries from oblivion, and to instill pride in the Spanish people who are among the most noble, generous, and heroic groups in the world.

MISSONARY

October 10, 1896: Reverend **Andrew Van der Wagen** and his wife, **Effa**, are unloading their possessions from a boxcar in Gallup when a group of horsemen surround them, guns drawn. The leader of the group challenges Andrew: *"You got any firearms and ammunition in that there freight car?"* Andrew says yes then fetches his Bible, saying, *"This is my ammunition. The spirit of this book is sharper than a double-edged sword and more powerful than any weapons you fellows possess..."* as related by Bernice Stock. The horsemen decide to leave the missionary alone.

Andrew Van der Wagen is sponsored by the Board of Heathen Missions of the **Christian Reformed Church** and Effa is a registered nurse. Together they work to improve the lives of the Navajo and Zuñi people. Andrew translates parts of the Bible into the Zuñi language and creates a dictionary of some 2,000 words.

1906: Andrew leaves the employment of the Christian Reformed Church. He becomes a trader and rancher, playing an active role in the community. He is the driving force behind building a wagon bridge over the Zuñi River in the heart of the village. Effa works to improve sanitary conditions and nurses the sick through the smallpox epidemic of 1898-1899 and the flu epidemic of 1919.

1897-1906
Miguel A. Otero (II) is Governor.

1897
LAND LAW

U.S. v. Sandoval is a landmark case used by the Court of Private Land Claims as the precedent for denying confirmation of common lands.

For example:

In 1879 the 300,000-acre **San Miguel del Bado** grant is surveyed
as a community grant and the Surveyor General
recommends its confirmation. The General Land Office
commissioner recommends that only the land occupied
by villages be confirmed, about 5,000 acres, rejecting
confirmation of the common lands, the bulk of the grant
and from which most settlers make their living. The
Court of Private Land Claims confirms the entire grant.

Government lawyers appeal to the Supreme Court which rules
that common lands belonged to Spain and Mexico,
therefore they now belong to the U.S.

[This vast acreage is now known as the **Carson** and **Santa Fe
National Forests.**)

Miguel A. Otero II (1902)
Courtesy Museum of NM, #47801

The Sandoval decision is not applied retroactively so past grants,
confirmed mostly to **speculators,** keep their common lands while Hispanic communities lose them.
According to V. Westphall, *"After the 1897 Sandoval decision, the land claims court rejected the
common lands of every community grant that came up for adjudication. ...In so doing it violated
international law"* which permits public domain to belong to the successor state while private
domain is still vested in communities and municipalities just like individuals retain their private
property. Usurping community land to the public domain *"was clearly an injustice to the owners of
these community grants."*

[Westphall ends the chapter by stating emphatically that the *"entire land grant story in N.M. under U.S.
control is surrounded by unsavory overtones,"* that this may be *"an unpalatable truth to Americans who
believe our brand of justice is a benevolent force."*]

LANGUAGE

An article in the *El Independiente* newspaper asserts that Hispanic New Mexicans must learn English well
or they will find themselves *"at the mercy of adventurers"* whose only superior talent consists of
knowing the English language.

SOCIETY

June 2: **Miguel "Gillie" Otero (II),** 38 years old, is the **first native-born New Mexican to be appointed
Governor** under the U.S. government. He is a staunch Republican but antagonistic to Old Guard
Republican T.B. Catron and in time an open, bitter feud breaks out between the two and their
partisans.

[Otero also has the distinction of being the first native governor to write an autobiography, *My Life on the
Frontier*.]

WATER LAW

Acequia statutes, the laws and traditions which had been in force for nearly three centuries in N.M., are codified. Salient statues decree that all rivers and streams belong to the public at large and can't be privatized; acequias are "bodies corporate, with power to sue or to be sued as such." The Mayor-domo (executive officer) and other acequia officers are elected annually and these "commissioners" can assess fatigue work.

[J.E. Holmes observes that *"political and administrative training received in the typical land grant community or irrigation enterprise must have been considerable."*]

1898
LAND GRANT LAW

Hayes v. United States is a landmark case because land grant claimants will henceforth have to prove that granting officials had the authority to award grants of land, and if copies were made of original documents, that the copier had authority to do so. The Government has sole authority over the land grant archives. Experts like **Will Tipton and Henry Flipper** [the latter is the first African-American to graduate from West Point and is said to be a handwriting expert] who have studied the archives and researched Spanish and Mexican law, work for the Government and are supported by all its resources.

Land claimants are usually unable to hire "experts" so they are dependent on the skill and honesty of their lawyers.

"Land grant lawyers are more often concerned with their own interests than with their basic duty to pursue their clients' interests..." while *"...the government pursued every case assiduously, appealing many on highly technical grounds..."*

U.S. Attorney for the Court of Private Land Claims is **M.G. Reynolds,** who has by now *"...acquired an arsenal of... technicalities, together with several procedural advantages, to aid him in the task of defeating land grant claims, which is the primary responsibility of his position. He also has assembled a superb team of experts to assist him in fashioning a defense to each claim..."*

Any adverse decision is appealed by Reynolds, forcing litigants to spend more time, energy, and money, until a "proper" verdict is decided. No such team of experts is provided by the Government for the people claiming their own land, though such a creation would have been in keeping with **responsibilities guaranteed by the Treaty of Guadalupe Hidalgo.** Once again New Mexicans are on their own, this time with the Government of the U.S. as adversary because it refuses to respect treaty stipulations.

EDUCATION LAW

June 21: **Harvey Fergusson** sponsors the **Fergusson Act** which passes both houses of Congress. *"The act probably did more than any other one thing to promote education and prepare the people of New Mexico for statehood."*

LAND GRANT

After confirmation of the **Jacona** land grant by the Court of Private Land Claims a re-survey is ordered and the grant is declared to contain about 7,000 acres (a significant difference from the 1878 survey which had it at about 40,000 acres).

Jacona attorney **Napoleon B. Laughlin** doesn't contest the second survey. Instead he files a lawsuit that will bring him ownership of one-third of the grant or a cash equivalent. **Defendants** are described as "**unknown heirs**" of the original grantee and legal notice is published in an English-language newspaper. **No living people are named as defendants and no one is served in person, especially not the people living on the land that will be taken.**

1908: Laughlin's legal notice goes unanswered so he petitions the court for a default judgment. The court grants his request to partition or sell the land grant. The **Referee** appointed by the court is (probably) **Laughlin's secretary.** The Referee's report contains a list of 170 "heirs" of Ignacio Roybal, but Laughlin is included as a one-third owner of the grant as payment for his confirmation fee and for handling the partition suit. The case is given to Commissioners for **recommendations**, which wind up being **to sell the grant.**

Judge **McFie** orders that Jacona be sold to the highest bidder.

Cosme Herrera discovers that the people's land is being sold from under them, without their knowledge.

PROFILE

José Montaner

JOURNALIST, EDUCATOR, LEGISLATOR

José Montaner (b. 1877 in Barcelona, Spain) arrives in the U.S., lives briefly in Tampa, Florida, where he files naturalization papers then relocates to Trinidad, Colorado, where he publishes the *El Tipográfico* newspaper.

1901: José moves to Taos where he publishes *La Revista de Taos* (which eventually has some 5,000 subscribers). He is very successful in his journalistic career and he also acquires much real estate and business property in Taos.

1904: He is a member of the Republican party and runs for public office, unsuccessfully.

1906: José marries **Mariquita Valdez**, daughter of Santiago Valdez y Martínez (biographer of Padre Martínez) who is brother-in-law to Larkin Read, Benjamin Read's brother.

1912: Montaner is appointed county school superintendent. He builds 40 new schools in Taos County and establishes the first high school.

1924: Montaner is elected to the state senate.

He rallies the villagers, collects $15 from each of them, and buys the Jacona land grant, whereupon he deeds it over to the villagers.

[It is unknown if Cosme Herrera availed himself of a lawyer.]

Villagers establish a three-man commission to administer the grant but as time goes by some villagers forget to pay their share of the taxes and the commission has no funds to pay them.

1919: A deed is executed under which 110 individuals agree to partition common lands among themselves, Each person gets title to about 60 acres of common land and is individually responsible for the taxes on it.

1928: Forty-six villagers (from the 1919 action) have not kept up with their taxes so a suit is filed, by those who are up to date, to declare that those forty-six have forfeited their interest in the Jacona grant and said interests should now pass to the plaintiffs. The court grants their petition and a deed is delivered to them.

1898 (con't.)
POLITICS
Pedro Perea is elected Delegate to Congress, defeating **Harvey Fergusson by** 2,163 votes. *"There was much ignorance at the national capital concerning the native people of New Mexico, and Perea's mild manner, although not attracting as much attention as Catron's or Fergusson's more forceful conduct, help to break down Eastern prejudices against his people"* according to R.W Larson.

LITERATURE
Porfirio Gonzáles writes a novel titled *Historia de un cautivo* (History of a Captive).

(L to R) E. Blumenschein, O.Berninghaus, E. Irving Couse, Bert Phillips Joseph Sharp, (front) Herbert Dunton
Courtesy Museum of NM, #28820

PAINTING

Artists **Ernest Blumenschein** and **Bert Phillips** travel south from Denver on a sketching trip after being told about Taos by Joseph H. Sharp. Tradition has it that a broken wagon wheel causes them to ride to Taos where they are so taken with the people and beauty of the landscape that they decide to settle there. They send out word of their newfound Shangri-La and in time are joined by Joseph Sharp, Oscar Berninghaus, Irving Couse, Walter Ufer, and Victor Higgins, all of whom form the **Taos Society of Artists.** *Los Ocho Pintores*, as they call themselves, create realistic and romanticized paintings of Indians, Hispanics, and the landscape.

1915: Because of their traveling exhibitions, the Taos painters are well known across the USA. During the summer over 100 artists are painting in Taos.

1917: The Taos Society of Artists has a show in New York City.

1922: Exhibitions have works of from 15 to 40 artists.

1927: The Taos Society of Artists is dissolved because its aims have been achieved.

OUTLAWS

William Walters and William Johnson, better known as **Bronco Bill** and **Kid Johnson** by law enforcement officers in Texas and N.M., ride into Belén appearing to be two ordinary cowboys. But their mission is to hold up the train that is carrying a large amount of Wells Fargo money so they hide their horses in the **Pueblitos** area then walk back to the railroad station and board the targeted train as passengers. They force the engineer to stop at Pueblitos, uncouple the money car from the rest of the train which they instruct to leave immediately, then they dynamite the Wells Fargo safe which turns out containing about $25,000. They take the money and ride for their hideout in the Ladrón Mountains southwest of Belén.

Deputy Sheriff **Francisco Vigil** is assigned to recruit a posse and apprehend the Texas desperadoes. But most citizens are unwilling to participate in the dangerous mission. Vigil is joined by his best friend, **Daniel Bustamante**, a crack rifle shot, and the two pick up the trail of the train robbers.

At the Indian community of **Alamo** two Apaches join Vigil and Bustamante. The Apaches want to take the two thieves in the middle of the night while they sleep but Vigil insists he must read the warrant for their arrest before taking them.

The bandits are approached early the next morning and taken completely by surprise. But when Vigil begins to read the warrant they shoot him dead and a brief gun battle breaks out in which Bustamante and one of the Apaches are killed. Bronco Bill is shot but both bandits get away.

[In a shootout with Wells-Fargo agents in Arizona some years later, Kid Johnson is killed and Bronco Bill is seriously wounded then sent to prison.]
Amalia Tafoya of Belén composes a corrido which relates the story of Vigil and Bustamante.

TIMELINE

April 25, 1898: The U.S. declares war against Spain when the Cuban revolt is depicted in hues of "yellow journalism," according to S.E. Morison, and the **U.S.S. Maine** is blown up in Havana harbor. **John Jay** refers to it as *"a splendid little war"* and the U.S. Congress *"hereby disclaims any disposition or intention to exercise sovereignty, jurisdiction, or control over said island except for its pacification and maintains a determination, when it is accomplished, to leave the govern-ment and control of the island to its people."* Popular support is strong and the few who speak out against the *"childish jingoism, the unjust blackening of Spain's noble history, and the needlessness of the war"* are ridiculed. Spanish authorities state they will meet all demands in order to avoid a useless war.

May: **Commodore Dewey** steams into Manila Bay with the Pacific squadron and destroys the Spanish fleet. Filipino leader **Emilio Aguinaldo** is invited to return from exile by Dewey. June: Some 15,000 Americans in the expeditionary force engage some 1,700 Spanish defenders on the battlefields of El Caney and San Juan. The war for Cuba is over within 10 weeks or so.

August: Filipinos organize a republic but Dewey reports he doesn't think the new government can keep order. Some American leaders believe a base should be obtained for Far East opera-tions and **President McKinley** decides to take the Islands *"and educate the Filipinos and uplift, civilize, and Christianize them..."* while he states emphatically that imperialism isn't America's intent.

February 4, 1899: The Filipinos under **Aguinaldo** demand control of their own government, self determination being the reason the Spanish had been thrown out, but the military is on orders not to allow it. On the grounds that Filipinos "aren't ready" to govern themselves, Americans take over all government authority. What is referred to in American history as the **Philippine Insurrection** breaks out and the bloody war lasts for two years and takes several hundred lives before the Filipino freedom fighters are defeated by American forces. In ceremonies ending the war, which was begun to free the Philippines from "Spanish bondage" and which lasted some two years longer than the war against Spain, **General Arthur MacArthur** states: *"We are planting the idea of personal liberty in the Orient. Wherever the American flag waves, that idea lives...The planting of liberty—not money—is what we seek."*

ROUGH RIDERS

May 6-7: The entire First New Mexico Cavalry, 14 officers and 342 enlisted men, is mustered into service for the Spanish-American War. The N.M. unit becomes part of the First U.S. Volunteer Cavalry Regiment, led by Colonels Wood and Roosevelt, popularly referred to as the Rough Riders, and wins acclaim at the battles of El Caney and San Juan Hill. George W. Armijo is selected as aide to Colonel Roosevelt.

SANTA FE STYLE ARCHITECTURE

"Anglo business leaders" want to modernize so they have Santa Fe platted as a conventional American city They want to build with red brick, Corinthian columns, false fronts, etc. Old adobe business buildings are razed and plans are finalized to tear down historic buildings on the Plaza, including the Palace of the Governors. **Carlos Vierra**, one of the founders of the Santa Fe art colony, speaks up against demolishing old-style, historic buildings.He leads the movement to preserve existing structures and urges that new ones reflect the historic style.

1909: Vierra is selected to direct the restoration of the Palace of the Governors as the Museum of New Mexico. Following guidelines established through the centuries of Hispanic N.M., the Museum becomes the model for what is called the **Santa Fe Style** of architecture. The cause for architectural restoration is substantially advanced. Along with artists like Edgar Spier Cameron, Vierra and others develop the theme of Santa Fe as the "City Different," asking that a city ordinance require all new buildings to maintain the historic style of architecture. Cameron writes: "The restoration of the charm ... that existed...in simple adobe cottages with their projecting vigas and portal will attract more people to Santa Fe than a pretentious brick box surmounted by the most elaborate galvanized iron cornice that money can buy."

Guarding Santa Fe's architectural integrity becomes a cause célèbre. A city ordinance restricts building to no more than three stories in order to protect the view in all directions. The local press supports the efforts of Carlos Vierra and native Hispanic architecture is considered almost an art form. John Gaw Meem becomes the premier architect for the Santa Fe Style.

1899

TIMELINE

1899: The *Atlantic Monthly* publishes an article titled *THE GREASER* in which the writer states the American domination of New Mexico is in the railroad, barbed-wire fences, and public schools. *"And the greaser is passing. It is now quite in order to write his obituary."* The author states emphatically that Anglo Americans are superior to Mexicans because the former are individualistic and heterogeneous while the latter *"are all alike,"* especially in their ignorance, poverty, backwardness, and lack of enterprise.

SOCIETY

Conrad Hilton, almost twelve years of age, attends the Goss Military Institute in Albuquerque. The following year he attends the New Mexico Military Institute in Roswell and then St. Michael's College in Santa Fe.

ROUGH RIDER REUNION

June: The first reunion of the Rough Riders is held in Las Vegas. The renowned bronc rider José González provides a rodeo exhibition for the Rough Riders. Theodore Roosevelt, now Governor of New York, promises to support New Mexico statehood if that is what people want.

[Roosevelt becomes President when McKinley is assassinated.]

1900

TIMELINE

1900: The buffalo (bison), once estimated to number anywhere from 50,000,000 to 125,000,000, are nearly extinct in the USA because hidemen have been allowed to slaughter the animals in

order to market their hides and as a way to destroy the Plains Indians. Buffalo are now estimated to number under 1,000 in the USA.

RELIGIOUS

There are 47 Catholic clergymen in N.M.; three reside in Pueblo villages.

CENSUS

Census figures state that N.M. has 8,488 Pueblo Indians living in 19 villages and at three schools: St. Catherine,
Indian Industrial, Albuquerque Indian.

The Territory has a population of 195,000, 67% of which a population of 195,000, sixty-seven percent of which
are Hispanic surnamed. Some 37,000 residents were born in other states. Texans settle in the southeast
corner and in time the area is referred to as "Little Texas."

NINTH CAVALRY

The last regiment of the Ninth Cavalry, the famous "Buffalo Soldiers" stationed at Fort Wingate, leaves N.M.

WEAVING

Chimayó blankets appear on the market because various curio dealers in and around Santa Fe want a moder-
ately priced article for tourist consumption. These blankets, pillowtops, and narrow runners are made
in the village of Chimayó and production is somewhat of a revival in Hispanic weaving.

Chimayó decorative design is unique, differing greatly from that used before in Río Grande blanketry.

["Altogether it begins to look as if this peculiar style must have sprung almost fully developed from the mind
of someone skilled in the adaptation of design, rather than having been the result of any orderly evolutionary
process" according to H.Y. Mera.]

CARPENTRY

Alejandro Gallegos of Peñasco is among the carpenters producing New Mexican furniture. Two new furniture
forms have developed by this time: the Taos-style bed and the combination chest-cupboard, an
amalgamation of the trastero and the harinero. But the railroad is bringing in factory-made furniture
and Ilfeld and Co. of Las Vegas becomes New Mexico's largest furniture wholesaler. The unique but
more expensive handcrafted New Mexican styles wane.

NEWSPAPERS

There are Spanish-language newspapers in every important town along the Río Grande from Trinidad in
Colorado to El Paso, Texas. The centers of journalistic production are Las Cruces, Albuquerque, Santa
Fe, and Las Vegas. Exchanges of articles and other writings are common and even reach into Mexico
and the rest of Latin America.

SOCIETY

The **Hispano "homeland"** (area settled and developed by N.M. Hispanics) is spread over five states in an area
about the size of Utah.

Santa Fe is the demographic center of the homeland and the largest Hispano community.

The interior half of the homeland (an area the size of Tennessee) is from 90% to 97% Hispano. "Rarely in America has so large an area had such uniformly high percentages so recently....few parts of America would have made more ideal states, were geopolitical boundaries to have been redrawn."

Racial intermixing between N.M. Hispanics and Native Americans is "…almost nonexistent."

Labor-intensive farming, like sugar beets in Colorado and Texas, cause Mexicans (from Mexico) to be recruited for work in the fields. Mexicans compete with New Mexicans for jobs and this brings them into conflict. Mexicans refer to New Mexicans as "pochos" (bleached, faded). New Mexicans refer to Mexicans as "surumatos" or "surumato manito," "southerners."

Women have a median age of 19 and 86% of all females live in rural communities according to R. Kern. Eighty-eight percent of women between 25 and 29 have been married. Rates for birth and death are higher than nationally so the average New Mexican female is rural, young, married with several children, and likely to see some of them die in infancy.

Santa Fe begins to have two distinguishable areas: the Hispano periphery and the city itself, 83.9% of the total population, which is ethnically diverse, though "Anglo" residences are perceptively clustered.

Las Vegas is in reality two communities separated by the Gallinas River: Old Las Vegas is 82.9% Hispanic and plaza-centered with 502 "Anglos" living in various residential clusters, the largest of which is around the plaza; East Las Vegas is 82.6% "Anglo" and railroad-centered with 622 Hispanics clustered "…mostly in one large segregated quarter which was clearly the creation of Anglo discrimination."

Albuquerque has heavily Hispano Old Town; to the east is depot-centered, heavily "Anglo" new town. Old Town (with 1, 191 people, 927 of whom are Hispanic) is characterized as congenial, mildly clustered, residentially integrated. New Albuquerque (with 6,238 people, 1,097 of whom are Hispanic) "…where Anglo intolerance and discrimination was open and overt," Hispanos and Mexican Americans live in strongly clustered patterns.

N.M. in 1900 is still a land of small villages containing overwhelmingly Hispanic populations. Santa Fe, Las Vegas, and Albuquerque are the largest population centers, the major areas of Hispano-Anglo inter-action, the seats of banking and commerce. These cities grow as urbanization begins to take place [especially noticeable after 1940.]

The Hispanic cultural impress of N.M. is identifiably distinctive:

Hispano villages, of which people are very proud as their patria chica, and dispersed ranchsteads dot the map. Farming lands described as "long-lots" are used to insure frontage to water sources. While adobe is the most common building material, Hispanos also build with logs. Hornos, outdoor ovens associ-ated with wheat culture, are in common use. Catholicism fosters churches, chapels, religious items, and celebrations, as well as myriad of place names. Accustomed to dealing with different kinds of people, Hispanos in general don't tend toward intolerance or segregation by race or ethnicity. Span-ish is an acceptable mode of communication.

Acculturation to U.S. society begins to accelerate for New Mexico's Hispanics and Native Americans after 1900. Brick begins to replace adobe for building. The use of Spanish is targeted as "unpopular" and the New Mexican newspaper is printed in English only as a remedy to the "evil" of teaching children in Spanish.

A large number of Mexican-born Hispanics are living in (the Mesilla Valley) Las Cruces, Doña Ana, Mesilla.

1900-1920
RELIGIOUS CRIMES

"Anglo" missionaries and Bureau of Indian Affairs officials cause the passage of a Religious Crimes Code in order to target for eradication "un-American" Indian customs and practices because investigators sent to study Indian life report immoral and anti-Christian practices according to L.R. Rudnick. The Code enables officials to prohibit ceremonial practices and punish tribal leaders or members who will not accept Christian doctrine and practice. Boarding schools are deliberately built far from tribal lands, children can be forcibly placed in them, with or without parental consent, because the goal is to separate them from tribal practices.

1900-1942
ART COLONIES

The Santa Fe and Taos art colonies are operating during this period. They attract "more creative folk ... than any other area in the U.S." according to A.M. Gibson. There were many enticements like the low cost of living but the most important were the natural, ethnic, and cultural environments. Particular attention is paid to the Vanishing American and artists want to preserve and conserve him. Many artists feel "at home" in Taos and Santa Fe, accepted by the community instead of being looked on as pariahs or refugees from Greenwich Village or the left Bank (sometimes characterized by deviant dress, promiscuous sex, eccentric personal habits, and vile language along with political radicalism).

1902: Fredric Remington spends most of the year painting in Taos, of which he writes: "Americans have gashed this country so horribly...I like to see a place which they have overlooked, some place before they arrive with their heavy-handed God of Progress."

1904: Carlos Vierra arrives in Santa Fe to recover from tuberculosis and becomes enamored of adobe architecture. He stays for the rest of his life and becomes a passionate advocate for preserving and restoring New Mexico's adobe buildings. Vierra, soon referred to as the "scenic architect," and Kenneth M. Chapman begin the Santa Fe art colony. In a short time they are joined by Gerald Cassidy, Sheldon Parsons, Paul Burlin, Olive Rush, Gustave Baumann, William P Henderson, and Robert Henri.

1907: Edgar L. Hewett moves to Santa Fe as director of the Museum of New Mexico (housed in the Governor's Palace) and School of American Archaeology (later the School of American Research) and serves until 1946. The museum includes laboratories for archaeologists and anthropologists but also studios for painters, sculptors, designers, and architects. He is greatly aided by Frank Springer who often provides cash advances for artists, takes painting or other art works as payment then donates the works to the Museum's permanent collections.

1908: Paul A.E Walter buys the *Santa Fe New Mexican*.

1913: Paul Walter founds *El Palacio*, the Museum of New Mexico magazine which achieves national circulation.

1914: N.M. has an exposition building in the Pacific Exposition being held in San Diego. Hewett, Springer, Vierra, and Jerry Nussbaum design the building according to N.M. mission architecture and the Santa Fe Style is publicized for the first time. N.M. receives the first-place award for originality and is rated the most popular of state exhibits.

New Mexican leaders in all walks of life now realize that the state's histories, cultures, arts, crafts, etc., are potentially profitable resources for the tourist business. Springer and Hewett receive support for Museum expansion in the form of the St. Francis Auditorium (so named to commemorate the martyrdom of the Franciscan missionaries in N.M.).

Ada and Carlos Vierra, 1932
Courtesy Museum of NM, #59762

1915: The Santa Fe Women's Club and the State Federation of Women's Clubs campaign for more exposure to art and literature.

1917: The St. Francis Auditorium is opened to the public and invites all artists to participate by exhibiting works of art.

1920: The Santa Fe Art Club is organized to sponsor exhibits throughout the country. Taos and Santa Fe are flourishing artistic communities, recognized nationally and internationally. Artists are often permanent residents or they own a second home in the community. Most have a stable family life rather than living permissive, reckless lifestyles. They become involved in civic and ethnic causes. Ernest L. Blumenschein is a leader in Taos, John Sloan in Santa Fe.

Artists socialize and the most important events are the Society of Taos Artists costume ball. In Santa Fe it is the Easter Week Artists' Ball. The more affluent artists regularly entertain in their homes.

In Santa Fe the most popular concentration of artist homes and studios is on Canyon Road then Camino del Monte Sol.
William R. Henderson and other artists create furniture inspired by the distinctive Hispanic New Mexican style of couches, chests, beds, tables, chairs, etc.
The Museum of New Mexico has become the patron agency for artists in Taos and Santa Fe, an intellectual guardian for the Southwest.

The Santa Fe Railway Co. promotes tourism across the Southwest with great emphasis on northern N.M. It purchases artistic works for display in waiting rooms and restaurants along the line. This causes an ideological split between commercial painters and those who create serious art. Besides those painters who live permanently in the area, from 100 to more than 150 arrive to work during the painting season.

New arrivals are still influenced by the land and its native people but new elements are introduced from the rest of the country and the world.

1923: The Harwood Foundation is the first gallery in Taos, founded by Elizabeth Harwood in honor of her husband Bert, upon his death.
The Society of New Mexico Painters is formed.

1925: Alice Corbin Henderson begins entertaining Santa Fe and Taos poets and other writers in her home which in time is called the Poets Roundup.

1928: The Santa Fe Summer School of Painting is founded.

1930: Taos is regarded as the most exploratory of American art colonies. The Taos Field School of Art is founded.
The Río Grande Painters (committed to Regionalism) is formed.

1931: The Santa Fe School of Music is founded.

1932: The Taos School of Fine Arts (art, dance, music, drama) is founded by Emil Bisttram.

The Society of Independent Artists is formed as an agency to barter members' work for food, shelter, and services.
1933: The Great Depression rages throughout the country and because of its large aesthetic community the N.M. New Deal is allocated five times the amount of funds for artist subsidy in proportion to population.

The Taos Guild and the Santa Fe Spanish Colonial Arts Society also display wood sculpture, colchas, blankets and other weavings, tin work, furniture, etc., produced by New Mexican Hispanics but they are "only momentarily recognized or have become virtually anonymous."
Writers' Editions is founded as a local and regional publishing outlet. (By 1942 it has published seventeen books.) Roberta Roby's Villagrá Bookshop in Santa Fe is the best known author's outlet in northern N.M.
1934: The Taos Little Theater is formed.

1935: Eidolon, a cooperative school for dance and music, is founded in Santa Fe.

1938: Raymond Jonson and Emil Bisttram found the Transcendental Painting Group in Taos in order "to express the spirit of form rather than form itself" and to "create forms that were cosmic, universal, and time-less."

The Arsuna School for the Arts is founded in Santa Fe.

1942: John Winchester and Scott S. Edmonds found the Conceptualism School at Taos.

1901
EDUCATION INEQUITIES
Territorial Superintendent of Public instruction **J. Francisco Chaves** reports to the Governor that a glaring inadequacy exists in school facilities for rural New Mexicans. Funding for the lower grades and primary schools is being neglected in favor of higher educational institutions where one finds more youth from Texas, Mexico, Arizona, California, "while our own New Mexican children are yet poorly served in the lower grade schools and therefore unable to qualify for admission to the higher institutions" as reported by G.I. Sánchez. Chaves contrasts what the federal government spends for Puerto Rico, Cuba, and the Philippines with the situation in N.M. where it is necessary to procure more public land "for so worthy a purpose as popular education of the masses of our people, so cruelly neglected by the parent government since as long ago as 1850."

November 2, 1901: **Eusebio Chacón** writes in *La Voz del Pueblo:* The government has done nothing to encourage education for New Mexicans. The few seats of learning that we have are what we created, which we paid for, and maintain at our own cost. No federal money is being expended for education in New Mexico while the feds talk about educating Cubans, Puerto Ricans, and Filipinos.

SOCIETY
Blackdom is founded, 16 miles south of Roswell, by **Francis Boyer**, "a college-educated descendent of black slaves who had walked all the way from Georgia to the Pecos Valley in 1896." Boyer's goal is to establish an economically independent farming community of black people from the South. After working for several years he obtains a loan with which to drill an artesian well and in time some 25 families, about 300 people, inhabit the settlement. But the new families need artesian wells and bankers won't loan them any money. Determined to succeed, the families work at dryland wheat farming while they haul water for domestic use, gardens, fruit trees, and stock. Local public schools refuse to admit their children so they build a community meeting house that serves as church and school.

When Boyer is unable to meet a payment on his loan the bank forecloses and the farm is lost. Laws are passed to restrict the drilling of wells and in 1916 the apple crop is nearly destroyed by worm infestation.

People begin leaving Blackdom (some of them moving to Roswell) and by the end of the 1920s it is only an historical memory.

CAVERNS
The **Carlsbad Caverns** are discovered by a cowboy named **Jim White** when he sees a large number of bats flying out of the caverns.

1930: The Caverns are made part of the National Park system.

1902
STATEHOOD

W.S. Knox of Massachusetts introduces an **Omnibus Bill** which would grant statehood to New Mexico, Arizona, and Oklahoma. **B.S. Rodey** is a force working for N.M. statehood.

Senator **Albert J. Beveridge** (R.-Indiana) opposes statehood, except for Oklahoma, because New Mexico's insufficient population is Spanish, they know little English, illiteracy is high, and the land too arid. Beveridge believes the Southwest to be a *"backward area...not equal in intellect, resources or population to the other states in the Union"* because its people are *"stifled"* by their Indian and Spanish heritage, therefore not *"sufficiently American in their habits and customs."*

[Senator Beveridge has been described as *"wrong for all the right reasons"* by W.A. Beck. He also relates that an investigation committee brought back the story that a county superintendent of schools *"expressed amazement"* when he was told that *"Christopher Columbus was dead."*]

Senator **Matthew S. Quay** (R. Penn.) attacks Beveridge's argument and spearheads passage of the statehood bill, presenting a number of arguments: the thousands and thousands of new immigrants to America are permitted in without an English-language requirement; New Mexico's population is larger than that of some other territories at the time of admission; no people were more loyal during the Civil War than New Mexicans...

March 4, 1903: The statehood bill is defeated by use of parliamentary maneuvers.

SOCIETY

Tenos Tabet and his wife, both born in Syria, open a general store in Manzano.

EDUCATION

Felipe Chávez founds a private school for girls (around this time). He establishes a $20,000 trust fund in his will to maintain the "Felipe Chávez School" and pay a teacher.

1903
T I M E L I N E

"The Great Train Robbery," the first western ever filmed, is produced by Thomas Edison.

ORGANIZATION

Nestor Montoya (1862-1923) is elected president of *La Prensa Asociada Hispano-Americana.*

NEWSPAPERS

1890: Nestor Montoya severs his partnership with Enrique H. Salazar and their *La Voz del Pueblo* newspaper.

1901: He takes over *El Nuevo Mundo*, an Albuquerque newspaper. He merges it with *La Bandera Americana,* which he controls until his death, and establishes the American Flag Publishing Company which has prominent leaders of the Republican party in Sandoval, Bernalillo, and Valencia counties on its board of directors.

1903: *La Bandera Americana* includes many cultural items as well as the writings of local literati like Eleuterio Baca, Felipe M. Chacón, etc., and of internationally famous writers like Rubén Dario, Ignacio Altamirano, etc.

1904
RAILROAD
Felipe Chávez, a large stockholder of the AT&SF railroad, and **John Becker** learn that a line will be laid from Amarillo to N.M., tentatively planned through Tijeras Canyon and Albuquerque. With Chávez in the background, which is the way El Millonario worked, Becker offers free land to the railroad if it will build to Belén. He buys up all land needed and donates it to the AT&SF after Chávez convinces the railroad people to lay track into Belén, which is done by 1905, making Belén the "Hub City" of N.M. with its roundhouse, shops, and railroad yards.

LAND GRANT
Heirs of the Cañon de San Diego Grant file a suit in District Court for title to their land grant. The suit is successful, the court decreeing that 88,000 acres belong to the heirs. The lawyer who presents the case is awarded ownership of 44,000 acres for his fee by the judge, according to O.E. Leonard, and a commission of three is appointed to decide how best to divide the remaining acreage, the recommendation later being that it be sold and the money divided equally.

1908: The land grant is sold at public auction for 45 cents per acre, netting approximately $20,000 which is divided among 200 legal heirs.

BANK ROBBERY
January 15: The National Bank of Belén is robbed at gunpoint by two men who then flee toward the Ladrón Mountains. A posse of some 50 men quickly gets on their trail.

COURT OF PRIVATE LAND CLAIMS
June 30: The Court of Private Land Claims ceases by law. During its tenure it has confirmed **six percent (6%)** of the acreage brought before it for adjudication in the N.M. district.

[In the contemporary period of avid tourist interest for things historical, the Museum of International Folk Art in Santa Fe, a unit of the Museum of New Mexico, displays an historical panel stating that most New Mexicans were allowed to keep their lands.]

[V. Westphall points out that up to June 30, 1904, officials had granted 33,440,482 acres of private land claims in the U.S. while in N.M. a total of 90 claims were confirmed for 2,051,625 acres and 33,239,404 acres were rejected. The Court has gone on record as claiming that the stringent congressional act left it no alternative but the only element in the act that wasn't open to interpretation was that all claims would be limited to 11 square leagues. Another stipulation, requiring that all grant titles must be "lawfully and regularly derived from the Government of Spain or Mexico," was not easily subject to discretionary interpretation, though one could argue as to what was "lawful and regular for that time and place." However, most other details, like if the granting document has been lost, become illegible, or copied but there is an original settlement on the grant, permitted discretionary powers in rendering decisions and the justices often held wide differences of opinion, proving that the congressional act was subject to their interpretation.

Justice Stone "had much foreknowledge of the subject" and was the most sympathetic toward confirmation, followed by Justice Sluss. Chief justice Reed was often the swing vote, with Justices Fuller and Murray being the least sympathetic to claimants.

But the Court as a whole viewed its task as "to defeat claims." It ruled, as did the Supreme Court, that treaty obligations were the domain of the "political department" of the American government, not the judiciary. If Congress chose to ignore treaty obligations then courts were powerless to enforce them. Treaties and international law were thus invalid if contrary to an act of Congress. **The result was the ignobility of two branches of a powerful government flouting the law...**" because the Constitution of the U.S. states in Article III, Section 1: The judicial Power of the United States, Shall be vested in one Supreme Court ... Section 2: The judicial Power shall extend to all Cases, in Law and Equity, arising under this Constitution, the Laws of the United States, and Treaties made, or which shall be made, under their Authority...]

ASSASSINATION

November 26: **J. Francisco Chávez** is murdered at Pino's Well (Torrance County). The distinguished rancher-soldier-lawyer-statesman was dining with friends when an unknown assassin shot him through a window, killing him instantly.

[The murder is said to have been politically motivated, the cowardly deed performed by a paid assassin. Chávez had been named to the post of Territorial Historian and at the time of his death was writing the history of N.M.]

PROFILE

J. Francisco Chávez

FATHER OF THE STATEIHOOD MOVEMENT

Col. J. Francisco Chaves
Courtesy Museum of NM, #146695

During his lifetime J. Francisco Chávez is regarded as a leader with strong convictions and indomitable courage. He combats political enemies and fights a notorious band of cutthroat livestock rustlers operating in the Río Abajo, some of whom he sends to jail. President Lincoln makes him a Lieutenant Colonel in the Army and later he represents Valencia County in the Legislature for 14 terms, is elected Delegate to Congress, serves as District Attorney for the Second Judicial District.

Chaves County is named in his honor.
A Republican, Chávez became involved in a bitter struggle with the Oteros and Lunas for leadership of the party.

[Father Railliere wrote in his diary: *The political fight between Col. Chávez and the Oteros worsens every day. I'm at the point that I don't even want to hear their confessions.*]
The feuding finally causes the creation of Torrance County so that each faction can have its own sphere of influence.

Chávez was an adamant advocate for statehood and served as President of the Constitutional Convention in 1889 and regarded by many as the "Father of the statehood Movement."

1905
TOURISM
The Mission-style **Alvarado Hotel** is completed in Albuquerque by the Fred Harvey Company. It becomes a
 famous "jewel" of the Fred Harvey system.

SOCIETY
Santero **Juan Miguel Herrera** dies.

George W. Armijo (grandson of Colonel J. Francisco Chávez) begins his political career when he is elected to the post of Probate Clerk for Santa Fe county. He becomes well known for his ability in extemporaneous speaking, in Spanish and English, and in succeeding years he is Chief Clerk for the House, school board member, and alderman; Speaker of the House (1939-1940), state senator from Santa Fe (1941-1944) and Corporation Commissioner until his death in 1947.

George W. Armijo
Courtesy Museum of NM,
#146679

  Felipe *El Millionario* **Chávez** dies.

SHEEP BUSINESS

Frank Bond, sheepman from Río Arriba County, begins operations in the Cuba (Espíritu Santo Grant) area. He deals in wool, hides, and lambs.

[Sheep have been the mainstay for New Mexican commerce through three centuries. C.F.Lummis described sheep husbandry as making life itself possible in N.M. Except for the excellent but short work by J.O. Baxter the subject hasn't been studied with enough depth or at least it hasn't been published in a form to get out among masses of students or readers.]

PROFILE

Felipe Chávez

THE MILLIONAIRE

1834: Felipe Chávez is born to José María Chávez and Manuela Armijo Chávez. He is educated at the Conciliar Seminary of Guadalajara, Mexico, where he receives awards for his academic talents.

1852: Felipe completes his education and returns to help his father in the management of the family's commercial operations. He works hard, displays much common sense, and is meticulous in his record keeping.

1856: Chávez is now in charge of the entire family business. He expands his business network but relies to a great extent on the Spanish firm of Peter Harmony and Nephews located in New York City.

The May invoice for this year reveals that Chávez bought 220 sacks of sugar, 71 barrels of whiskey, one of brandy, some cognac, claret, champagne, oysters, sardines, almonds, sacks of coffee, boxes of candles, soap, 3,000 cigars, etc., for a total of 64,298 pounds of freight.

June, 1858: Chávez makes purchases from Glasgow Brothers in St. Louis in association with Manuel Antonio Otero.

October, 30: José María Chávez dies. Felipe is now responsible for his mother, his sister Bárbara, and several other relatives. He is serious about his familial responsibilities. Mayordomo Atanacio Montoya is in St. Louis buying merchandise for Chávez from various wholesalers.

1859: Felipe becomes known for his massive purchases. One invoice lists the purchase of 80,000 yards of cloth, 1,092 pairs of boots, 540 pairs of shoes, 585 pairs of pants. The following year the March invoice enumerates 36 pages of items, including 200,000 yards of cloth.

1860: Mayordomo Antonio Robles is in New York buying merchandise for Chávez.

Felipe also loans money to family members and various friends, usually charging interest, though family members seldom pay it.
Chávez and other New Mexican merchants, especially those from the Río Abajo, cooperate with each other in order to promote business for everyone. Formal and informal arrangements are common. For example, Felipe works with the Delgado brothers, Simón and Felipe, for decades. 1870s: Chávez' shipments of wool are significant (192,668 pounds in 1878). He invests in U.S. government bonds.

1880s: Felipe Chávez believes in diversification. He owns about 500,000 sheep, is involved in mining activities, works with merchants in St. Louis, New York, Guadalajara, Zacatecas, Durango, Chihuahua, Manchester and Liverpool in England, and Canada, owns real estate in New York City, acts as banker, wholesaler, retailer. He has an agent on the Stock Exchange.

STATEHOOD
December 5: President Roosevelt calls for the admission of N.M. and Arizona as one state (and Oklahoma and Indian Territory as one). Residents of N.M. and of Arizona have never petitioned for jointure. (See **1906**.)

1906-1907
Herbert Hagerman is Governor.

1906
ARCHITECTURE
Five buildings on the University of New Mexico campus are in the Pueblo Mission style of architecture.

POLITICS
The period is one of prosperity and Old Guard Republicans control politics through men of vested interests like Holm Bursum and Solomón Luna (representing the livestock industry); H.L. Waldo and WA. Hawkins (railroads); Charles and Frank Springer (coal mining); Charles Spiess (mining); Albert B. Fall; etc.

Flamboyant Democrat Albert Bacon Fall turns Republican, explaining: "I know when to change horses."

STATEHOOD

Jointure debate rages in Congress. "New Mexico's predominantly Spanish-speaking population and Arizona's Anglo majority seem to many an incompatible combination…"

The *Pittsburgh Times* is quoted in the *El Paso Times* as referring "to the citizens of New Mexico as a mongrel population too ignorant and lazy to assume the privileges of full citizenship…"

July 19: An editorial in the Las Vegas *El Independiente* warns New Mexicans that they are presently being written out of the Southwestern historical record and that a vote for jointure will only speed up the process.

November 6: New Mexicans vote for jointure, Arizonans reject it, thus ending the movement forever. (See 1910.)

Solomón Luna
Courtesy Museum of NM, #7608

BLUE LAKE

President Theodore Roosevelt places the Taos Pueblo Blue Lake area (30,000 acres) under "protective custody" in an "…unfortunate but necessary sacrifice to progress…" and henceforth it will be regulated by the newly created U.S. Forest Service (an agency of the Department of Agriculture).

The Forest Service begins to interfere with the ancient Taos' religious observances.

June 26, 1908: Blue Lake is made a part of the Carson National Forest by executive order and therefore part of the public domain.

1912: Taos asks the Secretary of the Interior to declare Blue Lake an executive order reservation. The Secretary refuses.

1916: The 1912 petition is submitted again, and again rejected.

1919: There is so much encroachment on Taos land that intruders have to be forcibly ejected.

1928: Blue Lake is withdrawn from mineral entry, helping to preserve the terrain and stop further pollution of the Río Pueblo watershed. Non-Indians may acquire a permit for sightseeing, camping, fishing, etc., and ranchers may get a 10-year permit for grazing stock. Taos Pueblo may use Blue Lake for religious ceremonies for three days in August provided that permission is obtained from the Forest Service ten days in advance of actual use.

195 1: Taos Pueblo files with the Indians Claims Commission for the loss of Blue Lake. The Commission rules that Taos is entitled to compensation.

Taos refuses compensation, stating that Blue Lake must be returned. Senator Anderson of N.M. introduces a bill that will give Taos use of some of the land but which will also break it into parcels to be used for various purposes, including logging.

Senators Fred Harris of Oklahoma and Robert Griffin of Michigan amend the Anderson bill into the Harris-Griffin Bill and it passes.

November, 1970: President Richard Nixon signs it, returning Blue Lake to the Taos people after a fight of 64 years.

RAILROAD
The Eastern Railway is completed to Sunnyside, which continues to grow under the name of Fort Sumner.

SOCIETY
September 15: **Mateo Aragón** is born at Santo Domingo Pueblo.

October 6: **George I. Sánchez** is born (in Barelas) in Albuquerque.

1907
J.W. Raynolds is interim Governor.

WOMEN & LAW
The Legislature enacts a statute that abolishes community property rights that have been in force in N.M. for centuries under Spanish and Mexican laws and traditions. **In keeping with American jurisprudence, now only the husband can dispose of property and a woman's property prior to marriage can't be kept separate from that of her husband.** Women can no longer make a will or designate heirs for their property.

RAILROAD
Three pairs of transcontinental trains operate through N.M. and by the 1920s there are six. Famous steam trains on the Santa Fe include The Chief, the California Limited, and the Grand Canyon Limited. All pause in Albuquerque to allow tourists to shop.

1930s: The Super Chief is the first "name" train to be diesel powered.

1938: The Super Chief with its streamlined locomotive of silver, yellow and red, and El Capitán are now diesel powered as they operate through N.M.

1941: Freight trains are now diesel powered.

1946: The number of main line trains operating on the Santa Fe is at its greatest peak.

1970: The Santa Fe operates only three transcontinental trains: the combined Super Chief and El Capitán, Number 23, and Number 24.

May 1, 1971: Amtrak takes over Santa Fe passenger service and there is now only one transcontinental train, the Super Chief-El Capitán, Numbers 17 and 18, and its name is changed to the Southwest Limited and then, after Superliners cars are introduced, it is known as the Southwest Chief (in April, 1985).

T I M E L I N E

November 16, 1907: **Oklahoma becomes the 46th State in the Union.**

1907-1910

George Curry is Governor.

1908
KILLING
Pat Garrett and a friend named Carl Adamson are traveling by horse and buggy to Las Cruces,

They stop and Garrett leaves the buggy for a moment when one Jesse Wayne Brazel appears and begins to harangue Garrett violently. Shots ring out and Pat Garrett dies from a bullet in the back and another to the back of his head. (In a later court trial Brazel was acquitted of murder on the grounds of self-defense. It has been alleged that "supporters of Oliver Lee" hired Brazel to retaliate for Garrett's actions as sheriff.)

SOCIETY
June 25: Nina Otero marries First Lieutenant Rawson Warren.

[According to C. Whaley, "Changing her name from Otero to Warren offered advantages for Nina because prejudices had developed in New Mexico toward people with Hispanic surnames, particularly after the bitter war with Mexico in 1836 [sic]." The marriage ends within a short time because Otero discovers Warren has a common law wife and two children in the Philippines. Divorce not being permitted by her religion or culture, henceforth she refers to herself as a widow.]

1909
ARCHITECTURE
The Mission-style Los Chávez Hotel is completed in Vaughn by the Fred Harvey Company.

PRESERVATION
Dr. Edgar Lee Hewett, director of the Santa Fe Archaeological and Historical Society, persuades the Archaeological Institute of America to locate its School of American Research in Santa Fe. He also persuades the Legislature to give the Palace of the Governors to the Institute in order to house the new Museum of New Mexico. Hewett works for historical and cultural preservation. The Palace of the Governors is restored along Hispanic styles and he spearheads a movement to require all Santa Fe architecture to reflect "Spanish-Pueblo" styles. Sylvanus G. Morley, Kenneth Chapman, Carlos Vierra assist Hewett in his efforts, which are referred to as the "Santa Fe Style."

1909-1913
The Museum of New Mexico is founded and the Palace of the Governors is restored. Restoration is headed by archaeologist Jesse Nussbaum. The Fine Arts Museum is begun (in 1909).

1910
ARCHITECTURE
The El Ortiz Hotel at Lamy is the first built in the Spanish Pueblo style.

NEWSPAPERS
Saturnino Baca begins Belén's first successful newspaper, the *Hispano Americano*, written in Spanish, then follows it up with the *Belén News*, in English.
1925: The two newspapers merge into a bilingual newspaper.

EDUCATION
After teaching at the University of New Mexico for some years, **Aurelio Espinosa** accepts a position at Stanford University, where he teaches until his retirement in 1947. He becomes an acknowledged authority on New Mexican Spanish and folklore.

STATEHOOD
January 14: Representative Hamilton introduces an act [referred to as the Hamilton Bill] to enable N.M. and Arizona to form separate governments and become states "on equal footing with other States."

Senator Beveridge inserts an amendment that requires close federal government supervision of any proposed constitution. This has never been done with any other state, contradicting the enabling act which calls for New Mexico's entry into the union "on an equal footing with the other states." State land allotment is reduced (also a departure from procedures used with other states).

Senate restrictions have to do with language: "Whereas the House Bill permitted the teaching of languages other than English, the Senate version provided that schools should be conducted in English and struck out the provision 'that nothing in this act shall preclude the teaching of other languages in said public schools.' The Senate version requires state legislators as well as state officers to read, write, and understand the English language sufficiently well enough to conduct the duties of office without aid of an interpreter.

June 20: President Taft signs the (Hamilton Bill) Enabling Act of 19 10: New Mexicans can now form a government.
Despite the fact that the territorial legislature has never prescribed a literacy or language requirement for the right to vote or hold office, the Congress stipulates in the Enabling Act:

"That said state shall never enact any law restricting or abridging the right of suffrage on account of race, color, or previous condition of servitude, and that ability to read, write, speak, and understand the English language sufficiently well to conduct the duties of the office without the aid of an interpreter shall be a necessary qualification for all state officers and members of the legislature."

September: One-hundred Delegates are elected to the Constitutional Convention. There are 71 Republicans and 29 Democrats chosen to write a constitution.
Categories in the 100 include: 32 attorneys, 20 stockmen, 14 merchants, 7 farmers, 6 small businessmen 4 saloonkeepers, 3 bankers, 3 physicians, 3 editors, 3 territorial officers, 2 county officers, 1 college

president, 1 mining man, 1 lumber man.

Spanish-speaking delegates (32) are a sizable part of the Convention and the New York Sun remarks the
proceedings will resemble "...some bullfight in a Mexican village."

Spanish-speaking delegates provide for laws, and those speaking only English acquiesce to them, which
insure voting rights for everyone:

*"The right of any citizen of the state to vote, hold office or sit upon juries, shall never be restricted, abridged
or impaired on account of religion, race, language or color, or inability to speak, read or write the
English or Spanish languages except as may be otherwise provided in this constitution and the
provisions of this section and section one of this article shall never be amended except upon a vote
of the people of this state in an election at which at least three-fourths of the electors voting in the
whole state, and at least two thirds of those voting in each county of the state shall vote for such
amendment."*

Separate schools by race or ethnicity are made illegal, specifically stating that children of Hispanic descent
shall never be denied "the right and privilege of admission and attendance in the public schools ...
and they shall never be classed in separate schools."

[The *El Paso Times* warns the constitution will be rejected by Congress because it doesn't provide for separation of the races.]

Women are permitted to vote (only) in School Board elections.

A bill of rights is enacted: "The rights, privileges and immunities, civil, political and religious, guaranteed to the
people of New Mexico by the treaty of Guadalupe Hidalgo shall be preserved inviolate."

However, there is one more hurdle to overcome because Congress requires an English literacy qualification for
voting and/or office holding.

[Unless the Treaty of Guadalupe Hidalgo was to be disregarded altogether, which would cause vociferous
censure from the international community, the English language stipulation was the only leverage available to
neutralize Hispanic political strength and fortify "Anglo" privilege. Framers of the constitution refer to the
American guarantee of voting rights then state (Article XXI) "...and in compliance with the requirements of
the said act of congress, it is hereby provided that ability to read, write ... shall be a necessary qualification..."
in order to get the Congress to accept the constitution.

Charles Spies, "an able legislative draftsman and political strategist," commends the creators of the constitu
tion: "...You have by its provisions guaranteed the equal protection of the law to every citizen of New Mexico,
you have preserved the religious, political, social, and civic rights to every one of our citizens, and placed
them beyond the power of assault from any source whatsoever."]

November 21: The New Mexico Constitution is adopted by the Convention. (See **1911**.)

PROFILE

Isidoro Armijo

JOURNALIST AND TREATY ACTIVIST

1880(?): Isidoro Armijo graduates from the College of Agriculture and Mechanical Arts then teaches school in Doña Ana County for two years.

1882: Isidoro works for *El Tiempo*, Las Cruces' oldest newspaper, and learns the publishing business. For the next six years he travels widely in Mexico and the U.S.
1898: Isidoro Armijo is editor for El Progreso in Trinidad, Colorado.

1899: Isidoro returns to Las Cruces and becomes active in politics.

1900-1904: Armijo edits El *Eco* del Valle. Isidoro becomes the leading journalist in southern N.M.
1904-1908: He edits *La Flor del Valle.*

1908: Isidoro is elected to the territorial legislature and serves as Chief Clerk.

1910: Armijo is elected to the Constitutional Convention as delegate from Doha Ana County . He drafts the legislation which incorporates the Treaty of Guadalupe Hidalgo into the State Constitution.
[This has been singled out as one of Isidoro Armijo's greatest contribution to the people of N.M.]

1912: After this date Armijo lives in Santa Fe, Albuquerque, Taos, editing various newspapers.
1914: Isidoro serves a term in the House of Representatives.
1920s: Armijo edits the *Taos Valley News, La Revista de Taos, El Eco del Río Grande*, and establishes the Armijo Bureau, a clearinghouse and news service for Spanish newspapers throughout the state.
[He is described as a skilled orator and poet in both Spanish and English: *"He writes poetry like Keats, his prose is classic as Addison's and his humor is a combination of Josh Billings and Mark Twain combined,"* according to D. Meyer.]

Isidoro Armijo
Courtesy Museum of NM, #146678

1910-1912
William J. Mills is Governor.

1911
STATEHOOD
January 21: New Mexican voters ratify the proposed Constitution.

February 24: President Taft approves the N.M. Constitution.

March 1: The House approves the N.M. Constitution. When the Constitution gets to the Senate, Robert Owen of Oklahoma objects to N.M. being admitted without including Arizona's admission, causing Congress to meet in an extra session. The Flood Resolution is added, providing "....for the submission of amendments by a majority..." which would destroy the guarantees of equality for Hispanics.

August 15: President Taft vetoes the Flood Resolution.

August 21: President Taft signs a compromise resolution which insures N.M. statehood if voters accept it.
November 7: New Mexicans ratify the Constitution and elect State officials. (See *1912.*)

LAW
Priest v. Town of Las Vegas: The State Supreme Court rules that land grant property owners whose identity can be determined must be sued by name, not as "unknown heirs."

LITERATURE
Isidoro Armijo publishes his short story *"Sesenta minutos en los infiernos"* (60 Minutes in Hades) in *El Eco del Valle* of Las Cruces.
1924: The story is translated and republished in Santa Fe's Laughing Horse Magazine owned by Willard "Spud" Johnson.

BIOGRAPHY
José E. Fernández publishes *Forty Years as a Legislator, or The Biography of Casimiro Barela.* (The introduction is written by Benjamin Read who states Barela is one of the most "loyal and selfless" of citizens who should be emulated by all.)

1839: The Barela family moves from Tomé to Taos. The era is one of chaos because of the American invasion of Mexico, the Taos revolt, and its resultant persecutions and executions of Mexican citizens for "treason against the U.S."
March 4, 1847: Casimiro Barela is born in Taos. He studies with the Christian Brothers in Mora, apprentices under Reverend Juan B. Salpointe, and in time works as a freighter.

1871: Barela is elected to the Colorado legislature at the age of 25. Casimiro matures into a very good family man, an entrepreneur, civil libertarian, a stalwart leader of church and community, as well as a wealthy landowner and powerful politician who represents the Hispanic people of southern Colorado.

1893: Barela is elected President Pro Tempore of the Colorado Senate. He is appointed as Mexican Consul in Denver for the Mexican government and in 1897 Costa Rica also makes him its Consul.

PROFILE

Felipe M. Chacón

NEW MEXICO'S WORLD CLASS AUTHOR

Felipe Maximiliano Chacón (1873-1949) is born in Santa Fe and educated in public primary school then goes on to St. Michael's College for secondary studies. (His first cousin is poet and novelist Eusebio Chacón.) He is writing poetry and publishing it in *La Aurora* by the age of 14 writing in both Spanish and English.

[In time historian Benjamin Read lauds Chacón for his highly developed literary Spanish, the language of Cervantes and the noble Catholic Monarchs. Read believes Chacón is *"a genuinely American genius."*]

1886: Felipe's father dies suddenly (which Felipe later describes as the single most devastating loss during his lifetime).

1911-1918: Felipe works as an editor for various Spanish-language newspapers: Las Vegas: *La Voz del Pueblo, El Independiente*; Bernalillo: *El Faro del Río Grande; Mora, El Eco del Norte*.

1918-1922: Felipe dedicates himself to the world of business though he still does some newspaper editing.

1922: Chacón becomes the editor and general manager of *La Bandera Americana* in Albuquerque. He writes and publishes many of his more serious poems.

Ca.1924: Chacón continues writing for *La Bandera Americana* and publishes many of the items which become part of his Obras, but also including poems, translations of poets like Byron and Longfellow, short stories, and a novelette. Some of his work is printed in Albuquerque under the title of *Obras de Felipe Maximiliano Chacón, El Cantor Neomexicano: Poesía y Prosa* (Works of Felipe Maximiliano Chacón, The New Mexican Bard: Poetry and Prose).

[Doris Meyer believes this work is a part of American literary history "that has been denied mention in standard texts." Furthermore, her investigative studies indicate there were various other authors who were as literary in the quality of their work but are today basically unknown because they lacked a publisher.]

Chacón's poems have a variety of themes: The Fourth of July; on being admitted as a state; poems to family, especially children; to personalities like **Octaviano A. Larrazolo** (who was as eloquent in English as he was in Spanish, which was often denigrated by Anglos) and **Nina Otero-Warren**; and many merely to entertain the general population with literary poetry. Chacón's prose include short stories like "Un baile de Caretas" (A Masqued Ball) and "Don Julio Berlanga." His novelette (novelita) *Eustacio y Carlota* has to do with a brother and sister who are orphaned and separated while very young then meet each other in later life, marry, then learn they are brother and sister (said to be a true story).

July 10, 1949: Felipe Maximiliano Chacón dies in obscurity in El Paso.

[D. Meyer asserts Chacón's work "is as much sociohistorical as literary" and confirms the existence of a New Mexican literary tradition which has been ignored by scholars of American literature.]

PROCEDURE & LAW

Rodríguez v. La Cueva Ranch Co.: The State Supreme Court rules that persons [land grant heirs] in possession of land sought to be partitioned by a court have to be served personally instead of being so informed by publication of a legal notice in a newspaper.

[Before the Priest and Rodríguez cases a suit could be won by default because lawyers and judges saw to it that defendants weren't informed that they were defendants so the suit went against "unknown heirs" and therefore uncontested. The ruling is not retroactive, however, so those victimized by former courts aren't helped by this move toward justice after people have been dispossessed of their lands. The present owners of the land are now protected against a court of law taking their land without their knowledge so it could be observed that American law now upholds the land swindles of the past.]

POLITICS

Republican state chairman Colonel **Venceslao Jaramillo** addresses his party's convention by stating that the Republican party is dependent on Hispanic votes if it is going to win elections.

MISSIONARY

Reverend **John W. Brink**, his wife **Bertha**, and their four children arrive in Rehoboth. John is a highly successful minister in the Christian Reformed Church and his skills and dedication are put to immediate use at the mission church, school, and hospital five miles east of Gallup. He missionizes the Navajos at various locations like Tohatchi, Sheep Springs, Mexican Springs, etc., as well as Two Wells and Zuñi. The Brink and Van der Wagen families establish a relationship and in time two Brink daughters marry two Van der Wagen sons.

1912
STATEHOOD

January 6: At 1:35 p.m., President Howard Taft signs the proclamation making New Mexico the 47th State of the Union, and says, "Well, it is all over. I am glad to give you life. I hope you will be healthy." The effort has taken almost 64 years.

R.W. Larson sums up by asking: *"Why was N.M. so long denied statehood..."* despite increasing numbers of New Mexicans determined to rise above the colonial or second-class citizenship of territorial status? Scrutiny reveals... a small population, not developed economically...Factional strife and political discord...N.M. was never considered in the same light as other territories... because of a *"...strong prejudice toward the Spanish-speaking, Roman Catholic people of N.M .... [that] was thus the major obstruction to the territory's statehood aspirations ... a most unfair bias against a people labeled by one congressman 'a race speaking an alien language and not representing the 'best blood on the American continent'... the Catholic religion provoked the prejudice and dislike of a predominantly Protestant nation." It can be observed that an instinctive distrust of New Mexico's essentially Hispanic and Indian people and culture was "the last and most durable brick added to the strong wall of opposition that prevented the territory from becoming part of the Union until 1912."*

STATEHOOD

1912-1916

William C. McDonald is Governor.

1912
POLITICS

"Old Guard" Republicans dominate politics in the new state. This group includes T.D. Burns, Ed Sargent, and
    B.C. Hernández of Río Arriba County; Malaquías Martínez of Taos; Charles and Frank Springer of
    Colfax and Santa Fe ; Tom Catron and George Armijo of Santa Fe; Holm Bursum of Socorro; Felipe
    Hubbell of Bernalillo; Charles Spiess and Secundino Romero of San Miguel; Albert B. Fall of Doña
    Ana; Solomón Luna, Sylvestre Mirabal, and Eduardo M. Otero of Valencia. Republican power is based
    on the Hispanic vote but party management and owning newspapers are also considered crucial to
    success. (The *New Mexico Blue Book* regularly lists newspapers by party affiliation.)

U.S. SENATE

March, 1912: The State Legislature appoints **T.B. Catron** and **A.B. Fall** to the Senate. After their first term all
    Senators are to be elected by the people.
[The following compilation was prepared by Dr. Dan D. Chávez, Professor Emeritus from UNM.]

Catron Seat

Thomas B. Catron, (R) 1912-1917
Andrieus A. Jones, (D) 1917-1927
Bronson Cutting, (R) 1928
Octaviano A. Larrazolo, (R) Dec.'28-Mar.'29
Bronson Cutting, (R) 1929-1935
Dennis Chávez, (D) 1935-1962
Edwin L. Mechem, (R) 1963-1964
Joseph M. Montoya, (D) 1964-1977
Harrison "Jack" Schmitt, (R)1977-1983
Jeff Bingaman, (D) 1983-

Fall Seat

Albert B. Fall, (R) 1912-1921
Holm 0. Bursum, (R) 1921-1925
Sam G. Bratton, (D) 1925-1933
Carl A. Hatch, (D) 1934-1949
Clinton P. Anderson, (D) 1949-1973
Pete V. Domenici, (R) 1973-

U.S. HOUSE OF REPRESENTATIVES

Harvey B. Fergusson, (D) 1912-1913   George R Curry, (R) 1912-1913

[N.M. was allotted two Congressmen at first then due to population the two seats were cut back to one until
increased population warranted more representation.]

Harvey B. Fergusson, (D) 1913-1915
Benigno C. Hernández, (R) 1915-1917
William B. Walton, (D), 1917-1919
Benigno C. Hernández, (R) 1919-1921

Nestor Montoya, (D) 1921-1923
John Morrow, (D) 1923-1929
Albert G. Simms, (R) 1929-1931
Dennis Chávez, (D) 1931-1935
John Dempsey, (D) 1935-1941
Clinton P Anderson, (D) 1941-1943
Antonio M. Fernández, (D) 1943-1957
Joseph M. Montoya, (D) 1957-1961

Clinton R Anderson (D) 1943-1947
Georgia Lusk, (D) 1947-1949
John E. Miles, (D) 1949-1951
John Dempsey, (D) 1951-1959
Thomas G. Morris, (D) 1959-1961

Position 1
Joseph M. Montoya, (D) 1961-1965
Thomas G. Morris, (D) 1965-1969
District 1
Manuel Luján, Jr. (R) 1969-1991

Position 2
Thomas G. Morris, (D) 1961-1965
E.S. Johnny Walker, (D) 1965-1969
District 2
Ed Foreman, (R) 1969-1971
Harold Runnels, (D) 1971-1981
Joseph R. Skeen, (R) 1981-1983

District 1
Steve Schiff, (R) 1991-

District 2
Joseph R. Skeen, (R) 1983-

District 3
Bill Richardson, 1983-1997

1912 (con't)
BUSINESS
Isleta Pueblo organizes a business council and Pablo Abeita is chosen as its president.

MINING
The **Chino Copper Co.** begins production at Hurley because of an increase in the price of copper.

1914: About 1500 workers are involved at Hurley and the Santa Rita mine. Half of the labor force is Mexican and Mexican American, the other half "Anglo." "*As was common throughout the mining industry of the Southwest, Mexican Americans and Mexicans receive the lower paying unskilled jobs. Anglos are generally employed in the higher paying skilled and management positions ... Hurley is segregated*" according to J.B. Demark. Women are "virtually barred" from employment until the labor shortage caused by WW II.

1942: The War Labor Board forces Chino officials to sign a contract with the American Federation of Labor which, among other stipulations, calls for an end to discriminatory hiring practices. (The Chino Mine produces at least 90% of New Mexico's copper through 1945.)

LITERATURE
Antonio Lucero (1863-1921) publishes an article, "Virtues of the Hispanic American Hearth," in *Old Santa Fe* Magazine. (This is an example of what G. Meléndez refers to as a "cross over" into English language literary circles in N.M. in his classic *So All Is Not Lost*.)

SPORTS--BOXING

Las Vegas is the site of the world heavyweight title match between **Jack Johnson**, the first black fighter to hold the title, and Jim Flynn. The whole town takes on a holiday spirit as "fight trains" full of tourists arrive for the event. The scheduled 45-round fight is stopped in the ninth when Captain Fornoff of the N.M. Mounted Police jumps into the ring at the request of Governor W.C. McDonald who thinks Flynn can do nothing but headbutt. Johnson leaves Las Vegas with $36,000.

SOCIETY

August 30: **Solomón Luna**, political leader from Valencia County, dies in a tragic accident.

[Sister Lucretia Pittman wrote her M.A. thesis on New Mexico's Solomón Luna at St. Louis University in 1941. It hasn't been published in N.M.]

Aurora Lucero (1893-1964) is appointed by Governor MacDonald to assist with preparations for the state's exhibit at the San Diego Exposition.

PROFILE

Aurora Lucero

TEACHER AND WRITER

1893: Aurora Lucero is born. Antonio Lucero , her father, is associate editor at *La Voz del Pueblo* of Las Vegas. Aurora attends public schools in her home town.

1911: Aurora's essay, "Should the Spanish Language Be Taught in the Public Schools?" is published by Normal University.

1912: Aurora, age 19, is asked to help with the San Diego Exposition exhibit for N.M.

1915: Aurora, a student at New Mexico Normal (Highlands) University, is asked to serve as interpreter for William Jennings Bryan who is on a speaking tour through the West. She graduates from N.M. Normal.

1917: Lucero begins a lifelong career in teaching by accepting a job in Tucumcari. She marries **George D. White** of Santa Fe; they move to Los Angeles but later return to N.M.

1925: Aurora is awarded a B.A. degree from Highlands University.

1925-1927: Lucero serves as superintendent of schools for San Miguel County.

1927: She teaches Spanish at Highlands.

> 1929: Aurora completes requirements for the M.A. degree.
>
> 1934: Lucero accepts the position of assistant superintendent of instruction for the N.M. public schools, relocating to Santa Fe where she resides for the rest of her life.
>
> [G. Meléndez believes Aurora Lucero-White was the precursor of Hispanic female writers like Severina Esquibel, Frances Montoya, Herminia Chacón, Luz Elena Ortiz, Cleofas Jaramillo, Fabiola C. de Baca, Nina Otero, etc.]

1913
PUEBLOS & LAW

United States v. Sandoval: The Supreme Court decrees that the federal government has the right of jurisdiction over N.M. Pueblos, reversing the decision of the Court in *United States v. Joseph.*

The Government's attitude toward New Mexico's Pueblo people is mirrored in the decision: "Though they are sedentary and disposed to peace, they adhere to primitive modes of life, influenced by superstition and fetishism and governed by crude customs. They are essentially a simple, uninformed, and inferior people."

JUDICIARY

Pablo Abeita of Isleta is appointed as judge in the Indian court system.

TIMELINE

Twelve states/territories have granted suffrage to women.

[1869: Wyoming is the first to grant women the right to vote. The National American Woman Suffrage Association (NAWSA) was organized under the leadership of Carrie Chapman Catt and Anna Howard Shaw in 1890. Later the more militant Congressional Union (CU) is formed.]

CULTURAL PRESERVATION

The Society for the Preservation of Spanish Antiquities in New Mexico is incorporated by 72 signatories, among which are Archbishop Pitaval, L.B. Prince, B. Cutting, J.D. Sena, C. Padilla, A Chaves, A.B. Fall, B. Read, V. Jaramillo, T.D. Burns, A. Lucero, E. Lucero. Its purpose is "...the protection and preservation of churches, building, landmarks, places and articles of historic interest connected with the Spanish and Mexican occupation of New Mexico."

SOCIETY

The *Las Vegas Optic* criticizes Lt. Gov. Ezequiel C. de Baca, a Las Vegas native, for his involvement in the Las Vegas land grant issue. **Baca replies that his support of the community's cause to keep its land will be recorded by historians and remembered long after everything else is forgotten.**

FILM

August: **Romaine Fielding** arrives in Las Vegas and announces he will live and make movies in the area. He produces several movies, including one called "The Golden God," a five-reel action film. The winter weather makes Fielding move to a warmer climate, however.

Ca. 1914

WEAVING

Policarpio Valencia is producing embroidered quilts which contain dichos as well as Penitente Brotherhood alabados. His embroidery is done by candlelight after working at the lumber mill or on his farm land.

1914

AGRICULTURE LAW

The Smith-Lever Act provides for the establishment of agricultural extension services which will provide information for the betterment of agriculture and home economics. The New Mexico Agricultural Extension Service is instituted at New Mexico A&M at Las Cruces. County Agents go into the various New Mexican communities and begin programs in health, nutrition, farm and home education. Few Agents are bilingual or bicultural enough to work successfully with Hispanics until such individuals are hired later.

1929: **Fabiola Cabeza de Baca** is the first Hispanic to be employed as a Home Demonstration Agent.

WOMEN & SUFFRAGE

Senator T.B. Catron is adamantly opposed to women's suffrage and women asking for his help leave his office feeling all they are good for is staying home, having children, cooking, washing dishes, and having more children.

[New Mexico is the only western state that denies women the right to vote. The usual perception among suffragists in other parts of the USA is that the prejudiced attitudes of Hispanic men are responsible for the "...political ineffectiveness of New Mexico women."]

Congressional Union organizers Mabel Vernon and Ella St. Clair Thompson locate influential "Anglo" women in Santa Fe who establish a network of suffragists. Hispanic participation is encouraged by selecting well-known Hispanic women to help mobilize New Mexican females, including Nina Otero-Warren, Anita Bergere, Estella Bergere Leopold, Aurora Lucero.

TIMELINE

June 28, 1914: Archduke Francis Ferdinand, heir to the Austrian throne, is shot in Sarajevo by a young Bosnian fanatic, prompting the start of **World War I.**

1915

LABOR

Colorado sugar beet and smelting companies actively recruit seasonal laborers in N.M.

LAND & LAW

1915: The suit filed by S.B. Elkins and T.B. Catron in 1876 to partition the Mora Land Grant is revived in District Court. The 1912 Rodríguez v. La Cueva Ranch Co. decision requires that any person in possession of land sought to be partitioned by a court order must be served in person but lawyers and judges involved agree that the 1912 decision isn't binding in this 1915 case because the suit was instigated some 39 years before in 1876. The matter will affect virtually everyone living in Mora County so the action is kept as secret as possible by all lawyers and judges involved.

L. Bradford Prince writes: *The determination of the suit will affect the whole population. When the original suit was filed generations ago very few were notified of the pending action and in the present day no one is aware their lands are in jeopardy of being sold by order of the Court without individuals being notified and without being able to appear in their own defense. The Court should be a fountain of justice instead of the instrument of depriving these people of their property and rights ... the Judge should be a protector against oppression and against secret proceedings which ... work the rankest injustice.*

The Court orders that Mora common lands be sold.

February 22, 1916: The common lands are sold at the Mora courthouse door. The former Catron interests are bought by the State Investment Company (headed by George A. Flemming, William Shillinglaw, and Reeve Eagle) out of Las Vegas. When all Court actions are in place the people are informed that they do not own the land.

[Deprived of access to their ranch/grazing lands, the people of Mora County begin to seek work away from their ancestral lands and with factors like drought and the Great Depression the county becomes the poorest in the State, characterized by heavy population losses, poverty, and its attendant pathologies such as high unemployment, high rates of welfare payments, and poorly endowed county institutions.]

FILM

Summer: The annual Cowboys' Reunion in Las Vegas draws **Tom Mix** and his actress-wife Virginia Forde to town and he decides to live there and make westerns, which he does for about a year.

ORGANIZATION

The first New Mexico chapter of the **National Association for the Advancement of Colored People** (NAACP)is founded and it helps a black Texas woman to finish high school in N.M.

PROFILE

A F R I C A N - A M E R I C A N S   I N   N E W   M E X I C O

1920: The NAACP succeeds in the struggle to enable a black female to enroll at UNM.

1950s: **Edith Franks** becomes the first black operator to be hired by the Mountain Bell Telephone Company. ("Ma Bell" is described as "one of the worst discriminators" in N.M.)

1952: The NAACP lobbies the Albuquerque City Council which passes an ordinance that outlaws discrimination in places of public accommodations, the first such ordinance endorsed by any municipality. But many stores, hotels, and restaurants continue to refuse to serve blacks.

1953: A bill to abolish segregation in public schools is introduced to the Legislature but defeated. Among a few others, the towns of Clovis, Hobbs, Lovington, and Carlsbad steadfastly refuse to eliminate segregation.

1956: The Albuquerque Committee Against Discrimination in Housing is organized by H. La Grone, John Mills, G.C. Watson, Margaret Meade, and Mrs. R.E. Utter.

1960: The National Civil Rights Commission issues a report which names Albuquerque, Farmington, Alamogordo, Hobbs, and Tucumcari as the most difficult places in N.M. for blacks to obtain proper housing. It is especially critical of Albuquerque.

1961: Problems similar to those in Albuquerque are now observed in Santa Fe.

1963: Albuquerque passes a fair-housing ordinance. But five years later, it is estimated that Albuquerque's 10,000 to 12,000 blacks are still living in substandard neighborhoods.

1969: **Katie Pearl Jackson** of Alamogordo is the first to set up a Negro History Week in N.M. **Charles Becknell** sets up the first Afro-American history course in the state (at Albuquerque High School).

1972: The Sickle Cell Council of N.M. is formed.

1987: Charles Becknell is credited with coining the phrase: *"Racism is a sickness."*

1988: **C. Etta (Charlie) Morrissey** receives the Governor's Award for the Outstanding New Mexico Woman. (This is just one of the many awards garnered by New Mexico's beloved "Charlie" during the 1970s and 1980s.)

LEGISLATURE

The State Legislature is composed of 73 men: 24 represent the livestock (mostly sheep) industry; 17 are lawyers, 9 farmers, 5 doctors, 3 newspaper men, 1 banker, 1 capitalist, 1 industrialist, along with merchants, railroad men, real estate and insurance men. Forty-nine of the 73 are freshman.

1915-1927
ARCHAEOLOGY

Alfred V. Kidder [the sixth person in the U.S. to earn a Ph.D. in
archaeology] spends 10 summers at Pecos, making the
abandoned pueblo the most studied and reported upon
archaeological site in the country.

Alfred V. Kidder
Courtesy Museum of NM, #7600

1924: Kidder's *An Introduction to the Study of Southwestern
Archaeology, with a Preliminary Account of the
Excavations at Pecos* is published.

1927: At Kidder's invitation, the Pecos Conference is held
during which he and his colleagues reach basic
agreements on cultural sequence in the prehistoric
Southwest, definitions of stages in that sequence,
and standardization in the labeling of pottery types.

1977: The 50th anniversary Pecos Conference is convened. There is high praise for the pioneer work of A.V.
Kidder.

1916
SOCIETY

Alice Corbin Henderson arrives in Santa Fe with her artist husband, William Penhallow Henderson. As a
former associate editor of *Poetry: A Magazine of Modern Verse,* she has contacts with many poets,
especially Carl Sandburg, Vachel Lindsay, Harrier Monroe, who become frequent visitors in her
home.

LITERATURE

The *Telegraph-Herald* of Dubuque, Iowa, posthumously publishes the prose and poetry of **Vicente Bernal.**
His poetry, *Las primicias* (First Fruits), is written in English and in Spanish. One of his poems is set
to music and becomes the Alma Mater of Dubuque College.

COLUMBUS RAID

Mardi 9: **Pancho Villa** [or most likely, some of his men] conducts a predawn raid on Columbus. Eighteen
Americans die and others are wounded.

March 15: General John J. Pershing leads a fruitless punitive expedition into Mexico.

[Pancho Villa thus becomes the only leader in history to attack the U.S. and not be apprehended for it.]

PROFILE

Ezequiel C. de Baca

THE PEOPLE'S CHAMPION

Ezequiel C. de Baca (1864-1917) worked at La Voz del *Pueblo* as a reporter and then copy editor in Las Vegas. He was active in various groups: The Literary and Mutual Aid Society, The Society for the Protection of Education, and The Las Vegas Drama Club. These activities contrasted the realities of cultural conflicts, racial strife, territorial politics, and general lawlessness in Las Vegas. Ezequiel vowed to work for the good of poor people and supported the *Gorras Blancas* despised by his older brother, Manuel C. de Baca.

[Everyone knew of the rift between the two, who reconciled briefly over the Billy Green incident when Green was wanted for the murder of Nestor Gallegos. Marshall T. F Clay from **New Town** crossed into **Old Town** and took Green into protective custody, thus preventing Hispano lawmen from arresting him. When Hispanos became outraged the marshall called in Army regulars and accused the "Mexicans" of something akin to insurrection which incited a race war.]

Ezequiel worked for some 20 years as a journalist and the people's spokesman before seeking office in 1916 when he defeated Holm 0. Bursum for the governorship which he held for 49 days before dying of what was called "pernicious anemia." The eulogy delivered by colleague Antonio Lucero stressed Ezequiel's commitment to duty: *I die poor but I lived* in *honor*.

[A definitive biography is needed on New Mexico's valiant modern day champion, Ezequiel C. de Baca.]

Mr. and Mrs.
Eqequiel C. de Baca
Courtesy Museum of NM, #50332,
#7005

1917

Ezequiel C. de Baca is Governor (dies February 18 after some 49 days in office).

19I7-1918

Washington E Lindsey is Governor.

PROFILE

José Dolores López

FATHER OF NEW MEXICAN WOOD CARVING

April 1, 1868: **José Dolores López** is born to Nasario López and M. Teresa Bustos López, in Córdova. (Sons born to the couple become carpenters and weavers.)

1893: José Dolores marries **Candelaria Trujillo** and in time they have seven children: Nicudemos, Rafaél, George, Ricardo, María Liria; Epitacio and Alfredo die in childhood. The couple become land owners and build a goat herd of about 100 animals. José works as a carpenter, specializing in furniture, window and door frames, niches, roof beams and corbels, crosses for grave markers, coffins, and chests. He also becomes skilled in the making of filigree jewelry. He is very involved in the religious life of the Cordovan community.

1912: Candelaria dies.
1913: José marries **Demetra Romero**. (There are no children from this union.)

1917: José becomes depressed when his son Nicudemos is drafted to fight in World War I. José has trouble falling asleep at night so to pass the time he begins to whittle on wood. Nicudemos sends him a picture of his company and José carves a frame for it.

1919: Nicudemos returns from overseas to find his father very involved in the hobby of wood-carving. The carvings, everything from picture frames, clock shelves, and lamp stands to other types of utilitarian furniture, aren't sold but given as gifts to various villagers.

1920s: **Lorin W. Brown** introduces López' work to various Santa Fe personalities, including Frank Applegate and Mary Austin. López is "discovered" and encouraged. Applegate persuades José Dolores to sell his work at the Santa Fe fiesta, the Spanish Arts Shop, and the Native Market. López continues to create utilitarian items but he also produces items like small birds and animals for the tourist trade, as well as unpainted representations of the saints, the Virgin Mary, archangels, and Biblical personages.
[López is typically New Mexican: pious, related to other santeros by blood, serving the Church as a sacristan.]
José encourages his children to take up carving. Liria, George, Ricardo, and Nicudemos do so.

1933: López is in a serious accident which results in a curtailment of his carving production.

May 17,1937: José Dolores López dies. His grave is marked by the cross he had carved for himself early in his career.

[To this day José Dolores is remembered in prayers during Holy Week ceremonies in Córdova and his abilities continue to influence carving in this New Mexican center of the woodcarving industry.]

1917
SOCIETY

Mabel Dodge (Sterne) arrives in Taos. She begins immediately to serve as an apostle for artists and activists who expatriate themselves to Taos and Santa Fe because they feel alienated from Anglo-American society.

[**Erna Fergusson** later wrote of many new arrivals: *"Everybody had a pet pueblo, a pet Indian, a pet craft. Pet Indians with pottery, baskets, and weaving to sell were seated by the fire place, plied with tobacco and coffee, and asked to sing and tell stories."*]

Erna Fergusson
Courtesy Museum of NM, #59764
(Will Connell photo)

PROFILE

J.R. Willis

ART FOR THE TOURIST

J.R. Willis, illustrator, cartoonist, photographer, muralist, and painter, arrives in Gallup and sets up an art studio/curio shop business with emphasis on postcards. He becomes a successful entrepreneur of the tourist trade.

1931: Willis moves to Albuquerque and opens a business on Central Avenue.

1938: With the emergence of Old Town as a tourist center he moves his shop there. 1940s: Willis is highly successful and owns property around the Country Club area. He continues to promote art for tourist consumption, especially the postcard, until he retires in the 1950s.

EDUCATION

Nina Otero-Warren is appointed to the office of superintendent of public schools in Santa Fe County, an elective post which she wins in 1918 at the age of 37, making her the youngest superintendent in the State.

A teacher's annual salary is around $546 a year. Hispanic students are not permitted to speak Spanish in class or on the playground. Those who persist are punished.

WOMEN AND SUFFRAGE

March 1: Women's suffrage is rejected in the State legislature, *by four votes.*

MILITARY

April 21: The **N.M. National Guard** is activated for service in WW I. The entire state mobilizes to help in the victory effort: farmers plant more food crops, especially pinto beans, corn, and wheat; women's groups suggest effective ways to utilize female labor; and the state leads the way in developing medical care for wounded/injured soldiers. Out of a population of 354,000 there are 17,251 New Mexican soldiers in the War.

WOMEN

What comes to be known as the **Woman's Committee for the National Council of Defense** is organized and becomes *"a vast clearing house for women's activities..."*

TIMELINE

There is much **antipathy exhibited toward Germany** during WW I. The German language is taken out of the curriculum of N.M. schools. German-Americans [who are in reality the largest immigrant group in a country made up of many immigrant groups] are accused of blowing up factories, burning crops like wheat, poisoning food and water supplies, etc. On April 18, 1918, the *New Mexican* writes: *"The German is essentially a coward..."*

MUSEUM

November: The **Museum of Fine Arts** is dedicated in Santa Fe.

EDUCATION LAW

The **Smith-Hughes Act** provides federal funds for **vocational education** in agriculture, trades, industries, and the education of vocational education teachers. This infusion of money is slow to reach rural N.M. villages.

1918
RACISM & SOCIETY

The *North American Review* publishes a letter from **H.R. Walmsley** of Kansas City, Missouri, in which he declares that German officers with enough gold to gather a Mexican army would be aided and abetted by Spanish-Americans because *"...a state of treason exists in this part of our county and New Mexico confidently expects to arise and join the mother country..."* He further states that **Penitentes,** who *"keep the State loyally Mexican...are a strange sect, practicing weird religious rites, self-tortures, political oppressions and the elimination of enemies. The deserts are dotted with their Calvary crosses at which human crucifixions are annually carried out, despite the efforts of the Government to prevent them. The Penitentes are secretive, and will stone any unfortunate passerby who chances to witness one of their devotional marches. Americans who learn too much and become talkative are found on the highways, their hearts decorated with neat perforations. It is whispered that no one can talk against the conditions of New Mexico and live."* So much indignation is aroused that the *Review* is forced to print a retraction and apology.

FIESTA

The **Santa Fe Fiesta** is reinitiated. It is intended to be an historical pageant that celebrates the history and cultures of N.M.

WOMEN

Dolores García, *"a typical woman"* from Córdova, marries, bears four children, two of whom die in infancy, and works with her husband **Domingo** to raise their two sons and hold on to their land. She plasters their adobe house each year, raises hollyhocks and puts geraniums in the windows, plants a garden, dries fruit, chile, and meat, raises chickens and goats.

SOCIETY

Mary Austin arrives in N.M.

[Austin's abilities, talents, and energies, often described as causing much controversy, are to be a factor in New Mexico's history.]

Lillian Armijo
(Fiesta Season)
Courtesy Museum of NM, #41956

PROHIBITION

October 1: All saloons close their doors. **Prohibition** is in force [opening a 15 year period of illegal drinking in N.M. and the U.S.]. Alcoholic *"tea parties"* are fashionable in Santa Fe. **Bronson Cutting,** owner of the *New Mexican* who editorialized in 1917 that Prohibition would result in more happiness and prosperity, is reputed to *"...maintain perhaps the finest wine cellar in the Southwest..."*

1919-1920

Octaviano A. Larrazolo is Governor.

1919
RELIGIOUS

Fr. **Albert T. Daeger,** O.FM., becomes the **sixth Archbishop of**

Santa Fe. One of the most serious of Church problems

is the lack of clergy. After many years of no native

ordinations, three New Mexicans are ordained:

Fathers **José A. García, Juan T. Sánchez,** and **Philip J.**

Cassidy.

HISTORICAL SOCIETY

Ralph Emerson Twitchell is elected Director of the Historical
Society of New Mexico.

Octaviano Larrazolo
Courtesy Museum of NM, #47799

| PROFILE | |

Ralph Emerson Twitchell

AMERICAN HISTORIAN

November 29, 1859: **Ralph Emerson Twitchell** is born at Ann Arbor, Michigan.

In N.M. he is a practicing attorney, frequently representing the AT&SF Railway, president of the N.M. Bar Association, etc., and always a strong Republican. Throughout his adult life he is actively interested in the history, archaeology, reclamation, and conservation of N.M. His written works include:

1891: *The Bench and Bar of New Mexico During the American Occupation, A.D. 1846-1850.*

1909: *History of the Military Occupation of the Territory of New Mexico from 1816 to 1851 by the Government of the United States.*

1911-1912: *Leading Facts of New Mexican History*, Vols. *I and II.* [H.E. Bolton writes a *"devas-*

tating" review of this work.]
1913: *The Spanish Archives of New Mexico.*

1917: *Leading Facts of New Mexican History, Vols. 3, 4, 5* (consisting primarily of portraits and biographical sketches).

1919: *Spanish Colonization in New Mexico in the Oñate and De Vargas Periods.*

1924 (?): *Dr. Josiah Gregg, Historian of the Santa Fe Trail.*

1925: *Old Santa Fe.*

August 26, 1925: R. E. Twitchell dies.

POTTERY

The famous potters tradition of **San Ildefonso Pueblo** begins with **Santana Peña** then her daughters Nicolasa and Philomena:

Nicolasa's family: Isabel, Santana (and her Lupita), Rayita; Reyes Peña's family: Juanita, Desideria, María, Clara, Maximiliana; Philomenals: Rose Cata, Juanita (and her Adelphia);

Juanita's: Albert and Josephine (and their Charlotte), Carmelita;

Carmelita's: Gloria (and her Jessie, Angelina), Martha Apple Leaf (and her Eric Sunbird), Cynthia Star Flower, Jeannie Mountain Flower, Linda, Carlos;

María's: Popvi Da (and his Tony Da), Clara;

Isabel's: Tony, Gilbert, Angelita (and her Sandra), Helen (and her Kathleen, Geraldine, Carol and James, Rose).

Julian and María Martínez (Ca. 1941)
Courtesy Museum of NM, #68362

On the **Martínez** side the   pottery tradition begins with **Dominguita Pino Martínez** then her daughter Tonita Martínez Roybal (and her Margaret Lou);

Alfoncita Roybal's family: Lupita, Santana (and her Marie Anita), Viola (and her Beverly), Pauline;

Marie Anita's: Peter, Evelyn (and granddaughter Berlinda), Kathy (and her Wayland), Bárbara (and her Derek, Brandon, Aaron, Cavan).

María Martínez and her husband, Julian become famous potters in San Ildefonso Pueblo when Julian discovers the (now famous) matte black-on-black style of pottery. María's four sisters, Clara Montoya, Juanita Vigil, Maximiliana. M. Montoya, and Desideria M. Sánchez also work in pottery, as do members of their families:

María and Julian's family: Popovi Da (and his son Tony Da), Adam (and Santana, related to potter Tonita Roybal);

Juanita's family: Carmelita Dunlap (and her son Carlos);

Adam and Santana's family: George Martínez (and Pauline), Beverly Martínez, Marie Anita Martínez (and her daughter Tahn-Moo-Whe, Bárbara Gonzáles).

SOCIETY
Sabine R. Ulibarrí is born in Tierra Amarilla.

PROFILE

Sabine R. Ulibarrí

POET IN BILINGUAL WORLDS

1937: Sabine Ulibarrí graduates from high school and would like to attend Notre Dame but the cost is prohibitive. When invited by President James F. Zimmerman to enroll at UNM on a scholarship he accepts and graduates with majors in Spanish and English.

1942: He marries **María Concepción Limón** from La Mesilla.

1942-1945: Ulibarrí enlists in the Air Corps and flies **35 combat missions.** He is awarded the Distinguished Flying Cross and the Air Medal.

1949: Ulibarrí receives the M.A. degree in Spanish from UNM where he is hired to teach.

1958: Sabine is awarded a Ph.D. in Spanish from UCLA.

1961: Ulibarrí's book of short **poems,** Al *cielo se sube* a *pie,* is published in Mexico then in Spain.

1962: Sabine's **Ph.D. dissertation** on poet Juan Ramón Jiménez is published in Madrid, Spain. "Uli," as he is affectionately known by most of his students, becomes one of the few American Hispanic writers to be recognized as an influential literary figure in Spain, South America, and Central America while he is virtually unknown in his native land.

1964: *Tierra Amarilla: Cuentos de Nuevo México,* based on Uli's childhood experiences, is published. The work is translated into English in 1971 and the bilingual edition earns wide acclaim.

1973-1982: Ulibarrí is chairman of the Modern and Classical Languages Department at UNM.

1978: Ulibarrí is appointed to Spain's **Royal Academy of the Spanish Language.**

1920s
LABOR
It is estimated that from the upper Río Grande basin alone some 12,500 New Mexicans obtain seasonal work each year, most of them (7,000 to 10,000) going out of N.M. to Colorado, Utah, Wyoming, etc.

STUDIES
Toward the end of the decade New Mexican villages are "...*studied and analyzed by rural sociologist, psychologists, anthropologists, medical health and nutrition specialists, agricultural scientists, and educators...*" with their "...*survey sheets, questionnaires, diaries, cameras...*" etc., with which they record village life.

EDUCATION
Standardized tests are administered to urban and rural children of N.M. [and of Texas and Colorado]. "*Hispanic children were retarded by rates ranging from 89 percent in the fourth grade, to 63 percent in the eighth grade.*" These tests are challenged by some educators.

CULTURE & SOCIETY
Reformers want to preserve the cooperative, communitarian values of the Hispanic villages. They [purport to] value cultural pluralism and the Hispanic arts, crafts, music, folklore, etc., but they work to eradicate "*superstition ... irresponsibility*" in the forms of the Catholic Church, family ties, and every-day culture if they get in the way of making money. Hispanics are often described as "*docile,*" "*lacking ambition,*" and "*ignorant.*"
PRISONS
Conservative elements in New Mexican society **reject prison reforms** like parole, educational opportuni-

ties, work projects, etc., in the penal system, believing that prisoners should pay for their crimes with no "molly coddling."

1922: Convicts stage a revolt against prison conditions under the leadership of J.W Stocking. They demand a variety of food and the elimination of beans. When the cons refuse to return to their cells prison guards fire on them, wounding five and killing one. The prison commission censures the staff for the shooting, especially Warden Plácido Jaramillo. He is later replaced by John McManus.

1929: Executions are now required by electrocution instead of hanging.

1933: Prisoners work at manufacturing license plates.

1940: Convicts petition Governor Miles to allow them to join the military.

1944: Some inmates leave prison on a conditional release to work in war industries.

June 15, 1953: Overcrowding and other tensions lead to an eight-hour prisoners' riot. They hold Deputy Warden Ralph Tahash and 12 guards as hostages. There is a shoot-out and two convicts are killed.

August, 1956: Inmates are moved into a new prison 11 miles from Santa Fe. There are innovations in treatment and attitude toward prisoners. Each prisoner has a chance for educational programs, medical and psychological treatment, and vocational training. Residential units are still segregated by "race" for blacks, Hispanics, and "Anglo" whites.

February, 1980: Overcrowding, limited rehabilitation programs, and various tensions bring on the most destructive and brutal riot in the history of American penology. (See **1980.**)

SOCIETY & INTELLIGENTSIA
Artists and writers are attracted to Santa Fe from all over the USA. A partial list includes Mary Austin, Ruth Laughlin, Alice Corbin Henderson, Witter Bynner, Frank Applegate, Spud Johnson, Mabel Dodge, John Gaw Meem, Haniel Long, Randall Davey, etc., and painters like Josef Bakoz, Will Shuster, Willard Nash, Walter Mruck, Fremont Ellis, etc.

LAND GRANT
Most of the **La Joya land grant** is sold for back taxes due Socorro County.

1936: Socorro county sells 220,000 acres of the former La Joya grant to **Thomas Campbell** for 35 cents an acre. He fences off the land and local people begin moving away because they can no longer make a living without pastureland for their livestock.

1966: Thomas Campbell dies and his estate land is sold to the Nature Conservancy which in turn sells it to the U.S. government for use as a wildlife refuge. Some 2,500 acres are reserved for the use of the people of La Joya but even this acreage is endangered when several private parties file quiet title suits which challenge grantee ownership of portions of the land.

1973: Citizens form the *Merced de La Joya* corporation and purchase a backhoe with which to clear out a nine-mile-long ditch needed to make the land productive once more.

In time, water from the *acequia madre* reclaims the land and a **Viva La Joya Day** is celebrated every spring.

1977: The Merced issues a statement of solidarity to the people of Chililí that they will help them in their struggle to retain their grant lands.

1920
CENSUS
Some 325,000 people live in New Mexico which ranks 47th in per-capita income.

SOCIETY
John Collier accepts an invitation to visit **Mabel Dodge** [later **Luhan**] at her Taos home. He meets **Tony Luhan** and becomes enamored of Taos and Pueblo community life.

HEALTH
Sanatoria, which cater to health seekers with *tuberculosis* (also called *phthisis* or *consumption),* can be found around the state. "Climate therapy" is excellent in N.M. because of its sunshine, altitude, arid purity of its dry air.

1922: There are forty-eight officially recognized sanatoria in the state. There is an enormous increase in the number of physicians in N.M., with one doctor for every 693 citizens.

N.M. attracts many gifted health seekers like **physicians** Dr. W.H. Woolston, Dr. R.E. McBride, and Dr. W.R. Lovelace (founder of the **Lovelace Clinic** in Albuquerque). **Politicians** include Albert Fall, Bronson Cutting, Clinton R Anderson, the Simms brothers Albert and John, Clyde Tingley, etc. In **education** there are France V. Scholes, Dudley Wynn, John Winzirl, John Milne, etc. In the **arts** are Grace Thompson Edmister, Kathryn Kennedy O'Connor, architect John Gaw Meem, and many Taos and Santa Fe artists.

TEXANS
It is estimated that some 35,000 former Texans now live in N.M.

HIGHER EDUCATION
The **College of St. Joseph on the Río Grande** is founded in Albuquerque by the **Sisters of St. Francis.**

WOMEN & SUFFRAGE
February 19: N.M. becomes the 32nd state to approve the amendment which enables women to vote in the USA.

1920-1940
SOCIETY & LAND OWNERSHIP

Hispanic families in both the middle and lower Río Grande valley lose much of their land. This is accomplished by merchants foreclosing on land when credit buying can't be paid for and by establishing projects like the **Elephant Butte Irrigation District** and foreclosing over delinquent taxes, especially smaller plots which have been divided amongst several children.

"Anglo" farmers have easier access to financing through "Anglo-owned" banks and can buy out Hispanics, who then become tenants, sharecroppers, day laborers.

[Before 1911 when the construction of a dam is begun, 70% of all farms are owned by Hispanics. By 1929 "Anglos" own 60% of all farms and Hispanics are 80% of tenants and laborers.]

1921-1922
Merrit C. Mechem is Governor.

1921
SOCIETY
Frank Applegate arrives in N.M.

WOMEN & PUBLIC OFFICE

The State constitution is amended to permit women to hold public office. **Nina Otero-Warren** is encouraged to run for the U.S. House of Representatives and she wins the Republican nomination, becoming the first woman in N.M. to be so nominated.

Nina Otero-Warren
Courtesy Museum of NM, #30263

BUREAU OF INDIAN AFFAIRS

BIA Commissioner Burke issues regulations that Indian children in government boarding school attend church and Sunday school. He threatens to punish by fine and imprisonment anyone involved in any religious ceremony that involves drugs, self-torture, or idleness.

1923: Burke limits religious dances to one a month and strives to educate the general public against the dances.

[Allegations are made that Pueblo parents withdraw their children from government schools at puberty in order to give them a two-year course in sodomy.]

1925: The All-Pueblo Council denounces the BIA's efforts to destroy their self-government and when a small group goes to Berkeley to raise money to fight for their cause the BIA spreads the rumor that the Pueblos are being financed by Moscow's communists.

SOCIETY
Bill Mauldin is born in Mountain Park.

WOOD CARVING
José Dolores López, "...*a creative genius steeped in the traditional New Mexican Hispanic cultural system...*" woodcarver and furniture craftsman of **Córdova,** is "discovered" by Frank Applegate after an introduction by **Lorin W. Brown.** Applegate and other newly arrived artists are impressed with López' "*originality of artistic expression...*" and he proves to be "*...accomplished in several aspects of traditional Hispano...*" art forms. A revival of Hispanic arts and crafts begins.

SOCIETY
Gilberto Espinosa is awarded a law degree from Georgetown University. He practices law in Albuquerque where he earns a reputation as one of the leading authorities on Spanish and Mexican land grants. He works as an assistant U.S. Attorney while he writes and lectures on the history, culture, and folklore of N.M.

Espinosa is the first to translate into English the *Historia de la Nueva México* by **Gaspar Pérez de Villagrá,** New Mexico's epic founding chronicle. He co-authors *Río Abajo* with Judge **Tibo Chávez** of Belén.

1922
BURSUM BILL
The **Bursum Bill** is introduced by Senator **Holm Bursum** to "...*quiet title to lands within Pueblo Indian land grants.*" He tells Congress that Indians themselves favor the bill. The essence of the Bursum Bill is for non-Indians to secure title to Pueblo lands. It also provides that all future disputes over Pueblo water rights or land shall be adjudicated by State courts.

The existence of the Bursum Bill is unpublicized in N.M.

[M. Simmons writes that "*No reports of it appeared in the local press, no public official called it to their attention. In fact, it seemed there was a deliberate conspiracy of silence on the part of the Bureau of Indian Affairs to keep the measure quiet until it had become law.*"]

Holm Bursum
Courtesy Museum of NM, #51920

John Collier, a young poet from New York now living in Taos, informs the Pueblos about Bursum's pending legislation in Washington.

Leaders from all the Pueblos gather at Santo Domingo and unify in their fight against being swindled out of their lands by Government officials elected to represent them.
November 5: **Sotero Ortiz** of San Juan Pueblo is elected president of the modern **All Indian Pueblo Council.**

Pablo Abeita of Isleta is elected to the post of Secretary. Abeita is required to travel to Washington quite often in his duties for the AIPC.

Other Pueblo men begin to emerge as leaders and spokesmen: **Charlie Kie** of Laguna, **Alcario Montoya** of Cochití, and later younger men like **Porfirio Montoya** of Santa Ana, **Martín Vigil** of Tesuque, **Jesús Baca** of Jémez, and **Abel Sánchez** of San Ildefonso.

Artists and writers from Taos, then Santa Fe, join the Pueblo cause, unleashing a blitz of information across the USA, exposing the Bursum Bill. The **General Federation of Women's Clubs,** two million strong and led by a courageous **Stella Atwood** of California, causes other organizations to rally in support of the Pueblos. This is *"the first national campaign in United States history to protect Indian rights ... The protection of Indian lands and cultures became a national cause célèbre ... supported by progressives, radicals, artists, writers... committed to policies of ethnic and racial tolerance..."*

Bureaucrats like Secretary of the Interior **Albert Fall** are *"dumbfounded"* because *"it appears never to have occurred to him that anyone gave a penny for what happened to the Indians."*

The **Bursum Bill is recalled** from the House with the explanation that its intent has been misrepresented to national lawmakers. But the Senate comes up with the substitute **Lenroot Bill** which is intended to separate the coalitions which had united to defeat the Bursum Bill.

[There was much jealousy among N.M. "Anglos" as to who the "real Indian champions" were. John Collier came out on top and the Pueblos repudiated the Lenroot Bill, which was withdrawn. But a lawyer for the Justice Department now began to threaten the "champion" community by targeting individuals like Mabel Luhan, Alice Henderson, and Mary Austin.]

1924: The **Pueblo Lands Act** is passed, acknowledging that lands recognized by Spain and Mexico as belonging inviolably to Pueblo people shall be respected as perfect and unimpaired by the USA. (Pueblos still lose some of their ancient land holdings.)

POLITICS

Dennis Chávez is elected to the state House of Representatives. The first legislation he sponsors is to provide free textbooks for children in public schools.

AGRICULTURE

Farming in the Río Puerco area [once described as a "garden spot" of N.M.] has become a secondary activity because of soil erosion and deepening of the water table due to the cutting of arroyos. Villagers have to depend on their livestock and wage labor to make a living. (See **1928.**)

LABOR & ETHNICITY

Clinton Jencks states that "Mexican Americans" and "Mexicans" working in the **mining or railroad industries** are relegated to the difficult or dangerous jobs while "Anglos" get the better paid, semi-technical positions. *"Mining managers readily admitted that they encouraged and exploited ethnic divisions in their labor force to frustrate unionization. Separate payroll lines, washrooms,* *toilet facilities, and housing for Mexicans were commonplace."*

STRIKE

Gamerco miners go on strike in Gallup and work stops for several weeks. There is violence on the strike lines and in town so the state militia is called in. The **McKinley County Council of Defense** is involved in vigilante activities.

POLITICS

Nina Otero-Warren is defeated by **John R. Morrow** in her bid for a seat in the U.S. House of Representatives. Morrow carries the "*...majority of the votes in all the Little Texas 'Anglo' counties...*" which gives him the victory.

Democrat **Soledad Chávez Chacón** is elected to the office of **Secretary of State** [and becomes the first woman in the USA to serve as Acting Governor when the Governor and Lt. Governor are out of the State].

FESTIVAL

The **Inter-Tribal Indian Ceremonial** is established at Gallup.

WEAVING

Severo Jaramillo and his wife, **Teresita Trujillo,** open the **Severo Jaramillo Weaving Shop** in Chimayó. Severo builds looms for many weavers in the area and supplies them with wool yarn. He also serves as a distributor for the finished weavings. Chimayó weavers who appear on Severo's 1936 ledger include:

Córdova: Alfredo; Emilio;
Deaguero: José and Encarnación; Juan;

Durán: Josefina; Rosa; Teodoro;
Espinosa: Juan;
Jaramillo: Adelaida; H.M.; Victoriano; Willie;
Martínez: Bences; Benina;
Enriquez: Emilio; Fidelina; Frances; Lizardo; Marina; Pablo; Ricardo; Sotera; Ursulo; Victor; Mier: Antonio;

Montoya: Fesilano; Froilano; Lonjino; Macedonia; Silvia;
Ortega: Anastacio; Frank; Fransisquita;
Rodríguez: Frank;
Romero: Carpio;
Trujillo: Bernaida; Feliciana; Félix; Grabrelita; Marcos; Máximo; Nicolás; Ofelia; Jacobo; Rosinaldo;
Vigil: Esquibel; Isabel; Leonidez; María T.; Mercedes; Pedro.

1923-1924

James F. Hinkle is Governor.

1923
RECLAMATION
The **Middle Río Grande Conservancy District** is organized but lack of money prevents reclamation projects
until 1930.

INDIAN EDUCATION
Nina Otero-Warren is appointed inspector of Indian Schools in Santa Fe County, the first woman to hold
that post. She reports "*...scandalous conditions--overcrowded, fly-infested, disease-ridden
government boarding schools...*" where children are beaten for speaking their native tongues and
"*often roped like cattle*" if they attempted to run away Children forced from their Pueblo homes to
be indoctrinated in the "Anglo" way of life are malnourished, some even starving, on the "*...Indian
bureau's allotted seven to eleven cents a day for food...*"

TIMELINE
1923: The **Navajo Tribal Council** is created. **Chee Dodge** is the first Chairman.

POTTERY
The **Laurencita Herrera** family of Cochití Pueblo is creating pottery during this time. Working daughters are
Seferina (and some of her family) and Mary Francis.

Seferina's: Virgil, Inez (and her Krystal), Janice (and her Kimberly), Joyce (and her Leslie), and granddaughter
Amanda Ortiz.

SOCIETY
Mabel Dodge marries **Tony Luhan** from Taos Pueblo. Mabel believes she and Tony will function as a "bridge
between cultures" in order to build a society she refers to as a "cosmos." She seeks out and attracts
many "alienated white intellectuals," writers, artists, reformers, to Taos, including John Marín, Georgia O'Keeffe, Andrew Dasburg to paint the Taos landscape; Leopold Stokowski to build on Native
American music; D.H. Lawrence and Robinson Jeffers to interpret Taos to the world; John Collier to
champion Indian causes; Ansel Adams to photograph the "newfound Eden," Mary Austin, Leon
Gaspard, Willa Cather, etc.

Hundreds of artists and writers are drawn to Santa Fe, Taos and northern New Mexico (in the 1920s and 1930s)
in their search for inspiration and self-renewal. They look to Indian and Hispanic people to help break
the chains of empty, materialistic "Anglo" civilization and to create a "literature and art of affirmation"
instead of the alienation so prevalent in the rest of the country.

Mabel Dodge Luhan takes the lead in promoting the Southwest as a Garden of Eden which offers "cultural
renewal for the dying Anglo civilization."

March: Secretary of the Interior Albert B. Fall resigns in disgrace.

April 10: **Popovi Da** is born at San Ildefonso Pueblo to Julián and María Martínez, legendary potters of San Ildefonso.

1924
Mary Austin settles permanently in Santa Fe.

A very strong personality, Austin is sometimes called "God's mother-in-law" by her writer friends, but never to her face. Not to be outdone, other friends refer to her as the "Oracle of Santa Fe" or the "Prophet-at-Large to America." She devotes much of her time and energy to preserving and celebrating the native Indian and Hispanic cultures of N.M. and the Southwest. In spite of personality clashes with Mabel Dodge Luhan, Austin shares most of Mabel's goals, ideals, and activities. The two are friends despite many "stormy" incidents.

She has a house built on Camino del Monte Sol and names it *Casa Querida*. Alone because she is a divorcee, her brother's daughter, **Mary Hunter**, comes to live with her. Austin has financial independence and an international reputation as a writer and personality in public affairs, one of America's most interesting and creative females, despite her "air of infallibility and imperious outlook." She believes that women are more creative than men though she prefers the society of men. When she is not writing, lecturing, or leading some cause she is at home cooking or making jams and jellies for her friends.

During her 10 years in Santa Fe she writes eight books, including her autobiography, *Earth Horizon*.

Of all her "causes" she is most devoted to Indian welfare. She writes that "Protestant missionaries have always insisted that Indian drama, dance, music, poetry, and design must be totally destroyed" and replaced with a patchwork quilt of European cultures. "Missionaries have taught young Indians that the religion of their parents was not only contemptible but ridiculous."

Mary Austin also champions the Hispanic culture of northern N.M. She lectures on it all over the country and is very impressed with Hispanic theater which she wants to restore since "we Americans stupidly destroyed it." She believes that Penitente hymns have the same cultural value as Negro Spirituals. She wants to encourage use of the Spanish language: "Once Spanish speaking New Mexico produced interesting and vital literature of its own. Public speaking was an art and the common people composed songs and poems of genuine literary merit. But in the forced struggle to acquire an English vocabulary, this literary expressiveness has been completely lost."

AMERINDS & LAW
Native Americans are declared to be American citizens under American law.

POTTERY
Marie Z. Chino of Acoma Pueblo begins working in pottery and through the years her family, Carrie Chino Charlie (and her JoAnne, Corinne), Grace Chino (and her Gloria, Carol), Vera Chino Ely, Gilbert Chino,

Rose C. García (and her Tena) also learn the art of the craft. Marie works with traditional Acoma designs, especially the fine line, while Rose and Grace also experiment with design combinations.

ART PRESERVATION

The Spanish-Colonial Arts Society, dedicated to the preservation of traditional Spanish arts, is founded by a group which includes Mary Austin and Frank Applegate, who begin collecting Hispanic and Indian arts and crafts items. The society introduces an annual Spanish Market held in conjunction with the Santa Fe Fiesta. This provides incentive and a market for Hispanic crafts. Woodcarver Celso Gallegos is "discovered."

[The Spanish Market developed through the efforts "of Anglo artist and writer Frank Applegate and Anglo writer Mary Austin...," according to L.B. Kalb.]

LITERATURE

Felipe M. Chacón has his literary works published under the title of *Obras de Felipe Maximiliano Chacón, "El Cantor Neomexicano;" Poesía y Prosa*, 1924.

[New Mexican historian Benjamin Read refers to Chacón as the "New Mexican Bard" who wrote in "the beautiful language of Cervantes" in Modernist style. He declares that Felipe had an aversion to publicity. Chacón's father, Urbano, was an editor of Spanish language newspapers as well as serving as Public School Superintendent for Santa Fe County. Felipe followed in his fathers footsteps in journalism, editing Spanish language newspapers like *La Voz del Pueblo, La Bandera Americana, El Eco del Norte, El Faro del RíoGrande*.]

NEWSPAPERS

There are 87 newspapers in the state, 11 of which are printed in Spanish. Political affiliation is basic to most newspapers: 30 are Republican, 33 are Democrat, 8 Independent, 3 Independent Republican, 6 Independent Democrat, 2 Progressive, and 5 with unknown affiliations.

POLITICS

The Republican Party elects governors that function as party managers and execute policy that has been decided upon by "Old Guard" Republican leaders from around the state. If something new appears the governors must consult the Old Guard before taking any action. The Legislature is the instrument of the party, legislators serving as party functionaries, legalizing Old Guard policy in the form of statutes. Lobbyists are usually an extension of the Republican Party.

1925-1926

Arthur T. Hannet is Governor.

1925
ACTIVISM
Mary Austin helps to organize the Indian Arts Fund.
LITERARY SOCIALS

Alice Corbin Henderson and her husband open their home to writers who gather there one night a week. These "literary evenings" are in time referred to as the "Poets' Roundup" and include personalities like Oliver La Farge, John G. Fletcher, Mabel and Tony Luhan, Haniel Long, Willa Cather, Mary Austin, etc., with visits from Vachel Lindsay, Carl Sandburg, Robert Frost, Manuel (Angélico) Chávez, Erna Fergusson, Ruth Laughlin, etc. Witter Bynner (sometimes referred to as the "premier host of Santa Fe") calls them "mud-hut nuts."

POTASH

James Snowden and Henry McSweeney discover potash deposits while drilling for oil some 20 miles east of Carlsbad and a completely new industry is introduced to N.M. when they form the American Potash Co. (later called U.S. Potash Co., then the U.S. Borax & Chemical Corporation).

MAGAZINE

Camilo Padilla relocates his *Revista Ilustrada* magazine to Santa Fe. It is tailored for New Mexicans, a 16 page monthly Spanish language review for industry, commerce, literature, art, and the home. It becomes a showcase for Hispanic New Mexican writers and artists with its poetry, short stories, historical articles, essays, etc., enhanced with photographs, wood block prints, and other professional graphics. Padilla's association with established Hispanic publishers brings in items from the rest of the Hispanic world: Texas and the Southwest, Mexico, Latin America, and Spain.

La Librería de la Revista segment offered the readership an opportunity to buy popular books by international authors like Hugo, Dumas, Verne, Cervantes, Isaacs, Lizardí, etc., as well as local or regional authors like Benjamin Read, Eusebio Chacón, Aurelio Espinosa, etc.

1926: Camilo Padilla sees his dream come true: El Centro de Cultura (Culture Center) is opened in Santa Fe to showcase nativo art, music, and literature.

1933: Camilo Padilla dies at the age of 73 (after publishing the renowned Revista Ilustrada for 26 years).

[G. Meléndez states that the *Revista Ilustrada*, Camilo Padilla himself, as well as the work and members of his dynamic generation of writers and journalists soon passed into neglect and obscurity. He states even the highly successful *Revista Ilustrada* is for the most part "unknown in libraries and archival repositories across the Southwest."]

TOURISM

Americans begin to visit the Southwest and the AT&SF begins its "Santa Fe Indian Detours," a three-day trip through certain Indian Pueblos.

1927: Roads to Yesterday tours Taos, Truchas, Córdova, and Chimayó, the latter described as the "Lourdes of New Mexico."

1931: The Great Depression ends the railroad tours but tourism by motorcar continues to grow.

451

RECLAMATION
The Santa Cruz Irrigation District is begun over protests by Hispanos who claim that subsistence farming isn't lucrative enough to pay for the project of building a storage reservoir on the Santa Cruz River. Commercial farmers say they need the project. Bond issues are floated in 1926 and again in 1928.

1932: Tax delinquency is over 60% and the Irrigation District faces bankruptcy.

POLITICS
Governor Hannett takes a pro-labor stand, along with that of election reform. Ensuing controversies and opposition from the Ku Klux Klan cause his defeat for reelection.

POTTERY
The **Lucy Martín Lewis** family of Acoma is creating pottery during this time. Her family potters include Carmel (and her daughter Katerina), Delores, Mary, Emma, Andrew, Ann, Ivan and Rita (and grandson Kevin).

TOURISM
Elizabeth DeHuff presents lantern-slide lectures three to six times a week at La Fonda Hotel in Santa Fe as part of the Fred Harvey promotion called the "Indian Detour," [which she does from 1926 to 1941. Native American cultures are promoted, especially that of the Pueblos. These presentations "...reinforced cultural stereotypes..." and are highly commercial, promoting the buying of pottery, rugs, jewelry, crafted by Indians. Hispanic traditions are limited to architecture, old missions, chile ristras, etc., avoiding any mention of contemporary village life, which is not considered a commodity suitable for tourists. Spanish ties are acceptable, but not Mexican. DeHuff's presentation doesn't contain one slide on an Hispanic.

FILM
Movies in the silent era carry "...distorted cultural assumptions..." with heroes and villains painted in superlative hues:

1898: *Indian Day School* by the Edison Studios is the first movie on location (at Isleta) in N.M. European culture is portrayed as the ideal way of life.

1912: *A Pueblo Legend* by D.W Griffith, starring Mary Pickford, is filmed at Isleta. Pickford falls in love with the brave Pueblo hero who fights the "vile" Apache.

1917: *The Rattlesnake*: Hispanics are portrayed as vile Mexican bandits [along with the "popular" Mexican stereotype of taking a siesta under a large sombrero].

1917: *Adventures of Kit Carson,* produced by the N.M. Tourist Promotion Bureau, shows Taos artists in Indian headdress painting in the Taos plaza.

1926
FIESTA
Will Shuster creates **Zozobra** (Old Man Gloom) for the Santa Fe fiesta.

WOODCARVING

Celso Gallegos (1864-1943) takes first place in the woodcarving category of the 1926 (and 1927) Spanish Colonial Arts Competition. He is described as *"one of the best known and beloved of the native* **craftsmen, and one of the most skilled"** for his images and animal figures in wood and stone. He is also typically New Mexican: pious, serving the Church as a sacristan, and related to various santeros by blood.

[It is said Celso Gallegos was a big influence on José Dolores López.]

LAND FORECLOSURE LAW

A law is passed by the Legislature which enables foreclosure proceedings against land that has been tax delinquent for three years or more.

Celso Gallegos
Courtesy Museum of NM, #8991

[A definitive study is needed on how this law came to be enacted, if its basic intent was to divest people of their property by using tax laws, if its existence was kept hidden from the people whom it targeted, etc.]

1927-1930

Richard C. Dillon is Governor.

1927

BOOKS

Willa Cather publishes *Death Comes for the Archbishop* [and it goes on to become the best-selling book in the history of N.M. item publishing]. Highlights include:

Prologue: 1848: Three Cardinals and a Bishop are discussing the founding of an Apostolic Vicarate in New Mexico, "a part of North America recently annexed to the United States" and first "evangelized in fifteen hundred, by the Franciscan Fathers." Now that the area has been "taken over by a progressive government" the Church needs a good bishop there.

Book I: After a year of travel, **Jean Marie Latour**, Vicar Apostolic of New Mexico and Bishop of Agathonica in partibus, arrives in N.M. with his boyhood friend Father **Joseph Vaillant**, claiming it "for the glory of God."

Upon inspection of the Santa Fe church he is interested in the "wooden figures of the saints," [santos] which are "much more to his taste than the factory-made plaster images in his mission churches in Ohio." Father Martínez of Taos drops by "to receive the new Vicar and to drive him away," forcing Latour to go to Durango to show the bishop there his credentials from Rome. Upon his return to Santa Fe, Father Vaillant has already endeared himself to the local population.

Book II: Father Vaillant is out missionizing when he stops at the rancho of rich Mexican Manuel Lujon [sic] "to many his men and maid servants who were living in concubinage, and to baptize the children." While there, Vaillant adeptly separates his "swarthy host" from two prized mules which he and Latour will use henceforth on their missionizing journeys.

On one such journey, to Taos, they encounter Buck Scales and his wife, Magdalena, who saves the two by informing them that Buck plans to kill and rob them. Everyone knows Buck Scales "for a dog and a degenerate-but to Mexican girls, marriage with an American meant coming up in the world."

Magdalena is later saved by Christóbal [sic] Carson and the two missionaries become good friends with the famous Kit Carson, who informs them "Our Padre Martínez at Taos is an old scapegrace, if ever there was one; he's got children and grandchildren in almost every settlement around here. And Padre Lucero at Arroyo Hondo is a miser, takes everything a poor man's got to give him a Christian burial."

Book III: Bishop Latour visits Albuquerque where Padre Gallegos is pastor. Gallegos can "dance the fandango five nights running," play poker and go hunting with the best of them when he's not dancing with the merry ladies of Albuquerque. Latour decides to suspend Gallegos from all priestly duties as a warning to all native priests. Then he goes on to visit the Acoma church where he hears how the Acomas rid themselves of the "tyrannical and overbearing" Friar Baltazar, binding him hand and foot then tossing off the rock into the trash heap far below. "So did they rid their rock of their tyrant, whom on the whole they had liked very well."

Book IV: Father Gallegos is suspended and Father Vaillant takes charge of the parish. "The fickle Mexican population soon found as much diversion in being devout as they had once found in being scandal-ous." Vaillant the reformer wins Albuquerque's admiration.

The bishop visits Pecos, reduced from 6,000 to the present 100 adults, where he hears of Coronado's atrocities, "exacting a heavy tribute of corn and furs and cotton garments from their hapless hosts ... and taking with them slaves and concubines ravished from the Pecos people."

Latour and his Pecos guide get caught in a snowstorm and happen upon the ancient ceremonial cavern where the Pecos people held ceremonials which involved a huge snake.

Book V: Bishop Latour visits Taos and Padre Martínez who "hated the Americans," the "dictator to all the parishes in northern New Mexico, and the native priests at Santa Fe were all of them under his thumb."

Rumor has it that Martínez instigated the revolt of five years ago, causing the murders of Governor Bent and a dozen others. Seven Taos Indians were charged with the vile acts and sentenced to be hung. They send for Martínez who promises to save their lives if they deed him their farms, which they do, whereupon he leaves town and the Indians are executed. Now Martínez is one of the richest men in Taos.

Latour meets Trinidad, whom Martínez claims as his own son. During supper the "swarthy Padre" states that he doesn't favor celibacy for priests.

Later in his sleeping quarters Latour discovers a wad of woman's hair in a corner of the room, Martínez' snoring "like an enraged bull" keeping him awake from down the hall.

The next day Martínez celebrates mass with his "beautiful baritone voice ... Rightly guided, the Bishop *re-*flected, this Mexican might have been a great man. He had an altogether compelling personality, a disturbing, mysterious, magnetic power" But "his day was over." (In time Latour brings in a Spanish priest, Father Taladrid, to neutralize Martínez in Taos, and Martínez is excommunicated.)

PROFILE

Willa Cather

N O V E L I S T

Willa Cather
Courtesy Museum of NM, #111734

December 7, 1875: Willa Sibert Cather is born to Charles F. Cather and Mary Virginia Boak Cather in Winchester, Va.

1883: The Cather family moves to a ranch in Nebraska. She is described as a tomboy during this period, riding horses and socializing with children from other ranches, many of them foreign-born or second-generation Americans. Both of her grandmothers are members of the household and they tutor young Willa in the English classics and in Latin since there are no schools in the vicinity.

The family moves to Red Cloud where Willa graduates from high school after which she attends the University of Nebraska and does newspaper work for income.

1895: Willa graduates from the University of Nebraska, moves to Pittsburgh and works on the Daily *Leader* newspaper staff.

1901: Cather turns to teaching English at Allegheny H.S. She begins to write poetry.

1905: Willa publishes a collection of her short stories.

1906: She is hired to help edit McClure's *Magazine* in New York where she works until 1912 though she isn't in favor of its "muckraking, crusading methods." She travels in Europe and America, tries to live in France but becomes homesick for her prairie country and in time also becomes fond of the Southwest.

1913: Cather's 0 *Pioneers! is* published and well received, enabling her to write full time without the need of side employment.

> 1922: Willa's *One of Ours is* awarded the Pulitzer Prize.
>
> 1927: Cather publishes *Death Comes for the Archbishop* [described by some as the best novel written about New Mexico].

Latour visits Father Mariano Lucero, "the miser" at Arroyo Hondo. "He had the lust for money as Martínez had for women and they had never been rivals in the pursuit of their pleasures." When Father Lucero dies it is discovered that he has nearly $20,000 stashed away, a "great sum for one old priest to have scraped together in a country parish down at the bottom of a ditch."

Book VI: Bishop Latour goes about gathering funds for a cathedral in Santa Fe. One of the friends of "rich" Antonio Olivares met by the bishop is handsome Manuel Chávez "with delicately cut, disdainful features…one had only to see him cross the room, or to sit next [to] him at dinner, to feel the electric quality under his cold reserve, the fierceness of some embitterment, the passion for danger." Chávez "boasted his descent from two Castilian knights..." but "was jealous of Carson's fame as an Indian-fighter, declaring that he had seen more Indian warfare before he was twenty than Carson would ever see." He was expert with most weapons and "took a cool pleasure in stripping the Indians of their horses or silver or blankets, or whatever they had put up on their man" when they came by his hacienda for wagering. Chávez "never reconciled to American rule...was a Martínez man" and distrusted "the new Bishop because of his friendliness toward Indians and Yankees...he hated to spend an evening among American uniforms."

Book VII: Bishop Latour's diocese grows with the Gadsden Purchase and it becomes "no easy matter for two missionaries on horseback to keep up with the march of history." Father Vaillant is missionizing in Tucson and "restoring the old mission church of St. Xavier del Bac, which he declared to be the most beautiful church on the continent, though it had been neglected for more than two hundred years."

Latour goes to the Navajo country with his guide Eusabio [sic].

Book VIII: Father Vaillant is called back from Tucson only to be assigned to the gold fields of Colorado around Camp Denver. But his Denver congregation of miners and business owners would give him no money for church necessities so he had to return "to the Mexicans to beg for money .. to pay for windows in the Denver church."

Book IX: Latour remains immensely busy with his duties but he becomes a champion against "the persecution of the Navajos and their expulsion from their own country....it was his own misguided friend, Kit Carson..." who led forces which hunted them down during a terrible winter whereupon they were "driven by the thousands from their own reservation to the Bosque Redondo, three hundred miles away on the Pecos River Hundreds of them, men, women, and children, perished from hunger and cold on the way-driven by starvation and the bayonet; captured in isolated bands, and brutally deported."

Death finally overtakes Bishop Latour.

ARTIST

Russian émigré **Nicolai Fechin** is brought to N.M. by the Carnegie Institute. He builds a home in Taos [which is still a monument to his artistic genius] because *"he was in love with the land and the natives. He had found his place."*

PROFILE

Nicolai Fechin

"THE MODERN MICHELANGELO"

December 9, 1881: Nicolai Fechin is born in Kazan, Russia.

1895: Nicolai enters the Kazan Art School.

1900: Fechin graduates from the Kazan Art School and enters the Art Academy in Petrograd. He writes: *"Art demands the whole person and for the whole of his life. Don't think you are already an artist if you are standing only on one little step-the striving must be high, to heaven itself."*

1903: Nicolai makes two summer tours through Siberia.

1908: He is hired as an instructor in the Kazan Art School when he graduates with top honors from the Art Academy. He achieves the rank of "Master Scientist of All Arts" because he is acknowledged as a *Master of painting and drawing* as well as adept in sculpting, architecture, and woodcarving. He travels in Europe and is invited to enter international exhibits. He writes: *Art, like the whole of our life, submits to the eternal law of change, and attempts to stop it at any one particular level are like vain efforts to stop time itself. True art cannot belong solely to any one period or current in the evolution of art, life itself selects that which furthers its own purpose, discarding the superfluous. This process of selection of what is necessary to life remains ever our wise teacher. The experiences which we thus collect throughout the ages indicate the path into the unknown future.*

1910: Fechin participates in a Carnegie Institute exhibit in Pittsburgh, Pennsylvania.

1913: Nicolai marries Alexandra Belkovitch.

1914: Daughter Eya (their only child) is born.

August 1, 1923: Fechin arrives in New York and lives there four years.

1926: Nicolai visits Taos during the summer and moves there with his family the following year. He builds his "Fechin House" and studio over the years. He devotes himself to his art, loves Taos and its people but he never becomes part of the socialite crowd, preferring a quieter lifestyle.

1931: Fechin becomes an American citizen. (Over the years he exhibits his art work nationally and internationally. He wins awards too numerous to mention.)

1933: Alexandra decides she wants a divorce, telling Nicolai he can take his daughter with him. Fechin doesn't fight the situation, leaves his home, takes his daughter, returning to New York then relocating to southern California. In time he travels to Mexico, Japan, Java, Bali, etc.

1948: Nicolai creates a studio in Santa Monica, California.

1955: Nicolai Fechin, the "Living Old Master," the artists' artist, the "Modern Michelangelo," dies in his sleep.

1976: The Fechin ashes are returned to Kazan by his daughter Eya and granddaughter Nicaela.

1979: The *Fechin House and Studio* are placed on the National Register of Historic Places.

1981: The Fechin Institute is created. The Fechin House is used for educational and cultural activities.

POLITICS

Governor Dillon appoints **Bronson Cutting** to the U.S. Senate where he becomes a member of the Progressive bloc.

[Cutting is described as pertaining to the "patrician" class of Theodore and Franklin D. Roosevelt, receiving his education at schools like Groton and Harvard. When tuberculosis struck he came to N.M. seeking to regain his health, acquired a newspaper, the *New Mexican*, and turned his considerable wealth and talents to politics.]

RADIO

Roswell's KCRX-AM, owned by Rosendo Cesarez Jr., is the first radio station in the state to offer programming in the Spanish language. (It goes exclusively Spanish in the 1950s.)

1935: Santa Fe's KVSF-AM offers Spanish programming.

1940s: Albuquerque's KABQ-AM is the first all-Spanish station in N.M.

1950: KANW-FM is the first FM station to offer Spanish-language programming.

1963: KDCE-AM, the first all-Spanish station in northern N.M., begins broadcasting in Española. It becomes well accepted by the people of the area.

1996: Santa Fe's bilingual KSWV-AM is rated by Arbitron as the number one station in Santa Fe for people over the age of 12. (General Manager **George Gonzáles** says Spanish-language media is booming all over the USA.)

SOCIETY
May 12, 1918: **Manuel Luján** Jr. is born.

Manuel Luján Jr.

POPULAR STATESMAN

1948: Manuel marries **Jean Kay Couchman**.

1948-1968: Manuel works in the family insurance business.

1950: Manuel earns a B.A. degree from the College of Santa Fe

1964: The Luján family moves to Albuquerque.

Manuel Luján Jr.
Courtesy Museum of NM, #52338

1968: Running as a Republican, Manuel upsets five-term Congressman Thomas G. Morris, thus becoming the first Hispanic Republican in the U.S. House of Representatives where he serves until 1988 (when he decides to retire). He sponsors many bills on diverse issues like national health care, income tax credits for waste, wilderness areas, the elderly, radioactive waste, etc.

1988: Manuel states *"It's time to come home"* so he retires from the House but President Bush asks him to become his Secretary of the Interior and Manuel Luján can't refuse his President so he accepts the appointment.

ACTIVISM
February 23: **John Collier,** head of the **Indian Defense Association,** denounces the Bureau of Indian Affairs and Interior Department for the dictatorial policies they perpetrate on Native American peoples.

1928
TINSMITH
Benjamin Sweringen opens his Santa Fe shop **The Spanish Chest** and produces tinwork from 1928-1936.

RANCHING
Villagers in the **Río Puerco** areas lose nearly half of their sheep during a brutal winter. Wealthy sheepman **Frank Bond** survives and virtually monopolizes the range land, renting out sheep on shares to destitute Hispanos. Overgrazing denudes and erodes the soil even further.

POTTERY
The **Rosalea Medina Toribio** family of **Zía Pueblo** is creating pottery during this period. Her daughters working in the craft are Juanita (and her Sofía and some of her family) and María Bridgett (and her Candelaria; Trinidad),

Sofia's: Lois, Edna, Marcellus, and Elizabeth (and their Kimberly and Marcella).

CELEBRITY
Charles Lindbergh is charting a coast-to-coast airmail route when engine trouble forces him to land his plane near **Vaughn.** He has to wait three days for parts with which to repair the engine during which time Vaughn residents "visit" him and take souvenir pictures around his plane.

1929
SOCIETY
Governor Dillon states that N.M. has no unemployment problem because most of its people live pastoral, self-sufficient lives, which doesn't *"...bring them into sharp competition in the matter of earning a livelihood..."*

EDUCATION
The **Colonial Hispanic Crafts School** is founded in Galisteo by **Concha Ortiz y Pino.** It teaches weaving, leather working, and furniture making.

TINSMITH
Francisco Delgado (1858-1936) becomes owner of the **Colonial Tin Antiques** shop on **Canyon Road.** He is a collector of tinwork and also creates many pieces that gain much popularity. His son, **Ildeberto** "Eddie" **Delgado** (1883-1966) also becomes an outstanding tinsmith.

SOCIETY
E. Boyd arrives in N.M. (and in time becomes an internationally recognized authority on New Mexican Spanish colonial art).

PUBLISHING
The **University of New Mexico** begins a Press to promote communication among scholars, diffuse significant knowledge, and contribute to the development and enjoyment of regional culture. It plans to

publish scholarly works, especially in the *"fields of anthropology, Latin American studies, and the history and culture of the American West."*

1930s: During the Great Depression years Press Director **Fred Harvey** loads books in his car and drives throughout N.M. to sell them to bookstores and schools.

1933: The first (it is said) hardcover book to be published by UNM Press is *New Mexico History and Civics* by **Lansing Bloom**.

1934: *Practical Spoken Spanish* by Dr. **E.M. Kercheville** is published.

1984: UNM Press owns one computer.

1997: The Press now owns and utilizes 46 computers. All phases of the publishing process depend on them.

There are 748,447 books in the UNM Press warehouse.

Dr. Kercheville's *Practical Spoken Spanish* is still in print, making it the longest-running title on the UNM Press list.

POTTERY

Rose Gonzáles of San Ildefonso Pueblo creates carved-style pottery, the first in that Pueblo. Her son, Tse Pe (Eagle-Cane), and his wife, **Dora** (daughter of Candelaria Gachupin from Zía), and his second wife, Jennifer (from Santa Clara), learn the craft from Rose and they encourage their four daughters, Irene, Jennifer, Candace, and Gerri, to continue the family tradition.

ORGANIZATION

The **Spanish Colonial Arts Society** is incorporated by M. Austin, F. Applegate, F.I. Proctor, G.M. Bloom, F.E. Mera, M.A. Dietrich, Mrs. A.S. Alvord, J.G. Meem, J.D. DeHuff, and M.C. Bauer.

ARTIST

Painter **Georgia O'Keeffe** arrives in Taos after an invitation by Mabel Dodge Luhan.

[O'Keeffe goes on to define N.M. as symbolic of the Southwest with its semi-arid terrain, spectacular vistas illuminated by purified light, vast mountains, and sculptured mesas endowed with enduring beauty, which, possibly more than any other artist, she helped bring to the attention of the rest of the nation.]

PHOTOGRAPHY

Twenty-seven-year-old **Ansel Adams** arrives in Taos after an invitation by Mabel Dodge Luhan. Though he has prepared for a career as a concert pianist he agrees to collaborate with Mary Austin on a "verbal pictorial" celebration of Taos Pueblo (and he goes on to develop into one of America's greatest photographers).

ARTIST
Watercolorist **John Marín** arrives in Taos after an invitation by Mabel Dodge Luhan. He is *"captivateded by Taos Mountain"* and creates nearly 100 watercolors of the area.

BUSINESS
J.M. Ramiréz takes charge of the **Spanish Market.**

PRESERVATION
The **Santuario de Chimayó** is being dismantled piecemeal. **Mary Austin,** lecturing at Yale, finds an anonymous donor who buys it and gives it to the Church who must hold it and all contents in trust for worship and as a religious museum.

FLOOD
The **Río Grande** rages out of control and **floods** hundreds of farms in the densely populated Middle Río Grande Valley. Some villages, like **San Marcial,** are completely destroyed.

HEALTH
Infant mortality rates are 140 per 1,000 in N.M., compared to 61 per 1,000 in the nation as a whole, with Indians and Hispanics suffering the greatest losses. *"Anglo reformers"* begin a campaign against traditional forms of health care. Hispanic *parteras* (midwives) are attacked as *"superstitious, unclean, and uninformed."* Indian medicine men and women are also considered obstacles. But nurses with cultural sensitivity like Louise Kuhrtz, Elizabeth Forster (author of *Denizens of the Desert*), Eva Wade, etc., are quite successful in their field work.

1935: It is estimated that there are about 750 practicing *parteras* in the state.

1936: A rural demonstration unit to license and regulate midwives and teach modern techniques is set up in San Miguel County and is highly successful. Several female physicians (Nancy Campbell, Gertrude Light, Mary Lou Hickman, Marian Hotopp, Edith Millican, Mary Waddell) and as many as 10 nurses work through it. **Jesusita Aragón** graduates from midwife classes and becomes one of the most active workers in northern N.M.

1940: Infant mortality is now 100 deaths per 1,000 births.

1945: Some 800 midwives are practicing in N.M.,

1965: Less than one hundred midwives are practicing in N.M., most women giving birth in hospitals instead of at home.

1930s
BOOKS
Mabel Dodge Luhan writes her memoirs (*Background* in 1933, *European Experiences* in 1935, *Movers and Shakers* in 1936, *Edge of Taos Desert: An Escape to Reality* in '37) in an effort to unmask *"the*

system that produced her...a social system that taught her that the only way to succeed in life is by having power over other human beings." She feels "Anglo" American society rewards *"power, prestige, and possession"* while it hypocritically preaches love and brotherhood.

[Actress Cornelia Otis Skinner writes a parody titled *"A Brief Digest of the Intimate Memoirs of Mabel Fudge Hulan."*]

Mabel continues to attract *"great souls"* to Taos: Edna Ferber, Thornton Wilder, Leopold Stokowski, Thomas Wolfe, Robinson Jeffers, Myron Brinig, etc.

POTTERY

The Hopi-Tewa **Navasie** family is creating pottery during this period.

Paqua Naha's family: Helen Naha, Joy Navasie, Eunice, Pauline Setalla.
Helen's: Sylvia, Rainell, Burel.
Hugh's: Cynthia, Miltona.
Joy's: Grace, Loretta, Maynard (Veronica), Natelle Lee, Leona, Marianne (Harrison Jim and their Donna).
Eunice's: Fawn, Dawn, Dolly.
Pauline's: Karen, Gwen, Agnes, Stetson.
Loretta's: Lana, Charles, John Biggs.
Maynad's: Ray, Bill.
Leona's: Linda.

PROFILE

Robert H. Goddard

"FATHER OF AMERICAN ROCKETRY"

Dr. Robert H. Goddard leaves his hometown of Worchester, Massachusetts, and settles on a ranch in the Roswell area in order to work in *rocketry* (which most people consider to be *Buck Rogers stuff*). Ahead of his time, he manages to acquire enough funding to maintain a modest research program that results in discovering how to utilize gasoline instead of gunpowder as a fuel. His discoveries in the use of liquid fuel are unprecedented and his test flights reach thousands of feet.

1939: Dr. Goddard and his crew have uncovered the basic requirements necessary for high altitude rocketry, their last flight model capable of climbing perhaps six miles in altitude.

1940: Dr. Goddard seeks military funding for high altitude testing. The Army shows little interest in his work but the Navy wants to develop a rocket that can be attached to an airplane for additional thrust (JATO: Jet Assisted Take Off) when taking off with heavy loads or from short runways.

1941: Dr. Goddard leaves N.M. to work at Annapolis on the Navy contract. While the military goes with solid fuel instead of liquid as developed by Goddard, several engineering challenges are met for pumps, combustion chambers, thrust, engine cooling, etc., because of Goddard's work.

Dr. Goddard also serves as consultant for the powder rocket program which in time develops bazookas, depth charge launchers, and armor penetrating rockets.

1945: Dr. Robert H. Goddard dies just before V-J Day.

[His efforts have been described as the most *amazing lone-wolf development program in the history of technology.* Before his death he had written to H.G. Wells saying that he would work in rocketry as long as he lived with no thought of finishing because *"aiming for the stars is a goal to occupy generations."*]

1930
MIGRANTS
Increasing numbers of **impoverished migrants from Oklahoma, Texas, and Arkansas** enter N.M., looking for work.

1931: The Legislature limits to 15% the employment of nonresidents on public works projects.

ARTS & CRAFTS
The **Spanish Arts Shop** is established, with much credit due to **Mary Austin,** because of revived interest in old and new Spanish crafts.

EDUCATION
El Rito Normal School offers classes in traditional Hispanic crafts.

RECLAMATION
Construction begins on **Middle Río Grande Conservancy District.** Hispanic and "Anglo" farmers resist destruction of their irrigation ditches at the start of the planting season. **Heavy assessments** imposed on agricultural lands are impossible to pay.

1932: The Conservancy faces bankruptcy.

[Due to the efforts of New Mexico's congressional delegation, Senators Cutting and Bratton, Rep. Chávez, the **Reconstruction Finance Corporation** eventually finances the Conservancy and Santa Cruz projects, but only after bond holders have been forced into receivership.]

PROFILE

George I. Sánchez

E D U C A T O R ,   A U T H O R ,   A C T I V I S T

Educator George I. Sánchez has taught in rural elementary schools since 1923.

1930: Sánchez receives his bachelor's degree from the University of New Mexico.

1931: He is awarded a Master's degree from the University of Texas at Austin.

1934: George is awarded a doctor's degree from the University of California at Berkeley.

1935-1936: Sánchez conducts a survey on rural education in the southern states.

1937-1938: Sánchez works as *Asesor Técnico General* for the *Ministerio de Educación Nacional* in Caracas, Venezuela.

1938-1939: A Carnegie Corporation grant enables Sánchez to study the economic, social, and political conditions of Taos County, which will lead to the book titled *The Forgotten People*. Dr. Sánchez writes prolifically, producing many books and articles. *The People: A Study of the Navajos* is another of his well-known works.

1940: Sánchez is a professor at the University of Texas.

1951-1959: He chairs the Department of History and Philosophy of Education.

1963: Dr. Sánchez is Director of the Center for International Education at the University of Texas.

TINSMITH

Francisco Sandoval (1860-1944) of Santa Fe is producing **tinwork.** His work is described as excellent in craftsmanship and design. His art is characterized by trefoil scallops, repeated concentric circles of the finial, side rondels, and a distinctive shape of the base.

Francisco Delgado
Courtesy Museum of NM, #71180

EDUCATION

The **San José Experimental School Program** is begun in south Albuquerque, directed by Dr. **Lloyd S. Tireman.** Educator **George I. Sánchez** works with Tireman. The program lasts only five years but inspires other projects:

1936: **Taos Project,** headed by Professor J.T. Reid;

1937: **Nambé Project** (with Tireman as director).

LABOR ACTIVIST

Jesús Pallares, from Chihuahua, Mexico, is fired from his mining job for criticizing Gamerco. He finds employment as a coal miner in Madrid, later becoming the United Mine Mill and Smelter Workers of America representative.

1934: After a strike, Pallares is accused of being a communist agitator, evicted from his house, fired, and blacklisted. He helps to found *La Liga Obrera de Habla Española.*

1936: Pallares is jailed by immigration officials pending a deportation hearing as an undesirable alien. He is convicted of being a communist and deported *("...one of many ordered by the Immigration and Naturalization Service against Mexicans active in U.S. labor during this period..."* according to J.B. Demark).

1930-1935
GOVERNMENT
Dennis Chávez serves in the U.S. House of Representatives. He is a champion of reclamation and irrigation works like the Elephant Butte Dam and Carlsbad Irrigation Project. Ever sensitive to the needs of Indians, he is appointed chairman of the Indian Affairs Committee and in 1933 sponsors a bill authorizing compensatory payments of $750,000 to the Pueblo Indians for misappropriated lands.

1931-1933
Arthur Seligman is Governor.

1931
SOCIETY
The *Santa Fe New Mexican* reports that *"...several carloads of callow youths parked their autos close up against a morada or Penitente chapel at the settlement of Hernández the other night, commenced making merry and that when a group of natives appeared and asked them what they were doing, one bright boy drew a revolver and discharged the same in the general direction of the residents. 'Penitente chasers' are forming the habit of making a Roman holiday out of the Easter week observances of this religious sect and it is growing worse year by year."*

LITERATURE
The **New Mexico Quarterly,** intended for publication of regional literature, is funded at the University of New Mexico.

FOLKLORE
Mary Austin organizes the **New Mexico Folklore Society.**

POTTERY
The **Santana Melchor** family of **Santo Domingo** is creating pottery during this period. Santana's working daughters are Dolorita (and her Joann, Marlene, Darlene, Irene) and Crucita (and her granddaughters Marcella, Mandy).

GREAT DEPRESSION
Governor Seligman launches a $5,000,000 **highway construction** program to help combat unemployment. Twenty to twenty-five thousand New Mexicans are out of work. Highway construction rewards contractors and their use of machinery provides relatively few jobs for average New Mexicans.

PROFILE

Alberto O. Martínez

A TRI-LINGUAL NEW MEXICAN

February 18, 1932: **Alberto Onaldo Martínez** is born to Adelaido N. Martínez and Altagracia Martínez on the Jicarilla Apache Reservation.

1937: The family moves to **Santa Cruz de la Cañada.** Alberto attends the **McCurdy Mission School** where, despite being heir to a trilingual New Mexican heritage, he is severely punished whenever he is *"caught"* speaking Spanish, his native language. Summers are spent *"hoeing endless rows of corn"* and the corn is sold to pay for his education *"that is intended to abolish"* his Spanish and Indian heritage. He makes a vow that someday he will teach school and combat the racism that denigrates his New Mexican heritage.

1950: Alberto graduates from Española High School.

1940s: Martínez studies pottery making with **Fidel Archuleta,** a master potter from the Española Valley (who at the age of 15 studied with **María Martínez** from San Ildefonso). Archuleta is also trilingual, being able to speak Spanish, Tewa, and English.

1957: Alberto begins teaching Navajo, Apache, and Hispanic students, emphasizing their true history and the beauty of their cultures and traditions. He continues his language development, being fluent in Spanish, Navajo, English, and Tewa.

1959: Alberto Martínez receives a B.A. degree in Southwest History from Highlands University.

1960: Martínez receives an M.A. degree and develops a strong interest in anthropology. He goes to the National University of Mexico and does research in the *awesome* Museum of Anthropology.

1960-1970: Alberto works during the summers with Mr.. **J. Lee Correll** to produce the extensive six-volume history of the Navajo Nation. Because he can speak Athabascan (Navajo-Apache, a language which involves little lip movement compared to European languages) Alberto is instrumental in talking to older Navajos and convincing them to participate in the historical project. He also aids in identifying Anasazi ruins and is further attracted to the art of making pottery.

1981: Martínez retires from teaching and devotes himself to research, writing, and pottery making.

[His written work, which ranges from history to poetry, is copyrighted but unpublished.]

WATER LAW

Subterranean waters and their sources are adjudicated [becoming New Mexico's most important contribution to western water law], resulting in a statute which reads in part: *"The waters of underground streams, channels, artesian basins, reservoirs, or lakes, having reasonably ascertainable boundaries, are hereby declared to be public waters and to belong to the public and to be subject to appropriation for beneficial use."*

1932
POVERTY

Dispossessed of grazing lands and deprived of wage labor opportunities by the Great Depression, the heretofore self-sufficient **Hispanic villagers are in dire poverty.** Hispanos are 80% of New Mexico's relief load. Federal officials question whether they are eligible for emergency relief, believing their plight was caused by soil exhaustion, insufficient farm land, and long-term unemployment. *"They even question whether a population so backward and alien could be brought into the American fold."*

Margaret Reeves, director of the **Bureau of Child Welfare,** reports that relief needs are greater than anyone has imagined. In one rural county some children are found to be so undernourished they are emaciated. Some women and children wear clothing made from flour sacks. *"Despite their plight, Reeves reported, the Hispanic villagers were technically ineligible for relief since they were not victims of recent crop failures but had been made destitute through long term unemployment."*

Storekeepers throughout the State maintain they can no longer work on credit. One storekeeper closes all lines of credit unless people sign affidavits that they are starving.

Charles Ilfeld of Las Vegas loans seeds and insect poisons to villagers.

Counties most urgently in need of relief are Bernalillo, Colfax, Río Arriba, McKinley, Doña Ana, Valencia, Eddy, Curry, San Miguel, Socorro.

AMERIND

Pojoaque Pueblo *(P'-o-Suwae-Geh,* "Drinking Water Place") is revitalized by 14 original members of the community. They seek and obtain an official patent for their 11,593 acres of land.

POLITICS

November: Much to the dismay of Republicans, **F.D.R. wins New Mexico** as he does other Western states.

1933-1934

Andrew W. Hockenhull is Governor.

1933
GOVERNMENT

President Roosevelt appoints **John Collier** as **Commissioner of Indian Affairs.** Champion of Native
American causes, Collier now has access to federal funding. He is a proponent of cultural pluralism
and the rights of minorities, soil conservation, preservation of ethnic customs and revival of ethnic
arts and crafts. He introduces these ideas into the **New Deal** and its leaders (A.A. Berle, H.L. Ickes,
H.A. Wallace, R. Tugwell, H. Hopkins, R. Fechner, etc.)

Collier is successful in establishing an Indian Division of the Civilian Conservation Corps, the **Emergency
Conservation Works** program. Native American workers in this program build reservation roads,
storage dams, fences, wells, and structures to control erosion.

Collier is determined to improve and **expand Navajo and Pueblo land holdings,** even if it means altering the
balance of Indian/Hispanic/Anglo land relationships. **State officials** demand part of the federal pie
and **clash with Collier.**

The **Soil Erosion Service** is created with **H.H. Bennet** to direct it. From its funding base of $5,000,000,
$1,000,000 is earmarked for work on the **Navajo Reservation,** with labor supplied by the Civilian
Conservation Corps. Collier sees to it that his friends **H.G. Calkins** and **E. Shevky** are selected to
form part of the SES staff.

1934: The **Indian Reorganization Act** is passed, ending land allotments. it sets up a revolving fund for
economic development and gives preferential hiring to Indians within the BIA. It offers tribes the
opportunity to charter themselves as municipal corporations in order to compete in a modern
economy and encourages tribal nations to write constitutions that give them greater political
self-control. Collier adds 425,000 acres of *"eroded land"* from several of the old Spanish land
grants, **to the Navajo Reservation** and later he buys the Espíritu Santo and Montaño land grants for
exclusive use of **Laguna, Zía, and Jémez Pueblos.**

Villagers from the Río Puerco area protest the loss of their traditional grazing lands and wealthy ranchers
led by **Floyd Lee from San Mateo** call on the State's congressional delegation to put a stop to
Collier's activities. Senator **Dennis Chávez** demands an equitable federal land policy and blocks
legislation to expand Navajo Reservation boundaries. Collier describes Chávez as a sellout to
wealthy stockmen.

E. Shevky releases his **Tewa Basin Study** which reveals the acute suffering of Hispanic villagers, their
extremely limited agricultural resources, and their dependence on wage labor. Corroborating
studies show that **overstocked ranges** are used (50%) by large commercial (sometimes nonresi-
dent) stockmen, that if all are required to reduce stock numbers, the villagers with few animals
would be hardest hit.

[Shevky's reports threaten some of New Mexico's most powerful **stockmen.** *"Rumor has it that copies were ordered destroyed during the conservative, McCarthyite backlash of the 1950s. It appears that a number of monographs and others published by the Farm Security Administration no longer exist. Of those that do exist, very few copies remain..."* according to S. Forrest.]

1936: John Collier realizes that the struggle isn't really between Indian and non-Indian but **between "subsistence" populations and large commercial stock growers.** However, Indian lands receive *five times* the expenditures for soil conservation work as non-Indian lands. **Stock reduction** programs, referred to by government officials as *"livestock improvement programs,"* forever tarnish the reputation of John Collier in the minds of many Pueblos and Navajos and represent the low point of the Indian New Deal.

ART EDUCATION
Led by the talented **Dorothy Dunn,** a department of painting is established at the **Santa Fe Indian School.**

SOCIETY
Along with the State's congressional delegation, writers, artists, and progressive civic leaders influence public policy:

Mary Austin lectures about N.M. throughout the nation;

Paul A. Walter, business-man and long-time member of historical and archaeological societies, also edits *El Palacio,* the magazine of the Museum of N.M., and the *New Mexico Historical Review.*

E. Dana Johnson edits the *Santa Fe New Mexican* [from 1913 to 1937]. There is an amazing unanimity in what needs to be done in N.M.: roads have to be built throughout northern N.M. in order to link it with Santa Fe; village life needs to be revitalized by improving agricultural practices; cottage industries are necessary to supplement agriculture; land has to be restored; the various cultures of N.M. need to be revitalized and preserved for many reasons, including tourism and its monetary rewards.

New Deal programs come to N.M. when emergency education programs are begun under directors like:

Brice Sewell (Industrial Education and Rehabilitation), who institutes County Community Vocational Schools with classes in spinning, weaving, ironwork, tinwork, leather tooling, and Spanish furniture making for Hispanics.

For "Anglo" communities in the eastern and southern portions of the state he starts classes in auto mechanics, welding, woodworking, repair of farm equipment, commerce and finance;

Rebecca Graham (Adult Education), who spearheads introduction of classes in elementary education, English, homemaking, Spanish, art, music, dance, commerce, physical education, economics, government, etc.

Birdie Adams (Nursery Schools), seeks to introduce modern methods and concepts of child care, health, nutrition, and study of English at an early age.

The **Civilian Conservation Corps** is created by an act of Congress. Young men are recruited to work on the land: forest camps, soil conservation projects, grazing services, and the Bureau of Reclamation) and it becomes one of the most popular of New Deal programs. Only males aged 18 to 25 are allowed into the CCC; they are paid **$30 a month** and $25 of it is sent home to their families. The atmosphere is something akin to the military, the food nourishing, and at the end of the work day there is recreation in the form of educational and athletic programs.

There are 44 CCC camps in N.M. There are a few unpleasant incidents in southern counties when some individuals refuse to share tents with **"greasers."** A boxing match degenerates into a riot. Some "Anglos" "*....from Texas and eastern N.M.*" become infuriated when Hispanics speak in Spanish among themselves. New Mexico officials resist sending New Mexicans to out-of-state camps but it occurs and these young Hispanics vigorously fight the discrimination that targets them.

Federal Project One of the **Works Progress Administration** is begun and becomes as popular as it is effective in its various forms:

Federal Art Project hires 51 N.M. artists, including a number of Indian and a few Hispanics, to decorate public buildings and parks, paint murals in government buildings, and do sculptures. Individuals like **Patrocióño Barela,** a tremendously talented sculptor who gains national prominence, and **Juan Sánchez,** who can reproduce classic bultos with exactness are "discovered," and the project known as the Portfolio of Spanish Colonial Design becomes the forerunner of the Index of American Design.

Federal Writers' Project begins by translating the Public Survey Office Archives and the Historical Society Archives. The famed **1779 Miera y Pacheco map of N.M.** is discovered by a shepherd near the old Valverde battlefield then taken to the local WPA office. Production of a State guidebook is standard in all states but State Director **Ina Sizer Cassidy** emphasizes the collection of Hispanic folklore and appoints **Aurora Lucero-White** to supervise the collection. Federal officials and then **John Lomax** criticize the heavy emphasis on Indian and Hispanic folklore while "neglecting" that of "Anglos" so much of the Hispanic folklore is omitted in the 1940 volume titled *New Mexico: A Guide to a Colorful State.*

Federal Music Project, under the direction of **Helen Chandler Ryan,** emphasizes research and preservation by encouraging musicians and musicologists to transcribe, record, and revive New Mexico's Hispanic musical heritage

1942: An Hispanic New Mexican *Song and Game Book* is published and advertised as the *"oldest folk music in America"* after that of Native Americans. It includes *alabados* and traditional Hispanic musical forms like the *décima, cuando,* and *corrido.*

1942: A work titled *Spanish American Dance Tunes* is also published.

STRIKE

Gamerco workers in Gallup coal mines go on strike because the company refuses to bargain. Union leaders like **Eusebio Navarro** and organizers like **Bill and Martha Roberts** are arrested. Miners who still refuse to return to work are fired. The jailings and firings are vigorously protested. A fight breaks out in which the sheriff and three protesters are killed, several others being wounded. *Fifty-five miners* are arraigned for conspiracy to murder a peace officer. Defense lawyers are kidnapped and dumped on the Zuñi reservation (unhurt but badly frightened), which county officials describe as a *hoax*. Ten miners ultimately stand trial and seven are found guilty of second-degree murder. According to R. Kern, *"Labor simply could not withstand the combined forces of management and government."*

DISCRIMINATION AT UNM

January 26: **Juan A. Sedillo,** Senator from Santa Fe, introduces **Senate Bill** 71 *"To Prevent the Formation and Prohibit the Existence of Secret Fraternities and Sororities in State Educational Institutions, Universities, Colleges and Schools..."* to combat illegal discriminatory practices which target Hispanics at the **University of New Mexico,** according to P.B. Gonzáles.

1920s: The University of New Mexico begins to develop and attract more students. But its Hispanic enrollment is only around 3%.

1924: Upon graduating from the Georgetown School of Law, **Juan Sedillo** compiles the laws which govern the University of New Mexico, giving special emphasis to Article 8 of the state constitution which guarantees that citizens *"of Spanish descent shall forever enjoy perfect equality..."* in all state educational institutions.

1925: **Mela Sedillo,** Juan's sister and daughter of UNM regent **Antonio Sedillo,** and several "Anglo" women are successful in chartering the Chi Omega Sorority on campus.

1928-1935: Despite the Great Depression, various New Mexico business underwrite the building of fraternity/sorority houses and in time "Greeks" dominate student life at UNM.

1930: **Arthur Seligman** is elected Governor. UNM requests a "substantial" budget increase, this during the Great Depression. Rumor has it that UNM professors and administrators are directing taxpayer funded street improvements into their neighborhoods, the university president's tax-supported residence is built, and fraternities/sororities file claims for tax exemptions on their properties. Governor Seligman begins to view UNM as *"selfish, arrogant, and uncooperative."*

1932: UNM President **James Zimmerman** delivers a speech in California where he extols the value of exchange programs with Latin American countries. **J.J. Clancy,** a Spanish-speaking teacher at Antón Chico, criticizes Zimmerman for the hypocrisy of praising Latins from the other Americas while denigrating those in N.M. He charges that Hispanics are treated like foster children in the public schools and at UNM.

Independents win all student offices at UNM. And for two semesters in a row, Independents win the "Scholastic Cup" for the highest grade-point average among organized student groups. The (all male) **Bilingual Club** joins forces with the Independents in the status-significant athletic intramural contests, scoring well against the fraternities in the track and field meet. And the Bilingual Club basketball team wins the basketball championship.

The Bilingual Club of from 35 to 50 members do their utmost to promote Hispano welfare. Members discuss high dropout rates with educator **George I. Sánchez**. And they contact Santa Fe Senator **Juan A. Sedillo** in an effort to combat UNM's racism even though it is channeled through fraternities/sororities.

1933: **Juan A. Sedillo** introduces Senate Bill 71 to prohibit the formation of fraternities and sororities at any State educational institution. Pro and con petitions are sent to legislators:

Hispanics claim Greek organizations do harm to non-fraternity "Anglos" as well as to Spanish Americans, letters come from out-of-state Hispanics who declare they chose their schools because of the rampant racism at UNM; that fraternities/sororities foster a caste system, not democracy...

The **Inter-Fraternity Council** argues that their houses save the State thousands of dollars which would have to be spent for additional housing; that *"any barriers, racial or otherwise, the creation of which have been credited to fraternities and sororities, exist only in the minds of those students who are not members..."*

SB 71 dies in committee.

Within a month a professor at UNM is charged with fomenting racial discord and forced to resign.

1934: The all-female group called **Las Damitas** is organized by and for Hispanic young women at UNM. it is a subchapter of the **Phrateres** national organization [and is kept separate from **Laughlin,** the subchapter for "Anglo" young women at UNM, until 1943].

1934
ARTS & CRAFTS
June: The **Native Market** shop opens in Santa Fe (later with a branch store in Tucson) due to the efforts of **Leonora Curtin,** providing an outlet for Hispanic crafts. Goods sold include weaving, furniture, *colchas,* ironwork, religious carvings, tinwork.

LABOR
Workers in **Gallup** strike to protest wage cuts.

THEATER
The **National Little Theater Movement** comes to Taos with the formation of the **Taos Players.**

TIMELINE

June 18, 1934: The Indian Reorganization Act is passed (reversing the 1887 Dawes Act) but is "...now seen as destructive of traditional Indian government."

EDUCATION

Eastern New Mexico Normal School is founded at **Portales** (and later becomes **Eastern New Mexico University).**

SOCIETY

August 13: **Mary Austin** dies.

[Earlier she had placed a mark on a creviced rock on Picacho Peak in the Sangre de Cristos and her ashes are placed there and covered permanently with cement. She left her many causes and 34 books as her legacy to N.M. and the world. Most of her estate she bequeathed to the Indian Arts Fund, one of her most cherished causes.]

1935-1938

Clyde Tingley is Governor.

1935

TINSMITHS

Various tinsmiths are producing tinworks: Pedro Quintana, Robert Woodman, Juan García, David Laemmle, Bruce Cooper, Pedro Cervantes.

Clyde and Carrie Tingley
Courtesy Museum of NM, #56516, #7898

POLITICS

May 11: Governor Tingley appoints **Dennis Chávez** to the U.S. Senate upon the death of Senator Bronson Cutting and Chávez serves for the rest of his life.

POTTERY

Grace Chapella, a Hopi-Tewa, is creating pottery around this time, as do family members **Laura and Dalee.** Other potters in Grace's family include Alma Tahbo, Deanna Tahbo, Mark Tahbo, Dianne Tahbo, and adopted Mary Ami. Ethel Youvella and Verna Nahee are also part of this family of potters.

AMERIND

December 20: The **United Pueblos Agency** is established in Albuquerque by the Bureau of Indian Affairs.

1936
BOOKS

Old Spain in Our Southwest by **Nina Otero** is published.

[She doesn't use the name "Warren" for the book. But *"like several other well-educated Hispanic women involved at that time in the revitalization of their heritage--Concha Ortiz y Pino, Carmen Espinoza, and Fabiola Cabeza de Baca Gilbert--Nina has been criticized for not personally identifying with the class of Spanish Americans she was patronizing in the 1930s"* according to C. Whaley.]

PROFILE

Dennis Chávez

THE VOICE OF THE PEOPLE

April 8, 1888: **Dionisio (Dennis) Chávez** is born in Los Chávez, the son of David Chávez and Paz Sánchez Chávez.

1895: The Chávez family moves to Albuquerque.

1901: Dennis, the eldest of eight children, drops out of school because he must work to help support the family. After working at the same job for four years he is fired for refusing to deliver food to strikebreakers.

1911: Chávez marries **Imelda Espinosa**.

1916: He works as an interpreter for Senator A.A. Jones and is offered a clerkship in the U.S. Senate.

1918: At the age of 30, Dennis Chávez, a former school dropout and married man with two children, enters Georgetown Law School.

1920: Chávez receives his law degree.

1923: Dennis is elected to the State legislature. He introduces the first bill to provide New Mexico's students with free textbooks.

1930: Chávez is elected to the House of Representatives and re-elected in 1932.

1934: In one of the most acrimonious elections in N.M. history, Chávez fails to unseat Republican Senator Bronson Cutting [the only major election Chávez ever lost].

1935: After the death of Senator Cutting in a plane crash, Governor Tingley appoints Chávez to fill the vacancy in the U.S. Senate.

1936: Chávez is elected to the Senate (and re-elected in 1940, 1946, 1952, 1958). Throughout his career in the Senate, Dennis Chávez is concerned with development of resources in the West. He actively supports soil and water conservation programs, improved transportation, federal crop insurance, and rural electrification.

Dennis Chávez
Courtesy Museum of NM, #57271

1937: Dennis introduces the first of many bills to protect Native American lands, their citizenship and voting rights, their self-determination.

1940s: Chávez is a champion for improving American education. He favors America's entry into NATO. The only Spanish speaking Senator in Washington, he works with Secretary of State Cordell Hull in forming the Good Neighbor Policy for Latin America and in planning the Pan American Highway. He is very active with the concerns and aspirations of Puerto Rico.

He co-sponsors one of the first bills to prohibit discrimination in employment, the Fair Employment Practices Commission Bill, which prohibits discrimination based on race, religion, color, national origin or ancestry.

1950s: Dennis is among the first to denounce the tactics of Senator Joseph McCarthy, asking that the Senate return to *decency, sanity and the basic principles of due process.*

November 18, 1962: Senator Chávez dies. (At the time of his death he is the fourth ranking U.S. Senator.)

1966: The statue of Dennis Chávez is unveiled in Statuary Hall, the only New Mexican to be so honored. The inscribed plaque at the foot of the statue is in three languages, English, Spanish, and Navajo, and reads: *"We have lost our Voice. Our Voice is lost and gone forever."*

1991: The Dennis Chávez stamp is issued by the U.S. Postal Service as part of the Great American Series.

SCULPTOR
Patrociño Barela (Ca. 1900-1964) is one of the Federal Art Project artists displaying his work at the Museum of Modern Art when *Time* Magazine hails him as the *"discovery of the year"* for his wood sculptures.

POTTERY
The **Chavarría** family of **Santa Clara Pueblo** is creating pottery during this time. Pablita Chavarría's family working in pottery include Mildred, Stella, Mary, Florece, Elizabeth, Reycita, Clara Shije, and their families:

Stella's: Joey, Denise, Loretta;

Mary's: Fergus, Anna.

Elizabeth's: Yvette, Regina, Ernest, Betty;

Reycita's: Ernest, Jennifer.

LAND GRANT
The **Belén land grant** is taken over by the state due to **delinquent taxes.** Around 100,000 acres are sold for about 35 cents per acre. (Twenty-five years later one General Campbell sells the acreage for from $500 to $1,000 per acre.)

MURDER & MEDIA
Journalist **Carl N. Taylor,** who is working on an article on the Penitentes, is assaulted, shot to death, then robbed near **Cedar Crest.** The youthful killer is tried and convicted but popular psychology blames the **Penitentes.** The national media has a field day:

New Haven Evening Register: "Youth Confesses Killing, Absolving Torture Cult;"

Cleveland News: "Brutal Murder of Wandering Writer Unveils Weird New Mexico Torture Cult Rites He Was About to Expose;"

New York American: "Boy's Confession in Killing of Writer Fails to Calm Cult Vengeance."

POLITICS
New Mexican voters realign their loyalties to the Democratic Party.

EDUCATION

January: Under the directorship of **Tom L. Popejoy,** the National Youth Administration (NYA) enables young people between the ages of 16 to 24 to participate in the learning of crafts and to teach them along with other vocational subjects, in other communities. Popejoy champions educational opportunities that others haven't emphasized: his assistant is Hispanic; he takes pains to get programs to remote areas; he coordinates vocational and educational projects in order to develop the leadership qualities of young people in the communities being served. Popejoy's bureaucratic superiors question his approach to educational problems. As part of his explanation, Popejoy informs them as to the history of the State and the injustice inflicted on Hispanics since being taken over by the USA, freely quoting *The Forgotten People* by G.I. Sánchez.

PROFILE

Patrociño Barela

A M E R I C A ' S   G R E A T E S T   W O O D   S C U L P T O R

1900: **Patrociño Barela** is born to Manuel (who was born in Mexico) and Julia Barela around this time in Bisbee, Arizona. Patrociño has an older brother, Nicolás, and a younger sister.

1908: His mother, Julia, and infant sister die around this period so Patrociño, his brother Carlos and his father Manuel move to Taos. Manuel works as a *tamalero,* a sheepherder, and finally as a *curandero* herbalist. He places his sons in school but only for a few weeks, deciding it is a waste of time.

1911: Pat works as a laborer hauling stone.

1912: After quarreling with his father Patrociño leaves home around this time, looking for work on farms or anywhere that he can earn money. He is befriended by a black family in Colorado and begins to learn English. He works at railroad camps, army installations, coal mines, etc., but most often on farms. He roams through a number of states as an itinerant laborer. (It is said he becomes addicted to wine.)

[Portrayals of Barela often include negative characteristics. That is seldom done with most world-class artists.]

1930: Patrociño returns to Taos (Cañon). He is slightly over five feet tall and strongly built. He has thick black curly hair, large piercing but friendly eyes, and dark skin. He meets and (in 1931) marries **Remedios Josefa Trujillo y Vigil**, a widow with four children, and becomes

---

accustomed to the family life he never had. Pat and Remedios are happy for a time but then they begin a conflict that never ends. They have three children together: Luis, Julia Margarita, and Roberto Juan. Pat adores his children.

1931-1932: Patrociño is asked to repair a broken *santo* and something awakens in his creative soul: *could a santo be made out of one single piece of wood instead of putting it together in parts?* He becomes obsessed with carving figures out of one block of wood to the point that it appears to beckon him as a path to salvation. At the early stage of his career his work resembles Romanesque art, addressing morality through allegory and symbolism. He seeks inspiration from Bible stories and from his own life. His art begins to attract attention.

Patrociño Barela
Courtesy Museum of NM, #45749
(Mildred Crews photo)

1933: Pat visits Abad Lucero, a furniture maker from Santa Fe hired to teach his craft to people in Taos, to show him his sculptures.

1935: Doris Fish of the *Taos Valley News* writes that Barela's sculptures are really good because of their *"honest mysticism."*

1936: Barela is working for the government, hauling dirt at a salary of $80 a month. He is encouraged by **Vernon Hunter**, director of the Federal Art Project in N.M. (an artist himself and whose job it is to uncover new talent) to take a job creating wood sculptures instead, at a salary of $54 a month, which Patrociño accepts. During the month of March his work is put on display at the Museum of Fine Arts in Santa Fe where his creations are well received. Hunter tells his superiors in Washington, D.C. that Barela is the program's greatest find because he is a gifted sculptor of exceptional talent.

September, 1936: The Museum of Modern Art (MOMA) in New York puts on a WPA show called "New Horizons in American Art" which represents 171 artists from around the nation with some 400 items of their artistic creations on display. Barela has eight pieces in the show, more than any other artist, two of which are featured in the exhibition's catalog.

The *New York Times* and *Time Magazine* hail Patrociño Barela of Taos, New Mexico, as the outstanding artist of the WPA show at the MOMA. (The Taos art colony is *stunned*. Taos artists had been working for decades to achieve national recognition and suddenly not even one of their own had done it, and from a group considered of little worth to boot.)
The show in New York brings out several gallery owners who wish to represent Patrociño's work. Hunter now claims he will not permit the *exploitation* of Patrociño Barela, preventing the

artist from contact with gallery dealers, without Patrociño knowing about it. Hunter reports to his superiors that Barela hasn't produced enough of a significant body of work to show in a big city gallery but when lesser galleries request his work they are denied because of their lesser status. All information is kept hidden from Barela.

November, 1936: *New Mexico Magazine* features an article on Patrociño Barela and his highly acclaimed sculptures.

1939: Unable to live by his sculpting, Pat begins a period of about a dozen years in which he leaves Cañon to seek employment. This inhibits his artistic production.

1940: Due to Vernon Hunter's "protective" policy, Barela's sculptures are forgotten outside of N.M.

1943: Barela works with the Federal Art Project until this time, oblivious to the fame his art has earned him but kept hidden from him. He returns to working as an itinerant farm laborer.

1947: Mabel Dodge Luhan publishes *Taos and Its Artists*. Patrociño Barela is excluded from the work.

1951: Patrociño injures his back and returns to Cañon. A garage is converted into a studio where the artist, working with the simplest of tools, creates more than 1,000 sculptures (during his lifetime), the majority of them in cedarwood. The studio becomes a popular place to visit, especially attracting Pat's children and other young people. They like the sculptor's happy temperament and his sense of humor.

He sells his creations whenever possible but he also trades them or gives them to friends and family, still unaware that he is one of America's greatest sculptors. Various dealers cheat him by paying small amounts in cash then selling at a much higher price. Others get sculptures for a bottle of wine.

1953: Manuel Barela successfully removes his own appendix but an infection sets in and he dies.

1955: Mildred Crows, Judson Crows, and Wendell B. Anderson publish *Patrociño Barela, Taos Wood Carver*. Ernest Blumenschein berates Judson for referring to Barela as a great artist, saying *"None of us in our lifetime can ever say who the great artists are."*

Barela is prematurely aging and his health is deteriorating. His marriage and his drinking problem get worse. When he starts to lose his eyesight and can't carve as much because of it he seems to lose interest in living.

1963: Van Doren Coke publishes *Taos and Santa Fe: The Artist's Environment, 1862-1942*. Patrociño Barela isn't mentioned in the book.

October 24, 1964: A fire breaks out in the Barela garage studio and Patrociño perishes in it. Roberta K. Tarbell of the Los Angeles County Museum of Art later writes: *"The spirit of Barela's work spans centuries and* is *universally intelligible."*

1973: Jacinto Quirarte doesn't mention Pat Barela in his *Mexican American Artists.*

1996: Authored by Edward Gonzales and David L. Witt, Red Crane Books publishes *Spirit Ascendant: The Art and Life of Patrociño Barela.*

1937
BOOKS
Carmen Espinosa writes *New Mexico Tin Craft*, the first book on New Mexican tinsmithing.

DISCRIMINATION
Edgar L. Hewett accuses *"most Anglos of being hostile to New Mexico's native cultures."*

SOCIETY
Isidoro Armijo (1871-1949) is selected to *Who's Who in New Mexico*. He is credited with having authored more than 2,000 feature articles for English and Spanish newspapers in N.M. and Colorado.

RECLAMATION
Middle Río Grande Conservancy assessments (described as "exorbitant") are attached to and inseparable from **property taxes.** Farmers with the least productive lands and therefore the smallest cash reserves are required to pay the heaviest assessments. By the end of the year the State has taken over 2,000 properties due to **tax delinquencies** and another 9,000 are about to be sold for taxes.

Eighty-five percent of the delinquent tracts are under 10 acres and 89% of the owners being dispossessed are Hispanic.

Large land owners, with **Clinton P. Anderson** as their spokesman, complain that the entire burden for paying Conservancy costs is on their shoulders because small owners will not pay their share.

Small farmers are represented by the Liga Obrera and John Collier's **Committee for Spanish-American Affairs.**

The Conservancy District Board contends that any farmer who can't pay his taxes should be evicted and the land sold to others who will "recolonize" the area.

1947: The Conservancy District is taken over by the **Bureau of Reclamation** which observes that there is *"...no remedy to relieve the district from the effect of its original economically unsound basis of* *assessment of benefits...*" Most small farmers are forced off the land, some of them taking up residence in the community of **San José** in Albuquerque.

UN-AMERICAN ACTIVITIES

Professors **Arthur Campa** and **George I. Sánchez** announce plans to hold the first National Congress of Spanish-Speaking Peoples in the USA, to be celebrated on the campus of the University of New Mexico. Campa and Sánchez are quickly *"vilified as radicals and communists."* The **House of Un-American Activities** applies pressure to the University of New Mexico, which withdraws its support, squelching the conference.

SOCIETY

October 30, 1937: **Rudolfo Anaya** is born to Martín Anaya and Rafaelita Mares Anaya in Pastura.

PROFILE

Concha Ortiz y Pino de Kleven

A   PIONEERING   NEW   MEXICAN   WOMAN

Concha Ortiz y Pino is elected to the state House of Representatives where she serves through 1942 and becomes the first woman in the USA elected to the post of Majority Whip. She sponsors successful legislation to permit that Spanish be taught in the seventh and eighth grades [perhaps remembering the days when the nuns at Loretto Academy would force her to sit behind a statue as punishment for speaking Spanish?] as well as introducing a bill in the legislature for the establishment of the School of Inter American Affairs at UNM.

1943: Concha marries **Dr. Victor Kleven**, a former Rhodes Scholar and professor at UNM.

1950: Concha is appointed to the post of dean of women at the College of St.Joseph (later called the University of Albuquerque).

1951: Upon the death of her father, **José Ortiz y Pino,** Concha returns to Galisteo to manage the family ranch of 100,000 acres, which flourishes once again under her guidance.

1956: Husband Victor Kleven dies and drought strikes N.M. Concha returns to live in Albuquerque, burying herself in civic, cultural, and educational endeavors.

1966: Concha is the only woman appointed to the

National Commission on Architectural Barriers and

becomes the driving force behind the law requiring that

public buildings be accessible to the disabled. She also

is a member of the National Advisory Committee
for Project Upward Bound.

1977: The University of Albuquerque awards Concha
Ortiz y Pino de Kleven a Doctor of Humanities degree.

Concha Ortiz y Pino de Kleven
Courtesy Museum of NM, #59021

1938
LITERATURE
T.M. Pearce and Mabel Major publish *Southwest Heritage: A Literary History with Bibliographies.*

[E. Lomelí points out that this "otherwise authoritative" study consisting of 600 titles contains only seven
works by Hispanics. He states this is standard operating procedure and cites the following:

1934: *Writers and Writings of New Mexico* by Lester Raines mentions no Hispanic writers active during the
19th century;

1961: *The Early Novel of the Southwest* by Edwin W. Gaston doesn't mention one Hispanic novel.

1965: *Frontier American Literature and the West* by Edwin S. Fussell ignores all literature written before the
American takeover, thus promoting the implication that the "Anglo" American began Western
literature.

1972: The revised edition of *Southwest Heritage* contains some 850 titles; 21 are by Hispanics (for almost
three and a half centuries of Hispanic writing).

1974: *Southwest Classics: The Creative Literature of the Arid Land: Essays on the Books and Their Writers*
by Lawrence Clark Powell mentions one Hispanic work, the diary of the Franciscan missionary in
Arizona/California, Francisco Garcés.

Lomelí declares: *"This not-so-camouflaged ethnocentrism has become the measuring stick with which to
judge a people's literature."* He points to the writings of critics like **Luis Leal** and his
Hispanic-Mexican Literature in the Southwest, 1521-1848, published in 1985 by Greenwood
Press, to refute the ethnocentric writers mentioned above.]

SOCIETY

Governor **Clyde Tingley's** personality is expressed through a number of his projects while governor: he creates the **Carrie Tingley Hospital** for crippled children; he is responsible for building and financing the **State Fair,** with its **Tingley Coliseum,** which he locates permanently in Albuquerque; he obtains federal funds for **Tingley Park** and **Tingley Zoo.**

May 17, 1938: **E.A. "Tony" Mares** is born to Ernesto Gustavo Mares and Rebecca Devine Mares in Albuquerque.

1939-1942
John E. Miles is Governor.

1939
EDUCATION

Nina Otero-Warren, superintendent of the (Emergency Education Program) Literacy Program, describes observing one of her teachers, **Moises Romero,** in an isolated section of Mora County: Her car gets stuck twice and the final way up the mountain has to be climbed on foot. The classroom is an unheated room loaned by a student. Romero has 17 students, ranging in age from 17 to 65, to whom he teaches reading, writing, arithmetic in the form of agricultural figuring like how much seed is needed for a certain sized field, how much hay can be stored in a barn, etc. Instruction is in English while discussion is in Spanish.

TIMELINE

September 1, 1939: German forces invade Poland, beginning World War II.

ART COLONIES

Unable to support themselves through their art, many artists abandon the Santa Fe and Taos art colonies in the decade of the 1930s.

SOLDIER CARTOONIST

Bill Mauldin joins the Army.

[Mauldin spends most of his war years with the 45th Division. During WW II he sketched from foxholes for the *45th Division News* and matured from a gag cartoonist to a satirist of depth and stature. Later he served as cartoonist for *Stars and Stripes* and his cartoons were reprinted in hundreds of newspapers in the States where he was awarded the Pulitzer Prize in 1945 and 1959.]

BOOKS

Cleofas Jaramillo writes *The Genuine New Mexico Tasty Recipes* when she recognizes that much of what is being published on New Mexican food is inaccurate.

Bill Mauldin
Courtesy Museum of NM, #30194

1940s
WOODCARVERS
The sons of famed woodcarver José Dolores López, George, Rafaél, and Ricardo, are working at Los Alamos.

1937: **George López** does woodcarvings sporadically because the art doesn't provide a living. The same is true of Ricardo and Rafaél but at some point in time their wives, Benita and Precidez, also take up the art.

1952: George López: stops working at Los Alamos and devotes himself exclusively to carving. His wife, Silvianita, is completely in accord with the decision (the first time a Cordovan devotes himself solely to making a living through carving). Now he can greet customers in person and attend fiestas and shows to sell his works.

Ricardo and Rafaél work at Los Alamos until retirement but their wives, Benita and Precidez, sell their husbands' carvings.

1963: George and Silvianita move their shop from the central plaza to a more accessible homestead "rancho" in the valley.

1940
VOTING LAW
The **direct primary** law and the **permanent registration** statute go into effect.

SOCIETY
Congregation Albert is New Mexico's leading Jewish institution.

PROFILE

JUDAISM IN NEW MEXICO

1899: The cornerstone is laid for **Temple Albert**. Over the years a number of dedicated leaders work for the Congregation: Henry N. Jaffa, Berthold Spitz, Alphonse Fleischer, Samuel Neustad, Emil Uhlfelder, etc.

1900: There are 50 members in **Congregation Albert**.

1904: **Rabbi J.H. Kaplan** joins with Christian clergymen in establishing a nonsectarian charitable society to aid the sick. Methodists are permitted to use the temple while their church is under construction.

1907: Rabbi Kaplan writes an article against lynching. He is criticized in the newspaper for "maligning" Southerners and in time is forced to resign his position.

1909: The finance committee reports a revenue of $2,700.

1912: Rabbi Mendel Silber publicly supports the creation of a new high school for Albuquerque.

1912: There are 84 members in the Congregation.

1920: The Zionist Organization of America arrives in Albuquerque.

1921: **Congregation B'nai Israel** is formed by individuals who want a more traditional practice of Judaism, calling itself Orthodox.
1923: Congregation Albert celebrates its 25th anniversary and joins the Union of American Hebrew Congregations. The temple's Ladies Aid and Benevolent Society affiliates with the National Federation of Sisterhoods.

1931-1938: Rabbi **A.L. Krohn** is very active in the community. He teaches at UNM and is president of the Bernalillo County School Board. He is a strong advocate for the small farmers, mostly Hispanic, who are in conflict with the Middle Río Grande Conservancy District, while figures like Clinton P. Anderson sides with the large land owners. In 1937 Temple Albert's trustees order Krohn to desist and a special election is held to see if he should be retained as rabbi. He is retained by a small majority but Krohn resigns in protest.

1932: Due to the Depression the parsonage is put up for sale.

1933: Members are informed that unless all outstanding dues are paid the Congregation must be disbanded.

 1934: There are 64 members. The Ladies Auxiliary is formed.

1944: There are 87 members.

1951: A new temple is opened on Lead Avenue.

1952: The Men's Club is formed to stimulate Jewish religious activities and promote comradeship with the general community.

1953: About 172 families are members.

1958: Some 250 families are members.

1964: A Social Acton Committee is formed to address world problems and contemporary issues.

1973: Chavurat Hamidbar, **Fellowship of the Desert**, is started to encourage Jewish education and discussion in members' homes.

November 30, 1973 is declared "Rabbi David Shor Day" to honor his 30-year career.

> 1983: A controversy erupts at New Mexico State University when Paula Steinbach, a member of Hillel, calls for an end to using the swastika Indian logo on the Yearbook. Governor Anaya finally asks the board of regents to cease using the symbol and it complies.
>
> 1984: A new temple is dedicated. Some 400 families are members.

SOCIETY & FAMILY
Familial traditions are a contrast between "Anglo" and Hispanic groups.

Under "Anglo" family law, the husband is clearly the more powerful partner. "Anglo" husbands tend to will their property to sons. "Anglo" families are more isolated and therefore independent, not having kinship structures to rely on, more aggressive because of their isolation, and more inclined to creating formal community institutions. *"Anglos also support or allow discrimination in how these institutions care for Hispanic family members,"* according to J.B. Demark.

Hispanics provide for their sons and daughters on a more-or-less equal basis. Hispanic women benefit from the exalted status of holy women like Mary and various saints. Hispanic families also rely on extended family traditions, which include the *comadre-compadre* (godmother-godfather) support structure, along with kinship credit networks when finances are tight, repayment of loans forthcoming when things improve, without threats of foreclosure.

DISCRIMINATION
Río Puerco sheepmen ask that a grazing district be established for their use as has been promised to the impoverished *("subsistence populations")* **Río Puerco communities** of San Luis, Casa Salazar, Cabezón, and Guadalupe.
[Some Río Puerco children go to school with their feet wrapped in burlap sack because they have no shoes.]

A grazing district *isn't* established and the **Grazing Service** *has rules that bar these villagers* from federal grazing lands. The **Farm Security Administration** informs them they are *ineligible for loans*. The rules render them *ineligible for employment* on WPA road projects. The **State Welfare Board** can't assist them because it is out of funds.

1941: Río Puerco farmers and stockmen confront Governor Miles who promises to work for a solution to their very real problems. The solution never comes.

POVERTY AND LAND LOSS
Villagers at **El Cerrito** state that their economic problems began in 1904 when their common grazing land was taken away from them.

STUDY

Olen E. Leonard lives at **El Cerrito** (situated 30 miles southwest from Las Vegas, in the center of the "Upper Pecos Watershed," the east-central part of northern N.M., in one of the numerous land pockets formed at intervals by the Pecos River, on the San Miguel del Bado land grant) for around seven months in order to conduct an in-depth study of the village and its people. (His work is later published as *The Role of the Land Grant.*) Leonard has ample opportunity to make a number of observations:

The people: The first colonizers of N.M. were *"led by Don Christobal [sic] de Oñate."*

[Oñate's given name was *Juan* and "Christobal" doesn't exist in the Spanish language. Juan de Oñate had a son named "Cristóbal."]

The people of El Cerrito have *"racial characteristics"* that indicate most have varying degrees of Indian blood in their background though *"church records"* show that no marriages have taken place between Hispanics and Indians, a fact corroborated by findings of an investigator from the Soil Conservation Service. However, the *"...admixture had taken place prior to the migration from Mexico."*

[A few authors have pointed out that writers of these "studies" were going to come up with "accepted" views no matter what the investigation showed. In this case an "outdoors people" with "tanned skin" (because they live in "sun country") indicates *"Indian ancestry"* even if the written record doesn't corroborate the conclusion. The fixation on skin color has to be valid, so the "admixture" took place *centuries before* if it can't be documented in contemporary records *and the matter is closed.*]

Traditionally, the *"early economy seems to have been one of plenty."* Villagers in El Cerrito made their living from **stock raising** and irrigation **farming** (with a growing season of approximately 155 days). When the "commons land" was taken away from them by the **Court of Private Land Claims,** stock raising was made difficult to impossible and men had to seek wage labor outside the village. The Court reduced the land grant from approximately 400,000 acres to 5,024 acres. The national Depression deprived them of most of their work opportunities during the decade of the 1930s.

The Census of 1930 reveals that the **illiteracy rate** for the state of N.M. is 13.3%, one of the highest in the nation.

School in El Cerrito is for grades one through eight. Attendance is poor and isolation means that county supervision of instruction is rare. Girls usually attend school better than boys though completion of eight grades (18 girls, 16 boys in 1940) is almost equal. The study of English is considered highly important.

Fiestas are held for special occasions like the feast day for the village "Patron Saint," Holy Week, weddings, christenings, etc., and the most popular way to celebrate is to stage a **dance,** music being furnished by the guitar and violin, sometimes with an accordion. (In the old days dances would begin at 10 p.m. and last until "sunup" the next morning.) Spanish dances like the *raspa* and *varcoviano* [sic] are most popular. The schoolhouse becomes the dance hall and young and old participate. Females must come in groups or with their parents. No unmarried female would dare to come alone or in the company of an unrelated male. Men sit on one side of the hall, women on the other. Most of the music is fast and couples whirl around *"at an amazing speed."*

Horse racing is a popular amusement, especially the *corridas de gallo* where racing riders try to recover a rooster buried in soft dirt with only the head showing.

Religious plays are presented during Christmas and throughout the year there are religious processions, wakes, prayer meetings, etc.
This area is known to some as "Penitente Country" and *"Penitente hunting has become quite a popular sport for adventuresome Anglos during Holy Week..."*
Health and sanitary conditions are poor. Infant mortality is high.

All villagers are **Catholic** and though there is no resident priest there are services at least on Sunday and they are well attended. The priest has a high status in the community. Church services and dances are the basis for social life in the village.

Villagers rely on their neighbors when assistance is needed. Help is freely asked for and freely given in cases like sickness, peak work periods, building projects, harvesting, etc. Many of the villagers are related by blood and the parents' or grandparents' homes are centers for visitation, socializing, moral support, borrowing, etc. so everyone is aware of who is in need of what.

Marriage is a major event. The role of females is to become wives and mothers. Most young people are married by the age of 21. The family and the Church are probably the most important institutions in village life. A man is expected to support his family and help his parents or any other relative if the need should arise.

Politics are approached with tremendous enthusiasm. Until 1932 most voters were Republican but now they are Democrat.

Cash income for the average family in 1939 is about $294.

Land problems begin with the task of *"establishing definite boundaries and titles..."* Contributing factors are the lack of adequate records, people believe their titles will be purposely lost or destroyed in order to dispossess them of their land, and the many problems involved in changing from one type of land system to another.

[Leonard doesn't directly address the issue of Hispanic people being swindled out of their lands, though he does quote authors like **Frank W. Blackmar** and his *Spanish Institutions of the Southwest*, who observes: *"The original holders of lands have lost most of their properties either through misjudgments of the courts and commissions, or else by the wily intrigues of the Anglo-Americans, especially the latter. The Mexican has been no match for the invader in **business thrift and property cunning**."* Leonard doesn't explore the "misjudgments" and "wily intrigues," preferring, for example, to support the rulings of the Court of Private Land Claims which resulted in dispossessing New Mexicans for the benefit of the government's holdings. He sums up by saying, *"There is little doubt that the office of Surveyor-General and later the Court of Private Land Claims, tried to confirm all bona fide grants but lack of title papers, inexact acreage of grants, and disappearance of original boundary markers made the decisions in many cases largely a matter of opinion."* And it appears that he believes Hispanics would rather fight each other than unite to confront their economic problems, thus enabling *"...the sturdy Anglo-Saxons to over-power and dominate the Spanish people ... slowly absorbing or crushing the institutions of this romance people. Today the Anglo-Saxon exults in the strength of a predominant and united nation, while the Spanish-American yet within our borders deplores the failure of his people..."*]

BOOKS

Forgotten People: A Study of New Mexicans by educator **George I. Sánchez** is published and brings national attention to the plight of New Mexico's Hispanics. The 1940 Preface states the report *"is done in a spirit of constructive criticism ... the deficiencies are revealed and criticized with impersonal detachment and with all the scientific objectivity permitted to one who, at the same time, seeks emotional and mentalidentification with the mass of the people."*

Sánchez touches briefly on the Spanish and Mexican periods of New Mexican history which are ended by General Kearny who promises: *"We come among you for your benefit, not for your injury"* then he proceeds to document how New Mexicans have been treated like stepchildren of the officious government that came to plunder through "ruthless politicians," lawyers, judges, merchants, etc.

Education, especially in rural areas which have more than half of the territory's enrollment, has been woefully neglected from *"as long ago as 1850."* Though Hispanic students constitute better than half of public school enrollment they make up less than one-fifth of the enrollment in the 12th grade. More than 55% of Hispanic children beyond the first grade are at least two years over-age for their grade and scholastic achievement is below national and state averages. The explanation is found *"in the nature and quality of the educational facilities available to these children."* Handling of the "language problem" is illustrative of educational inadequacy: if students can't speak English it's their own fault.

Educational funding is *"startling in its ineptitude."* For the 1937-1938 school year N.M. spent $51 per pupil but in the four highest Hispanic counties the amount was under $35 per pupil. In distribution of the state public school equalization fund (1939-1940) the state average is $90, one county with very low Hispanic numbers getting $160 per unit, several others with low Hispanic numbers getting well over $100 while the four counties with the highest Hispanic numbers get $50 per classroom unit.

Infant mortality rates tell the story: for the nation it is 51 babies dead out of every 1,000 births; in N.M. it is 125.9 for every 1,000 and in the Hispanic counties it ranges from 104 to 167.

Hispanic loyalty to America has been firm from the beginning and proven militarily since the Civil War. Furthermore, during World War I, N.M. *"had more volunteers per capita than any other state."*

Yet Hispanics have been treated as "subject peoples" and left to shift for themselves, often with government officials, duty-bound to adhere to the Treaty of Guadalupe Hidalgo, preying on them. The *"inferior status held by the native New Mexican today is, in large measure, a result of the failure of the U.S. to recognize the special responsibility it assumed when it brought these people forcibly into the American society."*
The work continues with an in-depth study of Taos and its people.

[When *Forgotten People* was reprinted in 1967 G.I. Sánchez wrote that his initial *"modicum of optimism"* had been dashed since 1940 because more than a quarter century later nothing had changed for Hispanic New Mexicans. *"I had hopes, though very slim ones, that at the very least, a repentant nation would help us lift ourselves by our boot-straps. Instead, it took away our boots! Where are our land grants, for example?"* **Vicente Ximenes**, who knew Sánchez well, stated that George I. Sanchez must have become very disillusioned with American society and its realities. He got to the point where he would no longer accept speaking engagements and toward the end of his life became something of a recluse. Even close friends didn't know about his death until they read it in the newspapers.]

Angélico Chávez
Courtesy Museum of NM, #13217

LITERATURE
Fray Angélico Chávez from Wagon Mound begins a distinguished career as a scholar, historian, and general man of *belles lettres*

with the publication of works like his mystical ode *The Virgin of Port Iligat* and A *New Mexico Triptych*, a collection of short stories.

Many other works follow, including:
1954: *Origins of New Mexico Families* (printed by prepublication subscriptions);

1957: *Archives of the Santa Fe Archdiocese*;

1968: *Coronado's Friars*;

Family of Fabián Chávez Sr.
Courtesy Museum of NM, #13217

1974: *My Penitente Land;*

1981: *But Time and Chance: The Story of Padre Martínez of Taos;*

1985: *Tres Macho-He Said: Padre Gallegos of Albuquerque;*
and countless articles for various magazines.

WAR CORRESPONDENT
November: **Ernie Pyle** decides to live in Albuquerque and his wife, Geraldine (Gerry), supervises the
building of their home while Ernie is on assignment in Europe,
Africa, and the Pacific.

1944: Ernie receives the Pulitzer Prize for his reporting. He writes *Brave
Men* (which is published the following year).

April 18, 1945: Ernie Pyle is killed during the Battle of Okinawa. His wife,
Gerry, apparently loses her will to live and dies on November 3,
1945.

SOCIETY
December 17: Pueblo leader **Pablo Abeita** dies.

Ernie Pyle
Courtesy Museum of NM, #130793

1941
MILITARY
The Albuquerque **Army Air Depot** is established. In time two other bases are incorporated in to it to form
Kirtland Air Force Base (named after **Roy C. Kirtland**, a pioneer in the Army Air Corps).

[From 1941 to 1945 the War Department locates 21 separate military bases, training centers, prisoner-of-war
and Japanese internment camps, etc., within N.M.]

BOOKS
Cleofas Jaramillo publishes *Shadows of the Past* in which she presents unforgettable portraits of the
Hispanic women in her family.

EDUCATION
The **New Mexico Education Association** is successful in getting the state legislature to pass some 20 laws (a
tenth of all bills acted upon) during its session. No bill becomes law if seriously objected to by the
Association.

SOCIETY

August: **Thomas B. Campbell,** *"the Montana Wheat King,"* determines to buy up the 128,000 acres of tax delinquent land at auction around **Amalia** (by the N.M.-Co. border) for the amount due ($55,000). Amalia/Costilla families organize and apply for help from the Farm Security Administration, which makes loans with which villagers pay the delinquent taxes. Ousted State Extension Director **George Quesenberry** reports to the FBI that there is *"...suspicious political behavior"* on the part of one Alex Ortega from Amalia. FBI Director **J. Edgar Hoover** reports that the matter could be *"Communistically inspired..."* and Ortega's house is ransacked by FBI Agents looking for *"evidence."*

MILITARY

August: The **200th Coast Artillery,** formerly the 11th Cavalry and now acknowledged to be the premier anti-aircraft outfit in the U.S. Army, is taken to the Philippine Islands. It is said that when **General MacArthur** learned that his reinforcements were guardsmen he muttered, *"I asked for soldiers, not boy scouts."* (Before the war was over he would be asking for more New Mexicans, describing them as *"excellent jungle fighters."*)

PROFILE

Pablo Abeita

THE "GRAND OLD MAN" OF ISLETA

February 10, 1871: **Pablo Abeita** is born to José P. Abeita and Marcelina Lucero Abeita of Isleta. He grows up in traditional Pueblo fashion but the Isleta Catholic priest sees great promise in the youngster so he enrolls Pablo in a Jesuit school in Albuquerque and then later he attends St. Michael's College in Santa Fe. When Pablo returns to Isleta he is fluent in his Tiwa mother tongue but also in Spanish and English.

1889: The Governor of Isleta Pueblo appoints Pablo to serve on the **All Indian Pueblo Council**.

Pablo marries **María Dolores Abeita**. In time they have five sons: Juan Rey, José, Simón, Remijio, Ambrosio, Andrew. Pablo works as a typesetter on an Albuquerque newspaper. Later he works as a clerk for three years. In time he enters the Indian Service and works as an extension agent.

1905: Abeita manages the family general store at Isleta.

1912: Isleta Pueblo organizes a business council with Pablo Abeita as its first president.

1913-1923: Abeita serves as Judge in the Indian Court System of the Indian Service.

1919: Pablo serves as official translator when King Albert of Belgium and his Queen visit Isleta.

November 5, 1922: Abeita is elected to the post of Executive Secretary of the All Indian Pueblo Council. The main purpose at hand is to defeat the Bursum Bill. (Senator Holm Bursum of N.M. was trying to sneak his land bill through Congress so that it would give quiet title to non-Indians on Indian land.)

His work necessitates many trips to Washington D.C. He meets the Presidents starting with Grover Cleveland yet he never forgets his Isleta roots. For example, his spirituality and his native religion never change despite pressures exerted by the outside world: every morning, his little sack of corn pollen in hand, he gives thanks to the Great Spirit for his many blessingsand prays for the peace and prosperity for all mankind. His style of dress remains the same throughout his career: a tall, white,

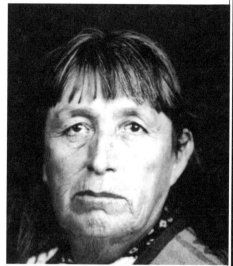

Pablo Abeita
Courtesy Museum of NM, #42286
(J.R. Willis photo)

creaseless Stetson with a straight brim, a red undershirt showing around the sleeves and collar of his lace front white shirt, a hand woven Pueblo red sash for a belt, the fringes hanging to his right side. During cold weather he drapes a blanket over his shoulders.

1926: Governor Hagerman calls Pueblo leaders to Santa Fe with the intention of forming a government-sanctioned Pueblo Council. The effort is construed as an attempt to destroy the existing All Indian Pueblo Council. Pablo Abeita uses all his diplomatic skills to avoid a confrontation and while the "United States Pueblo Indian Council" is formed it dies from lack of support.

1937: Pablo Abeita, the "Grand Old Man of Isleta Pueblo," is selected to *Who's Who in New Mexico*.
Pablo is admired and respected, not only for the many offices he has held during his life, but for being the champion of his Pueblo people.

TIMELINE

December 7, 1941 : In retaliation for the USA aiding China with military units like the **Flying Tigers,** Japanese bombers attack the military installation at Pearl Harbor, Honolulu, Hawaii. **The U.S. then declares war on Japan and Germany, entering WW II.**

WAR HEROS

The 200th Coast Artillery distinguishes itself against the Japanese in the **Bataan** and **Corregidor** campaigns and is described by General Jonathan Wainwright as "*the finest fighting unit in the Philippines, the unit first to fire and the last to lay down arms.*" These New Mexicans also experience the **Bataan Death March** and years of internment as prisoners of war during which some 11,107 die as POWs.

The 515th Coast Artillery Regiment, the 120th Combat Engineers, and the 804th Tank-Destroyer Battalion also distinguish themselves in combat.

During the war General **Douglas MacArthur** referred to the 200th Coast Artillery as "*...my New Mexico horse thieves. I knew them well and loved them ... and if I live I will return to save them.*" In 1945 he said that "*Bataan, with Corregidor, the citadel of its external defense, made possible all that has happened since. History, I am sure, will record it as one of the decisive battles of the world. Its long, protracted struggle enabled the united nations to gather strength to resist in the Pacific. Had it not held out, Australia would have fallen, with incalculable results. Our triumphs of today belong equally to that dead army. Its heroism and sacrifice have been fully acclaimed but the great strategic results of that mighty defense are only now becoming fully apparent. The Bataan garrison was destroyed due to its dreadful handicaps, but no army in history more thoroughly accomplished its mission. Let no man henceforth speak of it as anything other than an ultimate victory.*"

SOCIETY

December: Despite the stress and sorrows of World War II, **traditional Christmas customs** are observed around N.M. In Santa Fe *leñeros* (wood haulers) appear as always to sell wood; violins and guitars are played in **Sena Plaza** where there are bonfires of pyramided piñon wood. School children go through the area singing Christmas carols in English and Spanish while homes are lighted with *farolitos* (luminarias) and graced with nativity scenes.

1942
MILITARY

Holloman Air Force Base is established at Alamogordo and **Cannon Air Force Base** is established in Clovis.

POTTERY

The **Tenorio** family of **Santo Domingo Pueblo** is creating pottery during this time. Andrea Ortiz does pottery while Juanita Tenorio is a painter and jeweler.

Juanita's: Paulita, Robert, Hilda (and her lone).

Paulita and Gilbert Pacheco: Andrew.
From the Pacheco side: Lauencita Calabaza, Trinidad, Vivian.

PROFILE

Adelardo I. Sánchez

A N   U N S U N G   A M E R I C A N   H E R O

January 2,1918: **Adelardo I. Sánchez** is born in Belén to **Manuel G. Sánchez** and **Erinea Chávez Sánchez.** His school years are spent at Belén Elementary, St. Mary's, then Belén High School, though he drops out before graduation due to illness and disinterest. He becomes an apprentice butcher at Gilbert's Grocery Store and to strengthen his health he signs up for a Charles Atlas bodybuilding course.

March 22, 1941: Adelardo is drafted into the military and he reports to Fort Bliss, Texas, for induction and training. He is assigned to the **200th Coast Artillery, Battery D**.

August 26, 1941: Sánchez and his comrades sail out of Angel Island, California, on the *President Pierce* transport ship bound for Honolulu, Hawaii.

September 3, 1941: The *President Pierce* drops anchor at Honolulu. Adelardo takes pictures and sends them home but within 13 days he is on the island of Luzon in the Philippines, which he refers to in one of his letters as *"my home."* He writes home regularly because his family is so concerned for his welfare. He sends many pictures and informs everybody that he has *"lots more territory to cover."*

December, 1941: Manuel and Erinea receive Adelardo's last letter.

December 7, 1941: The Japanese attack the military base at Pearl Harbor.

May 7,1942: Bataan and Corregidor have fallen. The 200th Coast Artillery is among the 30,000 or so who are forced to surrender. (Adelardo is among those forced to make the Bataan Death March but he survives it.)

May 7,1942:Manuel and Erinea Sánchez are officially notified that their son Adelardo Sánchez is *"Missing in Action."*

July 14, 1944: The Sánchez family is informed by official telegram that Corporal Adelardo I. Sánchez, S.N. 38012204, died of malaria and dysentery on July 2, 1942, while a Prisoner of War. After much soul-wrenching anguish the family decides not to disturb their son's closed casket remains interred in the Philippines, which he had described in a letter as *"home."*

NAVAJO CODE TALKERS

Philip Johnston suggests to Major General **Clayton B. Vogel** of Camp Elliot that the Navajo language could be used as a code for communication during the war, as related by G.W. Thomas. Six Navajo shipyard workers are found and told to practice setting up a preliminary code and the brass thinks the experiment might work on the battlefield so recruiters go to the reservation in search of individuals who are adept in both English and Navajo. Twenty-nine men are selected. They enlist in the Marines and go through an eight-week boot camp like everybody else then three weeks of communications school after which they are assigned to Camp Elliot where the **Code Talker** school is set up. They work eight hours a day for eight weeks, memorizing the code of 412 words and 63 letters used in the Code alphabet. Most of the alphabet is represented by animals found on the reservation ("A" is *wol-la-che*, ant; "B" is *shush,* bear, etc.) and military terms like "dive bomber" becomes *gini*, the Navajo word for "chicken hawk," bombs are *ay-yay-gee,* eggs, etc. Nothing can be written down, everything has to be held strictly in memory. A message given to the Code Talker is in English, transmitted in Navajo, then translated into English at the receiving end. The Navajo Code is used only in combat and it is never broken by the enemy.

[The **Navajo Code Talkers Association** is in ceremonial existence to this day and **Albert Smith** and **Harold Y. Foster,** President and Vice-President, respectively, of the organization, are popular speakers at various ceremonies.]

PROFILE

James Williams

"AGAINST ALL ODDS"

James Williams of Las Cruces is drafted and later assigned as a pilot in the unit that comes to be known as the Tuskegee Airmen, the first black aviators to serve in the American armed services. They never lost a single bomber they escorted. (He remembers the irony of fighting for *freedom* while many of his own countrymen considered African Americans to be *"subhuman."*)

1947: James graduates from New Mexico A & M. (His mother, **Clara Williams**, was the first black graduate of N.M. A & M.)

1951: Williams graduates from the Creighton University School of Medicine.

1956: James Williams receives the "Master of Surgery" designation.

LAND GRANT

Grantees of the **Chililí** land grant apply for a $15,000 loan from the **Farmers Home Administration** (FHA) in order to finance a wood yard. The FHA approves the loan on the condition that the grant be deeded to an Albuquerque-based private corporation known as the **Chililí Cooperative Association** (which in effect abolishes the land grant's board of trustees and results in grantees eventually losing 80% of their land).

1970: The Chililí Cooperative has sold off more than 36,000 acres of Chililí grant land.

1971: A citizens committee known as *El Comité Para Reformar y Preservar Las Tierras de la Merced de Chililí* is formed in order to preserve the remaining 5,300 acres of grant land.

1977: After a demonstration outside the Bernalillo, County courthouse, Judge **Gerald Cole** orders the Chililí Cooperative to open its membership to 24 members of the Committee. But there is much struggling for control between the Cooperative and the Committee.

1981: El Comité members win control of the Chililí Cooperative board and form a policy that henceforth grant land will be leased only to community people living on the land.

MANHATTAN PROJECT

The U.S. Army informs the headmaster of the Los Alamos Ranch School that the facilities and area are needed for the national war effort. The top-secret **Manhattan Project** is put into operation under the overall direction of General **Leslie R. Groves** and hundreds of scientists and their families move into the new town of **Los Alamos** (or **Site Y,** as it is referred to officially). **J. Robert Oppenheimer** is the head of the new military installation and he recruits many of the top personnel himself. The men and women of Los Alamos are mostly young, the average age being 27, and nearly 1,000 babies are born on **"The Hill"** from 1943 to 1949; the 208 born during the war listed *"Box 1663, Sandoval County, Rural,"* as their place of birth. Nobel Prize winners and other brilliant minds come together to work on the Project, a list of which includes:

Robert Oppenheimer establishes the atmosphere at Los Alamos through his magnetic personality, brilliant mind, and administrative abilities;

Niels Bohr and his son **Aage** (from Denmark) escape from Nazi-occupied Denmark and in Los Alamos work under the names "Nicholas and Jim Baker." Both are later awarded Nobel Prizes;

Enrico Fermi (from Italy) is a gentle personality who escapes from Italy after being awarded the Nobel Prize in 1938, a master of theoretical as well as experimental physics and revered as much for his personality and balanced outlook;

Victor E. Weisskopf (from Germany) becomes renowned for his ability to solve an endless variety of problems;

Emilio Segre (from Italy) works with Fermi in the discovery of slow neutrons and of technetium, later writes Fermi's biographer. In 1959 he shares a Nobel Prize for the discovery of the antiproton;

Stanislaw M. Ulam, a mathematician, works closely with Edward Teller;

Edward Teller (from Hungary) labors with extremely complicated problems and later goes on to help develop the H-bomb;

I.I. Rabi is the main troubleshooter at Los Alamos;

John von Neumann is described by Oppenheimer as the brightest person he knows. John is a leader in creating the first large-scale computers;

Hans A. Bethe (from Germany) heads the Theoretical Division and helps predict how the atomic ball of fire will develop in the atmosphere.

In addition there were young scientists just beginning their careers: Marvin Wilkening, Louis Hempelmann, John Magee, McAllister Hull Jr., Val L. Fitch, Robert Wilson, etc.

[Los Alamos has been described as *"a hotbed of prima donnas"* and *"the largest collection of crackpots ever seen in one town"* as well as *"America's Athenian world."*]

1843: **Dorothy McKibbin,** *"one of the unsung heroines"* of the Project according to E.M. Szasz, runs its front office at **109 East Palace Avenue** in Santa Fe. Existence of the Manhattan Project remains one of the best-kept secrets of the war years.

July 16, 1945, at 5:29:45 a.m., the world's first atomic bomb is exploded at Ground Zero in Trinity Site. The explosion creates a blinding flash seen in three states, lighting up the sky like the sun for a few seconds. A mushroom-shaped, multicolored cloud surges some 38,000 feet into the air within minutes, changing colors from purple to green to orange as it expands. For over an hour the area is covered with smoke. Heat judged to be as hot as that in the center of the sun spreads through the site (and people 10 miles away feel it as if standing in front of a fireplace). The blast leaves a crater half a mile wide, burning the sand into greenish gray glass (later called *atomsite* or *trinitite*). Every living thing is destroyed *"and the stench of death lingers in the area for three weeks."*

After years of toil and the expenditure of $2,000,000,000 the **Atomic Age** begins, changing the history of the world forever. After the initial ecstasy of their success, the scientists return to Los Alamos in great solemnity. *They realize the power of the fissioned atom is now capable of destroying mankind.*

1942 (con't)
LAND GRANT
The Government acquires the **Juan José Lobato land grant** for "*...rural rehabilitation through preferential grazing rights to local residents...*" The Forest Service winds up administering the land grant.

1947: Forest Ranger **Paul Martínez** (from Vallecitos) files a report to his superior that state grant land isn't being used for the benefit of villagers. Forest Service practice is documented as favoring permits for large ranching operations and large timber sales to the wood products industry instead of emphasizing village needs.

NEW DEAL PROJECT

The **Taos County Project** begins and, all New Deal programs being considered, is very successful (until 1949 when funding is discontinued) because of its medical director and nurses who work with the community.

[S. Forrest sums up the Hispanic New Deal by stating that it failed because it wanted to create an economy minded individual who didn't desire profits; it wanted to create independent and resourceful people who would rehabilitate themselves, while they followed orders from their superiors in Washington; it wanted to develop "native creativity" without those developed questioning outsiders' ideas; it wanted people to improve themselves but remain content with poverty. Despite its failures and/or weaknesses, New Deal programs were a strong factor in preserving the physical existence of many Hispanic villages in N.M. and those programs must be lauded as one of the more humanistic efforts in the history of the U.S.]

MILITARY

The *U.S.S. New Mexico* is active in the Pacific Theatre of WW II. It logs 183,000 nautical miles, participating in most of the major campaigns from Guadalcanal to Okinawa. During its 544 days of combat it is damaged three times but fires some 13,000,000 pounds of ammunition during its tour of active duty.

August 27, 1945: The *U.S.S. New Mexico* drops anchor in Tokyo Bay to participate in the final operation of WW II.

INTERNMENT

March 14: A train arrives in Santa Fe with 425 Japanese Americans, *"alien enemies,"* middle aged Californians referred to as *"internees"* on their way to an *"internment camp"* located in the hills west of Santa Fe. The camp eventually houses 826 prisoners who are forced out of their homes after the Japanese attack on Pearl Harbor.

[**John Hersey** was later to describe this as "*...a mistake of terrifically horrible proportions...*" fueled by war hysteria and long-standing racist fear of *"yellow peril."*]

1943-1946

John J. Dempsey is Governor.

1943
MEDAL OF HONOR - JOE P. MARTINEZ

May 26, 1943: On Attu Aleutians, the assault to drive the enemy from a key defensive position high in the snow-covered precipitous mountains between East Arm Holtz Bay and Chichagof Harbor have failed. Troop readjustments were made and a reinforced battalion was included in a new assault but soon the forces were pinned down by severe machine-gun, rifle, and mortar fire. **Joe P. Martínez,** born in Taos, N.M. (entered the Service at Ault, Colorado), an automatic rifleman, rose to his feet and charged the enemy. At intervals he shouted for his comrades to follow, which they did. Martínez eliminated enemy resistance by lobbing hand grenades and burst after burst from his deadly BAR. He made his way up the snow-filled rocky ridges of the Hohz-Chichagof Pass, severe enemy fire barring his way from either flank and from tiers of snow trenches in front of him. Private Joe P. Martínez led his troops on and up the pass, personally silencing several trenches with BAR fire and ultimately reaching the top where he encountered the final enemy-occupied trench. He was firing into it when he was mortally wounded. The pass was taken, an important preliminary to capturing the entire island.

October, 1943: Private Joe R Martínez is awarded the Medal of Honor, "*For conspicuous gallantry and intrepidity above and beyond the call of duty in action with the enemy...*"

MEDAL OF HONOR - KENNETH N. WALKER

Kenneth N. Walker, born in Cerrillos, was Commander of the Fifth Bomber Command during the period from September 5, 1942, to January 5, 1943. Brigadier General Walker repeatedly accompanied his units on bombing missions deep into enemy-held territory. From the lessons personally gained under combat conditions he developed a highly efficient technique for bombing when opposed by enemy fighter airplanes and by anti-aircraft fire. On January 5, 1943, in the face of extremely heavy anti-aircraft fire and determined opposition by enemy fighters, he led an effective daylight bombing attack against shipping in the harbor at Rabaul, New Britain, which resulted in direct hits on nine enemy vessels. During this action his airplane was disabled and forced down by the attack of an overwhelming number of enemy fighters.

March 11, 1943: Brigadier General Walker is awarded the Medal of Honor for conspicuous leadership above and beyond the call of duty involving personal valor and intrepidity at an extreme hazard to life.

MEDAL OF HONOR - ROBERT S. SCOTT

Robert S. Scott entered the service at Santa Fe. On July 29, 1943, near Munda Airstrip, New Georgia, Solomon Islands, after 27 days of bitter fighting the enemy held a hilltop salient which commanded the approach to Munda Airstrip. Our troops were exhausted from the prolonged battle and heavy casualties, but Lieutenant Scott advanced with the leading platoon of his company to attack the enemy position, urging his men forward in the face of enemy rifle and machine-gun fire. He had pushed forward alone to a point midway across the barren hilltop within 75 yards of the enemy when the enemy launched a desperate counterattack which, if successful, would have gained undisputed possession of the hill. Enemy riflemen charged out on the plateau, firing and throwing grenades as they moved to engage our troops. The company withdrew but Lieutenant Scott, with only a blasted tree stump for cover, stood his ground against the wild enemy assault. By firing his carbine and throwing the grenades in his possession he momentarily stopped the enemy grenades aimed at him, suffering a bullet wound in the left hand and a painful shrapnel wound in the head after his carbine had been shot from his hand, he threw grenade after grenade with devastating accuracy until the beaten enemy withdrew. Our troops, inspired to renewed effort by

Lieutenant Scott's intrepid stand and incomparable courage, swept across the plateau to capture the hill and from this strategic position four days later captured Munda Airstrip.

October 14, 1944: Captain Robert S. Scott receives the Medal of Honor.

1944
BROTHERHOOD UNIFICATION

Due to the efforts of **Miguel Archibeque** and others, **all Penitente Brotherhoods are united** under the *Concilio Supremo*, Supreme Council. (The Supreme Council is endorsed by Archbishop Byrne in 1947.)

MEDAL OF HONOR - HAROLD H. MOON

Born in Albuquerque, Harold H. Moon fought with conspicuous gallantry and intrepidity when powerful Japanese counterblows were being struck in a desperate effort to annihilate a newly won beachhead at Pawig, Leyte, Philippine Islands on October 21, 1944. In a forward position, armed with a sub-machine gun, he met the brunt of a strong, well-supported night attack which quickly enveloped his platoon's flanks. Many men in nearby positions were killed or injured, and Private Moon was wounded as his foxhole became the immediate object of a concentration of mortar and machine-gun fire. Nevertheless he maintained his stand, poured deadly fire into the enemy, daringly exposed himself to hostile fire time and time again to exhort and inspire what American troops were left in the immediate area. A Japanese officer, covered by machine-gun fire and hidden by an embankment, attempted to knock out his position with grenades but Moon, after protracted and skillful maneuvering, killed him. When the enemy advanced a light machine gun to within 20 yards of the shattered perimeter and fired with telling effects on the remnants of the platoon, he stood up to locate the gun and remained exposed while calling back range corrections to friendly mortars which knocked out the weapon. Momentarily he killed two Japanese as they charged him. By dawn his position, the focal point of the attack for more than four hours, was virtually surrounded. In a fanatical effort to reduce it and kill its defender, an entire platoon charged with fixed bayonets. Firing from a sitting position, Private Moon calmly emptied his magazine into the advancing horde, killing 18 and repulsing the attack. In a final display of bravery he stood up to throw a grenade at a machine gun which had opened fire on the right flank. He was hit and instantly killed, falling in the position from which he had not been driven by the fiercest enemy action. Nearly 200 dead Japanese soldiers were found within 100 yards of his fox hole. The continued tenacity, combat sagacity, and magnificent heroism with which Private Moon fought on against overwhelming odds contributed in large measure to breaking up a powerful enemy threat and did much to insure our initial successes during a most important operation.

November 15, 1945: Private Harold H. Moon is posthumously awarded the **Medal of Honor.**

SOCIETY
Miguel A. Otero II dies.

Miguel Archibeque

LEADERSHIP IN THE BROTHERHOOD

July 1, 1883: **Miguel Archibeque** is born in San Miguel del Barrio (Vado?).

1990: Miguel works in Colorado, Wyoming, Idaho, Montana, and Utah as a shepherd, miner, and railroad hand.

1910: Archibeque joins the Brotherhood.

1916: Miguel is in N.M. and marries **Esquipulita Salazar.** They buy a ranch in Palma.

1922: The drought forces the Archibeques to move to Santa Fe where Miguel works for various state and municipal agencies until retirement.

1938: Miguel is a member of the Ministerial Council of the Alliance Fraternity of Our Father Jesús of Colorado and New Mexico (which becomes the Archbishop's Supreme Council after 1947).

Archibeque protests the *New Mexico Sentinel* articles written by Msg. **Philip F. Mahoney** as *"slanderous, offensive, and defamatory inasmuch as they besmirch the character and good name of our fraternal organization."* (This public admonition of a Church figure is rare but Mahoney replies in a conciliatory manner.)

1943: Archibeque leads the movement to have the Brotherhood officially recognized by the Church.

1946: Miguel begins a seven-year term as the first *Hermano Supremo Arzobispal*. With the exception of one year in which Román Aranda of Las Vegas serves, Archibeque is reelected as Hermano Supremo until 1960 when his health begins to fail.

1947: The Brotherhood is officially recognized by the Church. Due to the efforts of Archibeque and others, local moradas and councils are now organized into districts which are under the jurisdiction of the Archbishop's Supreme Council.

1956: Esquipulita dies and for a time Miguel lives at the Velarde Nursing Home until he returns to stay with his family in Santa Fe.

1958: A limited edition of *The Way of the Cross:* **A New Mexico Version,** edited by Reginald Fisher, is inscribed: *For Don Miguel Archibeque ... in appreciation of the important role his Brotherhood has had in development and preservation of this beautiful expression of the true vocation of New Mexico Spanish people.*

June 16, 1970: Miguel Archibeque dies.

BOYS RANCH

Led by concerned members like **Al Buck, Cecil Pragnell**, and Judge **Albert R. Kool**, the **Albuquerque Kiwanis Club** organizes a Boys Rehabilitation Committee that, using Father Flanagan's example of "Boys Town," comes up with the concept of "**New Mexico Boys Ranch.**"

September, 1944: Boys Ranch is incorporated and the general working guidelines are: our purpose is to rehabilitate, educate, and provide vocational training for underprivileged boys and to serve *in loco parentis* to boys between the ages of seven and fourteen; all races will be served, it will be interdenominational and non-political; funding will be from private sources, no funds will be taken from state or federal governments. President of the Board of Directors is **Albert E. Buck.**

1945: The Chadwick property in Socorro County, some 2,000 acres, becomes the site of Boys Ranch.

March, 1946: The first actual work is done at the site of Boys Ranch when a water well is drilled.

1947 (the first full year of operation): Boys Ranch calendars are distributed after being printed by **R.P. Woodson** at his own expense. **Albert Mitchell** gives Boys Ranch its foundation herd of Herefords, which is augmented by five more from **George Currier** of Artesia.

Thirteen boys are living on the ranch, most of whom attend school at La Joya.

1948: There is a dire shortage of help, constant turnover of personnel, and not enough money to meet basic expenses. Al Buck makes a personal loan to Boys Ranch and saves the entire operation.

1950: The Expansion Fund Campaign is successful and brings much needed capital to Boys Ranch. The probation officer of Doña Ana County requests that admission age be raised to at least 17.

1952: There are 77 boys living at Boys Ranch.

1954: **Walker Hubbard** becomes superintendent of Boys Ranch. His dynamic leadership, along with a very positive influence from the Baptist Church, saves the operation from financial collapse.

1970: **Dr. and Mrs. (Jackie) Spencer** of Carrizozo donate $50,000 toward the cost of a new cottage that will house 16 boys, to be named the *Bancroft Cottage* in honor of Jackie's former husband, Dr. Bancroft.

The ranch manager reports that Boys Ranch livestock includes 133 head of cattle, 25 horses, 2 mules, 5 sows and 1 boar, 50 chickens, 10 sheep, and 1 registered goat.

1970s: **Celebrities** like Larry Mahan (six-times All Around World Champion Cowboy), Don Perkins (Dallas Cowboys football star), actor Ernest Borgnine, singers Burl Ives, Charlie Pride, Roy Clark, and Glenn Campbell, etc., help Boys Ranch whenever possible.

1971: Better than 80% of the youth at BR have had no encounters with law enforcement officers in the past six years.

1975: Boys Ranch has 16 full-time employees, 230 head of cattle, 47 horses and mules; there are 150 acres in wheat grass, 17 acres of oats, 45 acres of corn, 130 acres of winter wheat; some 500 tons of ensilage corn have been put up, along with 100 tons of alfalfa and about 1,000 bales of oat hay and wheat grass; there is a bank balance of $58,375; and the entire operation is valued at $1,139,016.

1979: The mission of Boys Ranch continues to expand: a need is stated to expand boys' facilities but also to see to the possibility of a *Girls Ranch.*

August 1, 1981: In a piñon meadow southeast of Santa Fe near Lamy ground is broken for **Girls Ranch.**

1982: With the invaluable help of a $200,000 matching grant from the Mabee Foundation of Tulsa, Oklahoma, the new Girls Ranch is off to a promising start. There are 12 girls in residence and a wide variety of civic organizations, especially women's groups, render aid to the venture.

Beulah May Hart wills the Hart Ranch in the Melrose area to Boys Ranch, stipulating that it be used to help children from troubled backgrounds.

1983: Boys Ranch is now authorized to set up Foster Care Programs which results in the outreach effort known as "Families for Children."

1984: The first building is erected at *Hart Youth Ranch* and is designed to accommodate 10 to 12 boys and one house parent couple.

June 1, 1985: Hart Youth Ranch celebrates its grand opening. Over 200 guests from New Mexico, Colorado and Texas are in attendance.

September 2, 1989: Boys Ranch celebrates its 45th Anniversary Reunion.

1945
ARTS & CRAFTS
There are only two art galleries in Santa Fe.

POTTERY

Sarafina Tafoya of **Santa Clara Pueblo** is creating pottery during this period [exact dates unknown]. Her offspring, **Margaret, Camilio** (and **Agapita**), and **Christina,** learn the craft from her. Their families also become accomplished in the field of pottery:

Margaret's family: Shirley, Mary Esther Archuleta, Tonita Roller, Luann (and her Michelle Tapia), Betty, Virginia, Jennie Trammel, Lee (and his Linda), Mela Youngblood;
Camilio and Agapita's family: Grace Medicine Flower, Joseph Lonewolf, Lucy Year Flower;

Christina Naranjo's family: Mary Cain, Mida Tafoya, Claudio Naranjo, Teresita Naranjo;

Tonita Roller's family: Clifford, Tim, Susan (and her Charles Lewis), Morning Star, Jeff;
Betty (and Lee): Melvin;
Virginia Ebelacker: Richard, James;
Mela Youngblood: Nancy, Nathan;
Joseph Lonewolf: Rosemary Apple Blossom (and her Adam Speckled Rock), Susan Romero, Gregory Lonewolf;
Lucy (and Joe): Myra Little Snow (and her Quincy Nolona Eagle Feather), Shawn, Kelli Little Kachina, Forrest Red Cloud;
Mary Cain: Doug, Joy (and her Edward), Linda (and her Autumn, Tammy), Billy, Warren, Tina Díaz (and her daughter Rosemary);
Mida Tafoya: Ethel Vigil (and her Ginger Willow), Dona (and her Valerie Ochoa), Sherry (and her Leslie), Red Bird, Robert, Philis (and her Lorraine), Cookie Pérez (and her Robert Maurice);

Cecilia Naranjo: Sharon, Judy and Lincoln (and their Sarah);
Teresita Naranjo: Georgia Wyasket, Mildred Moore, Stella Chavarría (and her Denise, Joey, and Loretta "Sunday").

AMERIND-MILITARY

Thousands of **Native Americans** serve in the **Armed Forces:** 21,767 in the Army, 1,910 in the Navy, 121 in the Coast Guard, 723 in the Marines [figures don't include officers]. They receive many decorations for valor, including Air Medals (71), Silver Stars (51), Bronze Stars (47), and the Distinguished Flying Cross (34).

MEDAL OF HONOR - JOSÉ F. VALDEZ

January 25, 1945, Rosenkrantz, France: José E. Valdez (born in Governador, N.M., entered Service at Pleasant Grove, Utah) was on outpost duty with five others some 500 yards from American lines when the enemy attacked with overwhelming strength. Valdez saw a German tank some 75 yards away so he raked it with automatic rifle fire until it withdrew. Then three enemy soldiers came out of the thick woods and directed heavy automatic weapons fire at him from 30 yards away but José came out of his cover and killed all three. The enemy then launched an attack with two full companies of infantrymen, some 200 men, blasting the American patrol with murderous concentrations of automatic and rifle fire in an encircling movement which forced the patrol leader to order a withdrawal. Private Valdez volunteered to cover the maneuver and as the patrol plunged through a hail of bullets toward American lines he fired burst after burst into the swarming enemy. Three Americans were struck as they withdrew then José Valdez was struck down by a bullet that entered his stomach and, passing through his body, emerged from his back. Despite his agonizing wound, José resumed firing on the charging enemy, delivering a protective screen of bullets until the patrol was safe behind American lines. By field telephone he called for artillery and mortar fire on the Germans, correcting the range until he had shells falling within fifty yards of his own position. The American barrage broke the counterattack whereupon Valdez dragged himself back to his own lines where he later died from his wounds.

February 8, 1946: José E Valdez is posthumously awarded the Medal of Honor *"for his valiant, intrepid stand which enabled his comrades to escape, at the cost of his own life..."*

MILITARY
February: **White Sands Missile Range** is established.

MEDAL OF HONOR - ALEJANDRO R. RUIZ
April 28, 1945: Okinawa, Ryukyu Islands: Alejandro R. Ruiz (born in Loving, entered Service at Carlsbad) was in an attacking unit that was halted by severe enemy fire coming from a skillfully camouflaged pillbox. The unit was suddenly pinned down under a hail of machine-gun fire and a deadly grenade attack. Private Alejandro (Alexander) Ruiz jumped to his feet, seized an automatic rifle, and charged through the flying grenades and rifle and automatic fire to the top of the camouflaged pillbox. An enemy soldier charged Alejandro, who fired only to learn his rifle was jammed, so Ruiz used it as a club and downed his enemy. He retreated to the American position, grabbed another automatic rifle and more ammunition, and again charged to the top of the enemy pillbox. Leaping from one opening to another, he sent burst after burst into the pillbox, killing a dozen of the enemy and completely destroying the position. His unit was now able to advance without casualties.

June 26, 1946: Alejandro R. Ruiz is awarded the Medal of Honor *"for heroic conduct in the face of overwhelming odds ... which saved the lives of many comrades..."*

ATOMIC AGE
July 16: Ranchers in the areas around White Sands feel they are witnessing the end of the world but the *New Mexican* runs a story titled *"Magazine Lets Go at Alamogordo"* to hide the fact that the first **atomic bomb** was tested at *"the strangely named"* **Trinity Site** on the White Sands Missile Range, according to R.E. Etulain. Scientists working in the Manhattan Project out of Los Alamos make N.M. *"the birthplace of the atomic age"* and within days of dropping atomic bombs on Hiroshima and Nagasaki, **Los Alamos** is the only New Mexican city to achieve a *"worldwide reputation."*

TIMELINE
August 6, 1945: **A United States bomber plane drops an atomic bomb on the city of Hiroshima, Japan.**

August 9, 1945: **An atomic bomb is dropped on the city of Nagasaki, Japan. Japan announcesits surrender on August 14. World War II is over.**

1946

BOOKS

Saints & Saintmakers of New Mexico ("...the first truly scholarly and well-researched book on santos...") is published by **E. Boyd**.

OIL & GAS

Four Corners oil and gas discoveries stimulate much interest from the nation top petroleum producers.

WOMEN IN POLITICS

Georgia Lusk is the first New Mexican woman to be elected to the U.S. House of Representatives.

GOVERNMENT

October 12: **Sotero Ortiz** steps down from his leadership role with the **All Indian Pueblo Council** after 24 years of service to the Pueblo people.

E. Boyd
Courtesy Museum of NM, #160379
(Lansing Brown photo)

1947-1950

Thomas J. Mabry is Governor.

1947

T I M E L I N E

President Harry S. Truman integrates all military forces of the U.S.

RANCHING

The **Moise Livestock Company** owns 72,000 acres and is typical of large ranching concerns. [Between 1900 and 1960, many small ranches go out of business because of increased mechanization and insufficient water.]

SOCIETY

Millicent Rogers, granddaughter of Henry Huddleston Rogers, founder of Anaconda Copper, takes up residence in Taos after traveling all over the world. "*The discovery of Taos changed Millicent's life. It seemed to her a romantic outpost, outside of time, with its ease, its soft climate, its native American spirit, and the beautiful mountain that overlooked it.*" She finds a rambling adobe to renovate and names it *Turtlewalk*. Millicent becomes interested in the region's arts and cultures and begins collecting fine Hispanic

Millicent Rogers
Courtesy Museum of NM, #

and Native American art in an effort to prevent its disappearance. An intelligent, multitalented, energetic woman, she loves spectacular clothes and in Taos often dresses in moccasins, Indian skirt and blouse, a shawl, and superb Indian jewelry.

1953: Millicent Rogers dies after an accidental fall and is buried in a tiny cemetery in the shadow of the mountain she loved so deeply.

1956: Family members found the **Millicent Rogers Museum** in her memory and to enable everyone to enjoy the items collected by Millicent during her lifetime.

1996: The Millicent Rogers Museum celebrates its 40th anniversary with a special exhibition from the permanent collection of its namesake as well as more recent acquisitions.

MILITARY-INDUSTRIAL
Sandía Laboratories is founded in Albuquerque and quickly becomes one of the biggest employers in the state.

FOREST SERVICE
March: A forest ranger at Vallecitos declares that the **policy** of favoring local residents in allotting grazing and timber resources is a fallacy and should be changed to **favor the large operator.** The Regional Forester in Albuquerque agrees but warns *the change must be a slow process.*

RELIGIOUS
The **Monastery of Via Coeli** is established at Jémez Springs in order to render aid to priests with personal and spiritual problems.

ROSWELL INCIDENT
July 2, 1947: **Dan Wilmot** and his wife are sitting on the front porch in their Roswell home at about 10 p.m. when they spot an enormous glowing object heading in a northwesterly direction. They observe it for almost a minute: the thing is oval shaped, appearing to be linked inverted saucers. The light seems to emanate from within and there is no noise.

Some 10 miles northwest of Roswell a sheep rancher named **W.W. Mac Brazel** is at home waiting out a lightning storm. He hears an explosion that doesn't sound like thunder.

July 3: Mac Brazel saddles a horse and rides out to check his sheep. He comes upon what he later describes as a long swathe of wreckage spread out across land owned by his neighbor.

There are pieces of metal all over the place, along with tin foil, wood, etc. The metal is very lightweight but he can't bend it and he can't tear the tin foil either. The wood has some sort of colored symbols on it, something like chicken scratchings. He picks up various items for souvenirs and returns home.

G.L. Barney Barnett, who works with the U.S. Soil Conservation Service, notices sunlight being reflected from metallic objects in the distance. Fearing airplane wreckage he goes to investigate, as does a separate archaeological research group working in the area. They find a dull grey, disc-shaped object about 30 feet across. It appeared to have burst on impact because there are dead bodies on the ground. The bodies have some human features but they are small, three to four feet tall, heads much larger than their torsos. They are hairless, their eyes slanted and wide apart. They all wear a type of one-piece jumpsuit with no visible buttons or zippers.

A military truck drives up and an Air Force officer gets out and orders everyone to leave the area since this a matter of national security. Neither are they to discuss *with anybody* what they have seen. As the civilians leave more trucks arrive and guards encircle the area.

July 4: Mac Brazel drives into Corona and tells some of his friends what he has seen. They suggest he go into Roswell and report it to the sheriff.

July 6: Roswell **Sheriff Wilcox** hears what Mac has to say and reports it to Major **Jesse A. Marcel**, the intelligence officer at Roswell Army Air Base. Marcel leads a squad of men to the site and gathers everything. A two-foot piece of metal as thin as a sheet of paper can't be dented with a hammer blow ... a cigarette lighter can't ignite the wood-like material...

Brazel is told he must give up all the souvenirs he picked up, his duty as a patriot, so he does,

All wreckage is taken to Roswell Army Air Field and one Lieutenant **Walter Haut** issues a statement that there has indeed been an alien spacecraft wreck with dead aliens in it The story appears in newspapers across the nation. The following day the story is denied. (Haut is reassigned to another base and he resigns his commission within a few months).

July 9: All wreckage is flown to Fort Worth Army Air Base and General Roger Maxwell Ramey states in a press conference the whole thing was just a downed weather balloon. (See **1964.**)

June, 1997: An Air Force spokesman confirms that the "alien space craft" of 1947 was in fact an experimental weather balloon and the "dead aliens" were merely test dummies. He says the case is closed.

July, 1997: A festival is held in Roswell to celebrate the 50th Anniversary of the *Roswell Incident*. Journalists from all over the world are on hand, part of the estimated crowd of 30,000 that sets attendance records at the UFO Museum & Research Center as well as those who attend lectures, the festival's trade expo, and visit many booths where alien-oriented items are on sale.

CULTURE - MATACHINES

Flavia Waters Champe and her husband see the **Matachines dance** for the first time at San Ildefonso Pueblo. Enthralled, Flavia begins to study and research everything on the presentation that reminds her of a well choreographed ballet.

1983: Flavia publishes *The Matachines Dance of the Upper Río Grande: History, Music, and Choreogra-*

phy. It becomes the acknowledged classic on the Matachines.

History: No one knows where the term *Matachines* came from. It could be from Arabic *mutawajjihin,* Italian *mattacinos,* French *matassins,* Mexican Nahuatl *matlachines,* from the Spanish *matar,* etc.

Characters: *El Monarca* (Monarch, King) is the leading figure and dances throughout the presentation. His costume includes a headdress resembling a crown, a cape, ribbons, fringed shawl, etc.

Los Capitanes: are four dancers who dress like El Monarca.

Los Matachines: (usually) 12 dancers dressed basically like El Monarca except for the headpiece.

La Malinche: is a very young girl dressed in white, the only female dancer in the production.

El Abuelo (Grandfather): is a sort of clowning master of ceremonies.

El Toro (Bull): to simulate a humorous bullfight.

Assistants: to help as needed.

Music: Produced by violin and guitar, tunes are short and repeated over and over.

Choreography: Dancers turn, move backward, forward, bow, etc., in basic steps.

1948
AMERIND SUFFRAGE
Native Americans are given the right to vote in state as well as national elections because of the activism of **Miguel Trujillo,** a World War II veteran, of Isleta Pueblo.

BOOKS
Southwest Heritage: A Literary History with Bibliography ("a book about books and the place in which they were written") is published by **Mabel Major, Rebecca W, Smith, and T.M. Pearce.** The authors state that because of limited space *"...we can include only works written in English or those available in translation..."* because *"...the dominant strain seems clearly to be Anglo American."*

Part One: Literature before the coming of the Anglo-American, to 1800:

In some 36 pages the authors cover Indian prose and poetry (10 pages) as well as Spanish chronicles, dramas, songs, and folktales: *The Narrative of Alvar Nuñez Cabeza de Vaca,* Castaneda's *Narratives of the Coronado Expedition,* Villagrá's *History of New Mexico,* Benavides' *Memorial, Los Moros y los Cristianos, Los Comanches, Las Posadas, Pastorelas,* and names of various kinds of songs, poetry, and stories are mentioned. *"It would be desirable and profitable to include in this guide..."* the literature of the *"Indian, Spanish, English, and other tongues, that have sprung from the section. Some day we shall attain that breadth of vision."* The work then continues with:

Part Two: Literature of Anglo-American adventurers and settlers, 1800 to 1918: and

Part Three: Literature of the Contemporary Scene, 1918-: Among the authors and books mentioned are:
Louise Abeita writes *I Am a Pueblo Indian Girl* (1939).

Hartley B. Alexander emphasizes the aesthetic elements of Indian dance, painting, and myth in his *God's
Drum and Other Cycles From Indian Lore* (1927) and *Pueblo Indian Painting* (1932).

Ruth Laughlin Alexander publishes *Caballeros* (1931).

Mary Austin publishes *The Land of Journey's Ending* (1924), *Earth Horizon* (1932, described by the
authors as the "most significant autobiography that the Southwest has produced."

Hubert Howe Bancroft writes many volumes on the history of the Southwest, including *History of Arizona
and New Mexico* (1889).

Ethnologist **Adolph Bandelier** writes *The Delight Makers* (1890), a novel dealing with ancient Cliff Dwellers
in Frijoles Canyon. **Walter Noble Burns** writes *The Saga of Billy the Kid* (1925).

Witter Bynner writes poetry: *Indian Earth* (1929).

Willa Cather publishes *Death Comes for the Archbishop* (1927), described by the authors as "the finest
novel that has come from the Southwest."

Fray **Angélico Chávez** publishes *New Mexico Triptych* (1945) as well as poetry collections like *Eleven
Lady-Lyrics (1945), The Single Rose* (1948).

Agnes Morley Cleaveland publishes *No Life for a Lady* (1941).

Leo Crane writes *Desert Drums* (1928).

Kyle S. Crichton publishes *Law and Order Limited, The Life of Elfego Baca* (1928).

Frank Cushing publishes *Zuñi Folk Tales* (1931).

W.W.. H. Davis writes *El Gringo, or New Mexico and Her People* (1857).

Harvey Fergusson writes *Wolf Song* (1927), *Río Grande* (1933).

Erna Fergusson writes *Dancing Gods* (1931), *Our Southwest* (1940).

Lewis H. Garrard publishes *Wah-To-Yah and the Taos Trail* (1850).

Josiah Gregg publishes his ("handbook for travelers over the Santa Fe Trail") *Commerce of the Prairies* (1844).

Alice Corbin Henderson writes *Brothers of Light* (1937).

Archaeologist **Edgar Lee Hewett** writes *Ancient Life in the American Southwest* (1930), *Indians of the Río Grande Valley* (1937), and many other works.

Anthropologist **Frank C. Hibben** writes *The Lost Americans* (1946).

Paul Horgan writes a trilogy of novels: *Main Line West* (1936), *A Lamp on the Plains* (1937), and *Far From Cíbola* (1938).

Julia Keleher and Elsie Ruth Chant write *The Padre of Isleta* (1940).

George W, Kendall (acknowledging "help from Mr.. Gregg...and Mr.. Pike") describes the "ill-advised Texas-Santa Fe Expedition" of *1841* in his *Narratives...*

Mabel Dodge Luhan writes the autobiographical *Edge of Taos Desert* (1937).

Charles F. Lummis, a New Englander by birth, comes to N.M., marries an Isleta woman, and writes many items about the land and its people, including *A New Mexico David* (1891) which tells of the exploits of the people of Cebolleta (Seboyeta), *The Land of Poco Tiempo* (1893*), Pueblo Indian Folk Tales* (1894*),* and 11 other books dealing with the Native American/Spanish Southwest. (In 1915 Lummis was knighted by the King of Spain for his work on the Southwest.)

Susan Shelby Magoffin, said to be the first American female to cross the plains, publishes her diary *Down the Santa Fe Trail and Into Mexico, 1846-1847*. (She refers to the books of Kendall and Gregg in her work.)

Dr. **Washington Matthews** publishes *Navajo Legends* (1897).

Three-term Governor of New Mexico **Miguel Otero** writes *My Life on the Frontier* (1936), the only native New Mexican governor to write an autobiography.

Nina Otero publishes *Old Spain in Our Southwest* (1936).

James O. Pattie sets down his adventures "with a simple, straightforward style" in his *Personal Narrative of James 0. Pattie of Kentucky* (1831).

Zebulon M. Pike: *The Expedition of Zebulon Montgomery Pike ...* (1805-1807) is the first "Anglo-American' chronicle of N.M.

Albert Pike writes *Prose Sketches and Poems* (1834) which include N.M.

Eugene Manlove Rhodes writes books and stories based on his experiences while living in N.M., including Good *Men and True* (1911), *Desire of the Moth* (1916), *Once in the Saddle* (1927), *Trusty Knaves* (1933), etc.

Englishman **George Ruxton** writes (1848) a fictionalized serial, *Life in the Far West*, that is later published in book form as *In the Old West, As it Was in the Days of Kit Carson and the "Mountain Men"* (1920).

Sister **Blandina Segale** arrives in Santa Fe in 1877. She keeps a journal of her many activities (which are published as *At the End of the Santa Fe Trail* in 1932).

Ernest Thompson Seton republishes *Wild Animals I Have Known* (1942).

R. E. Twitchell compiles *The Spanish Archives of New Mexico* (1914).

Howard N. (Jack) Thorp writes many cowboy ballads. His first collection is published in 1908, his *Songs of the Cowboys* in 1921.

Stanley Vestal [Walter S. Campbell] writes *Kit Carson* (1928).

Susan Wallace arrives in N.M. in 1878 and while her husband, Lew Wallace, is finishing his *Ben Hur* (1880) she writes articles for Eastern magazines (which are later republished as *The Land of the Pueblos*).

Frank Waters writes *People of the Valley* (1941), *The Man Who Killed the Deer* (1942).

TELEVISION

Stanley Hubbard (from Minnesota) brings the first television station to N.M.: **KOB-TV.**

1950s: **Vergie Abeyta** begins work as a receptionist with KGGM-TV and during her 22 years with the station she serves in many capacities, including hosting the Sunday morning "News From A Woman's Point of View" and sitting on the board of directors for the station.

1967: **Mary Noskin** takes a part time job with KOB-TV and over the years becomes one of a handful of Hispanics to be promoted into management.

1968: The **Val De La 0** show is syndicated in 52 markets. (It is said that Val's show was the first to attract the attention of mega-advertisers to the Hispanic market.)

1970: **Jim Baca** is the first Hispanic to work as (weekend) news anchor in N.M.

1949
BOOKS

Fabiola Cabeza de Baca publishes *The Good Life* which contains stories about an imaginary family, with recipes for the preparation of traditional New Mexican foods. One of the principal characters is **Martina**, the village *curandera.* Hispanic feminine traditions and rituals are portrayed with fidelity.

STUDIES

Los Atarqueños: A Study of Patterns and Configurations in a New Mexico Village is written by **Florence R. Kluckhohn** as a Ph.D. dissertation. Much of this work appears later in the 1961 *Variations in Value Orientations* by Kluckhohn and E.L. **Strodtbeck.**

[These and *"a number of sociological and anthropological studies"* are singled out by **J.E. Holmes** as being of *questionable accuracy* with regard to New Mexican political institutions. Holmes relates that these studies agree on the importance of family, church, and patrón-peón, that all stress the "infrequency" of other types of groups and organizations found in typical American communities. But the various authors (*"Writings based upon firsthand knowledge are not numerous"*) disagree as to the extent of Hispanic knowledge, interest, and effectiveness in N.M. politics, some writers showing negative bias when describing its workings. Nevertheless, from these efforts *"has been derived a somewhat Procrustean synthesis exemplified in works of* **Margaret Mead and Lyle Saunders.**" Accordingly, Hispanic New Mexicans live in cultural isolation as per the customs of Spain and Indian America. Villages are isolated not only from Spain and Mexico but from other villages. Business enterprise is rudimentary to nonexistent. Agriculture is a family or communal effort Village communities are highly self-sufficient but individuals are adjudged not self-reliant. Religion is paramount and politics are based on the patrón system where the most powerful individual in the community is looked to for assistance and dependency.

Margaret Mead writes (in *Cultural Patterns and Technical Change*) that the patrón is the supreme father figure: *"To be Spanish American is to be a father or to be dependent, or both, in different contexts. For most fathers, it is to be dependent upon a patrón."* Holmes asserts that if such studies were valid, the history of N.M. politics would show how a patrón could control village votes or move them from one party to another, and accurate history doesn't reflect such patterns. So he concludes that *"...the villages studied comprise by quite improbable chance a statistical oddity producing a skewed result,"* that the patrón-peón concept is more scriptography than valid history.]

Holmes cites a number of studies that have been conducted in or about rural Hispanic villages:

Sigurd Johansen, *Rural Social Organization in a Spanish-American Culture Area;*

Paul A.E Walter, Jr., *A Study of Isolation and Social Change in Three Spanish-Speaking Villages of New Mexico;*

Olen Leonard and **C.P. Loomis,** *"Culture of a Contemporary Rural Community: El Cerrito, New Mexico,"* in **Charles P. Loomis** *"Studies of Rural Social Organization in the United States, Latin America and Germany."* Holmes reports that Leonard and Loomis find no evidence of patrón domination in San Miguel county;

Olen E. Leonard, *The Role of the Land Grant in the Social Process of a Spanish-American Village in New Mexico;*

Donovan Senter, *Acculturation Among New Mexican Villages in Comparison to Adjustment Patterns of*

Other Spanish-Speaking Americans;

Lyle Saunders, *Cultural Difference and Medical Care: The Case of the Spanish-Speaking People of the Southwest*;

Suzanne Forrest remarks in *The Preservation of the Village* that *"The skewed results, which suggested the existence of great social inequality within the Hispanic rural community gave rise to the concept of a passive, one-sided, patrón-peón relationship. Once in the literature, the idea gained strength through repetition."* She cites **Charles Briggs,** author of *Our Strength*, as agreeing with Holmes that *"hierarchy and equality coexisted in traditional Hispanic society in a set of paired and shared duties and obligations."*

RANCHING

The ranching industry has experienced profound changes: pickup trucks are used more than horses; Hereford and Durham cattle have taken the place of Longhorns; fewer employees are needed due to mechanization; story-oriented Western songs of the land, elements, and animals, are being replaced by Nashville-style *country music.*

The **ranching image** is "primarily Anglo" in music, movies, and the media, though the industry (roundups, roping techniques, mounted herdsmen, rodeos, attire, etc.) was created by Hispanics, who are now often portrayed as villains or jolly sidekicks.

[A few exceptions are The Cisco Kid, Zorro, and Walt Disney's "The Nine Lives of Elfego Baca" which makes no mention of Elfego's heroic gunfight against 80 to 84 cowboys.]

Billy the Kid is a popular character in the movies while the other personalities of the Lincoln County War are virtually ignored. Hollywood sets stereotypes for ranch culture and New Mexican ranching diversity is not reflected in those stereotypes.

Ranch women *"...have not received their due..."* from traditional western writers like J. Frank Dobie, C.L. Sonnichsen, D. Dary, etc. In N.M. ranch women are an integral part of the culture and they work on the ranch as well as in the home. From the turn of the century to the beginning of WW II women participate in New Mexican rodeos. Individuals like **Fern Sawyer** and **Goldy Smith** earn reputations as top rodeo athletes.

STRIKE

Miners, most of whom are Hispanic, **strike at Empire Zinc** in Hurley. The International Union of Mine, Mill, and Smelter Workers' charges that Empire Zinc is *"...fostering division between Mexican Americans and other workers to break labor unity."* The extended strike has novel characteristics: for the first time in its history the IUMMSW takes a pro-Hispanic position; and when strikers are arrested their **wives and daughters** take over the picket lines and other strike-related activities, a first in labor history.

Salt of the Earth is filmed on location about the strike (the producer and writer of the movie are already blacklisted as radicals by the Hollywood establishment).

Reviewing the history of labor in the first part of the 20th century, Robert Kern states that "...*race and radicalism animated labor and troubled ethnic groups as much as any single issue...*" Despite the numerical superiority of Hispanics they have been considered marginal to the labor movement, with "*Anglo racial attitudes*" forcing them into the most difficult and low-paid jobs, often excluding them from union membership, especially craft unions.

POPULATION
New Mexico's population is 37% Hispanic surnamed.

POTTERY
Lucy Martín Lewis of **Acoma Pueblo** is becoming famous for her pottery which utilizes the Mimbres design. Her daughters, Dolores Lewis García, Mary Lewis García, Emma Lewis Mitchell, and Anne Lewis Hansen, also create this popular pottery.

GOVERNMENT
November 2: **Popovi Da** is elected chairman of the **All Indian Pueblo Council.** He is elected to the governorship of **San Ildefonso** three times (1958, 1959, 1963).

URANIUM
Paddy Martínez, a Navajo sheepherder, discovers uranium near Grants.

CELEBRITY
A small cub is rescued after losing its mother in an El Capitán Mountain forest fire. He is named **Smokey Bear** and becomes famous by reminding Americans, "*Only you can prevent forest fires.*"

[Surveys claim that some 95% of American children can identify Smokey Bear, giving him the distinction of the most recognized "New Mexican" celebrity of all.]

1951-1954
Edwin L. Mechem is Governor.

1951
SOCIETY

The **Forest Service** denies **Juan Lucero** a permit to graze his cattle on the former common lands of **Placitas** [which the family had done for generations]. The Lucero family moves to California, though ties are maintained in Placitas. In California Juan's son **Tony** recalls his family attending the **New Mexico Clubs** where former New Mexicans gather to talk about their villages "back home." Tony remembers that his father would often repeat the dicho (saying), "*Grulla, grulla. A tu tierra, grulla. Porque esta no es tuya...*" when he saw geese in the sky

1975: **Tony Lucero** returns permanently to N.M., as does a married sister in 1985.

RELIGIOUS
Brother Mathias Barrett establishes his first house of the **Little Brothers of the Good Shepherd** in Albuquerque. Brother Mathias dedicates his life to helping the desperately poor [and in time the order of the Little Brothers of the Good Shepherd spreads throughout the world].

MEDAL OF HONOR - HIROSHI H. MIYAMURA
April 24-25, 1951, near TaeJon-ni, Korea: On the evening of the 24th, Hiroshi H. Miyamura (from Gallup) and his Company H were in a defensive position when the enemy began a surprise mass attack, threatening to overrun the position. Corporal Miyamura, a machine-gun squad leader, jumped up from his shelter and wielding his bayonet in close hand-to-hand combat, engaged and killed some 10 enemy soldiers. Then he returned to his position, administered first aid to the wounded and directed their evacuation. Another assault wave then hit his position so he manned his machine gun and delivered withering fire until his ammunition was expended. He ordered his squad to withdraw while he stayed behind to render the gun inoperative. As the enemy infiltrated the position he bayoneted his way through enemy soldiers to a second gun emplacement and assisted in its withering fire. But the attack continued and Hiroshi saw his men would have to withdraw or be overcome by sheer force of numbers. Miyamura ordered his men to fall back while he covered their escape. Though wounded, he continued firing on the enemy, killing scores of them in his magnificent one-man stand until his ammunition was depleted. When last seen he was engaging the overwhelming enemy in ferocious hand-to-hand combat until the position was overrun.

November 4, 1953: Hiroshi H. Miyamura is awarded the Medal of Honor *"for indomitable heroism and consummate devotion to his comrades and duty, reflecting the utmost glory on himself and his country.*

[Hiroshi was taken prisoner and kept as a POW. His citation was written as if it was a posthumous award and not publicized so as not to motivate retribution by the enemy.]

1952
GOVERNMENT
Martín Vigil of Tesuque is drafted to serve as chairman of the **All Indian Pueblo Council.** Vigil is persistent in the drive for Pueblos to acquire community centers.

SOCIETY
Edward Pasqual Dozier from Santa Clara Pueblo is the first New Mexican Native American to receive a Ph.D. degree (from UCLA).

URANIUM MINING
Laguna **Pueblo** is offered a lease with Anaconda Corporation to mine **uranium** deposits discovered on Pueblo land.

1953
ARTS & CRAFTS

Thomas A. Valdez sells four embroideries done by **Policarpio Valencia**, *The Embroiderer,* to the Museum of New Mexico.

BOOKS
Aurora Lucero-White Lea publishes *Literary Folklore of the Hispanic Southwest.* It is divided into five parts:

> I: Dramas; II: Ballads, Corridos; III: Folkstories; IV: Folkways; V: Folksay

LAND & FOREST SERVICE
The Forest Service now has administrative authority over lands, to be used *"in the public interest"* previously regulated by the Soil Conservation Service and the Farm Security Administration, as well as the greater part of the northern N.M. grant lands.

[S. Forrest writes: *"To the many New Mexicans, Hispanic and otherwise, who have come to see U.S. forest rangers as uniformed occupational troopers guarding the spoils of the Treaty of Guadalupe-Hidalgo, it will come as no surprise that the Forest Service subverted so soon the intentions of the Land Utilization program in whose trust its new lands had been acquired..."*]

URANIUM MINING
Laguna Pueblo signs an extensive lease with **Anaconda Copper** for uranium mining. In time the Jackpile Mine provides jobs for workers from Laguna, Paguate, Bibo, Cebolleta, etc.

1970s: Radioactive dust endangers the surrounding areas and various cancers are predicted because of exposure. Blasting from the mine also destabilizes many people's homes. When Anaconda lets it be known that it intends to stop production within 10 years, people become militant and demand better royalties. The lease is renegotiated and the royalty schedule improves but Anaconda downplays health hazards.

July 16, 1979: United Nuclear's tailings pond in the Church Rock area bursts, sending more than 90,000,000 gallons of radioactive water into the Río Puerco. Navajos have to haul in purified water, feed for their stock, etc., and United Nuclear reports a $25,0000,000 loss to rectify the situation.

1954
BOOKS
Fabiola Cabeza de Baca publishes *We Fed Them Cactus.* It provides historical perspectives on the land, Hispanics who are able to survive calamities like drought (by feeding cactus to their cattle), erosion, and thick clouds of dust. Then the land is lost forever when taken over by "Anglos." The work also depicts how Hispanic women nourish ranching and community life.

TIMELINE
Plessy v. Ferguson, the 1896 decision that legalized "separate but equal" racial segregation in America, is overturned by the Supreme Court in **Broom v. Topeka Board of Education.**

[With the exception of towns like Hobbs, Clovis, Lovington, Carlsbad, etc., black students in most of N.M. had been attending schools with everybody else for decades.]

BOOKS

Philip Stevenson begins publication of *The Seed*, an "epic" account of the Gallup coal mining strike.

Part One: 1954: Vol. 1: *Morning, Noon, and Night*. 1956: Vol. 2: *Out of the Dust*.

Part Two:
196 1: Vol. 1: *Old Father Antic* and Vol. 2: *The Hoax*.

SKIING

May: **Ernie Blake** (born Ernest Herman Block in 1913 in Frankfurt, Germany) and **Peter Totemoff** (an Aleut Indian) sight the Twining Mining Camp and decide it is a perfect site for an Alpine ski resort.

1955: Using a mule and the help of 18 Indians from Taos Pueblo, Blake and Totemoff place a 2,000-foot diesel-driven T-Bar in operation. **Taos Ski Valley** is born and in time the industry begins to attract skiers from all over the nation and the world.

1995: The "ski boom" causes the creation of other ski areas which include: Angel Fire; Enchanted Forest (XC); Red River; Sandía Peak; Santa Fe; Sipapu; Ski Apache; Ski Río; Snow Canyon; Sandía Peak; Taos Ski Valley.

1955-1956

John F. Simms is Governor.

1955
BOOKS

Cleofas Jaramillo publishes *Romance of a Little Village Girl*, an autobiography of growing up in a northern N.M., steeped in highly developed Hispanic traditions and culture, then changing into loss.

CHILE

New Mexico No. 9, the most popular chile grown in the state, is proving too "hot" for outside consumption so **Roy Nakayama** and **Paul Bosland,** botanists at New Mexico State University, work in conjunction with various chile growers to improve the strain.

1974: NuMex **Big Jim** is on the market in the fall with its long pods and reduced hotness. It is an immediate success.

1980s: New Mexico grows more acres of chile than all the other states combined. The annual **Hatch Chile Festival** achieves national recognition and chile is an acknowledged part of folklore, as acknowledged by the following poem by New Mexican writer **Alberto O. Martínez:**

We Love it Hot

Chile is the food New Mexicans eat,
This cure-all food is really a treat,
A food so good it makes you sweat,
And a runny nose is more proof yet!
New Mexico farmers labor and toil,
In special ways they prepare the soil,
And when they plant the seed they say:
"We love it Hot," both green and red.
In early August, along with corn,
Our tables green chile will adorn,
Its fragrant aroma does fill the air,
For green chile pods roast everywhere.
Take one good bite and you're chile afflicted,
Take two more bites and you're chile addicted.

Alberto O. Martínez

Harvest in Santa Cruz
Courtesy Museum of NM, #8088

BOOKS
Paul Horgan is awarded the Pulitzer Prize for *Great River: The Río Grande in North American History.*

PROFILE

Paul Horgan

A M E R I C A N   A U T H O R

August 1, 1903: Paul Horgan is born in Buffalo, New York, to Edward D. and Rose Marie Rohr Horgan, *"first generation Americans, of English-Irish and French-German blood."*

1915: The Horgan family moves to Albuquerque. His education, begun at the Nardin Academy in Buffalo, is continued in the Albuquerque Public Schools, New Mexico Military Institute, the Eastman School of Music and the Eastman Theatre (in Rochester, New York). In N.M. he lives in the towns of Albuquerque, Roswell, and Santa Fe.

1926: Horgan accepts the post of librarian at N.M. Military Institute and pursues his interest in writing.

1933: His first novel, *The Fault of Angels*, receives the Harper Prize.
1942-1946: Paul serves in the Army General Staff Corps. He receives the Legion of Merit for his work as chief of the Army information Branch in the Information and Education Division.

1946: Horgan returns to N.M. and devotes himself full time to writing.

1955: Paul receives the Pulitzer Prize for *Great River: The Río Grande in North American History.*

1956: Paul Horgan receives an honorary doctorate from Wesleyan University.

1962: Paul becomes the director of the Center for Advanced Studies at Wesleyan University. In time he is an adjunct professor, professor emeritus, and author in residence at Wesleyan.

1975: His biography, *Lamy of Santa Fe, is* awarded the Pulitzer Prize, as well as the Bancroft Prize,

1976: Paul is awarded the Laetare Medal by the University of Notre Dame.

1977: Horgan receives an honorary doctorate, his 20th, from Yale.

1981: Paul is awarded the Baldwin Medal of Wesleyan University.

1982: Paul's 17th novel, Mexico *Bay, is* published in his 79th year. His works are being distributed in 17 countries. He lives in Middletown, Connecticut.

1956
ARTS & CRAFTS
Studio of Indian Arts is opened by **Popovi Da** and his mother, **María Martínez,** the potter of San Ildefonso.

PHOTOGRAPHY
The first **New Mexico Photographers Exhibition** is staged. Photographers working in N.M. include John Candelario, Ernest Knee, Laura Gilpin, Anne Nogle, Betty Hahn, Todd Webb, Meridel Rubenstein, Paul Caponigro, Patrick Nagatani, Ansel Adams, Eliot Porter, and the state's photography output is described by a New York art critic as of *"very high calibre--as good as anything in the country."*

AMERIND
Forty percent of the **Navajo Nation** lives in N.M. and 80% of them vote regularly in county, state, and federal elections.

ORGANIZATIONS
Individuals who have portrayed don **Diego de Vargas** in past Santa Fe Fiestas gather to form an organization which comes to be known as *Los Caballeros De Vargas.*

June, 1956: **Johnny Valdés** is sworn in as the first *Presidente General* of the *Los Caballeros De Vargas.*

The Caballeros De Vargas are involved in events like celebrating "sister city" status with Santa Fe de la Vega de Granda, Spain; Santa Fe Trail festivities; distributing food baskets for Thanksgiving and Christmas; putting on the Fiesta Entrada, etc.

1960: Santa Fe's 350th anniversary is celebrated with Los Caballeros crowning *La Conquistadora.* They also host María Luisa and María Teresa Pérez Balsera of Madrid, 12th generation descendants of don Diego de Vargas.

1957-1958
Edwin L. Mechem is Governor.

1957
MUSEUM
The **Gadsden Museum** is opened by **Aureliano and Elizabeth** (Fountain) **Armendáriz** in La Mesilla in an
effort to preserve the Hispanic arts of the area. They emphasize folk music, corridos, the décima, as
well as santos and other items from the general Hispanic history and traditions of La Mesilla.

[Elizabeth is a great-great-granddaughter of santero José Aragón and some of his work is displayed in the
museum. The Doña Ana Historical Society elects her to their "Hall of Fame."]

MILITARY
May 22: An Air Force B-36 from Kirtland Air Force Base accidentally drops a ten-megaton hydrogen bomb
five miles south of Albuquerque. A nuclear disaster is averted only because the bomb is not fully
armed at takeoff.

MUSIC - OPERA
July 3: Under the leadership of founder and director **John Crosby,** the **Santa Fe Opera** opens its doors with
a company of 67 people, a 480-seat Theater, and a budget of $110,000.

1967: Fire completely destroys the Theater but within a year it is rebuilt to seat 1,889 [its present capacity].

1995: Attendance for the season reaches 72,397 (or 89% of Theater capacity),

1996: The SFO counts over 600 company members at the height of its summer season and operating
expenses are estimated at around $9,000,000. By the end of the 1996 season 114 different operas
have been presented since 1957, including 8 world and 35 American premieres.

An SFO seasons includes five operas but also a variety of special activities like A Day at the Opera Ranch
(open house and entertainment for the community), Gala Opening Weekend, Supper Preview on the
Grounds, Picnics in the Orpheus Grove, and Grand Finale Fiesta, to bid farewell to the season.

[The world renowned Santa Fe Opera also sponsors educational programs related to opera and theater: the
Apprentice Program for Singers assists young American singers in making the transition from student to
professional; the **Apprentice Program for Theater Technicians; the Youth Night at the Opera** offers an
opportunity for young people to see entire operas at special prices; the **Pueblo Opera Program** brings opera
to the Pueblos of N.M. and Pueblo children to the SFO; the **Opera Insights Discussion Series;** and guided
Backstage Tours.]

1958
NEWSPAPERS
April 30, 1958: After 67 years of continuous publication in the Spanish language, *El Nuevo Mexicano* closes its
doors. **Pedro R. Ortega,** the newspaper's last editor, states there is little interest in Spanish language
publications because young people now read only English.

SOCIETY

November 7: The *Albuquerque Journal* quotes Senator **Dennis Chávez** as to how Hispanics are considered in their native state: *"If they go to war they're Americans; if they run for office, they're Spanish Americans; and if they looking for a job, they're damned Mexicans."*

1958-1982
HEALTH

Mortality rates are studied during this period by **T.M. Becker, C.L. Wiggins, R.S. Elliott, C.R. Key,** and **J.M. Samet.** Statistics for incidence or death (presented from the highest to lowest number) from:

CANCER

Stomach: Indian mortality rates are stable, non-Hispanic whites have slightly lower rates than whites nationally; Hispanic New Mexicans have a rate similar to blacks nationally, which is nearly double that of whites nationwide.

Colon/Rectum: mortality increased among N.M. males, especially among Hispanics and Indians.

Pancreas: Males: increased by 88% for Hispanics, 78% for Indians, 48% for non-Hispanic whites. Rates also increased for females but on a smaller scale.

Prostate: increased 74% for Hispanics, 37% for n-H whites, 24% for Indians.

Bladder: increased the most for n-H whites, then Hispanics, and lowest for Indians.
Breast: Hispanic, Indian, n-H white.

Cervix uteri: Mortality rates declined during the study period but they are still patterned Hispanic, Indian, n-H white.
Leukemia: n-H white, Hispanic, Indian.

DIABETES

Indian, Hispanic, n-H white. *("The prevalence of diabetes and obesity in southwestern American Indians is much higher than with U.S. whites.")*

Ischemic heart disease (frequent cause of death for persons with diabetes): n-H white, Hispanic, Indian.

INFECTIOUS DISEASES

Tuberculosis: Indian, Hispanic, n-H white.

Meningitis: Indian, Hispanic/h-H white.

Pneumonia and Influenza (the sixth leading causes of death in N.M. in 1987): Indian, Hispanic/n-H white.

RESPIRATORY DISEASE

Lung cancer: n-H white, Hispanic, Indian (*"older Hispanic women have had particularly high mortality*

from lung cancer").
Chronic obstructive pulmonary disease: n-H white, Hispanic, Indian.

ALCOHOL RELATED
For all three ethnic groups, mortality rates for males exceed by at least a twofold margin those for females.

"Mean rates of alcohol metabolism are almost identical between American Indians and whites ... and there
are no racial *differences in* hepatic alcohol dehydrogenase activity and isoenzyme pattern in liver
biopsy specimens."

Illness: Indian, Hispanic, n-H white.

INJURY
Male & Female: Indian (two to three times higher than the other groups), Hispanic, n-H white.

"Injuries are the third leading cause of death in N.M. and the leading cause for persons aged 1 to 44."
Males in all ethnic groups die from injuries more than females.

Motor vehicle fatalities: Indian (two to four times higher than whites), Hispanic (20% to 50% higher than
n-H whites), n-H white. (*"Alcohol is involved in 55% to 65% of all motor vehicle fatalities...N.M.
ranks highest in motor vehicle accident fatalities in the U.S. for 1989 ... Alcohol abuse is a major
public health problem in N.M., ranking second to Nevada in the rate of alcohol-related mortality."*)

Exposure: Indian.
Suicide: Indian (by hanging, especially in jail), n-H white, Hispanic.

Homicide: Indian, Hispanic (*"two- to threefold higher than n-H white rates"*), n-H white.

1980: N.M. whites (Hispanic and n-H whites combined) have the nation's highest homicide rate among white
Americans.

*"The minority populations of N.M. are at high risk for violent death ... their rates of violent death will
increase through the next decades unless effective preventive strategies can be put into place."*

Drowning: Indian, Hispanic, n-H white,

SYMPTOMS, SIGNS, AND ILL-DEFINED CONDITIONS ("CAUSES UNKNOWN," ETC.)
Male & Female: Indian (females have a rate 21 times higher than white women nationally), Hispanic (males
have a rate 10 times higher than white men nationally), n-H white.
*"The mortality rates attributed to this category exceeds national rates for blacks and for whites
in each of the stat6 major ethnic groups...which probably is an indicator of health service access
and use."*

WOODCARVERS

The village of Córdova is New Mexico's center for woodcarvers.

1940s: Juan Sánchez, said to be from Mexico when he lived in Córdova for a few years, can copy bultos and retablos with amazing exactness. He doesn't develop a style of his own.

1959: José and Alice Mondragón are among the first carvers in Córdova who aren't related to the famous López family. Their craftsmanship is well developed and their repertoire extensive.

1960: George López is considered to be Córdova's leading woodcarver.

1963: George López and his wife **Silvianita** move out of town and open a studio closer to the highway, a move that proves commercially successful. The couple's adopted daughter, **Savinita** (the eldest daughter of George's brother Ricardo) learns to carve and influences her husband, **Cristóbal** (junior) **Ortiz,** to take up the craft.

George's younger brother **Ricardo López** markets his carvings under his wife's name, **Benita Reino.** They concentrate on the production of small trees, birds, and animals. Their married daughter **Nora Cerrano** becomes an accomplished carver, as does a son, **Eurgencio.**

1964: Apolonio Martínez and his wife (from Chimayó), weavers by profession, also turn to carving.

1970-1971: Eluid L. Martínez, son of Liria López, exhibits his work in the Spanish Market after being influenced by Uncle George and Aunt Silvianita López.

1973: Gloria López Córdova, daughter of Rafaél and Precidez López, sets up a studio in her home and she and her husband **Herminio** sell their carvings to tourists. Their images take first prize in the Spanish Markets of 1975 and 1976.

1975: Sammy Córdova, a distant relative of the López family and Herminio Córdova's nephew, sets up his own workshop near the plaza and devotes himself exclusively to carving.

1976: Lina Ortiz de Córdova (Sammy's grandmother, who along with her husband **Federico** helped Sammy in various ways) markets her work in the 1976 Spanish Market.

1977: The entire village of Córdova mourns the death of Benita Reino López.

1959-1960

John Burroughs is Governor.

1960
HISPANICS AND POVERTY
While New Mexican Hispanics comprise 28% of the population, Census figures show that **Spanish-surnamed families** account for 41.6% of New Mexicans living in poverty. The median family income for New Mexicans is $5,371; in Los Alamos the median is $9,269, though 44% of Los Alamos families have incomes in excess of $10,000.

1961-1962
Edwin L. Mechem is Governor.
(Resigned and appointed to the U.S. Senate in November, 1962).

1962
Tom Bolack is Governor. (Serves through December, 1962).

1962
MUSEUM
Ross Ward begins carving miniature wood figures which he later puts in a turn-of-the-century general store which he opens in Sandía Park east of Albuquerque. With lots of help from his wife **Carla,** the general store becomes the **Tinker Town Museum.**

1998: Tinker Town is a 22-room museum (surrounded by walls made of some 51,000 glass bottles) filled with items like miniature wood carvings, wagon wheels, old-fashioned store fronts, "wacky" western memorabilia which includes a western town, a miniature circus, antique tools, an international doll collection, swords, a one-man band, etc., etc., and a 35 foot wooden sailboat that made it around the world.

LAND ACTIVISM
February 2: **Reies López Tijerina** founds the *Alianza Federal de Mercedes* with 15 people as members. Within one year there are 800 people attending the Alianza's first convention in Albuquerque.

SOCIETY
August 18: **Mabel Dodge Luhan** dies.

November 18: Senator **Dennis Chávez** dies.

[Though he is immortalized in Statuary Hall, no biography has been commissioned by State publishers or written on Dennis Chávez.]

1963-1966
Jack M. Campbell is Governor.

1963

TIMELINE

American military advisers for the army of Ngo Dinh Diem in **South Vietnam** number 16,000. (There were only 100 in 1961.)

SOCIETY

The Albuquerque City Commission enacts the Albuquerque Fair Housing Practices Ordinance (predating the federal and state civil rights laws that would later prohibit housing discrimination on the basis of race that is rampant throughout most of the country).

1964
POLITICS

Navajo candidates from San Juan and McKinley counties win seats in the state legislature. The New Mexico Cattle Growers Association leads an unsuccessful movement to unseat them through a technicality.

UFO

April 25: At around 5:50 p.m. a Colorado family in a green 1955 Cadillac sights "an oval-shaped, metallic object" which is flying so low it hits the car's radio antenna as it is traveling on Highway 85 just south of **Socorro.** The flying object drops out of sight west of the highway. Within a few moments a police car appears on the scene and heads in the direction of the object. Driving is Officer **Lonnie Zamora** who had been driving south of town when he heard a huge roaring noise and saw a blue flame to the southwest of his location. He thought maybe the dynamite storage shed in the area had exploded so he drove onto the rough path that led to the shed, coming to a stop on a low ridge from which he sees a white metal object "parked" in the arroyo below. At first he presumes it's an overturned vehicle then he becomes aware of the odd shape and that it's balanced on four "lee supports. Then he spies two small figures standing next to the object ... they're wearing something like white coveralls ... they seem startled by Zamora's arrival. He radios the sheriffs office and asks that state Police Sergeant **Samuel Chávez** be sent to the scene. He exits his car for a closer look: the two figures are gone and there is some kind of red insignia on the side of the craft Suddenly there is a sound like a closing heavy steel hatch and a second final slam when a bright blue flame bursts forth from beneath the object. The roar is deafening and Zamora throws himself to the ground. The object is rising now and Zamora expects an explosion so he gets up and runs behind his car. But the roar stops, the flame disappears, and the object begins moving away at the height of perhaps twenty feet for maybe a mile. Then its shoots upward and disappears in a southwesterly direction.

Sergeant Chávez arrives and the two officers go down into the arroyo: a large greasewood bush is smoldering; four depressions pushed into the ground by an apparently enormous weight are found in a quadrangular pattern; in the burned area the sand has been melted into glass. Other officers are converging on the area and the sheriffs office receives three calls from Socorro residents who report a bright blue light in the area south of town.

April 26: The news is officially released to the press and scores of reporters descend on Socorro. Upon further examination of the site various little "shoeprints" are discovered as well as parallel indentations that might have been made by some kind of ladder.

Within a few days the country's top UFO experts arrive in Socorro: **James** and **Carol Lorenzen,** independent civilian researchers; Dr. **J. Allen Hynek** from Northwestern University; **Ray Stanford** of the National investigations Committee on Aerial Phenomena; as well as Air Force officers.

Stanford visits the site with Hynek, Zamora, and Chávez. The vitrified sand had never been there or had already been removed. Zamora points to a fractured rock that had been broken by the weight of the object and after more inspecting the group returns to town. But Stanford, bursting with excitement, later hurries back to the site and digs out the broken rock, wraps it in a newspaper, stashes it under the seat of his car and drives back home to Phoenix. Upon arrival he inspects the rock and discovers bits and slivers of some sort of metal imbedded in the stone. While he hates to part with his find he knows that a thorough analysis can be done only by a government agency like NASA so he ships it to the NICAP representative in Washington D.C. The results of the test are reported by Dr. **Henry Frankel:** *the metal is an alloy of zinc and iron not manufactured anywhere in the world.*

Within a few days Frankel is removed from the Socorro rock sample study and NASA issues a formal report stating the rock contains nothing more than common silica.

1966: **Phillip J. Klass** arrives in Socorro and spends his time asking about the UFO incident. He writes that nothing ever really happened, that the hoax had been merely a publicity stunt to attract tourists.

LAND GRANT ACTIVISM

Reies López Tijerina takes petitions signed by thousands of New Mexicans to Mexico City in an effort to get the Mexican government to demand that the Treaty of Guadalupe Hidalgo be fulfilled by the U.S. Neither govenment does anything.

July: Tijerina is arrested in Mexico while speaking at a students' meeting. He is released from jail and continues his trip to Mexico City in preparation for a caravan he is planning. But in Mexico City he is deported and threatened that if he returns he will be imprisoned for ten years. Convinced that he has been "set up" by the U.S. government, Tijerina realizes that the Mexican government will not act as an advocate for land claims, guaranteed by the Treaty of Guadalupe Hidalgo, in the United Nations.

SOCIETY

July 28: Pueblo leader **Sotero Ortiz** dies at the age of 86.

1965
SOCIETY

January 3: **Nina Otero-Warren** dies.

1966
SISTER CITIES
Ruth Hashimoto is instrumental in bringing the *Sister Cities* program to N.M. when Sasebo and Albuquerque become Sister Cities.

MEDAL OF HONOR - DANIEL FERNÁNDEZ
February 18, 1966: While serving in Cu Chi, Hau Nghia Province in the Republic of Vietnam, **Daniel Fernández** (born in Albuquerque) *"demonstrated indomitable* courage*"* when his patrol was ambushed by a Viet Cong rifle company and driven back by intense enemy automatic weapons fire before it could evacuate an American soldier who had been wounded in the attack. Fernández was among the four volunteers who fought their way through devastating enemy fire and exploding grenades to reach their fallen comrade. The officer in command was seriously wounded by machine gun fire so Fernández took charge. The patrol now had two men down and intense enemy fire forced the volunteers to drag their fallen comrades to cover where first aid was administered but an enemy grenade landed in their midst. Perhaps Danny was the only one who saw it but unhesitatingly he jumped over the wounded men and threw himself on the grenade moments before it exploded. The lives of his four comrades were spared.

1967: Danny Fernández is posthumously awarded the **Medal of Honor,** America's highest award, *"For conspicuous gallantry and intrepidity at the cost of his life, above and beyond the call of duty...."*

SOCIETY
March 3 1: The statue of **Dennis Chávez** is unveiled in **Statuary Hall** in Washington D.C.

LAND ACTIVISM
October 15, 1966: Some 100 Alianza members and their families set up camp at the **Echo Amphitheater** campground south of **Tierra Amarilla.** They declare they are now in charge of the area, calling it the *"People's Republic of San Joaquín."* There are no incidents.

The following weekend when a 50-car caravan returns to **Echo Amphitheater** the people are met by state policemen and two forest rangers who tell them to pay the camping fees or leave. After an "argument" in which a ranger reportedly runs to get a gun the man is "arrested" by the people, given a "trial" in which he is found guilty of trespassing, given a suspended sentence and released.

[A charge of "trespassing" from government officers would have had to address the issue of land titles. Instead, Tijerina. and others are charged with assault on federal officers, thus preventing the land issue from being opened up in court.]

May, 1967: Some 500 Alianza members gather at the **Tierra Amarilla** courthouse and proclaim the area a free city-state within the *"People's Republic of San Joaquín."* They elect city officials then hold a conference and barbecue outside the village of **Coyote.**

Rumors are spread that the Alianza is looking for a *"showdown"* and *"armed takeover of the National Forest."*

District Attorney **Alfonso Sánchez** goes on the radio to denounce the *"bunch of commies"* that are projecting *"the wrong image of our people."* He sends State Police to Coyote with orders to arrest anyone who is involved in *"unlawful assembly and extortion."*

[The legal basis is an old anti-riot act that says three or more persons planning to take over property on which they are assembled constitutes "unlawful assembly;" extortion is communicating threats to take over said property.]

June 2, 1967: State police roadblocks are set up around Coyote. Police *"swarmed through people's homes"* in Coyote [which isn't state or federal land]. Eleven Alianza members are arrested and jailed in the Tierra Amarilla courthouse pending arraignment.

June 5, 1967: Armed *"People's Deputies"* go into the courthouse intending to make a citizens' arrest on Alfonso Sánchez for "tampering with and abusing the constitutional rights" of the jailed citizens. A State patrolmen is shot and panic sweeps through the courthouse as many shots are fired. Elogio [sic] Salazar is shot twice and courthouse employees jump out of windows or run for cover, Judge J.M. Scarborough locking himself in the men's room.

Other state police arrive at the scene but are driven off with gunfire. Raiders take two hostages, who are later released unharmed, and dash for the safety of the mountains.

The courthouse raid makes headlines nationwide and reporters swarm into Río Arriba.

The **New Mexico National Guard** under the command of Adjutant General **John P. Jolly** is ordered into the area. Some 350 Guardsmen capable of firing 20,000 rounds of ammunition [and Jolly orders another 20,000 from Ft. Bliss because *"twenty-thousand rounds won't last long if we start shooting"*] are deployed, **along with jeeps armed with machine guns, two M-42 tanks, and a spotter plane and helicopters.** There are also scores of state police, sheriffs and deputies, forest rangers, some 80 N.M. Mounted Patrol, and even armed officers from the N.M. Game and Fish Department, a force estimated at around 500 men intent on capturing nineteen (19) *"raiders."*

The manhunt begins in the 25,000 acre area of Río Arriba backcountry but the "raiders" seem to have vanished. From his command headquarters in the Forest Service ranger station at Canjilón, General Jolly sends tanks and troops into the village to round up "suspected Alianza sympathizers" who are herded into a barbed wire sheep pen. Most are women, children, or elderly and it is hoped the raiders will give themselves up or try to rescue the "detainees." When a reporter asks about the detainees rights, Jolly answers: *"Let's don't get involved in civil liberties."* After 36 hours of bad publicity, Jolly orders the release of the detainees.

No *raiders* are caught until they walk up to authorities and turn themselves in.

June 10, 1967: A car pulls into a Bernalillo service station and a suspicious attendant alerts the State Police. When the vehicle is stopped down the road **Reies Tijerina** is taken into custody.

Tijerina is charged with two counts of assault to commit murder, two counts of kidnapping, damage to state property and possession of a deadly weapon.

Nine others are indicted by a grand jury: Reies H. Tijerina Jr., Baltazar Martínez, Ezequiel Domínguez, Tobias Leyba, José Madril, Moises Morales, Juan Valdez, Salomón Velásquez, and Gerónimo Borunda, who are later released on bond.

1967: The **John Birch Society** distributes 50,000 pamphlets denouncing the land grant issue as a *"Communist plot to grab the Southwest."*

Attempts are made to bomb Alianza headquarters in Albuquerque and the windows are shot out so many times they are finally bricked in.

Reies Tijerina and the other Echo Amphitheater defendants are convicted of assault and released pending appeal.

PROFILE

Nancy López

REVOLUTIONIZING THE GAME OF GOLF

Nancy López from **Roswell** wins her first golf tournament at the age of 9, beating her closest competitor by a by an 110-stroke margin. Her father gives her a *Barbie* doll for the win.

1969: Nancy wins the New Mexico Women's Amateur Tournament at the age of 12.

1971: As a freshman at Goddard H.S. Nancy petitions for permission to play on the boys' golf team but the New Mexico High School Athletic Association won't permit a female to compete on male teams. A threatened lawsuit overturns the decision and she gets to play during her sophomore and junior years, Goddard H.S. winning the State golf title those two years. During her senior year in high school, Nancy finishes second in the New Mexico Women's Open and later that summer she garners another second in the U.S. Women's Open.

1978: Nancy wins her first professional tournament at the age of 21 then goes on to win five consecutive tournaments to set a record as the **all-time Rookie money winner** in the 20-year history of the Ladies Professional Golf Association. And Nancy wins nine of the next twenty-five tournaments she enters, causing her to be selected as **Pro-Golf Player of the Year** *and* **Female Rookie of the Year,** as well as being awarded the **Vare Trophy** for the lowest scoring average of the season.

1983: Married to **Ray Knight**, Nancy leaves the pro tour (a total of three times) to have a child.

1985: After leaving the pro tour to have her first daughter, Nancy captures the LPGA championship.

1987: Nancy is elected to the **LPGA Hall of Fame,** one of the youngest inductees on record.

1992: Nancy rejoins the pro tour.

[Nancy López is credited with revolutionizing golf for women, proving that you don't have to be male or born to privilege to participate in the sport. Her place in sports history is assured.]

November, 1968: Charges stemming from the courthouse raid come to trial. Tijerina is charged with leading the raid and ordering that hostages be taken. (First-degree kidnapping charges carry a possible death penalty.)

Saying that the day of lawyers is over, Tijerina conducts most of his own defense. When the case goes to the jury it returns after four hours of deliberation with a verdict of "**not guilty**." Jubilant supporters go outside with him only to be met with shouts of *"We'll get you yet, Tijerina!"*

[It was later brought out that Tijerina's acquittal came about because he was incorrectly charged. **If he had broken land law it had nothing to do with the kidnapping charge leveled against him, so he was found innocent.**]

January 19, 1969: Alianza headquarters are bombed again.
February, 1969: The Alianza culture center is burned to the ground.

June, 1969: On the anniversary celebration of the courthouse raid a Forest Service sign is burned near Abiquiú then later another at Coyote as *"a symbolic act of protest against the occupation of our peoples' lands."* Armed Rangers descend on the crowd and make arrests.

Reies Tijerina is found guilty of helping to burn the signs and sentenced to three years in prison. Later he is found guilty of other charges from the courthouse raid. He serves his time in prison.

1967-1970

David E. Cargo is Governor.

1967
PAINTING
Painter **Peter Hurd** finds himself in the national spotlight when President Lyndon Johnson rejects Hurd's commissioned portrait of the Chief Executive. Undaunted, Hurd and his wife **Henriette Wyeth** continue to paint along Southwestern themes.

SPORTS
The UNM **Sports Arena** known as **The Pit** is completed.

1983: The NCAA Basketball Finals are held in The Pit.

1968
The **Pan American Center,** an ultra modern sports complex, is completed on the campus of New Mexico State University.

FILM COMMISSION
Gov. Cargo directs the establishment of the first state film commission [the first in the nation, which serves as a model for other states].
1968-1988: Hollywood movie makers produce more than 150 films on location in N.M. and by the end of 1988 they have spent more than $30,000,000 in the state.

SOCIETY
September 16: **Mateo Aragón,** the gentle, persistent promoter of Indian education, dies at the age of 62.

1969
SOCIETY
Beryl Blue Spruce, whose parents are from **Paguate and San Juan,** is licensed as a medical doctor, the first Pueblo New Mexican to achieve that distinction.
BOOKS
N. Scott Momaday, a Kiowa who grew up at Jémez Pueblo, is awarded the Pulitzer Prize for his novel *House Made of Dawn.*

MUSIC
Richard B. Stark researches and writes books on **New Mexican music:**

> 1969: *Music of the Spanish Folk Plays in New Mexico;*
> 1973: *Juegos infantiles cantados en Nuevo México;*
> 1978: *Music of the Bailes in New Mexico;* and *Music of the Alabados in NewMexico.*

RELIGIOUS

Benedictine Monks purchase the Trappist Monk retreat property in the Pecos Mountains and convert it into the **Pecos Benedictine Abbey,** the only coed Catholic monastery in the nation. They also establish the more traditional monastery known as **Christ in the Desert** near **Abiquiú,** which has a nationally famous chapel designed by architect **George Nakashima**.

AGRICULTURAL COOP

An agricultural cooperative known as the *Cooperativa Agrícola de Tierra Amarilla* is created by community people coming together and farming some 600 acres of land collectively. Corn, wheat, beans, and many other vegetables are planted. Most of the labor is voluntary and president **Gregorita Aguilar** observes that people work *"because it's like it used to be."*

A medical clinic, *La Clínica del Pueblo de Río Arriba,* is opened by the Cooperative because there is no doctor between Española and Durango, Co.

Arsonists set a fire which guts all rooms and destroys most of the equipment and medicine. It takes 10 months to reopen to serve the community.

1970
HERITAGE RAZED

February: Albuquerque's **Alvarado Hotel,** built in the California Mission Revival style of architecture and considered a jewel of the Fred Harvey system, is demolished to make way for a parking lot.

MEDAL OF HONOR - FRANKLIN D. MILLER

Franklin D. Miller entered the service at Albuquerque. On January 5, 1970, at Konturn Province, Republic of Vietnam, Staff Sergeant Miller distinguished himself while serving as team leader of an American-Vietnamese long-range reconnaissance patrol operating deep within enemy controlled territory in Konturn Province. Leaving the helicopter insertion point, the patrol moved forward on its mission. Suddenly one of the team members tripped a hostile boobytrap which wounded four soldiers. Sergeant Miller, knowing that the explosion would alert the enemy, quickly administered first aid to the wounded and directed the team into positions across a small stream bed at the base of a steep hill. Within a few minutes Sergeant Miller saw the lead element of what he estimated to be a platoon size enemy force moving toward his location. Concerned for the safety of his men, he directed the small team to move up the hill to a more secure position. He remained alone, separated from the patrol, to meet the attack. Miller single-handedly repulsed two determined attacks by the numerically superior enemy force and caused them to withdraw in disorder. He rejoined his team, established contact with a forward air controller and arranged the evacuation of his patrol. However, the only suitable extraction location in the heavy jungle was a bomb crater some 150 meters from the team location. Sergeant Miller reconnoitered the route to the crater and led his men through the enemy controlled jungle to the extraction site. As the evacuation helicopter hovered over the crater to pick up the patrol, the enemy launched a savage automatic weapon and rocket propelled grenade attack against the beleaguered team, driving off the rescue helicopter. Sergeant

Miller led the team in a valiant defense which drove back the enemy in its attempt to overrun the small patrol. Although seriously wounded and with every man in his patrol a casualty, Miller moved forward again single-handedly to meet the hostile attackers. From his forward exposed position, Sergeant Miller gallantly repelled two attacks by the enemy before a friendly relief force reached the patrol location. Sergeant Miller's conspicuous gallantry, intrepidity in action and selfless devotion to the welfare of his comrades at the risk of his life above and beyond the call of duty are in keeping with the highest traditions of the military service and reflect great credit on him, his unit, and the United States Army.

SOCIETY
June 16: **Miguel Archibeque,** spiritual leader of the **Penitente Brotherhood,** dies.

Archbishop Davis states that Archibeque *"was very instrumental in bringing some very good leadership into the Penitentes."*

Governor Cargo says Archibeque *"had a tremendous impact on N.M., particularly in the northern part of the state because of his activities among the Penitentes. Few people were aware of his influence."*

Congressman Manuel Luján says, *"If I were to name the men who have had the greatest influence on my life, I think Miguel Archibeque would be high on the list."*

STATE GOVERNMENT
The State constitution is amended to permit a single four-year term for state executives but they can't be candidates for successive terms (excepting the lieutenant governor).

POLITICS
Enthusiasm for politics and the workings of government are so pervasive in the state, especially among Hispanic New Mexicans, that N.M. is described as *"the political state."* Politics are at once personal and prominent, influencing economics, education, and virtually every aspect of major activities.

[We are informed by **W.A. Beck** that to *"properly understand"* N.M. politics one must realize that N.M. is *"in the U.S. but not of the U.S."* The opposite of political indifference is the problem: *"…how to keep the politically enthusiastic…so-called natives … from voting several times in the same election."* Furthermore, *"Spanish-Americans enthusiasm isn't always matched with an understanding of democratic practices"* because they were accustomed to the *"tyranny of Spain and Mexico."* There are many tales about this or that patrón voting his sheep to deliver an election; buying votes continues, with the price of one dollar going up to 10 dollars *"more recently."*]

SOCIETY & POVERTY
New Mexico's poverty rate is 22.8%. A fourth of the counties have poverty rates of 32% or higher (the

highest is 57% in Mora county); 47.7% of female-headed families live in poverty and among the western states N.M. ranks last in per-capita income.

BOOKS

Tony Hillerman publishes his first mystery novel, *The Blessing Way.*

MEDAL OF HONOR - LOUIS R. ROCCO

May 24, 1970: In the northeast of Katum, Republic of Vietnam, Louis R. Rocco (born in Albuquerque, entered the Service in Los Angeles) volunteered to accompany a medical evacuation team on an urgent mission to evacuate eight critically wounded Army of the Republic of Vietnam personnel. As the rescue helicopter approached the landing zone it became the target for intense enemy automatic weapons fire and crash-landed ablaze while Sergeant Rocco identified and directed accurate suppressive fire on the enemy positions. Rocco sustained a fractured hip, wrist, and severely bruised his back but he pulled the survivors from the burning wreckage, sustaining burns to his own body. Though enemy fire continued intensely, Louis carried to safety each unconscious survivor across some 20 meters of exposed terrain, making it to a friendly position. Inside the position Louis Rocco helped to administer first aid to his wounded comrades until his own wounds and burns caused him to collapse and lose consciousness.

Warrant Officer Louis R. Rocco received the Medal of Honor for courage *"far above and beyond the call of duty ... in keeping with the highest traditions of sacrifice and courage of the military service."*

PROFILE

Tony Hillerman

B E S T - S E L L I N G   A U T H O R

May 27, 1925: **Tony Hillerman** is born in Sacred Heart, Oklahoma.

1930-1938: Tony attends St. Mary's Academy.

1939-1942: He attends Konawa High School.

December 25, 1941: Gus Hillerman, Tony's father, dies.

1942: Tony enrolls at Oklahoma State University. The following year he quits school to manage the family farm. When he turns 18 he joins the Army.

1944: Hillerman lands in France on D-Day.

1945: Tony is awarded the Silver Star. Later he is wounded by an enemy grenade while on patrol in Alsace. He is returned to the U.S. on a convalescent furlough, staying in Oklahoma. He drives a truck to the Navajo Reservation.

1945-1948: Hillerman attends the University of Oklahoma.

August 16,1948: He marries **Marie Elizabeth Unzner.**

1948-1949: Tony writes for the *New Herald* in Borger, Texas.

1949-1950: Hillerman is the News editor for the *Morning Press* in Lawton, Oklahoma.

1950-1952: He becomes a reporter for the United Press International in Oklahoma City.

1952-1954: Hillerman is UPI bureau chief in Santa Fe.

1954-1962: Tony works as reporter and editor for the Santa Fe *New Mexican*.

1963: He attends UNM and is hired as assistant to President Tom Popejoy. He buys a house in Albuquerque.
1964: He is hired as associate professor in Journalism at UNM.

1966: Hillerman becomes the Chair of the UNM Journalism department.
1970: His first novel, *The Blessing Way, is* published, "launching" the career of **Lt. Joe Leaphorn** of the Navajo Tribal Police. He receives $3,500 for the book.

Many books follow and several make the New York Times Best-Seller list.

1973: *The Great Taos Bank Robbery.*
Dance Hall of the Dead (winner of the Edgar Allan Poe Award from the Mystery Writers Assoc.).

1974: Hillerman resigns the chairmanship of the Journalism Department.

1975: Tony is awarded the Dan Burrows Memorial Award for Journalism.

1976: He becomes assistant to UNM President William Davis.

1985: Hillerman retires from the UNM Journalism Department.

1986: *Skinwalkers;*

1988: *A Thief of Time;*

1989: *Talking God;*

1990: *Coyote Waits;*

1991: *Hillerman County;*

1993: *Sacred Clowns.*

1971-1974
Bruce King is Governor.

1972
SANTOS & THEFT
Recovery is made of 76 **religious artifacts** which have been stolen over a two-year period from more than 23 moradas and chapels.

[Hispanic folk art now has a high monetary value.]

BOOKS
Rudolfo Anaya publishes *Bless Me, Ultima,* and the novel becomes the second most popular bestseller in the history of New Mexican literature.

PROFILE

Rudolfo A. Anaya

N E W   M E X I C O ' S   A U T H O R   A N D   E D I T O R

October 30, 1937: **Rudolfo A. (Alfonso) Anaya** is born to Martín Anaya and Rafaelita Mares Anaya (both from the farming community of Puerto de Luna) in the small village of Pastura. The family, which uses the Spanish language almost exclusively, moves to Santa Rosa where Rudy experiences his childhood. The large family and the much larger extended family as well as neighbors often drop by to visit, stop over during a trip, celebrate holidays together, etc., and to relate stories and adventurous tales. Rudy loves to hear their stories. When Rudy is old enough to attend school he learns to love it though he has little knowledge of the English language. He also loves nature and in the summer he spends as much time as possible in the mountains, hills and riverbanks of his world.

1952: The Anaya family relocates to Albuquerque, taking up residence in the historic Barelas neighborhood. Street life is something new for a country boy, sometimes exciting, sometimes dangerous. He attends Albuquerque High School.

1954: Rudy suffers a serious back injury while swimming. He spends an entire summer at Carrie Tingley Hospital.

1956: Anaya graduates from high school and enrolls in the Browning Business School from which he graduates in 1958.

Rudolfo A. Anaya

1963: Rudy graduates from the University of New Mexico with a B.A. in Literature (to which he adds an M.A. in 1968, a second M.A. in Guidance and Counseling in 1972). He begins teaching in the Albuquerque Public Schools.

1966: Rudolfo marries **Patricia Lawless.**

1972: Rudy's first novel, *Bless Me, Ultima, is* published by Quinto Sol Publications of California and becomes a best-seller. The characters and adventures in the novel are based on those of Puerto de Luna and Pastura.

[It has been written that 100,000 copies of the book were sold during its first 10 years, despite being published by a very small regional press.]

1974: Anaya becomes an associate professor of English at UNM.

1976: The novel *Heart of Aztlan is* published in California (UNM later picks it up for re-release). It is said the work is based on the Barelas years. Rudy also begins work as an editor with *Voices from the Río Grande.*

1979: *Torturga,* based in part on his experiences/impressions while convalescing at Carrie Tingley Hospital, is published in California (later picked up by UNM).

1982: Anaya publishes his short story collection, *The Silence of the Llano,* in California.

1984: The German edition of *Bless Me, Ultima is* published by Nexus Verlag of Frankfurt.
1988: Rudy is elevated to the rank of Full Professor at UNM.

1989: Anaya edits *Tierra, Contemporary Short Fiction of New Mexico* [sometimes described as the best anthology of fiction in N.M.].

1989-1993: Anaya founds and edits the *Blue Mesa Review.*

1993: The Spanish edition of *Bless Me, Ultima is* issued by Editorial Grijalbo of Mexico City.

1995: The *Anaya Reader is* issued by Hyperion as is his novel *Zía Summer.*

1996: *Río Grande Fall* is Rudy's latest novel, published by Warner Books.

[Rudolfo A. Anaya's works have been translated into German, Italian, French, Japanese, Russian. He continues to write, edit, lecture, etc., and encourage the development of new writers.]

BALLOON FIESTA

April: Thirteen balloonists ascend from an Albuquerque shopping center parking lot while an estimated 20,000 people watch. (It is said there are about 30 hot air balloons in the entire USA.)

1996: The **Kodak Albuquerque International Balloon Fiesta** takes place in October and is a tremendous tourist attraction. It is advertised as the most photographed event in the world and features more than 800 hot air balloons in its mass ascensions which are watched by more than a million people. (It is estimated that there are now some 5,000 to 6,000 balloons in the USA.)

WOMEN & EDUCATION

The first **Women's Studies Center** is founded at UNM.

1973: The New Mexico Commission on the Status of Women is created by an executive order of Governor King. The chairperson is **Dorothy L. Cline,** one of New Mexico's most honored and respected activists.

The Rape Crisis Center is founded at the Women's Center at UNM. The Sex Crime Prosecution and Treatment Act is finally passed by the legislature in 1978 and other centers are started in various towns.

1975: **Mary Helen Carroll** and her sister **Dorothy** buy a house with their own money (because bureaucrats won't help them) and open the **Southwest Maternity Center.** The first baby is born there on Christmas Eve, 1975.

1976: The Albuquerque Women's Community Association founds the **Albuquerque Shelter for Victims of Domestic Violence,** the first in the state.

1977: **Millie Arviso** and **Alva Bensen** found the Native American Women's Coalition at UNM.

1978: Under the leadership of **Tasia Young,** a study on the sufferings of displaced homemakers is distributed to the Legislature. The Displaced Homemakers Act is enacted in 1979.

1981: A chapter of the Mexican American Women's National Association is formed for N.M.

1986: Albuquerque is hosting the **Miss USA Pageant** (in February) and feminists organize a *No More Miss USA* protest of the event because they say it promotes *"a racist, sexist ideal."*

1973
ACTIVISM
May: **Navajos** hold marches on each Saturday in Farmington.

[This is to protest the inhuman cruelties perpetrated on Navajos: three were found with hands tied behind their backs, mutilated, disemboweled, throats cut from ear to ear (there were no suspects and no one was ever arrested); Farmington teenagers set two Navajos on fire as they slept *"in a state of unconscious drunkenness,"* and three teenagers are sent to reform school; a Navajo's body, decomposing due to weeks of exposure, is discovered in a desolate arroyo in the Farmington foothills.]

SOCIETY
September 24: Pueblo leader **Martín Vigil** of Tesuque dies of a heart attack while working on his farm.

1974
GOVERNMENT LAND GRANT
Embudo grant lands are being administered by the **Bureau of Land Management.** Private land is acknowledged to be that which is occupied, improved, or cultivated by citizens. The BLM informs the residents of **Apodaca, Cañoncito, and Montecito** that land on which their homes, churches, cemeteries, gardens, etc., are situated, **is BLM land.** Residents protest but they are merely told they can buy the land from the BLM, at current market value, for a clear title. Residents of Apodaca raise the money and buy the land on which their people have lived for a century and a half. A tremendous public outcry and publicity result from BLM actions so it cancels plans to require residents of Montecito and Cañoncito to buy back their private property.

COMPUTERS
Ed Roberts is producing *Altair* desktop computers. **Paul Allen** and **Bill Gates** develop software for them.

BOOKS

Popular Arts of Spanish New Mexico by **E. Boyd** is published and quickly becomes a fundamental resource for the study of Hispanic arts of N.M. The book is divided into Architecture, Domestic and Religious; Graphics; Paintings on Hides; Panels in Gesso Relief; Textiles; Woodworking and Decoration; Metals, Their Uses and Re-uses; Opas y Ramilletes; The Santero; Penitentes.

RELIGIOUS

Father **Robert E. Sánchez,** a native New Mexican, is installed as Archbishop of Santa Fe.

TIMELINE

1974: The Federal government establishes guidelines with which to decide which people have **Native American status**: an individual must have a full-blooded ancestor no further away than a grandparent to qualify for Native American standing and a permanent **Census Number** is issued to that person.

[Tribal membership is acknowledged according to requirements decided upon by the individual tribes. Some tribal membership requirements are very demanding: one well known "Indian" artist was denied participation in certain village rituals because, while her mother was full blooded, her father was a non-Indian. Claiming "Indian" heritage from relatives beyond a grandparent isn't recognized by the federal government or any acknowledged Native American nation.]

BANKING

Despite various obstacles, **Sósimo Padilla** leads the effort to create the **El Valle State Bank** in Albuquerque.

PROFILE

Sósimo Padilla

" B A R E F O O T   B O Y   W I T H   C H E E K   O F   T A N … "

November 1, 1929: Sósimo Padilla is born to **Sósimo Padilla Sr.** and **Felicita Sánchez Padilla.**

1934: Sósimo goes to live with his grandparents, **J. Manuel Padilla** and **María Sánchez Padilla**, on their farm in Los Chávez. Young Sósimo learns how to raise vegetables, especially chile, and a variety of fruits. He has three horses that are used for plowing as well as "Pintito" used only for riding. When he is strong enough he plows with horses until his grandfather buys a tractor.

1936(?): For all eight years Sósimo attends St. Mary's Grade School in Belén.

1941-1945: During the war years Sósimo sells rabbits, for a dollar each, to local supermarkets.

1944: Sósimo attends Belén High School. He earns varsity letters in football all four years.

1948: Sósimo graduates from high school. He briefly attends UNM to become a teacher but then decides his destiny is not in the classroom.

January 19, 1950: Sósimo marries **Ruth Córdova** of Jarales. In time they have three children. All three attend St. Anne's in Albuquerque, then Harrison Mid School and Río Grande High School.

Sósimo Padilla

1950: He is working as a boiler maker for the Santa Fe railroad.

1951: With $5 in his pocket, Sósimo drives to Clayton for training as a Port of Entry Inspector. *"Starting out Hispanic, Catholic, Republican…and broke…I told myself right then and there I would never be broke again."*

1951-1954: Padilla works as a Port of Entry Inspector for the State of N.M.

1952: His mother, **Felicita Sánchez Padilla**, dies.

1954-1986: Sósimo works as a mailer for the Albuquerque Publishing Co. for 32 years. His hours are from 8 p.m. to 4 a.m.
During "regular" hours he is President of Westland Security Transportation which involves contract hauling everything from auto parts to newspapers. *"Usually you've got to go out and get it done for yourself."*

1954-1964: Sósimo is elected and reelected president of Local 56 of the International Mailers' Union.

1962: **Sósimo Padilla Sr.** dies in Albuquerque.

1970 to present: Padilla serves on the Board of Directors for the Westland Development Corporation.

1974: Sósimo leads the effort that creates the **El Valle State Bank** in Albuquerque. (A State Comptroller had told him: *"Poor people don't start banks."*) He serves as Chairman of the Board of Directors. El Valle grows into the **Bank of Albuquerque** and then the **Bank of New Mexico.**

1975-1977: Padilla is Director of the Westside Association.

1975-1978: He serves for three years as a member of the Board of Directors for the Greater Albuquerque Chamber of Commerce.

1977-1980: Padilla is Director of the Hispano Chamber of Commerce, in which capacity he serves again from 1996-1999.

1978-1986: Sósimo serves for 8 years on the Board of Directors for the N.M. State Highway Commission.

1979-1981: Padilla is a Trustee for the University of Albuquerque.

1982: Governor Toney Anaya appoints Sósimo to chair the State Highway Commission, in which capacity he serves for three years.

Padilla vows that the Paseo del Norte Bridge will be built before the end of the Anaya administration. Ground breaking ceremonies are held before the end of Anaya's term of office.

1985: Governor Bruce King appoints Sósimo to the State Highway Commission.
One of Belen's three exits on I-25 is named "Sósimo Padilla Boulevard."

1986: Padilla falls on some ice and suffers a serious shoulder injury that ends his career at the Albuquerque Publishing Co.

1990: Sósimo, a founding member of the Bank of New Mexico, has served on the Board of Directors for 24 years.

1992: Westland Corporation earns 9.3 million dollars. (Westland Corporation is the only corporation to be created out of a Spanish land grant.)

1998: Sósimo serves as Director of the Barelas Community Center and continues as Director and Chairman of the Board for Westland Corporation.
Retirement is enjoyable because Sósimo can travel with his wife Ruth. He continues as Director and Chairman of the Board for Westland Corporation. Despite his many business successes he maintains that his family and extended family including his in-laws are his greatest achievements.

1975-1978

Jerry Apodaca is Governor.

1975
ELECTIONS

Delfine Lovato (from San Juan-Santo Domingo) is elected Chairman of the **All Indian Pueblo Council** (to which he will be re-elected through 1984). Paul Bernal (from Taos) is second-in-command (through 1982).

LAND GRANTS
Senator **Joseph Montoya** introduces a bill in the U.S. Senate to create a Special Commission on Guadalupe Hidalgo Land Rights. Representative Manuel Luján introduces a similar bill in the House of Representatives.

Montoya's bill proposes that a temporary commission review violations of property rights guaranteed by the treaty and make recommendations to Congress for restitution where it is merited, stating:
"If certain lands have been wrongfully taken from people, we must make amends."

Jerry Apodaca
Courtesy Museum of NM, #166715

Representative (from California) Augustus Hawkins proposes that Congress establish a Community Land Grant Act relating to Hispanic villages of N.M. where lands might have been lost through deceit or corruption.

Both bills die in committee. R. Griswold del Castillo writes: "That these measures were defeated is not too surprising since any federal investigation into land tenure in N.M. would be bound to unsettle powerful commercial and speculative interests."

1977: Representative **Henry B. González** of Texas introduces a resolution to create a special congressional committee "to investigate the legal, political, and diplomatic status of lands which were subject to grants from the King of Spain and the Government of Mexico prior to the acquisition of the American Southwest as a result of the Treaty of Guadalupe Hidalgo." The resolution is rejected.

1979: Representative Ronald V. Dellums of California introduces a proposal similar to that of Gonzáles but it is also rejected in committee.
1979: The N.M. legislature asks congressional representatives to introduce legislation to permit a board of review to investigate theft of communal lands in northern N.M. but the effort is killed in Congress.

[Richard Griswold del Castillo sums up his study of the Treaty of Guadalupe Hidalgo by stating that its stipulations are "largely unfilled...it joined the ranks of hundreds of other treaties the U.S. made with Native Americans... that have been almost totally ignored" since they were signed.]

BUSINESS ORGANIZATION
May: Salvador "Sal" Nuñez calls Ed Romero and two others then some 31 business people come together to form the Albuquerque Hispano Chamber of Commerce with the avowed purpose of promoting small

business.

1995: The AHCC is acknowledged as one of the largest and finest chambers in the USA.

WILDERNESS

Governor Apodaca creates the nation's first State Wilderness Commission to study how best to preserve wild lands and handle pro-extractive industries.

1976: The Bandelier Wilderness Area is signed into law.

1978: The Sandías, Manzanos, and the Chama River Basin are protected by law.

1984: Representative Bill Richardson's Bisti and Den-na-zin Badlands bill is passed. New Mexico's wilderness areas now total 1,535,000 acres (1.9% of the entire state).

GOVERNMENT

By the end of Governor Apodaca's administration some 200 agencies are consolidated into 12 major cabinet departments headed by a secretary appointed by the governor.

ACTIVISM

February 21, 1975: The Fairchild Semiconductor Plant in Shiprock assembles its employees, mostly Navajo females, and informs them that 140 of them will be laid off effective immediately

February 25: Some 20 members of AIM arm themselves with high-powered rifles, occupy the plant and swear they will remain until the workers are rehired. More than 200 Navajos gather outside the plant in support of the AIM warriors led by Larry Anderson.

Fairchild demands that a BIA swat team be sent to storm the plant. Chairman Peter MacDonald refuses to take such an action and AIM issues a list of grievances above and beyond those against Fairchild, who threatens simply to abandon the plant altogether.

March 3: Tribal elders counsel with the AIM riflemen and get them to end their occupation. Within days Fairchild's president, Wilford Corrigan, announces the permanent closing of the Shiprock plant. Many Navajos turn against AIM, blaming it for their loss of employment, but AIM asserts that Fairchild files prove the Shiprock plant was slated for closure before the occupation, the basic reason for the layoff in the first place.

RADIO ASTRONOMY

September: The first telescope in the **Very Large Array** (VLA) project is completed on the 7,000-foot elevation Plains of San Agustín 50 miles west of Socorro.

1961: The National Radio Astronomy Observatory begins planning for a large array of radio telescopes which will produce "photographs" of the radio sky. Preliminary design radio telescopes are built in Green Bank, West Virginia.

1967: The NRAO submits a formal proposal for funding to the National Science Foundation for construction of the VLA.

1972: Congress appropriates initial funding and construction begins west of Socorro on the estimated $76,000,000 project. The Socorro site is ideal because of its altitude and desert climate, low atmo**spheric water** vapor and thus minimum blurring by clouds of the radio photography. Surrounding mountains tend to block out interfering radio signals from TV, radio, and military bases. The large flat plain facilitates movement of the telescopes. Its latitude of 34 degrees is sufficiently south to permit astronomers to observe 85% of the sky as well as the center of the Galaxy.

1977: Five telescopes are operational and serious astronomical observations begin. (Each telescope weighs 235 tons, has a diameter of 82 feet, the top is 94 feet above the foundations, and each costs $1,150,000.)

1979: The last telescope, number 28, is in place and the VIA is complete.

October 10, 1980: The VLA is officially dedicated. It is essentially within budget with a total cost of $78,600,000. Even during the ceremony the VLA is producing radio images of unparalleled quality and in record time.

1976
ACTIVISM & NUCLEAR WASTE

Over 100 Albuquerqueans join to form CANT (Citizens Against Nuclear Threats) to combat the building of a nuclear Waste Isolation Pilot Plant (WIPP) in N.M. Similar groups organize throughout the state and come together under the umbrella organization known as CARD (Citizens for Alternatives to Radioactive Dumping).

1979: Congress authorizes WIPP. Nuclear waste is scheduled to arrive within nine years.

CRIME & SOCIETY

Greg MacAleese of the Albuquerque Police Department conceives the program of CRIME STOPPERS through which citizens can deliver information to law enforcement authorities without revealing their own identity. (CRIME STOPPERS spreads throughout the USA.)

CULTURE

August: The Indian Pueblo Cultural Center opens its doors to the public. Created by New Mexico's 19 Pueblos, the center is unique in the USA.

1977
HISTIOGRAPHY

The States and the Nation Series publishes **New Mexico: A Bicentennial History** by Marc Simmons.

PROFILE

Marc Simmons

N E W   M E X I C O ' S   H I S T O R I A N

May 15, 11937: Marc Simmons is born in Dallas, Texas. His parents are Julian Marion Simmons and Lois Skielvig Simmons. Marc grows up to be involved in a wide variety of activities: he works as a ranch hand in Wyoming, a horseshoer in Arizona, movie extra at Warner Brothers, adobe maker and plasterer in New Mexico, etc.

1958: Simmons earns a B.A. degree at the University of Texas.

1961: M.A., University of New Mexico.

1965: Ph.D., University of New Mexico.

1967: Marc translates and edits *Border Comanches*.

1968: *Two Southwesterners: Charles Lummis and Amado Chaves*.

1969: Simmons completes Spanish studies in Guanajuato and North Texas Farrier's School. He publishes *Yesterday in Santa Fe*.

1974: *The Little Lion of the Southwest*. Also *Witchcraft in the Southwest*.

1977: Marc is selected to write *New Mexico: A Bicentennial History*.

1979: *People of the Sun*.

1980: *Southwestern Colonial Ironwork*.

1982: *Albuquerque: A Narrative History*.

1986: *Along the Santa Fe Trail*.

November 14, 1986: A car whose driver has suffered a seizure plows into Simmons' vehicle in a head-on collision. Marc suffers a broken neck, broken hip, broken legs, crushed foot, and a battered face. While still in the car after the crash the only thing he remembers is someone tugging on his coat. He looks to the seat beside him: two little angels are telling him,

---

"Comewith us, come with us, come with us over the Great Divide." Marc replies, **"No, I can't, I'm booked to speak in Hutchinson."** More than a year is spent in convalescence and many friends let him know he is in their prayers.

1987: *Murder on the Santa Fe Trail.*

Spring, 1988: "Normal" life resumes for Marc Simmons.

1991: *The Last Conquistador - Juan de Oñate and the Settlement of the Far Southwest.*

1994: *Treasure Trails of the Southwest.*

DIPLOMACY
September 26: **Dr. Mari-Luci Jaramillo** from Las Vegas is sworn in as U.S. ambassador to Honduras.

1979-1982
Bruce King is Governor.

1979
POVERTY & ETHNICITY
The ethnicity and percentage of New Mexico families living below the
poverty line is:
Indian: 37.9%
Hispanic: 20.7%
Non-Hispanic White: 7. 1 %

ARTIST
Federico Vigil and **Luis Tapia** from Santa Fe co-found *La Cofradía de Artes y Artesanos Hispánicos* (The Brotherhood of Hispanic Arts and Artists). The group promotes artistic independence by organizing numerous exhibitions of their work, which inspires and encourages Hispanic artists to draw on their culture, history, and traditions as well as their own abilities.

Bruce King
Courtesy Museum of NM, #50280

PUBLISHING
Tomás Atencio founds and edits **Academia Publications** (later renamed **Del Norte Publications**) which specializes in bilingual (Spanish/English) regional literature.

DISASTER
July 16: The **United Nuclear Corporation Church Rock Mill** tailings pond ruptures, releasing 94,000,000 gallons of radioactive liquid waste into the Río Puerco.
[It is "*the worst radiation accident in all American history*," releasing far more radiation into the

atmosphere than the more publicized **Three Mile Island** disaster in the same year.]

Ca. 1979
COMPUTER BUSINESS
Bill Gates and **Paul Allen** found Microsoft Corporation in Albuquerque.

1980: Microsoft software is licensed by IBM but Microsoft retains ownership of software systems like DOS and WINDOWS.

1980
CENSUS
The census states that the N.M. population has 364,545 Hispanos (20% of the total State population); 200,991 Mexican Americans (11%); 1,260,300 "Anglos" and Native Americans (69%). Pueblo Indians number 35,932.

PROFILE

Tomás Atencio

COMMITMENT TO COMMUNITY

1932: **Tomás Atencio** is born in Dixon (formerly Embudo) to **Tomás Atencio Sr.** and **Bernardita Roybal Atencio.** His father is a native Hispano Presbyterian clergyman. Tomás attends community schools and from the 7th to 12th grades is in Presbyterian Mission boarding schools in Santa Fe and Albuquerque.

1951: Tomás graduates from high school and enlists in the Marine Corps.

1951-1954: Atencio is in the Corps and serves in Korea.

1954: Tomás enrolls at UNM and studies there for one year then moves to San Diego where he goes to school during the day and works at night.

1958: Atencio receives a B.A. degree from California Western in San Diego.

1959: Tomás begins his professional career as a child welfare worker.
Tomás Atencio Sr. dies.

1962: Atencio receives an MSW degree in social work from USC.

1963-1965: Tomás is a community mental health consultant for three counties in northern New Mexico.

1966: Tomás is director of the Colorado Migrant Council with a keen interest in organizing farm workers in the migrant stream from Texas to the East Coast.

1968: Atencio returns to New Mexico and co-founds *Academia de La Nueva Raza* as the vehicle for developing and testing the **Resolana** concept (which is explored for a ten-year period).

He works as a trainer, evaluator, and program development consultant for mental health and social services.

1977: Tomás begins work on a Ph.D. at UNM.

1985: Tomás is awarded a Ph.D. in Sociology from UNM. His dissertation is awarded the George I. Sánchez Award for Outstanding Dissertation.

He directs the Southwest Hispanic Research Institute (until 1989).

1987: Because of his interest in forced religious conversions, Tomás joins a project to examine the possible crypto-Jewish presence in New Mexico. His paper *"The Impact of Crypto-Judaism on Contemporary Indo-Hispano Culture"* is the result of that interest.

1989: Atencio's lecture *"Resolana, A Chicano Pathway to Knowledge"* is published by the Stanford Center for Chicano Research. (The concept of *Resolana* is based in part on the teaching techniques of Socrates and *"to bring to light the story of a community through discourse and dialogue."*)

1989-present: Tomás is a Lecturer III in the Department of Sociology at UNM.

1989-1992: Tomás directs a four-year seminar series for the Río Grande Institute at the Ghost Ranch Conference Center on the theme of *"The Indo-Hispano Legacy After Columbus."*

1993: Tomás is a panelist at the Cesar Chávez Social Justice Convocation on Racism.

1994: Atencio receives the Eagle Feather Award for Outstanding Services to American Communities from the National Indian Youth Leadership Project.

1994-1996: Tomás initiates and Coordinates the Río Grande Institute's Resolana Learning Centers which emphasize utilizing "modern technology to expand the base of community knowledge while at the same time validating traditional values" and *Resolana Electrónica* (both of which are hosted by the UNM College of Education).

1997: Tomás receives the Maclovio Barraza Leadership Award from the National Council of La Raza.

1998: Atencio is a Lecturer at UNM, specializing in programs for television and computers. He appears weekly on Channel 19. He continues with his research, writing, speaking, consulting, seminars, etc. His vision is still to create a "learning society" in every community because *"equity in the Information Age will rest on knowledge, information, and a well developed consciousness. Without these our society will be more repressive of humanistic values than in the Industrial Age."*

POVERTY
The poorest counties and their ethnicity are:

> Mora (86.6% Hispanic, 38% living in poverty);
> McKinley (65.7% Indian, 36% living in poverty);
> Guadalupe (82.7% Hispanic, 30% living in poverty);
> San Miguel (81.4% Hispanic, 30% living in poverty);
> Río Arriba (74.4% Hispanic, 28% living in poverty);
> Taos (69.1% Hispanic, 27% living in poverty).

[*"These figures compare to a 1986 national average of 29% of Hispanics living in poverty."*]

DEMOGRAPHY
Some 54% of resident New Mexicans were born in N.M. Urban areas are the fastest growing parts of the state and a majority of urban dwellers were born in other states.

BOOKS
Simon J. Ortiz publishes *Fight Back: For the Sake of the People, For the Sake of the Land.*

PROFILE

Simon J. Ortiz

I H A V E   F E A R E D   D E A T H   A N D   I   H A V E   F E A R E D   L I F E

May 27, 1941: **Simon J. Ortiz** of Acoma is born in Albuquerque. Simon attends the BIA school in McCarty, then St. Catherine, then the Albuquerque Indian School.

1962-1963: Ortiz is a student at Ft. Lewis College.

1966-1969: Simon studies at the University of New Mexico then at the University of Iowa.

1974: Simon teaches at San Diego State then at the Institute of American Indian Arts.

1974-1975: Ortiz undergoes treatment at the Ft. Lyons VA Hospital.

1975-1979: Ortiz teaches at various institutions of higher learning (Navajo Community College, College of Marin, University of New Mexico) while speaking to various groups and doing lecture tours.

1976: His poetry collection, *Going For The Rain*, is published.

1977: *A Good Journey is* published.

1978: Ortiz publishes *Howbah Indians*.

1980: Simon's stories about "now-day Indians" and their Cajun, Okie, black, Mexican, etc., co-workers are published under the title of *Fight Back: For the Sake of the People, For the Sake of the Land*. They have to do with the struggle against government and corporate exploitation.

1981: Simon's chapbook, *A Poem Is A Journey*, is published and *From Sand Creek* follows.

1983: Simon publishes *Fightin': New and Collected Stories* in which he speaks for "respect, compassion, and the promise of hope."

[Ortiz is an Acoma New Mexican who personifies storytelling in the Indian oral tradition. He has held a wide variety of jobs but has gained special renown as a poet, writer of fiction, and one who is committed to the welfare of humanity. He puts some of his stories into poetry but his primary concern is what he writes about, not style and form. He has the moral courage to combat popularly held but erroneous beliefs. Following are some of the essential ideas in Ortiz' writings:

LOVE is Simon's greatest inspiration as a writer. He writes for his son, Raho and his daughter, Rainy Dawn. He writes for his father, an elder of the Antelope People who are in charge of the spiritual practice and philosophy of the Acomas. Acoma people are taught to love grandparents, parents, the home, the land, and to have compassion for all human beings.

CONTEMPORARY ISSUES are crucial to Simon for he believes that for Indians to refuse to take part in things like politics is the path to destruction. Assimilation became government policy only after extermination was no longer feasible. *"There are always those who would annihilate us, whether politically, socially, or culturally."*

WATER is the lifeblood of all tribes in the arid Southwest but water and most of nature's resources are threatened by the Department of the Interior, the U.S. Army Corps of Engineers, and the Department of Agriculture.

NEW MEXICO is virtually the only place in the USA where native tribes still live on lands settled before the arrival of Europeans.

RACISM is part and parcel of the American consciousness. American schools don't teach you to think for yourself. The Bureau of Indian Affairs fears the loss of control over our minds and our communities.

COOPERATION is at the heart of Indian society. The popular mind still doesn't know us because capitalism encourages the acquisition of material goods even if you have to step on others to acquire them.

LIFE & DEATH: *"I have feared death and I have feared life ... but I continue to love, to teach, and to write."*

HISTORIOGRAPHY- LAND
The **Center for Land Grant Studies** of Santa Fe publishes *The Tierra Amarilla Grant: A History of Chicanery* by **Malcolm Ebright.** The author states that the work is written in response to the challenge issued by **Victor Westphall** in an article published in the *New Mexico Historical Review* where he says: *"This writer renews his long standing invitation for interested persons to submit documented evidence of land grant chicanery"* in New Mexico.

SOCIETY
The Pueblo people observe the 300th anniversary of the **Pueblo Revolt.**

FAMILY
Nearly one-quarter of New Mexican children, 23%, live in single-parent families.

RESEARCH
The **Southwest Hispanic Research Institute** is established at the University of New Mexico. It is intended to serve as an interdisciplinary center to promote scholarly discourse, conduct research, and disseminate information concerning historical, contemporary, and emerging issues which impact on Hispanic communities of the greater Southwest.

EDUCATION
New Mexico *"lags behind most other states in the performance of its educational system;"* 18.3% of all 16 to 24 year-olds in the state aren't in school nor are they high school graduates. The pupil-teacher ratio is ranked 40th in the nation.

HISTORIOGRAPHY

Dr. John L. Kessell establishes the **Vargas Project** at the University *of* New Mexico. Its purpose is to collect, translate, edit, and publish information related to Diego de Vargas in a projected six-volume *Vargas Series* edited by Kessell, **Rick Hendricks,** and **Meredith D. Dodge.**

ENVIRONMENT

Earth First! is founded by **Dave Foreman,** a native New Mexican from Glenwood. The organization attracts many people who wish to be active in the defense of Mother Earth and combat *"eco-terrorism being committed daily by corporate America."*

ART GALLERIES

There are about 90 **art galleries in Santa Fe** and Fenn Galleries claims an annual volume of $6,000,000.

Old Town in Albuquerque has some 24 galleries and the Albuquerque art market is valued at $12,000,000 annually.

1990: Santa Fe has around 200 art galleries and is ranked third in the nation in art, behind New York and Los Angeles, but first in the selling of art to buyers from outside the region. Santa Fe is "sold" as *"America's Salzburg"* and achieves an international reputation.

[Some residents complain that Santa Fe has been *"Aspenized"* or turned into an *"adobe Disneyland."*]

PRISON RIOT

February 2, 1980: Convicts seize control of the New Mexico State Penitentiary outside of Santa Fe and take 12 guards as hostages. During the 36 hours of their control the inmates murder and mutilate at least 33 other cons, torture eight of the hostages, and terrorize scores of other inmates as they destroy much of the prison in *"the most savage penal riot"* in the history of the USA, according to R. Morris.

PROFILE

"This prison is going to blow."

1948: A food riot breaks out at the end of the year, followed by another six months later.

1950: Several guards are hurt during the November riot.

June 15, 1953: In the fourth violent incident of the year, convicts seize the prison hospital and

---

take 21 hostages. The situation is quelled only after a hostage deputy warden gets a rifle and shoots two of the riot leaders. There are demands to build a new prison.

1956: A new, $8,000,000 penitentiary is built south of Santa Fe and considered *"among the most advanced correctional institutions in the country."*

1968 -1977: Seven inmate deaths are reported as suicides.

1971, 1973, 1976: Minor uprisings are repressed.

1977: **Dwight Durán,** S. Towers, L. Durán, H. Ellits, among others, file a suit against the State of New Mexico to protest prison conditions. Judge Santiago Campos suggests mediation which is tried until the effort is cut off.

1979: Durán informs Governor King that the failure to reform prison conditions will result in *terrible consequences* because the situation will soon go beyond control.

January, 1980: Rumor has it that plans are being made to take over the prison and kill all the *"snitches"* working for the system. There is a shakedown but no *shanks* (homemade knives) are confiscated.

February 2, 1980: The riot is on and its 36-hour duration is referred to as *payback time* by the cons.
[Of the 33 reported dead by officials, 24 are Hispanic, 7 are "Anglo," 1 black, 1 Indian. A report from the Justice Department later summarizes that the N.M. penitentiary is *"one of the harshest, most punitive"* in the country.]

SWAT teams finally regain control of the prison and National Guardsmen secure it.

1981
HEALTH
New Mexico's first AIDS case is reported.

1988: AIDS cases now number 132, sixty-nine (69) of which result in death. Some 3,000 New Mexicans are reported to be infected with the human immunodeficiency virus (HIV).

Governor Carruthers abolishes New Mexico AIDS Services.

COUNTIES
N.M. now has 33 counties with the creation of **Cíbola County** on June 19, 1981. The counties (listed sequentially) are: **1850:** Socorro; **1852:** Bernalillo, Doña Ana, Río Arriba, San Miguel, Santa Fe, Taos, Valencia; **1860:** Mora; **1868:** Grant; **1869:** Lincoln, Colfax; **1884:** Sierra; **1887:** San Juan; **1889:** Chaves, Eddy; **1891:** Guadalupe; **1893:** Union; **1899:** Otero, McKinley; **1901:** Luna; **1903:** Quay,

Roosevelt, Sandoval, Torrance; **1909:** Curry; **1917:** De Baca; Lea; **1919:** Hidalgo; **1921:** Catron; **1949:** Los Alamos; **1981:** Cíbola.

1983-1986
Toney Anaya is Governor.

1983
ORGANIZATION
Arturo G. Ortega founds the **Hispanic Culture Foundation** as a non-profit corporation. Its mission is to identify, preserve, and enhance the arts and humanities rooted in New Mexico's long Hispanic history. It publishes a newsletter called *El Puente*.

Toney Anaya
Courtesy Museum of NM,
#166710

ACTIVISM
Peace activists led by individuals like **Blanche Fitzpatrick, Dorie Bunting**, and **Kent Zook** are responsible for the founding of the Albuquerque Center for Peace and Justice.

The *peace walk* known as the **Prayer Pilgrimage** from Chimayó to Los Alamos is initiated by **Joan** and **John Leahigh** of Albuquerque.

DRAMA
E.A. "Tony" Mares writes and performs his one-act play, *Padre Antonio José Martínez de Taos* as part of the Chautauqua Series of the New Mexico Endowment for the Humanities.

1985
MURALIST
Frederico Vigil, a fresco muralist, completes two murals at St. Michael's High School, his alma mater. Vigil believes that *"True fresco is the ultimate and noblest form of painting,"* though at first his art is patterned after the traditional masters of New Mexican religious art: Fresquis, R. Aragón, Molleno, etc., and he especially enjoys church commissions. By the age of 45 he has won many awards for his mural art and quips that he is *"always looking for another wall."*

SOCIETY & CULTURE
1985: **Francisco LeFebre** goes to San Antonio, Texas, to visit a friend who is director for the Guadalupe Cultural Arts Center. Impressed with the varied artistic activities in the San Antonio area, Francisco feels the same kind of center is needed in N.M. Upon his return to Albuquerque he discusses the situation with **John García** of the **Hispano Chamber of Commerce** who informs him that **Representative Al Otero** is interested in such a project.

1986: LeFebre and other artists organize a non-profit group to encourage the creation of a cultural center that is tentatively named *El Centro Cultural de Nuevo México.*

1986-1992: *Noches de Cultura,* a monthly gathering of artists and other interested community people, are held at different artists' studios and/or homes. There are readings from prose and poetry, theatrical shows, dances, etc., which promote networking, mingling, socializing, etc., with a drive to create a Hispanic Cultural Center added to the artistic bond of the group. The core group of artists include **Francisco Lefebre** (painter), **Rudy Anaya** (writer), **Irene Blea** (writer), **Francisco Ortega** (actor), **Ricardo García** (painter), **Eva Lovato** (sculptor), **Leonor Armijo** (musician), **Victor Padilla** (musician), **Bernadette K. Rodríguez** (painter), **Cecilio García Camarillo** (writer). Artists from other states are also invited to attend.

1987-1989: Albuquerque Mayor **Ken Schultz** is approached with the idea that a permanent committee should be formed and the City Council selects one person from each district to pursue the creation of a Cultural Center. When **Louis Saavedra** is elected mayor he disbands the committee and gives governance to the Hispano Chamber of Commerce.

1991: **Dan Hernández** donates space for the Noches de Cultura group at the Sheraton Old Town Hotel complex. There is space for a gallery, working studios, etc., for various artists to reach out to the community from children to senior citizens.

PROFILE

E.A. "Tony" Mares

"THE CENTER IS EVERYWHERE"

1920s: The Mares family of Ratón is dispossessed of its ancestral land holdings. The Mares relocate to Albuquerque, hoping to find work with the railroad.

May 17, 1938: **Ernesto Antonio "Tony" Mares** is born to **Ernesto Gustavo Mares** and **Rebecca Devine** in Old Town Albuquerque. Tony is thus the product of an Hispanic family (related to Padre Martínez of Taos) and an Hispanicized Irish family. He attends San Felipe de Neri Elementary School, then St. Mary's High School where he graduates.

1956: Ernesto Antonio enrolls at the University of New Mexico where he studies with professors like Spanish novelist Ramón Sender and New Mexican author Sabine Ulibarrí.

1960: Tony receives his B.A. degree and goes to Florida State University for graduate work.

1962: Mares receives an M.A. degree from Florida State. His thesis is titled *The Philosophy of José Ortega y Gassett: Towards an Ultra-Utopian Society*.

1962-1964: Tony teaches Spanish courses at North Texas State University. It is during this period that he becomes vitally interested in history and political activism.

1965: Tony returns to UNM as a doctoral student in History. He helps organize the UNM chapter of Students for a Democratic Society.

1967-1969: Mares teaches at the University of Arkansas. He develops a deep love of poetry and devotes much time and energy to poetry workshops conducted by men like Jim Whitehead.

1972: The Chicano Movement lauds the Aztec influence and Mares proclaims *"We aren't Aztecs and we're far from Aztlan"* though the following year he acknowledges how unifying has been the central concept of Aztlan in his essay "Myth and Reality."

1974: Mares receives his Ph.D. His dissertation is titled *Elements of Myth In Spanish Thought and in the Writings of the Generation of 1898*.

1979: Tony begins his career as dramatist when Albuquerque's **Compañia de Teatro** produces his bilingual comedy *Lola's Last Dance*.

1980: Tony's various poems are published under the title *7he Unicorn Poem*. He helps to edit *Ceremony of Brotherhood*.

1981: Mares writes the teleplay *New Mexico and the Multilingual Experience* for KNME-TV.

1982: In "**The Center is Everywhere: Hispanic Letters in New Mexico**," Mares declares the end of the colonial status of literary creation in the Southwest.

1983: Tony writes the book-length text for *Las Vegas, New Mexico: A Portrait*, a book of photographs by Alex Traube.

Mares adapts and translates into Spanish Arthur Miller's *View from the Bridge* for a La Compañia production set in Barelas.

1984: Ernesto writes the drama *El Corrido de Joaquín Murieta*.

1986: The autobiographical short story "Florinto" is published. Mares explores his roots from the Mares and Devine families: *"I knew what is was to be a coyote..."*

1987: Tony marries **Carolyn Meyer.**

1988: Mares edits *Padre Martínez: New Perspectives from Taos.*

1989: Tony writes the script and lyrics for the musical *Santa Fe Spirit* as well as *The Shepherd of Pan Duro* (which incorporates elements of New Mexico's traditional *Los Pastores* and *Las Posadas)* about the plight of the homeless. *I Returned and Saw Under the Sun,* a bilingual play about Fr. Martínez *of* Taos, is published.

[Dr. Mares' work as poet, historian, dramatist, and actor have been described by Enrique R. Lamadrid as *"a chapter in the intellectual history of the Hispanic Southwest" which explores the themes of mestizaje, cultural resistance, and intellectual independence."*]

1995: E.A. Mares teaches Creative Writing in the English Department at UNM. His poetry and fiction writing work shops are extremely popular.

LAW
January 4, 1985: **José Abeyta,** an Isleta Pueblo Indian, is charged by the Department of the interior with violating the Bald Eagle Protection Act because he killed an eagle to use its feathers in religious ceremonies. Abeyta testifies before the U.S. District Court that his right to exercise his religion is guaranteed by Article IX of the **Treaty of Guadalupe Hidalgo.** Judge Burciaga rules in his favor [thought to be the first time that treaty language is the primary basis for a legal decision].

POLITICAL SANCTUARY
Governor Anaya declares New Mexico to be a sanctuary state (the first in the USA) to protest the atrocities in Central America.

1987: Newly elected Governor Carruthers rescinds Anaya's proclamation.

ARTS & CRAFTS
Orlando Romero and other Santa Feans create a **Contemporary Hispanic Market** to coincide with the traditional Spanish Market. The exhibition proves successful.

1989: A Winter Market is held in December at a downtown hotel.

1990: The Contemporary Hispanic Market is moved to Lincoln Avenue to make it more visible for buyers.

1986
MUSEUM
The New Mexico Museum of Natural History and Science, a division of the Office of Cultural Affairs and the first major state-funded natural history museum to be constructed in the U.S. in 50 years, is opened to the public. Visited by more people than any other in N.M., the museum's theme is *"Timetracks:*

A Journey Through the Natural World," and it displays the third largest Triassic vertebrate fossil collection in the nation as well as permanent exhibits titled *Origins, Age of Giants, New Mexico's Seacoast, Age of Volcanoes, Evolving Grasslands, New Mexico's Ice Age, Fossil Works, Naturalist Center,* and the *Dynamax Theater.*

1987-1990
Garrey Carruthers is Governor.

1987
POLITICS

Raymond G. Sánchez is elected as New Mexico **Speaker of the House of Representatives** (a post to which he will be reelected as New Mexico looks into the new millennium).

PROFILE

Raymond G. Sánchez

THE POWER OF THE VOTE

September 22, 1941: **Raymond G. (Gilbert) Sánchez** is born to Gil and Priscilla Sánchez of Belén. (Raymond is heir to the family political tradition because both his father and grandfather were very active in politics.)

1946: Raymond enters the pre-first grade of Mrs. Sánchez at St. Mary's Elementary in Belén.

1960: Raymond graduates from Belen High School (*"where I received as excellent a public school education as anyone in the country"*) and enrolls at UNM with a desire to study government.
1964: Sánchez is awarded a B.A. degree at UNM.
He marries and in time his son, **Raymond Michael,** is born, and later Raymond M. has three children: the twins **Dyland** and **Chelsea,** and then **Gavin.**

1967: Sánchez is awarded a *Juris Doctorate* from the UNM School of Law. He begins to practice, specializing in trial and transportation law. He buys a home in the North Valley.

1969: Raymond is elected to the New Mexico Constitutional Convention.

1970: Sánchez is elected to the House of Representatives from **District 15** in the far north Valley (to which he is reelected going into the new millennium).
1973: He serves as House Chairman of the Judiciary Committee. (Through the years he serves on many committees of State and national importance, is chosen for many *Who's Who* selec-

tions, public service awards, "Legislator of the Year" recognition, etc., and is a member of various organizations from the Knights of Columbus, etc., to the National Federation of the Blind.)

1983: Raymond is elected Speaker of the House for the first time.

1987-1998: Sánchez is elected Speaker and remains in that post.

Raymond G. Sánchez

As a well-known political personality, Raymond is often in the news (although he is not considered an extroverted individual). He wants to serve the State in the House, which must be elected every two years, because it is the people's branch of government. He believes that the **VOTE** is representative of well-being for the child and his parents, that a good education is the cornerstone of economic betterment. While politics are always complex, Raymond is reinvigorated by his constituents who appreciate what he does on their behalf. He feels he is elected as Speaker because he respects the minority party and does his best to be fair with them. He believes in equality even when people have differing ideas on an issue. Politicians are generally civil, though he believes that some people hired to run a campaign sometimes display values that aren't well thought of in New Mexico.

Sánchez remains popular with his constituents and his colleagues. He considers ignorance, bigotry, and racism to be his avowed enemies.

LEGISLATION
Alfonso "Al" Otero introduces the legislation to fund a study to determine the feasibility of a private, non-profit **Hispanic Cultural Center**.

WOMEN & ELECTIONS
January: **Vera Olguin Williamson** is elected **Governor of Isleta Pueblo**, the **first woman** ever to win that office. She serves for four years.

SANTA FE TRAIL
May 8: Due to legislation sponsored by **Representative Bill Richardson,** President Reagan designates the **Santa Fe Trail** as one of America's National Historic Trails.

ROYAL VISIT
September: During his visit to N.M., **King Juan Carlos of Spain** gives a silver-crowned cane to each of New

Mexico's Pueblo governors.

[Each Pueblo governor now has **four canes:** Spanish, Lincoln, State of N.M., and the Juan Carlos. The canes are blessed every January 6, feast day of the Three Wisemen, as dictated by tradition.]

1988
HEALTH

Some 20% to 25% of New Mexicans have no health insurance (compared to 10% to 13% nationwide). Hispanics are twice as likely as non-Hispanics to be without health insurance (33% compared to 15%).

Nearly one-third of all babies in N.M. are born to unmarried mothers and more than 10% of all babies are born to unmarried teenagers. More than 45% of New Mexican infants are born to mothers who receive no prenatal care during the first trimester of pregnancy and overall N.M. is at the bottom of the nation when it comes to prenatal care.

WOMEN

The **Hispanic Women's Council** is founded. With a membership that includes women from all walks of life, its goal is to promote unity and the participation of Hispanic women in setting policy, passing laws, and making decisions that impact society, community, and family ... and always **"to promote, empower, support and create opportunities for Hispanic women."**

1989: The Hispanic Women's Summit is held in Albuquerque. Those in attendance are offered various training workshops and motivational speakers from across the country are featured.

1990: A training conference titled "Maximizing Women's Potential" is co-sponsored with **Las Mujeres de LULAC** and **MANA del Norte.**

1992: The HWC completes a book titled *Nuestras Mujeres,* a volume of excellent photos and essays which highlight the lives of many New Mexican women.

1997: The HWC has a membership of almost 100 women. To commemorate the group's 10th anniversary in 1998, an original painting titled *Mañana Viene Mi Hija* is commissioned from artist **Rosa María Calles.** Commemorative posters are printed for sale to the general public.

STATE GOVERNMENT

The State constitution is amended to permit two successive four-year terms for all state executives.

POLITICS

Manny M. Aragón is elected *President Pro Tempore* of the Senate.

WOMEN & LITERATURE

Las Mujeres Hablan: An Anthology of Nuevo Mexicana Writers is published. Edited by **Tey Diana Rebolledo, Erlinda Gonzáles-Berry,** and **Teresa Márquez,** the work is comprised of writings by some of the area's most talented female writers.

1989
HISTORIOGRAPHY
The **Vargas Project** at the University of New Mexico begins publication of the **Vargas Series**:

1989: Vol. 1: **John L. Kessell,** ed., *Remote Beyond Compare: Letters of don Diego de Vargas to His Family from New Spain and New Mexico, 1675-1706.*

1992: Vol. 2: John L. Kessell and **Rick Hendricks,** eds., *By Force of Arms: The Journals of don Diego de Vargas, New Mexico, 1691-1693.*

1995: Vol. 3: John L. Kessell, Rick Hendricks, and **Meredith D. Dodge,** eds., *To the Royal Crown Restored: The Journals of don Diego de Vargas, New Mexico, 1693-1694.*

Projected volumes: Vol. 4: Struggling to coexist; Santa Cruz founded; a second Pueblo Revolt; the Pueblo-Spanish war ends; Vargas replaced, 1694-97.

Vol. 5: The administration of Governor Pedro Rodríguez Cubero; Vargas is charged and held in New Mexico, tried and exonerated in Mexico City, and reappointed, 1687-1703.

Vol. 6: Vargas's return to office; the colony's slow growth; death of Vargas and aftermath, 1703-04.

MUSIC ORGANIZATION
The **New Mexico Hispanic Music Association** is founded to promote Hispanic music, heritage, and culture by recognizing various artists with awards. Current or former residents of N.M. are eligible for recognition in 26 categories, including Female/Male Vocalist of the Year, Mariachi Song of the Year, Upcoming Artist/Group, Song Writer of the Year, Junior Artist, Cumbia/Salsa/Tropical, Progressive and Traditional Ranchera, two People's Choice Awards, etc.

PROFILE

Manny M. Aragón

" O N   T H E   S I D E   O F   W H A T   P E O P L E   N E E D "

March 22, 1947: **Manny M. Aragón** is born to **Mel** and **Charlotte Aragón** in the historic **Barelas** section of Albuquerque. Involvement in politics is part of the Aragón family tradition: father Mel Aragón is elected to the Albuquerque City Council and the State Legislature where he is chosen as Majority Whip in the House. Manny grows up in Barelas, attends Sacred Heart Elementary and then St. Mary's High School where he is greatly influenced by his teachers, especially coach **Babe Parenti**.

1965: Manny graduates from St. Mary's.

1967: Aragón marries and in time two children, **Greg** and **Angela,** are born.

1968: Manny begins his political career as a delegate to the 1968 Democratic Convention in Chicago.

1973: Aragón graduates from the University of New Mexico School of Law and begins his practice.

1975-1998: Manny is elected to the **State Senate** to represent **District 14** in Albuquerque's **South Valley.**

Manny M. Aragón

Through the years he chairs, co-chairs, or is a member of committees like Legislative Council, Rules, Finance, Radioactive and Hazardous Materials, etc.

He is a member of various organizations: the N.M. Bar, Legislative Leaders Foundation, Southwest Voters Project, Energy Council, etc.

His stated goals are to provide more educational opportunity and jobs for more people, to improve health care and the quality of life, to see to it that necessities like infrastructure aren't ignored, etc. He earns a reputation as the Legislature's "leading advocate for the poor, for minorities, working class people, for women and children and others who are underrepresented or not represented at all."

For relaxation he plays golf, reads, goes fishing.

1988: After a 13-year struggle against the Senate's seniority system, Aragón forges a coalition of Democrats and Republicans to become *President Pro Tempore* of the Senate. Changes are then enacted that allow freshmen senators to serve as members or vice chairmen of key committees.

April 2, 1989: Manny writes to the *Santa Fe New Mexican*: *"I have tried to help with some of the problems in the Corrections Department but I have been told to 'butt out and mind your own business.' State business and clients on the receiving end of state services **are my business.**"*

1991: Aragón sponsors and/or co-sponsors a variety of legislation: **Minimum Health Care Protection Act** and the **County Maternal and Child Health Plan Act** which authorize affordable health care plans for individuals and families; **Tutor-Scholars**

Program Act which enables high school students to earn credit toward college scholarships by tutoring academically at-risk classmates; etc.

1992: Manny sponsors a constitutional amendment that provides crime victims with specific rights to confer with prosecutors, receive restitution from offenders, and to be notified when offenders escape or are to be released. He sponsors the **Public Employee Bargaining Act** which grants state and local government workers the right to collective bargaining.

1992-1996: As a well known political figure people are constantly making observations on Manny Aragón:

Duncan Scott, a Republican: *I've seen him go without sleep and deliver a better speech than most of us can when we're rested up.*

Albuquerque Tribune (May 14, 1992): Aragón ... can be credited with some of the biggest gains made by organized labor and human services programs in the last four years.

Bob Giannini: A lot of people think he's complex but ... when you get right down to it ... he's always on the side of what people need.

Tom Rutherford, a Democrat: His words have a special strength and meaning for people.

Albuquerque Journal (February 11, 1996): Aragón is high-strung, big-hearted, emotional and outspoken ... capable of single-handed legislative endeavor.

BOOKS
Pasó Por Aquí: Critical Essays on the New Mexican Literary Tradition, 1542-1988, is published by UNM Press. Edited by **Erlinda Gonzáles-Berry,** the work is a scholarly investigation of New Mexican writings.

MILITARY
Cannon Air Force Base in Clovis is selected to house the country's extensive F-111 fighter-bomber fleet.

1990
BOOKS
Carlos LoPopolo, historian and genealogist, begins publication of the book series titled *The New Mexico Chronicles* which have to do with original settlement of various areas, first settlers, their genealogy and history. Primary source documents are utilized throughout, with many included in the projected publications, which are:

1990: *Valencia* Edition;
1991: *Tomé* Edition;
1992: *Belén* Edition;

1994: *Los Lunas/Los Chávez* Edition;
1995: **Foundations Edition**.

Other projected volumes include the Albuquerque/Atrisco, Bernalillo, Española, Taos, and Santa Fe
Editions.

EDUCATION
There are **88** school districts operating in the state.

PROFILE

M. Teresa Márquez

LIBRARIAN AND RESEARCHER

María Teresa Huerta [Márquez] is born to **Juan and M. Zenaida Huerta** in El Paso, Texas. In time she has three brothers and two sisters. The family lives in typical El Paso neighborhoods: El Segundo, Del Pujido, Del Diablo. She attends San Jacinto and Zavala elementary schools then attends and graduates from Bowie High School (*"La Bowie"*) where she is active in the Student Council, Spanish Club, The Bowie Growler newspaper, and the National Honor Society.

Teresa attends and graduates from the University of Texas at El Paso. She teaches at Alamo Elementary then moves with her husband, **Antonio Márquez,** and son, **Christopher Alexander,** to Bay City, Michigan.

Within a couple of years the Márquez family relocates to Albuquerque where Teresa teaches at Carlos Rey Elementary while Antonio does graduate work at UNM.
In two years Teresa moves to Fullerton, California, where she receives a degree in Library Science and Information then returns to Albuquerque where she works in the department of Public Administration at UNM. In time she earns a degree from the Graduate School of Library Science and Information Management at the University of Illinois.

1993: Márquez heads the Information Department at **Zimmerman Library** at UNM (which is one of the 14 regional federal depository libraries in the Government Printing Office's Federal Depository Library Service Program).

1998: Teresa is the only Hispana heading a regional federal depository at a designated Association of Research Libraries (ARL) academic library.

At Zimmerman Library she has been elected as officer of the library faculty and served on or coordinated numerous important committees and/or projects: fund raising events, Premio Aztlan Literature Award and Crítica *Nueva*, Critical Literary Series, events sponsored by Rudolfo and Patricia Anaya, Southwest Hispanic Research Speakers series, events in honor of Rudolfo Anaya and Sabine Ulibarrí, the Visiting Scholar Program, etc. Among many other activities Teresa is the bibliographer for Chicana/o Studies and has helped develop the collection of cookbooks and publications on Nuevo Mexicano Culinary Arts. Her scholarly research is in Chicana literature with a specialization in the Chicana/o detective/mystery novel and she continues to edit, compile bibliographies, do book reviews and articles for various publications as well as to involve herself in community activities.

In scholarly circles around the region and on the UNM campus M. Teresa Márquez is considered a highly accomplished exponent of the librarian's profession.

POPULATION
The population of N.M. is 1,515,069, nearly **tripled from 1940:**

1940: 531,818;
1950: 681,187;
1960: 951,023;
1970: 1,017,055;
1980: 1,303,393;
1990: 1,515,069. Bernalillo County has 480,577 residents.

Pueblo Indians number 55,776 according to the 1990 census.

PROFILE

John L. Kessell

HISTORIAN
FOUNDER OF THE VARGAS PROJECT

April 2, 1936: **John L. (Lottridge) Kessell** is born to John S. Kessell and Dorothy Lottridge Kessell in East Orange, New Jersey. Both parents are medical doctors.

1943: The Kessell family relocates to Fresno, California. John attends the public schools and the field of medicine is a strong pull when he starts to consider career choices.

1954: John graduates from high school and enrolls at Fresno State College.

1958: John Kessell graduates from Fresno State with a B.A. degree.

1958-1959: John travels to Australia to renew ties with his father's side of the family. He stays there for seven months then tours the Far East, travels west into the Mediterranean through the Suez Canal. He spends a couple of months in Spain then goes on to Rome from where he decides to head for home in an Italian liner which finally anchors at Halifax. He makes his way across the country and decides to do graduate work at Berkeley.

1961: Kessell graduates from Berkeley with an M.A. degree in History and Latin America.

1961-1962: He works as Historian for the National Park Service at Saratoga National Historical Park.

1963-1966: He is transferred to the Tumacacori National Monument in Arizona and becomes fascinated with Southwestern colonial history.

1967: Kessell is recruited to the University of New Mexico.

1969: John receives a Ph.D. in History from the University of New Mexico.

1970: Kessell's *Mission of Sorrows: Jesuit Guevavi and the Pimas, 1691-1767* is published by the University of Arizona Press.

1970-1980: John works as a self-employed contract historian.

1976: University of Arizona Press publishes his *Friars, Soldiers, and Reformers: Hispanic Arizona and the Sonora Mission Frontier, 1767-1856* .

1979: John's *Kiva, Cross, and Crown: The Pecos Indians and New Mexico, 1540-1840 is* published by the National Park Service (reprinted by UNM Press in 1987).

1980: Kessell founds the Vargas Project at UNM and teaches at the university. His *Missions of New Mexico Since 1776* is published by UNM Press.

1982: John receives a *Comité Hispano-Norte Americano* Travel Grant.

1990: *Remote Beyond Compare is* selected as the best non-fiction book of the year by the Historical Society of New Mexico.

1996: John semi-retires from UNM in that he discontinues teaching regular classes though he continues to work with graduate students and the Vargas Project. He spends most of his time writing.

1997: Dr. Kessell is Visiting Professor at Ft. Lewis College in Durango, Colorado.

PUEBLO LAND HOLDINGS
Northern Pueblos maintain ownership of land as follows (in acres):

Nambé	19,124
Picurís	14,947
Pojoaque	11,601
San Ildefonso	26,197
San Juan	12,236
Santa Clara	45,827
Taos	95,341
Tesuque	16,813

Southern Pueblos maintain ownership of land as follows (in acres):

Acoma	378,113
Cochití	50,681
Isleta	211,103
Jémez	89,623
Laguna	484,495
Sandía	22,870
San Felipe	48,929
Santa Ana	61,931
Santo Domingo	71,092
(Ysleta del Sur, Texas)	97
Zía	121,599
Zuñi	409,344
(in Arizona)	10,085

PROFILE

Erlinda Gonzales-Berry

SCHOLAR, EDITOR, WRITER

1942: Erlinda Gonzales is born to **Carlota** and **Canuto Gonzales** in Roy. Canuto is a rancher and Carlota is a school teacher. Erlinda is one of five Gonzáles daughters. She attends local schools and graduates from El Rito High School.

1964: Erlinda graduates from the College of Education at UNM.

1964-68: She teaches in public schools in California and New Mexico.
1970: Gonzales becomes a Teaching Assistant at UNM.

1971: Erlinda is awarded an M.A. in Spanish from UNM.

1974-83: Erlinda is an Assistant Professor at different universities.

1978: She receives her Ph.D. in Romance Languages from UNM.

1983-84: Erlinda receives the UNM President's Award for Outstanding Teacher of the Year.

1983-91: Erlinda is an Associate Professor at UNM.

1988: She co-edits *Las Mujeres Hablan* and the following year edits *Pasó Por Aquí.*

1992: Erlinda is a Professor and Chair of the Department of Spanish and Portuguese at UNM.

1996: She co-edits *Recovering the U.S. Hispanic Literary Tradition* (for Arte Público Press).

1997: Gonzales-Berry is Chair of the Department of Ethnic Studies at Oregon State University.
She continues to write, lecture, and conduct special seminars.

SANTERO ARTISTS

The creation of religious figures continues in contemporary N.M. Among the various artists involved in this tradition are: Frank Alaríd, Luis Barela Jr., Frank Brito, Charlie Carillo, Marie Romero Cash, Gloria López Córdova, Victor Goler, Anita Romero Jones, Félix López, George López, José B. López, Nicolás Herrera, Luisito Luján, Wilberto Miera, Eulogio Ortega, Zoraida Ortega, Guadalupita Ortiz, Lawrence Ortiz, Sabinita López Ortiz, Alcario Otero, Marco Oviedo, Patricia Oviedo, Paul Pletka, Enrique Rendón, Max Roybal, Leo Salazar, Arlene Cisneros Sena, Luis Tapia, Horacio Valdez, etc.

1991-1994

Bruce King is Governor.

1991
POLITICS

January: **Patrick Baca** of **Sandía Pueblo** is appointed to the office of Secretary of Labor by Governor Bruce King.

SOCIETY

January: The Democratic Party (posthumously) inducts **Augustine Sando** of Jémez Pueblo into its **Hall of Fame.**

INCOME
New Mexico ranks 46th in the nation in per-capita income.

TIMELINE

Jan.-Feb., 1991 : The United States and its allies liberate Kuwait from Iraq in the Gulf War which lasts some 100 hours.

ASTRONAUT
June 5: Colonel **Sidney Gutiérrez** from Albuquerque pilots the space shuttle Columbia on its 11th flight from Kennedy Space Center, thus making Gutiérrez the first native-born Hispanic astronaut on a space mission.

MEDAL OF HONOR - RECIPIENTS
The following individuals, directly or indirectly associated with New Mexico's history, have been awarded the nation's highest award for valor, the Medal of Honor:

Recipients, where born, war and locale, date of action:
Sp/4 **Daniel Fernández,*** Albuquerque, Vietnam, Cu Chi, 2-18-66;
Pvt. **Joe R. Martínez,** Taos, W.W. II, Aleutians, 11-22-43;
Cpl. **Hiroshi Miyamura,*** Gallup, Korea, 4-24/25-51;
Pvt. **Harold Moon, Albuquerque, W.W. II,** Phil. Is., **10-21-44;**
WO **Louis Rocco,** Albuquerque, Vietnam, Katum, 5-24-70;
Pfc. **Alejandro Ruiz,*** Loving, W.W. II, Okinawa, 4-28-45;
Pfc. **José E. Valdez,** Governador, W.W. II, France, 1-25-45;
Brig. Gen. **Kenneth Walker,** Cerrillos, W.W. II, New Britain, 1-5-43.
(*Also entered the Service in N.M.)

Recipients who entered the Service in N.M.:
1st Lt. **Alexander Bonneyman, Atlanta,** Ga., W.W. II, Tarawa, 11-2-1943;
l/Lt. **Robert McDonald,** New York, Indian Wars, Wolf Mt., Montana, 1-8-1877;
S/Sgt. **Franklin Miller,** Elizabeth City, NJ., Vietnam, Kontum, 1-5-70;
1st Sgt. **Francis Oliver,** Baltimore, Indian Wars, Chiricahua. Mts., Arizona, 10-20-1869;
Capt. **Robert Scott,** Washington, D.C., W.W. II, Solomon Is., 7-29-43;
Pvt. **Ebin (Eben) Stanley,** Decauter City, Iowa, Indian Wars, Turret Mt., Arizona, 3-25/26/27-1873.

Recipients living in N.M. [at the time of publication of this book] include:
Cpl. (USA) **Hiroshi Miyamura;**
Capt. (Ret., USMC **Raymond J. Murphy;**
Col. (Ret., USA) **Robert Scott.**

1992
MUSEUM

The **Albuquerque Hispano Chamber of Commerce** hires **Loretta Armenta** to promote the Hispanic Cultural
Center. The following year Loretta meets and begins to collaborate with Ron Vigil (the primary
catalyst of the center).

PROFILE

Manuel T. Pacheco

U N I V E R S I T Y   P R E S I D E N T

Manuel Trinidad Pacheco is one of 12 children in the Pacheco family of Maxwell, N.M., all of
whom have earned bachelor's degrees, several of whom have received master's degrees, and
four who have earned doctorates.

1958: Manuel Pacheco finishes high school in his junior year at Maxwell and qualifies for early
entrance to Highlands University. His roommate is (Governor-to-be) Toney Anaya.

1961: Pacheco begins teaching at Carlsbad High School.

1962: Manuel is awarded a bachelor's degree. Dr. Jean Johnson encourages him to apply for a
Fullbright Fellowship, for which he is selected, becoming one of the first New Mexicans to be so
honored.

1963: Pacheco is awarded an M.A. degree from the Universite de Montpellier in France.

1964-1980: Manuel works as lecturer, professor, chairman, dean, at various institutions like
Western N.M. University, Florida State, U. of Colorado, San Diego State, Texas A& I (Laredo
State U.), U. of Texas-El Paso, Middlebury College, Indiana U., and Elmira College.

1969: Manuel Pacheco receives his Ph.D. degree.

1971: Acknowledged as an authority on bilingual education, Dr. Pacheco publishes *Approaches
to Bilingualism: Recognition of a Multi-Lingual Society.*

1982: After raising and educating all the Pacheco children, Manuel's mother, Mary Elizabeth,
in her 50s, receives a B.A. degree from Highlands University.

1984: Dr. Pacheco becomes President of Laredo State University. He is also named to the list of
the 100 most influential Hispanics in the USA.

1988: Manuel becomes President of the University of Houston--Downtown.

1991: Dr. Pacheco becomes President of the University of Arizona, one of the largest universities in the Southwest.

[Manuel's brothers also achieve academic excellence: Dr. Mario Pacheco is a medical doctor and Dr. John Pacheco is academic vice-president of Highlands University.]

BOOKS

Tey Diana Rebolledo edits *Nuestras Mujeres: Hispanas of New Mexico, Their Images and Their Lives, 1582-1992* (with Erlinda Gonzales-Berry and Millie Santillanes as associate editors). The work puts a face on the feminine side of New Mexican history with scores of anecdotes and pictures about:

Heroines: Refugio Gurriola, Gertrudis Barceló, Lola Chávez de Armijo, Beatriz Nuanes Salas;

Teachers: Carlota Gonzáles, Rafaelita L. Chávez, Mary Mariño Sánchez, Celestina Padilla-López;

Folklorists: Carmen G. Espinosa, Aurora Lucero-White Lea, Dora Ortiz Vásquez, Josephine M. Córdova, Elba C. De Baca;

Writers: Cleofas Martínez Jaramillo, Nina Otero-Warren, Fabiola Cabeza de Baca, Margarita Arellano;

Rural Prototypes: Estefanita Montoya Turrietta, Rachel Sánchez Olivas, Mary Gherardi, Celestina and Cleo Padilla, Angie Carrillo-Mariño;

Entrepreneurs: Annie Chávez-Sánchez, Josie Turrietta;

Artists: Rosa María Calles, Pola López de Jaramillo, Anita Rodríguez;

Photographers: Dolores Ortiz, Kozlowski, Lindsa Montoya, Soledad Marjon;

Santeras: Gloria López Córdova, Marie Romero Cash;

Weavers: Agueda Salazar Martínez, Teresa Archuleta-Sagel;

Musicians: Julia Jaramillo, Genoveva Chávez, Yvonne Ulibarrí;
Writers: María Esperanza López de Padilla, Jo Roybal Izay, Denise Chávez, Erlinda Gonzales-Berry, Demetria Martínez;
Producers: Irene Oliver-Lewis, Margarita Martínez, Catalina Gonzáles;

Dancer: Lili del Castillo;

Careers: Leonila Durán Serna, Veronica García, Mari-Luci Jaramillo;

Politics: Soledad Chávez Chacón, Julia Tenorio, Concha Ortiz y Pino de Kleven, Patricia Madrid, Petra Jiménez Maes;

Business: Rosalia Durán Urrea, Flossie Córdova, Clarita Serna McBride, Teresa McBride, Beverly Durán, Beatriz Betty Rivera, Millie Santillanes;

Activists: Otilia De La 0 Montoya, Virginia Chacón, María Gutiérrez Spencer;

Military: Carmelita Vigil-Schimmenti:

Healers: Jesusita Aragón, María Margarita Jaramillo y Mascareñas, Leonora López, Conchita Paz;

Ranchers: Alicia Quintana, María Martínez Sánchez;

Religious: M. Rita and M. Dolores Sánchez, Mary Nolasco (M. Josephine Sánchez).

AMERINDS & POLITICS
Seven Native Americans have been elected and are serving in the state legislature.

BOOKS
Joe Sando of Jémez Pueblo publishes Pueblo *Nations: Eight Centuries of* Pueblo History. The work is written from a Native American perspective and provides unique cultural as well as political views.

BUSINESS
December: Sales receipts for the State total $11.75 billion.

N.M. has the highest percentage of Hispanic-owned businesses in the USA. There are some 107,377 business firms in N.M., 20% (21,586) of which are owned by Hispanics, who comprise 38% of the population.

PUEBLO FESTIVALS - SAINTS' DAYS
There are a number of celebrations held by the Pueblos throughout the year, including:

Acoma-San Esteban, September 2;

Cochití-San Buenaventura, July 14;

Isleta-San Agustín, September 4;

Jémez-San Diego, November 12;

Laguna
   -at Mesita Village, Our Lady of the Ascension, August 15;
   -at Encinal Village, Nativity of the Blessed Virgin, September 8;
   -at Old Laguna, San José, September 19;
   -at Paguate Village, St. Elizabeth, September 25;
   -at Paraje Village, St. Elizabeth, October 17;

Nambé-San Francisco, October 4;

Pecos-at Jémez, Our Lady of Portiuncula (Persingula)[no date provided];

Picurís-San Lorenzo, August 10;

Pojoaque-Our Lady of Guadalupe, December 12;

Sandía-San Antonio, June 13;
San Felipe-May 1;

San Ildefonso-January 23;

San Juan-June 24;

Santa Ana-July 26;

Santa Clara-August 12;

Santo Domingo-August 4;

Taos-San Gerónimo, September 30;

Tesuque-San Diego, November 12;

Zía-Our Lady of the Ascension, August 15;

Zuñi-Our Lady of Guadalupe, December 12 (not observed due to Shalako ceremonies).

[These feast days/festivals are renowned throughout the USA among people who are interested in different cultures, especially those which can be described as aboriginal. Since there are no "native villages" (villages or towns which have existed since Europeans landed on eastern shores of what is now the USA) east of the Mississippi River, their existence in New Mexico is of tremendous interest to many people who have never seen "Indians" with their native culture as part of a contemporary lifestyle. With the exception of Spain and usually France, Europeans generally viewed "Indians" as people to enslave or exterminate under the guise of "racial superiority" or "progress."]

PROFILE

Tey Diana Rebolledo

A   V O I C E   F O R   " W O M E N   S I N G I N G   I N   T H E   S N O W "

April 29, 1937: **Tey** (Esther) **Diana Rebolledo** is born in Las Vegas, N.M.

1947: The Rebolledo family moves to New London, Connecticut. There is a tremendous mix of people and cultures in New London but no Hispanics. Diana attends local schools.

1955: Tey enrolls in Connecticut College in New London, majoring in Spanish.

1959: Diana is awarded a B.A. degree. She still misses New Mexico and the Southwest so she goes to Albuquerque for graduate study at the University of New Mexico.

1962: Rebolledo is awarded an M.A. in Latin American Studies.

1963: Diana's daughter, Tey Marianna, is born.

1973: Diana marries Michael Passi.

1977-1978: Tey is an instructor at the University of North Carolina at Chapel Hill.

1979: Tey is awarded a Ph.D. in Spanish at the University of Arizona in Tucson.

1978-1984: Diana is an Assistant Professor at the University of Nevada at Reno.

1984 to present: Dr. Rebolledo is on the faculty at the University of New Mexico as Director of Women's Studies, Associate Professor of Spanish, and then Professor of Spanish. She is the recipient of dozens of Academic Honors, Awards, and Grants. She authors and contributes scores of scholarly papers and articles for various Journals and books and is a very popular Lecturer.

1988: Diana (et al.) edits *Las Mujeres Hablan: An Anthology of Nuevo Mexicana Writers.*

1992: Tey (et al.) edits *Nuestras Mujeres: Hispanas in New Mexico, Their Images and Their Lives, 1582-1992.*

1993: Dr. Rebolledo (et al.) edits *Infinite Divisions: An Anthology of Chicana Literature.*

1995: Tey publishes *Women Singing In The Snow: A Cultural Analysis of Chicana Literature.*

1997: Dr. Rebolledo is working on a new book to be titled *I Am As Good As She* having to do with recovering women's cultural history from 1650 to 1950.

Joe S. Sando

HISTORIAN OF THE TIMELESS PUEBLO INDIAN

August 1, 1923: **Joe S. (Simon) Sando** is born to Juanito Sando and Leonor Yepa Sando of Jémez Pueblo. When he is of school age he attends the San Diego Mission School at the Pueblo then later the Santa Fe Indian School.

1943-1946: Joe is in the Navy. He serves on the *USS Corregidor.*

1949: Sando attends Eastern New Mexico University.

1960: Joe attends Vanderbilt University.
1976: Sando publishes *Pueblo Indian Biographies* and *The Pueblo Indians.*

1982: Sando becomes a popular lecturer in West Germany, Switzerland, Italy, Spain, as well as in N.M.
He publishes *NEE HEMISH: The History of Jémez Pueblo.*

1986: Joe retires as Instructor from the University of New Mexico.

1992: He publishes *Pueblo Nations.*
Sando assists in the production and appears in various television documentaries: *Surviving Columbus* (PBS), *American Encounters: Pueblo Resistance* (Smithsonian Institute); *Cavalcade of Enchantment* (KOB-NBC); *Southwest Missions* (Discovery Channel); *War on the American Indians* (BBC), etc.

1997: Joe Sando is director for the Institute for Pueblo Indian Research and Studies at the Pueblo Indian Cultural Center in Albuquerque.
His new book *Pueblo Profiles: Cultural Identity Through Centuries of Change* is soon to be published.

MUSEUM

The legislature passes and Governor King signs enabling legislation that creates the **Hispanic Cultural Division,** the ninth division of the Office of Cultural Affairs, whose mission it is to plan, design, and build the New Mexico **Hispanic Cultural Center.** The Center is intended as a mecca for tourists, artists, educators, scholars, genealogists, etc., and an example of American cross-cultural understanding.

[*No other state in the USA has a state owned and operated Hispanic center.* Inquiries about it have come in from the rest of the USA and many countries throughout the world.]

The other eight divisions of the Office of Cultural Affairs include the Museum of New Mexico, State Library Historic Preservation, Space Center, Natural History & Science, New Mexico Arts Division, Administrative Services, Farm and Ranch.

TOURISM

Foreign travelers visit N.M. from many countries but especially from:

Canada: 53,000;
Germany: 31,833;
Mexico: 26,000;
United Kingdom: 21,877;
South America: 15,720;
France: 9,301;
Japan: 6,419.

NEW MEXICO FACTS

Founded: July 11, 1598, at *San Juan de los Caballeros* (**Knights of St. John**) by San Juan Pueblo in the **Española Valley** (oldest colony of Europeans in the USA).

Founder: Juan de Oñate.

First History: *Historia de la Nueva Mexico, 1610,* by Gaspar Pérez de Villagrá.

Population: 1,616,000 (1993 estimate).

Official Languages: English, Spanish.

Land Area: 122,666 square miles (fifth largest state in area in the USA with the federal government owning more than half of the state).

Area Code: 505.

Highest Point: Wheeler Peak (northeast of Taos), 13,161 feet above sea level.

Lowest Point: Red Bluff Reservoir (south of Carlsbad along the Texas border), 2,842 feet above sea level.
State Capital: Santa Fe (oldest capital in the USA).

Statehood Day: January 6, 1912 (the 47th state).

State Flag: Zía symbol denoting the four winds, four directions, four elements, etc.

State symbols are:
> State Flower: Yucca;
> State Tree: Piñon;
> State Grass: Blue Grama;
> State Bird: Roadrunner;
> State Fish: Río Grande Cutthroat Trout;
> State Animal: Black Bear;
> State Vegetables: Chile and Pinto Beans;
> State Gem: Turquoise;
> State Fossil: Coelophysis;
> State Insect: Tarantula Hawk Wasp;
> State Cookie: Bizcochito.
> Best known personalities: Smokey Bear, Billy the Kid.

Characteristics: N.M. is known for its climate, bilingual and trilingual people, military installations, birthplace of the atomic bomb, Indian and Hispanic arts and crafts, and its unsurpassed civil rights record.

RELIGIOUS
March 20: Archbishop **Robert F Sánchez** resigns his post over allegations of sexual impropriety with various women.

Michael Jarboe Sheehan is installed as the 11th **Archbishop of Santa Fe.** His predecessors are:

> Robert Fortune Sánchez, 1974-1993;
> James Peter Davis, 1964-1974;
> Edwin Vincent Byrne, 1943-1963;
> Rudolph Aloysius Gerken, 1933-1943;
> Albert Thomas Daeger, 1919-1932;
> John Baptist Pitaval, 1909-1918;
> Peter Bourgade, 1899-1908;
> Placid Louis Chapelle, 1894-1897;
> John Baptist Salpointe, 1885-1894;
> John Baptist Lamy, 1875-1885.

TIMELINE

A National Adult Literacy Survey is published by the U.S. Department of Education after having been administered by the Educational Testing Service in 1992. The intent of the survey is to profile the English literacy of adults in the United States by testing some 26,000 adults. Findings are as follows:

LEVEL I:
From 21% to 23%, representing some 40,000,000 to 44,000,000 American adults, fall into this the lowest level of prose, document, and quantitative proficiencies because of their limited literacy skills. Some could find the time or place of a meeting on a paper notice and some couldn't. From 66% to 75% of people scoring in Level I describe themselves as being able to read or write English "well" to "very well."

LEVEL II:
From 25% to 28%, representing about 50,000,000 adults, demonstrate skills in the next higher level of proficiency. They can accomplish routine tasks like calculating the total cost of a purchase. They aren't successful, for example, if a task requires two sequential steps in order to arrive at a proper conclusion. From 93% to 97% of people scoring in Level II describe themselves as being able to read or write English "well" to "very well." (Individuals in Levels I and II aren't very successful in tasks that require higher level reading and problem-solving skills.)

LEVEL III: About 33%, representing some 61,000,000 adults, perform at this level. Respondents can perform tasks like integrating information from long texts or documents and can utilize basic analytical skills.

LEVELS IV and V:
From 18% to 21%, representing some 34,000,000 to 40,000,000 adults, perform at the two highest levels of prose, document, and quantitative literacy.

1994
MUSEUM

The Legislature appropriates $12,000,000 for the **Hispanic Cultural Center**. A site at 4th and Bridge in southwest Albuquerque is selected and the City of Albuquerque donates approximately 11 acres of land for the Center. Mayor Martín Chávez and City Counselors Vince Griego, Alan Armijo, and Steve Gallegos are instrumental in the land acquisition.

EDUCATION & THE ALBUQUERQUE PUBLIC SCHOOLS

Dr. Moises Venegas releases his report In Search of a Workforce for the 21st Century commissioned by the Albuquerque Hispano Chamber of Commerce. The report is an in-depth study of academic achievement in the Albuquerque Public Schools, the largest school district in the State. The research presented includes the following data:

According to 1993 statistics compiled by the Albuquerque Public Schools, "minority" (Hispanic, Indian, Black) students constitute the majority, or 53%, while "majority Anglos" are 47%.

Significant correlations exist between race-ethnicity/ socioeconomic level-dropout rates and academic achievement: the higher the minority enrollment in a school, the higher the dropout rate and the lower the student achievement.

There is a wide range of achievement in standardized tests:
 elementary schools: from the 70th to 79th percentile to the 10th to 19th percentile;
 middle schools: from the 65th percentile at Eisenhower to the 27th percentile at Ernie Pyle and Harrison.

Dropout rates for APS high schools district-wide is 22.6%, with Valley and Del Norte having the highest rate of 27.8%, the lowest being La Cueva at 6.4%.

[APS altered the reporting format in its report titled A Longitudinal Report on Graduation, Transfer, and Withdrawal Rates for the Graduating Class of 1993. Albuquerque High School thereby lowered its 1992 dropout rate of 33.3% to 17.7% and Río Grande went from 29.4% to 15.4%.]

Graduation (1993) rates by ethnicity/race are: "Anglo," 64.3%; Asian, 64.1%; Hispanic, 55.3%; Native American, 50.9%; African American, 50.9%.

Of the 11 APS high schools, the schools producing the lowest number of 1994 freshmen at UNM are West Mesa (57), AHS (53), Río Grande (42).
Dr. Venegas finalizes his research with a 1996 addendum:

"Minority" students are still the majority in the Albuquerque Public Schools and if a school has a high minority enrollment it has a high dropout rate and low academic achievement;

Around 2,600 students drop out of the Albuquerque Public Schools each year;

Achievement in standardized tests for grades three, five, and eight still show a wide disparity with no significant changes from three years ago;

"Will our Albuquerque student population be prepared for the workforce? Are the Albuquerque Public Schools capable of educating poor and minority children? The Albuquerque Public Schools record for the last thirty years certainly does not provide a sense of hope."

BOOKS
Victory in World War II: The New Mexico Story, lists New Mexican WW II recipients of the Medal of Honor as follows:
Alexander Bonnyman, Jr.;
John C. Morgan (in an Editor's note it is explained that Morgan was born in Vernon, Texas, was a 1934 graduate of New Mexico Military Institute, and that "he is attributed to England" for Medal of Honor purposes yet Morgan appears for N.M. in *Victory*);
Alejandro R. Ruiz;
Robert S. Scott.

[New Mexican Medal of Honor recipients for WW II include Joe P Martínez and José E. Valdez, who are not mentioned in *Victory.*]

CAR CLUB
The Española Valley Arts Festival includes a Car Show with 12 different categories.

MAGAZINE
Spring: **Ana Pacheco** of Santa Fe begins publication of the quarterly magazine *La Herencia Del Norte* in an effort to preserve and document the Hispanic culture and history of N.M. in a popular format.

SANTERA
Arlene Cisneros Sena is the 1994 Spanish Market poster artist. The poster is a reproduction of her retablo depicting Our Lady of the Rosary.

[Arlene was born in San Luis, Colorado, but grew up in Santa Fe. At the age of 15 she did a drawing of a music star which her father showed to "a nice man" who drew corrections over it, infuriating the teenaged artist. The "nice man" turned out being Josef Bakos, one of the original Cinco Pintores who started the Santa Fe art colony. Today the "corrected" drawing is treasured by Arlene, who also cites santero Bernardo Miera y Pacheco as an inspiring influence in her artistic development. Arlene also studied with santeros Charles Carrillo and Ramón José López. She believes her family history of faith and religion are the cornerstone of her work and artistic creations.]

ONATE MONUMENT
April: The Oñate Monument and Visitors Center opens to the public under the directorship of Estevan Arellano. (Building of the Monument to honor New Mexico's founder was spearheaded by Emilio Naranjo and funded by Río Arriba County.)

1994-1995
PRISON REPORT
The N.M. Corrections Department Annual Report is issued for the Ninety-Fifth Fiscal Year (between July 1, 1994 through June 30, 1995): Adult Prison Facilities are located at:

Santa Fe - Penitentiary of N.M.;
Grants - Western N.M. Correctional Facilities for Men and Women;
Los Lunas - Minimal Restriction Unit; Ft. Stanton - Camp Sierra Blanca;
Roswell - Correctional Center;
Las Cruces - Southern N.M. Correctional Facility;

Hobbs and Santa Rosa (projected sites for future prisons).

Ethnicity of Inmate population:
"Anglo"	35.09%
Black	11.63%
Hispanic	51.09%

Native Am.   2.18%

Native Americans by tribal membership are:

Navajo	129	78%
Pueblo	19	12%
Other Ntns	17	10%

Age Range of Inmate population:

Under 18	0.18%
18-25	20.90%
26-30	18.54%
31-40	36.18%
41-55	18.72%
Over 55	5.45%

The Probation and Parole Division supervises 17,590 offenders during this period. Under the Intensive Super-vision and House Arrest Program are 987 offenders.

Private firms are operating community corrections programs in Roswell, Las Vegas, Raton, Taos, Grants, Río Rancho Delancey Street, Socorro, Silver City, and Los Lunas.

Most commonly committed crimes and number of inmates serving for them are:

MALES

Burglary	880
Traffic Control Substance	692
Armed Robbery	529
Aggravated Battery	419
Receiving Stolen Property	312
Forgery	290
Aggravated Burglary	268
Possession Control Substance	267
Murder, First Degree	243
Second Degree	243
Robbery	243
Sexual Penetration, Second Degree	220
Theft/Larceny	217

FEMALES

Forgery	52
Traffic Control Substance	48
Burglary	33
Violation	24

Shoplifting	22
Murder, First Degree	12
Second Degree	12
Evidence Tampering	12
Robbery	11
Armed Robbery	10
Credit Card Fraud	10

Expenditure per inmate:
    1986: $33,176.57
    1995: $28,137.80

Number of escapes from 1985 to 1995 are: 1985 - 48; 1986 - 36; 1987 - 33; 1988 - 19; 1989 - 14; 1990 - 11; 1991 - 16; 1992 - 33; 1993 - 36; 1994 - 22; 1995 - 16.

Projected growth of inmate populations from Fiscal Year 1995 through Fiscal Year 2000:
    Male: 117.96%
    Female: 135.76%

1995

Gary Johnson is Governor.

1995
GAMING COMPACTS
Indian gaming compacts are ratified by Governor Johnson then declared illegal by the State Supreme Court.

MILITARY - INDUSTRIAL
Kirtland Air Force Base is slated for closure. Community efforts and the congressional delegation labor vigorously and the Base remains intact.

Gary Johnson

1995: Kirtland AFB: consists of 82 square miles (one-third larger than Washington, D.C.); is the largest employer in N.M. (with 19,900 employees, 4% of all employees in N.M.); has a combined payroll (fiscal year 1995) of $870.7 billion; had a $1.6 billion impact on the city of Albuquerque (in FY 1995); Department of Defense agencies on Kirtland spent $245.4 million in the local area.

TERRORISM
January 6: A Forest Service office in Española is bombed, destroying a wall and roof.

CULTURE
February: **Prem Gabaldón** of Albuquerque holds his annual matanza to honor his mother, Delfina Sedillo Gabaldón, on her birthday and as a celebration of community. He states: "*I want to continue the old cultural ways of community solidarity as an example to young people.*"

POST-SECONDARY INSTITUTIONS
State universities include:

Eastern New Mexico University (Portales);
    Branches: Roswell Campus, Ruidoso Instructional Center;

New Mexico Highlands University (las Vegas);

New Mexico Institute of Mining and Technology (Socorro);

New Mexico State University (Las Cruces);
     Branches: Alamogordo, Carlsbad, Doña Ana Community College, Grants;

University of New Mexico (Albuquerque);
    Branches: Gallup, Los Alamos, Valencia; Western New Mexico University (Silver City).

Private colleges are:
    College of Santa Fe;
    College of the Southwest (Hobbs);
    St. John's College (Santa Fe).

Vocational-Technical school:
    Job Training Services (Albuquerque)

Junior Colleges and/or Vocational-Technical Schools:
    Albuquerque T-VI: A Community College;
    Clovis Community College;
    Crownpoint Institute of Technology;
    Luna Voc.-Tech. Institute: A Community College (Las Vegas);
    Mesa Technical College (Tucumcari);
    New Mexico Junior College (Hobbs);
    Northern New Mexico Community College (Española);
    Northern New Mexico Community College (El Rito);
    San Juan College (Farmington);
    Santa Fe Community College.

Junior Colleges/Community Colleges for Native Americans are:
> Institute of American Indian Arts (Santa Fe);
> Navajo Community College (Shiprock);
> Southwestern Indian Polytechnic Institute (Albuquerque).

1996
EDUCATION
Public school districts in N.M. are
> Alamogordo, Albuquerque, Animas, Artesia, Aztec, Belén, Bernalillo, Bloomfield, Capitán, Carlsbad, Carrizozo, Central, Chama Valley, Cimarron, Clayton, Cloudcroft, Clovis, Cobre, Corona, Cuba, Deming, Des Moines, Dexter, Dora, Dulce, Elida, Española, Estancia, Eunice, Farmington, Floyd, Fort Sumner, Gadsden, Gallup, Grady, Grants/Cíbola, Hagerman, Hatch, Hobbs, Hondo Valley, House, Jal, Jémez Mountain, Jémez Valley, Lake Arthur, Las Cruces, Us Vegas City, Las Vegas West, Logan, Lordsburg, Los Alamos, Los Lunas, Loving, Lovington, Magdalena, Maxwell, Melrose, Mesa Vista, Mora, Moriarty, Mosquero, Mountainair, Pecos, Peñasco, Pojoaque, Portales, Quemdado, Questa, Ratón, Reserve, Río Rancho, Roswell, Roy, Ruidoso, San Jon, Santa Fe, Santa Rosa, Silver City, Socorro, Springer, Taos, Tatum, Texico, Truth or Consequences, Tucumcari, Tularosa, Vaughn, Wagon Mound, Zuñi.

Non-public schools are found in:
> Alamogordo, Albuquerque, Animas, Belén, Bernalillo, Bloomfield, Capitán, Carlsbad, Central, Clovis, Cuba, Des Moines, Duke, Española, Eunice, Farmington, Gadsden, Gallup, Grants/Cíbola, Hobbs, Jémez Valley, Las Cruces, Las Vegas City, Los Alamos, Los Lunas, Magdalena, Moriarty, Mountainair, Pecos, Pojoaque, Portales, Questa, Ratón, Reserve, Río Rancho, Roswell, Ruidoso, Santa Fe, Silver City, Socorro, Taos, Tucumcari, Tularosa, Zuñi.

MUSEUM
Ronald Vigil of the State Hispanic Cultural Division of the Office of Cultural Affairs coordinates all activities pertaining to the **Hispanic Cultural Center** to be built in Albuquerque. The project is condemned as unnecessary by some but there is also overwhelming support for the Center emanating from thousands of New Mexicans who work to realize the project, including legislators like Manny Aragón, President Pro Tempore of the Senate, and dedicated community people like **Loretta Armenta** of Albuquerque. Vigil, later appointed to the post of Director, states the Center's first phase is slated for a grand opening in 1998, the 400th anniversary of the founding of N.M.

[The Center is the focus of aspirations for many people with its projected outdoor theater, genealogical resource library, a publishing unit, museums, a small railroad line to connect with the Botanical Gardens and Zoo, etc., and plans for a River Walk, nature trails, garden exhibits, picnic grounds, Sister City exhibits, large sculpture gardens, etc., and events like international film, music, and theater festivals, the Hispanic Games modeled after the Olympics, as well as historical festivals and celebrations of the arts.]

PROFILE

J. Ronald Vigil

B R I N G I N G   T O   F R U I T I O N :
A   1 2 T H   G E N E R A T I O N   N E W   M E X I C A N

December 6, 1942: **J. Ronald Vigil** is born. His roots are in Española with the families Vigil, Martínez, Ferrán, Sena, Salazar, Ortiz. He attends the public schools.

1960: Vigil graduates from Santa Fe High School

1964: Ron is shift supervisor to build the optical simulation system for the NASA Lunar Excursion Module Apollo Project at Tinsley Laboratories, Berkeley, California.

1967: Vigil earns and is awarded a Bachelor of Arts degree from New Mexico State University. He is then hired as a Resource Specialist by the U.S. Department of the Interior, Bureau of Land Management, in Washington D.C.

1968-1969: Ron is hired by the New Mexico State Highway Department to work in Right of Way, researching and analyzing data to be used in writing appraisals. He is involved in much field work and many negotiations.

1969-1970: Vigil works as a Research Analyst for the City of Santa Fe Demonstration Agency. He supervises eight personnel in the unit.

1971: Ron is voted into the position of Sergeant at Arms of the New Mexico State Senate. He becomes intimately acquainted with the varied Legislative processes from the practical as well as theoretical points of view.

1971: Ronald attends Southern Methodist University to study the field of Real Estate Appraisal.

1971-1972: Ron works as the Relocation Officer for the New Mexico State Highway Department.

1872-1973: Ronald is a Research Associate for the National Economic Development Association (NEDA) out of Los Angeles.

1973-1974: Vigil studies Management and Organizational Dynamics with McBer & Company in Boston. (The intermittent seminars are to become a highlight of his professional education.)

1973-1975: Ronald is National Director of Training for NEDA.

1975: His son **David** is born.

1975-1976: Vigil is a Management & Business Consultant for NEDA in San José. He also works as an Independent Contractor, providing consultation services to small businesses (1976-77).

1976: Ron attends the University of West Los Angeles School of Law then the following year he is in the Lincoln University School of Law.

J. Ronald Vigil

1977: His daughter **Carin** is born.

1977-1983: Vigil is Deputy Secretary of the New Mexico Department of Hospitals and Institutions. After the state reorganization of 1978 his duties remain the same under the title of Deputy Director for Behavioral Health Services Division, Health and Environment Department.

1983-1987: Ron is Deputy Director for the New Mexico Property Control Division, General Services Department. During these years he is responsible for, among other things, overseeing the construction of the South Capital Complex (a $27,000,000 project).

1987-1991: Vigil becomes Director of the Property Control Division, General Services Department, thus in charge of capital projects totaling some $400,000,000.

1991: Ronald becomes Deputy Director of the Office of Cultural Affairs for the State of New Mexico.

January, 1993: Vigil conceptualizes and initiates the statutory enactment of the Hispanic Cultural Division within the Office of Cultural Affairs. Shortly thereafter he is appointed Interim Director to manage the creation and development of the New Mexico Hispanic Cultural Center to be located in Albuquerque.

Vigil writes the enabling legislation that becomes known as Senate Bill 739.

March, 1993: Senate Bill 739 is introduced by Senators Manny M. Aragón, Pete Campos, Martín J. Chávez, Tito D. Chávez, Fernando R. Macías. It is passed by the Legislature and signed by

Governor Bruce King. Start-up funding is appropriated: $410,000 to begin planning and design, $116,000 for operating costs. Making the Hispanic Cultural Center a reality is now the primary responsibility of Ronald Vigil.

January, 1998: The amount of $17,000,000 has been appropriated for the HCC by the State Legislature. (Another $17.8 million is being pursued by Senators Domenici and Bingaman at the Federal level.)

J. Ronald Vigil is elected Board Emeritus to New Mexico First.

SOCIETY
March 18, 1996: **Fray Angélico Chávez**, one of the most versatile and distinguished artists and man of letters in 20th century N.M., dies in Santa Fe. The History Library at the Palace of the Governors is renamed the *Fray Angélico Chávez History Library and Photographic Archives* in his honor.

[Among the many eulogies of Fray Angélico one of the most poignant is: *"We'll miss you, little Father."*]

LAND OWNERSHIP
The federal government owns more than half of New Mexico's 122,666 square miles.

RECREATION SITES
Federal and State agencies manage a variety of recreational sites, facilities, and activities in New Mexico:

Bureau of Indian Affairs (all Pueblo, Apache, and Navajo lands);

Bureau of Land Management (22 sites);

Forest Service (five national forests: Carson, Cíbola, Gila, Lincoln, Santa Fe);

Museum of New Mexico State Monuments (five);

National Park Service (16 federal parks/monuments);

New Mexico Department of Game and Fish (30);

New Mexico Department of Tourism (10 Welcome Centers: Anthony, Aztec, Chama, Gallup, Glenrio, La Bajada, Lordsburg, Raton, Santa Fe, Texico);

New Mexico State Parks (40);

U.S. Army Corps of Engineers (seven lakes/dams);
U.S. Fish and Wildlife Service (eight wildlife refuges and/or hatcheries).

PROFILE

Guadalupita Ortiz

S A N T E R A

Santera Guadalupita Ortiz is a successful female artist, in a traditionally male dominated art form, who has won top awards in the Spanish Market.

December 12, 1950: **Guadalupita María Francisca Herrera** is born in Santa Fe to **Procopio** and **Adela Herrera**. The newborn is taken home to El Rancho (where ancestor Santiago Roybal grew up and became the first native New Mexican ordained to the priesthood). The Herrera children are raised with a religious orientation.

1955: The Herrera family moves to California where Guadalupita is attracted to art activities. The family returns to N.M. and Guadalupita attends schools at El Rancho then Pojoaque. She works at a tourist shop at San Ildefonso Pueblo and meets people like famous potter María Martínez, who inspire her.

1970: Guadalupita marries **Tony David Ortiz** from Pojoaque.

1974: While working at the Museum of International Folk Art the vast collection of art pieces have a powerful effect on her, especially the *retablos*.

Guadalupita Ortiz

1978: Guadalupita studies the lives of the saints and begins to paint.

1979: Ortiz exhibits her work at the Spanish Market, comprising some 30 artists, for the first time.

1987: The Ortiz family moves to Palm Springs, California, but after an earthquake they return to N.M.

1989: Guadalupita Ortiz is awarded a First Place award in the Spanish Market in the *retablo* category.

1991: Guadalupita wins another *retablo* first place for her *Our Lady of the Rosary*.

1994: "Pita" is awarded First and Second awards at the State Fair for her *retablos* of St. Joseph and the Madonna.

EDUCATION & ALBUQUERQUE PUBLIC SCHOOLS

April 28, 1996: The *Albuquerque Journal* prints a front page article exposing educational inequalities in the **Albuquerque Public Schools,** the largest school district in the state. Standardized test scores show that students in heavily Hispanic areas rank at the bottom of the district while students from "Anglo" sections of Albuquerque score at national averages or higher. An unnamed teacher is quoted as saying she transferred from her (predominantly Hispanic) school to one in the east side of town after teaching *"became a nightmare."* APS officials are quoted as maintaining that most teachers transfer to be nearer to home.

Dr. Moises Venegas, who prepared a report on three years of APS test scores for the Albuquerque Hispano Chamber of Commerce, is quoted as stating : *"There's a significant correlation between ethnicity, socioeconomic level, school achievement, and dropout rates. In Albuquerque the tests show that the higher the Hispanic or minority enrollment in a school, the lower the student achievement and the higher the dropout rate."*

An APS spokesman states that low scores are attributed to lower income levels more than to ethnicity.

A *"talented"* [westside] teacher reports that her school is *"plagued by theft and vandalism,"* that she's disheartened because *"district administrators don't provide the school with basic necessities."*

May 17, 1996: The *Albuquerque Journal* reports that a teacher at Alameda Elementary has been suspended (with pay) *"because she left her classroom while on duty."* Alameda, with a high percentage of Hispanic students and ITBS scores well below national averages, was the scene of a protest by *"the activist group Vecinos United"* who wished to draw attention to the problems at the school. After the staff was instructed to refer all *"media and parent"* questions to an APS spokesman, the teacher talked to a television reporter during her lunch break and that evening (Wednesday) she was served by APS police with papers charging her with insubordination. The acting principal reported to the media that the offending teacher *"left her classroom while on duty"* and was suspended, referring all further questions to the APS spokesman *"who could not be reached for comment Thursday night."* November 16, 1996: The *Albuquerque Tribune* runs a front page article titled "School Supplies May be Restored," relating that when the insurance fund turns up with extra money some of it is earmarked for supplies, the list for which includes *eight new cars* for upper echelon superintendents, administrators, and the district's truant officer.

November 28, 1996: The *Albuquerque Journal* lists all APS administrators who have **"take-home cars:"** the superintendent (with a salary of $115,442), the deputy superintendent ($81,000), northwest superintendent, northeast superintendent, south superintendent, curriculum superintendent, human resources superintendent (with salaries of $66,881 each) and 14 other directors, coordinators, etc. Superintendent **Horoschak** tells the School Board that the cars are necessary because administrators *"are often called out to meetings during off-duty hours."* Board member **Robert Lucero** is quoted as saying that administrators providing cars for themselves "is *a huge waste of taxpayers' money."*

[The Superintendent can assign a car to whomever he wishes and at a later meeting the School Board votes 4-2 to let the district buy new cars for various individuals. In time it is also alleged that APS administrators are abusing the purchase and use of cellular phones and no mention is made of how many have had the district purchase laptop computers for their own use.]

April 10, 1997: The *Albuquerque Journal* runs a story titled "Dropout Rates Alarming," presenting statistics that show the six Albuquerque high schools with the highest percentage of Hispanic students have had the highest annual dropout rates for the past two years, despite "a real effort" by APS to combat the trend.

May 10, 1997: The *Albuquerque Tribune* discloses that "since last summer" the Albuquerque superintendent, drawing a salary of about $115,000 per year, has been interviewed for superintendent jobs in Tampa and Orlando, Florida; Toledo, Ohio; Denver, Colorado; Albany, New York. He is quoted as being "happy to be here" in Albuquerque.

May 20, 1997: The Albuquerque Superintendent writes a letter to the School Board requesting that his contract not be renewed in 1998. The Board complies and prepares to search for a new superintendent.

August 29, 1997: The *Albuquerque Journal* remarks in an editorial that **seventy-four (74) take-home** cars, with all maintenance expenses paid by the tax-supported Albuquerque Public Schools, is an administrative perk that can't be tolerated.

December 20, 1997: The *Albuquerque Journal* runs a front page article titled "Closed Doors At APS Cited" in which **Moises Venegas** observes that APS administrators make it difficult to investigate educational progress at schools where achievement is low while such investigations are received positively in schools where achievement is high. Venegas, who heads **Albuquerque Partnership** which was created to improve schools and neighborhoods, says it is made difficult to observe in schools in the South Valley.

[The *Journal* later does an article that states that from among the various groups working for APS, people being served by the District have the lowest esteem for APS administrators.]

CHIMAYÓ WEAVERS: Families

TRUJILLO
The centuries-old **Trujillo family** tradition of weaving continues in Chimayó:

Seventh generation: Karen Vigil, Velma Vigil; Elisha Vigil; Lourdes Vigil;

Sixth generation: Irvin L. Trujillo and Lisa D. Rockwood (of **Centinela Traditional Arts**, **Río Grande Weavings**); Jerry & Marie Trujillo; Dulcinea Trujillo & Dimas Vigil;

Fifth generation: Albino Trujillo; Juan Trujillo, Mercedes Trujillo, Antonio Trujillo, Rosinaldo Trujillo; Nicolás Trujillo; Alfredo Córdova, Harry Córdova; Teresita Trujillo & Severo Jaramillo;

Fourth generation: Isidoro Trujillo;
Third generation: Concepción Trujillo;

Second generation: José Rafaél Trujillo;

First generation: Diego Trujillo.

ORTEGA
Robert Ortega of the **Ortega's Weaving Shop** is the eighth generation of Ortega weavers in Chimayó upon
the retirement of his father **David Ortega**.

Ca. 1985: Andrew and Evita Ortega open **Galería Ortega** (in the old home of José Ramón Ortega).

Ca. 1975: David and Jeanine Ortega (joined by sons Andrew and Robert) maintain the family weaving
tradition and David's brother, Merardo, opens a branch shop in Albuquerque's Old Town.

Ca. 1910: Nicacio Ortega and his wife Virginia (**Trujillo,** of the famous Trujillo family of weavers) open a
general store in Chimayó. Weavings are popular items and family members join the business until it
becomes strictly a weaving shop with the help of Nicacio's sons José Ramón and David and their
wives, Bernie and Jeanine.

1885: The railroad comes to Española and visitors want to buy local weavings.

Ca. 1710: Gabriel Ortega settles in Chimayó and makes a living by farming and weaving. Many of his
descendants, like his son Manuel, Manuel's son José Gervacio, and J.G.'s son José Ramón, follow
in his footsteps.

VIGIL
Eugene D. Vigil and **Rose Bartlett Vigil**, owners of **Los Vigiles Living Traditions**, are generational heirs to
the Trujillo and Ortega families of Chimayó weavers:

TRUJILLO	ORTEGA
Seventh generation:	Eugene D. Vigil
Sixth generation: Eugene D. Vigil	Ercilia Trujillo Vigil
Fifth generation: Ercilia Trujillo Vigil	Toribio Trujillo
Fourth generation: Toribio Trujillo	José Concepción Trujillo
Third generation: José Concepción Trujillo	María Francisca. Ortega
Second generation: José Carmen Trujillo	Pedro Asencio Ortega
First generation: Miguel Trujillo	Nicolás Gabriel Ortega

TIMELINE

August 11, 1996 : The *Albuquerque Journal* runs a front page story on the eve of the Republican
Convention regarding a poll commissioned by Porter-Novelli, a New York public relations firm
investigating the **credibility of American institutions**. Eleven hundred Americans are polled:

92% state the government is not a reliable source of information, 98% don't believe the major political parties, nearly 50% think political reporters are less believable than they were even five years ago, and 70% believe politicians are less reliable than five years ago, undermined by insincerity, broken promises, and mudslinging campaigns.

PUBLIC ART at UNM

The University of New Mexico has been adding to its walking tour and now has 17 works of public art on its main campus, which include:

1910: *Kwakiutl Totem*, paint on carved cedar pole by Charlie James;
1940: *Three Peoples Panels*, oil on canvas by Kenneth Adams;
1943: *Union of the Americas*, fresco by Jesús Guerrero Galván;
1963: Untitled, French stained glass by John Tatschi;
1968: Untitled, cast concrete forms by Paul Wright;
1976: *Static Motion*, by John Keyser;
1985: *Modulator*, Corten steel by Ed Vega;
1987: *Dreams and Nightmares: Journey of a Broken Weave*, steel by Dennis Oppenheim;
1987: *Cosmos Historia*, fresco by Federico Vigil;
1988: *Center of the Universe*, concrete and sodium vapor lights by Bruce Nauman;
1994: *Parade*, ceramic tile by Beverly Magennis;
1994: *Homage to Grandmother Earth*, granite by Youn Ja Johnson;
1996: *Spirit Mother*, by Michael Naranjo;
1996: *Cultural Crossroads of the Americas*, by Bob Haozous;
1996: *Fiesta Dancers*, fiberglass by Luis Jiménez.

INDIAN GAMING

Indian casinos are operating at Acoma, Isleta, Jicarilla Apache (Dulce), Mescalero Apache (Ruidoso), Pojoaque, Sandía, San Juan, Santa Ana, and Tesuque.

EDUCATION

August 22: Governor Johnson suggests that all students be tested in all grades, instead of just the third, fifth, eighth, in order to track educational progress more effectively.

RACISM

October 19: The *Albuquerque Journal* runs a front page article titled "Hate Letter Stirs Rival Schools:" A letter attributed to the cheerleaders of a northeast Albuquerque high school is received by the coach of a cross-town rival school just before their football teams are to meet in an important district game. A copy of the letter isn't released but it is said to include *"We're superior because you eat beans and rice and we eat steak and lobster."* APS officials state the letter probably came from someone totally unrelated to either school.

EDUCATION
Roy Stogner scores a perfect *1600* in his SAT college-entrance exam.

DIPLOMACY
December 13: **Bill Richardson, Representative** of the 3rd Congressional District and renowned for his ability to negotiate the release of various hostages throughout the world, is selected by **President Clinton** to fill the post of Ambassador to the United Nations.

1997
LAND CLAIMS
Representative **Bill Richardson** introduces a bill titled the *"Guadalupe Hidalgo Treaty Land Claims Act of 1997"* in an effort to establish a presidential commission to study and determine the validity of land claims throughout New Mexico. Descendants of New Mexicans living at the time of the Treaty maintain their families were defrauded by land grabbers, lawyers, judges, and/or government authorities, despite the Treaty that assured everyone legitimate land titles would be protected.

[In previous years **Senator Joe Montoya** had introduced legislation to investigate Hispanic land claims but it failed to get out of committee. With Richardson going on to be Ambassador to the United Nations the claimants hope his successor and others in the congressional delegation will work for the legislation to go through.]

Senator Joseph Montoya
Courtesy Museum of NM, #166715

INDIAN GAMING
Casino-style gaming is now operating legally in all Amerind casinos with the State taking *16%* of the profit.

QUALITY OF LIFE
The **Albuquerque Biological Park** consists of the *Río Grande Zoo* (established in 1927), the "state-of-art" *Albuquerque Aquarium*, the 10-acre *Río Grande Botanic* Garden, and the Tingley Aquatic Park.

1987: Albuquerque voters pass a "Quality of Life" sales tax to be used for the Biological Park.

December 4, 1996: The Aquarium and Botanic Garden are opened for the public. The biggest draw is to the Aquarium's 285,000-gallon shark tank which houses 16 sharks. Visitors observe the sharks and thousands of other ocean fish through large viewing windows. The 16-acre facility, which costs $34,000,000 but opens free of debt due to the sales tax, includes a lagoon outside the Aquarium, a glass conservatory which displays Mediterranean and desert plant species, a special walled rose garden with a wedding chapel, and a Spanish Moorish garden.

EDUCATION

Coached by **Linda Davey,** the *Academic Decathlon* team from **Belén High School** places 16th out of 37 states in the national competition, second in the Midwest Region (to Texas, the ultimate overall national winner). The group of nine members and two alternates wins more medals (eight) than any other team in the history of N.M. participation:

Joe Williams: Gold Medal in Fine Arts, fifth place medal for Economics;

Grant Farnsworth: three third place Bronze Medals for Economics, Science, Fine Arts, fifth place in Language and Literature;

Will Gabaldón: fifth place in Speech;

James Knecht: fourth place in Social Science.

SANTERO EXHIBITION

March: The University of California at Los Angeles (UCLA) presents an exhibition of some 90 items of New Mexican religious art in its Fowler's Museum. The exhibition is titled **"When the Saints Speak: Contemporary Santero Traditions from Northern New Mexico"** and includes art works from Charles Carrillo, Marie Romero Cash, Gloria López Córdova, Gustavo Victor Goler, Anita Romero Jones, Félix López, Manuel López, José Benjamin López, Leroy López, Ramón José López, Luisito Luján, Sabinita López Ortiz, Luis Tapia, as well as creations by members of some of their families.

SOCIETY

World-renowned painter **Henriette Wyeth,** daughter of master **N.C. Wyeth,** dies at the age of 89.

CULTURE & COMMUNITY

A donation of $30,000 is made by **Sandía National Laboratories** and **Lockheed Martín Corporation** (the largest single donation to date) for the Hispanic Cultural Center to be built in Albuquerque. Department of Energy Secretary **Federico Peña** is on hand for the presentation. Peña declares: *"It is crucial that we inform all Americans and the rest o the world of the extraordinary contributions and impact Hispanic people have made for many centuries in the Southwest. When the Center is finished it will be the largest, most important project of its kind in the USA."*

LAND GRANT

May 10- 11: **Ezequiel L. Ortiz** writes a synopsis of the Tomé Land Grant for the *Valencia County News-Bulletin:*

Ca. 1659: Tomé Domínguez is awarded a grant of land totaling some 371,000 acres which extend from the east bank of the Río Grande to the Manzano Mountains, the north boundary at Tomé Hill, south to the *Cerro de la Casa Colorado.*

1680: The Pueblo Revolt forces all Hispanics out of N.M.

1693: Governor Diego de Vargas leads colonists back to N.M. Neither Tomé Domínguez nor his direct heirs return with Vargas so the land is unoccupied.

Ca. 1750s: Various families from Albuquerque petition for permission to occupy the entire Tomé Land Grant and the governor accedes to their request. It is awarded as a community grant and administered by a Board of Trustees.

1846: The USA takes the northern half of Mexico in the Mexican War. Under the American system of land ownership taxes must be paid on the land. (Under the Hispanic system land wasn't taxed, just what it produced. With the U.S. in power much land is taken over by the government when land taxes can't be paid.)

1913: The southern portion of the Tomé Grant, some 200,000 acres is sold to the Fegue Land and Cattle Company in order to obtain money with which to pay land taxes. The money is placed in a trust account which accrues interest and is added to when small parcels of grant land are sold to private individuals for development as farms or ranches. Heirs have unrestricted use of the 47,000 acres designated as "common usage lands."

1950s: Non-heirs of the Tomé Grant begin acquiring acreage within grant boundaries. In time they demand use of the commons grazing lands. Former Trustee Esteban Torrez informs his nephew and current Board of Trustees member Pablo Torrez that the grant will be threatened by the non-heirs if immediate action isn't instituted. In time the Tomé Land and Improvement Company becomes a legal entity with power over all aspects of the grant. A corporate body is elected and stock certificates are issued to all heirs/property owners.

Through the years some of the ranchers (referred to as "cowboys") section off large tracts of grazing land for exclusive use of their own cattle, denying entry to anybody else's stock. If another's cattle roam onto their sections the cattle disappear. Yet the ranchers agree that all land taxes and maintenance fees should be paid by the communal trust fund.

Two antagonistic factions are now identifiable, loosely referred to as "cowboys" and "farmers." There are innumerable disputes over fair and equitable land rights.

1950s: Headed by businessman **Gillie Sánchez** the Progressive Committee is formed to study how best to pursue development of the Tomé Grant and its 47,000 acres of commons land. The "cowboy" faction opposes the Progressive Committee and the community is split, not knowing who to believe. Despite the conflict, some heirs are disinterested and sell their shares of stock, some for as little as $15 per share.

1960s: Rumors have it that various buyers are interested in purchasing the 47,000 acres of disputed land, that each share could be worth around $ 10,900. After much heated discussion a vote is in favor of finding a buyer for the acreage. An offer is made to the **Horizon Land Company** which bids $4,500,000 for the land. The bid is accepted and each registered shareholder, 275 in total, is to receive $5,000 during the first three years of payments by Horizon.

Some shareholders now reject the conditions of the sale and file suit. There are numerous lawsuits, injunctions, pleadings and counter-pleadings, etc., and the matter winds up in the New Mexico Supreme Court, Judge Sosa presiding, who rules that not all heirs have been properly identified, that more time is necessary to prove if others are entitled to receive money from the sale; heirs who have received payments must now return said payments, that if payments weren't returned then liens could be filed on their property wherever it happened to be located.

(Heirs who had received money suffered extreme hardship if they didn't have it to return immediately, some having to mortgage their property to raise the money.)

Judge Sosa rules (at various hearings) that all heirs must be properly identified, that all funds be equally divided, that no statutory provisions existed for a land grant to dispose of its land via a corporate entity of its own making, that the sale was legal and the money thus acquired would be placed in a trust fund *that would be administered by the courts.*

The Court decrees that legal heirs number in excess of 500, that after *legal fees and administrative costs* are paid each heir is entitled to about $4,000 as his/her fair portion.

[Author E.L. Ortiz states that the only "bright side" in the entire history is that land from the Tomé Grant was donated to the University of New Mexico which established the UNM branch Valencia Campus in Tomé.]

POLITICS
May 13: Republican **Bill Redmond** wins the seat for the 3rd Congressional District in a close election. Registered Democrats outnumber Republicans two to one in the 3rd District and it had been held by Democrat Bill Richardson since its creation in 1982 but the final vote by percentages is 43% for Redmond, 40% for Democrat Eric Serna, 17% for Green Party Carol Miller.

ATHLETICS & ACADEMICS
Bobby Newcombe finishes a high school athletic career that saw him earn a strong "B" average academically while he was selected to **All-State** honors in football, basketball, and track in his Senior year as well as **Gatorade Player of the Year** in all three sports. In football he was selected to the **Parade All American** team. (People who know him personally also describe him as "one great guy.")

TIMELINE
The demise of Affirmative Action in California is being felt in the university system: Hispanic and black ("minority") admissions to the freshman class at UCLA and Berkeley's law school have dropped by 80%. The surge is also felt at the University of Texas where "minority" admission is down 85% in the law school and 20% in undergraduate schools.

PRIVATE LAND & OWNERSHIP

June: *Crosswinds,* an Albuquerque monthly magazine, publishes an article titled "Who Owns New Mexico?" which lists the forty (40) largest private land owners in the State. Written/researched by W.R. Barrett, J. Casey, D.J. Chacón, N. Kryloff, D. McKay, S. Montoya, and M. Salazar, the following are listed as the largest private land owners in N.M.:

NAME	RESIDENCE	ACREAGE
Henry Singleton	Beverly Hills, CA.	1,200,000
R.E. "Ted" Turner	Georgia	1,150,000
Lee family	San Mateo, N.M.	300,000
Lane family	(Various)	290,000
Bidegain family	Tucumcari, N.M.	180,000
King family	Stanley, N.M.	170,000
Huning family	Los Lunas, N.M.	160,000
Michael Mechenbier	Albuquerque, N.M.	135,000
Leslie and Lisa Davis	Cimarron, N.M.	125,000
Bogle family	Dexter, N.M.	100,000
John Yates family	(Various)	100,000
Dunigan family	Abilene, Texas	95,000
Wesley D. Adams	Logandale, Nevada	95,000
Butler heirs	(Various)	95,000
J.A. Whittenburg III	(Various)	85,000
Corn family	Roswell, N.M.	85,000
R.A. "Hap" Canning	Capitán, N.M.	65,000
Brittingham family	Antón Chico, N.M.	60,000
Doherty family	Folsom, N.M.	60,000
Jay Taylor family	(Various)	60,000
Baeza family	Chihuahua, Mexico	55,000
Mitchell family	Albert, N.M.	55,000
Colin McMillan, Benjamin Rummerfield	(Various)	55,000
Sam Brit	Grenville, N.M.	50,000
Moise family	Albuquerque, N.M.	50,000
Sam Donaldson	Virginia	45,000
William D. Sanders	(Various)	45,000
Cain family	(Various)	45,000
Baldridge family	(Various)	45,000
Edmund E Ball	Indiana	45,000
Mike and Deborah Smith	Pampa, Texas	40,000
David Salman family	Mora, N.M.	40,000
Frank Chappell	Connecticut	40,000
Mike Fitzgerald	Mosquero, N.M.	40,000
James family	Logan, N.M.	40,000

Huling "Jupe" Means	Logan, N.M.	40,000
Spires family	(Various)	40,000
Wootten family	Springer, N.M.	35,000
Floyd Blackburn	Dumas, Texas	35,000
Carl Lane Johnson	Tatum, N.M.	35,000

TIMELINE

July 12, 1997 : The *Albuquerque Journal* publishes an article written by **Frank S. Lechuga** titled "Mexican American 'Conspiracy' Incites Citizens Group" on its Op-Ed Page. **Voices of Citizens Together,** a group based in Sherman Oaks, California, asserts that Mexicans and Mexican Americans are struggling to regain domination of the Southwest. They attack President Clinton and VP Gore for "supporting" Latinos and demand that Mexicans not be included in the national conversations on race because Hispanics are after reconquest to recover the lands taken from Mexico in the Mexican War, according to the **Plan de Aztlan which is central to the Chicano movement**. Writer F.S. Lechuga believes the group feeds on nationalism and xenophobia because it considers Chicanos a threat to the security and sovereignty of the U.S. **Morris Janowitz** of the University of Chicago is cited as asserting that Mexican-American empowerment in the Southwest should be considered an extension of Mexican culture and the Mexican nation. **David Kennedy** of Stanford University is quoted as saying: *The possibility is very real that in the next generation or so we will see a kind of Chicano Quebec take shape in the Southwest.*

ART MUSEUM

July 17: The **Georgia O'Keeffe Museum** opens to the public in Santa Fe. More than 5,000 art enthusiasts see a collection of Georgia's paintings on opening day.

BOXING

July 18: Two Albuquerque professional title holders, **Johnny Tapia and Danny Romero,** meet in a highly publicized boxing match held in Las Vegas, Nevada. The entire sport is hurting because of a previous debacle in the heavyweight division and the subsequent destructive actions of fight fans at a Vegas hotel. Crowd-pleasing Tapia wins a unanimous decision over a gallant Romero in what ring sportscasters describe as one of the most professional boxing matches of recent times. The caliber of the Albuquerquean's boxing skills is complimented by famous heavyweight champion George Foreman and mention is made of the positive manner in which the thousands of Albuquerque fight fans in Vegas have conducted themselves.

BUSINESS ORGANIZATION

August: **Loretta A. Armenta** is selected as President and CEO of the Albuquerque Hispano Chamber of Commerce.

MUSIC

Angel Espinoza is selected "Female Vocalist of the Year" during the **New Mexico Hispano Music Awards** ceremonies. Her *"El Corrido de don Juan de Oñate" is* named the official song for the **Cuarto**

Centennial by the City of Española and Río Arriba County.

SOCIETY

August 29: The *Albuquerque Journal* publishes an article titled **"Poll: Lawyers Not Trusted in N.M."** It states that more than half of New Mexicans from differing ethnicities, genders, education levels, income levels, ages, etc., have negative attitudes about lawyers and the legal system. A majority believe that lawyers' fees are exorbitantly high, even for routine services; that lawyers manipulate the law, drag out court proceedings as a strategy, etc., that lawyers are *"dishonest"* and have *"low standards as a profession."*

N.M. lawyers have a 54% negative rating compared to 34% nationwide.

Fifty-nine percent (59%) of those polled said the legal system *"needs a complete overhaul."*

PROFILE

Loretta A. Armenta

AN OUTSTANDING WOMAN OF NEW MEXICO

1974-1979: **Loretta A. Armenta** is Chief Operating Officer for all local fund raising programs for the March of Dimes, increasing its income from $34K to $360K in five years. She designs and produces the award-winning slide presentation "This Child of Mine."

1979-1980: Loretta is State Director for the New Mexico March of Dimes.

1980-1981: Armenta is the Account Executive for KRDM Radio in Albuquerque.

1981-1993: Loretta is a Special Agent for Prudential Financial Services. She is awarded the National Sales Achievement Award five years in a row. She is the first woman to qualify for the Million Dollar Round Table Award and wins it four years in a row.

1986-1991: She is the Owner/Operator of Snow Goose Gift Baskets. She is selected to share her expertise in the Soviet Union for a "Women In Business" seminar.

1992-1995: Armenta handles the Special Projects/Cultural Office for the Albuquerque Hispano Chamber of Commerce. She lobbies for the building of the Hispanic Cultural Center.
1995: Loretta receives the Governor's Award for Outstanding Women In New Mexico.

1995-1996: Armenta is Interim President of the Albuquerque Hispano Chamber of Commerce.

May, 1996: Loretta is Vice President of the AHCC, one of the premier Hispano chambers in the USA.

August, 1997: Loretta A. Armenta is selected President and CEO of the Albuquerque Hispano Chamber of Commerce.

CULTURE

September 2: The *Albuquerque Journal* runs a front page article on the commemorative issue of the **Calendar of the Great Southwest: The New Mexico Edition** which celebrates the 400th anniversary of the founding of N.M. The issue is structured around uniquely New Mexican calendar art which includes petroglyphs, painting reproductions, portraits, missions, etc.; informative historical sidebars; 15 facsimile autographs from personalities out of **New Mexico's rich history;** and a **Hall of Fame** listing. Alternating at the bottom of each page is Happy 400th Anniversary New Mexico!/ *¡Feliz Cuatro Centenario Nuevo México!*

October: The State of New Mexico issues two calendars: **New Mexico Treasures** by the Office of Cultural Affairs and **Enchanting New Mexico** by *New Mexico Magazine.* **Treasures** is an engagement calendar while **Enchanting** commemorates the 75th anniversary of *New Mexico Magazine.* Neither of these tax-funded publications is dedicated to New Mexico's 1598 founding nor does either even mention New Mexico's 400th anniversary.

PUBLISHING

October 22: The Board of Directors for the **Hispanic Cultural Center** approves the creation of a publishing unit as mandated by the Hispanic Cultural Center Act of 1993. By way of commemorating New Mexico's 400th anniversary in 1998 the Board votes (with only one negative vote) to publish the general history titled *New Mexico: A Brief Multi-History* by Rubén Sálaz Márquez.

TIMELINE

November 2, 1997: The *Sunday Journal* publishes an article titled "Nonprofits Part of Secret GOP Funding" which relates how Republicans, who are investigating Democrats for using illegal campaign contributions, use nonprofit organizations to gather the millions of dollars needed to run their political campaigns. Organizations like Americans for Tax Reform, the National Right to Life Committee, Citizens for Reform, Citizens for the Republic Education Fund, Coalition for Our Children's Future, etc., are used illegally but cloaked by extreme secrecy, to attract corporate donations which are then channeled into use by the Republican party.

1998
CUARTO CENTENNIAL

February 5, 1998: The Albuquerque Journal reports that Native Americans, "*particularly those from Acoma*," are against any memorial to **Juan de Oñate,** founder and colonizer of New Mexico in 1598. Various speakers address the gathering sponsored by the **Albuquerque Arts Board:** Oñate shouldn't be honored because of the atrocities he committed against the Acomas; the Acoma war faction ruled the Pueblo and led it to destruction by ambushing a Spanish trading party then refusing to surrender before the war was fought; the Spanish colonists would never have survived if it hadn't been for Pueblo help; the memorial is being erected to commemorate the Hispanic presence in N.M., not the multicultural society we now have; the monument will not last if it glorifies Oñate; Oñate brought the colonization that led to the preservation of Pueblos and other Native Americans. If Captain John Smith or the Puritans had been the first ones in N.M. there would be no Indians as there aren't any "native villages" in Jamestown, Virginia, or Plymouth, Massachusetts...

Millie Santillanes, a well-known business woman involved in many community projects, spoke on the theme that Oñate, not a saint but neither the vile sinner as some are depicting him, led the Hispanic founding of N.M. therefore he is the logical figure on which to focus since there are financial constraints which preclude a more ambitious memorial.

SOCIETY & TELEVISION MEDIA

February: **KOB-TV** is in need of a sponsor to continue its New Mexico series "*Cavalcade of Enchantment.*" The following items have been filmed:

Acoma; Petroglyphs; Chaco Canyon; Historic Santa Fe; Navajo Code Talkers; Los Alamos; Mysteries of the Sky; Legends of the Mining; Caves; Santuario de Chimayó; Taos Artists; Ghost Town; Billy the Kid; Río Grande Valley (North; South); Zuñi Pueblo, Santa Fe Trail; Early Albuquerque; Copper Mining-, Forts of New Mexico's Frontier; Bosque del Apache; Railroads; Keepers of the Range; The Bisti; Route 66; Storytellers; Lure of the San Juan; Georgia O'Keeffe; Expresiones de La Raza-Hispanic Art; Bandelier National Monument; Río Grande Northern Pueblos; Carved in Stone; Sandía National Laboratories; A Place to Dwell; White Sands; Bats; Philmont Scout Ranch; Silver City; Behind the Scenes at the Zoo; Carlsbad Caverns; White Sands Missile Range; Turquoise Trail; Resurrection-Saving New Mexico's Historic Adobe Churches; Ghosts, Spirits, and Mysteries of New Mexico; Albuquerque Bio-Park; Zozobra; N.M. Vineyards; Albuquerque International Balloon Fiesta.

[With 1998 being Hispanic New Mexico's 400th anniversary a spokesman from KOB answers in the negative when asked if the station is planning some sort of "Cavalcade" programming with which to commemorate the state-wide celebration. KNME, the PBS station supported by viewer contributions as well as New Mexico and federal tax dollars, has no plans for anniversary programming either.]

ORGANIZATION

February 22, 1998: The group that comes to be known as the **New Mexican Hispanic Culture Preservation League** is formed when its bylaws are presented to a committee of the whole and adopted virtually as presented. **Millie Santillanes** is a driving force in the creation of NMHCPL which has as its primary goal "*to end the defamation of the Hispanic culture and history of New Mexico. NMHCPL opposes negative stereotyping, racism, prejudice and bigotry of all kinds whether overt or covert. NMHCPL will promote an appreciation of our Hispanic New Mexican heritage and culture.*" Santillanes is elected to Chair all meetings until elections for officers are held.

PROFILE

Millie Santillanes

"WITH THE CONQUERING SPIRIT OF OLD"

1910: **Francisco Urrea** from the province of Huesca in Spain arrives in N.M. because of a sheep contract n Vaughn, N.M.

1927: Francisco marries **Rosalie Durán** (of the Durán and Montoya branches of New Mexico families who were in on the 1706 founding of Alburquerque). In time the couple is involved in business, Francisco in sheep husbandry and Rosalie as a shop owner in Old Town.

September 9, 1932: **Emilia Durán Urrea (Millie Santillanes)** is born to Francisco Urrea and Rosalie Durán Urrea in Old Town, Albuquerque.

1941: Millie is struck with a severe case of scarlet fever which results in the affliction of *narcolepsy* [which affects the sleep center of the brain] which isn't properly diagnosed until she is in her 30s.

1938-1946: Millie attends San Felipe School in Old Town.

1950: Millie graduates from St. Mary's High School.

December, 1950: Millie marries **Vidal Santillanes** who works in the family plastering contractor business.

1951-1966: Eight children are born to Vidal and Millie: **Abe, James, Valerie, Eugene, Francine, Renee, Dominic, Marina.**

1956: The Santillanes family relocates to Midland, Texas, for economic reasons. They encounter entrenched discrimination against Hispanics in housing, church, and school. When Millie is ready to give birth (to Valerie) she is refused a bed in the hospital so Valerie is born in a bed placed in a hallway at Midland Memorial Hospital.

1957: The Santillanes return to Albuquerque but now, because of her experiences in Texas,

Millie recognizes the subtle discrimination that exists in her own town and State.

1964: Millie opens her first Old Town shop, **Candies Unlimited,** with $800 borrowed from her life insurance policy. She is fascinated by the business career of **Conrad Hilton,** who becomes one of her favorite role models.

1970: Millie opens her **Potpourri** shop in Old Town, the first complete gourmet cookware shop in Albuquerque.

1972: Millie opens **Wickery and Cookery** at Winrock Center.

Millie Santillanes

[Over the years Millie becomes involved in politics in order to improve the business climate in Old Town. She lobbies the City Council for public parking lots, the purchase of land for the Albuquerque Museum, placement of the Natural History Museum in Old Town, promotes the creation of honors programs at Albuquerque High School, etc. Through the years she receives more than 30 awards, certificates of appreciation and/or recognition plaques, etc.]

1982: Millie serves as the first president of the **Hispano Chamber of Commerce.** An article in the *New Mexico Business Journal* refers to her affectionately as "La Jefa."

She attends the University of Albuquerque.

1983: Millie is the first woman to serve on the board of the **National Hispanic Chamber of Commerce.** (Over the years she serves on dozens of bureaus, chambers, boards, etc.)

1985: Millie runs for the office of Mayor in an effort to effect needed reforms. She isn't successful but the experience provides her with many insights into the political process.

1985-1989: Millie is an Administrative Assistant to Mayor Ken Schultz.

1987: Millie studies at the University of Phoenix.

1989: Millie is a founding member and first president of the **Hispanic Women's Council.**

1992 - 1994: Millie is a freelance writer and Junior Stringer for the *Albuquerque Journal.*

1993-1994: Millie works as a real estate agent.

1994-1997: Mayor Martín Chávez appoints Millie to the post of Albuquerque City Clerk. He also appoints her Director of the Cuarto Centenario Project intended to celebrate the founding of Hispanic New Mexico and the four centuries of Hispanic presence in the State.

1998: Millie and Vidal continue their commitment to community affairs, now focusing on Cuarto Centenario projects, Millie as spokesperson and Vidal as "spear carrier." When asked about the greatest influences in her life she declares that her mother Rosalie continues to be her greatest inspiration because of her faith in God and belief that one must use God-given talents for the benefit of community. She considers Conrad Hilton to be her business role model and the writings of Dr. Wayne Dyer have helped her cope with the demands of community involvement as well as her responsibilities as human being, woman, wife, and mother.

SOCIETY

March 25, 1998: Steve Schiff (1947-1998), the popular and highly regarded five-term Congressional Representative from District 1, dies of cancer. President Bill Clinton is among those who feel that New Mexicans *"have lost an effective legislator and an honorable public servant."*

PUEBLO POPULATION

The Pueblo people of New Mexico number around 35,000.

MUSEUM

April 28, 1998: Project Preview ceremonies are held at the site of the **Hispanic Cultural Center** in Albuquerque. Local, State, Federal, and European dignitaries are in attendance.

DIPLOMATIC CORPS

Ed Romero is nominated by President Clinton as **Ambassador to Spain**. (The Senate later confirms the nomination.)

TIMELINE

July, 1998: *Ventana* Magazine publishes a short article concerning a **Fordham Foundation** study that evaluated school systems throughout the nation. The study focused on public laws which guide school districts as well as State policy clarity.

New Mexico was adjudged a "B" in Math, an "F" in Science, an "F" in Geography (scoring 41 out of a possible 90 points), **an "F" in History (scoring 2 [two] out of possible 60 points).** According to the Fordham Expert Advisory Committee *"...most States don't have good history standards ... barely a third of the States received grades of C or better."*

GLOSSARY

acequia - irrigation ditch
alcabala - sales tax
alabado - prayer or hymn associated with the Penitente Brotherhood
Alcalde Mayor - chief magistrate with judicial and executive powers
alcaldía - district of the alcalde mayor
arriero - muleteer; transporter who used mules to move freight
Audiencia - high court of appeals
ayuntamiento - municipal council

Black Legend - stereotypical villainies attributed to Spanish/Hispanic people (see White Legend)
BLR - Bandelier-Lummis-Read
borreguero(s) - shepherd(s)
bulto - statue carved from wood

cabildo - town council; meeting hall
cacique(s) - leader(s)
Camino Real – King's Highway, Royal Road
capilla - chapel
carreta - cart
Cibolero - Hispanic buffalo hunter who generally used a lance
ciudad - city
Comanchero - Hispanic or Pueblo businessman who traded with Plains Indians
Cortes - Senate and Congress of Deputies in Spain
corrido - ballad that tells a story
curandera (-o) - healer who utilizes herbs
Cuaresma - Lent
Custos - Custodian (head of the Church in a certain area)
charquí (tasajo) - jerky, *carne seca*

doctrinario - an Indian boy who is educated by missionaries to help spread Christian doctrine
dicho - saying; proverb

encomienda - a formal grant of Indians entrusted to a certain Spaniard
escopeta - flintlock musket
escultor - sculptor

fandango - a type of dance; the event of gathering for dancing
fanega - a dry measure consisting of 1.5 to 2.5 bushels
farolitos - brown bags with sand in which lighted candles are set (popularly referred to as *luminarias* in
        much of N.M.) during the Christmas holidays
fawner - someone in a targeted group who tries to "curry favor" from a dominant or "in-group"

genízaro - an Indian, usually from the plains, raised by or living among Hispanics

hacienda - an estate or large ranch
hoaxistory - misinformation presented as historical fact
horno - outdoor baking oven
hypistory - scripted writing, often characterized by "heroes vs. villains," presented as "history'
hypoics - heroics created for effect; more "hype" than real

igug - person who utilizes ignorance and ugly morality
indio(s) - Indian(s)
Inscription Rock - El Morro National Monument

jefe - boss

KGD - Kendall-Gregg-Davis (part of the White Legend cycle of writing)
kiva - Indian ceremonial chamber

ladino - an educated Native American who can read and write Spanish
luminarias - bonfires; the name has been popularly applied to brown bags with sand in which lighted
        candles are set (which were referred to as farolitos in Hispanic N.M.)
llanero - plainsman
llano estacado - a plain with escarpments that from a distance could appear to be stockades (often mistrans-
        lated as "staked plains")

maestro - master
matanza - to slaughter a pig or cow, usually in a group of friends and neighbors
mayordomo - supervisor
mesteñero - wild horse (mustang) cowboy
mesteño – mustang
Mt. Olympus history – to write history with the benefit of hindsight and maintain that the people of the past
        "*should have known*" that a situation would turn out the way it did

nicho - a hollow or shelf in a wall in which to locate a statue
Norte Americanos - North Americans
novio - betrothed; boyfriend
novia - betrothed; girlfriend

partera - midwife
pastor(es) - shepherd(s)
patrón - large land owner; patron; boss
peón - (literally: foot soldier) worker; yeoman
peonada - tradition of mutual work assistance
presidio - fort; garrison of soldiers

punche - homegrown tobacco

ranchería - encampment (usually designating an Indian camp)

rancho - ranch

reredo - altar screen

residencia - official investigation of a former official's administration

retablo - painting on a wood panel

rico(s) - rich person (people)

Río Abajo - down river; area south of La Bajada

Río Arriba - up river; area north of La Bajada

santero - saint maker

scriptography (see also White Legend) - writing designed to promote certain ends; it is characterized by *hoaxistory* (misinformation/disinformation), *hypistory* (promotion), *hypoics* (larger-than-life heroics), *selectistory* (pick and choose what you want readers to know and ignore everything else, even if documented), *spinistory* (to channel people's thinking).

Semana Santa - Holy Week

[sic] - shows that a quoted passage, especially one containing some error or something questionable, is precisely reproduced

simpático - likeable, winsome

spinistory - to endow an historical event or personality with a designed portrayal or "spin"

Teniente Alcalde - subordinate or assistant of the Alcalde Mayor

teguas - hard-soled moccasins

trovador - poet who could rhyme

troubador - minstrel

Vaquero Apache - plains Apache

vecino - colonist (settler, neighbor)

visitas - missions

White Legend - "hype" promoted as history; "heroic good guys and villainous bad guys" scriptography with the usual groups in each category

ANNOTATED BIBLIOGRAPHY

The following is a limited but generally available bibliography for the interested reader to study further (but shouldn't be confused with the *Recommended Books and Authors of New Mexico* listed with the *Hall of Fame* section):

Allport, Gordon W. *The Nature of Prejudice.* Reading, Massachusetts: Addison-Wesley Publishing Company, 1979.
This classic study of the sickness of prejudice is indispensable and has been used widely in college-level courses. Allport discusses practices that are almost startling: "official morality" is what is espoused in the Declaration of Independence but day-to-day reality includes the psychology that motivated the Dred Scott Decision; to meet a *Jewess* or a *Negress* (a condescending label that works to deprive an individual of basic human worth because some other factor is being emphasized) in literature isn't rare but when was the last time we met a *Protestantess?* Allport doesn't discuss the term *Anglo,* the linchpin for racism in New Mexico, but he does describe the forming of "in-groups/out-groups" represented by the label because, while Hispanics are the largest ethnic group in the State, the many other ethnic/racial groups "club together" to call themselves *Anglos* in order to become the "majority" in-group. Ethnocentric history, which I refer to as "scriptography" or the "White Legend" because it is generally underscored by exaggerated larger-than-life achievement, morality, heroics, etc., of someone who represents a favored "in-group," is a product of "official morality." Allport doesn't provide a label for someone in a targeted group who tries to "curry favor" from a dominant or "in-group" ("Uncle Tom" to some African-Americans) but perhaps *fawner* will do.

Alperovitz, Gar. *The Decision to Use the Atomic Bomb and the Architecture of an American Myth.* New York: Alfred A. Knopf, 1995.
This most disturbing volume documents that Japan was ready to surrender, that the atomic bomb was unnecessary, that censorship played an enormous role to conceal the heinous brutality from the American people after two bombs were used on Japanese civilian, not military, populations.

Anaya, Rudolfo A., Ortiz, Simon J. (eds.). *Ceremony of Brotherhood.* Albuquerque: Academia, 1981.
This anthology was compiled in observance of the anniversary of the 1680 Pueblo Revolt. Its weakness is implying this revolt against European people was the first of its kind, thereby ignoring the earlier revolts against the English on the eastern seaboard. Its pages do celebrate the blend of cultures in N.M. but the English extermination of Indians is ignored while "harsh" Spanish rule is emphasized despite the historical fact of Amerind survival under Hispanic sovereignty. Anaya, part of "Generation C," can be credited with helping many writers to get published with works like this. His first novel, the classic *Bless Me, Ultima,* had to go out of N.M. to find a publisher.

Andrist, Ralph K. *The Long Death--The Last Days of the Plains Indians.* New York: Macmillan Company, 1964.
Andrist documents how the USA brutally destroyed Indians of the plains. He exposes the atrocities of leaders like General Custer and Reverend Chivington to the point that one understands that only in an Orwellian society replete with "Doublethink" can these types be hailed as heroes. We can also begin to clarify why the Spanish in North America are made out to be "cruel villains" where Indians are concerned: after initial atrocities, Hispanics preserved Indians living under Spanish rule, as in N.M., while no original aboriginal settlement exists east of the Mississippi due to English and USA extermination/removal policy.

Arias, Bishop David. *Spanish Roots of America.* Huntington, Indiana: Our Sunday Visitor, Inc., 1992.
This work approaches Hispanic history in a positive way and is thus open to charges of apologist for the more popular "Black Legend" of "cruelty, greed, fanaticism," attributed to Spanish/Hispanic people. Serious students should be knowledgeable in both camps so Arias is worth reading.

Bancroft, H.H. *History of New Mexico and Arizona.* Albuquerque: Horn and Wallace, 1963.
Bancroft is often but not always a reliable English-language source for history of the Southwest. He isn't as culturally biased as some historiographers who are more aptly described as scriptographers because they promote "official morality" instead of documented scholarship. It takes courage to tell the truth and scriptographers posing as historians prefer the primrose path.

Bandelier A. *The Delight Makers.*
This is a fictional account of Precontact people who, as the story emerges, are human beings who functioned in their society just like everybody else. Bandelier, from Switzerland, doesn't promote the cultural bias that is so popular in some quarters.

Bannon, John Francis. *Herbert Eugene Bolton: The Historian and the Man, 1870-1953.* Tucson: University of Arizona Press, 1978.
_____. (ed.) *Bolton and the Spanish Borderlands.* Norman: University of Oklahoma Press, 1964.
These excellent volumes tell us about the man, the archivist, the teacher, the student of the Spanish borderlands and its personalities, the scholar who stands with the greatest of American historians. Perhaps, from a native Southwestern point of view, he stands alone for writings like "The Epic of Greater America" in Borderlands which heightens appreciation of a more complete understanding of the human experience in the Western Hemisphere.

Baxter, John O. *Las Carneradas.* University of New Mexico Press, 1987.
Sheep were the cash crop of Hispanic New Mexico and *Carneradas* is perhaps the best study of sheep husbandry. Much needs to be done in uncovering more information on New Mexico's many sheep kings and this basic New Mexican industry..

Beck, Warren A. *New Mexico: A History of Four Centuries.* Norman: University of Oklahoma Press, 1961.
This work, in its seventh printing when I bought it, libels many aspects of Hispanic New Mexico and is often an example of scriptography. It makes observations like: Hispanics vote three or four times in every election, N.M. is in the U.S. but not of the U.S., etc., Spaniards like Vargas were more foolhardy than brave, etc. It is a wonder how such a work ever got published or how the author and/or the publisher haven't been slapped with a class action libel suit.

Becker, Thomas M. (ed., et al.). *Racial and Ethnic Patterns of Mortality in New Mexico.* Albuquerque: University of New Mexico Press, 1993.
Anyone targeted as a "minority" in N.M. will be very disturbed when s/he sees documentation on who suffers the most from various diseases and untimely death. The work is also a bit unique in that it doesn't use "Anglo" to group ethnic groups that aren't Amerind or Hispanic. (Use of Anglo is the linchpin of racism in the Land of Enchantment, encouraging ethnic/racial groups from the rest of the world to be the "Anglo majority" and make Hispanics, the largest ethnic group in the State, a "minority.")

Bertlitz, Charles, and Moore, William L. *The Roswell Incident.* New York: Berkley Books, 1988.
This is an interesting "documented" account of the nation's most famous UFO incident that officially "never happened."

Bolton, H.E. *Coronado: Knight of Pueblos and Plains.* Albuquerque: University of New Mexico Press, 1949.
Bolton approaches his subjects with marvelous documentation and an open mind that is quite unique among English-language historiographers. Because he isn't biased against Hispanics he has been criticized for not promoting the Black Legend but to my knowledge no one has ever refuted his documentation. He seems to have genuine respect for subjects like Coronado, Kino, Anza, etc. The students he trained in historiography have often followed in the master's footsteps. The Bolton school is generally the opposite of the KGD cycle of Hispanophobic English-language writers. It is possible that more than 90% of English-language writers are Hispanophobes who lace their work with popularly accepted cultural bias.

Boorstin, D.J. and Kelley, B.M. *A History of the United States.* Lexington, Mass.: Ginn and Co., 1986.
It is difficult to encounter a public school textbook that doesn't promote official morality because it won't get published if the truth is told. So we have nonsensical hypistory that promotes Orwellianisms like *Spanish women didn't come to the New World with their men* thereby pandering to prejudices like the idea that Hispanics are "inferior halfbreeds" with no rights anyone has to respect as per the Dred Scott Decision.

Boyle, Susan Calafate. Los *Capitalistas: New Mexican Merchants and the Santa Fe Trade.* Albuquerque: University of New Mexico Press, 1997.
Before this introductory work was published many people had the impression the Santa Fe traders were mostly from the States. Calafate Boyle shows that Hispanics controlled more than half of the trade because of their numbers and abilities. Much needs to be brought out on this subject.

Briggs, Charles L. *The Wood Carvers of Córdova, New Mexico.* Knoxville: University of Tennessee Press, 1980 (UNM, 1989).
Sculpting in wood is one of the talents of some New Mexicans and Córdova was and is the center of the art. Other cultural and historical items come forth at the same time.

Briggs, Charles L. and **Van Ness, John R.** (eds.). *Land, Water, and Culture: New Perspectives on Hispanic Land Grants.* Albuquerque: University of New Mexico Press, 1987.
Not very many writers have had the intestinal fortitude to bring forth documented studies on the land. These authors have the abilities to expose land grant history and put it in a true light.

Bryan, Howard. *Wildest of the Wild West.* Santa Fe: Clear Light Publishers, 1991.
_____. *Incredible Elfego Baca.* Santa Fe: Clear Light Publishers, 1993.
Former newspaper man Howard Bryan has been one of New Mexico's treasures and as a writer he is quite dependable to going where the documentation leads him. For example, he is one of the few to describe how New Mexicans who fought against the U.S. invasion in 1846 were hung for *treason* against the U.S. Such revelation smacks of "treason" in the minds of scriptographers.

Bunting, Bainbridge. *Of Earth and Timbers Made.* Albuquerque: University of New Mexico Press, 1974.

Buntings work isn't in the Orwellian genre and worth studying. New Mexican architecture was universally criticized by English-language observers but then it became "fashionable" with certain of their cultural descendants to the point that one author now claims the "Santa Fe Style" of architecture was really created by "Anglos."

Campa, Arthur L. *Hispanic Culture in the Southwest.* Norman: University of Oklahoma Press, 1979.
Campa is one of the icons of Southwestern historiography. As a member of "Generation B" he was in the crucible of acculturation pressures but he produced writings that are valid to this day. He also has the courage to refuse to get on bandwagons; for example he believes the term *Chicano* is political, not ethnic, that Chicanos lauding their "Indian" past would have been targeted by raiders during New Mexico's frontier era right along with those who used the term "Hispano."

Cather, Willa. *Death Comes for the Archbishop.* New York: Vintage Books, 1971.
This is said to be the most widely read book in the history of New Mexican publishing. It slanders Hispanic New Mexicans like Father Martínez, Manuel Antonio Chaves, etc., as well as its women who are portrayed as believing that *Marriage to an American was coming up in the world.* A fictional pair of French priests, thought to be patterned after Lamy and Machebeuf, are portrayed as moral champions who are there to lead the *immoral and ignorant New Mexicans out of their miseries now that a progressive country dominates New Mexico.* Manuel Antonio Chaves is portrayed as anti-American and despoiler of the Indians while heroic Kit Carson, *of whom Chaves is totally jealous,* leads the destruction of the Navajo Nation only because he has been duped. People like Mary Austin didn't like the book and it's a wonder that Cather's estate hasn't been sued for all its worth. From the native New Mexican point of view this Orwellian work doesn't deserve anything but negative plaudits.

Cave, Dorothy. *Beyond Courage: One Regiment Against Japan, 1942-1945.*
World War II was the USA's most popular war and much has been written about it. This work is worth studying because of the many New Mexicans who served their country as Americans.

Chávez, Fray Angélico. *But Time And Chance: The Story of Padre Martínez of Taos, 1793-1867.* Santa Fe: The Sunstone Press, 1981.
_____. *Origins of New Mexico Families.* Santa Fe: William Gannon, 1954.
_____. *My Penitente Land.* Museum of New Mexico Press, 1974.
_____. *Très Macho--He Said.* Santa Fe: William Gannon, 1985.
Fray Angélico is New Mexico's distinguished man of letters, certainly one of the most talented writers in our history. As a part of "Generation B" he had to achieve publication of the classic *New Mexico Families* through pre-publication subscriptions which goes far to document that Hispanic writers aren't sought out by tax supported State presses like UNM Press and the Museum of N.M. Press (to my knowledge there has never been an Hispanic director of a State-funded press) until one is a super-star who can't be ignored as in the case of Rudy Anaya. Generation B was pressured with subtle pitfalls like "If they were all like you there wouldn't be any problem" and I don't know that Chávez was ever able to help his fellows get published. (Being "published" is crucial because it is a form of "self determination.") His *Penitente Land* is perhaps the best work ever written on N.M. but it is beyond the scope of most general readers. One can only wish Angélico had written a documented or popular history of the N.M. he loved so much. But he did leave a most impressive body of work

that will survive and he appears to have recognized the plight of Hispanics in *Très Macho*.

Chávez, Dan D. *Soledad Chávez Chacón, A New Mexico Political Pioneer, 1890-1936.*
This monograph explodes the myth that Hispanic women were kept at home, "chained" to cooking and child bearing. While New Mexico was undeniably dominated by males it must be observed that, unlike their sisters east of the Mississippi, Hispanic women could own land within the law and Soledad proves that women were also involved in politics.

Commager, Henry Steele (ed.). *Documents of American History.* New York: Appleton-Century-Crofts, Inc. 1958.
This popular volume is a wealth of information that reflects the true history of the USA.

Coulter, Lane, and Dixon, Maurice. *New Mexican Tinwork, 1840-1940.* Albuquerque: University of New Mexico Press.
Like sculpting in wood, tinwork became one of New Mexico's distinguishing arts. It became more widespread after the American takeover of the Southwest because tin became more readily available.

Crow, John A. *The Epic of Latin America.* Garden City, New York: Doubleday & Company, Inc., 1946.
 This standard classic is still a treasure house of information on Latin America.

Cummins, Light Townsend. *Spanish Observers and the American Revolution, 1775-1783.* Baton Rouge, Louisiana State University Press, 1991.
This book is a good introduction to the role of Spain in achieving American independence. After the use of "Observers" in the title is explained, Cummins shows that Spain, its money, diplomats, and soldiers were an integral factor of George Washington's final victory at Yorktown.

Cutter, Charles R. *The Protector de Indios in Colonial New Mexico, 1659-1821.* University of New Mexico Press, 1986.
This marvelous short item documents how Native American groups, especially the Pueblos, were protected through the Hispanic legal system. And it proves the Pueblos were excellent students in learning how to protect themselves.

Davis, W.W.H. *El Gringo, or New Mexico and her People.* Santa Fe: Rydal Press, 1938.
Davis, the first U.S. Attorney, disappeared from New Mexico after he was charged with embezzlement. However his "Black Legend/White Legend" book is read to this day despite the fact that it says more about Davis and American racism than New Mexico. The embezzlement charges have more validity than many of his impressions, most of them based on his own omniscient ignorance, of Hispanic New Mexicans.

DeBuys, William. *Enchantment and Exploitation: The Life and Hard Times of a New Mexico Mountain Range.* Albuquerque: University of New Mexico Press, 1985.
This work is a bit unique in that the author speaks well of the Forest Service in northern New Mexico. And he doesn't believe returning the land to its rightful owners is feasible, though his presentation of the Las Trampas land grant swindle appears to be historically accurate. The historical overview is written as if from Mt. Olympus

and other items seem like essays.

DeMark, Judith Boyce (ed.). *Essays in 20th Century New Mexico History*. Albuquerque: University of New Mexico Press, 1994.
These informative essays have to do with a variety of items like family farm life, groundwater, mining, military impact, labor, tourism, etc.

Dickey, Roland F. *New Mexico Village Arts*. Albuquerque: University of New Mexico Press, 1990.
Dickey reviews the arts but he also feels the need to throw in hypistory like the misinformation that New Mexicans became citizens of the USA because General Kearny so decreed. The work is seriously weakened because of such forays though it was published by the scholarly UNM Press, of which Dickey was once Editor.

Dobie, J. Frank. *The Mustangs*. Boston: Little, Brown and Co., 1952.
_____. *Coronado's Children*. New York: Grosset & Dunlap, 1930.
_____. *The Longhorns*. New York: Bramhall House, 1941.
Much information on Hispanic plainsmen (llaneros) can be gleaned from the inimitable Dobie, especially in the *Mustangs* volume, certainly one of his best efforts. It must also be pointed out that Dobie is a product of his era, attested to by the title of one of his mining tales, "The Lost Nigger Mine," in *Coronado's Children*. He also writes that Comanches distinguishing "Texans" from other "whites" is something to be proud of. Perhaps he is confident that no one will learn the "distinction" is based on Texan treachery at the Council House Massacre of 1840 when the Texans gunned down their Comanche guests who had been invited to come in and talk peace. Dobie's pride might be an example of Orwellian "Ignorance is Strength."

Drumm, Stella M. (ed.). *Down the Santa Fe Trail and into Mexico: The Diary of Susan Shelby Magoffin, 1846-1847*.
Magoffin's impressions of N.M. and its people are interesting reading because young Susan isn't plagued by as much igug mentality which characterizes so many of her countrymen during the era of world-conquering Manifest Destiny.

Ebright, Malcolm. *Land Grants and Lawsuits in Northern New Mexico*. Albuquerque: University of New Mexico Press, 1994.
_____. *The Tierra Amarilla Grant: A History of Chicanery*. Santa Fe: Center for Land Grant Studies, 1980.
_____. *Spanish and Mexican Land Grants and the Law*. Journal of the West, 1989.
If one is interested in the history of land ownership in N.M. there is no one more crucial than Ebright. My grandparents and their generation, individuals coming of age around 1900 and whom I refer to as "Generation A," knew they had been swindled out of their lands but they couldn't prove it. Ebright's documentation does. His *Land Grants and Lawsuits* is a classic, certainly one of the best books ever done on N.M.

Encinias, Miguel; Rodríguez, Alfred; and Sánchez, Joseph P. (trans. and eds.). *Historia de la Nueva México by Gaspar Pérez de Villagrá*. Albuquerque: University of New Mexico, 1992.
This annotated, bilingual edition is certainly the best rendition of Villagrá's epic founding chronicle of N.M. and the first historical account of the entire USA. Villagrá's unique (the only one of its kind in world history) epic is all but unknown, reflective of New Mexico's Hispanic history.

Espinosa, Gilberto and Chávez, Tibo. *El Río Abajo.* Portales: Bishop Publishing Co. (No date.)
This popular history provides many interesting stories that need to be investigated further because they could be very important with additional documentation.

Espinosa, J. Manuel. *The Pueblo Indian Revolt of 1696 and the Franciscan Missions in New Mexico.* Norman: University of Oklahoma Press, 1988.
This volume is well documented and provides much information for that period in our history. While it wasn't their intent, the missionaries' correspondence demonstrates their heroic stature. Due to cultural bias, these knights of Christendom aren't often portrayed as the heroes that many of them actually were.

Etulain, Richard E. (ed.). *Contemporary New Mexico.* University of New Mexico Press, 1994.
Writing contemporary history has many pitfalls but these essays on politics, economics, ethnicity, and culture are informative and not intended to be the last word on any issue.

Faulk, Odie B. *Arizona: A Short History.* Norman: University of Oklahoma Press, 1970.
Official morality is the key to understanding this work.

Florian, Sister M. O.S.E. *The Inexplicable Stairs.*
The "miraculous stairway" is one of New Mexico's most enduring tourist attractions. This monograph provides a very basic introduction to the stairs.

Forrest, Suzanne. *The Preservation of the Village.* Albuquerque: University of New Mexico Press, 1989.
This is an excellent study of Hispanic N.M. and the New Deal but it also perpetuates the racism that people who aren't Indian or Hispanic are "Anglo," i.e., one ethnic or racial group, thus projecting the majority/minority fallacy. The use of "Anglo" is the linchpin for racism in N.M.

Frank, Larry. *New Kingdom of the Saints: Religious Art of New Mexico, 1780-1907.* Santa Fe: Red Crane Books, 1992.
This is one of the best, if not *the* best item on the religious art of N.M. An introductory note on the dust jacket refers to New Mexico's Spanish pioneers as "immigrants" (as if somehow the "real" settlers were yet to arrive?) but the book itself is a beautiful, informative creation that is indispensable to anyone serious about *santero* art and the religiosity it symbolizes.

Frazer, Robert W (ed.). *New Mexico in 1850: A Military View. Col. George Archibald McCall.* Norman: University of Oklahoma Press, 1968.
McCall's reports to the Secretary of War (now called the Secretary of Defense) are dry but they present an unvarnished picture of the ineffective military in N.M. Frazer's introduction and general guiding hand is excellent.

Friedenberg, Daniel M. *Life, Liberty, and the Pursuit of Land: The Plunder of Early America.* Buffalo, New York: Prometheus Books, 1992.
This is an excellent introduction to the nature of American land greed, fraud, and swindles later perpetrated on New Mexicans. Friedenberg writes that fraud, treachery, and deceit rule supreme when it comes to American land history.

Fulton, Maurice G. *History of the Lincoln County War.* Tucson: University of Arizona Press, 1968.
The violence of the Lincoln County War has always attracted interest because of personalities like Billy the Kid. Fulton's narrative includes information on the Hispanic personalities who took part in the conflict whereas most writers have a predilection for ignoring them. This episode in New Mexican history still needs to be done from the Hispanic point of view.

Gallegos, Bernardo P. *Literacy, Education, and Society in New Mexico, 1692-1821.* Albuquerque: University of New Mexico Press, 1992.
This short volume dispels the hoax history that Hispanic New Mexico relied basically on oral skills instead of the written word. Not only were the missionaries highly literate, the study shows many people owned books and read various magazines when available in a basically frontier society. Many Indian youngsters, called *doctrinarios* and trained by missionaries, were also literate in the Spanish language.

García, Nasario. *Recuerdos de los Viejitos: Tales of the Río Puerco.* Albuquerque: University of New Mexico Press, 1987.
This collection of stories and reminiscences from people who lived in western N.M. rings true because they have the grass roots flavor of oral history. The Río Puerco area was once described as the garden spot of N.M. and most of its history and culture has yet to be told.

Garrard, Lewis H. *Wah-To-Yah and the Taos Trail.* Norman: University of Oklahoma Press, 1955.
Young Garrard, perhaps 17 years of age, is generally considered a primary source for the era when the U.S. took N.M. and the Southwest from Mexico. He is a reflection of his society but he doesn't deny he is swept up in the evils of aggressive warfare.

Gates, Zethyl. *Mariano Medina, Colorado Mountain Man.* Boulder: Johnson Publishing Co., 1981.
This work emphasizes the fact that little has been done on mountain men who are not considered "Anglo." Racism has perverted historiography into scriptography so the popular mind hasn't been exposed to accomplished individuals like Mariano Medina.

Gavin, Robin Farwell. *Traditional Arts of Spanish New Mexico.* Santa Fe: Museum of New Mexico Press, 1994.
This is a beautiful but short item. New Mexican arts and crafts have received much attention while items like the Santa Fe Ring and the Court of Private Land Claims swindles are ignored.

Gibson, Arrell Morgan. *The Santa Fe and Taos Colonies: Age of the Muses, 1900-1942.* Norman: University of Oklahoma Press, 1983.
This is an excellent work to learn about all the artists who came into N.M. to enhance their artistic abilities. It all but ignores the native people of the State so the work must be described as ethnocentric but it is loaded with information on the newcomers.
_____. *The Life and Death of Col. Albert Jennings Fountain.* University of Oklahoma Press, 1965.
Fountain was a real hero who stood up to the entrenched villainy of New Mexico's Territorial period. The era should be researched and studied but most writers steer clear of the Santa Fe Ring and its manipulation of American democracy.

Gonzáles-Berry, Erlinda (ed.). *Pasó por Aquí: Critical Essays on the New Mexican Literary Tradition, 1542-1988*. Albuquerque: University of New Mexico Press, 1989.
These scholarly, magnificent essays are of utmost interest. Their only weakness is that they are written for academics, not the masses of readers, so circulation is hindered. They need to be published in popular culture magazines so that more people can be aware of New Mexico's rich history and culture.

Gonzáles, Edward & Witt, David L. *Spirit Ascendant: The Art and Life of Patrociño Barela*. Santa Fe: Red Crane Books, 1996.
This book is a work of art in and of itself. The contents, replete with marvelous color photos and a very realistic text, are also exceptional. For example, Ernest Blumenschein, Laurie Kalb, Mabel Dodge Luhan, etc., are unmasked. I am surprised that Vernon Hunter is portrayed with such a light hand. It is also disappointing that America's greatest wood sculptor is portrayed through his "pidgin English." Spanish, not English, was his native language. But the authors do appear to consider Barela, one of America's greatest sculptors and perhaps the greatest wood sculptor, as representative of the burdensome plight of Hispanics in the USA.

Gonzáles, Phillip B. "Spanish Heritage and Ethnic Protest in New Mexico: The Anti-Fraternity Bill of 1933." New Mexico Historical Review: October, 1986.
This article exposes the racism and discrimination that has been part and parcel of the University of New Mexico's history. While such behavior is strictly prohibited by the State constitution, UNM has been able to flaunt the law with astounding success. Dr. Gonzáles is among the younger generation of highly prepared and respected scholars.

Gregg, Josiah. *Commerce of the Prairies.* (Edited by M.L. Moorhead.) Norman: University of Oklahoma Press, 1954.
This "White Legend" work is usually referred to as the "classic" account of the Santa Fe Trail and Trade. While full of detailed information that all investigators relish it must be pointed out that even the generally reserved Fray Angélico Chávez considered Gregg a racist bigot. I feel Gregg is generally unreliable when discussing the Hispanic and/or Indian people of N.M.

Griswold del Castillo, Richard. *The Treaty of Guadalupe Hidalgo: A Legacy of Conflict*. Norman: University of Oklahoma Press, 1990.
The treaty that took almost half the country of Mexico and made it "American" is studied and analyzed. The plight of Hispanics who remained in the conquered lands is also touched upon. The work is an excellent beginning to a situation that most authors studiously avoid.

Gutiérrez, Ramón A. *When Jesús Came, the Corn Mothers Went Away.* Stanford: Stanford University Press, 1991.
This controversial work is as powerful as it is vicious. For example, the paladin missionaries are referred to as "fools for Christ" because they often suffered martyrdom. Kendall, Gregg, and Davis have nothing on Gutiérrez.

Hackett, C.W. *Revolt of the Pueblo Indians of New Mexico and Otermín's Attempted Reconquest, 1680-1682*, (two vols.) Albuquerque: University of New Mexico Press, 1942.
These volumes are acknowledged to be the most complete study of the Pueblo Revolt but unfortunately they are accessible only in Special Collections of certain libraries.

Hammond, G.P and Rey, A. *Don Juan de Oñate, Colonizer of New Mexico, 1595-1628.* Albuquerque: University of New Mexico Press, 1953. (two vols.)
This is the classic study of Oñate and the colonization of N.M. but available only in Special Collections of large libraries. The authors report the punishment for ambushing Acoma rebels was to have a foot cut off but contemporary researchers maintain it was toes and was even that sentence actually carried out? Paleography is no simple task. (A popularly accepted mistranslation is "Staked Plains" for *llano estacado* which in reality is "stockaded" or "palisaded plains.")

Hanke, Lewis. *The Spanish Struggle for Justice in the Conquest of America.* Boston: Little, Brown and Co., 1965, p. 151.
_____. *All Mankind is One: A Study of the Disputation Between Bartolomé de Las Casas and Juan Ginés de Sepúlveda in 1550 on the Intellectual and Religious Capacity of American Indians.* DeKalb, Ill.: Northern Illinois University Press, 1974.
Hanke's scholarship is magnificent and not marred by cultural bias. These items should be part of the groundwork for anyone who wishes to study Hispanic America or Hispanic N.M.

Handlin, Oscar. *Truth In History.* Cambridge, Mass.: Belknap Press of Harvard University Press, 1979.
This marvelous item is for professionals and serious students of history. There is much here with which to agree or disagree: the continent was "all but empty" when the English landed; American history is a discipline in crisis because it has slipped into "the hands of propagandists, politicians, dramatists, novelists, journalists, and social engineers;" American history is generally written within the framework of a grand mission *(progress, freedom, democracy)* and conflict between heroes and villains, etc. He mentions that Jared Sparks "took the liberty" of improving the grammar in George Washington's personal letters which is to me symptomatic of the "crisis" I refer to as *scriptography.*

Henderson, Alice Corbin. *Brothers of Light: The Penitentes of the Southwest.*
Henderson wrote about the Penitente Brotherhood with the sensitivity and understanding of the poet she was. It is doubtful anyone has penned a better portrayal.

La Herencia del Norte.
This popular quarterly provides many articles on a wide variety of topics and issues.

Hill, Gene. *Americans All/Americanos Todos.* Albuquerque: Añoranza Press, 1997.
This bilingual effort relates historical anecdotes on Hispanic contributions to America. It can be used to good advantage in the schools but wide dissemination will be a problem.

Hilton, Conrad. *Be My Guest.* New York: Simon & Schuster (Fireside Book), 1994.
Hilton's autobiography shows a man of faith, business acumen, family ties, and ultimate "American dream" success.

Hoffman, Virginia, and **Johnson, Broderick H.** *Navajo Biographies.* Rough Rock, Arizona: Dine, Inc., 1970.
Biographies are always interesting and those of Navajo leaders are not generally encountered so this is an invaluable resource for anyone interested in the various cultures of the Southwest.

Holmes, Jack E. *Politics in New Mexico.* Albuquerque: University of New Mexico Press, 1967.
Politics are a passion in N.M. and, while a bit dry, this is perhaps the best study to date. Holmes also has the courage to assert that peonage wasn't a form of slavery, quite a contrast to most writers.

Horgan, Paul. *Lamy of Santa Fe.* New York: Farrar, Straus and Giroux, 1975.
_____. *Great River: The Río Grande in North American History.* Wesleyan University Press, 1984.
_____. *The Heroic Triad.* University of New Mexico Press, 1970.
_____. *Conquistadors in North American History.* University of Texas at El Paso: Texas Western Press, 1982.
Though Horgan wasn't born in N.M. he is considered one of the State's most brilliant men of letters. His abilities are beyond question yet it appears he is ever a proponent of Manifest Destiny, evil or not. In *Triad* he writes of "Anglo-American Sons of Democracy" as if he had never heard of the USA's extermination of Indians or African-American slavery. (Use of "Anglo" in this fashion is typical of New Mexican racism; when a group sponsored a Town Hall meeting on the subject of Education a flyer listed an ethnic checkoff list with the following choices: *Anglo, Hispanic, Native American, African American, Asian American, Other...*Acknowledged "minorities" are therefore targeted while ethnicities from all over the world are the "Anglo" majority, i.e., dominant group.) He never mentions realities like the Santa Fe Ring, which was the State's introduction to "democracy." Bishop Lamy is heroicized by denigrating New Mexican Hispanics a la Willa Cather. In *Conquistadors* ("pidgin English" for *conquistadores*) he states that all Acoma men were sentenced to having a foot cut off when in reality it was toes of 24 warriors, if the sentence was actually carried out. Horgan perpetuates the Black Legend against Hispanics and the White Legend for anyone considered part of the "sons of democracy" and his society has honored him with various literary prizes. Perhaps that's what it takes? A comparative study of the lives and careers of Horgan and Angélico Chávez would be most interesting.

Jacobs, Wilbur R. *Francis Parkman, Historian as Hero: The Formative Years.* Austin: University of Texas Press, 1991.
From the title one would think this would be a laudatory work about an American icon but it might be safe to say it is almost opposite. While Parkman made history more popular he also believed Indians to be racial inferiors and he fought against women's suffrage because he harbored a deep-rooted belief they could never handle the responsibility. The book is a must for anyone interested in the basics of how American history is written by people like Parkman, Turner, Bancroft, Beard, etc.

Jenkins, Myra Ellen, and Schroeder, Albert H. *A Brief History of New Mexico.* Albuquerque: University of New Mexico Press, 1974.
This short volume is a general introduction to the history of N.M. Jenkins, the State archivist, also wrote *Guides to the Spanish and Mexican Archives of N.M.*

Johnson, Byron A. and Sharon P. *Gilded Palaces of Shame: Albuquerque's Redlight Districts.* Albuquerque: Gilded Age Press, 1983.
Fans of the KGD cycle of writers won't be pleased to learn that organized prostitution entered N.M. with the railroad, according to this short study.

Jones, O.L. *Pueblo Warriors and Spanish Conquest.* Norman: University of Oklahoma Press, 1966.
This excellent volume explores the military alliance between Hispanic and Pueblo people of N.M. It also

documents that the Pueblos were masterful warriors when the situation demanded.

Josephy, Jr. Alvin M. *500 Nations: An Illustrated History of North American Indians.* New York: Alfred A. Knopf, 1994.
Josephy is usually reliable when writing about Native Americans and this item is no exception. Further, he describes how the English enslaved the coastal Indians in such a brutal manner that it resulted in their extermination, which is why there is no Indian base in those areas today. Spanish atrocities aren't ignored but it is rare for an English-language writer to focus on how the English brutalized then exterminated the Indians and how the USA followed in their footsteps.

Kalb, Laurie Beth. *Crafting Devotions: Tradition in Contemporary New Mexico Santos.* Albuquerque: University of New Mexico Press, Gene Autry Western Heritage Museum, 1994.
This book about contemporary santeros is informative and beautiful but marred by an ethnocentric fixation on things "Anglo." It is almost as if there would be no santeros or santero art if it wasn't for "Anglo newcomers, Anglo patrons, Anglo writers, Anglo artists, Anglo scholars, Anglo museums, Anglo 'modes,' Anglo control, Anglo marketing techniques, Anglo notions, etc." It would appear that everyone who came through Ellis Island automatically becomes an "Anglo" in New Mexico. Perhaps the author and/or publisher are promoting "Ellis Island Anglos"? Someone should tell them the term is akin in usage to Hitler's "Aryan" super race, therefore more racist than ethnic.

Keleher, William A. *Turmoil in New Mexico, 1846-1868.* Santa Fe: Rydal Press, 1952.
_____. *Memoirs: 1892-1926 A New Mexico Item.* Santa Fe: Rydal Press, 1969.
_____. *The Maxwell Land Grant.* Albuquerque: University of New Mexico Press, 1942.
_____. *The Fabulous Frontier. Twelve New Mexico Items.* Albuquerque, University of New Mexico Press, 1945, 1962.
Attorney Keleher has been described as an "amateur historian" but his works are generally well done and worthy of study. He had much experience with land grants because of his law practice and he met many celebrities like Elfego Baca during his long career. His perspectives are still of interest to the general reader. Keleher's research is generally strong but it is obvious he prefers to write in a positive vein, whatever his subject.

Kenner, C.L. *A History of New Mexican-Plains Indian Relations,* Norman: University of Oklahoma Press, 1969.
This item is a must for anyone interested in *llaneros* (Hispanic plainsmen) like *ciboleros* and comancheros. It is one of the most important books ever written on N.M.

Kern, Robert (ed.). *Labor in New Mexico: Unions, Strikes, and Social History since 1881.* Albuquerque: University of New Mexico Press, 1983.
This study of labor is also an investigation of its people. It is amazing how those in power often managed to brand their enemies as "communists and troublemakers" and win the day, indicating the thought control of an Orwellian society. It is also interesting to see how ethnic groups were set against each other in order to neutralize both.

Kessell, John L. *Kiva, Cross, & Crown: The Pecos Indians and New Mexico, 1540-1840.* Tucson: Southwest Parks and Monuments Association, 1987.

_____. *Letters from the New World.* Edited by John L. Kessell, Rick Hendricks, Meredith D. Dodge. Albuquerque: University of New Mexico Press, 1992.

Dr. Kessell's contribution to New Mexico and the Southwest has been enormous. *Kiva* is a classic so can *Mission of Sorrows* or *Missions of New Mexico* or *Friars, Soldiers, and Reformers* be far behind? Kessell's documentation is always superb and his writing brings subjects to life. His work and that of his associates Hendricks and Dodge on the Vargas Project are of utmost interest and enthusiasm. *Kiva* is perhaps the best history of Spanish colonial N.M.

Klaits, Joseph. *Servants of Satan: The Age of the Witch Hunts.* Bloomington: Indiana University Press, 1985. Klaits considers the "witch craze" to be the deadliest instance of mass persecution in Western history before the 20th century. That it was directed mostly against women leads him to believe it had misogyny as a base. While the Spanish Inquisition and its Inquisitors have often been written about very little is publicized concerning the **Witch Finder General** and the witch trials. A documented historical comparison of these two institutions would be most interesting.

Kolchin, Peter. *American Slavery 1619-1877.* New York: Hill and Wang, 1993.

This documented study reveals much about the "peculiar institution" and the mentality that sought to preserve it. It is sobering to learn how pervasive and brutal it was: eight of the first 12 American Presidents were slave owners; punishments for slaves included *castration* [in New Mexico Hispanophobes make much of Oñate ordering that *puntas de pies*, toes, be cut off for punishment after the Acomas ambushed a trading party] and it was against the law to teach a black slave to read or write. Contrary to impressions in popular entertainment like the movie "Amistad," England dominated the business of trafficking in slaves with many of the leading families of England and New England getting richer because of it.

Kutz, Jack. *Grassroots New Mexico, A History of Citizen Activism.* Albuquerque: The Inter-Hemispheric Education Resource Center, 1989.

_____. *Mysteries & Miracles of New Mexico.* Corrales: Rhombus Publishing Co., 1988.

Grassroots is an account of citizen activism probably inspired by the civil rights movement and of great interest because of its perspectives. These items aren't found in standard textbooks. *Mysteries* is engaging for anyone who enjoys folklore.

Lambdin, William. *Doublespeak Dictionary.* Los Angeles: Pinnacle Books, 1979.

The entries are often humorous but one can understand much "American history" by going through this volume. It's a good companion to Lutz' *Doublespeak* below.

Larson, Carole. *Forgotten Frontier: The Story of Southeastern New Mexico.* Albuquerque: University of New Mexico Press, 1993.

Larson writes basically about the people, mostly Texans and their Southern heritage, who entered southeastern N.M. after the Civil War but especially in the 1880s. She describes these newcomers as *courageous Anglo pioneers*, giving the work its fatal flaw of ethnocentrism because, among other things, Ft. Stanton, established in 1855 and not mentioned by Larson, was already in the area for protection of the *"courageous pioneers."*

Somehow, the European Hispanic people who settled there before the 1880s aren't "the pioneers" of the area. Such is the way of scriptography.

Larson, Robert W. *New Mexico's Quest for Statehood, 1846-1912*. University of New Mexico Press, 1968. This is the classic study of how N.M. was kept in colonial status so long as Hispanics had a good opportunity to control powerful elective office such as the Governor's chair, etc., and nationally the Senate and House of Representatives. This work attests to the fact that studies could be made of the Santa Fe Ring, the Court of Private Land Claims, and colonialist attitudes that encourage the use of N.M. as the place for the country to dump its nuclear waste.

Lecompte, Janet. *Rebellion in Río Arriba, 1837*. Albuquerque: University of New Mexico Press, 1985. While this is an informative volume the author appears to have unabashed admiration for writers in the KGD (Kendall-Gregg-Davis) or White Legend cycle which I believe are mired in racism, bigotry, and ignorance. Embracing these igug perspectives weakens the overall impact of the work.

Lederer, William J. and **Burdick, Eugene.** *The Ugly American*. New York: Fawcett World Library, 1958. This work "unmasks" official morality to expose opportunism, deceit, incompetence, etc., in the diplomatic corps and in the character of so many people. It inspired the "igug" label to describe the "ignorant and ugly" personality convinced of its own superiority.

Leonard, Olen E. *The Role of the Land Grant in the Social Organization and Social Processes of a Spanish American Village in New Mexico*. Albuquerque: Calvin Horn Publisher, Inc., 1970. This work is often referred to as a gem but I found it quite ordinary, accepting biases of the day, bringing out aspects of surface culture, jumping to established conclusions. For example, when his research turns up not a single instance of intermarriage with the Indians, Leonard says, without documentation to verify his opinion, the mixture occurred in Mexico before his subjects came to N.M. This implies Leonard can't verify the situation in 1940 but he can do so for 1598.

Lister, Robert H. and Florence C. *Those Who Came Before*. Southwest Parks & Monuments Association. This is for individuals who want to begin the study of precontact civilizations in N.M. and the Southwest. The pitfall in such studies is that human beings are investigated as anthropological specimens.

Loomis, Noel M. and **Nasatir, Abraham R.** *Pedro Vial and the Roads to Santa Fe*. Norman: University of Oklahoma Press, 1967. This well-documented account of the Southwest's most accomplished trail-blazer is flawed by ethnocentricity, which one might expect from the author of *The Texan-Santa Fe Pioneers*. Despite the authors' use of sources like Gregg and Davis one can glean a wealth of information about Vial and his times so long as the reader can handle Orwellian speculation and approval of "restless," hard driving "Anglo American pioneers" who were ready to dispossess people of their land *for freedom and democracy*.

Lopopolo, Carlos. *Foundations*. Los Lunas: Cincar Publishing, 1995. Lopopolo's works, based on painstaking research, are indispensable to historians and genealogists alike. They will become classics to people attracted by culture and documented historical awareness. He isn't intimidated by tenets of popularly accepted racism and will explore wherever the documentation takes him.

Lucero, Donald L. *The Adobe Kingdom: New Mexico 1598-1958 as experienced by the families Lucero de Godoy y Baca.* Pueblo: El Escritorio, 1995.
While the general focus is on specific families there is also much valuable historical information in this popular history.

Lummis, Charles F. *A New Mexico David.*
_____. *The Land of Poco Tiempo.*
Lummis is one of the Southwest's most engaging personalities. He was genuinely impressed with the native people of New Mexico, for which he has been criticized as merely trying to promote the area. While he took prohibited pictures of Penitente rituals and such, Lummis remains a bright light in the firmament of America's grandeur and maturity. A "Lummis Reader" should be created and published.

Lutz, William. *DOUBLESPEAK.* New York: Harper Collins Publishers, 1989.
This popular work gives example after example of how language is manipulated to distort and subvert in order to sell this or that. Only the details are new if one is a student of American history. George Orwell has been alive and well long before and after *1984*.

Madariaga, Salvador de. *The Rise of the Spanish American Empire.* New York: The Free Press (Macmillan Co.), 1947.
Don Salvador, the incomparable bilingual scholar of Europe and the Americas, is read by Europeans and Americans alike because most of his works are classics. He has been described by a few critics as the "apologist" for the Black Legend and Spanish history because they have difficulty with his documentation and abilities which are phenomenal. The writings of Madariaga, professional in every sense of the word, are vital to understanding America's Hispanic people and the age-old cultural bias that affects them to this day.

Major, Mabel (et al.). *Southwest Heritage - A Literary History.* Albuquerque: University of New Mexico Press, 1948.
It would have been more accurate to name this otherwise interesting work "Anglo-American Southwest Heritage Literary History" because the authors ignore most of what hasn't been written in English or available to them in English translation. Perhaps they can't be blamed for being ignorant of what was in the archives all along but it must be pointed out that in the introduction the authors crow that where matters of language and civilization are concerned "...the dominant strain seems clearly to be Anglo-American, with its ever increasing tendency to spread its influence and to absorb its competitors." I don't know if this is condoning ignorance but no one can deny the authors are products of their era and their scholarship is skin-deep.

Mallo, Jerónimo. *España: Síntesis de su civilización.* New York: Charles Scribners Sons, 1957.
Esta obra breve resulta de los cursos creados por el Profesor Mallo durante su carrera de enseñanza. Se concierne de los temas fundamentales y predominantes de la historia y cultura española.

Marks, Paula Mitchell. *And Die in the West: The Story of the O.K. Corral Gunfight.* Norman: University of Oklahoma Press, 1989.
This is a prime example of the White Legend in action: the heinous buffalo slaughter was "hunting;" prostitution paid much better than doing laundry; violence at the base of society makes for "interesting" reading; etc.

The work is quite a contrast to the tenets of how Hispanic New Mexican history is generally written. The 15-second gunfight at the OK is often considered the most "famous" in the West but then the popular mind probably has never heard of Elfego Baca.

Meketa, Jacqueline Dorgan (ed.). *Legacy of Honor. The Life of Rafaél Chacón, A Nineteenth-Century New Mexican.* Albuquerque: University of New Mexico Press, 1986.
This good work needs better organizing. The study of biography is certainly a step in the right direction and Meketa usually has the moral courage to confront entrenched cultural bias.

Meléndez, A. Gabriel. *So All Is Not Lost: The Poetics of Print in Nuevornexicano Communities, 1834-1958.* University of New Mexico Press, 1997.
Destined to be a classic, this volume identifies and documents the Spanish-language literary tradition as exemplified in newspapers. It explodes the igug myth that Hispanics are heirs only to oral literature. Typos, which indicate editorial problems and usually not found in books released by a scholarly press, mar this fine, hard-hitting work. It is one of the best books ever written on N.M.

Mera, H.R. *Spanish-American Blanketry.* Santa Fe: School of American Research Press, 1987.
I grew up with the "Río Grande blanket" in my grandparents' abodes but I never knew it was a New Mexican creation. I'm probably typical so this work is most interesting on several planes.

Meyer, Doris. *Speaking for Themselves: Neomexicano Cultural Identity and the Spanish Language Press, 1880-1920.* Albuquerque: University of New Mexico Press, 1996.
Like the Meléndez book, this wonderful volume is destined to be a classic because it fills in aspects of New Mexican culture that nefarious forces have tried to suppress. Meyer sometimes tends to "argue" with her sources but the book should be studied by anyone interested in N.M. culture.

McKay, John P (et al.). *A History of Western Society.* Boston: Houghton Mifflin Company, 1991
This work is used as a text at the university level.

McNitt, Frank. *Navajo Wars: Military Campaigns, Slave Raids, and Reprisals.* Albuquerque: University of New Mexico Press, 1972.
This well-documented work is important because it presents information on western N.M. and the Navajo Nation. He talks about Cebolleta, uses sources like scornful Thomas James and so labels him, talks about Manuel A. Chaves, provides much information on Cebolla Antonio Sandoval, etc.

Moorhead, Max L. *New Mexico's Royal Road: Trade and Travel on the Chihuahua Trail.* Norman: University of Oklahoma Press, 1958.
_____. (ed.) *Commerce of the Prairies.* Norman: University of Oklahoma Press, 1954.
While Moorhead's works are well documented he is just too ethnocentric to accept much of what he writes. For example, the purpose of the Texan-Santa Fe Expedition of 1841 was to invite Mexicans to "share in the blessings of Texas freedom" though history shows Texas was a slave republic and inimical to "Mexicans."

Morison, Samuel Eliot. *The Oxford History of the American People.* New York: Oxford University Press, 1965.

This is a well-known history found in most libraries. When dealing with "things English," the work is suspect due to propaganda like "the energy and gallantry of the English nation" or "striking proof of English capacity for self government...." Perhaps the unreliability of much English-language historiography stems from this legacy? Because of the power of scriptography, the popular mind has it that the English came to America for *freedom* but the reality is that they came, often forced, to make money for stockholders. Many didn't want to migrate to the Americas at all and had to be kidnapped. That's the psychology loosed on the Indians.

Morris, Richard B. (ed.). *Encyclopedia of American History*. New York: Harper & Row, Publishers, 1965. This standard reference work is found in most libraries. It has an excellent chronological structure.

Morris, Roger. *The Devil's Butcher Shop: The New Mexico Prison Uprising*. New York: Franklin Watts, 1983. The hideous brutality of the USA's most violent prison uprising is emphasized in this well-documented book.

Motto, Sytha. *More Than Conquerors: Makers of History, 1528-1978*. Albuquerque: Adobe Press, 1980. Motto is the only writer of my acquaintance to reject the slanders that have long been leveled against Manuel Armijo, New Mexico's last Mexican governor before the American conquest. The book contains much interesting information that needs to be investigated professionally.

Myrick, David E. *New Mexico's Railroads: A Historical Survey*. Albuquerque: University of New Mexico Press, 1970 and 1990. The book supplies basic information on railroads in our State.

New Mexico Blue Book. The Blue Book provides a compilation of State facts.

New Mexico Historical Review. (See Vol. X, April, 1935; Vol. XII, Jan., 1937.) This publication specializes in scholarly articles.

Nostrand, R.L. *The Hispano Homeland*. Norman: University of Oklahoma Press, 1992. This should be considered a classic for anyone interested in New Mexico's Hispanic population because of the varied information it contains on so many topics. It is one of the most important books ever written on New Mexican Hispanos.

Noyes, Stanley. *Los Comanches: The Horse People, 1751-1845*. Albuquerque: University of New Mexico Press, 1993. This well-documented and informative volume supplies much history on the "Horse People" so long as the reader is aware of the author's admission that "we norte Americanos, ethnocentric as most peoples, evidently prefer history in which our forefathers played leading roles." Pedro Bautista Pino describes the Comanche as a handsome people and Noyes calls Pino a "prejudiced" observer, preferring Catlin's description of "unattractive and slovenly-looking." As is not uncommon, things Spanish are often portrayed as villainous in order to camouflage atrocities like the Texas Council House murders.

Orwell, George. *1984*. New York: Signet, 1949.
_____. *Animal Farm*. New York: Signet, 1945.

These classics about "Negative Utopia" might have been models for White Legend scriptography where "Ignorance is Strength" and "Truth is Treason."

Padilla, Genaro M. *My History, Not Yours: The Formation of Mexican American Autobiography.* Madison: University of Wisconsin Press, *1993.*
If this classic has a flaw it's that it's written for scholars, not the general reader. Dr. Padilla's work brings out much documented information like the story of Angustias de la Guerra Ord's comment: "*La toma del país no nos gustó nada a los Californios, y menos a las mujeres*" which translates **We Californios didn't at all like the taking of the country** [by the U.S.], **least of all the women.** Then Padilla points out that Francis Price and William Ellison's translation has her saying "The conquest of California didn't bother the Californians, least of all the women," exactly the opposite. The disinformation was then picked up by (among others) Dr. David Weber for his well-known *Foreigners in Their Native Land*, emphasized in a picture gallery and the section called "Angustias de la Guerra Ord, 1878." Is it any wonder such writings are referred to as scriptography? And it's as old as Capt. John Smith and his Pocahontas hoaxistory.

Pearce, T.M. (ed.). *New Mexico Place Names - A Geographical Dictionary.* Albuquerque: University of New Mexico Press, 1965.
A more recent effort isn't as well done as this standard reference.

Pino, Pedro Bautista. *The Exposition on the Province of New Mexico, 1812.* Translated and edited by Adrian Bustamante and Marc Simmons. Albuquerque: University of New Mexico Press, 1995.
Representative to the Spanish Cortes, Pino wrote a good description of the N.M. of his day. It has been a standard reference work used mostly by scholars but now available in this very readable edition.

Pletcher, David M. *The Diplomacy of Annexation: Texas, Oregon, and the Mexican War.* Columbia: University of Missouri Press, 1973.
This highly documented work is a wealth of information though some of it is couched in language designed not to offend official morality.

Powell, Philip Wayne. *Tree of Hate: Propaganda and Prejudices Affecting United States Relations with the Hispanic World.*
Dr. David Weber feels this is the best presentation of the Black Legend written in English. He also says that *The Black Legend: Anti-Spanish Attitudes in the Old World and the New* by Charles Gibson is a good collection of anti-Spanish authors and writings. The techniques used by the writers in Powell's book are those later utilized by Nazi Germany but I know of no author who has made that observation.

Quaife, M.M. (ed.). *The Diary of James K. Polk During His Presidency, 1845 to 1849* (four vols.).
Polk and his times are authentically portrayed here if you can get an edition that hasn't been scripted.

Robinson, Cecil. *With the Ears of Strangers: The Mexican in American Literature.* Tucson: University of Arizona Press, 1963.
This classic work portrays the igug mentalities who wrote about Mexico and what is now the Southwest. Robinson believes they said more about themselves than what they wrote about. Agreed.

Rogozinski, Jan. *PIRATES! Brigands, Buccaneers, and Privateers in Fact, Fiction, and Legend. An A-Z Encyclopedia.* New York: Da Capo Press, 1996.
It is indeed astonishing how many pirates came out of England and/or the British Isles. While there also appear to be an inordinately large number from the Barbary states of Africa it seems that the more successful of the British pirates (Sir Francis Drake [Caribbean, Atlantic, Pacific], Sir Henry Morgan [Caribbean], Sir John Hawkins [Atlantic, Caribbean], Sir Richard Hawkins [Atlantic, Caribbean, Pacific] etc.) were also knights of the realm.

Rudnick, Lois Palken. *Mabel Dodge Luhan: New Woman, New Worlds.* Albuquerque: University of New Mexico Press, 1984.
While Mabel always kept money coming in from her former life she turned her back on "civilization" as she knew it and wanted to establish a new order in N.M. A non-conformist in many things, D.H. Lawrence was aghast that Mabel would actually marry an Indian. It has been said that by introducing so many "famous" people to N.M. she helped to destroy what she loved most about.

Sálaz M., Rubén. *Cosmic: The La Raza Sketchbook.* Santa Fe: Blue Feather Press, 1975.
_____. *The Truth About American Education.* Albuquerque: Cosmic House, 1991.
_____. *New Mexico: A Brief Multi-History.* Albuquerque: Cosmic House, 1999.
Cosmic contains information on southwestern founding fathers and items like arrieros, ciboleros, comancheros, mesteñeros, machismo, etc. *Truth* is written from a classroom perspective. The author hopes to complete his *Multi-History* with a short volume tentatively titled *The Polemics of New Mexican History* which were edited out before publication.

Sánchez, George I. *Forgotten People: A Study of New Mexicans.* Albuquerque: Calvin Horn, 1940.
More than half a century ago Sánchez protested what is still happening today. Perhaps in those days he was guided by official morality but toward the end of his life he seemed to become a recluse, perhaps as a defensive posture.

Sando, Joe. *Pueblo Nations.* Santa Fe: Clear Light Publishers, 1992.
Sando writes from Pueblo perspectives and would be interesting for that feature alone if there weren't others, which there are. He is one of the few authors to provide biographical information for various Pueblo leaders and personalities.

Silverberg, Robert. *The Pueblo Revolt.* Lincoln and London: University of Nebraska Press, 1970 (Bison Book: 1994, Introduction by Marc Simmons).
This reprint belongs on the "Black Legend Bookshelf." It is merely another leaf on the "tree of hate" because it promotes the idea that the "conquistadores" treated the Indians *"with chilling inhumanity ... converted them to Christianity, by force if necessary, and turned them into slaves ... terror was a routine instrument of Spanish policy ... martyrdom of the Indians at the hands of Spain was one of history's darkest episodes."* Sir Jeffrey Amherst isn't mentioned and the author doesn't mention that Indians still live in their native villages in N.M. while none exist east of the Mississippi, which is perhaps why Hispanics are painted "with chilling inhumanity"? Targeting Hispanic people for villainy is alive and well in the Southwest while documented history is routinely ignored. For example, when one travels in Colorado there is no talk about Sand Creek; in San Antonio, Texas, there is no talk about the Council House murders of Comanche chieftains; in California the near

extermination of Indians by the 49ers isn't a topic for discussion; but in New Mexico the Acoma war of 1599 appears to have occurred just a few years ago and is publicized as if it was a holocaust. Because of Orwellian history, few stop to observe that if it had been a matter of extermination there would be no Acomas or any othr Pueblos living here today. (Few realize why there are so many Indians in Oklahoma: Andrew Jackson and the forces of "ethnic cleansing" sent them there.) The author also informs us that the Spanish missionaries introduced orchards of *"oranges, lemons, nectarines, pomegranates, olives, figs, dates..."* to the Pueblo people of N.M.

Simmons, Marc. *The Last Conquistador: Juan de Oñate and the Settling of the Far Southwest.* Norman: Universsity of Oklahoma Press, 1991.
_____. *Coronado's Land.* Albuquerque: University of New Mexico Press, 1991.
_____. *Spanish Government in New Mexico.* Albuquerque: University of New Mexico Press, 1968 and 1990.
_____. *Little Lion of the Southwest: A Life of Manuel Antonio Chaves.* Chicago: Swallow Press, 1973.
_____. *Ranchers, Ramblers & Renegades.* Santa Fe: Ancient City Press, 1984.
_____. *The Fighting Settlers of Seboyeta.* Cerrillos: San Marcos Press, 1971.
_____. *New Mexico.* New York: W.W. Norton & Co., 1977.
Although born a Texan, Simmons got most of his higher education in N.M. and has since become one of its best-known historians. The Oñate biography is especially crucial in understanding documented (i.e., valid) historical perspectives, especially concerning the Acoma war. Simmons' work is well researched and often enlightening though on occasion he panders to popularly held beliefs like the idea that New Mexicans have an *"inbred fear of Texans."* Perhaps this kind of hypistory is necessary Orwellian salve because New Mexicans defeated/ helped defeat the Texans in two separate invasions. Then there are personalities like Elfego Baca, Rafaél Chacón, Manuel Antonio Chaves, etc., if one is a student of documented history. But Simmons is usually reliable and all his works are worth reading/studying.

Smith, Bradley *Spain: A History In Art.* Garden City, New York: Gemini-Smith, Inc. by Doubleday & Co. (no date).
This provides popular history as well as color photographs of Spanish art through the ages. The combination proves to be excellent.

Southwestern Mission Research Center Newsletter. Arizona State Museum, University of Arizona at Tucson.

Spicer, Edward. *Cycles of Conquest: The Impact of Spain, Mexico, and the United States on the Indians of the Southwest, 1533-1960.* Tucson: University of Arizona Press, 1981.
This work is well known and often cited by other writers. The book is really a comparison of Spanish and U.S. Indian policy because Mexico held the "Southwest" for a mere 25 years. Cultural bias aside, the missionaries were heroic figures who are mainly responsible for preserving the Indians through the training ground of mission communities intended to give way to the usual Hispanic town. By contrast, the American reservation system and its dependency was intended to be permanent. But it just isn't acceptable to write that there was never much "ethnic cleansing" or there is no such thing as an "Hispanic Oklahoma."

Spielvogel, Jackson J. *Western Civilization: Volume I to 1715.* Minneapolis/St. Paul: West Publishing Company, 1997.

This book is a popular introductory history text generally used at the college level.

Steele, Thomas J. *(S.J.). Santos and Saints.* Santa Fe: Ancient City Press, 1994.
This work on santos is perhaps more intellectual than most treatments, which is good for investigators doing research.

Sunder, J.E. (Ed.). *Matt Field on the Santa Fe Trail.* Norman: University of Oklahoma Press, 1960.
The best thing about Matt Field is that he isn't part of the KGD cycle of writers who came into N.M. and denigrated virtually everything they saw. His impressions on the Trail are still interesting.

Sunseri, A. *Seeds of Discord.* Chicago: Nelson-Hall, 1979.
Sunseri writes about New Mexican conflicts that some writers refuse to acknowledge. This perspective can't be ignored if one sincerely wishes to know the State.

Szasz, Ferenc Morton. *The Day the Sun Rose Twice: The Story of the Trinity Site Nuclear Explosion,* July 16, 1945. Albuquerque: University of New Mexico Press, 1984.
The creation of the atom bomb is often considered the "greatest" achievement since the U.S. takeover of N.M. and the Southwest. J. Robert Oppenheimer himself was sobered by the "achievement" that could well destroy the world and it is ironic that so many brilliant minds came together in Los Alamos to create such destructive force. Los Alamos has been described by some unthinking writers as "America's Athenian World." The Athenians would surely have objected to threatening the destruction of mankind as an "achievement."

Taylor, Lonn, and **Bokides, Dessa** (Curators). *Carpinteros and Cabinetmakers: Furniture Making in New Mexico, 1600-1900.* Santa Fe: Museum of International Folk Art, Museum of New Mexico Press, 1983.
This is perhaps the best volume on carpentry in N.M. Its pages contain almost as much history as beautiful photographs.

Terrell, John Upton. *Land Grab: The Truth About "The Winning of the West."* New York: The Dial Press, 1972.
There is no ethnocentricity in this volume. Terrell believes massacres like those at Camp Grant, the Washita, and Sand Creek were "typical" of how the West was won and that "No nation on earth can boast of breaking so many treaties solemnly executed under oath." The mountain men and the fur trade were precursors of "corruption, disease, and ruination." The so-called cattle barons were "despots and tyrants" who operated "by force of arms and criminal violence" and resulted in a ruination of the land.

Thomas, G.W. (ed., et al.). *Victory in World War II: The New Mexico Story.* Las Cruces: New Mexico State University, 1994.
While it contains a variety of informational tidbits, the section which discusses N.M. Medal of Honor recipients for WW II excludes Joe P. Martínez and José F. Valdez, which is unpardonable and makes one wonder how accurate are the other sections.

Tobias, Henry J. *A History of the Jews in New Mexico.* Albuquerque: University of New Mexico Press, 1990.
The work starts with what Tobias refers to as "Hispanic New Mexico and Its Jewish Question," adding the crypto-Jew" identity to some people's confusion. (Hispanic identity is approaching schizophrenic proportions with some writers. Hispanics appear to be everything but Hispanic.) Then the book provides much interesting

information on Jews who came into the area after the U.S. takeover and to about 1940.

Trafzer, Clifford E. *The Kit Carson Campaign: The Last Great Navajo War* Norman: University of Oklahoma Press, 1982.
This documented, brutal account of the destruction of the Navajo Nation is blamed more on General Carleton than Kit Carson, the man who led it. Carleton is supposed to have instructed concerning the Navajo people: "You are to be punished for your crimes ... you cannot make peace ... you will be killed wherever you are found." This sounds like Hitler talking to the Jews but such analogy isn't acceptable in the popular mind unless Hispanics are the perpetrators of the villainy.

Twitchell, R.E. *Leading Facts of New Mexican History.* Vols. 1 & 2 Albuquerque: Horn & Wallace, 1963.
Twitchell is generally an unreliable source for New Mexican history when it has any relation, directly or indirectly, to Manifest Destiny. His art is scriptography for it appears he condones virtually anything done by "Americans" and should be considered part of the KGD cycle of writers. His *Leading Facts* is a misnomer: heroic events like the defense of Cebolleta (Seboyeta) in 1804 and Elfego Baca's gunfight aren't mentioned in his selectistory and one doesn't have to wonder why.

Udall, Stewart L. *Majestic Journey: Coronado's Inland Empire.* Santa Fe: Museum of New Mexico Press, 1987.
This positive work is a "must" study and far more than a report on Coronado's expedition because it promotes a healthy appraisal of history as it should be written. It underscores the fact that English writers like the Reverend Richard Hakluyt wrote anti-Hispanic propaganda "that distorted 16th century history and robbed us of the Spanish part of our national American history." Udall credits Hakluyt with a marvelously skillful ability to convince the world of the fantasy that English explorers could be compared to "Spain's great discoverers." Perhaps the feat isn't so marvelous if one considers the precedent of promoting an imaginary Camelot presided over by an imaginary King Arthur who had a round table populated by imaginary knights. Have many movies been made about Charlemagne and his knights, a real medieval king and his paladins?

Waldman, Carl. *Atlas of the North American Indian.* New York: Facts On File Publications, 1985.
Waldman's history isn't new but it must continue to be addressed because the popular mind has never really considered the extermination of Native Americans east of the Mississippi or in California after it became part of the Union in 1850. (Ethnic cleansing isn't confined to Europe.) Few people even think of what happened to the Indians in what is now the USA, perhaps believing they just "went away," except in N.M. "where the Spanish were brutal and cruel to them." Doublethink has done the job.

Weber, David J. *The Mexican Frontier, 1821-1846: The American Southwest Under Mexico.* Albuquerque University of New Mexico Press, 1982.
_____. *Foreigners in Their Native Land.* Albuquerque: University of New Mexico Press, 1973.
_____. *Myth and the History of the Hispanic Southwest.* Albuquerque: University of New Mexico Press, 1988.
_____. *The Spanish Frontier in North America.* New Haven: Yale University Press, 1992.
Dr. Weber is one of the best-known historians in the Southwest. His *Spanish Frontier* is a tour de force. And he has the moral courage to address loaded issues as in *Foreigners* and *Myth,* both of which are among the most important books written on the Southwest. A disturbing feature of Weber's style is to use Spanish words like *pobladores* instead of English *colonists/settlers,* implying a begrudging acknowledgment or "softening"

effect. (One can only wonder why Hispanic history is so immensely popular with highly accomplished historians like Bolton, Kessell, Weber, Simmons, etc., and why the Territorial/Statehood periods haven't been so attractive. No book has been written on the workings of the Court of Private Land Claims or the Santa Fe Ring, for example, implying there are taboo items in New Mexican history if one wants to "publish.")

Weigle, Marta. (ed., et al.). *Hispanic Arts and Ethnohistory in the Southwest.* Santa Fe: Ancient City Press, 1983.
_____. *Brothers of Light, Brothers of Blood.* Albuquerque: University of New Mexico Press, 1976.
Weigle's many works are always extremely well researched and documented so they are well worth studying.

Weinberg, Albert K. *Manifest Destiny: A Study of Nationalist Expansionism in American History.* Chicago: Quadrangle Paperbacks, 1935, reprint 1963.
This volume lays bare the truth about Manifest Destiny. It isn't popular reading.

Westphall, Victor. *Mercedes Reales: Hispanic Land Grants of the Upper Río Grande Region.* Albuquerque: University of New Mexico Press, 1983.
_____. *The Public Domain in New Mexico, 1854-1891.* Albuquerque: University of New Mexico Press, 1965.
_____. *Thomas Benton Catron and His Era.* Tucson: University of Arizona Press, 1973.
Westphall is always documented and often dependable. He has laid the foundation for land grant studies and the swindles that characterized Hispanics' dispossession of their land. Sometimes it appears he is torn between official morality and recognizing historical truth. The only volume I have trouble with is the Catron biography.

Whaley, Charlotte. *Nina Otero-Warren of Santa Fe.* Albuquerque: University of New Mexico Press, 1994.
While Nina is a fitting New Mexican personality for a biography (one out of many, it should be said) it appears the author needs to get in the way with ideas of ethnicity espoused by individuals like Willa Cather and her generation. The work would have been better without igug thrusts and one wonders if the work would have been written if Nina hadn't carried the name "Warren."

Wilson, John P. *Merchants, Guns & Money: The Story of Lincoln County and Its Wars.* Santa Fe: Museum of New Mexico Press, 1987.
The Lincoln County War appears never to fade in interest. While this volume adds to the literature it certainly isn't the final word on the era or its personalities.

WPA. New Mexico: A Guide to the Colorful State. New York: Hastings House, 1953.
This informational guide intended for tourists has a history just as interesting as the book itself. The material is perhaps a notch above that put out by the local chamber of commerce but ethnocentrism is a discernible guide.

New Mexico's Hall of Fame

Louise Abeita of Isleta Pueblo is the first N.M. Native American female writer to author a book.

Pablo Abeita was a renowned leader from Isleta Pueblo.

J.M. Hilario Alaríd is representative of the poet-troubador as well as the written Spanish-language tradition of New Mexico.

All Indian Pueblo Council, having its beginning in 1598, is unique in the history of New Mexico and the USA.

Brad Allison is representative of public school superintendents who realize personnel in Administration can't be exempted if legitimate educational reform is to take place.

Amerind pioneers were prehistoric people known as the Sandía, Clovis, Folsom, Cochise, Anasazi Mogollón, the first human beings in the New Mexico area.

Rudolfo Anaya is the first Hispanic New Mexican to write a "best seller" and even more far-reaching has been his work as an Editor which enabled many talented writers to be published (which generally wasn't accomplished in "Generation B").

Toney Anaya, Jerry Apodaca, Octaviano A. Larrazolo, Ezequiel C. de Baca, and (appointed) **Miguel A. Otero (II)** are the only Hispanics to serve as Governors of N.M. (excluding Donaciano Vigil who was a figurehead appointee by Gen. Kearny) since it became part of the USA in 1846 (Larrazolo and C. de Baca serving very short terms).

Dr. **Frank Angel** was the first N.M. Hispanic to serve as president of a major university.

Juan Bautista de Anza, a military and diplomatic genius who served as governor of New Mexico and established the Comanche Peace (1786-1846), explored the frontier and led successful overland colonizations that have never been equaled.

Jesusita Aragón, Ignacia Chávez, are representative of New Mexican midwives.

Dr. **John A. Aragón** was a famous educator and champion of cultural awareness.

Manny Aragón, Raymond Sánchez, E. Chris García are representative of New Mexico's passion for politics.

Miguel Archibeque brought unifying leadership to the Penitente Brotherhoods.

Anselmo Arellano has earned renown as the people's historian.

Elizabeth Fountain Armendáriz was a cultural force in the Mesilla Valley.

George W. Armijo was a Rough Rider and famous politician.

Isidoro Armijo was responsible for the legislation that made the Treaty of Guadalupe Hidalgo part of the New Mexico State Constitution.

Manuel A. Armijo, Adelardo Sánchez, are representative of the heroes of Bataan during WW II.

Manuel Armijo, the last governor before the American takeover, is perhaps the most unjustly maligned personality in New Mexican history.

Arrieros were the valorous and honest muleteers, the teamsters of the Southwest who never turned their backs on friend or foe.

Art colonies in Santa Fe and Taos became well known all over the USA.

Artists who have demonstrated commitment to community include Cleofas Vigil, Roberto Martínez, Leonor Armijo, Bernadette Rodríguez, Carlos Ortega, Samuel Sisneros, Rudolfo Anaya, Irene Blea, Selia Cortez, Arnold Trujillo, Regina Chávez, Ricardo García, Adán Sánchez, Jaime Chávez, Eva Lovato, Demetria Martínez, Daniel Ortega, Irene Oliver Lewis, Francisco Ortega, Victor Padilla, Frances Rivera, Concha Padilla, Aron Rael, Arnold Trujillo, María Elena Frésquez West, Monica Espinoza, Gloria Miera, Francisco LeFebre.

Jesús Arviso rendered invaluable service to the **Navajo Nation** during the most critical period of its existence.

Professional **artists/entertainers and athletes** associated with New Mexico include Tommy McDonald, Don Perkins, Mel Daniels, Michael Cooper, Luc Longley, Art Aragón, Bobby Foster, the Unser brothers Bobby and Al, Al Unser Jr., Nancy López, Sam Lacey, Charlie Crisp, Randy Brown, George Knighton, Notah Begay, Rob Evans, Don Woods, Kathy Whitworth, Danny Romero, Johnny Tapia, Preston Dennard, Terance Mathis, Jim Everett; Demi Moore, Kathy Baker, Kim Stanley, Vivian Vance, Mike Judge, Madolyn Smith, Patrice Martínez, Neil P. Harris, French Stewart, Dennis Hopper, Paul Smith.

Tomás Atencio is representative of individuals who have founded organizations like La *Academia de la Nueva Raza* and the *Río Grande Institute* which promote New Mexican culture.

François X. Aubry holds the record for traversing the 780-mile trail from Santa Fe to Independence Missouri, in five days, 16 hours.

Mary Austin did much to preserve aspects of New Mexican life and cultures.

Eleuterio Baca was a translator famous for his skills with English and Spanish.

Elfego Baca defended himself single-handedly against 84 cowboys in the most heroic, incredible gunfight in the history of the West.

Ezequiel C. de Baca was the people's champion.

Albuquerque **International Balloon Fiesta** is said to be the most photographed event in the world.

Adolf E. Bandelier gained world renown as ethnologist, archaeologist, and writer.

Casimiro Barela was the "Father of the Colorado Senate."

Patrociño Barela is New Mexico's world-class wood sculptor, quite possibly the greatest in American history of art.

Antonio Barreiro, attorney and writer, published the first newspaper in N.M., El *Crepúsculo de la Libertad* (The Dawn of Liberty).

John Becker and Felipe Chávez were instrumental in bringing the AT&SF railroad into Belén.

Charles Becknell was the first to develop courses on African Americans.

William Becknell is considered to be the first trader to bring American trade goods to N.M. and is often referred to as the American Father of the Santa Fe Trade.

Fr. **Alonso de Benavides,** Custodian of the New Mexico Missions, was typical of missionary scholarship, zeal, and dedication.

Batsinas, **Jason Betzinez,** rode with Gerónimo and later wrote a most interesting autobiography.

Blackdom, founded by **Francis Boyer,** was the only African-American community in N.M.

Borreguero: Sheep husbandry was the most important industry in the historical Southwest and the sheepherder was responsible for this "cash crop."

Boys Ranch/Girls Ranch has been a positive community force in the lives of innumerable young people, without receiving funding from State or Federal governments.

E. Boyd authored the first systematic study of N.M. arts and crafts.

Brotherhood of Our Father Jesús, often referred to as **Penitentes,** supplied religious guidance to communities when there were few clergymen in N.M.

Lorin W. Brown recorded much folklore during the WPA years.

Howard Bryan has written about New Mexico and its people for many decades.

Josefa Bustamante was the wealthiest woman in N.M. in 1769.

Alvar Nuñez Cabeza de Vaca experienced an eight-year odyssey of overland wandering explorations that started in Florida, possibly included a part of N.M. and the Southwest, and ended in northern Mexico.

Fabiola Cabeza de Baca wrote about N.M. and portrayed its people, especially Hispanic women, with sensitivity and accuracy.

Arthur L. Campa is a renowned folklorist and historian on New Mexican themes.

Caravan: The only way in or out of early New Mexico was the mission supply caravan, financed by the Spanish Crown, that brought in items for the missionaries. In time its appearance was a joyful event.

The best known **celebrities** to come out of N.M. are Smokey Bear and Billy the Kid.

Christopher "Kit" Carson was a scout, guide, and mountain man.

Cebolla, Antonio Sandoval, was the incomparable leader of the **Cañoncito Navajos.**

Felipe Maximiliano Chacón was a world-class New Mexican author.

Phil Chacón, Robert Rosenbloom, and Shawn McWethy represent law enforcement officers who died in the line of duty.

Rafaél Chacón was a Civil War hero and author of an autobiography.

Soledad Chacón, Georgia Lusk, Adele B. Hundley, Heather Wilson, Verna Williamson-Teller, Lela Kaskala, were/are political pioneers.

J. Francisco Chaves, "Father of the Statehood Movement," was a long-time business, education, and political leader of New Mexico. He was murdered by an unknown assassin said to have been hired by members of the Santa Fe Ring.

Manuel Antonio Chaves was the Southwest's greatest real-life hero whose feats rival those of the valiant Spanish knight, *El Cid.*

Fr. **Angélico Chávez** is New Mexico's most famous man of letters, a "Renaissance man" combination of genealogist, historian, scholar, author, poet and patriot.

David Chávez, Ramón Flores, are representative of New Mexico's artistic directors.

Senator Dennis Chávez was the first native Hispano elected to national office and the longest serving (1931-62). He emphasized education for native people of New Mexico and achieved important positions of leadership in the U.S. Senate.

Genoveva Chávez is representative of New Mexico's fabulous female singers/musicians.

Linda Chavez holds controversial opinions and is a nationally recognized personality.

Wendell Chino and Jacob Viarrial are representative of New Mexico's modern tribal leaders.

John Chisum was New Mexico's acknowledged cattle king.

Ciboleros were New Mexican plainsmen and master horsemen who hunted buffalo with a lance and utilized virtually every part of the animals they brought down.

"Los Cinco Pintores" (The Five Painters) who popularized the Santa Fe art colony were Jozef Bakos, Fremont Ellis, Will Shuster, Walter Mruk, Willard Nash.

John Collier was a champion of Native American causes.

Comancheros were courageous Pueblo and Hispanic businessmen who traded with warrior Indian nations on the plains.

Comanches at one time were fearsome enemies but they became stalwart allies after the Comanche Peace (1786-1846) was established by Governor Anza and Chief Ecueracapa. During the American period they wanted lands to build their villages in eastern N.M.

Pedro Córdova is representative of New Mexico's patrón class.

Kandy Córdova, Richard Romero, Rick Miera, Kiki Saavedra, are representative of New Mexico's popular and competent elected officials.

Vincent Córdova, Dan D. Chávez, Richard Toledo, A.B. Chávez, Bill Rothanbargar, Ernest Stapleton, are representative of New Mexico's career educators/administrators.

Francisco Vásquez de Coronado entered the Southwest in 1540 and blazed paths which others would follow, discovered lands that others would settle.

Don **Benito Crespo,** 12th Bishop of Durango, was the first (1730) bishop to set foot in N.M.

Cuerno Verde was a warrior Comanche chieftain.

Dance was New Mexico's favorite social activity.

Dates that are especially significant to New Mexicans include:

April 30, 1598, is the official day of New Mexico's coming into being when Oñate and his colonists stopped by the Río Grande in the vicinity of (present) Juárez/El Paso to celebrate their **Thanksgiving** with a formal ceremony taking possession of New Mexico, a solemn high mass with everyone in attendance, and then much merrymaking throughout the rest of the day which closed with the enactment of an original drama written by Captain Farfán de los Godos.

July 11, 1598: *San Juan de los Caballeros* (**Knights of St. John**) is founded in the Española Valley.

August 18, 1598: The main caravan arrives at San Juan de los Caballeros. This is the first colony of European people in the present USA.

September 11, 1694: The Vargas reconquest of New Mexico is complete. In 1696 some Pueblos rise in rebellion while Pecos, Tesuque, San Felipe, and Zía remain loyal to the Spanish; by December there is peace in Pueblo land and Hispanic and Pueblo people forge an alliance that is never broken.

February 28, 1786: The Comanche Peace is begun by Governor Anza and Chief Ecueracapa, thus insuring the survival of New Mexico.

April, 1787: The Comanche Peace is finalized when all branches of the Comanche nation have signed the peace treaty with Governor Anza. Comanches become staunch allies of New Mexicans and the Peace holds for generations.

January 6, 1912: New Mexico becomes a State in the American Union.

The **décima** was New Mexico's favorite poetical form.

Valentino De La O was a popular New Mexican television personality, the first to be nationally syndicated.

Samuel Delgado is representative of those New Mexicans who left the state to make a living but was pulled back permanently by New Mexican history and culture.

Tow Diem is representative of highly regarded athletic trainers.

Sister Dolores, Manuela Antonia Chávez, was New Mexico's first native nun.

Senators **Pete Domenici and Jeff Bingaman** have served New Mexico and the USA for decades.

Malcolm Ebright is bringing forth the true history of New Mexican land grants.

Ecueracapa was a Comanche chieftain who helped establish the Comanche Peace with Governor Anza.

Editors of popular Spanish-language newspapers include Isidoro Armijo, Ezequiel C. de Baca, Manuel C. de Baca, José Antonio Escajeda, José Escobar, Pedro García de la Lama, Antonio Lucero, Félix Martínez, José Montaner, Frances Montoya, Nestor Montoya, Teófilo Ocatia Caballero, Victor L. Ochoa, Hilario L. Ortiz, Camilo Padilla, Rafaél Ronquillo, Enrique H. Salazar, Manuel Salazar y Otero, José Segura, Nepomuceno Segura, Enrique J. Sosa, Francisco de Thoma, Severino Trujillo.

Manuel Simón Escudero was the "Hispanic Father of the Santa Fe Trade," the first individual to take a significant amount of trade goods to Missouri, opening what was described in the States as a "new era" in trade utilizing the Santa Fe Trail.

José Julián Espinosa and **Rufina Montoya Espinosa** are the progenitors of one of the most educated families in N.M.

Capt. **Marcos Farfán de los Godos** wrote the first drama performed on what is now U.S. soil.

Erna Fergusson wrote without cultural bias about N.M.

José Emilio Fernández authored *Forty Years a Legislator, or the Biography of Casimiro Barela,* one of the most important biographies written in the Southwest.

Harold Y. Foster is representative of the Navajo Code Talkers of WW II.

Albert J. Fountain was a courageous attorney who fought corruption in high places and, along with his young son, was murdered because of it.

Frenchmen who became an integral part of Hispanic New Mexico are represented by Carlos Beaubien, Ceran St. Vrain, Antoine Robideaux, Maurice Ledoux, Manuel LeFebre. Their many descendants are represented by individuals like Francisco LeFebre, Eugene (Jean) Ledoux, Gene Hill, Clyde Archibeque.

Frontiersmen already famous in their own lifetimes include Antonio Alonso Baca, Francisco Luján, Gaspar Pérez, Diego Romero, Marcelino Baca, El Carpintero from Pecos Pueblo, Chato Aragón, Redondo Gallegos, Domingo Baca, Pedro Chaves, Román Baca.

Celso Gallegos was a highly esteemed woodcarver.

Prem Gabaldón is representative of the small businessman who has built a most positive rapport with his community.

Ignacio V. Gallegos and **Stella Sánchez Gallegos** were parents of a large New Mexican family that produced three priests: Fr. **Moises Gallegos,** Fr. **Albert Gallegos,** and Fr. **David Gallegos.**

(Padre) **José Manuel Gallegos** was New Mexico's first Delegate to Congress.

Marty García, a former Golden Gloves champion and professional prize fighter, has earned renown in the field of community service.

Cecilio García Camarillo is a well-known poet who also utilizes his skills in diplomacy on behalf of the community while working in the Mexican Embassy.

Rey Garduño, Arturo Atencio, John Candelario, Miguel Gandert, are representative of New Mexico's artistic, professional photographers.

Pat Garrett was a real life incorruptible lawman.

Reverend **Donato M. Gasparri** founded the Jesuit Missions in New Mexico-Colorado as well as the Catholic press when he became the first editor of *La Revista Católica.*

Genealogy researchers who have devoted themselves to help their communities include Angélico Chávez, Ernie Tafoya, Luis Padilla, Paul Horvat, David Gonzáles, Jonathan Ortega, Ronaldo Miera, Carlos Lopopolo.

Robert H. Goddard became the "Father of American Rocketry" during his years in N.M.

Catalina Gonzáles, Irene Oliver-Lewis, Margarita Martínez, are representative of New Mexico's producers.

Mildred M. Griffo is representative of competence at government installations like Sandía National Laboratories.

Col. **Sidney M. Gutiérrez** was the first Hispanic New Mexican on a space mission.

Harwood Foundation was founded by Elizabeth Harwood in memory of her husband Bert.

Alice Corbin Henderson did much to promote poetry and she was one of the first English-language writers to portray the Penitente Brotherhood in a true light.

The Hermit, **Giovanni María Agostini,** was an unusual personality.

Cosme Herrera learned of the judiciary swindle of the Jacona land grant, rallied community support and "bought it back" to prevent villagers from being dispossessed of their land.

The **Herrera brothers** Juan, José, Pablo, and Nicanor were activists in defense of the people's land.

Lloyd Herrera is representative of the public school principal who is committed to his students and their community.

Edgar L. Hewett was a powerful influence on New Mexican culture.

Gene Hill, first president of the **Hispanic Culture Preservation League**, has demonstrated a life-long commitment to the history, culture, and people of New Mexico.

Tony Hillerman, New Mexico's best-selling author, creates and immortalizes Navajo law enforcement officers in his popular writings.

Conrad Hilton is the internationally renowned hotel owner whose motto became "*Be My Guest.*"

Hispanic Cultural Center in Albuquerque is the only institution of its kind in the USA.

Historia de la Nueva México, an epic poem in rhyming verse by Gaspar Pérez de Villagrá, is New Mexico's founding chronicle, the first history in the USA and unique in the world because no other colony has ever been chronicled by an epic poem.

The **Horned Saddle,** an Hispanic creation funded by Viceroy Antonio de Mendoza, revolutionized the ranching industry which in turn created the American West.

Huning brothers Franz, Charles, and Louis were very active merchants in N.M.

Al Hurricane, Eraclio Pérez, Genoveva Chávez, Jerry Jaramillo, Miguel Archibeque, Angel Espinoza, José M. Trujillo, Roberto Mondragón, Israela, Andrea Gallegos, Lorenzo Martínez, Juan Ortega, Roberto Martínez, Nick Branchal, Pedro Sepúlveda, Hector Pimentel, Darren Córdova, Stefani Sullivan, Jerry and Gilbert López, Ernie Montoya, Luis Sánchez, Debbie Martínez, Ernie Márquez, Freddie Brown, David Salazar, Sunny Ozuna, Freddie Chávez, Vicente Saucedo, Los Hermanos Baca, Roberto Griego, Eddie Roybal, Mathew Martínez, Mona Montoya, Michael Silva, Nena García, Iv6n Ulibarrí, Viento, Los Chavos, Purple Haze, La Iluvia, Apache Spirit, Lumbre, Persuasion, La Compañia, Los Reyes de Albuquerque, Red Wine, La Raza Unida, Los Quickies, Sound FX, Brown Sugar, are representative of New Mexico's talented bilingual individual and group musicians. Dick Bills, Glen Campbell, are representatives of the country music genre.

Charles Ilfeld was one of New Mexico's most famous businessmen.

Indian Pueblo Cultural Center is a unique creation by the 19 Pueblos of New Mexico.

Katie Pearl Jackson was the first to set up a Negro History Week in N.M.

Dr. **Mari-Luci Jaramillo** is the first New Mexican female to be appointed as Ambassador.

Margarita Jaramillo y Mascareñas is representative of New Mexico's *sobadoras.*

Myra Ellen Jenkins, Marina Ochoa, José Villegas, Arthur L. Olivas, Richard Rudisill, are well-known archivists.

Fr. **Andrés Juárez** supervised construction of the grandest mission church in all N.M. at Pecos Pueblo.

John Kessell, founder of the Vargas Project, has brought to light much New Mexican colonial history.

Alfred V Kidder laid the foundation for the study of archaeology in New Mexico.

Bob King and **Lou Henson** took N.M. college basketball into national prominence.

Bruce King and Manuel Armijo are the only Governors of N.M. who served three separate terms.

Kirtland Air Force Base is the largest military installation in N.M. and one of the largest in the USA.

A.L. Krohn, David Shor, are representative of New Mexico's rabbis.

Our Lady of the Rosary, La *Conquistadora, also referred to as Our Lady of Peace, is* New Mexico's famous patron and most renowned statue.

Jean Baptiste Lamy was the first Archbishop of Santa Fe.

Lincoln LaPaz founded and directed the Institute of Meteoritics at UNM.

Octaviano Larrazolo was a crucial influence in writing of the New Mexico Constitution and is the only person in New Mexican history to be elected as Governor and Senator.

José Dolores López was one of the first woodcarvers from Córdova, the New Mexican mecca of wood-carvers.

Delfine Lovato chaired the All Indian Pueblo Council for 19 years.

Lovelace Medical Center: Dr. William R. Lovelace came to New Mexico seeking health and with Dr. Edgar T. Lassetter founded one of the state's largest health care institutions.

Mabel Dodge Luhan was a writer and celebrity Taos personality who introduced many highly accomplished people to the state.

Ed Luján was appointed to chair the first Board of Directors for the Hispanic Cultural Center.

Manuel Luján Jr. possibly had more bipartisan respect than any statesmen ever elected to the House of Representatives.

Charles Fletcher Lummis sincerely admired the Southwest and its people, whom he portrayed according to their true accomplishments.

Maximiliano Luna is the personification of patriotism.

Greg MacAleese conceived of CRIME STOPPERS, a way for anonymous citizens to help law enforcement officers, which has spread throughout the USA.

Roque Madrid wrote one of the first descriptions of the Navajos and their homeland.

Susan Magoffin is well known for her diary and is thought to be the first U.S. female in N.M.

Manuelito was a Navajo warrior and chieftain who would fight for the freedom of his people.

E. A. "Tony" Mares is representative of New Mexico's bilingual poets and dramatists.

José Mares, famous scout and soldier, also blazed a trail from Santa Fe to San Antonio.

Eloy Márquez is representative of the respect and admiration which many Hispanic New Mexicans have for Native Americans.

Gerónimo Márquez was one of Oñate's most stalwart captains.

Teresa Márquez, Cecilia Casaus, Linda Avery, Orlando Romero, are representative of N.M. librarians.

Brother Mathias is the immortal founder of the Brothers of the Good Shepherd

Alberto O. Martínez, a professional potter, fluent in Spanish, English, the Apache-Navajo language known as Athabascan, with an understanding of spoken Tewa, is representative of trilingual New Mexicans.

Fr. Antonio J. Martínez, "Curate of Taos," was one of the finest minds of New Mexico and a social and religious force to be reckoned with.

Demetria Martínez, Leslie Marmon Silko, Denise Chávez, Luci Tapahanso, are representative of New Mexico's highly accomplished female writers.

Elmer Martínez is representative of New Mexico's great interest in the field of heraldry.

Félix Martínez was a multi-talented force in New Mexican society who, among many other things, sponsored the legislation that created Highlands University.

María Martínez is representative of our famous potters.

Paul Martínez (Medanales/Santa Fe) is representative of competence in State government as well as in traditional skills in New Mexican farm/ranch as well as city lifestyles.

Gino J. Matteuci, Benjamin Silva Jr., are representative of trustworthy New Mexican lawyers.

Martyrs in religious orders who gave their lives as the price to assimilate New Mexico's Amerinds into the Christian community include **Juan Bernal, José Espeleta, José Figueroa, Juan de Jesús María, Francisco Lorenzana, Lucas Maldonado, José Montes, de Oca, Antonio Mora, Luis Morales, Juan Pedrosa, Juan Bautista Pino, Matías Rendón, Antonio Sánchez, Agustín de Santa María, Juan Talabán, Manuel Tinoco, José Trujillo, Tomás Torres, Juan del Val, Fernando Velasco, Domingo Vera,** all of whom died in the Pueblo Revolt of 1680. Equally heroic were missionaries who were slain during other times, which include **José Arbizu, Martín Arvide, Pedro Avila, Antonio Carbonell, Francisco Casañas, Cristóbal de Concepción, Francisco Corvera, Juan de la Cruz, Luis Escalona, Alonso Gil, Antonio Guerra, Andrés Gutiérrez, Simón de Jesús, Francisco Letrado, Francisco López (1581), Francisco López (1682), Antonio Moreno, Pedro Ortega, Francisco Porras, Agustín Rodríguez, Juan de Santa María, Domingo Saraoz.**

Bill Mauldin was a morale builder with his satirical war cartoons and is now said to be the best of all war cartoonists.

Medal of Honor recipients:
(*Born in N.M.*): Daniel Fernández, Joe R Martínez, Hiroshi Miyamura, Harold Moon, Louis R. Rocco, Alejandro R. Ruiz, José E Valdez, Kenneth Walker;
(*Entered Service in N.M.*) Alexander Bonnyman Jr., Robert McDonald, Franklin Miller, Francis Oliver, Robert S. Scott, Ebin (Eben) Stanley;
(*Living in N.M.*) Hiroshi Miyamura, Raymond J. Murphy, Robert Scott.

Media personalities who have earned a reputation for being responsible are represented by Tom Doyle, Carlos Salazar, Dick Knipfing, David Steinberg, Liz Otero Vallejos, Chris Schuler, Bill Hume, Howard Morgan, Dan Herrera, Anthony DellaFlora.

Mariano Medina and **Marcelino Baca** are representative of Nuevomexicano mountain men.

John Gaw Meem was the most celebrated architect of the Santa Fe Style of architecture.

Mesteñeros were New Mexican plainsmen who captured wild horses and trained them to the saddle for use in the ranching industry.

Microsoft Corporation was founded in Albuquerque by **Bill Gates and Paul Allen.**

The **"Mighty Midgets"** from St. Michael's were New Mexico's most remarkable high school basketball team.

Minero: The miner and his technology were a path to riches in New Mexico and the New World.

Misionero: The *missionary* in New Mexico and the Americas was a Christian, teacher, civilizer, and Defender of the Indians. No other individual has done more for New Mexico and the Americas.

Joseph M. Montoya served the people of N.M. for decades in national elective office.

C. Etta (Charlie) Morrissey has been recognized with a number of awards for her dedication to the people of N.M.

La Mujer: Without the Hispanic woman as the heart of the pioneering New Mexican family unit, new lands, settlements, and colonies would never have survived. She suffered hardships alongside her man and prevailed or lost her life with him.

Botanists **Roy Nakayama** and **Paul Bosland** worked with chile farmers to create the "Big Jim" strain which became the most popular chile export in the state.

Emilio Naranjo, while often described as "controversial," has served the people of New Mexico for decades.

José (López) Naranjo was a famous ladino, scout, and interpreter from **Zuñi Pueblo.**

Narbona was a valiant Navajo warrior and headman who could also work for peace, though the effort cost him his life.

Bobby Newcombe forged a high school athletic career that few have or will ever equal while maintaining a solid "B" average in his academic studies.

"New Mexicans" who experienced highly successful collegiate athletic careers include Toby Roybal, Paul Tapia, Willie Banks, Tony Sandoval, Ray Gianni, Bobby Santiago, Abie Paez, Chuck Hill, Greg Brown, Rob Robbins, Trent Dimas, Randy Rich, Tom Walker, Blake Irwin, John Bell, Walt Arnold, Jason Bloom, Larry White, Stan Quintana, Houston Ross, Jerry Nesbitt, Jack Abendschan.

The **New Mexico Constitution** is unique among State constitutions for its safeguards against depriving Hispanics of their human and constitutional rights.

New Mexico Volunteers fought valiantly for the Union during the Civil War.

Newspapers in the Spanish language like *La Voz del Pueblo, El Independiente, El Nuevo Mexicano, La Opinión Pública,* etc., featured renowned writers José Escobar, Luis Tafoya, Manuel C. de Baca, Felipe M. Chacón, etc.

Salvador "Sal" Nuñez was instrumental in founding the Albuquerque Hispano Chamber of Commerce.

"Los Ocho Pintores" (The Eight Painters) are credited with starting the Taos art colony: J.H. Sharp, B.G, Phillips, E. L. Blumenschein, O.E. Berninghaus, 1. Couse, WH. Dunton, V Higgins, W. Ufer.

Bartolomé de Ojeda from **Zía** and **Picurís Pueblos** was a *ladino* who became instrumental in stabilizing and preserving New Mexico by helping the Spaniards' return in 1693 when raiders now mounted on horseback were on the verge of destroying the people of Puebloland.

Georgia O'Keeffe is representative of the artist whose deepest creative instincts were brought forth by the New Mexican landscape and ambiance.

Rachel Sánchez Olivas, Estefanita Montoya, are representative of the *comadre* system in Hispanic society.

Juan de Oñate is the founder of New Mexico (1598), the oldest colony in the USA. His efforts also helped to found Santa Fe, the oldest capital (1608-1610?), and he is the first authority figure in New Mexican government who labored to preserve the Indians and their way of life (which is why Indians have survived in N.M.).

Oñate Memorial and Visitors Center, a project of Río Arriba County and situated in the Española Valley, is unique in that it honors an heroic personality from New Mexico's long history.

Padre **Ramón Ortiz** was a humanitarian as well as beloved activist on both sides of the American/Mexican border.

Simon J. Ortiz, Harold Littlebird, are representative of Pueblo writers and intellectuals who maintain their cultural ties.

Alfonso "Al" Otero introduced the legislation to fund a study to determine the feasibility of a private, non-profit Hispanic Cultural Center.

Miguel A. Otero (II) was New Mexico's first and only native territorial governor and the only native governor to write an autobiography.

Nina Otero-Warren was a multi-talented individual.

Gabriel Ortega is the progenitor of the Chimayó Ortega family of weavers.

Concha Ortiz y Pino de Kleven, member of the famous Ortiz family, is a well-known educator, legislator, and rancher.

Ana Pacheco is the founder and editor of *La Herencia del Norte*, a quarterly magazine that promotes New Mexican culture.

Fr. **Juan de Padilla,** the *"Fighting Friar"* of the Coronado expedition, was the first missionary martyr in the Southwest.

Pete Padilla, Manuel Mora, Anthony Aragón, are representative of New Mexicans who were wounded or died serving their country in Vietnam.

Pastor or *borreguero,* the sheepherder was a master of sheep husbandry who tended New Mexico's most important stock animal.

Juan Patrón, a renowned community leader during the Lincoln County War of 1878, was assassinated by a gunmen said to have been contracted by the Santa Fe Ring.

Juan José Peña, Samuel Adelo, are representative of contemporary professional translators and champions of community activism.

Fr. **Estevan Perea** is considered to be *"Father of the New Mexican Church."*

Larry Perea, Ramón Herrera, Conchita Lucero, Moises Venegas, Juanita Sánchez, Max de Aragón, Rozanne Chávez Hurst, Richard Quintana, Ernest Hill, Juan Chacón, Priscilla Lucero, Robert Rodríguez, Virginia Rael, Vidal Santillanes, Chano Merino, Dennis Sánchez, Grace Olivares, Angel Collado, Juan Cruz-Solano, Ben Hernández, Alberto Sandoval, are representative of unsung individuals dedicated to community action and participation.

Pedro Bautista Pino was New Mexico's representative to the Spanish *Cortes* parliament.

Pobladores *(vecinos)* colonists *(settlers)* were pioneering New Mexican men, women, and children who experienced untold hardships that often cost them their lives. Ancestors of the Pueblo people were the first and foremost pioneers then Hispanics with Oñate and later Vargas were the first of European pioneers.

Popé was one of the principal leaders of the Pueblo Rebellion of 1680. Other leaders included Luis and Lorenzo Tupatú, Antonio Malacate, Francisco El Ollita, Nicolás Jonva, Domingo Romero, Antonio Bolsas, Cristóbal Yope, Alonzo Catiti, El Jaca, Domingo Naranjo.

Tom Popejoy is representative of competent educational administration at the university level.

Ernie Pyle, perhaps the most famous reporter of WW II, chose to make his home in N.M. in 1940.

Juan José Quintana from Cochití Pueblo was a champion of Native American rights as guaranteed through the Spanish legal system.

Miguel de Quintana was a popular writer of the 1730s and a champion of freedom of expression.

Juan B. Railliere was the highly accomplished, energetic priest at Tomé,

Rancho de las Golondrinas is typical of a New Mexican hacienda.

Benjamin Read was an historian who emphasized documentation instead of cultural bias in the writing of New Mexican history.

Researchers who have or are bringing out much valuable information on New Mexico are represented by Tibo Chávez, Robert Hemmerich y Valencia, Patrick Beckett, J. Benito Córdova, Rose Díaz, Meredith D. Dodge, Rick Hendricks, Sandra Jaramillo, Carlos Lopopolo, Sylvia Rodríguez, Maurilio Vigil, C.R. Cutter, Nasario Garcia, Eloy Gallegos, Julián Josué Vigil, Alvin Korte, Galindo Rendón, Adrian Bustamante, Alfred Córdova, Ray John de Aragón, David Sandoval, Daniel Valdes y Tapia, Carolyn Zeleny, Frances Swadesh, Guadalupe Tafoya, Moises Venegas.

Revista Ilustrada, edited by **Camilo Padilla** for more than a quarter century, was New Mexico's most popular magazine.

Pedro Ribera y Ortega is representative of New Mexico's bilingual scholars.

Bill Richardson represented N.M. in the 3rd Congressional District, achieved notable successes in freeing hostages around the world and then was appointed American Ambassador to the United Nations.

Río Grande Blanket is a unique style of weaving that developed in New Mexico.

Charlie Romero is representative of an individual who forged a highly successful business career despite a serious physical handicap.

Ed L. Romero is representative of New Mexico's businessmen. He was selected to serve as Ambassador to Spain.

Vicente Romero is representative of the plainsmen of his day.

Santiago Roybal was the first native New Mexican ordained to the priesthood.

Runners have been a part of New Mexican cultures for many centuries and are represented by **Steve Gauchupin, Jerry García, John Baker, Adolph Plummer.**

George I. Sánchez was a noted activist, educator, and author.

Joe Sando is an historian of New Mexico and its Pueblo people.

Bonifacio E. Sandoval was a master tinsmith and progenitor of a family of tinsmiths.

Felipe Sandoval and **Felipe Tafoya** are representative of the men who held the post of *Protector of the Indians* in colonial N.M.

San Juan Pueblo hosted the first Hispanic colonists in New Mexico in 1598 and is still an integral part of New Mexican history.

Santa Fe Opera, founded **by John Crosby,** is famous the world over.

Santa Fe Style New Mexican architecture is famous throughout the USA.

Santeros are artists who create religious art for New Mexican communities. The most famous santeros out of history include B. Miera y Pacheco, Fr. A. García, 18th Century Novice, Laguna Santero, R.A. Fresquis, A. Molleno, José Aragón, "A.J.," Quill Pen Santero, Santo Niño Santero, J.R. Aragón, Arroyo Hondo Santero, J. de G. Gonzáles, J.M. Herrera, J.R. Velázquez, J.B. Ortega.

Millie Santillanes, Tana Alexander, Loretta Armenta, are typical of highly successful businesswomen who are also dedicated to the community.

Santuario de Chimayó is often referred to as the *"Lourdes of America."*

Scholars who have made or are making a difference in New Mexican society are represented by Erlinda Gonzáles-Berry, Tobias Durán, Felipe Gonzáles, Enrique Lamadrid, Francisco Lomelí, A. Gabriel Meléndez, Doris Meyer, Jacqueline Dorgan Meketa, Raymond MacCurdy, Genaro Padilla, Tey Diana Rebolledo, José Rivera, Joseph T. Sánchez, Tom Chávez, David Weber, Felix Almaráz, Samuel Cisneros, Guillermo Lux, Miguel Encinias, Richard Melzer, Felipe Mirabal, Richard Salazar, Alfred Rodríguez.

France V. Scholes was a transplanted scholar who investigated New Mexico's Spanish colonial history and became an authority in it.

Sisters **Blandina Segale, Catherine Mellon, Emerentiana Corby,** were teachers and healthcare workers who laid the foundation for what is today the St. Joseph Healthcare System.

José D. Sena was a Civil War hero.

Sheep kings who could club together and drive 50,000 to 100,000 animals to market in any given year are represented by ranchers (and other members of their families) like Clemente Gutiérrez, Juan Miguel Alvarez de Castillo, Joseph de Reaño 11, Mateo J. Pino, Manuel Delgado, Francisco Xavier Chaves, José Chaves y Castillo, Pedro José Perea, Juan Rafaél Ortiz, Manuel Armijo, Juan Est6van Pino, Antonio José Luna, Mariano Chaves y Castillo, José Leandro Martínez, Antonio Sandoval, José Jaramillo, Santiago Ulibarrí, etc. Among many others, the Otero, Luna, Ortiz, Pino, Perea, and Armijo families were masters of sheep husbandry.

"Simpáticos" emanating from other states who became enamored with New Mexico are represented by Stan Aglen, Marty and O.C. Brown, Mike Bridge, Becky Steinkueller, Ted Turner and Jane Fonda.

Eshref Shevky exposed land abuses in his **Tewa Basin Study.**

Marc Simmons is a professional historian who has also written important biographical works.

Sisters of Charity worked for the good of the people of New Mexico.

Solomon Jacob Spiegelberg was one of the first Jewish merchants in N.M. and the Spiegelberg clan became an integral part of New Mexican history.

Doña **Eufemia Sosa Peñalosa** represents the early pioneer women who came to N.M.

Southeastern New Mexico produced leaders and pioneers like J.C. Lea, M. Corn, J. Poe, J.T. White, and J.J. Hagerman.

Spiral Staircase is considered one of New Mexico's miracles.

Catherine Stinson-Otero was a famous aviatrix who settled in New Mexico.

St. Michael's is the oldest extant secondary school in N.M.

José Tafoya is called the "Prince of Comancheros" because of the magnitude of his highly successful trade with plains Indians like the Comanches.

Taos Fair was the most popular of New Mexican trade fairs and possibly the first "state fair" in the USA.

Ralph Tasker, Babe Parenti, Jim Hulsman, are typical of New Mexico's master high school coaches.

Master **Teachers** of N.M. are represented by individuals like Sister Albert, E.R. "Doc" Harrington, Dolores Gonsález, Pauline Peck, Herb Graubard, Rose M. Zamora, Daniel Dooley, Rita Minkin, George Fishbeck, the Córdova sisters Patsy and Nadine, Robert Smolich, the Figge brothers Robert and Roger, María Gutiérrez Spencer, Larry Torres, Benjamin Sachs, William Dabney, Ramón Sender.

Temple Montefiore was New Mexico's first synagogue and **Congregation Albert** is New Mexico's largest Jewish community.

Theater has always been a passion of Hispanic New Mexico starting from the time of Oñate's colonization with the presentation of Capt. Farfán's drama, as well as works based on religion or history such as **Las Posadas, Los Pastores** (La Pastorela), **Los Reyes Magos, El Niño Perdido, Los Comanchos** (religious), **Los Matachines** (dance drama), **Los Comanches** (historical), to *Así Es Nuevo México* of the present day.

Clyde Tingley was a positive political and social force from the governor's office.

Tinsmiths produced treasured works of art.

Trinity Site saw the explosion of the first atomic bomb and the beginning of the Atomic Age.

Trovadores were folk poets and masters of rhymed verse.

Miguel Trujillo of Isleta Pueblo demanded and got the right for Native Americans to vote in all elections as of 1948.
José Concepción Trujillo was the first of the Trujillo family weavers from Chimayó.

Along with men like **Teodoro Gonzáles,** the brothers **Pedro and Celedón Trujillo** were the most famous mustangers on the Great Plains.

The **200th Coast Artillery** fought heroically in Bataan and Corregidor and experienced the Bataan Death March.

Sabine R. Ulibarrí, educator, poet, and author, has touched the lives of many people in New Mexico and the Hispanic world.

Diego de Vargas led the Reconquest and recolonization of New Mexico.

Vaquero became the *"American cowboy,"* the greatest mythical hero of the USA.

Pablita Velarde is a world-renowned artist.

Tomás Vélez Cachupín is representative of talented governors during Spanish colonial times.

Pedro Vial, New Mexico's and the Southwest's most famous trail-blazer, was the first to map important southwestern trails, including the Santa Fe Trail.

Carlos Vierra was one of a group that helped popularize the *Santa Fe Style* of architecture.

Capitán Vigil, **José Antonio Vigil** from Cundiyó, was a renowned frontiersman and *llanero.*

Cleofes Vigil was a sculptor, story teller, musician, activist, and personality of northern N.M.

J. Ronald Vigil conceptualized and initiated the statutory enactment of the Hispanic Cultural Division within the Office of Cultural Affairs. He also wrote the enabling legislation known as SB 739 which structured the creation of the Hispanic Cultural Center in Albuquerque and served as its founding Director.

Brigadier General **Carmelita Vigil-Schimmenti** is representative of New Mexican females in the military.

Gaspar Pérez de Villagrá chronicled the founding of N.M. in the rhyming epic poem titled *Historia de la Nueva México,* and N.M. is the only colony in the history of the world that can claim that distinction.

Volunteerism is represented by Tracey Almond, Toby Chávez, Sharon Billings, Jean Brody, Carey Carleton, Kathie Buchanan, Luis Abeyta, H.R. Humphrey, Paul Kinsella, Lewis Lubers, Dolores Michutka, Gilda Montaño, Geri Garrison, Virgil H. Reynolds, Arthur Romero, Bruce Seligman, Mary Karp, George Valtierra, Israel and Ernestine Morales.

Annie Wauneka was a most positive force in the Navajo Nation of New Mexico-Arizona.

Weavers in N.M. are famous for their creations.

Marta Weigle is producing New Mexican works based on sound documentation and scholarship.

Victor Westphall, founder and builder of the Vietnam Veterans Memorial Chapel in Eagle Nest, has laid the groundwork for serious study of New Mexican land grants.

Vicente Ximenes was a part of President L.B. Johnson's administration that was so successful with Civil Rights legislation.

Juan de Ye was the heroic leader of **Pecos Pueblo** who helped prevent full-scale warfare during Vargas' reentry into New Mexico. Other renowned leaders from Pecos include Felipe Chistoe and Juan Tindé.

Norman Zollinger is representative of booksellers with community commitment and is a well-known author in his own right.

Frank Zúñiga is representative of accomplished New Mexicans working in the film industry.

RECOMMENDED
BOOKS AND AUTHORS OF NEW MEXICO*

R. Anaya: Bless Me, Ultima; *Tierra* (ed.).

A. Arellano: Las Vegas Grandes on the Gallinas.

J.E. Arellano: *Entre Verde y Seco.*

M. Austin: Earth Horizon.

E. Baca: Santa Fe Fantasy: Quest for the Golden City.

J.S. Baca: Black Mesa Poems.

M. C. de Baca: Vicente Silva and his 40 Bandits.

H.H. Bancroft: History of Arizona and New Mexico.

A. Bandelier: The Delight Makers.

J.E Bannon: Bolton and the Spanish Borderlands.

I. Barraza Sánchez, G. Sánchez Yund: *Comida Sabrosa.*

J.O. Baxter: *Las Carneradas:* Sheep Trade in New Mexico, 1700-1860.

T.M. Becker (ed., et al.): Racial and Ethnic Patterns of Mortality in New Mexico.

H.E. Bolton: Coronado: Knight of Pueblos and Plains.

E. Boyd: Popular Arts of Spanish New Mexico.

C.L. Briggs, J.R. Van Ness: Land, Water, and Culture.

H. Bryan: Wildest of the Wild West.

F. Cabeza de Baca: We Fed Them Cactus.

S. Calafate Boyle: *Los Capitalistas:* New Mexican Merchants and the Santa Fe Trade.

A. Campa: Tales of the Sangre de Cristos.

B. Candelaria: Inheritance of Strangers.

F.M. Chacón: Works of F. M. Chacón.

F.W. Champe: The Matachines Dance of the Upper Rio Grande: History, Music, and Choreography.

A. Chávez: Origins of New Mexico Families.

D. Chávez: The Last of the Menu Girls.

R. Cobos: *Refranes:* Southwestern Spanish Proverbs.

G.B. Córdova: Abiquiú and Don Cacahuate, A Folk History of a New Mexican Village.

R. Cutter: Protector of the Indians.

M. Ebright: Land Grants and Lawsuits in Northern New Mexico.

A. Espinosa: Los Comanches: A Spanish Heroic Play of the Year 1780.

G. Espinosa, T. Chávez: The *Río Abajo.*

J.E. Espinosa: Saints in the Valleys.

J.M. Espinosa: The Pueblo Indian Revolt of 1696 and the Franciscan Missions in N.M.

M. Evans: Blue Feather Fellini.

E. Fergusson: Dancing Gods.

L. Frank: New Kingdom of the Saints.

M.G. Fulton: History of the Lincoln County War.

E.J. Gallegos: Jacona: An Epic Story of the Spanish Southwest.

M. García: *Recuerdos de los Viejitos:* Tales of the Río Puerco.

E. Gonzales-Berry (ed.): Pasó Por Aquí: Critical Essays on the N.M. Literary Tradition, 1542-1988.

E. Gonzales, D.L. Witt: Spirit Ascendant: The Art and Life of Patrociño Barela.

A. Griego: Good-bye, My Land of Enchantment.

A.C. Henderson: Brothers of Light.

G. Hill: Americans All/*Americanos Todos*.

T. Hillerman: Coyote Waits.

V. Hoffman, B.H. Johnson: Navajo Biographies.

J.E. Holmes: Politics in New Mexico.

B. Jaramillo: Shadows of the Past/*Sombras del Pasado*.

O.L. Jones: Pueblo Warriors and Spanish Conquest.

W.A. Keleher: Turmoil in New Mexico, 1846-1868.

C.L. Kenner: A History of New Mexican-Plains Indians Relations.

J. Kessell: Kiva, Cross, and Crown.

J. Kutz: Grassroots New Mexico.

R. Larson: New Mexico's Quest for Statehood.

A.S. López: Blessed Are The Soldiers.

C. Lopopolo: The New Mexico Chronicles.

A. Lucero-White Lea: Literary Folklore of the Hispanic Southwest.

C.E Lummis: A New Mexico David.

H. Luna: *San Joaquín del Nacimiento.*

E.A. Mares: The Unicorn Poem.

A.G. Meléndez: So All Is Not Lost: The Poetics of Print in Nuevomexicano Communities, 1834-1958.

J. D. Meketa: Legacy of Honor: The Life of Rafaél Chacón.

D. Meyer: Speaking for Themselves.

S. Motto: More than Conquerors: Makers of History, 1528-1978.

R. Morris: The Devil's Butcher Shop.

S. Niederman, M. Sagan (eds.): New Mexico Poetry Renaissance.

R. Nostrand: The Hispano Homeland.

M. Otero: My Life on the Frontier.

N. Otero: Old Spain in Our Southwest.

S.J. Ortiz: Fight Back: For the Sake of the People, For the Sake of the Land.

A. Ortiz: The Tewa World.

G. Padilla: My History, Not Yours.

Pasó Por Aquí Series, University of New Mexico Press.

A. Peña: Memories of Cíbola.

B. & M.R. Porter; J. Sunder (eds.): Matt Field on the Santa Fe Trail.

L.V. Quintana: Sangre.

B. Read: Illustrated History of New Mexico.

T. D. Rebolledo, E. Gonzales-Berry, T. Márquez (eds.): *Las Mujeres Hablan*: An Anthology of Nuevo Mexicana Writers.

M. Rhodes: The Little World Waddies.

C. Robinson: With the Ears of Strangers: The Mexican in American Literature.

O. Romero: Adobe.

J. Sando: Pueblo Nations.

R. Sálaz M.: New Mexico: A Brief Multi-History.

G. I. Sánchez: Forgotten People.

M. Simmons: The Little Lion of the Southwest.

A.R. Sunseri: Seeds of Discord.

L. Taylor, D. Bokides: New Mexican Furniture: 1600-1940.

H.J. Tobias: A History of the Jews in New Mexico.

S.L. Udall: Majestic Journey.

S. Ulibarrí: My Grandmother Smoked Cigars and Other Stories.

A. Vigil: *Una Linda Raza:* Cultural and Artistic Traditions of the Hispanic Southwest.

J.J. Vigil: *Arse Poética.*

E. Waters: People of the Valley

D. Weber: Foreigners in Their Native Land.

M. Weigle: The Lore of New Mexico.

V. Westphall: *Mercedes Reales.*

N. Wood: Many Winters.

N. Zollinger: Riders to Cíbola.

*Most authors will have several books that readers will find interesting. Many of these volumes will contain a wealth of additional bibliography. For example see the "Bibliography of New Mexican Hispanic Literature" by Teresa Márquez in *Pasó Por Aquí* mentioned above.

INDEX